Oxford Studies in European Law

General Editors: Paul Craig and Gráinne de Búrca

ACCOUNTABILITY AND LEGITIMACY
IN THE EUROPEAN UNION

A

13

Accountability and Legitimacy in the European Union

Edited by

ANTHONY ARNULL and
DANIEL WINCOTT

OXFORD
UNIVERSITY PRESS

OXFORD

UNIVERSITY PRESS

Great Clarendon Street, Oxford OX2 6DP

Oxford University Press is a department of the University of Oxford.
It furthers the University's objective of excellence in research, scholarship,
and education by publishing worldwide in

Oxford New York

Auckland Bangkok Buenos Aires Cape Town Chennai
Dar es Salaam Delhi Hong Kong Istanbul Karachi Kolkata
Kuala Lumpur Madrid Melbourne Mexico City Mumbai Nairobi
São Paulo Shanghai Taipei Tokyo Toronto

Oxford is a registered trade mark of Oxford University Press
in the UK and in certain other countries

Published in the United States
by Oxford University Press Inc., New York

© Anthony Arnull and Daniel Wincott 2002

British Library Cataloguing in Publication Data

Data available

Library of Congress Cataloging in Publication Data

Data available

ISBN 0–19–925560–1 (hbk.)
ISBN 0–19–925710–8 (pbk.)

1 3 5 7 9 10 8 6 4 2

Typeset by Kolam Information Services, Pvt. Ltd, Pondicherry, India
Printed in Great Britain
on acid-free paper by
T.J. International Ltd, Padstow

FOREWORD

I am delighted to commend this important and stimulating book.

The accountability and legitimacy of the European Union is a huge subject. It touches on the lives of all our citizens. It goes to the heart of the governance of the 15 democracies that make up the EU today, and which will soon be joined, we hope, by many more.

But it is no secret that the accountability of the EU institutions, and their legitimacy in the eyes of the people they are created to serve, leaves a great deal to be desired. 'Brussels' is seen as remote and out of touch. The European Commission is seen as a vast bureaucracy, intervening in what Douglas Hurd called the 'nooks and crannies' of our national life. The European Parliament does valuable and important work—but it has hardly captured the public's imagination.

These impressions are unfair. But it is a fact that at present some people feel sullen and alienated from the EU, not just in Britain, but more widely. And it is dangerous, because it could eventually lead people to question their political obligation. If people feel that they have no say; that policy is being made over their heads; that the law is a scourge rather than a protection, they will eventually revolt. As Edmund Burke said: 'People crushed by law have no hopes but from power. If laws are their enemies, they will be enemies to laws.'

How to build affection for international institutions is not just a European conundrum. It is a problem for the United Nations, for the IMF, for the World Bank, for the World Trade Organization. People accept intellectually the need to pool sovereignty in Europe, as they accept the need for a World Trade Organization. But they feel little affection or loyalty towards the institutional structure created for the purpose. Critics preach endlessly about the need to create democratic legitimacy, as if leaders and élites were obstinately refusing to face the problem.

I hope the issues *are* now starting to be addressed. That, after all, is a major theme of the work of the Convention being chaired by Valéry Giscard d'Estaing. Working out how to fix these problems is, of course, much more of a challenge than identifying them in the first place. It is clear that we have to get away from the impenetrable jargon and lengthy discussions about labyrinthine institutional structures. We have to talk more about subjects that *really* interest people, and less about the minutiae of comitology or qualified majority voting.

It is a paradox of our time that, while there are more nations in Europe than ever before, it is also more widely accepted than ever that in the modern world those nations need to pool their sovereignty if only in response to the process of globalization. That is why most of these states are already members of the European Union or hoping to join it. The problem is how to control and legitimize the structures created for this purpose. There is no European 'demos' nor, for reasons of language and culture, is there likely to be one. So if we want to increase democratic control we have to find better ways of connecting the national political institutions with the supranational ones.

This book suggests some ways in which that might be achieved, and I warmly welcome it.

The Rt Hon Christopher Patten European Commissioner for External Relations
July 2002

GENERAL EDITORS' PREFACE

Accountability and legitimacy are perennial concerns of the EU, and no more so than at present. The very future of the EU is being considered at the Laeken Convention, the conclusions of which will shape the discussions leading to the intergovernmental conference in 2004. Accountability and legitimacy feature prominently in these debates. The addition of this thought-provoking, interdisciplinary collection of essays to the series is, therefore, timely.

The editors have done an excellent job in bringing together contributions that relate to many of the major areas of the EU. Part I deals with accountability and legitimacy in relation to the institutions and decision-making structure of the EU. It is particularly helpful for this discussion to range over decision-making under the Second and Third Pillars, as well as under the Community Pillar. It is equally important that the analysis includes topics such as the judicial architecture and the European Central Bank, reflecting as it does the centrality of the Community Courts and the ECB to the operation of the EU as whole. The discussion in Part II shifts to issues of constitutionalism, and includes topical issues such as the delimitation of Community competences, the development of an EU Constitution, and the rule of law. The significance of the EU Charter of Rights, and the relationship between traditional rights and social and economic rights, is the subject of Part III. The penultimate section, Part IV, focuses upon issues of accountability and legitimacy as they arise in areas such as social policy, Economic and Monetary Union and the Commission's Governance White Paper. The last part of the book is devoted to the implications of enlargement, both in general terms and more specifically for free movement, the management of the Community's borders, and immigration.

This book will be of enduring interest to all those concerned with the continuing debate about accountability and legitimacy within the EU.

Paul Craig
Gráinne de Búrca
November 2002

PREFACE

This book examines from an interdisciplinary perspective the accountability and legitimacy deficit from which the European Union is now widely thought to suffer. It is based on the papers presented at a conference entitled 'Legitimacy and accountability in the European Union after Nice' organized by the Institute of European Law, University of Birmingham, in July 2001. There was not room in the conference programme to cover the theme from more than a limited number of angles, so several additional contributions were subsequently commissioned in an attempt to ensure that the book would be properly rounded.

Our aim was not to produce a textbook, but to compile a collection of authoritative yet accessible analyses of the general theme from a variety of perspectives. We did not ask contributors to range outside their specialisms, but to address a multidisciplinary audience from within their specialisms. These include political science, law, economics and geography. We hope the book will be of interest to anyone concerned with the future of Europe, from students and academics, whatever their discipline, to policy-makers, journalists and perhaps even the general reader. Because several of the chapters deal with legal topics, numbered footnotes have been used throughout rather than the Harvard referencing system, which can be hard to adapt to academic writing about the law. However, the book is not aimed exclusively—or even mainly—at lawyers. It does not therefore contain some of the standard furniture of law books, such as tables of cases and legislation.

We would like to express our thanks to the contributors for agreeing, in spite of their many other commitments, to address the overall theme of the book from their own particular perspectives. We would also like to thank Commissioner Patten for writing a foreword to the collection at a particularly busy time. We are grateful to Mohammad Idriss, Research Associate at the School of Law in Birmingham, and Nadene Bryan, Secretary to the Institute of European Law at Birmingham, for their help in getting the typescript ready for publication. Finally, we wish to acknowledge the support of those who sponsored the 2001 conference which constituted the prototype for the book: Martineau Johnson, solicitors; the Jean Monnet

European Centre of Excellence, University of Birmingham; and the University Association for Contemporary European Studies.

AA DW
Birmingham, May 2002

TABLE OF CONTENTS

LIST OF CONTRIBUTORS

Fabian Amtenbrink is Lecturer in European and Economic Law in the Faculty of Law, Rijksuniversiteit Groningen.

Anthony Arnull is Professor of European Law and Director of the Institute of European Law, University of Birmingham.

Judy Batt is Senior Lecturer in Central and East European Politics in the Centre for Russian and East European Studies, European Research Institute, University of Birmingham, and a member of the Committee of Advisers on Transfrontier Cooperation of the Council of Europe.

Sophie Boyron is Senior Lecturer in the School of Law, University of Birmingham.

Alan Dashwood, Barrister, is Professor of European Law and Fellow of Sidney Sussex College, Cambridge.

Gráinne de Búrca is Professor of European Union Law, European University Institute, Florence.

Fiorella Dell'Olio is Research Officer in the Department of Politics and International Relations, University of Oxford.

Bruno de Witte is Professor of European Union Law, European University Institute, Florence.

Peter Dyrberg is Head of the Legal Service, EFTA Surveillance Authority.

Evelyn Ellis is Professor of Public Law, University of Birmingham.

Brigid Fowler is Honorary Research Fellow at the Centre for Russian and East European Studies, European Research Institute, University of Birmingham.

Lothar Funk is Head of the Industrial Relations and Trade Union Economics Section at the Institut der deutschen Wirtschaft, Cologne, and lectures in economics at the University of Trier.

Laurence W Gormley, Barrister, is Professor of European Law and Jean Monnet Professor, Rijksuniversiteit Groningen, and Visiting Professor, Universität Bremen and Katholieke Universiteit Leuven.

Christophe Hillion is Deputy-Director of the Centre for European Legal Studies at the Faculty of Law, University of Cambridge.

Adrian Hyde-Price is Professor of Politics and International Relations in the Department of Politics, University of Leicester.

FG Jacobs, QC is an Advocate General at the Court of Justice of the European Communities.

Julian Lonbay is Senior Lecturer in the School of Law, University of Birmingham.

Ronald L Martin is Professor of Economic Geography and Professorial Fellow of St Catharine's College in the University of Cambridge. He is also a Fellow of the Cambridge-MIT Institute.

Jeremy McBride is Reader in International Human Rights Law, University of Birmingham and consultant on human rights to the Council of Europe and the Organization for Security and Co-operation in Europe.

Anand Menon is Professor of European Politics and Director of the European Research Institute, University of Birmingham.

Jörg Monar is Professor in Contemporary European Studies, Jean Monnet Professor and Co-Director of the Sussex European Institute, University of Sussex.

Andy W Mullineux is Professor of Global Finance in the School of Business, University of Birmingham.

Nanette Neuwahl is Professor of European Union Law, University of Liverpool and University of Montreal, where she is currently holder of the Jean Monnet Chair.

Cillian Ryan is Senior Lecturer in the Department of Economics and Director of the Jean Monnet European Centre of Excellence, University of Birmingham.

Erika Szyszczak is Jean Monnet Professor of European Law *ad personam*, Professor of European Competition and Labour Law and Director of the Centre for European Law and Integration, University of Leicester.

John A Usher is Salvesen Professor of European Institutions and Honorary Jean Monnet Professor of European Law in the University of Edinburgh, where he is Director of the Europa Institute.

Frank Vibert is Director and Co-Founder of the European Policy Forum.

Stephen Weatherill is Jacques Delors Professor of European Law and Fellow of Somerville College, Oxford.

Steven Wheatley is Lecturer in the School of Law, University of Liverpool.

Daniel Wincott is Senior Lecturer in the Department of Political Science and International Studies, European Research Institute, University of Birmingham.

LIST OF ABBREVIATIONS

AC	Appeal Cases
ACE	Applicant Countries Eurobarometer
AFSJ	Area of freedom, security and justice
AG	Advocate General
APEC	Asia-Pacific Economic Cooperation; Asia-Pacific Economic Cooperation Forum
Art	Article
ASEAN	Association of South East Asian Nations
CAP	Common Agricultural Policy
CEE	Central and Eastern Europe/European
CEECs	Central and Eastern European countries
C4ISR	Command, control, communications, computers intelligence, surveillance and reconnaissance
CFI	Court of First Instance of the European Communities
CFSP	Common Foreign and Security Policy
CIREA	Centre d'information, de réflexion et d'échange en matière d'asile (Centre for Information, Discussion and Exchange on Asylum)
CIREFI	Centre d'information, de réflexion et d'échanges en matière de franchissement des frontières et d'immigration (Centre for Information, Discussion and Exchange on the Crossing of Frontiers and Immigration)
CJTF	Combined Joint Task Force
CLP	Current Legal Problems
CMLR	Common Market Law Reports
CMLRev	Common Market Law Review
COREPER	Committee of Permanent Representatives
COREU	Réseau telex des correspondants européens (Telex Network of European Correspondents)
Court of Justice	Court of Justice of the European Communities
CSCE	Conference on Security and Cooperation in Europe
CYELS	Cambridge Yearbook of European Legal Studies
Dir	Directive
Dec	Decision
EAEC	European Atomic Energy Community (EURATOM)
EBLR	European Business Law Review
EC	European Community

ECB	European Central Bank
ECHR	European Convention on Human Rights
ECR	European Court Reports
ECSC	European Coal and Steel Community
EEC	European Economic Community
EES	European Employment Strategy
EFA Rev	European Foreign Affairs Review
EHRR	European Human Rights Reports
EIoP	European Integration online Papers
EJIL	European Journal of International Law
ELJ	European Law Journal
ELRev	European Law Review
EMS	European Monetary System
EMU	Economic and Monetary Union
EPC	European Political Cooperation
EPL	European Public Law
ERM	Exchange Rate Mechanism
ESCB	European System of Central Banks
ESDI	European Security and Defence Identity
ESDP	European Security and Defence Policy
EU	European Union
EUMC	European Union Military Committee
EUMM	European Union Monitoring Mission
EUMS	European Union Military Staff
EUSA	European Union Studies Association
FRY	Federal Republic of Yugoslavia
FYROM	Former Yugoslav Republic of Macedonia
GAC	General Affairs Council
GATS	General Agreement on Trade in Services
GATT	General Agreement on Tariffs and Trade
GDP	Gross domestic product
HICP	Harmonized Index for Consumer Prices
HRLJ	Human Rights Law Journal
HRQ	Human Rights Quarterly
ICJ Rep	International Court of Justice Reports
ICLQ	International and Comparative Law Quarterly
IGC	Intergovernmental conference
ILJ	Industrial Law Journal
ILM	International Legal Materials
IRAs	Independent European regulatory agencies
JCMS	Journal of Common Market Studies
JHA	Justice and home affairs

JEPP	Journal of European Public Policy
JESP	Journal of European Social Policy
LI	Liberal Intergovernmentalist
LIEI	Legal Issues of European Integration
MEP	Member of the European Parliament
Mercosur	Mercado Común del Sur (Southern Cone Common Market)
MJ	Maastricht Journal of European and Comparative Law
MLR	Modern Law Review
NAFTA	North American Free Trade Agreement
NATO	North Atlantic Treaty Organization
NGO	Non-governmental organization
NAPs	National Action Plans
NJB	Nederlands Juristenblad
OCA	Optimum currency area
OHIM	Office for Harmonization in the Internal Market (Trade Marks and Designs)
OJ	Official Journal
OJLS	Oxford Journal of Legal Studies
OMC	Open method of coordination
OSCE	Organization for Security and Cooperation in Europe
PHARE	Pologne-Hongrie: aide à la restructuration économique (Action plan for coordinated aid to Poland and Hungary)
PJCCM	Police and Judicial Cooperation in Criminal Matters
PL	Public Law
PPS	Purchasing power standards
PSC	Political and Security Committee
PTA	Policy Target Agreement
QMV	Qualified majority vote; qualified majority voting
Reg	Regulation
SCR	Supreme Court Reports
SEA	Single European Act
SIS	Schengen Information System
SPA	Social Policy Agenda
TACIS	Technical Assistance to the Commonwealth of Independent States
TARGET	Trans-European Automated Real-Time Gross Settlement European Transfer System
TEU	Treaty on European Union (Maastricht Treaty)
TRIMS	(Agreement on) Trade Related Investment Measures
TRIPS	(Agreement on) Trade Related Aspects of Intellectual Property Rights
WEU	Western European Union
WTO	World Trade Organization
YEL	Yearbook of European Law

Introduction: The European Union's Accountability and Legitimacy Deficit

Anthony Arnull

The constitutional and political health of the European Union

The rejection by the Irish people of the Treaty of Nice in June 2001 underlined the extent to which the European Union has become disconnected from its citizens. Ireland seems, at least to an outsider, to be one of the Member States which has gained most from Union membership and all the main political parties supported ratification of the Treaty, yet nearly 54 per cent of those who took part in the referendum voted against it. The turnout was admittedly very low and the precise reasons for the outcome were difficult to establish.[1] Nonetheless, the result seemed symptomatic of a profound malaise. It does not just afflict the European Union: many domestic political institutions seem to have lost their capacity to mobilize and inspire; the WTO is increasingly contested. Be that as it may, it is a malaise to which the Union is particularly vulnerable because of a widespread feeling that it is insufficiently *accountable* and lacks *legitimacy*.

Accountability was identified by the Nolan Committee as one of seven principles applicable to all aspects of public life. That meant, according to the Committee, that 'Holders of public office are accountable for their decisions and actions to the public and must submit themselves to whatever scrutiny is

---

[1] See B Laffan, 'The Nice Treaty: the Irish vote', http://www.notre-europe.asso.fr/ Quoideneuf.html. Cf the National Declaration by Ireland and the Declaration of the European Council, both annexed to the Conclusions of the Seville European Council, 21 and 22 June 2002. The Taoiseach (Prime Minister of Ireland) announced at Seville that his Government intended to hold a second referendum on the Treaty in the autumn of 2002. The Irish electorate approved the Treaty on 19 October 2002.

appropriate to their office'.[2] Similarly, in the context of the EU the European Commission has singled out accountability as one of five principles underpinning good governance, observing: 'Roles in the legislative and executive processes need to be clearer. Each of the EU institutions must explain and take responsibility for what it does in Europe. But there is also a need for greater clarity and responsibility from Member States and all those involved in developing and implementing EU policy at whatever level'.[3] Neither of those statements really amounts to a definition, but each reflects what Mulgan calls the 'the original or core sense' of accountability, 'that associated with the process of being called "to account" to some authority for one's actions'.[4]

But the term may also be understood more broadly. Oliver comments: 'Accountability has been said to entail being liable to be required to give an account or explanation of actions and, where appropriate, to suffer the consequences, take the blame or undertake to put matters right if it should appear that errors have been made'.[5] She points out that accountability is 'closely related to responsibility, transparency, answerability and responsiveness, and these terms are often used interchangeably'.[6] The term responsibility was used by the Committee of Independent Experts in the famous final paragraph of its first report, which led to the resignation of the European Commission in March 1999. The Committee observed:

The responsibility of individual Commissioners, or of the Commission as a body, cannot be a vague idea, a concept which in practice proves unrealistic. It must go hand in hand with an ongoing process designed to increase awareness of that responsibility. Each individual must feel accountable for the measures he or she manages.

The Committee described a sense of responsibility as 'essential', but found 'a growing reluctance among the members of the hierarchy to acknowledge

---

[2] First Report of the Committee on Standards in Public Life chaired by Lord Nolan (Cm 2850-I), 14.

[3] European Governance: A White Paper, COM(2001)428, 25 July 2001. Cf the First Report of the Committee of Independent Experts on Allegations Regarding Fraud, Mismanagement and Nepotism in the European Commission (15 March 1999) para 9.3.3.

[4] See R Mulgan, ' "Accountability": an ever-expanding concept' (2000) 78 Public Administration 555.

[5] D Oliver, *Government in the United Kingdom* (1991) 22.

[6] ibid. Cf Mulgan (n 4 above) 558. The Committee of Independent Experts drew a distinction between 'accountability' and 'political responsibility' in its Second Report on Reform of the Commission (10 September 1999) para 7.14.1.

their responsibility'.[7] Lord calls this sense of responsibility 'internal accountability'.[8]

There are a number of channels by which accountability in its extended meaning may be achieved.[9] Some may be more appropriate than others in particular contexts. One channel is accountability to politicians, whose scrutiny will be politically motivated. Another is accountability to the general public. For those who are elected, this means accepting the verdict of the voters. But not all public bodies are elected and even those that are must be accountable between elections. This implies that ordinary people have access to the information they need to hold to account those to whom power and resources have been entrusted in the general good.[10] It may also imply that institutional and decision-making structures should be kept as simple as possible. Otherwise, it may become hard to present issues comprehensibly and decision-makers may find themselves in 'the unhappy predicament of being submitted to unfocused and uninformed criticism by press and public opinion'.[11] A third form of accountability is legal accountability to the courts, an aspect of the rule of law. This channel may be used to require a public body 'to explain and justify its actions in legal terms in the courts and to make amends if found to have transgressed'.[12] Legal accountability typically entails the possible imposition of coercive remedies and sanctions. Oliver sums up by saying that accountability is about establishing a framework:

within which public bodies are forced to seek to promote the public interest and compelled to justify their actions on those terms or in other constitutionally acceptable terms (justice, humanity, equity); to modify policies if they should turn out not to have been well conceived; and to make amends if mistakes and errors of judgment have been made.

The concept of legitimacy is equally elusive. It is useful to distinguish between formal legitimacy and social legitimacy, a wider notion.[13] The former is concerned with the extent to which all the applicable legal

---

[7] n 3 above, para 9.4.25.

[8] C Lord, *Democracy in the European Union* (1998) 80. See also Mulgan (n 4 above) 556.

[9] See Oliver (n 5 above) 23–28. Cf Lord (n 8 above) ch 3. Additional or extended mechanisms of accountability are discussed in C Scott, 'Accountability in the regulatory state' (2000) 27 Journal of Law and Society 38.

[10] cf the Second Report of the Committee of Independent Experts (n 6 above) para 7.6.3.

[11] Second Report of the Committee of Independent Experts, ibid para 7.14.3. Cf Lord (n 8 above) 94.

[12] Oliver (n 5 above) 26.

[13] See JHH Weiler, *The Constitution of Europe* (1999) 77–86.

requirements were satisfied when the entity in question was set up, the latter with the extent to which the allocation and exercise of authority within it commands general acceptance. The formal legitimacy of the EU is unimpeachable: it is based on a series of treaties validly entered into by the High Contracting Parties, each of which they have ratified in accordance with their own constitutional requirements. Indeed, it may have been assumed until relatively recently that the formal legitimacy of the EU (and, before that, the European Community) was enough. But it is now almost universally recognized that formal legitimacy, while essential, is not sufficient. A healthy Union also requires social legitimacy if the fruits of its decision-making processes are to enjoy broad societal acceptance.

Because it is a more nebulous concept than formal legitimacy, social legitimacy is more difficult to acquire and retain. In its White Paper on European Governance, the Commission acknowledged that 'many Europeans feel alienated from the Union's work'. That feeling, it said, 'reflects particular tensions and uncertainty about what the Union is and what it aspires to become, about its geographical boundaries, its political objectives and the way these powers are shared with the Member States'.[14] It may well be unlikely that people will ever identify as closely with the Union as they do with more familiar domestic institutions that can draw on a developed sense of social cohesion and loyalty. Indeed, the Union is pledged to respect the national identities of its Member States[15] and to respect their history, culture and traditions.[16] But if the social cohesion of increasingly pluralistic States can be exaggerated, so Europe's common cultural background and shared historical experiences should not be dismissed. In that context, the process of working together, within the framework of the EU Treaties, to address common problems may in time serve to reinforce the Union's legitimacy by inculcating a sense of shared destiny and making people more willing to assent to the burdens the Union will sometimes need to impose on them.[17] That outcome is unlikely to materialize if the Union is widely perceived as insufficiently accountable. To counter that perception, the Union needs to do more to involve the public in articulating its

---

[14] n 3 above, 5. Cf G de Búrca, 'The quest for legitimacy in the European Union' (1996) 59 MLR 349.

[15] See Art 6(3) TEU.

[16] Preamble, TEU.

[17] See JHH Weiler, 'Does Europe need a constitution? Reflections on demos, telos and the German Maastricht decision' (1995) 1 ELJ 219; J Habermas, 'Remarks on Dieter Grimm's "Does Europe need a constitution?"' (1995) 1 ELJ 303; Lord (n 8 above) ch 4.

underlying values and formulating its substantive policies. But enhancing what is sometimes called the Union's 'input legitimacy' in this way must not be allowed to jeopardize its 'output legitimacy', that is, its capacity to achieve its objectives. The balance can be a difficult one to strike.[18]

In the first of the five parts into which this book is divided, the Union's institutions and decision-making processes are considered. What mechanisms should the Union employ to determine when and how to exercise its powers? How open should its decision-making be? What is the right relationship between accountability and making sure the Union is equipped to carry out its tasks effectively? To what extent should the uniformity which the European Community traditionally sought now give way to greater flexibility? How should the Union's two Courts and the European Central Bank be structured? The subject of Part II is 'Constitutionalism and the future of Europe'. Would giving the Union a formal constitution help make it more accountable and legitimate? What is the best way of allocating powers between the Union and its Member States? How can respect for democracy and the rule of law in the Union best be ensured? Part III looks at the protection of fundamental rights and social rights in the Union and Part IV at the 'new governance' agenda, which is concerned with finding new ways of reconciling competing policy priorities. Part V is concerned with the challenge of enlargement and the movement of people in the Union of the 21st century. The questions addressed in each part of the book are difficult ones on which people, however reasonable and well-informed, may differ. If the Union is to be truly accountable and legitimate, they must feel that they have had an opportunity to participate in the process of finding the answers, even if they do not always agree with them.

The origins of the Union's accountability and legitimacy deficit

What are the origins of the Union's current accountability and legitimacy deficit? The answer lies, at least in part, in the changed climate in which the Union now operates. Today's Europe bears little resemblance to the Europe of the 1950s which gave birth to the Union's precursor, the European

---

[18] cf K Lenaerts and A Verhoeven, 'Institutional balance as a guarantee for democracy in EU governance' in C Joerges and R Dehousse (eds), *Good Governance in Europe's Integrated Market* (2002) 35, 49.

Community. There are obvious political differences. Then, the Second World War was fresh in people's memories and the Cold War made a new conflagration seem a real possibility. The need to avoid further conflict between the countries of Europe that remained outside the Soviet sphere of influence, and to enable their economies to compete with that of the United States, had an obvious resonance. Moreover, the pre-war spirit of deference to those in authority had not yet broken down, so that grand schemes devised by politicians and civil servants could be put into effect without worrying too much about the reaction of ordinary people.[19] It is also true to say that, of the three original Communities, the Coal and Steel Community and the Atomic Energy Community were rather technical and limited in scope. The Treaty establishing the European Economic Community (as it was originally called) was much more ambitious, but even its authors may not have foreseen quite how vigorously it would develop.

That backdrop is apparent in the system put in place by the EEC Treaty. A central role in shaping and policing the common market was to be played by the appointed Commission. Although there was to be an Assembly (not then called the European Parliament), it would not initially be directly elected and its role would be purely advisory and supervisory. Notwithstanding the scope of the legislative powers conferred on the Council, that institution was not required to meet in public or to reveal how its members had voted, even after the anticipated transition to qualified majority voting. Acts adopted by the institutions were only to a limited extent subject to judicial review at the suit of private parties, who were apparently to have no right to challenge important categories of Community act, however adverse their effects and however doubtful their legality. By contrast, the Member States, the Council and the Commission (though not, significantly, the Assembly) would have unlimited standing to challenge all Community acts.

Twenty-first century Europe is quite different. The Union is on the verge of an unprecedented enlargement which will bring in many of the countries of central and eastern Europe. The prospect of healing the continent's post-war division would have been unthinkable to the authors of the original Community Treaties. The enlargement process offers the Union an historic opportunity, but is at the same time fraught with danger because of the immature political and legal institutions of many of the candidate States and their relatively underdeveloped economies. If the Union is to be account-

---

[19]   See P Craig, 'The nature of the Community: integration, democracy, and legitimacy' in P Craig and G de Búrca (eds), *The Evolution of EU Law* (1999) 1, 5–7.

able to the citizens of those States and retain legitimacy in their eyes, it will have to show that it can help them achieve Western levels of prosperity and respond to their particular concerns.

Meanwhile, in Western Europe memories of the Second World War and even of the Cold War have faded. Developments in science and technology have, as elsewhere, transformed the economic, political and social landscape. Many of the Union's citizens now enjoy unprecedented prosperity. People have become less willing to accept passively government by unaccountable élites. Public institutions and those who hold public office have become subject to an increasing level of critical scrutiny. People have become more litigious. The implications of these changes for the process of European integration began to emerge during the Maastricht ratification process. Ordinary people had started to pay more attention to the European Community with the growth of qualified majority voting and the advent of the single market programme in the 1980s. However, that programme, though ambitious, was limited by the scope of the Treaty to which it was designed at long last to give effect. The Treaty on European Union signed at Maastricht in February 1992, with its arrangements for economic and monetary union and its creation of a European Union subsuming the existing Communities into a new entity with a much broader substantive ambit, represented a quantum leap, but it was a leap with which many ordinary people were uncomfortable.

The degree of public unease became clear during the exceptionally difficult ratification process which the Treaty underwent. It was rejected by the people of Denmark in a referendum less than six months after it was signed and later secured only a narrow majority in a referendum held in France. It was the subject of legal challenges in the national courts of the United Kingdom,[20] Germany[21] and Denmark.[22] Although those challenges were unsuccessful and the Danish people were persuaded to vote in favour of the Treaty in a second referendum in May 1993, it had become apparent that there were widespread public misgivings about the nature of the Union and an unwillingness to entrust the continued governance of Europe to the élites by whom it had hitherto been dominated.

---

[20] *R v Secretary of State for Foreign and Commonwealth Affairs, ex parte Lord Rees-Mogg* [1993] 3 CMLR 101.

[21] *Brunner v European Union Treaty* [1994] 1 CMLR 57.

[22] *Carlsen and Others v Prime Minister Rasmussen* [1999] 3 CMLR 854.

The quest for accountability and legitimacy

The lesson took time to sink in. The failure of the European Commission, which took office in 1995 under the Presidency of Jacques Santer, to recognize the change in climate contributed to its collective resignation in 1999 amid allegations of fraud, mismanagement and nepotism. But the Commission is now engaged in a process of internal reform and in its White Paper on European Governance[23] it made a number of recommendations on how to enhance democracy in Europe and increase the legitimacy of the Union's institutions. The Member States, too, are taking steps to make the Union more accountable and to improve its legitimacy. At Amsterdam, the Treaty on European Union was amended so that it now declares[24] that the Union 'is founded on the principles of liberty, democracy, respect for human rights and fundamental freedoms, and the rule of law…' A procedure was introduced for suspending the Treaty rights of Member States found to be in 'serious and persistent breach' of any of those principles.[25] Moreover, the position of the European Parliament under a legislative procedure introduced at Maastricht was improved, so that, where the procedure applies, it is now a genuine co-legislator with the Council.[26] At the Cologne European Council in June 1999, the protection of fundamental rights was identified as an 'indispensable prerequisite' to the Union's legitimacy. Accordingly, the decision was taken to establish a charter of fundamental rights 'in order to make their overriding importance and relevance more visible to the Union's citizens'. The Charter of Fundamental Rights of the European Union was solemnly proclaimed by the European Parliament, the Council and the Commission in Nice in December 2000.[27]

The Treaty of Nice itself, signed in February 2001, was designed essentially to make various institutional changes considered necessary in view of the forthcoming enlargement of the Union. However, in a Declaration on the Future of the Union, the Member States called for 'a deeper and wider debate' on four questions in particular:

(a) how to establish and monitor a more precise delimitation of powers between the European Union and the Member States;

---

[23] n 3 above.

[24] Art 6(1).

[25] See Art 7 TEU; Art 309 EC; Art 204 EAEC.

[26] See Art 251 EC.

[27] [2000] OJ C364/20.

(b) the status of the Charter of Fundamental Rights;

(c) simplifying the Treaties to make them clearer and easier to understand; and

(d) the role of national parliaments.

The Member States recognized 'the need to improve and to monitor the democratic legitimacy and transparency of the Union and its institutions, in order to bring them closer to the citizens of the Member States'. They agreed to convene a new intergovernmental conference (IGC) in 2004 in order to agree the necessary changes to the Treaties.

At its meeting in Laeken in December 2001, the European Council took the process forward by issuing a further declaration on the future of the Union. The Laeken Declaration sketched out a series of additional questions prompted by those identified at Nice, each of them touching the account-ability and legitimacy of the Union. The innovative step was taken of establishing a Convention with the task of paving the way for the 2004 IGC by considering the key issues raised by the future development of the Union. Modelled on the body which drew up the Union's Charter of Fundamental Rights, the Convention was to be chaired by a former French President assisted by two Vice-Chairmen. It would also comprise one representative of each Head of State or Government, two members of each national parliament, 16 members of the European Parliament and two representatives of the Commission. Candidate countries would be represented in the same way as current Member States, although they would not be entitled to block any consensus which might emerge among the latter. Others, such as the European Ombudsman and representatives of the Economic and Social Committee and the Committee of the Regions, would be invited to attend as observers. The Convention's final document, to be produced in 2003, would provide a starting point for discussions at the IGC, where the final decisions would be taken.

The Nice and Laeken Declarations put the future of the Union and its accountability and legitimacy at the top of the political agenda. However, it seems doubtful whether, as the Union embarks on the most ambitious process of enlargement it has ever undertaken, it will be possible to settle these matters definitively in 2004. As a result, the debate is likely to preoccupy everyone with an interest in the Union's constitutional and political health for many years to come.

Part I

Institutions and Decision-making

It is crucial to the Union's accountability and legitimacy that its decision-making processes and ultimate objectives should be properly understood. Moreover, the institutions of the Union need to be responsive to the wishes of those affected by the measures they adopt. This means allowing people access to information about the reasons underlying such measures. Where the normal decision-making mechanisms become deadlocked due to a divergence of views among the Member States, it is possible to envisage that some of them might use the Treaty procedures to move forward on their own. However, a potential drawback of that approach is that it could have the effect of undermining the Union's cohesion and adding undue complexity. It also needs to be recognized that the drive to enhance the Union's accountability and legitimacy could compromise the ability of some of its institutions to carry out their tasks effectively. This raises the question whether accountability and legitimacy as commonly understood are the most important criteria by which to judge the Union.

The Court of Justice played a pivotal role in the rigorous development of the European Community and has become an essential component of the Union's institutional framework. In 1988, a Court of First Instance was established to help reduce the workload of the Court of Justice. However, that workload has continued to grow to the point where the rule of law is now threatened. This was recognized by the Member States at Nice, where important changes to the relevant Treaty provisions were made. The judicial architecture of the Union may as a result be on the verge of a period of profound change. Whether it emerges better equipped to cope with the demands which will be made of it remains to be seen.

The capacity of a political system to increase the prosperity of its people is another important component of its claim to legitimacy. The Union is more likely to be regarded as legitimate by its citizens if it can make—and be seen to make—a decisive difference to employment rates and the competitiveness of the European economy. Absolutely fundamental in this context is the success of Economic and Monetary Union. The European Central Bank occupies a powerful position in that process and must demonstrate not just technical competence but also that it is responsive to political demands about the issues to which it should attach priority.

Issues of Decision-making in the European Union after Nice

Alan Dashwood

Introduction

The shape and substance of this chapter have been inspired not so much by the Treaty of Nice itself as by what may be termed 'the post-Nice process'. The debate that was invited by the Declaration of Nice on the Future of the Union,[1] and given a more substantial agenda by the Declaration of Laeken,[2] gathered momentum within and around the Convention brought together under the chairmanship of Mr Valéry Giscard d'Estaing. The developments in the law and practice of decision-making which are discussed here are thought to be interesting in themselves, but even more so because they shed light on issues at the heart of that debate, and about which the IGC, scheduled to foregather in 2004, will have to make up its mind. Those issues are:

- the possibility of abolishing the distinction between the Community and the Union;
- the possibility of modifying the Union's 'pillar structure'; and
- ways of enhancing the legitimacy of the Union order.

Towards an integrated Union structure

An integral Union would clearly be one with its own set of institutions and its own legal personality. These are necessary but not, of course,

---

[1] Declaration No 23 annexed to the Final Act of the Conference.
[2] SN 273/01. See chapter by Vibert in this volume.

sufficient conditions for the subsumption of the Communities into the Union.

Whose decision-making institutions?

In the period following the signature of the Maastricht Treaty, when commentators were struggling to explicate the new dispensation, it was sometimes said that the European Union had only one organ it could call its own, namely the European Council: the 'institutions' in the sense of Article 7 EC, which are listed in Article 5 TEU, could be 'borrowed' when action was being taken for the purposes of Title V or Title VI of the latter Treaty, but they retained the legal character of institutions of the European Communities. That view drew plausibility from the fact that the TEU did not expressly amend the references found in Article 1 and Article 9 of the Merger Treaty to, respectively, '[a] Council of the European Communities' and '[a] Commission of the European Communities'. It went with a conception of the Union as amounting to little more than a framework for enhanced cooperation between the Member States.[3]

The alternative view is that institutions 'born' under the European Community Treaties have been 'legally adopted' by the European Union. The transfer of the institutions to the Union is consistent with a conception of the latter as a complex constitutional entity distinct from its Member States, into which the three Communities have been integrated as a distinct sub-order.

There is textual support for that view in the drafting of Article 3 and Article 5 TEU. Article 3 says '[t]he Union shall be *served* by a single institutional framework' (emphasis added), not an apt choice of words if intended merely to give permission for the use of institutions regarded as belonging to the Communities. According to Article 5, the institutions there listed 'shall exercise their powers under the conditions and for the purposes provided, *on the one hand*, by the provisions of the Treaties establishing the European Communities… and, *on the other hand*, by the other provisions of

---

[3] An early exponent of the 'loan' theory was C Timmermans in P de Schoutheete and J-V Louis (eds), *L'Union européenne après Maastricht* (1992) 49. See also M Pechstein and C Koenig, *Die Europäische Union* (1998). For a contrary view, see B de Witte, 'The pillar structure and the nature of the European Union: Greek temple or French gothic cathedral?' in T Heukels, N Blokker and M Brus (eds), *The European Union After Amsterdam* (1998) 57, and the references there cited. The writer originally inclined to the 'loan' theory, but does so no longer: see AM Arnull, AA Dashwood, MG Ross and DA Wyatt, *Wyatt and Dashwood's European Union Law* (4th edn, 2000) (hereinafter 'Wyatt & Dashwood') ch 8.

this Treaty' (emphasis added). As the writer has noted elsewhere, the grammatical construction of the Article places the powers derived by the institutions from the TEU and those derived from the Community Treaties on the same footing.[4] If Articles 1 and 9 of the Merger Treaty are read in the light of those provisions, the intention of the constitution-making authority seems clear: to endow the Union as such with a single set of institutions, whose functioning depends on the particular arrangements applicable pursuant to the Treaty under which they are acting.

Further support can be found in the existence of powers exercisable by the institutions, not for the specific purposes of the European Communities or of Title V or Title VI TEU, but at the level of the Union itself (in the customary architectural jargon, powers located within the 'pediment', rather than under one of the 'pillars'). The original examples of such powers were provided for by what is now Article 48 TEU, laying down a common procedure for the amendment of 'the Treaties on which the Union is founded',[5] and Article 49 TEU, laying down a common procedure for accession to the Union. A significant addition by the Treaty of Amsterdam was Article 7 TEU, which establishes machinery enabling action to be taken against individual Member States in order to enforce compliance with the fundamental political values of the Union stated in Article 6(1) TEU. The machinery is to be reinforced under the Treaty of Nice.[6]

The Council has expressly acknowledged its 'adoption' by the Union by officially renaming itself 'Council of the European Union'.[7] Its example has not been followed by the Commission, which retains the official designation 'Commission of the European Communities', while favouring the style 'European Commission'—a touch grandiose, perhaps—in less formal contexts.

An interesting case is that of the European Court of Justice, which continues to call itself 'Court of Justice of the European Communities'. It might seem justified in so doing, since that designation appears in the very provision, Article 46, which defines the Court's strictly circumscribed

---

[4] Wyatt & Dashwood, 178–179.

[5] The 'foundational' Treaties are not specifically identified. They comprise, presumably, the Community Treaties, as amended, and the TEU, together with any surviving fragments of other amending Treaties such as the Merger Treaty and the Single European Act.

[6] See the new para (1) of Art 7, which will enable preventive action to be taken if it is determined that a clear risk exists of a serious breach by a Member State of the Art 6(1) principles.

[7] Council Dec 93/591 [1993] OJ L281/18.

jurisdiction under the TEU. The relevant passage reads: 'The provisions of the Treaty establishing the European Community, the Treaty establishing the European Coal and Steel Community and the Treaty establishing the European Atomic Energy Community concerning the powers of *the Court of Justice of the European Communities* and the exercise of those powers shall apply only to the following provisions of this Treaty...' (emphasis added). How can such wording be reconciled with that of Articles 3 and 5 TEU which include the Court of Justice within the single institutional framework serving the Union? The explanation, it is submitted, lies in the particular drafting technique employed in Article 46. The Article refers to the application to certain TEU provisions of the provisions governing the powers of the Court which are contained in the EC, ECSC and EAEC Treaties. Since those Treaties pre-date the establishment of the Union, and each is concerned exclusively with the particular Community it establishes and organizes, it would have been inappropriate, indeed inaccurate, in the context of Article 46 to speak of 'The Court of Justice of the European Union'. No inference can be drawn from the status of the Court under the former dispensation of the European Communities, which is recalled here, as to its status under the new constitutional order which the TEU has brought into being. Accordingly, in the writer's respectful view, a name change for the Court of Justice is called for, no less than in the case of the other institutions mentioned in Article 5 TEU.

The latest development is the inclusion in the text of the Treaty of Nice of express allusions to the institutions as belonging to the Union. One example is found in the second recital of the preamble to the Treaty, which speaks of the signatories' desire 'to complete the process started by the Treaty of Amsterdam of preparing *the institutions of the European Union* to function in an enlarged Union' (emphasis added). Another is in Article 24 TEU, which is about the negotiation and conclusion of international agreements in second and third pillar matters (its effect regarding the issue as to whether the Union has international legal personality is considered below). A new paragraph (6), to be added to Article 24, provides that the agreements in question 'shall be binding on *the institutions of the Union*' (emphasis added).

Those explicit references in the new Treaty are a clear indication that the institutions are thought of as the Union's by the constitution-making authority itself. Taken together with the considerations previously mentioned, they appear to settle the issue.

Legal personality and decision-making

There is no provision in the TEU stating that the European Union shall have legal personality.[8] Proposals for texts on the legal personality of the Union were put forward by the Irish and Dutch Presidencies in the course of the IGC that was negotiating the Treaty of Amsterdam, but these failed to win acceptance. All that could be agreed was the insertion into Title V TEU of a provision, now Article 24, which on its face is a purely procedural legal basis. The Council is given power to authorize the Presidency, assisted by the Commission as appropriate, to open negotiations on international agreements necessary for the implementation of the common foreign and security policy (CFSP); and power, on a recommendation from the Presidency, to conclude such agreements. Those powers of the Council are extended by the second paragraph of Article 24, in conjunction with Article 38, to agreements on police and judicial cooperation in criminal matters (PJCCM), which is the subject of Title VI TEU. However, Article 24 contains this proviso: 'No agreement shall be binding on a Member State whose representative in the Council states that it has to comply with the requirements of its own constitutional procedure; the other members of the Council may agree that the agreement shall apply provisionally to them'.

Article 24 TEU, in its Amsterdam version, is ambiguous as to the nature of the decision-making power which it confers on the Council.[9] On the one hand, the proviso allowing a Member State to avoid being bound by an agreement concluded under Article 24 unless and until the requirements of the domestic constitution have been complied with, could be taken as an indication that the Council has been empowered to act on behalf of the Member States collectively; if so, then they, and not the Union, would be parties to any agreement. On the other hand, the fact that the power of

---

[8] cf Art 281 EC. The Court of Justice has interpreted the bare reference to legal personality in Art 281 as meaning that 'in its external relations the Community enjoys the capacity to establish contractual links with third countries over the whole field of objectives defined in Part One of the Treaty...': see Case 22/70 *Commission v Council (AETR)* [1971] ECR 263, para 14. On the international legal personality and capacity of the former ECSC and of the EAEC, see, respectively, Art 6 ECSC and Arts 101 and 184 EAEC.

[9] The ambiguity of Art 24 TEU has previously been noted by the writer in 'External relations provisions of the Amsterdam Treaty' (1998) 35 CMLRev 1019, 1038, reprinted as ch 13 of D O'Keeffe and P Twomey (eds), *Legal Issues of the Amsterdam Treaty* (1999). See also Wyatt & Dashwood, 184–187. A similar point is made in an editorial entitled 'The European Union—a new international actor' (2001) 38 CMLRev 825.

decision has been given, not to the representatives of the governments of the Member States meeting within the Council, but to the Council as such, would suggest that decisions are being taken on behalf of the Union.

Support for the latter interpretation can be found in amendments which the Treaty of Nice will bring to the text of Article 28.[10] One such amendment consists of the deletion of the words 'to them' at the end of the proviso.[11] The only apparent reason for this would be to make clear that it would be the Union, and not the Member States, on which an agreement could be made provisionally binding, were the representative of any Member State to invoke the right to complete requisite national procedures. Another relevant amendment is the alteration of the Council's voting rule from unanimity in all cases, as the Amsterdam version of Article 24 requires, to allow qualified majority voting (QMV) under certain circumstances.[12] This change of voting rule would seem anomalous, if Article 24 were conceived as a vehicle for the exercise by the Council of powers belonging to the Member States.

Since the Court of Justice has no jurisdiction to interpret Article 24 TEU,[13] the ambiguity of the Article could finally be resolved only by waiting to see how practice would develop. Which, as between the Union and the Member States, would formally be identified as the party on the EU side in agreements negotiated and concluded pursuant to the powers of decision conferred by the Article upon the Council?

The answer is now becoming clear. The year 2001 saw the adoption by the Council, pursuant to Article 24, of two Decisions concluding Agreements with third countries explicitly on behalf of the European Union.[14] The Agreements were concerned with the detailed arrangements governing

---

[10]   The existing Art 24 is to be replaced by a new version of the Article, divided into six numbered paragraphs.

[11]   See the new para (5) of Art 24.

[12]   Regarding the CFSP, the drafting of the new paras (2) and (3) of Art 24 leaves it uncertain whether QMV is to apply in all cases where it is prescribed for the adoption of internal decisions, or only for the implementation of joint actions or common positions. For present purposes, nothing turns on this. Regarding PJCCM, the rule in the new para (4) is clear: QMV is to apply wherever required for the adoption of internal decisions or measures.

[13]   Art 46 TEU.

[14]   See Council Dec 2001/352 of 9 April 2001 concerning the conclusion of the Agreement between the European Union and the Federal Republic of Yugoslavia (FRY) on the activities of the European Union Monitoring Mission (EUMM) in the FRY, [2001] OJ L125/1; Council Dec 2001/682 of 30 August 2001 concerning the conclusion of the Agreement between the European Union and the Former Yugoslav Republic of Macedonia (FYROM) on the activities of the European Union Monitoring Mission (EUMM) in the FYROM, [2001] OJ L241/1.

the activities of the European Union Monitoring Mission (EUMM) in, respectively, The Federal Republic of Yugoslavia (FRY) and the Former Yugoslav Republic of Macedonia (FYROM).[15] In both instances, the party on the EU side was identified, by the Agreement as well as in the Council's own Decision, as the Union, with no equivocation. The Agreements are described as being 'between the European Union' and, respectively, the FRY and the FYROM; and the Union is included in the collective designation, 'the Participating Parties'. The relevant Council Decisions were adopted under the existing rule of unanimity and none of the Member States invoked the proviso.[16]

In the light of those developments, it can be asserted with some confidence that Article 24 TEU should be interpreted as conferring on the Council decision-making powers exercisable on behalf of the European Union, with a view to the negotiation and conclusion of international agreements covering matters within the scope of Title V and Title VI TEU, to which the Union is intended to be party. So understood, Article 24 may be seen as a procedural legal basis performing a function in respect of the so-called second and third pillars (the CFSP and PJCCM) similar to that performed by Article 300 EC for the purposes of the Community.

That conclusion is of constitutional moment, because of the bearing it has on the issue as to whether the Union has international legal personality and capacity and, if so, as to the extent of its capacity. Such matters, it is worth recalling, fall to be determined in accordance with public international law; and in the case of entities like the European Union the criteria to be applied are those that were identified by the International Court of Justice in its Advisory Opinion of 1949 on *Reparation for Injuries Suffered in the Service of the United Nations.*[17]

Even before the developments considered above, it seemed clear to the writer that, at least with respect to the performance by the Union of its tasks under Title V and Title VI TEU, the criteria of the *Reparation for Injuries* case were amply fulfilled.[18] The ambitious objectives set for the CFSP could only be attained by a Union capable of acting as a subject of the international

---

[15] The Agreements implement Art 6 of Council Joint Action 2000/811 on the European Union Monitoring Mission, [2000] OJ L328/53.

[16] Since the Decisions relate to Agreements implementing a Joint Action, they fall into the category which, once the Treaty of Nice enters into force, the Council will be able to adopt by QMV.

[17] ICJ Rep 1949 174.

[18] Wyatt & Dashwood, (n 3 above) 186–187.

order; and the same appeared true (if less self-evidently) of PJCCM object-ives such as combating terrorism and other serious international crimes. Moreover, in the Council, the Presidency, the Commission, and latterly the Secretary General/High Representative for the CFSP, the Union has been well equipped institutionally and procedurally to tackle such tasks. If any doubts lingered they must surely have been dissipated, now the Member States have manifested their intention, through the interpretation being given to Article 24, that the Union should operate on the international plane as an entity independent of themselves.

The European Union must accordingly be recognized as possessing international legal personality and capacity for the purposes of the CFSP and of PJCCM. That raises the ulterior issue of the relationship between such 'limited' Union personality (as it will here be called) and the separate personalities of the three Communities, more particularly that of the EC which is becoming ever more active in the field of external relations.

A first point to make is that there is no reason in law why the Union's 'limited' personality should not co-exist with the Community's personality. If an international agreement relates to matters governed by the EC Treaty, it will fall to be concluded in the name of the Community by the Council acting under the appropriate substantive legal basis of that Treaty, in conjunction with its Article 300; while if an agreement relates to the CFSP or to PJCCM, it will fall to be concluded in the name of the Union, again by the Council, acting this time under Article 24 TEU (where appropriate, in conjunction with Article 38). The possibility, therefore, exists that complex international agreements, combining EC elements with CFSP or PJCCM elements, may in future have both the Community and the Union as parties, which would be a new form of 'mixed agreement'; and if there were reasons for the Member States to be parties in addition, the agreement would be 'doubly mixed'.[19]

A second point is this. For specialists in EU law, what was said in the previous paragraph may make perfectly good sense; but the different legal identities under which the Union functions in the external sphere are a source of confusion and frustration for its international partners, let alone its own citizens. In the submission of the writer, a basis exists, even under the present Treaty structure, for the recognition of a 'general' Union personal-ity, which has subsumed the 'limited' personality charged with the tasks of

---

[19] A possibility that was noted in the CMLRev editorial cited in n 9 above. See also what is said there about giving the Union a single legal identity, an idea which is discussed below.

Title V and Title VI TEU, together with the personalities of the European Communities. A single international identity may be seen as a corollary of the conception of the EU as an integrated constitutional order with a single institutional framework designed to ensure, among other things, 'the consistency of its external activities as a whole'.[20] Such an analysis would, indeed, seem already to be reflected in diplomatic practice, particularly the practice, which is now well established, of third countries accrediting their representatives to the Union, rather than to the European Communities. Acceptance of the analysis, it must be stressed, need not in any way affect the balance of power between the Member States and the Union, or the internal balance of power between the institutions. In any situation where international action by the Union were contemplated, the necessary decisions would have to be taken under the conditions, and in accordance with the procedures, prescribed by the applicable Treaty.

The establishment of a 'general' Union personality may seem too radical a result to be achieved by way of interpretation. If so, then hopes must be pinned on the Convention on the Future of Europe, which has within the remit it received from the European Council of Laeken the question of a possible review of the distinction between the Union and the Communities,[21] and subsequently on the 2004 IGC.

Decision-making and the pillar structure

A tale of two tendencies

Another item on the agenda of the Convention is the possible simplification of the Union's 'pillar structure'. The Union is a complex constitutional order made up of three sub-orders or 'pillars'—the European Communities based on their respective Treaties as the 'first pillar', the CFSP based on Title V TEU as the 'second pillar', and PJCCM based on Title VI TEU as the 'third pillar'. The complexity is explained by the wish of the Member States, or some of them, at the time of the Maastricht Treaty, to bring within the single institutional framework of the Union 'the policies and forms of cooperation' covered by the second and third pillars, but to keep them outside a Community order owing its unique character to principles which have been elaborated by the Court of Justice reading between the lines of the EC

---

[20] Art 3, second para TEU.   [21] See SN 273/01.

Treaty.[22] The 'pillar structure' is a conventional way of referring to the different sets of arrangements allocating powers between the institutions, and between the Union and the Member States, for the purposes, respectively, of the Communities, of the CFSP and of PJCCM. The differentiation means, in crude terms, that the pooling of Member States' sovereignty goes less far under the second and third pillars than under the first. The task of simplification sets the challenge of determining how far it may be possible or desirable to reduce or even eliminate the differentiation between the pillars, or any two of them.

Developments which have taken place since Maastricht show a tendency of the third pillar to converge on the first pillar. The clearest manifestation of this was the transfer, effected by the Amsterdam Treaty, of a great swathe of policy areas from Title VI TEU to Title IV of Part Three of the EC Treaty on visas, asylum, immigration and other policies related to the free movement of persons ('the Free Movement Title'). In the case of the second pillar, an opposite tendency, of ever greater divergence from the first pillar, is discernible. A realistic objective for the Convention and the 2004 IGC might, therefore, be to 'go with the flow', attempting to complete the assimilation of the third pillar to the first, while allowing the second pillar to retain its specificity; and thus to bring about a two-pillar Union.

The discussion that follows is devoted to one aspect of the pillar structure, namely the differentiation, in comparison with the Community model, of the rules and practices of decision-making under, respectively, the third and the second pillars. Those rules and practices, it will be contended, display the convergent and divergent tendencies which have been remarked on.

The Community model of decision-making

The model referred to is that of the European Community. The institutional arrangements under which decisions are taken for the purposes of the EAEC reflect the sectoral specificity of that Community. Even with respect to the EC, however, the notion of a 'model' or standard method of decision-making gives a false impression of uniformity.

---

[22]   The classic statement by the Court of Justice as to the nature of the 'new legal order' to which the EC Treaty has given rise is in Case 26/62 *Van Gend en Loos* [1963] ECR 1, 12. An updated formulation is found in Opinion 1/91 [1991] ECR I-6079, para 21. On the background to the Maastricht Treaty, see J Cloos, G Reinesch, D Vignes and J Weyland, *Le Traité de Maastricht: Genèse, Analyse, Commentaires* (2nd edn, 1994).

A complicating factor affecting the model itself has been the introduction of new procedures designed to enhance the role of the European Parliament in decision-making, first cooperation and subsequently co-decision.[23] The familiar interaction—between the Commission as the instigator of proposals and the Council wielding the power of final decision—remains central under EC procedures that either do not involve the Parliament at all, or merely give it the right to be consulted and to render a non-binding Opinion.[24] In such cases, the Parliament can contribute to the moulding of a decision only indirectly, by prevailing upon the Commission or the Council to incorporate elements of the Opinion into the proposal, by exercising their respective powers of amendment.[25] Under the co-decision procedure, in the refined version laid down by the Treaty of Amsterdam, the interaction between the institutions is quite different. The Commission has its customary right of initiative, but the Parliament has been put on an equal footing with the Council as co-legislator: a measure can only be adopted if it receives the positive approval of both Parliament and Council, at first or second reading where the co-legislators act at arm's length, or after a joint text has been thrashed out by their representatives in a conciliation committee, with the Commission acting as honest broker. Instead of the classic 'dialogue', therefore, there is a 'trialogue'; and indeed that is the name which has been given to the organized contacts which take place between the three institutions at the different stages in the passage of a measure which is subject to co-decision.[26]

When the assent procedure applies, the Council must obtain the assent of the European Parliament, that is, its positive approval, before acting. The procedure differs from co-decision in that no opportunity is provided for formal interaction between the institutions. That makes the procedure appropriate only for matters requiring a simple 'yes' or 'no' from the Parliament, such as the conclusion of important international agreements.[27]

Moreover, a range of procedures that deviate from the Community model have been admitted into the system of the EC Treaty.[28] An example that goes back to the original EEC Treaty is what may be termed the 'organic law

[23] See respectively, Art 251 and Art 252 EC.
[24] The so-called 'consultation procedure' is discussed in Wyatt & Dashwood, 40–43.
[25] See Art 250 EC.
[26] On the co-decision procedure, see Wyatt and Dashwood, (n 3 above) 43–47. On the characteristic interactions between the institutions involved in decision-making, see ibid, 52–56. The success of the reformed co-decision procedure is noted by the writer in 'The constitution of the European Union after Nice: law-making procedures' (2001) 26 ELRev 215.
[27] See Art 300(3), second subpara EC.
[28] On variant EC procedures, see the writer's article, cited in n 26 above, at 231–237.

procedure', since it is appropriate for decisions which are structural in character: the Council, acting on a proposal from the Commission, and after consulting or, as the case may be, with the assent of, the European Parliament, takes a decision which it must then recommend to the Member States for adoption in accordance with their respective constitutional requirements.[29] However, most variant procedures date from the TEU and the Treaty of Amsterdam. They are especially prolific in the Title on Economic and Monetary Policy. The deviation is explained in some instances by the extreme political sensitivity of the decisions to be taken. For instance, the Commission's right of initiative under the procedure of Article 104 EC for dealing with excessive government deficits is exercisable by way of a recommendation: that avoids the rule in Article 250(1) EC which requires the Council to act by unanimity when amending a Commission proposal. In other cases, the explanation lies in the specificity of monetary policy and of the tasks which have been entrusted to the European System of Central Banks: hence the fact that, under some legal bases, the European Central Bank (ECB) has been given a right of initiative as an alternative to the Commission;[30] and it also enjoys autonomous power to take decisions for carrying out its tasks, including power to make regulations for certain purposes.[31]

The variant of the consultation procedure applicable under Article 67(1) EC during a transitional period of five years for the purpose of taking action under the Free Movement Title, is considered below.

Third pillar decision-making

The tendency towards the convergence on the Community model of the third pillar arrangements on decision-making is here considered with respect, first, to the forms of instrument which are available to the Council when acting for the purposes of Title VI TEU and, secondly, to the procedures that have to be followed when such action is taken.

Under the original Title VI, the Council was authorized by the then Article K.3(2) to act by the following methods: the adoption of 'joint positions' and the promotion, 'using the appropriate form and procedures', of any cooperation contributing to the pursuit of Union objectives; the

[29] A provision surviving from the original EEC Treaty, which prescribes the organic law procedure, is Art 269 EC on the system of own resources.

[30] See, eg, Art 107(5) and (6) EC; Art 111(1) and (2) EC. The ECB exercises its right of initiative by way of a recommendation.

[31] See Art 110 EC.

adoption, subject to a subsidiarity test, of 'joint action'; and the drawing up of conventions to be recommended to the Member States for adoption in accordance with their respective constitutional requirements. The difference between 'joint positions' and 'joint action' as instruments of decision-making was left obscure; but it seemed to reflect a distinction also found under the provisions of Title V TEU, between an act expressing an agreed point of view, and an act organizing collective behaviour by the Member States.[32] Nor was it clear what legal effects, if any, the instruments were intended to have—in contrast to the definitions of Community instruments contained in Article 249 EC.[33] As for the third form of instrument mentioned by Article K.3(2), inter-Member State conventions, these are, of course, known to the EC Treaty as a complement to the normal legislative activity of the institutions in the areas specified by Article 293.

The Treaty of Amsterdam replaced the provisions of the former Article K.3(2) with those of Article 34(2) TEU, which the Treaty of Nice will leave intact. The Council has been equipped by Article 34(2) with four kinds of instrument:

(a) 'common positions'. These have the function of 'defining the approach of the Union to a particular matter';

(b) 'framework decisions'. The function of framework decisions is 'approximation of the laws and regulations of the Member States'. Their legal effects are described in language identical in substance to that used by Article 249 EC, third paragraph with respect to directives: '[f]ramework decisions shall be binding upon the Member States as to the result to be achieved but shall leave to the national authorities the choice of form and methods'. However, it is explicitly stated that '[t]hey shall not entail direct effect';

(c) 'decisions'. This form of instrument is available 'for any other purpose consistent with the objectives of [Title VI], excluding any approximation of the laws and regulations of the Member States'. Decisions are stated to be binding but, like framework decisions, they do not entail direct effect;

(d) 'conventions'. As previously under Article K.3(2), a convention established by the Council must be recommended to the Member States for adoption in accordance with their respective constitutional require-

---

[32] Respectively, 'common positions', as defined by Art 15 TEU and 'joint action', as defined by Art 14 TEU. See below.

[33] cf also the definition of a CFSP joint action in the then Art J.3 TEU.

ments. New elements are the requirement that Member States begin the procedures applicable within a time limit to be set by the Council; and that, unless they provide otherwise, conventions shall, once adopted by at least half of the Member States, enter into force for those Member States.

We have seen already that conventions between the Member States are an instrument of decision-making common to the first and third pillars. On analysis, the other three instruments provided for by Article 34(2) also exhibit similarities to familiar instruments available under the system of the EC Treaty.

The resemblance is most obvious in the case of framework decisions as provided by Article 34(2)(b) TEU. These have been conceived, like EC directives, as legislative acts which are indirectly applicable: the Member States are obliged to achieve a prescribed legal outcome by taking appropriate action within their respective national orders. One difference as compared with EC directives (that framework decisions are defined as having the approximation of laws and regulations of the Member States as their sole purpose) is more apparent than real. Approximation, it can be argued, is the only job which directives, by their very nature, are capable of doing. They can only apply to matters which are regulated, or liable to be regulated, at the national level: for instance, the creation of a new form of intellectual property in Community law has to be done by means of a regulation.[34] The other difference (no direct effect of framework decisions) is significant; though less so, perhaps, than might be thought, given the limitations the case law places on the direct effect of directives, and because the duty of courts in the Member States to interpret national provisions, if they possibly can, consistently with any applicable EC directive, regardless of direct effect, seems capable of being extended to framework decisions.[35]

According to the definition in Article 34(2)(c), third pillar decisions are general purpose instruments which do not entail direct effect. They differ, therefore, from the EC decision in the sense of Article 249, fourth paragraph EC, which is an act 'binding in its entirety upon those to whom it is addressed'—in other words, specifically designed for making binding determinations in individual cases. There is, however, a Community instrument corresponding quite closely to the third pillar decision, namely the so-

---

[34] On the scope of a power of 'approximation', see A Dashwood, 'The limits of European Community powers' (1996) 21 ELRev 113, 120–121.

[35] See Case 14/83 *Von Colson* [1984] ECR 1891; Case C-106/89 *Marleasing* [1990] ECR I-4135; Case C-91/92 *Faccini Dori* [1994] ECR I-3325.

called 'decision *sui generis*' or 'innominate decision'.[36] It was recognized for the first time by the Court of Justice in the *AETR* case[37] that an act of an institution not falling under any of the definitions in Article 249 EC might nevertheless produce legal effects and so be challengeable in Article 230 proceedings. Over the years, the adoption under formal Council procedures of acts which are designated 'decisions', although they do not have a specific addressee, has become a regular practice. This form of instrument is used where the intended legal effect is something other than the laying down of rules (whether directly, as under a regulation, or indirectly, as under a directive). Decisions *sui generis* are, for example, the standard instrument for establishing programmes of so-called 'incentive measures', where EC funding is made available in order to encourage activities within or between the Member States, which are considered conducive to some objective of the Treaty.[38] Similar programmes 'of incentives, exchanges, training and co-operation' have been established by third pillar decisions.[39] Other examples of the use of third pillar decisions have been to supplement the arrangements on the protection of the euro against counterfeiting,[40] and to set up a European crime prevention network.[41]

It is uncertain whether third pillar common positions have been conceived as acts capable of having binding legal force. The silence of Article 34(2)(a) would suggest not, given that the binding quality of, respectively, framework decisions and decisions is expressly referred to under points (b) and (c) of the same paragraph.[42] As formal acts which are non-binding and have the

---

[36] The most authoritative treatment of decisions *sui genesis* is still that of R H Lauwaars, *Lawfulness and Legal Force of Community Decisions* (1973).

[37] Case 22/70 *Commission v Council* [1971] ECR 263.

[38] Notably, the Erasmus Programme, to promote the mobility of students (Dec 89/489 [1989] OJ L239/24) and the Lingua Programme, to promote foreign language competence (Dec 94/819 [1994] OJ L340/8). These Programmes have been brought together under the umbrella of the Socrates Programme (Dec 95/819 [1995] OJ L87/10), which is now in its second phase (Dec 253/2000 [2000] OJ L28/1).

[39] The following third pillar programmes of incentive measures are now in their second phase: Grotius II, for legal practitioners (Dec 2001/512, [2001] OJ L186/1); Oisin II, for law enforcement authorities (Dec 2001/513 [2001] OJ L186/4); Stop II, for persons responsible for combating trade in human beings and the sexual exploitation of children (Dec 2001/514 [2001] OJ L186/7). See also the new Hippokrates Programme for the prevention of crime (Dec 2001/515 [2001] OJ L186/11).

[40] Dec 2001/887 [2001] OJ L329/1.

[41] Dec 2001/446 [2001] OJ L153/1.

[42] cf also Art 15 TEU, where it is provided: 'Member States shall ensure that their national policies conform to the [second pillar] common positions'.

function of defining the Union's approach to different matters, common positions would appear quite readily assimilable to first pillar 'opinions'.

Recommendations are not among the instruments listed in Article 34(2) TEU. This is in contrast to Article 249 EC, which mentions them (along with opinions) as a form of non-binding Community act. Nevertheless, it has become an established practice of the Council to make recommendations under its third pillar powers.[43] The adoption of Council resolutions is also a practice common to the first and third pillars.[44] These are instruments not formally recognized by either Article 249 EC or Article 34(2) TEU, which are typically used to give a light steer by the Union in policy areas where Member States are particularly jealous of their sovereignty.

Turning to the decision-making procedures of the third pillar, developments that have occurred since the Maastricht Treaty concern three things in particular: the power to initiate the adoption of measures by the Council; the Council's voting rules; and the involvement of the European Parliament in the adoption process.

Under the original Article K.3(2) the Commission shared the power of initiative with the Member States in only some of the policy areas then subject to Title VI—mostly ones which are now covered by the Free Movement Title of the EC Treaty.[45] In other areas—those of judicial co-operation in criminal matters, customs cooperation and police cooperation in preventing and combating serious forms of international crime—the power of initiative belonged exclusively to the Member States.[46] As part of the reform which refocused Title VI on those very areas, the Treaty of Amsterdam altered the rule on the initiation of Council measures, Article 34(2) TEU giving the Member States and the Commission shared power to set the decision-making process in motion for all third pillar purposes.

It has always been, and remains, the general rule that primary powers under Title VI are exercised by the Council acting unanimously. However,

---

[43] Recent examples of third pillar recommendations are: Council Recommendation of 25 June 2001 on contact points maintaining a 24-hour service for combating high-tech crime, [2001] OJ C187/5; Council recommendation of 6 December 2001 setting a common scale for assessing threats to public figures visiting the European Union, [2001] OJ C356/1.

[44] Recent examples of third pillar resolutions are: Council Resolution of 25 June 2001 on the exchange of DNA analysis results, [2001] OJ C187/1; Council Resolution of 6 December 2001 concerning a handbook with recommendations for international police cooperation and measures to prevent and control violence and disturbances in connection with football matches with an international dimension, in which at least one Member State is involved, [2002] OJ C22/1.

[45] See former Art K.1(1) to (6), referred to in former Art K.3(2), first indent.

[46] See former Art K.1(7) to (9), referred to in former Art K.3(2), second indent.

the Amsterdam Treaty brought a change of voting rule in relation to implementing measures. Previously, it was for the Council itself to decide (by unanimity) whether a measure implementing joint action could be adopted by qualified majority voting (QMV):[47] post-Amsterdam, QMV applies automatically to Council acts implementing at the level of the Union decisions in the sense of Article 34(2)(c) TEU. Similarly, measures implementing conventions which have been established under Article 34(2)(d) are adopted within the Council by a majority of two thirds of the Contracting Parties: the option of specifying in a convention that such decisions be taken by unanimity is no longer available.[48]

In the Maastricht version of Title VI TEU, the European Parliament had the right to be consulted by the Council Presidency 'on the principal aspects of activities referred to in this Title', but it had no formal role in the procedure for the adoption of particular measures.[49] That was changed by the Treaty of Amsterdam, which gave the Parliament the right to be consulted by the Council 'before adopting any measure referred to in Article 34(2)(b), (c) or (d)'.[50] So the consultation of the European Parliament has become 'an essential procedural requirement' for the adoption of third pillar framework decisions, general decisions and conventions, but not of common positions; and, regarding the first two of those forms of instrument, failure to comply with the requirement would be an infringement providing grounds for the Court of Justice to review the legality of the measure in question, in proceedings brought by a Member State or the Commission (though the Parliament itself has no right of action).[51] The Council may set a deadline of not less than three months within which the Parliament must deliver its opinion, and may act in the absence of an opinion if none is forthcoming in the specified period.[52] It has a similar power under the first pillar when consulting the Parliament on the conclusion of an international agreement, but not when acting for legislative purposes.[53]

---

[47] See former Art K.3(2)(b).

[48] See former Art K.3(2)(c).

[49] See former Art K.6 TEU.

[50] Art 39(1) TEU.

[51] Art 35(6) TEU. On the truncated jurisdiction of the Court of Justice under the Third Pillar, see A Arnull, 'Taming the beast? The Treaty of Amsterdam and the Court of Justice' in D O'Keeffe and P Twomey (eds), *Legal Issues of the Amsterdam Treaty* (1999) 109, 117.

[52] Art 39(1) TEU, second and third sentences.

[53] See Art 300(3), first sub para. Where the consultation procedure applies in the legislative sphere, the Council is required, in principle, to be seised of the Parliament's opinion before its acts: Case 138/79 *Roquette Frères v Council* [1980] ECR 3333. However, it has been

To sum up on the present legal framework of third pillar decision-making:

(i) The Council has been equipped with a set of instruments having legal force, which are broadly equivalent to instruments available under the first pillar. However, directly applicable instruments, whether of a general nature (like EC regulations) or of an individual nature (like decisions in the sense of Article 249, fourth paragraph EC) are lacking.

(ii) The Council assumes it has power to adopt, in a third pillar context, any of the non-binding instruments of the first pillar.

(iii) The standard decision-making procedure of the third pillar is a variant of the consultation procedure with the Council acting by unanimity. The variation consists of the fact that the right of initiative is shared between the Member States and the Commission.

(iv) The Commission has not been given power to adopt binding acts. Where primary third pillar acts call for implementation at the level of the Union, this has to be done by the Council itself. In such cases, the Council acts by QMV.

In contemplating a strategy for completing the assimilation of the third pillar into the first, inspiration can be drawn from the transitional regime on decision-making which was provided by the Treaty of Amsterdam in order to facilitate the transfer of competences to the Free Movement Title. The procedure laid down by Article 67(1) EC, which is applicable for a period of five years from the entry into force of the Treaty, is effectively that of the Third Pillar: the Council acts by unanimity on a proposal from the Commission *or on the initiative of a Member State* and after consulting the European Parliament. At the end of the five-year period (ie from 1 May 2004), pursuant to Article 67(2), the Commission will recover its monopoly of the initiative, and the Council will have power, acting unanimously after consulting the Parliament, to introduce co-decision as the procedure for legislating under the Free Movement Title, or parts of it.[54]

---

accepted by the Court of Justice that the Council may act in the absence of an opinion, if the Parliament's failure to adopt one amounts to a breach of the duty of loyal cooperation between institutions: Case C-65/93 *European Parliament v Council* [1995] ECR I-643.

[54] There are derogations from the regime of Art 67(1) and (2) EC with respect to the adoption of rules on short term visas: see paras (3) and (4) of the Article. The derogation is explained by the fact that aspects of the rules on visas were already within the scope of the EC competence before the Amsterdam Treaty: see the former Art 100c EC.

Evidently, it was not thought necessary to preserve the special characteristics of third pillar instruments under the Free Movement Title, even on a transitional basis. The Council acts for the purposes of the Title using the normal set of instruments provided by Article 249 EC.

The attractiveness of a solution like that provided by Article 67, when the incorporation of further third pillar elements into the first pillar comes to be considered, has been enhanced by the Treaty of Nice. One of the successes of the Treaty is the package of measures intended to speed up the 'communitarization' of decision-making under a number of the legal bases provided for by the Free Movement Title.[55] The package has three main constituents: a new paragraph (5) to be inserted into Article 67, which will substitute co-decision for the variant procedure of paragraph (1) of the Article in certain cases, without it being necessary to wait for the end of the transitional period;[56] a Declaration which, in certain other cases, commits the Council in advance to make use of its power under Article 67(2), exercisable once the period ends, to introduce co-decision;[57] and a Protocol which will replace the procedure of Article 67(1) from the end of the period, in one case, not by co-decision but by the consultation procedure with the Council acting by QMV.[58] This development should help assuage fears that procedural abnormalities, tolerable if purely transitional, are liable to become permanent exceptions.

Second pillar decision-making

The decision-making process of the second pillar has not undergone the reforms which provide the best evidence of convergence on the Community model in the case of the third pillar. There is no instrument corresponding to the framework decision (or the EC directive) which has been provided under Title V TEU for the purpose of approximation of the laws and regulations of the Member States. Nor has the European Parliament been given a right to be consulted before second pillar decisions are taken. Its formal involvement in decision-making remains as originally defined by the Maastricht Treaty: to be consulted by the Council Presidency 'on the main aspects and the basic choices' of the CFSP, and have the Presidency ensure

[55] For a detailed analysis of the package, see the writer's article cited in n 26 above.

[56] The relevant legal bases are Art 63(1) and (2)(a), and Art 65 EC.

[57] See Declaration No 5. The relevant legal bases are Arts 62(3) and 63(3)(b) EC, as well as Art 62(2)(a) EC.

[58] See Protocol No C.2. The relevant legal basis is Art 66 EC.

that its views are 'duly taken into consideration'; and to be kept regularly informed by the Presidency and the Commission of the development of the CFSP.

Such reforms were not necessarily to be expected, however, since the conduct of foreign, security and defence policy is essentially an executive activity. The formal instruments of the CFSP are perfectly suitable for carrying on such activity: common strategies, to ensure the overall coherence of Union policies 'in areas where the Member States have important interests in common'[59]; joint actions, to 'address specific situations when operational action by the Union is deemed to be required';[60] and common positions, to 'define the approach of the Union to a particular matter of a geographical or thematic nature'.[61] What is more, the Council seemingly does not regard the list of instruments in Article 12 TEU as exhaustive. Acts in the form of decisions *sui generis* have, for example, been used to set up various CFSP bodies, including the powerful Political and Security Committee[62] (as to which, see below). The limited role accorded to the European Parliament, too, seems unexceptional. There is no general practice in Member States of requiring the legislature to be consulted in advance when action is contemplated at national level in the policy areas covered by the CFSP. Moreover, even in the sphere of the common commercial policy, where the EC is exclusively competent, the Council is empowered to act on a proposal from the Commission without any legal requirement that the Parliament be consulted.[63]

Nevertheless, evidence of a continuing tendency to diverge from the Community model is abundantly available in a series of developments which have taken place in the law and practice of decision-making under the second pillar.

One example concerns the conditions under which second pillar decisions can be adopted by QMV. In the Maastricht version of Title V TEU, QMV was the voting rule in one case only, where it was provided for in a joint action (itself adopted by unanimity) for taking implementing decisions.[64] The Treaty of Amsterdam, while retaining the unanimity rule for

---

[59] Art 13(2) TEU, first para.

[60] Art 14(1) TEU.

[61] Art 15 TEU.

[62] [2001] OJ L27/1.

[63] Art 133 EC. In practice, it is common for the European Parliament to be consulted on an optional basis, when the matter is not urgent.

[64] See former Art J.3(2), first subpara TEU.

primary measures under Title V, made QMV automatically available in respect of measures adopted in the framework of a common strategy and measures implementing joint actions or common positions;[65] and the Treaty of Nice will add one further case, that of the appointment of special representatives, as provided for by Article 18(5) TEU.[66] Resort to QMV in those cases is subject to two limitations, however. The first limitation is that decisions having military or defence implications must still be taken by unanimity.[67] The second limitation consists of the procedural device which the writer has dubbed 'the Luxembourg Compromise Mark II'.[68] This gives any member of the Council a right to oppose the taking of a decision by QMV 'for important and stated reasons of national policy'; in which event, the Council may, acting by QMV, request that the matter be referred to the European Council for decision by unanimity.[69] The purpose of the device is to preserve a Member State's right of veto (as long as it is prepared to make a reasoned case based on national policy), while giving an opportunity for peer group pressure to be exerted at the highest political level in order to promote a compromise. The device is not exclusive to the second pillar: it was also introduced by the Treaty of Amsterdam into the EC Treaty and Title VI TEU,[70] but in respect of one category of decisions only, those on the approval of measures of closer cooperation (or 'enhanced cooperation', as the Treaty of Nice will re-christen it). In those cases, moreover, the device is to be modified by the Treaty of Nice: the right of an objecting Member State will be confined to having the matter 'raised before the European Council', after which it will be open to the Council to proceed to a decision by QMV. So, once the Treaty of Nice enters into force, avoidance of QMV by invoking the Luxembourg Compromise Mark II will be possible only under the second pillar.

A second indicator of divergence from the Community model has been the gradual establishment within the Council of an infrastructure for managing the different phases of the CFSP, from planning and the formulation of specific proposals, through decision-making, to the ultimate execution of policy. The starting point of this development was the choice made at

[65] Art 23(2), first sub para TEU.
[66] A third indent will be added, ibid.
[67] Art 23(2), fourth sub para.
[68] See 'States in the European Union' (1998) 23 ELRev 201, 215. Reprinted in B Rider (ed), *Law at the Centre* (1999) 235.
[69] Art 23(2), second sub para TEU.
[70] Respectively, Art 11(2) EC and Art 40(2) TEU (which, pursuant to the Treaty of Nice, will become Art 40a(2)).

Maastricht to accord the Council's Presidency a uniquely active role in the conduct of second pillar business. The Presidency was mandated to represent the Union internationally in CFSP matters, and was made responsible for the implementation of decisions taken under Title V TEU.[71] The Commission was, and remains, entitled to be 'fully associated' in those tasks,[72] but its role has clearly been conceived as that of a supporting actor.

The Treaty of Amsterdam took the further step of creating the post of Secretary-General/High Representative for the CFSP, with two main functions: that of 'contributing to the formulation, preparation and implementation of policy decisions'; and that of representing the Union in CFSP matters on the world stage.[73] It was also agreed in Amsterdam to set up a 'policy planning and early warning unit', having within its remit the production of 'argued policy options papers to be presented under the responsibility of the Presidency as a contribution to policy formulation in the Council, and which may contain analysis, recommendations and strategies for the CFSP'.[74]

Recently, with the rapid progress made in equipping the Union to carry out the so-called 'Petersberg tasks'[75] in the framework of a European Security and Defence Policy (ESDP), the Council's infrastructure has been substantially reinforced through the establishment of new political and military bodies.[76] Among these, the Political and Security Committee (PSC) has been described as the 'linchpin' of the ESDP and of the CFSP.[77] Besides helping generally in the formation of Council policy and in the co-ordination of activities in the areas falling under the CFSP, the PSC has been charged with exercising 'political control and strategic direction of crisis management operations'. Once the Treaty of Nice enters into force, the Council will be empowered to authorize the taking of decisions by the PSC for the purposes of such operations.[78] That amounts to the conferment

---

[71]   See the provisions now contained in Art 18 TEU.

[72]   ibid, para (4).

[73]   Art 26 TEU.

[74]   Declaration No 6 to the Final Act of the Conference.

[75]   Those are the tasks defined in Art 17(2) TEU.

[76]   Notably, the Political and Security Committee (see Council Dec 2001/78, [2001] OJ L27/1); the Military Committee (see Council Dec 2001/79, [2001] OJ L27/4); and the Military Staff of the European Union (see Council Dec 2001/80, [2001] OJ L27/7).

[77]   In the opening paragraph of the Annex to Dec 2001/78, above.

[78]   The Treaty of Nice will add two further paragraphs to the text presently found in Art 25 TEU. That text will be amended so as to refer to the PSC instead of, as now, to the 'Political Committee'. Dec 2001/78 describes the PSC as 'the standing formation of the Committee referred to in Article 25 of the Treaty'.

of executive powers on a Council body—a novel departure, and unthinkable in the system of the EC Treaty.

A third indicator of divergence is the decision-making role assumed by the European Council in the development of the ESDP,[79] which has no specific legal basis but is clearly dictated by the political preference of the Member States (or, perhaps more accurately, of those among them most influential in this field). A favourable political climate was created for the ESDP by the joint Declaration of the Union's leading military powers, France and the United Kingdom, which was issued after their summit meeting in St Malo on 4 December 1998.[80] The first steps in the formation of the new Policy were taken under the German Presidency which entered office at the beginning of 1999, and the results of the work were set out in a 'Presidency Report on strengthening of the Common European Policy on Security and Defence', which was presented to and approved by the European Council of Cologne in June of that year.[81] The incoming Finnish Presidency was invited to take the work forward and to report to the European Council of Helsinki in December 1999.

The pattern was thus set for the elaboration of the ESDP by successive Presidencies. Papers are prepared by the Presidency and discussed in the appropriate Council bodies (now including the PSC and the Military Committee, which were established, initially on an interim basis, pursuant to a suggestion originating in the Cologne Report). The European Council at the end of each semester (in June or December, as the case may be) receives and endorses a Report from the Presidency on the ESDP, and this is annexed to the Presidency Conclusions. The detailed arrangements that comprise the ESDP are almost entirely contained in the series of Presidency Reports. Whether consciously or not, the Member States have chosen not to incorporate the organizing principles and concepts of the ESDP into formal CFSP instruments, which manifestly they could have done.[82] In effect, the Reports are a new form of decision-making instrument, and as such they are open to a number of criticisms.[83] They are written in diplomatic language,

[79] On the ESDP post-Nice, see S Duke, 'CESDP: Nice's overtrumped success' (2001) 6 EFA Rev 155.

[80] The Declaration of St Malo was welcomed by the Vienna European Council, which took place a week later: Vienna Conclusions, point 76.

[81] Cologne Conclusions, Annex III.

[82] The only such instruments relate to the establishment of the Political and Security Committee, the Military Committee and the Military Staff: see above.

[83] These criticisms are more fully developed by the writer in 'The legal framework of the European Security and Defence Policy' (forthcoming).

and the normative elements are not sufficiently distinguished from policy positions which can be expected to evolve over time. Nor is there any mechanism for resolving conflicts between different texts. The Nice Report of the Presidency, with its seven annexes, contains the most complete statement to date of the ESDP, but its status is no different from the Reports that preceded and followed it. Those are criticisms that need to be addressed by reforms which must, however, be crafted to go with the grain of the second pillar.

From the developments which have been discussed, it is apparent that, as the CFSP acquires more substance, particularly in the areas of security and defence, so the decision-making process of the second pillar is tending to diverge further from the Community model. That suggests that the divergent tendency may reflect profound political reality, and that efforts to check or reverse it would not only be misguided but futile.

Making decision-making legitimate

The success of co-decision

The Treaty of Nice is the first in the series of reforming Treaties which began with the Single European Act, not to provide for any reform of the decision-making process designed to give a greater role to the European Parliament. It did not need to do so, because the co-decision procedure had been radically reformed by the Treaty of Amsterdam. The procedure of the first and second readings was streamlined, so as to facilitate the early adoption of proposals. More significantly, the third Council reading, provided for under the Maastricht version of the procedure, was abolished,[84] with the result that measures subject to co-decision require the approval of both the Parliament and the Council. Practical arrangements for the implementation of the reformed procedure were laid down by a Joint Declaration of the European Parliament, the Council and the Commission, dated 4 May 1999.[85]

The co-decision procedure, in the form resulting from the Treaty of Amsterdam, can be judged a success in constitutional terms. As was noted

---

[84] The effect of the third reading procedure was that, if conciliation failed, the Council could act unilaterally, subject to a possible European Parliament veto. On the reform of co-decision by the Treaty of Amsterdam, see A Dashwood, 'European Community legislative procedures after Amsterdam' (1998) 1 CYELS 25.

[85] [1999] OJ C148/1.

above, in the discussion of the Community model, the procedure gives the European Parliament real partnership with the Council in shaping the measure finally adopted. It is well adapted to a constitutional order like that of the Union, where the Member States remain the principal forum of democratic activity, since it provides a system of dual legitimation: indirectly, through the political processes of the Member States, because ministers are responsible to their national parliaments for Council decisions in which they take part; and directly, through the still-embryonic political process of the Union, which links Members of the European Parliament—albeit tenuously—to their electors.[86]

At the same time, the procedure has had a generally favourable reception from the politicians and civil servants professionally engaged in the decision-making process of the Union, although the burdens it places on them are considerable. A report presented to the European Council of Nice by the French Presidency and the Council's General Secretariat referred with satisfaction to the rate of legislative output (demonstrating this with some impressive statistics), and spoke of an evolving 'culture of negotiation and compromise' between the co-legislators.[87] Similarly positive sentiments can be found in documents emanating from the European Parliament.[88]

Ideas for further improvements

Nevertheless, the perception of a legitimacy-deficit lingers, even in the most august circles, as demonstrated by the Nice Declaration which speaks of 'the need to improve and to monitor the democratic legitimacy and transparency of the Union and its institutions, in order to bring them closer to the citizens of the Member States'. There are four kinds of improvement which, it is thought, are clearly necessary to enhance the legitimacy of Union decision-making.

A first improvement would relate to the level of real democratic accountability achieved under the reformed co-decision procedure. If the level is unsatisfactory, that is not because of any defect in the procedure itself which could be cured by the 2004 IGC. One part of the problem lies in the failure of parliaments in most of the Member States to hold ministers effectively to

[86] See the article cited in n 26 above.
[87] Press Release: Brussels (28.11.2000)–Nr: 1336. 1/00.
[88] See, eg, the Press Release which was issued following the Joint European Parliament/Council/Commission Seminar of 6 and 7 November 2000 on the functioning of the co-decision procedure since the Amsterdam Treaty.

account for what they get up to in the Council.[89] Ways need to be found of improving the flow of information from the Union's institutions to the national level; however, the task is mainly for the authorities and parliamentarians of the Member States to put in place adequate arrangements for scrutinizing the conduct of ministers and their officials in Union matters. The other part of the problem is the failure of MEPs thus far to establish themselves in the eyes of their electorates as politicians with a specific job to do at the level of the Union, rather than as supernumeraries of national political parties.

A second improvement would be to ensure a better match between the procedure provided for under a given legal basis, and the substance of the acts whose adoption is authorized. The writer shares the view of the Commission that, in principle, all measures which are legislative in character ought to be adopted by co-decision.[90] The Commission has provided a working definition of a legislative act as comprising 'rules of general scope based directly on the Treaty and which determine the fundamental principles or general guidelines for any Community action, and the essential aspects to be implemented'.[91] Though the definition refers only to EC acts, it is submitted that the same issues of legitimacy apply to third pillar acts which are genuinely legislative, such as framework decisions. Even under the EC Treaty, there remain major policy areas where legislation is still enacted under procedures other than co-decision: for instance, in the two areas in which by far the greatest part of the Union's budget is spent, namely agriculture and regional aid. Primary legislation on the CAP (and also on fisheries matters) is adopted under the consultation procedure,[92] while the assent procedure (which, we have seen, is unsuitable for enacting legislation, because there is no structured interaction between the Council and the Parliament) applies to regional aid.[93] It is not, however, intended to suggest crudely that co-decision should be made available ever more widely. Acts of an executive character should be adopted under the consultation procedure;[94] or, in cases of urgency, without consultation,[95] but perhaps with a

---

[89] Despite Protocol No 9 on the role of National Parliaments in the European Union.

[90] This was expressed in the Opinion which the Commission submitted pursuant to Art 48 TEU on the calling of the IGC (Adapting the Institutions to Make a Success of Enlargement, 26 January 2000). See Section 11, point (a).

[91] ibid.

[92] See Art 37 EC.

[93] See Art 161 EC.

[94] See, eg, Art 83 EC.

[95] An example would be the decisions provided for by Art 100 EC.

subsequent report to the European Parliament. An idea perhaps worth considering, where different kinds of power may be exercisable under a single legal basis, would be to prescribe more than one procedure, for example, co-decision when the Council is called upon to legislate, consultation when it is deciding on a particular action to be taken.[96]

A third improvement would be to give the system a thorough pruning. The cooperation procedure, which has outlived its usefulness, should finally be abolished.[97] Variant procedures should be allowed to survive only if they can be justified constitutionally: those that undoubtedly can be, would include the power of the ECB to initiate, and even to adopt, legislation on some aspects of monetary policy; and the procedures reflecting the particularity of the second pillar. An attempt should also be made to bring order into the wild profusion of procedures for carrying out minor amendments to the Treaties.[98]

A fourth improvement would be to enhance the transparency of decision-making by opening up the Council process, if not to the public, at least to television cameras, when legislation is being considered. Support for such a move has been expressed by various powerful figures,[99] and the issue was raised in the Report on Preparing the Council for Enlargement, which was submitted by the Secretary General of the Council to the President of the European Council in March 2002.[100] As noted in that Report, it would be necessary, if the idea were taken up, to distinguish clearly between the Council's working methods, depending on whether or not it was legislating.

Conclusion

To continue to insist, in the face of recent Treaty language referring to 'the institutions of the Union', that somehow the institutions are only on loan from the Communities, would seem perverse. However, in order to remove

---

[96] There is full consideration of the procedural changes that will result from the Treaty of Nice, and of disappointments, in the article cited in n 26 above.

[97] Cooperation survives only in four legal bases which are found in the Treaty Title on economic and monetary policy, ie: Art 99(5); Art 102(2); Art 103(2); Art 106(2) EC.

[98] See, eg, Art 17(1) TEU; Art 13 EC; Art 22, second para EC; and the new Art 10(6) of the Statute of the European System of Central Banks.

[99] Including Prime Minister Blair and Chancellor Schröder: see *Financial Times*, 25 February 2002.

[100] Doc 1636/1/02 Rev 1.

even unreasonable doubts, the opportunity should be taken of amending (or preferably abolishing) Articles 1 and 9 of the Merger Treaty. If, in any reorganization of the Treaties, the option of a basic treaty with supporting texts were chosen, a provision establishing the institutions of the Union should be included in the basic treaty.

That the Council enjoys what has been described as 'limited' legal personality now appears incontestable, and the case for a 'general' Union personality is a strong one. Again, doubt could be laid to rest by an express provision creating a single Union personality (and suppressing those of the Communities). A basic treaty would be the appropriate locus for this.

The tendency of the arrangements on decision-making under the third pillar to converge on the Community model of the first pillar, and of the arrangements under the second pillar to diverge from that model, has been demonstrated. That means a Union comprising at least two pillars is likely to continue. Assuming that would be the case, it will be a question for the Convention, and eventually for the 2004 IGC, whether the abolition of the distinction between the Union and the Communities is conceivable, while maintaining the particularity of the Community model, on the one hand, and the CFSP model, on the other.

There is no need to tinker any further with the elements of the co-decision procedure, but action should be taken to ensure that the co-legislators strengthen their links of political accountability. The standard procedure for adopting legislative acts should be co-decision, and for adopting executive acts, consultation. Variant procedures should be reduced to the minimum, and the Council process be made more transparent.

That set of improvements would be unlikely to bring cheering crowds onto the streets. But they should help, over time, to bring about a gradual accretion of legitimacy to the Union.

3

Decision-making under the Second Pillar

Adrian Hyde-Price

The common foreign and security policy shall include all questions relating to the security of the Union, including the progressive framing of a common defence policy, which might lead to a common defence, should the European Council so decide… (Article 17(1) of the Treaty on European Union, as amended at Nice).

Introduction

The second pillar—comprising the Common Foreign and Security Policy (CFSP), including its more recent European Security and Defence Policy (ESDP) component—is often regarded as a somewhat esoteric area, separate and apart from pillar one 'Community' business, widely seen as the 'real' substance of the EU. In important respects, this is the case. The second pillar is certainly distinctive in terms of its decision-making structures, its forms of accountability and the sources of its legitimacy. It is also frequently seen as having insubstantial policy output, with declaratory policy over effective action being the rule rather than the exception. Once again, there is some truth to this.

Since late 1998, however, dramatic developments have begun to transform the character and profile of the second pillar. Indeed, the last few years have seen more progress in European security and defence cooperation than in all the decades since the failure of the European Defence Community (EDC) in 1954. Whilst talk of a 'revolution in European military affairs'[1] may be overstated, significant policy innovation has occurred, the implications of which are manifold and potentially far-reaching. The EU has taken a 'Great Leap Forward' in defence and security cooperation. First, after decades as a 'civilian power'[2] in which it functioned as an 'economic giant

[1] N Gnesotto, 'Preface' to J Howorth, 'European integration and defence: the ultimate challenge?' (Chaillot Paper 43, Paris, WEU Institute for Security Studies, 2000), v.

but a political dwarf', the EU is now seeking to define for itself a role as a consequential international actor with a capacity for conflict prevention and crisis-management. Second, the EU's project of creating an ESDP, including an autonomous military capability, has implications for the European security system, particularly in terms of the NATO alliance and the future role of the USA in Europe. Third, it has implications for the European integration process as a whole, and will both affect, and be affected by, parallel developments in the first and third pillars. The transformation of the second pillar thus raises questions that are central to the future of the European Union and its role in the European order in the 21st century.

Background and history

Although none of the founding treaties of the European Community dealt with foreign policy, let alone security or defence policy, the European integration process itself was primarily motivated by foreign and security policy concerns. These focused on the need to overcome the legacy of intra-European conflict—particularly that between France and Germany—that had ignited three major wars since 1870. European integration thus began with defence, in the shape of the Treaties of Dunkirk (1947) and Brussels (1948).[3] The EEC's external relations were limited to the 'low politics' of commercial diplomacy. An ambitious attempt to forge a European Defence Community (the Pleven Plan) was killed off by the French National Assembly in 1954, much to the chagrin of the Americans. West European security and defence concerns—the sphere *par excellence* of 'high politics'[4]— were henceforth met by the North Atlantic Treaty Organization (NATO), with the Western European Union (WEU) playing a minor role in fostering

---

[2] This notion was originally applied to the EC by F Duchêne: see 'The European Community and the uncertainties of interdependence' in M Kohnstamm and W Hager (eds), *A Nation Writ Large? Foreign-Policy Problems before the European Community* (1973) 19–20. For a critique, see H Bull, 'Civilian power Europe: a contradiction in terms?' (1982) 20 JCMS 149.

[3] For details of the Treaty of Brussels, the EDC, the Washington Treaty, the Treaty of Rome and other relevant documents, see C Hill and K Smith (eds), *European Foreign Policy: Key Documents* (2000) section 1, 1–70.

[4] S Hoffmann, 'The European process at Atlantic crosspurposes' (1964) 2 JCMS 85, 89. Stanley Hoffmann argued that high politics concerned the realm of 'traditional interstate politics' where 'grandeur and prestige, rank and security, domination and dependence are at stake'. In this policy area, national governments were the decisive actors, and the 'spillover effect' identified by neofunctionalists did not and could not apply. On this point, he insisted, neofunctionalism was 'essentially mistaken'.

security dialogue between a core group of seven countries. It was only after the resignation of De Gaulle in June 1969 that the European integration process was deepened to include limited foreign policy coordination in the shape of European Political Cooperation (EPC).[5]

From the very start, EPC was separate and distinct from the European Community. It was an entirely intergovernmental process, outside the treaties, and managed by diplomats rather than the Commission. It acquired its first legal, treaty-based identity in 1986, as a result of Title III (Article 30) of the Single European Act (SEA). This created a two pillar structure for EC cooperation, with EPC forming the second—and much smaller and weaker—pillar under the 'single' framework of the European Council. One important consequence of this was the development of the Council presidency into a key Community institution. The SEA also created a small EPC Secretariat which was to 'assist the Presidency in the organization of EPC meetings, including the preparation and circulation of documents and the drawing up of minutes'.[6] The EPC Secretariat was based in Brussels, and initially it was separate from the Council of Ministers' Secretariat, although in the early 1990s it became an autonomous unit within the Council Secretariat. Last but not least, the SEA took the important step of including the 'political and economic' aspects of security within the ambit of the EPC. This reflected the self-image of the EC as a 'civilian power', committed to using political, diplomatic and economic instruments to pursue its external goals, rather than military power projection (which was seen as the preserve of individual Member States acting alone or in concert through NATO).

Despite its intergovernmental character, EPC transformed the diplomatic working practices of Member States. 'By the end of the 1980s', William Wallace has written, 'the procedures of EPC had evolved into an extensive network, drawing in some thousands of diplomats in the foreign ministries of the member states, in their embassies outside the EU, and in missions to international organisations'. Traffic around the COREU telex network grew from 2,000–3,000 telegrams a year to some 9,000 in 1989. Desk officers in foreign ministries met regularly together in working parties, and were in constant contact by telephone and telegram. 'The habits and assumptions of a generation of national diplomats were thus reshaped, reinforced by joint

[5] Two good accounts of the EPC are P Ifestos, *European Political Cooperation* (1987) and S Nuttall, *European Political Cooperation* (1992).

[6] Press and Information Office of the Federal Government of Germany, *European Political Cooperation (EPC)* (5th edn, 1988), 87–92.

training courses, exchanges of personnel, even sharing of embassy facilities in some third countries'.[7] The effect of this institutionalized cooperation was to encourage a gradual convergence of views on key foreign policy issues among Member States. This can be observed from an analysis of voting behaviour by Member States in the United Nations between 1979 and 1995.[8] This increase in foreign policy coordination occurred despite the fact that the EU enlarged during this period from ten to twelve and then to fifteen members, and suggests that the existence of a common institutional framework has contributed to a pronounced learning and socialization process in the foreign ministries of all Member States.

CFSP

The second pillar formally came into existence as a result of the Maastricht Treaty on European Union (TEU), which in Article J grandly announced that 'A common foreign and security policy is hereby established'.[9] More controversially, it referred to 'the eventual framing of a common defence policy, which in time might lead to a common defence' (Article J.4.1 TEU). The institution that was expected to give substance to this 'common defence' was the WEU, which had long occupied an ambiguous and ill-defined place between the EU and NATO.[10] This body was designated 'an integral part of the development of the Union', which could be requested 'to implement the decisions and actions of the Union which have defence implications' (Article J.4.2 TEU). However, the precise policy implications and modalities of Article J remained shrouded in ambiguity given the

[7] A Forster and W Wallace, 'Common Foreign and Security Policy' in H Wallace and W Wallace (eds), *Policy-Making in the European Union* (4th edn, 2000) 461, 465.

[8] P Luif, *On the Road to Brussels: The Political Dimension of Austria's, Finland's and Sweden's Accession to the European Union* (1995) and (by the same author) *The Common Foreign and Security Policy of the European Union: Theoretical and Empirical Issues* (1997), 26–33. The only exception to this general trend was Greece under the PASOK government, but by the late 1980s it, too, had adjusted to the EC mainstream.

[9] For details of the negotiations leading to the agreement on Title V of the TEU, see P de Schoutheete de Tervarent, 'The creation of the Common Foreign and Security Policy' in E Regelsberger, P de Schoutheete de Tervarent and W Wessels (eds), *Foreign Policy of the European Union: From EPC to CFSP and Beyond* (1997) 41.

[10] On the ambiguities surrounding the WEU's place in Europe's security architecture, see W Rees, *The Western European Union at the Crossroads: Between Transatlantic Solidarity and European Integration* (1998) and Anne Deighton (ed), *Western European Union 1954–1997: Defence, Security, Integration* (1997).

continuing lack of consensus between Member States (notably the UK and France) on the desirability and achievability of a common European foreign, security and defence policy.[11]

The TEU thus modified the EPC's existing institutional arrangements rather than fundamentally reshaping them.[12] The intergovernmental principle remained sacrosanct, with national governments retaining the initiative operating through the European Council. Policy initiative, representation and implementation were explicitly reserved to the Council Presidency, 'assisted if need be by the previous and next member states to hold the Presidency' (the 'troika' principle). CFSP issues were the preserve of Foreign Ministers operating in the monthly General Affairs Council (GAC). Their meetings were prepared by the Political Committee (PoCo), which met fortnightly at the level of foreign ministry Political Directors, with the assistance of COREPER (the Committee of Permanent Representatives). The Commission was to be 'fully associated' with discussions in this intergovernmental pillar (Articles J.5 and J.9), and the views of the European Parliament were to be 'duly taken into consideration' (Article J.7). The WEU Secretariat was strengthened and relocated from London and Paris to Brussels. 'Joint actions' in pursuit of agreed common aims were possible (Article J.3).

The ink was barely dry on the Maastricht Treaty when the CFSP confronted—and spectacularly failed—its first major test. Faced with the break-up of the Yugoslav Federation, Jacques Poos of Luxemburg, in his role as President of the Council of Ministers, grandly proclaimed 'this is the hour of Europe'.[13] Hubris, however, was followed by the shame and frustration of failure. To be fair, the 'wars of Yugoslav succession' presented complex legal, political and moral problems, and none of the leading powers in the international community possessed either the necessary understanding or political will to find a solution.[14] The fledgling CFSP was thus ill-prepared to manage let alone resolve the Yugoslav conundrum, not least because of policy disputes between Western Europe's major powers.[15] At the same

[11] For details of the wider European security context, see A Hyde-Price, *European Security Beyond the Cold War: Four Scenarios for the Year 2010* (1991).

[12] L Aggestam, 'The EU at the crossroads: sovereignty and integration' in A Landau and R Whitman (eds), *Rethinking the European Union: Institutions, Interests and Identities* (1997) 75, 90. On the institutional structure of the CFSP, see B White, *Understanding European Foreign Policy* (2001) 11.

[13] Quoted in C Hill, 'Closing the capabilities–expectations gap?' in J Peterson and H Sjursen (eds), *A Common Foreign Policy for Europe? Competing Visions of the CFSP* (1998) 3.

[14] On this see J Gow, *Triumph of the Lack of Will: International Diplomacy and the Yugoslav War* (1997) and more generally L Freedman (ed), *Military Intervention in European Conflicts* (1994).

time, NATO was successfully repositioning itself as Europe's dominant security organization, thereby further reducing the scope for the CFSP to develop into an effective instrument for crisis management.

The Amsterdam European Council and Treaty

The early and mid-1990s witnessed a wide-ranging discussion on the future evolution of the EU in preparation for a new intergovernmental conference (IGC). This culminated in the European Council in Amsterdam in June 1997, at which a 'consolidated' TEU was agreed.[16] In terms of the CFSP, little substantive progress was made at Amsterdam, in part because the newly elected 'New Labour' government of Tony Blair in Britain had yet to work out its policy on the CFSP and the WEU. A number of incremental changes were made at Amsterdam, adding some new institutional capabilities and giving the Council the task of defining EU 'common strategies'.

One significant development was the Amsterdam Council's endorsement of a Swedish–Finnish proposal to include the WEU's 'Petersberg tasks' in the Treaty. These were originally formulated in the Petersberg Declaration of 19 June 1992 by WEU foreign and defence ministers and referred to 'humanitarian and rescue tasks, peacekeeping tasks and tasks of combat forces in crisis management, including peacemaking' (Article 17(2) TEU). The Petersberg tasks clearly fell far short of a commitment to a 'common defence',[17] but they did include the use of military force in crisis management—a new and increasingly important aspect of European and international security. The Petersberg tasks embrace both the first and second 'generation' of UN peacekeeping: in other words, both traditional 'blue-helmet' operations undertaken under Chapter VI of the UN Charter, which typically take place with the consent of the parties involved (usually following a ceasefire or a peace deal, as in Cyprus), and peace-enforcement or humanitarian operations undertaken under Chapter VII, which may

[15] A prime example of this is Germany's clumsy handling of the recognition of Croatia and Slovenia. See M Libal, *Limits of Persuasion: Germany and the Yugoslav Crisis, 1991–1992* (1997). On German CFSP policy more generally, see L Aggestam, 'Germany' in I Manners and R Whitman (eds), *The Foreign Policies of European Union Member States* (2000) 64.

[16] See A and D Spence, 'The Common Foreign and Security Policy from Maastricht to Amsterdam' in KA Eliassen (ed), *Foreign and Security Policy in the European Union* (1998) 43.

[17] Although Art 17 TEU, as amended at Amsterdam, does speak of 'the progressive framing of a common defence policy' in contrast to the Maastricht version of the TEU, which referred only to its 'eventual' framing (see Art J.4).

involve the limited use of military coercion against one or more of the parties involved (as in Bosnia, Somalia, Rwanda or Albania).[18] Their inclusion in the Amsterdam Treaty indicated that Member States felt that the EU needed to go beyond *conflict prevention* and take on responsibility for *crisis management*.[19] This would involve engaging in what were dubbed 'Chapter VI and a half' type missions which occupy a legal and conceptual 'grey zone'—albeit an increasingly important one—between peace-enforcement and limited war.[20]

The Amsterdam Treaty was also significant for the second pillar in that it introduced a distinctive element of 'flexibility' into the CFSP, in the form of a 'constructive abstention' (Article 23 TEU). The dominance of the intergovernmental principle in the second pillar means that responsibility for defining the principles, general guidelines and common strategies of the CFSP lies with the Council. Decisions are generally taken by unanimity. However, unless a Member State invokes 'important and state reasons of national policy', the Council can act by qualified majority 'when adopting joint actions, common positions or taking any other decision on the basis of a common strategy' or 'when adopting any decision implementing a joint action or a common position' (Article 23(2) TEU). The Amsterdam Treaty introduced a new principle, that of a 'constructive abstention'. This gave Member States the right to opt out of specific policy decisions 'having military or defence implications' by abstaining from voting on a decision by formally declaring that it will not contribute to the decision, whilst accepting that the decision commits the entire EU.[21] Constructive abstention is a decision-making mechanism that provides for an element of flexibility in the second pillar, and was regarded as essential if the CFSP was not to be hamstrung by the veto of one or more states. It might serve to facilitate a more effective international presence for the EU, particularly in

[18] See E Schmidl and R Oakley (eds), *Peace Operations Between War and Peace* (2000).

[19] As C Hill has noted, the EPC/CFSP has primarily been concerned with conflict prevention, and indeed this notion has become 'a binding concept in the discussion of the CFSP'. The end of the cold war generated a belief that the EU had an opportunity, indeed a responsibility, to make a major contribution to a new and more cooperative system of international order. Given the EU's self-perception as a 'civilian power' relying on the 'soft' instruments of power such as diplomacy and economic leverage, conflict prevention and—in the wake of the Bosnian war—post-conflict resolution became the central focus of the CFSP. See C Hill, 'The EU's capacity for conflict prevention' (2001) 6 EFA Rev 315.

[20] On the blurred boundaries between intervention and limited war, see C Bellamy, *Knights in White Armour: The New Art of War and Peace* (updated edition, 1997).

[21] For details see A Missiroli, 'CFSP, defence and flexibility' (Chaillot Paper 38, Paris, WEU Institute for Security Studies, 2000) 10.

the context of an enlarging Union. However, it could introduce new sources of tension. One potential problem is the finance of policy activities approved through constructive abstention: they are to be financed by the participating members and not by the Community budget, unless the Council explicitly decides otherwise. This raises the potential problem of 'free-riding' if some members abstain for purely financial reasons.[22]

The 'Great Leap Forward': Cologne and Helsinki

In late 1998 and 1999, a 'Great Leap Forward' occurred in the EU's CFSP. Against a background of persistent 'European' failure in the Balkans and simmering tensions in transatlantic security relations, EU Member States finally committed themselves to the historic task of supplementing the CFSP's commitment to *conflict prevention* by adding a military capacity for *crisis management*. The impetus for this Great Leap Forward was the Franco–British St Malo Declaration of 4 December 1998. This policy initiative had been presaged by a more constructive attitude to European security and defence cooperation on the part of the UK government at the informal European Council held in Pörtschach (Austria) and the first ever (informal) meeting of EU Defence Ministers in Vienna (both held in October 1998).[23] St Malo itself paved the way for the historic decisions on European security and defence cooperation laid out at the Cologne and Helsinki European Councils in 1999.

Europe's Great Leap Forward was made possible by a convergence of British and French thinking on security policy around that of Germany, which had long argued that a strong NATO and more robust European security and defence cooperation were complementary, not conflicting objectives.[24] By a fortuitous coincidence, Germany held the Presidencies of both the EU and the WEU in the first half of 1999, and was thus able to forge a new consensus around the ESDP. At the landmark Cologne European Council (3–4 June 1999), the EU announced its resolve to 'play a full role on the international stage' and to equip itself 'to take decisions on the full range of conflict prevention and crisis management tasks defined in the Treaty on European Union, the "Petersberg tasks"'. Echoing the words used

---

[22]   Missiroli (m21 above) 14–15.
[23]   M Jopp, *European Defence Policy: The Debate on the Institutional Aspects* (1999).
[24]   A Hyde-Price, *Germany and European Order: Enlarging NATO and the EU* (2000) 195.

at St Malo, the Council declared that 'the Union must have the capacity for autonomous action, backed up by credible military forces, the means to decide to use them, and a readiness to do so, in order to respond to international crises without prejudice to actions by NATO'. Underlying its determination 'to launch a new step in the construction of the European Union', the EU committed itself to preparing 'the modalities for the inclusion of those functions of the WEU which will be necessary for the EU to fulfil its new tasks and responsibilities in the area of the Petersberg tasks'.[25]

The implications of Cologne for the wider European security system were twofold. First, after years if not decades in which it had been assumed that the WEU would provide the defence arm of the EU, this body was simply bypassed and its functions absorbed into the EU's second pillar. A major reason for this was the baroque complexity of the procedural steps necessary for the EU to activate the WEU for military crisis management operations.[26] Second, Cologne indicated that European defence and security cooperation would be constructed within the EU framework, and not within NATO. Since 1994, NATO had been working towards the creation of a European Security and Defence Identity (ESDI) as the Alliance's European pillar. Considerable energy had been focused on operationalizing the Combined Joint Task Force (CJTF) concept as a means by which the EU, through the WEU, could use NATO assets for European operations not involving the Alliance as a whole. Cologne signalled a new resolve by EU Member States to build a European crisis management capability within the second pillar, thereby potentially marginalizing NATO's ESDI in favour of the EU's ESDP.

The aspiration to give the EU the ability to conduct autonomous military crisis management operations within the framework of the Petersberg tasks was given concrete expression at the Helsinki European Council (10–11 December 1999). The Kosovo war had exposed the inability of European countries to back up their political and diplomatic aspirations with credible military force. In recognition of the need to address this weakness in the

---

[25] Declaration of the European Council on Strengthening the Common European Policy on Security and Defence, Cologne European Council, 3–4 June 1999, reprinted in M Rutten (ed), 'From St-Malo to Nice. European defence: core documents' (2001) Chaillot Paper 47, Paris, WEU Institute for Security Studies, 41–45.

[26] A tentative 'flow-chart' drawn up on the occasion of a joint exercise in June 1998 identified no less than 25 distinct procedural steps necessary to utilize the WEU as an agency of the CFSP. These steps increased to 37 (or even 45, depending on the type of interface) if NATO assets were to be used. See S De Spiegeleire, 'The European security and defence identity and NATO: Berlin and beyond' in M Jopp and H Ojanen (eds), *European Security Integration: Implications for Non-alignment and Alliances* (1999) 57.

EU's common foreign and security policy, the European Council in Helsinki adopted the 'headline goals'. These specified that in order to conduct EU-led operations, 'Member States must be able, by 2003, to deploy within 60 days and sustain for at least one year forces of up to 50,000–60,000 persons capable of the full range of Petersberg tasks'.[27] In establishing these headline goals, the EU committed itself to establishing a military crisis management capability, not for territorial *defence* of the Union, but for Petersberg-type operations, 'including the most demanding'. The force concerned would be of corps size (up to 15 brigades), and 'should be militarily self-sustaining with the necessary command, control and intelligence capabilities, logistics, other combat support services and additionally, as appropriate, air and naval elements'. In order to sustain this force in the field for up to a year 'an additional pool of deployable units (and supporting elements) at lower readiness to provide replacements for the initial forces' would be required (totalling about 200,000 personnel, or up to 45 brigades).[28]

It is important to note that this rapid reaction corps is explicitly *not* designed to be a 'European army', and—given the Atlanticist security orientation of many EU members, coupled with the national security policies of the EU's 'post-neutral' members (Sweden, Finland, Austria, Ireland)—it is not tasked with collective territorial defence (which remains the preserve of Article V of the NATO Washington Treaty). Rather, it is an instrument of power projection designed to give the EU an autonomous military capability to back up its diplomacy with force in the context of its Petersberg tasks, 'including the most demanding'.[29] As noted above, this means that the EU will be able to conduct 'Chapter VI and a half' operations, involving peace-enforcement or humanitarian intervention missions. The EU will only be able to conduct small-scale operations using its own designated forces. For more substantial operations (similar in scope to those in Bosnia and Kosovo) where NATO as a whole is not engaged, EU-led operations will involve the use of NATO assets (using the so-called 'Berlin plus' procedure, named after the NATO ministerial meeting in June 1996 which launched the ESDI project and called for the creation of CJTFs as a way of operationalizing it).[30]

[27]   Presidency Conclusions, Helsinki European Council, II ('Common European Policy on Security and Defence') in Rutten (n 25 above) 82.

[28]   Annex 1 to Annex IV, 'Presidency Progress Report to the Helsinki European Council on Strengthening the Common European Policy on Security and Defence' in Rutten (n 25 above) 84.

[29]   On the need for military force to give diplomacy credibility, see C Bildt, 'Force and diplomacy' (2000) 42 Survival 141. On the wider issue of strategic coercion, see L Freedman (ed), *Strategic Coercion* (1998).

The Headline goals specified at Helsinki are ambitious, but not unrealistic given the military capabilities of EU Member States. As various defence analysts have noted, the UK and France alone should be able to field almost 100,000 fully professional troops by 2002, whilst Germany aims to have up to two divisions (comprising approximately 20,000 troops) following its military restructuring.[31] Nonetheless, the ESDP project will have significant resource implications. If the EU is to conduct autonomous military crisis management, it will need to improve its strategic assets, above all its capacity for C4ISR, strategic lift and planning). The problem is, however, that European defence budgets have been contracting for most of the last decade. This contraction has been most marked in Germany, which, given its size and political importance, is a key player determining the success or failure of the ESDP. Klaus Becher has estimated that unless the German defence budget increases 'by about 10 percent or DM4–5 billion per year, the announced reforms [to the Bundeswehr] will not be achieved'.[32] The difficulties Germany experienced in deploying its military forces to Kabul in January 2002[33] exposed Europe's chronic shortage of strategic air-lift capability, and illustrated why many Americans are sceptical that the ESDP will amount to more than an exercise in rhetoric and a new set of institutional structures.

The institutions of the second pillar

The ESDP project has led to the creation of a number of new institutions within the second pillar. The first of these is the High Representative for CFSP, a post that was created by the Amsterdam Council, and eventually filled in October 1999 by Javier Solana (NATO's former Secretary-General). The High Representative for CFSP also serves as Secretary-General of the Council and Secretary-General of WEU, thus giving him a pivotal position within the decision-making structures of the second pillar. His task is to assist the Council in the formulation, presentation and implementation of policy decisions, and to engage in dialogue with third parties, thus contributing 'to the effectiveness and visibility of the Union's action and policy'.[34]

[30] See M Ortega, 'Military intervention and the European Union' (2001) Chaillot Paper 45, Paris, WEU Institute for Security Studies.

[31] For details see Howorth (n 1 above) 40.

[32] K Becher, 'Reforming German defence' (2000) 42 Survival 164, 167.

[33] 'Deutsches Vorauskommando in Kabul', Frankfurter Allgemeine Zeitung, 12 January 2002, 6.

In this he is assisted by the Policy Planning and Early Warning Unit, a body also created by the Amsterdam Council.

The most important new committee established by the Helsinki Council was the Political and Security Committee (PSC). This body is designed to serve as 'the linchpin of the European security and defence policy (ESDP) and of the common foreign and security policy (CFSP)'. In terms of the EU's crisis management mechanism, the PSC has 'a central role to play in the definition and follow-up to the EU response to a crisis'.[35] The PSC will deal with all the tasks defined in Article 25 TEU, and may convene in Political Director form. The PSC may be chaired by the High Representative for CFSP, 'especially in the event of a crisis', and, most importantly, the PSC will exercise 'political control and strategic direction' of the EU's military response to a crisis. In addition, it receives reports and advice from the other bodies created as a result of the ESDP initiative.[36]

These include the European Union Military Committee (EUMC) and the European Union Military Staff (EUMS). The former, which is a 'source of advice based on consensus', is responsible for 'providing the PSC with military advice and recommendations on all military matters within the EU' and exercising 'military direction of all military activities within the EU framework'.[37] The latter's task is to perform 'early warning, situation assessment and strategic planning for Petersberg Tasks including identification of European national and multinational forces', and to implement policies and decisions as directed by the EUMC.[38]

The Feira European Council

The launch of the ESDP project immediately sent shock-waves through the transatlantic relationship, with the then US Secretary of State Madeline Albright insisting on the '3 Ds'—no decoupling, no duplication, no discrimination. NATO Secretary General Lord Robertson quickly refor-

[34] Nice European Council, Annex VI, (Presidency Report on the European Security and Defence Policy) in Rutten (n 25 above) 172.

[35] Rutten (n 25 above) 171.

[36] Nice European Council Nice, Annex III to Annex VI, 'Political and Security Committee' in Rutten (n 25 above) 191.

[37] Nice European Council, Annex IV to Annex VI, 'European Union Military Committee (EUMC)' in Rutten (n 25 above) 193–96.

[38] Nice European Council, Annex V to Annex VI, 'European Union Military Staff Organisation (EUMS)' in Rutten (n 25 above) 196–99.

mulated these more positively in terms of the '3 I s'—indivisibility of the Alliance, improved European capabilities, inclusiveness of all partners. In order to address the thorny problem of the relationship of the ESDP to NATO, the Feira Council agreed a mechanism for political discussions with the six non-EU NATO European countries[39] and the additional nine EU candidate countries[40] ('the 15'). This involved regular meetings in the 15-plus-15 format and at least two meetings per Presidency in the 15-plus-6 format.

In addition, the Feira Council addressed the concerns of some of the 'post-neutrals' that the ESDP was giving undue weight to the military rather than the civilian aspects of crisis management. A Swedish–Finnish initiative was adopted that established four priority areas for developing civilian crisis management capabilities: policing, strengthening the rule of law, strengthening civilian administration, and civil protection. At Feira, Member States committed themselves 'to providing by 2003, by way of voluntary cooperation, up to 5,000 police officers, 1,000 of them to be deployable within 30 days, for international missions across the full range of conflict-prevention and crisis-management operations'.[41] It also established a Committee for Civilian Aspects of Crisis Management, which has met twice monthly since May 2000 and specified that the General Secretariat of the Council is to be given a permanent expertise on police matters.

The purpose of this new initiative was to ensure that the EU developed an *integrated approach* to crisis management: 'European Union action on Petersberg-type assignments requires a strong synergy between the military component and the civilian component (police, rule of law, civilian administration, civil protection). The military and police components must therefore, where necessary, be part of an integrated planning process and should be used on the ground in a closely coordinated manner, making allowance for the constraints on deployment of Member States' police forces'.[42]

---

[39] Norway, Iceland, Turkey, Poland, Czech Republic and Hungary.

[40] Slovakia, Slovenia, Bulgaria, Romania, Estonia, Lithuania, Latvia, Cyprus and Malta.

[41] Nice European Council, Annex II to Annex VI, 'Strengthening of European Union Capabilities for Civilian Aspects of Crisis Management' in Rutten (n 25 above) 185.

[42] Rutten (n 25 above) 186.

The Nice European Council

'In the end', Nicole Gnesotto has argued, 'it was defence policy that was the major achievement of the European Council in Nice'.[43] The Nice Treaty amended Articles 17 and 25 TEU, thereby doing away with the requirement to resort to the WEU for military operations and giving the PSC, like the ESDP, the necessary legal authority. Article 25 is particularly important because it gives executive powers to the PSC for crisis management operations and gives the PSC the power to take legally binding decisions. This is a sign that the CFSP will be run from within the Council, and thus reinforces its distinctiveness vis-à-vis the first pillar.[44] The Treaty of Nice also amends Article 23(2) TEU to enable the Council to act by qualified majority (unless important national policy reasons are invoked) when appointing a special representative under Article 18(5) TEU with a mandate relating to particular policy issues.

The Nice Treaty does not itself deal with the question of the status of the ESDP vis-à-vis NATO. Instead, this question is dealt with in a report attached to the Presidency Conclusions of the European Council, while a Declaration annexed to the Final Act of the Conference calls for the ESDP conclusions of that report to be implemented 'as soon as possible in 2001' (ie, without waiting for formal ratification). However, there are differing interpretations of the report's conclusions and it is not clear how they can be resolved, nor what the statement that EU-led military operations will take place only 'where NATO as a whole is not engaged' will mean in practice.

As the Presidency Report on the European Security and Defence Policy approved at the Nice European Council noted, 'The aim of the efforts made since the Cologne, Helsinki and Feira European Councils is to give the European Union the means of playing its role fully on the international

---

[43] N Gnesotto, 'An ever closer Union?' (2001) WEU Institute for Security Studies Newsletter, no 32, 1. For a less sanguine assessment see S Duke, 'CESDP: Nice's overtrumped success?' (2001) 6 EFA Rev 155.

[44] See chapter by Dashwood in this volume. Dashwood also notes that the Preamble to the Nice Treaty and Art 24(6) TEU, introduced at Nice, speak of the institutions of the European Union, reflecting the EU's status as a new legal entity with legal capability. In the Mostar international agreement on the EU police presence, the agreement referred to the Member States acting in the EU framework. The recent EU Treaty with Yugoslavia, however, specified the EU as the legal actor. For an analysis of these and related issues see T Tiilikainen, 'To be or not to be? An analysis of the legal and political elements of statehood in the EU's external identity' (2001) 6 EFA Rev 221, and R Wessel, 'Revisiting the international legal status of the EU' (2000) 5 EFA Rev 507.

stage and of assuming its responsibilities in the face of crises by adding to the range of instruments already at its disposal an autonomous capacity to take decisions and action in the security and defence field'. The EU now aspires to mobilize 'a vast range of both civilian and military means and instruments' in order to give itself 'an overall crisis-management and conflict-prevention capability in support of the objectives of the Common Foreign and Security Policy'.[45] Once the decisions taken at Helsinki and Feira are implemented, the EU will be in an even stronger position to exert a stabilizing influence on its 'near abroad'. Few international organizations possess the wealth of resources and instruments available to the EU: these range from diplomatic initiatives in the shape of Joint Actions, Common Positions and Common Strategies, through economic sanctions and conditionality clauses, to military and civilian crisis management. Given the Union's 'power of attraction',[46] coupled with the political, technical and administrative capabilities it has developed through its intense engagement with Central and Eastern Europe (including the Balkans),[47] the EU is well situated to play a major role in shaping the system of international order emerging in post-cold war Europe. Whether it does so or not will depend both on the political will of Member States and on the decision-making capacity of the second pillar.

Accountability and legitimacy in the second pillar

The distinctive character of decision-making in the second pillar raises a number of questions concerning the principles of accountability and legitimacy that govern its functioning. The first point to note is that the second pillar is distinctive because of its substantive concerns. Foreign, security and defence policies are the classic exemplars of 'high politics' and are traditionally the preserve of small élite groups. In comparison to public policy issues like social welfare, employment policy and immigration, they generate relatively little public interest. Mechanisms for accountability in foreign policy are consequently fairly rudimentary, and parliamentary control relatively limited. This is particularly the case for much of the routine

[45] Rutten (n 25 above) 168.
[46] G Munuera, 'Preventing Armed Conflict in Europe: Lessons from Recent Experience' (1994) Chaillot Paper 15–16, WEU Institute for Security Studies, 91.
[47] See K Smith, *The Making of European Union Foreign Policy: The Case of Eastern Europe* (1998).

work of quiet diplomacy and conflict prevention that is the bread-and-butter of the CFSP. Moreover, transparent decision-making procedures and public access to documentation can be incompatible with the requirement for confidentiality that effective diplomacy requires—particularly conflict prevention and crisis management where undue publicity can be highly counter-productive.[48]

Given the intergovernmental character of the CFSP/ESDP, accountability in the second pillar primarily takes the form of accountability to national parliaments and electorates through Member States acting in the framework of the European Council. The role of the European Parliament in the second pillar is limited, although the Parliament's right to scrutinize the EU budget gives it some rights to discuss external relations. From one perspective, therefore, the extension of the Community method into the second pillar could be seen as undermining the accountability of the CFSP to national governments. Antonio Missiroli, for example, suggests that 'the democratic element represented by the rotational presidency may be easily offset by the [High Representative for CFSP] and the new Commissioner in charge of external relations as a whole, Chris Patten'.[49] On the other hand, Jolyon Howorth argues that, given the EU's self-image as the institutional embodiment of a new approach to international relations (based on democracy, cooperation, tolerance and humanitarian principles), 'issues of transparency, legitimacy and even democratic accountability are likely to be central to the success of EU defence and security policy, even though they have traditionally been absent from classic state-based policy in these areas'. He therefore suggests that it may be necessary 'formally to involve some degree of parliamentary oversight if the EU is not to be perceived as preaching one thing and practising another'.[50] One interesting suggestion has been to constitute a Foreign Relations Committee of the Union, drawing its members from both the European Parliament and national parliaments.[51]

---

[48] From this perspective, it is instructive to note the controversy surrounding the decision by the High Representative for CFSP/Secretary General, Javier Solana, to amend the rules for the protection of classified information applicable to the General Secretariat. He called for the introduction of the grade 'très secret/very secret'. This was adopted in the face of opposition from Finland, the Netherlands and Sweden, and was strongly criticized by the leader of the Green Group of MEPs as heralding 'the imposition of the security state in the EU with all the paranoia that goes with it'. For details see S Duke, 'CESDP: Nice's overtrumped success?' (2001) 6 EFA Rev 155, 168.

[49] Missiroli (n 21 above) 44.

[50] Howorth (n 1 above) 90.

[51] D Hannay, 'Europe's Common Foreign and Security Policy: Year 1' (2000) 5 EFA Rev 275, 279.

Whatever the merits of developing mechanisms for parliamentary accountability within the second pillar, the fact is that the legitimacy of the EU's CFSP/ESDP will depend primarily on its effectiveness—in other words, on output legitimacy rather than process legitimacy. Nothing produces an upsurge in public interest in international affairs better than a good crisis, thanks in no small part to the 'CNN effect'. The legitimacy of the EU's common foreign, security and defence policy will depend primarily on how well it handles future crisis situations. In this respect, the failure of EU Member States to take common action during the Albanian crisis of April–August 1997 (in which Italy took the role of 'lead nation' in Operation Alba on the basis of a UN/OSCE mandate) was, with hindsight, a missed opportunity. It was a crisis of relatively short duration that proved relatively easy to tackle.[52]

The importance for the perceived legitimacy of the CFSP of successfully managing crisis situations and projecting stability into its immediate neighbourhood highlights one potential problem, namely the coherence and efficiency of decision-making procedures in the second pillar. The rash of new bodies created to oversee the ESDP has complicated the institutional architecture of the second pillar. An impressive 'wiring diagram' is taking shape specifying the role and responsibilities of these new bodies and their various inter-relationships. The precise functions of the Brussels-based bodies (PSC, PoCo, COREPER, PPEEW, EUMC, EUMS) need further clarification. More importantly, there is a possibility for tension between the High Representative and the External Affairs Commissioner (representing a tension between the intergovernmentalism and supranationalism in the second pillar). Nonetheless, despite these potential sources of clashing competences, on paper a viable structure for decision-making within the second pillar is taking shape. The problem is that the formal procedures and institutional forums of the second pillar might not function effectively under pressure, and that therefore in a crisis situation the connecting wires might, in effect, blow a fuse. Indeed, Simon Nuttall has suggested that crisis situations require a high degree of improvisation and ad-hoc behaviour because of their complex and multi-faceted nature, and that the more the EU specifies precise procedural and institutional relationships, the less effective its efforts at crisis management are likely to be.[53]

[52] As Hill notes, 'the CFSP failed to act when the situation might have seemed ideal for it to engage its multiple, but limited resources' (n 19 above) 318. See also Missiroli (n 21 above) 22.

[53] Quoted in Missiroli (n 21 above) 22.

The problem is complicated by the fact that effective crisis management involves the use of a mix of different policy instruments, from diplomacy and economic inducements, to policing and military force. This means that not only will decision-making procedures in the second pillar have to work efficiently, but the second pillar will have to be coordinated with the Commission and, most probably, the third pillar. At the same time, the EU will have to coordinate its multiple activities with those of other international organizations—most importantly, NATO, the UN and the OSCE—and possibly NGOs (for example, in the distribution of humanitarian aid). This means that the output legitimacy of the EU's second pillar is dependent on a wide range of factors beyond its control.

The tension between legitimacy based on effective policy output, and legitimacy based on transparent and inclusive decision-making structures, is also highlighted by the issue of informal *directories* within the second pillar. The experience of much crisis management and preventive diplomacy by the international community over the last decade suggests that there is a tendency for larger powers to coordinate their foreign policy activities in informal groupings (a phenomenon sometimes termed 'mini-lateralism'[54]). Examples include the 'Contact Group' and Prime Minister Blair's attempt to convene an informal meeting of Europe's 'Big Three' during the 'war on terrorism'. The enlargement of the EU might encourage the emergence of such informal 'inner cores' within the CFSP involving the larger and more powerful Member States.[55] This would undermine the accountability and formal legitimacy of the second pillar because it would sideline the influence of smaller states. Once again, there is a tension here between accountability and efficiency.

Conclusion

Foreign, security and defence policy—the substantive concerns of the second pillar—intrude into Member States' core national interests, involving as they do sensitive issues of status, power and influence. Not surprisingly, therefore, the integration process in the second pillar has differed markedly

---

[54] M Kahler, 'Multilateralism with small and large numbers' (1992) 3 International Organization 681.

[55] On the role of a directorate within the second pillar, see S Keukeleire, 'Directorates in the CFSP/CESDP of the European Union: a plea for restricted crisis management groups' (2001) 6 EFA Rev 75.

from that of the first pillar, primarily in terms of its inter-governmental character. The national sensitivities surrounding the 'high politics' with which the CFSP deals are reflected historically in its relatively weak institutionalization and marginal policy output, especially when compared to the first pillar. Despite these limitations, however, the existence of common institutions and procedural mechanisms has acted as a constraint on the national foreign policies of Member States and means that 'the European Union's foreign policy is more than the sum of the foreign policies of its member-states'.[56] Indeed, for diplomats in the foreign ministries of Member States, 'styles of operating and communicating have been transformed':

The COREU telex network, EPC working groups, joint declarations, joint reporting, even the beginnings of staff exchanges among foreign ministries and shared embassies: all these have moved the conduct of national foreign policy away from the old nation-state national sovereignty model towards a collective endeavour, a form of high-level networking with transformationalist effects and even more potential.[57]

In addition to this gradual and long-term process of socialization and integration, there can be little doubt that, in the two years between St Malo and Nice, the character of the European Union began to change. The decision to build a military power projection capability marked a major watershed in the European integration process. The 'civilian' nature of the EU as an international actor was put to one side as Member States committed themselves to the historic, and for many decades, unthinkable, goal of acquiring a strategic capacity for military and civilian crisis management.

Coupled with the introduction of the euro and the fashioning of a sphere of 'freedom, security and justice' in the third pillar, the commitment to build a more effective European crisis management capability suggests that the EU is on the cusp of transforming itself into a qualitatively new Euro-polity.[58] This 'new model Union' will have a more pronounced identity and a stronger international presence, particularly in its immediate neighbourhood. The prospects for this new Euro-polity are dependent, first and foremost, on the success of Economic and Monetary Union, rather than the

---

[56] B Soetendorp, *Foreign Policy in the European Union* (1991) 155.

[57] C Hill and W Wallace, 'Introduction: actors and actions' in C Hill (ed), *The Actors in Europe; Foreign Policy* (1996) 1, 6.

[58] P van Ham, *Europe's New Defense Ambitions: Implications for NATO, the US and Russia* (the Marshall Center Papers, no 1, 2000) 35.

achievement of the 'Headline goals' set by the Cologne Council. Nonetheless, if the EU fails to develop the capabilities to carry out crisis management operations in the framework of the Petersberg tasks effectively, the political credibility and legitimacy of the Union will be called into question. To a significant extent, therefore, the prospects for building 'an ever closer union' depend in no small part on the success of the CFSP, including its defence component.

Looking to the immediate future, the effective development of the second pillar depends on two key factors. The first concerns resources. Will Member States make available the necessary resources needed to prepare and implement military operations over the whole range of Petersberg tasks, particularly given the monetary constraints of EMU and the preference of European electorates for 'welfare not warfare'. As former US Secretary of Defence William Cohen asked in December 1999, 'Where are the resources to match the rhetoric?'[59] The problem here is not simply one of gross resources, although Germany's shrinking defence budget has already been mentioned as a source of concern. What is certainly required is a 'more efficient, more focused, better-planned and co-ordinated use of resources'.[60] EU countries already spend 60 per cent of that of the US on defence, without having the latter's global responsibilities and superpower aspirations, and yet in some areas they only have 10–15 per cent of the assets available to the Americans.[61] Addressing this capabilities deficit will require the development of much more formalized procedures for defence policy harmonization, along with the political will to invest in areas where Europe is particularly weak, such as strategic intelligence, operational planning and airlift capacity.

The second factor determining the success of the ESDP project is the forging and cultivation of a common foreign policy vision and strategic culture, comparable to that which has developed in NATO. The finest military forces in the world, one commentator has noted, 'would serve little purpose if there were no common foreign policy to define the "why" and "how" of their possible use'.[62] The EU is equipping itself with the instruments for crisis management in the framework of the Petersberg tasks, but

---

[59]   Quoted in Howorth (n 1 above) 41.

[60]   W Slocombe, US Under Secretary of Defense for Policy in the Clinton Administration, quoted in F Heisbourg (ed), 'European defence: making it work' (2000) (Chaillot Paper 42, Paris, WEU Institute for Security Studies), 40.

[61]   Heisbourg (n 60 above) 84.

[62]   Gnesotto (n 43 above) 1.

there is no conceptual or operational consensus on when, why and how they might be used. To paraphrase Clausewitz, crisis management is the continuation of politics by other means. EU Member States need to develop a much clearer understanding of the relationship between the CFSP—with its emphasis on long-term conflict prevention—and the ESDP, which is more concerned with the short-term requirements of crisis management. This will involve a clearer consensus on how to combine instruments of persuasion and coercion into an integrated foreign, security and defence policy. EU Member States will therefore need to develop the equivalent of NATO's 'Strategic Concept' in order to establish clear political criteria specifying how and when to intervene in crisis situations, and with what mix of civilian and military instruments.[63]

The difficulty here is that the EU contains a diverse group of states with very different strategic cultures, from former colonial powers like Britain and France with a long history of military power projection, through 'civilian power' Germany, to the Scandinavian and post-neutral countries. This diversity will grow as the EU expands to include new members from central and eastern Europe and the Mediterranean. It may be that the ESDP project will provide the catalyst for a distinctly European approach to international security and that the EU will generate 'a new model of crisis management that is more appropriate to the complexities of the 21st century than military interventionism alone'.[64] However, it might also be the case that Europe's growing diversity will prove a major impediment to the development of a shared foreign policy vision and a common strategic culture, and that Europe's nascent crisis management capabilities will remain mired in political controversies over the guiding principles and policy objectives of the CFSP. Only one thing is certain: now that the EU has committed itself to launching a common security and defence policy within the framework of the CFSP, its credibility is on the line. Should the ESDP project fail and the EU prove unable to carry out Petersberg missions, the consequences will be dire, not just for the EU, but, more importantly, for international peace and security more broadly.

[63] See P Cornish and G Edwards, 'Beyond the EU/NATO dichotomy: the beginnings of a European strategic culture' (2001) 77 International Affairs 587.

[64] N Gnesotto in Howorth (n 1 above) vi. On the diverging international security agendas of the US and the Europeans, see I Daalder, 'Are the United States and Europe heading for divorce?' (2001) 77 International Affairs 553, 559.

4

Decision-making in the Area of Freedom, Security, and Justice

*Jörg Monar**

Introduction

At the beginning of the 1990s justice and home affairs (hereinafter JHA) did not yet exist as a policy-making area; since then it has been the fastest growing such area of the EU. Now—under the ambitious title of an 'area of freedom, security and justice' (hereinafter AFSJ)—it has become a major integration objective, codified in Article 2 TEU, to which the Tampere European Council of October 1999 has added a very ambitious political agenda. Since the entry into force of the Treaty of Amsterdam more than 200 Council acts regarding the development of the AFSJ have been adopted. In the aftermath of the unprecedented terrorist attacks of 11 September 2001 the speed of decision-making has again increased in certain areas, especially in judicial cooperation in criminal matters. At first sight all this looks quite impressive, but decision-making in the context of the AFSJ is also affected by a number of deficits and problems, some of which are also of considerable relevance to accountability and legitimacy in the post-Nice EU as a whole. However, before taking a closer look at the decision-making system within the AFSJ through an analysis of the role of the main political institutions, it seems useful to highlight three distinctive features which make it a special area of EU decision-making. These features, which make the AFSJ subject to a number of specific conditions and constraints, are its hybrid character, which combines elements of the Community and

* This chapter is based on research carried out in the context of the ESRC project 'Towards a new European governance of internal security' (Award L213252011) at the Centre for European Politics and Institutions of the University of Leicester.

Intergovernmental Methods, its high degree of 'flexibility' and the continuing predominance of unanimity in the Council.

Distinctive features of the AFSJ as an area of EU decision-making

Decision-making in the AFSJ as a hybrid of the Community and the intergovernmental method

The Treaty of Amsterdam has split EU JHA between one group of newly communitarized areas under Title IV TEC (asylum, immigration, external border controls and judicial cooperation in civil matters) and another group which remains within the intergovernmental context of Title VI TEU (police and judicial cooperation in criminal matters). Yet this division of the AFSJ into 'communitarized' and 'intergovernmental' policy-making areas, which is fully maintained by the Treaty of Nice, is much less clear-cut in pratice than theory. The communitarized areas (asylum, immigration, external border controls, civil law matters) retain strong intergovernmental features such as the continuing predominance of unanimity, the non-exclusive right of initiative of the European Commission, a very limited role for the EP and a number of limitations imposed on the role of the European Court of Justice. If the communitarized parts of the AFSJ do not fit convincingly under the heading of the 'Community method' neither do the areas remaining under Title VI TEU (police and judicial cooperation in criminal matters) fit easily under the 'intergovernmental method'. Elements such as the mandatory role given to the Court of Justice, mandatory consultation of the European Parliament on all legally binding acts and the strong link established with the provisions on the AFSJ under Title IV TEC (Article 61 TEC) make what is left of the old 'third pillar' much less intergovernmental than the CFSP. At least until 2004, when the transitional period ends, decision-making in the AFSJ is best described as a hybrid between the Community and the intergovernmental method.

It should be added that because of the legal divide between the first and the third pillar the development of the AFSJ is a natural domain for 'cross-pillar' action which further reinforces its hybrid character. For example, in the fight against drugs, measures against drug trafficking continue to fall under Title VI TEU whereas action against drug addiction has to be based on Article 152 TEC.

Schengen and other cases of 'flexibility'

A further distinctive feature of the AFSJ is its high degree of 'flexibility' generated by the incorporation of the Schengen acquis and the range of 'opt-outs' negotiated at Amsterdam. Only twelve EU Member States currently participate fully in the Schengen system. Denmark is a signatory of the Schengen Convention, but secured an opt-out possibility in respect of any Council decision building on the Schengen acquis in the context of Title IV TEC.[1] The United Kingdom and Ireland negotiated a full opt-out from both Schengen and measures adopted under Title IV TEC at Amsterdam. Yet they reserved the possibility of a total or partial opt-in. That option was used by the British Government in May 2000 when it secured the agreement in the Council to participate in substantial parts of the Schengen acquis, in particular, the ensemble of the provisions regarding the establishment and operation of the Schengen information system. A similar move was made on the Irish side, and both governments have already opted into a number of individual EC acts under Title IV TEC which are linked to the Schengen acquis. As a result both Ireland and the United Kingdom are now both partial Schengen members and partial participants in measures under Title IV TEC.

To complicate matters even further two non-Member States, Norway and Iceland, had to be closely 'associated' with the incorporated Schengen acquis because of the 1957 Nordic Passport Union and, more practically, because of the largely uncontrolled 1,650 km land border between Norway and Sweden. The EU insisted on its complete institutional autonomy for the further development of the Schengen acquis. The agreed solution was that Norway and Iceland would apply most of the operational parts of the Schengen acquis but content themselves with 'decision-shaping' instead of 'decision-making' in the context of a special 'Mixed Committee' (see below).

Voting rules: the intergovernmental legacy of the third pillar

The issue of voting rules is obviously crucial for any consideration of decision-making in the AFSJ. The transfer of most areas of the 'old' Title VI into the EC framework agreed on at Amsterdam could have caused a decisive change in this respect. Yet the intergovernmental legacy of the third pillar has proved to be rather tenacious. At Amsterdam, German Chancellor

---

[1] Art 5 of the Protocol on Denmark (Protocol No 5).

Helmut Kohl effectively blocked the introduction of qualified majority voting in the areas of asylum and immigration. This position was rooted in anxieties about the particular asylum and immigration pressures on Germany and the involvement of *Länder* interests in this area. Yet there were other advocates of unanimity in the newly communitarized areas. The British Government, for instance, insisted on unanimity in the area of judicial cooperation in civil matters. As a result Article 67(1)–(2) TEC, which establishes the decision-making rules for Title IV TEC, provides that the Council shall act unanimously for a five-year transitional period ending in 2004. After this period the Council will decide (by unanimity) whether to govern some or all parts of the Title on free movement by the Article 251 ('co-decision') procedure which provides for qualified majority voting. This two stage approach applies to all measures provided for by Title IV with the exception of visa policy as governed by Article 62(2)(b) TEC. Whether majority voting will be extended in 2004 is still an open question. It cannot be taken for granted that the unanimity required on this point will be achieved in the Council. Among former 'third pillar' policies, majority voting based on the Article 251 procedure applies only to measures against fraud affecting the financial interests of the Community (Article 280 TEC) and customs cooperation (Article 135 TEC), both of which are located outside of Title IV TEC.

As regards the areas remaining under Title VI TEU, all of the different types of acts mentioned above must be adopted by unanimity. However, Article 34(2)(c) states that measures implementing a 'decision' shall be taken by qualified majority, although Article 34(3) TEU creates the 'special hurdle' of a 'double' qualified majority requiring not only 62 votes but also that these are cast by at least ten Member States. This provision has never been used so far because 'decisions' tend to be drafted in such a detailed way that implementing measures are not needed.

The negotiations on the Treaty of Nice provided an opportunity to revise this continuing predominance of unanimity that tends to cause major delays in the decision-making process and least common denominator decisions. Yet the opportunity for a breakthrough towards qualified majority has, again, been missed. It is true that new Article 67(5) TEC introduces qualified majority voting in the context of the co-decision procedure (Article 251 TEC) for asylum policy measures and civil law cooperation. Yet this progress looks much less impressive because the German Government—again very much under pressure by the German *Länder*—successfully insisted that measures in these areas only be adopted by qualified majority after agreement on 'common rules and basic principles' by unanimity. The importance of the extension of qualified majority voting to judicial cooperation in civil matters is also considerably diminished by the fact that family law matters—arguably the most substantial part of civil law cooperation—remain excluded. A major discrepancy remains between on the one hand, the extensive range of objectives set for the AFSJ by the Amsterdam Treaty and the Tampere European Council Conclusions and, on the other, the limitations imposed on the decision-making capacity entailed by the continuing predominance of the unanimity principle. The report on the implementation of the Tampere agenda submitted by the Belgian Presidency and endorsed by the Laeken European Council of 14–15 December 2001 described the problem unusually clearly, stating that 'maintaining the unanimity rule is clearly a serious hindrance to progress'.[2]

The decision-making system of the AFSJ

Although the decision-making system of the AFSJ obviously consists of the same principal institutions as in other EU policy-making areas, their respective roles are slightly different, and there are also a number of problems specific to the AFSJ.

The European Council

Although Article 4 TEU gave the European Council an important role in JHA, for a long time there was little evidence of it giving any special 'impetus' in these areas. Even after Maastricht most of the issues were still regarded as rather technical and a matter for ministers. These ministers wished to keep developments in this field under their own control. This changed with the Treaty of Amsterdam which gave the Heads of State a huge new potential for EU action in JHA. As well as considering how they might use this potential, by the end of the 1990s the Heads of State or Government had become acutely aware that issues such as the combat against illegal immigration, drugs and crime were of major concern to EU citizens. They required more visible action by the European Council. During 1998 the feeling grew that the JHA ministers—often under the influence of conservatively minded senior officials—were taking up the challenge of implementing the Amsterdam potential only slowly. They

---

[2] Council document 14926/01.

were proceeding largely on the basis of 'business as usual'. This impression was only confirmed by the second, operational part of the December 1998 'Vienna Action Plan',[3] which hardly went beyond the pre-Amsterdam agenda. The decision to hold a special European Council on JHA matters can therefore be seen as an attempt of the Heads of State or Government to do two things. First they sought to assert their leadership role in what had now become a major EU policy-making area. Second, they wished to avoid losing the impetus and potential of Amsterdam because of widespread conservatism and inertia at the ministerial level.

The Tampere European Council of 15–16 October 1999 was a landmark for both the political and the institutional development of EU JHA. Launched in March 1999 by a joint letter of German Chancellor Gerhard Schröder and Finnish Prime Minister Paavo Lipponen, the preparations carried out under both the German and the Finnish Presidencies were among the most extensive of recent European Councils. Contrary to some predictions that the Heads of State or Government would spend most of the actual meeting on burning international problems and unresolved EU business, the Tampere summit did indeed focus on key issues of the further development of the AFSJ. The Heads of State or Government agreed on the introduction of a 'common asylum system' including a range of precise targets. Additionally they covered, at least partially, new ground as regards future EU action in areas such as access to justice and mutual recognition of judicial decisions; and they agreed to create two new institutions, the cross-border prosecution agency Eurojust and a European Police College. They also set several target dates for Commission and Council to implement the Tampere agenda. The new impetus provided by Tampere was felt almost immediately. By the end of 2000 key compromises had been achieved on the establishment of a European Refugee Fund, the creation of Eurojust and the European Police College, and major proposals in the area of asylum and immigration, most of them tabled by a more active Commission, were all under serious negotiation.

The Tampere summit was a 'special session' of the European Council, and the following meetings from Helsinki inevitably gave less prominence to AFSJ. Nonetheless, at Tampere the AFSJ was clearly at the top of the European Council's agenda, and every European Council meeting since then has included discussion of JHA matters in the Presidency Conclusions.

---

[3] On priorities and measures regarding the implementation of the Treaty of Amsterdam provisions on JHA [1999] OJ C19.

The European Council again exercised a strong leadership role in the aftermath of the terrorist attacks of 11 September 2001. A special European Council on 21 September endorsed the hastily prepared but substantial Action Plan agreed on by the JHA Council on 17 September. In addition it also instructed the Justice and Home Affairs Council to agree on the relevant arrangements at its meeting of 6–7 December 2001 at the latest. The ministers have never before been put under so much time pressure. When progress seemed rather slow (especially on the proposed European Arrest Warrant and the framework decision defining a terrorist act) the Heads of State or Government[4] felt the need for unusually strong language urging speedier decision-making in the JHA Council. Without the strong pressure by the European Council it seems unlikely that agreement on the common definition of terrorist acts and the introduction of the European Arrest Warrant would have been reached so quickly.

The results of the Nice Summit also suggest that the new leadership role assumed by the European Council in JHA matters will remain an important factor in the construction of the AFSJ. With the Treaty of Nice making little progress towards more majority voting (see above) the European Council will need to provide forceful guidelines and, occasionally, even to intervene in the decision-making process to prevent crucial progress from being blocked in the JHA Council because of the unanimity requirement.

From the perspective of accountability, the European Council's major role in the construction of the AFSJ is not unproblematic. European Council decisions are not subject to direct parliamentary control at either the European or the national level. Traditionally, the acceptability of this situation has rested on the fact that European Council decisions are not legally binding, together with the accountability of the Heads of State or Government to their own parliaments. However, European Council decisions can pre-determine the content of legally binding acts later adopted by the JHA Council to a considerable extent. The impact of Tampere on mutual recognition in judicial cooperation and the creation of Eurojust demonstrates this effect. Full democratic accountability should start where the substance of the decisions is taken, and not only at the implementation stage. Moreover, the Heads of State or Government tend to report back only rather generally to their national parliaments on European Council meetings. Their reports are rarely followed by in-depth parliamentary scrutiny of the results.

---

[4] At their meeting in Ghent on 19 October 2001. See Council document SN 4296/2/01.

The impact of the leadership role of the European Council on the European Commission's traditional right of initiative in the European construction also requires attention. Much of the Tampere agenda could—and should—have been formally proposed by the Commission. This is not entirely the fault of the European Council, but it means that the Commission (which is directly accountable to the European Parliament) has not shaped the main programmatic elements of the AFSJ's further construction.

The Council of the European Union

The Council of the European Union remains the main decision-making body of the AFSJ. Since 1994 the Justice and Home Affairs Council has been in *formal* session three to four times each year. It has become customary to hold in addition one *informal* Council meeting during each Presidency to allow for the discussion of strategic issues outside the normal procedural constraints. Under the Belgian Presidency of the second half of 2001—mainly because of the 11 September events—the total number of meetings rose to eight, and from 2002 onwards the JHA Council will in principle be convened on a monthly basis. The total number of texts adopted by the JHA Council has grown from 54 in 1994 to 99 in 2001, but more important than the numbers is the fact that since Amsterdam a much larger percentage are legally binding.

The incorporation of Schengen has added a considerable degree of complexity to the Council's business. The British and Irish 'opt-outs' mean that ministers of the two countries do not vote on certain Schengen issues and are not bound by certain Schengen decisions of the Council. By virtue of its special Amsterdam Protocol, Denmark may also not participate in decisions building on the Schengen acquis in the context of Title IV TEC. The Agreement of 18 May 1999[5] associating Norway and Iceland with the Schengen system gives these countries the right to express their views on proposed new measures in the context of a Mixed Committee at ministerial level. This Committee regroups the members of the EU Council and the ministers of Norway and Iceland. For obvious practical reasons these Mixed Committee meetings are held 'in the margins' of the JHA Council. The ministers representing Norway and Iceland join their EU colleagues at a pre-agreed time in the meeting room (before or after the normal Council meeting) to deal with any Schengen aspects concerning all of them. Unsur-

[5] [1999] OJ L176/36.

prisingly the Schengen members (plus the United Kingdom and Ireland where applicable) have normally already 'pre-agreed' on the issues at stake and in practice the representatives of Norway and Iceland have little chance to influence the final shape of the decisions adopted by the Council effectively. All these features of post-Amsterdam 'flexibility' complicate the Council's proceedings, reduce transparency and increase the difficulties of effective parliamentary control at both the national and the European level. For members of the European Parliament and national parliaments it is not always evident which members of the Council participated in a given decision and to which countries it is going to apply.

As in other areas of EU policy-making the decisions taken on AFSJ matters at the ministerial level are prepared and in most cases pre-determined by the work of a considerable number of bodies which operate within the Council framework below the ministerial level. The first and foremost is the Committee of Permanent Representatives (COREPER), which for JHA matters meets in the composition of the Permanent Representatives themselves (COREPER II) and is in charge of overall coordination. COREPER's role in JHA was initially a contested one, as national ministries of interior and justice associated with the 'old' third pillar tried to bypass it by establishing the former 'Article K.4 Committee' as the key decision-making body below the ministerial level. Yet the COREPER's central role has not only been reconfirmed in the Treaty of Amsterdam but it has also become clear that a strong COREPER input is very often needed to find political compromises when certain texts are blocked in the specialized JHA committees and working parties. In this respect the Permanent Representatives rely heavily on the work of their 'JHA advisers' who also meet regularly to prepare JHA points on the COREPER's agenda.

As a result of the communitarization of a major part of the AFSJ by the Treaty of Amsterdam, substantial changes had to be made to the Council working structures. One inevitable effect of the Amsterdam reforms was the limitation of the remit of the former 'Article K.4 Committee', now the 'Article 36 Committee', to the few areas still covered by the 'third pillar' (Title VI TEU).

Several Member States insisted, however, on also retaining a special coordinating body for matters of asylum, immigration and external border controls. This eventually took the form of a Strategic Committee working directly under the authority of COREPER. This solution was mainly due to the unwillingness of several national ministries to see certain supervisory and coordinating powers transferred to the Permanent Representatives. It leaves the newly communitarized areas of asylum and immigration with a similar four level structure as the remaining intergovernmental areas within the remit of the Article 36 Committee (see Figure 4.1). In spite of the SIS functions in the communitarized areas of external border controls, asylum and immigration, the working parties dealing with the functioning of the SIS have all been included in the police and customs cooperation part of the working structure. This represents a further 'intergovernmental' feature in the revised working structure of the Council. Equally noteworthy, the working party on customs cooperation remains within the 'third pillar' working structure although customs cooperation falls formally under Title X TEC. Some Member States took the view that this area was so closely related to police cooperation it should remain in the context of the Title VI TEU working structures.

Decision-making on JHA encounters most of its difficulties at the committee or working group level. In many national ministries the ambitious objectives of Amsterdam and Tampere have been received with scepticism. This attitude has been further fuelled by lack of knowledge of and/or lack of confidence in procedures and judicial and policing structures in some of the EU countries. The political impetus provided by the European Council and (more rarely) by the ministers is frequently lost on the Council committees, where the forces of inertia represented by officials from the national ministries of justice and the interior wanting to protect their own legal systems against change rarely fail to raise objections of principle and to the details of legal implementation.

A number of management problems also reduce the efficiency of the Council. Concerned about the slowness of progress in several JHA areas, in January 2001 the Swedish Presidency felt the need to start a critical evaluation of the working methods in JHA, known as the 'Haga process' after the Swedish castle where it began. Problems identified by this 'Haga process' include: deficits in the coordination and preparation of initiatives and meetings, a lack of prioritization of objectives, absence of longer term planning, frequent failures of senior Council committees to manage and concentrate the activities of working groups effectively, and weaknesses in the follow-up of decisions.[6] A number of suggestions to improve working methods have been made. Some have already found their way into the Belgian Presidency's report of December 2001 on the implementation of the Tampere agenda.[7]

---

[6] Council document 10336/01.   [7] Council document 14926/01.

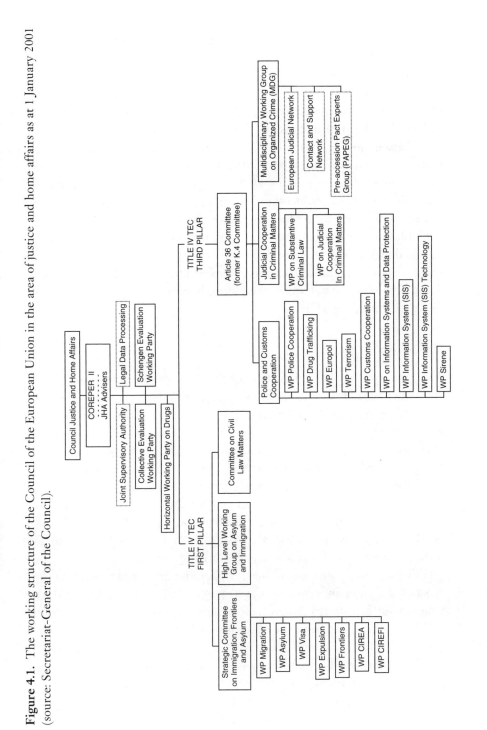

Figure 4.1. The working structure of the Council of the European Union in the area of justice and home affairs as at 1 January 2001 (source: Secretariat-General of the Council).

National legislative initiatives are a particular feature of decision-making on the AFSJ in the Council. Since 1999 Member States have made an increasing use of their shared right of initiative. While in some cases—such as the establishment of Eurojust—these have driven the process forward, they have caused a number of problems, such as the legal quality of the national proposals. Several of those submitted by Member States since 1999 lacked quality as in the form, legal basis and consistency of the terminology used. In the context of the 'Haga process' it has been suggested that Member States should follow the Council's legal service's guidelines, assess the legal situation in other Member States more carefully and circulate preliminary drafts to other delegations before taking formal initiatives. Examples of overlapping and competing initiatives have complicated and slowed down the decision-making process. Some Member States have also failed to provide timely and comprehensive information to the European Parliament on their initiatives, thereby adding to the democratic accountability deficit of the AFSJ.

The European Commission

The Treaty of Nice has left the Commission's role in the construction of the AFSJ unchanged from the slightly strengthened provisions of the Treaty of Amsterdam. According to Article 67(1) and (2) TEC the Commission still has to share the right of initiative with the Member States in all the communitarized areas under Title IV during the transitional period of five years, and only after this period will its right of initiative become exclusive. This is clearly a serious restriction, made worse by the limitation of the Commission's margin to manoeuvre due to the maintenance of unanimity in these areas during the transitional period. Under Title VI TEU the Commission still has to share its right of initiative with the Member States, but by virtue of amended Article 34(2) TEU it now extends also to matters of police and judicial cooperation in criminal matters.

Since the entry into force of the Treaty of Amsterdam (May 1999) the Commission has started to play a more active role in the JHA area. On the basis of the increased in-house expertise provided by the new Directorate-General Justice and Home Affairs it has submitted a range of legislative proposals—especially on asylum, immigration and judicial cooperation issues—and has adopted a number of 'Communications' outlining the main challenges the EU is facing in these areas and sketching out fundamental strategies and policy options. This increase in activity can be partially ascribed to the obvious upgrading of the importance of JHA by the Treaty of Amsterdam which was reconfirmed by the Tampere European Council in October 1999. From the outset, the new Prodi Commission placed JHA much higher on its agenda, as demonstrated by the 2000–2005 legislative programme.[8] Yet there is also a certain personality element. The Portuguese Commissioner Antonio Vitorino, who took over responsibility for JHA from Anita Gradin when the new Commission came into office, brought with him a far greater expertise in the area and adopted a much more ambitious and dynamic approach.

Apart from making an increasing number of formal legislative proposals the Prodi Commission has also made greater efforts than its predecessor to act as a policy initiator, through the adoption of a number of substantial analysis and programme documents. A major example is the Commission's Communication on a European migration policy of November 2000[9] which, rejecting the 'zero immigration' principle traditionally adopted by the Council, suggested a 'new approach' with a more positive, flexible and proactive approach towards immigration.[10] This initiative was well timed. The previous months had seen a growing debate on immigration in some Member States in the light of specific labour market skill shortages and the problem of ageing EU populations. The prevailing unanimity requirement in the Council, however, seriously limits the Commission's tactical possibilities to steer proposals through the Council. Several of its legislative proposals—especially on asylum and immigration matters—are currently blocked in the Council.

With Member States making extensive use of their right of initiative in AFSJ matters the Commission clearly has to struggle to live up to its traditional role as policy initiator. The Commission often finds its potential initiative partially or totally pre-empted by Presidency or Member State initiatives. This can reduce the impact of the Commission's own proposals on negotiations in the Council. In some cases the Commission has little option but to base its own proposals or general ideas on previous Member States initiatives. An interesting example in this context were the negotiations during 2000 on the establishment of Eurojust. In June 2000 Germany submitted a first formal initiative on the composition and tasks of the unit.[11]

[8] COM(2000) 154.
[9] COM(2000) 757.
[10] See chapter by Dell'Olio in this volume.
[11] Council document 8938/00.

This was followed in July by a joint initiative—a quite innovative feature—of the 'four Presidencies' (ie the current French one plus the preceding Portuguese and the two succeeding Swedish and Belgian).[12] There were significant differences between the two texts: the German initiative, aimed at avoiding delays in the setting up of the unit, proposed a very light structure with liaison officers from the Member States which would serve primarily as information exchange agents. The 'four Presidencies' initiative, however, gave the central role to the institution as such rather than to the liaison officers. It also envisaged that the operational functions for Eurojust should include such things as the power to ask a Member State to undertake an investigation or to prosecute specific acts. The Commission could then only build upon these initiatives in its own Communication on Eurojust.[13] As a compromise between the German and the 'four Presidencies' proposal it backed a two stage approach with a lighter provisional unit in the first stage and a fully fledged Eurojust with tasks of its own, a legal personality and an appropriate infrastructure to follow in the second stage. The Commission came firmly out in favour of Eurojust being more than just a documentation and information centre and suggested various ways in which it should become actively involved in cross-border criminal investigations. Nevertheless, in this case it acted as hardly more than a follow-on initiator to the Member States.

The non-exclusivity of the Commission's right of initiative may be justified in two ways. First, national administrations continue to have much greater expertise in the JHA area and, second, the implementation of JHA decisions continues to be largely in the hands of the Council and the national governments. Some element of competition may also be good in the sense that it forces the Commission to come up with potentially better ideas than the Member States and to introduce them before the Member States may pre-empt the field. The Commission also has a chance to make its proposals prevail through more extensive prior consultation with Member States and better legal quality than some of the national proposals. Yet pre-emptive and competing initiatives by Member States clearly reduce both the Commission's role overall and its capacity to steer negotiations towards outcomes above the least common denominator. There is also an issue of democratic accountability. The Commission—subject to a more direct control by the European Parliament—tends to inform the Parliament about its initiatives in a more timely and comprehensive manner than Member States.

---

[12] Council document 10356/00.   [13] See COM(2000) 746 (November 2000).

The European Parliament

The AFSJ has been branded repeatedly as a project for the European citizen. Some measures can also have major implications for the rights of individuals. These include measures such as those aimed at limiting abuses of the asylum system, the transfer of personal data in the context of police cooperation and external border controls, and rules on the interception of telecommunications and on money laundering in the fight against organized crime. Effective parliamentary control should therefore be one of the priorities of decision-making in the AFSJ.

The Treaty of Amsterdam strengthens the position of the European Parliament in the construction of the AFSJ by granting it a formal right to be consulted on all legally binding acts, both under Title IV TEC and Title VI TEU. This improved markedly on the previous situation under which the Council had only a vaguely phrased obligation to consult Parliament on the 'principal aspects' of JHA cooperation. By virtue of Article 67(2) TEC, co-decision by the European Parliament could be introduced on all the 'communitarized' matters under Title IV TEC after the end of the transitional period in 2004, but this remains subject to a unanimous decision by the Council. Its formal consultative role has significantly increased the amount of information provided to the Parliament by the Council, and since 1998 the Parliament has adopted full legislative reports with the corresponding resolution on all legally binding Council acts.

The Parliament's 'Committee on Citizens' Freedoms and Rights, Justice and Home Affairs' has (in spite of its cumbersome title) become quite an effective scrutiny body. Its procedures on JHA business are well developed, through contacts with the appropriate units in Council and Commission, which are marked by regular attendance of senior Commission and Council officials at its meetings, and frequent appearances of political representatives of Presidency and Commission on upcoming Council acts. The Committee's reports normally provide a detailed critical evaluation of the proposed acts with a range of suggested amendments and a presentation of broader political perspectives in the explanatory and resolution texts.

Major problems of democratic control through the Parliament persist, however. Its powers are currently limited to legislative consultation. The Council is not compelled to consider fully amendments suggested by the Parliament. In practice the impact of the Parliament's opinions on the Council's final decisions tends to be very limited, although Commission proposals have increasingly referred to positions adopted by the Parliament.

A further problem is that the Council continues to adopt strategy documents on which the Parliament is not consulted. As these are not legally binding the Council is not forced to consult, but the Parliament resents this practice as strategy documents often predetermine future EU action. The Action Plans on Afghanistan, Iraq, Morocco, Somalia and Sri Lanka, as major countries of origin and transit, adopted by the Council in October 1999 and implemented during 2000 are examples of such documents. The Parliament, which had not been consulted in advance on them, sharply criticized these Action Plans.[14] It detected an imbalance between the provisions on punitive action and those concerning integration as well as the absence of an adequate distinction between immigration and asylum issues. An increasing number of Member State legislative initiatives also make effective scrutiny more difficult (see above). These often lack the legal clarity of Commission initiatives, are frequently submitted belatedly to the Parliament and create some confusion as to which proposals are going to be the basis for final decision in the Council. There have also been controversies between Parliament and Council over the re-submission for consultation of substantially amended Council texts and the use of EC funds for JHA programmes under Title VI TEU.

In spite of a remarkable internal adaptation to the challenges of a relatively new policy-making area, the Parliament is clearly struggling, both at the plenary and the committee level, with the enormous workload resulting from the rapid development of the AFSJ and the large number of new initiatives. If a considerable number of measures is coming up in a relatively short period—as it happened with the post-11 September Action Plan—the Parliament can clearly only focus on the most important aspects. This may then leave some issues largely outside effective scrutiny, as happened, for instance, with the important first cooperation agreement between Europol and the United States.[15]

Conclusions

As a result of the extraordinary growth of the EU's JHA agenda during the last few years, and the complexity generated by the high degree of 'flexibility' and the challenge of adapting EU decision-making to the requirements of the

[14]   Bulletin of the EU 3–2000, 1.4.3.
[15]   Signed in the margins of the JHA Council of 6–7 December 2001 (Council document 13359/01).

AFSJ was greater than in any other area of EU policy-making. In terms of 'output', so far this challenge seems to have been met reasonably well. The large number of new initiatives launched since the entry into force of the Treaty of Amsterdam and the shift from 'soft' to 'hard' instruments of law justify the assumption that the AFSJ, in spite of all obstacles, will become much more of a reality during the next few years. After some near failures, the fact that the EU has been able to agree on two major groundbreaking judicial cooperation instruments—the European Arrest Warrant and the Framework Decision on the fight against terrorism—in just three months, under the impact of the 11 September attacks,[16] proves that the decision-making system can produce substantial results even under major time constraints.

Yet there are also a number of problems. The high degree of fragmentation caused by Schengen and the range of opt-outs complicates decision-making, leads to legal fragmentation and reduces transparency. The political guidance provided by the European Council in the JHA area poses problems of democratic accountability. It also tends to lose impetus at the level of the Council committees where objections from national ministries and management problems slow down the decision-making process. The predominance of unanimity encourages least common denominator agreements in the Council, and negotiations are made more complex by an increasing number of initiatives from Member States, some of which have been lacking in quality. In this context the Commission has clear difficulties in attempting to play its traditional role as a driving force in terms of policy initiation. The European Parliament's powers of democratic control continue to be limited to consultation, the weakest form of parliamentary participation in the legislative process, and often do not extend to important strategy documents. At the committee level its scrutiny capacity is often stretched to its limits because of the large number of new initiatives coming up in the Council and the often very limited time for consideration of Council texts, especially if these emanate from Member States.

The Treaty of Nice has brought only very limited progress in terms of the EU's decision-making capacity in the AFSJ—through a slight extension of the possibility of majority voting—and has not addressed the problems of accountability. With the agenda for the next Intergovernmental Conference still being largely a matter for speculation it seems that the end of the transitional period in 2004 will be a crucial moment for the further development of the AFSJ. Should the Member States then fail to make use of

[16] September–December 2001.

Article 67(2) TEC to extend the co-decision procedure to all or most of the Title IV TEC areas the opportunity to increase significantly the Union's decision-making capacity in justice and home affairs could be lost for a long time, perhaps even forever. It is far from certain that many of the applicant countries will be willing to give up national 'veto' possibilities on crucial parts of the AFSJ—such as external border controls and money-laundering— which are of special sensitivity to them. The use of 'enhanced cooperation', which will be made easier by the Treaty of Nice, could then provide the only way out of protracted deadlocks in the Council, but this would come at the price of further fragmentation, complexity and reduced transparency of the AFSJ.

5

Accountability and Legitimacy: What is the Contribution of Transparency?

*Peter Dyrberg**

Transparency, democracy, accountability and legitimacy

Since the term 'transparency' emerged in a European Union context approximately ten years ago, its use has become widespread. The term commonly appears in the company of other positive terms and expressions such as 'openness', 'democracy', 'close to the citizens', 'accountability' and 'efficiency'. As this list illustrates, transparency has links to ongoing debates in the European Union such as those on the democratic deficit, good governance and administrative reform. Therefore, a few clarifying remarks should be made about the term.

It is often said that transparency and, in particular, access to information is based on the democratic principle. Such a proposition is both right and wrong at the same time. Thus, it must be qualified. The proposition is wrong in the sense that transparency does not necessarily have a link with the classical and still-popular perception of Western democracy. In that perception, the administration is part of the executive, which is an emanation of the legislature. That being so, the legislature is capable of monitoring the administration. Core elements of transparency—such as public access to information held by the administration and an ombudsman to monitor the administration—came about historically in a different setting, in Sweden in the eighteenth and nineteenth century. The Swedish administration was meant to be independent, hence the need to develop other mechanisms of control and accountability, such as public access to information and an

---

* The opinions expressed are personal and cannot be attributed to the institution I serve. My thanks go to Peter Bonnor, Strasbourg, for comments on this chapter. I am solely responsible for any errors.

Ombudsman Office.[1] The reason for the increased interest in and adoption of these institutions in most Western societies is the recognition that, in complex modern societies with huge public sectors, the legislature cannot do the day-to-day monitoring of the administration, and that the classical model must be reviewed.[2]

The proposition is also right, first, in the sense that a well-functioning democracy depends on public and informed debate. The debate may be fuelled by the information that citizens, and in particular journalists and researchers, may obtain from public authorities through rules on public access to information. It may also be fuelled by the contributions that public servants may independently make through their use of the freedom of expression. This consideration does not imply that a well-functioning democracy is conditioned by the availability of rules on public access. It implies that, all things being equal, public access may contribute to such functioning.

If one is a supporter of participatory democracy, the proposition is also right in the sense that mechanisms of transparency, such as public access to information, may enhance the possibilities for civil society to participate in the authorities' decision-making. This does not mean that transparency necessarily implies participatory democracy. Whether one wants participatory democracy or not is a distinct question. It means that, if one wants to arrive at participatory democracy, transparency may offer tools to get there.

Likewise, the transparency debate does not imply a stand on the question whether the democratic anchorage of the Union should lie mainly with the European Parliament or with the domestic parliaments, whether national or regional. However, transparency is democratic and at odds with intergovernmentalism in the sense that the latter often brings with it working practices stemming from classical diplomacy, such as closed doors and secrecy. While it has to be recognized that, to some extent, there still has to be room for such practices in the Union, it appears unacceptable to the quest for transparency that, as a rule, provisions governing citizens' lives should be made under such conditions.[3] It seems understandable that citizens react adversely if

---

[1] For a comparison of the Swedish model with the standard European model of governance, see J Ziller, 'European models of government: towards a patchwork with missing pieces' (2001) 54 Parliamentary Affairs 102.

[2] See equally R Dehousse, 'European institutional architecture after Amsterdam: parliamentary system or regulatory structure' (1998) 35 CMLRev 595, 615.

[3] See equally K St C Bradley, 'La transparence de l'Union européenne: une évidence ou un trompe l'œil?' (1999) Cahiers de Droit Européen 283, 358.

policy areas that had hitherto lain in the public domain on a domestic level are made subject to secrecy because of Europeanization of the policy area. Secrecy may foster anti-internationalist and anti-globalization sentiments amongst citizens.

Transparency may be considered part of accountability or a prerequisite to it: how can the public hold public authorities accountable if the public is not allowed to know what goes on within the public authorities, or if what goes on is obscure?[4] In the words of the Community judiciary: '... the transparency called for by European Councils, in order to allow the public "the widest possible access to documents" ... is essential to enable citizens to carry out genuine and efficient monitoring of the exercise of the powers vested in the Community institutions ...'.[5] Thus, transparency and accountability go hand in hand. Likewise, it is doubtful that the exercise of public authority may be perceived as legitimate if it is not understood.

Lastly 'transparency' seems increasingly to become synonymous with 'good administration'. The European Ombudsman has defined 'transparency' in the following way: '... [P]rocesses of decision-making should be understandable and open. The decisions themselves should also be reasoned and based on information that, to the maximum extent possible, is publicly available.'[6] Another definition is that transparency in decision-making covers at least the following four principles: '(1) the right to a statement of reasons for a decision, (2) the right to be heard before a decision is taken, (3) a party's right of access to the file, and (4) the public's right of access to information.'[7] The elements of these definitions can largely be found in Article 41 of the Charter of Fundamental Rights of the European Union which enshrines the 'Right to good administration'. According to paragraphs 1 and 2 of the Article:

1. Every person has the right to have his or her affairs handled impartially, fairly and within a reasonable time by the institutions and bodies of the Union.

---

[4] To be allowed to see what is going on in public authorities is sometimes referred to as 'openness' as opposed to 'transparency', which then is concerned with the question whether what one sees is obscure or clear. See for instance the OECD paper 'European principles for public administration', available at http://www1.oecd.org/puma/sigmaweb/pubs/ENGPDF/SPNO27.pdf/. The distinction is not used in this chapter.

[5] Case T-92/98 *Interporc v Commission* [1999] ECR II-3521, para 39.

[6] J Söderman, 'The role and impact of the European Ombudsman in access to documentation and transparency of decision-making' in V Deckmyn and I Thomson (eds), *Openness and Transparency in the European Union* (1998) 75.

[7] B Vesterdorf, 'Transparency—not just a vogue word' (1999) 22 Fordham International Law Journal 902, 903.

2. This right includes:
   —the right of every person to be heard, before any individual measure which would affect him or her adversely is taken;
   —the right of every person to have access to his or her file, while respecting the legitimate interests of confidentiality and of professional and business secrecy;
   —the obligation of the administration to give reasons for its decisions.

In a separate provision, Article 42, the Charter enshrines the right of access to documents. The similarity of the definitions given suggests that the quest for transparency will increasingly be occupied with the topic of good administration.[8]

Different elements in transparency

In the European Union, there is a cluster of elements under the heading 'transparency'. These are, amongst others, clear drafting, simplification of the founding Treaties, simple legislation, the debate on comitology, efforts to trace the influence of interest groups in the decision-making process, transparent enforcement procedures, public access to documents, freedom of expression of servants and whistle-blower protection. A selection has to be made. Even on the selected subjects this chapter cannot be exhaustive.

The chapter will mainly deal with public access. The reason is that public access has been at the core of transparency efforts. Before that, the issue of simplifying the Treaties will briefly be dealt with. The reason is that this issue of transparency has been considered sufficiently important to be mentioned in the Declaration on the Future of the Union, annexed to the Nice Treaty. Finally, the chapter will briefly present the issue of transparency in the Commission's enforcement procedures. That subject may be at the forefront of transparency in the years to come, as good administration is increasingly focused upon.[9]

---

[8] See also A Tomkins, 'Transparency and the emergence of European administrative law' (1999/2000) 19 YEL 217, 245.

[9] As for the debate on comitology, the myriad committees assisting the Commission in policy formulation and implementation, see amongst others R Dehousse, 'European governance in search of legitimacy: the need for a process-based approach' in O De Schutter, N Lebessis and J Paterson (eds), *Governance in the European Union* (a study from the Commission's Forward Studies Unit) (2001) 169, 176; W Sauter and E Vos, 'Harmonisation under Community law: the comitology issue' in P Craig and C Harlow (eds), *Lawmaking in the European Union* (1998) 169; and the special issue of ELJ on the subject, (1997) 3 ELJ. For the drafting and the quality of Community legislation, see amongst others H Xanthaki,

Simplification of the Treaties

In the process leading to the Amsterdam Treaty simplification of the Treaties figured as an issue.[10] The Amsterdam Treaty made a first 'spring-cleaning' of the founding Treaties—obsolete expressions and provisions were removed. Next, the Amsterdam Treaty proceeded to renumber the remaining provisions. In declaration 42 to the Treaty, it was stated that one should continue work on the consolidation of the Treaties. Point 5 in the Nice Declaration on the Future of the Union specifically mentions simplification of the Treaties as one of the topics to be dealt with in the process leading to the next Treaty revision. It is stated that the simplification of the Treaties should be made 'without changing their meaning'.

Simplifying the Treaties should, albeit not being an uncomplicated task, in principle be a manageable 'technical' task.[11] It is also a laudable task. Bringing order and legibility into a normative document is in itself positive. However, one should certainly not overestimate the importance such an exercise may have in bringing the Union closer to its citizens. Next, one should not be unaware of the possibility that another agenda lies behind the simplification issue. Although it is stated that there should be no change in the meaning of the Treaties, the following point 6 in the Nice Declaration provides that 'Addressing the abovementioned issues [ie including the simplification of the Treaties] the Conference recognises the need to improve and to monitor the democratic legitimacy and transparency of the Union and its institutions, in order to bring them closer to the citizens of the Member States.' Thus, it cannot be excluded that those who find a merely technical simplification of the Treaties unsatisfactory from a democratic point of view, will argue that further simplification is required. All things being equal, drafting a Constitution will normally, legally speaking, be a simpler exercise than drafting Treaties in which the interests of many States have to be accommodated. This slippage from simplification of the

'The problem of quality in EU legislation: what on earth is really wrong?' (2001) 38 CMLRev 651; T Burns, 'Better lawmaking? An evaluation of lawmaking in the European Community' in Craig and Harlow (this note above) 435 and C Timmermans, 'How can one improve the quality of Community legislation?' (1997) 34 CMLRev 1229.

[10] See for instance the Commission's Report on the Functioning of the Treaty on European Union (SEC (95)731 final) 4. The Parliament commissioned a report on the subject which was made by R Bieber. The report is part of the Parliament's project file IV/95/25. See also chapter by Vibert in this volume.

[11] The necessary work is currently being undertaken at the European University Institute, see the website http://www.iue.it/RSC/Treaties.html/.

Treaties to the drafting of a Constitution now also appears in the Laeken Declaration on the Future of the Union: 'If we are to have greater transparency, simplification is essential.... The question ultimately arises as to whether this simplification and reorganization might not lead in the long run to the adoption of a constitutional text in the Union.'

This shows clearly one of the risks to the transparency debate: it is taken hostage by other discourses. It is perfectly legitimate that some people may want to discuss the idea of a Constitution of Europe. If that is the case, however, it is submitted that it would be better that the idea is not introduced through a back door called 'transparency'.

Public access to documents

Public access to documents is the field where transparency efforts have been most successful. The latest success was the enactment of Regulation 1049/ 2001, of 30 May 2001, regarding public access to European Parliament, Council and Commission documents.[12] In what follows, the developments until now will be described so that the question of what remains to be done after the enactment of the Regulation can be considered.

Before the Maastricht Treaty secrecy was the norm in the institutions. Reflections of this may be found for instance in the case of *BEUC v Commission*, in which the European Office for Consumer Organizations was denied access to the non-confidential documents in an anti-dumping file held by the Commission.[13] This official stand was not entirely translated into the practice of the institutions: lobbyists and journalists based in Brussels found it relatively easy to obtain information through contacts as long as the identity of the supplier was kept anonymous: the 'culture of leaks'.[14] Lobbyists and journalists not based in Brussels were less happy with this culture which was problematic from a number of angles, including the principle of equality of citizens before public authorities. The Maastricht Treaty itself did not alter this situation. Declaration 17 to the Treaty limited itself to providing that transparency strengthens the democratic nature of the institutions and the public's confidence in the administration and that, accord-

[12] [2001] OJ L145/43.

[13] Case C-170/89 *BEUC v Commission* [1991] ECR I-5709.

[14] Bjorn Kassoe Andersen and Ole Vigant Ryborg, 'EF og Offentlighed i Forvaltningen'—a report established for the Danish Association of Journalists and the Confederation of the Danish Press—(1993) 6.

ingly, the Commission should submit to the Council a report on public access.

The Danish and French referenda, as well as opinion polls in other countries which demonstrated scant popular support for the Union, made it urgent to act upon this Declaration, and transparency found its way onto the agenda of European Council meetings. Following a number of preparatory works [15], in December 1993 the Council and the Commission adopted a common Code of Conduct on public access to documents which each of them then implemented through a decision.[16] As a result of an own initiative inquiry by the European Ombudsman, the other institutions and bodies adopted similar rules, with the exception of the Court of Justice.[17]

The rules provided, in short, that members of the public should have the widest possible access to documents held by the institutions without having to show any particular interest. The rules thus implied a radical change in the hitherto official stand. 'Documents' meant any written text, whatever its medium, containing data and which had been established by the institution in question. As in any other regime on public access, the rules laid down a number of grounds on which access to documents could be refused, for instance public security or individual privacy. Public access rules are not enacted to reveal security measures installed in public buildings or to enable neighbours to 'nose' into the medical record of an individual. Given that the institutions were venturing into hitherto unknown territory and given the vast range of the institutions' activities, the grounds for refusing access

[15] See in particular the Commission communications in [1993] OJ C63/8, C156/5 and C166/4.

[16] Decision 93/731 on public access to Council documents and Decision 94/90 on public access to Commission documents, respectively [1993] OJ L340/43 and [1994] OJ L46/58. The Council adopted the rules on the basis of its Rules of Procedure. This legal basis was subsequently contested before the Court of Justice which dismissed the action, Case C-58/94 *Netherlands v Council* [1996] ECR I-2169. The ruling has been extensively commented upon in legal literature, see amongst others F Sejersted *Innsyn og Integrasjon* (1997) 127–130 and U Öberg, 'The EU citizens' right to know: the improbable adoption of a European Freedom of Information Act' (1999) 2 CYELS 303, 312.

[17] In my submission the Court should adopt rules so as to enable its servants to handle requests for access to its administrative documents. However, it must be accepted that the public's interest in these would be rather limited. On the other hand, as concerns judicial documents covered by the Rules of Procedure, the lack of public availability of some categories of documents seems to merit reflection, in particular as concerns requests for preliminary rulings. The legal community as a whole would appear to have a justifiable interest in the availability of these. The Rules of Procedure are in principle no obstacle to a party itself making public its pleadings, see Case C-376/98 *Germany v Parliament and Council* [2000] ECR I-2249.

were drafted in a rather abstract and thus generous way. Thus, the extent of the openness that the rules would effectively create depended, to a large extent, on the interpretation given to the rules in practice. The rules also laid down the procedure to be followed in order to obtain a document: in short, the institution had 30 days to take a stand on an application for access. Where the application was refused, a 'confirmatory application' could be lodged, upon which the institution again had 30 days to decide. The rules also provided for information on remedies: where the 'confirmatory application' was refused, the applicant had to be informed about the possibility of lodging a complaint with the Ombudsman or bringing an action before the Court of First Instance. These rules were thus an illustration of good legislative drafting: they included the principle, the exceptions, the procedure to be followed and the remedies.

The application of the rules in practice was less fortunate. It appeared that the Council, the Commission and/or their servants had a restrictive view of what could be disclosed to citizens.[18] It is understandable that the inhabitants of the two institutions needed time to adjust to the radical change of culture that the rules implied. However, their restrictive attitude discredited the two institutions in the public's view and led to a hardening of the tone in the transparency debate. An inevitable outcome of the restrictive view was litigation before the Community Courts and the Ombudsman. It did not help the two institutions' reputation that the Community judiciary overwhelmingly annulled refusals to disclose documents, although the annulment often occurred on the ground of lack of reasoning. The Community judiciary and the Ombudsman contributed significantly to the early development of transparency.[19] Amongst the achievements one may mention that the public access rules were held to apply to all documents established by the institutions, thus including documents related to the

---

[18] See equally the open letter of 30 April 1996 addressed to the Secretary General of the Council by the European Federation of Journalists, stating 'grave reservations about the Council's interpretation and practice of the code of conduct concerning access to documents', and H Ragnemalm, 'The Community Courts and openness within the European Union' (1999) 2 CYELS 19, 29–30. In one case, the Court of First Instance even took the unusual step of applying its rules on unreasonably or vexatiously caused costs and ordered the Community institution to bear all the costs of the proceedings: see Case T-311/00 *British American Tobacco (Investments) Ltd v Commission*, judgment of 25 June 2002, paras 62–67.

[19] See equally, as concerns the Court of Justice, RW Davis, 'The Court of Justice and the right of public access to Community-held documents' (2000) 25 ELRev 303, 308 and as concerns the Ombudsman, U Öberg, 'Public access to documents after the entry into force of the Amsterdam Treaty: much ado about nothing?', available at http://eiop.org.at. For a more hesitant view see A Tomkins (n 8 above) 224–245.

second and the third pillars, and the ruling that documents established by the Commission in the framework of comitology equally were covered.[20]

The Amsterdam Treaty brought improvements in respect of transparency, including a provision on public access, Article 255 EC, which provides that the European Parliament and the Council shall lay down rules on public access.[21] The rules are contained in the above-mentioned Regulation which applies to the Parliament, the Council and the Commission.[22] It overcomes shortcomings in the previous rules. In the first place, the Regulation covers both documents established by the institution to which the application for access is addressed and incoming documents. This is of great importance to the extent that users of public access rules, ie journalists, researchers and professionals, find it valuable to compare authorities' output with the input they have had. In the second place, the Regulation provides for the creation of public registers of documents. Registers of documents are supposedly an important tool for any public authority to keep track of its files. Making them public enhances the public's opportunity to access the documents. In providing for this, the Regulation promotes order, ie efficiency, and transparency in the institutions.[23] In the third place, the Regulation makes more stringent the grounds for refusing access. Next, the Regulation shortens the deadlines within which the institutions have to

---

[20] Respectively Case T-174/95 *Tidningen Journalisten v Council* [1998] ECR II-2289 and Case T-188/97 *Rothmans International v Commission* [1999] ECR II-2463. These results had also been assumed in legal literature, respectively N Fenger, 'Aktindsigt i EU-sager' (1996) Juristen 205 and P Dyrberg, 'Current issues in the debate on public access to documents' (1999) 24 ELRev 157, 167.

[21] Legal literature appears to be uncertain on whether Art 255 EC enshrines public access as a constitutional right, see D Curtin, 'Citizens' fundamental right of access to EU information: an evolving digital *passepartout*?' (2000) 37 CMLRev 7, 14, and C Harlow, 'Freedom of information and transparency as administrative and constitutional rights' (1999) 2 CYELS 285, 295. As to the question whether public access should be considered a fundamental human right, see RW Davis, 'Public access to Community documents: a fundamental human right?', available at http://eiop.or.at. Legal literature is divided on the question whether the current case law enshrines public access as a fundamental general principle of Community law; for an affirmative answer see amongst others U Öberg (n 16 above) 314 and for a more hesitant view see amongst others M Broberg, 'Retten til Aktindsigt hos Fællesskabets Institutioner' (2001) Ugeskrift for Retsvæsen 329, 336. In its latest ruling concerning public access, the Court of Justice did not address the question but decided the case on other grounds, Case C-353/99 P *Council v Hautala*, judgment of 6 December 2001, para 31.

[22] Implementing rules have been laid down by each of the three institutions, respectively [2001] OJ L374/1, OJ L313/40 and OJ L345/94.

[23] The Council has, since 1999, maintained a remarkable register on its website. It ensures, amongst other things, that once a document has been disclosed to one citizen under the rules on public access, the document is accessible on the website.

act on an application for access to documents: the 30 days mentioned above are reduced to 15 working days. That delay may still appear long to a journalist. What is more important is, therefore, that the Regulation provides that in principle an application for access shall be handled promptly. Thus, if the institutions take the full 15 working days in handling a request, without justifiable reasons, they may expose themselves to criticism from the Ombudsman. Finally, the Regulation addresses the thorny subject of its relationship with national rules on public access as concerns documents originating in the Union institutions and in the possession of national authorities. Member States with a liberal regime of public access had feared that Community standards could be imposed upon them as concerns such documents, and they had reasons for these fears.[24] The Regulation solves the issue by providing that the national authorities shall consult with the Union institution in question before taking a decision of disclosure, unless non-disclosure/disclosure is clear. The provision must imply that in case of disagreement, the national authorities are entitled to go ahead with disclosure. In that case, the Commission or another Member State may then consider bringing infringement proceedings before the Court of Justice against the Member State in question where the applicant would have to prove its case for confidentiality. The provision appears to be a fair compromise between the interests at stake.[25] Thus, an overall assessment of the Regulation must be positive.[26]

---

[24] For instance in the *Tidningen Journalisten* case (n 20 above) it was argued that Community rules should regulate national authorities' disclosure of documents, established by the institutions. The Court of First Instance did not rule on the question.

[25] The category of documents which is most affected in practice appears to be letters of formal notice and reasoned opinions, issued by the Commission to the Member State before possibly taking the Member State to Court for its alleged failure to comply with Community law. In Sweden, for instance, it is normal practice for these documents to be disclosed after consulting the Commission, which does not disclose such documents itself and does not believe Member States should do so. In the EEA, it is standard practice in Norway and Iceland for such documents, issued by the EFTA Surveillance Authority, to be disclosed. Following the Commission's practice, the Surveillance Authority itself does not disclose the documents. On the other hand, the Surveillance Authority has hitherto not considered that it has any interest in preventing disclosure by the aforementioned EFTA States.

[26] See equally the European Ombudsman's speech 'Transparency as a Fundamental Principle of the European Union', given at the Humboldt University, Berlin, on 19 June 2001, available through the Ombudsman's homepage; B Wägenbauer, 'Der Zugang zu EU-dokumenten—Transparenz zum Anfassen' (2001) 12 Europäische Zeitschrift für Wirtschaftsrecht 680, 685 and O Abrahamsson, 'Obefogad Ängslan för den svenska offentlighetsprincipen' (2001) 4 Europarättslig Tidskrift 391. For a different view, see U Öberg, 'Sura svenska krusbär' (2001) 2 Europarättslig Tidskrift 155.

The remedies have also been improved in the sense that an amendment to the Rules of Procedure of the Court of First Instance permits the Court to take knowledge of the document at issue without having to communicate it to the other party to the procedure.[27] It remains to be seen whether this will lead the Court of First Instance to enter more into an assessment of the merits of a refusal to disclose a document.[28] As concerns the Ombudsman, an amendment to the Statute of the Ombudsman is currently on its way through the legislative machinery. It will improve the Ombudsman's right to inspect documents held by the institutions. This coupled with a possible acceleration of the Ombudsman's procedures in cases concerning refusal to grant access to documents would enhance the attractiveness of the Ombudsman Office as a remedy for applicants whose requests for documents have been turned down. All things being equal, the 'division of labour' that one should attempt to bring about in practice is that normally the cases go to the Ombudsman, not to the Community judiciary. Amongst the reasons for such a 'division of labour' one may mention that the scarce resources of the Courts could be deployed to other effects and that Ombudsman procedures are normally speedier.

What remains to be done? Not much, when compared with the work accomplished since Maastricht. An outstanding issue is whether documents related to the Commission's infringement proceedings against Member States, in particular reasoned opinions and letters of formal notice, should continue to be secret. Another issue is the relationship with rules on data protection. These rules are to a large extent based on the same concerns which lie behind the exceptions to the main rule on public access to documents: protection of justifiable public and private interests in confidentiality. However, there are signs that the institutions are taking an excessive view of what requires data protection.[29] It is therefore worth recalling that, put very simply, the origin of data protection rules is to protect citizens against undue intervention by public authorities, not to protect public authorities against scrutiny by citizens.

On the other hand, there are also encouraging signs as concerns attitudes in the institutions. For instance, the figures that the Commission and Council publish on the percentage of documents disclosed out of all

---

[27] Art 67(3) of the Rules of Procedure, [2000] OJ L322/5.

[28] It was the use of this new procedural tool which enabled the Court of First Instance to quash a refusal to grant access, because of a manifestly incorrect assessment of the facts, in Case T-211/00 *Aldo Kuijer v Council*, judgment of 7 February 2002, paras 69 and 70.

[29] See the European Ombudsman's special report on complaint 713/98/IJH, available on the Ombudsman's website: www.euro-ombudsman.eu.int/.

documents requested is continuously increasing. Thus, the two institutions are becoming familiarized with public access. Against this background, it appears understandable that the transparency debate is partly moving on to the subject of good administration.

Transparent enforcement procedures

Under Article 211 EC, the Commission is responsible for monitoring compliance by Member States with their obligations under Community law—it is the so-called 'Guardian of the Treaty'. Its ultimate tool in performing this task is to bring infringement proceedings before the Court of Justice under Article 226 EC. Bringing a case is preceded by an administrative phase which may roughly be divided into two stages. First, there is a so-called informal stage where the Commission may have contacts with the national authorities to verify whether an infringement is actually occurring and, if so, to see whether the Member State may be brought into line with its obligations under Community law. This stage is followed by the so-called formal stage, the elements of which are the Commission's letter of formal notice, its reasoned opinion and the Member State's replies.

Citizens and firms have always been around on the fringes of the procedure outlined above. The Commission's knowledge of possible infringements stems mainly from complaints lodged with it by citizens and firms. The Commission may even have encouraged such complaints by publishing a complaint form in the Official Journal.[30] However, legally complainants have no place in the procedure. This is related to the fact that the Community Courts have consistently held that complainants have no locus standi to challenge the Commission's decision on their complaint, the Commission's power to bring a case against a Member State being discretionary.[31] This case law is not borne of an attitude hostile to citizens. Rather it is borne of concerns to ensure that the Commission remains firmly in control

---

[30] Originally [1989] OJ C26/6, now [1999] OJ C119/5.

[31] Case C-87/89 *Sonito and Others v Commission* [1990] ECR I-1981. Legal literature appears divided and uncertain as to what exactly the discretion implies and under what circumstances it applies, see A Dashwood and R White, 'Enforcement actions under Articles 169 and 170 EEC' (1989) 14 ELRev 388, A Evans, 'The enforcement procedure of Article 169 EEC: Commission discretion' (1979) 6 ELR 442, A Mattera, 'La procedure en manquement et la protection des droits des citoyens at des opérateurs lésés' (1995) Revue du Marché Unique Européen 137 and P Dyrberg, 'Medlemsstaternes traktatbrud—Kommissionens skon og forklaringspligt i forhold til private klagere' (2001) EU-ret & Menneskeret 241.

of this crucial part of its institutional position. The Court of Justice has therefore also persistently dismissed submissions of Member States that could encroach on the Commission's discretion.[32] The same concerns may underlie the Courts' acceptance that documents concerning infringement proceedings are not disclosed to complainants under public access rules.[33]

Nonetheless, citizens and firms continue in growing numbers to complain to the Commission about Member States and the complainants increasingly make demands of the Commission. They expect the infringement complained of to be pursued to its end and without delays, that they will be heard and kept informed throughout the procedure and that they will receive a reasoned decision on their complaint. Thus, complainants expect the Commission to act, not just as 'Guardian of the Treaty' but as some sort of 'Protector of Citizens'. There is a tension between the two roles and it is not clear how they can be reconciled.[34] Furthermore, the fact that the Commission's procedure lies in the dark and that it is not legally bound to give explanations as to what it does or does not pursue may nurture beliefs that infringement proceedings are subject to illegitimate political considerations.[35]

Citizens and firms who have considered the Commission's handling of their complaint unsatisfactory have sometimes gone to the European Ombudsman with their grievances. Furthermore, the Ombudsman decided,

---

[32] See for instance Case 416/85 *Commission v United Kingdom* [1988] ECR 3127.

[33] Case T-105/95 *WWF UK v Commission* [1997] ECR II-313 and Case T-309/97 *Bavarian Lager Company v Commission* [1999] ECR II-3217.

[34] This tension between the two roles may be reflected in the internal divisions, which there reportedly have been in the Commission, on how to handle infringement proceedings, see European Voice, 2–8 March 2000 under the heading 'Commission's legal chief sparks infringement row'. See also the European Parliament's Resolution of 14 January 1999 concerning commercial communications in the internal market, Parliament document number A4-0503/98, available through the Parliament's website (www.europarl.eu.int), which seems to blame the Commission's Legal Service for the failures of infringement proceedings. It may be that operational departments, dealing directly with complainants, have a more liberal view on what should be pursued than legal services, which have the task of bringing the case in Luxembourg. Complaints may concern failure to comply in individual cases, without general implications, or may be 'facts heavy' and thus not suitable for court proceedings in Luxembourg, see equally C Timmermans, 'Judicial protection against the Member States: Articles 169 and 177 revisited' in D Curtin and T Heukels (eds), *Institutional Dynamics of European Integration—Essays in Honour of Henry G Schermers* Volume II (1994) 391, 399.

[35] See also R Williams, 'The European Commission and the enforcement of environmental law: an invidious position' (1994) 14 YEL 351, 372.

in 1997, to conduct an own initiative inquiry into the Commission's procedures for dealing with complaints against Member States. As to the Commission's discretion in the matter, the Ombudsman stated that the case law did not prevent the Commission, on its own initiative, from adhering to standards of good administration. The result of the inquiry was in essence that the Commission committed itself to informing complainants of its provisional decision to close the file on their complaint, providing them with the reasons for this decision and enabling them to give their comments before the final decision is taken.[36] It appeared from the Commission's comments to the Ombudsman that all complaints are registered. Thus, no discretion appears to be exercised on reception of the complaint. In practice discretion as to what to pursue appears to be exercised mostly at the transition from the informal stage to the formal one.

The Ombudsman considers that there is still scope for improvement in the Commission's procedures. He advocates that the Article 226 complainant should have the status of a party in infringement proceedings—if need be, through a Treaty amendment—and that the administrative stage of infringement proceedings should be regulated.[37] He is receiving support from the Parliament.[38] The Ombudsman's latest proposal is that a Chancellor of Justice within the Commission should be in charge of Article 226 cases.[39] The Ombudsman's proposals may reflect the changing perception of infringement proceedings in a changing environment: these have evolved from being delicate matters pertaining to the constitutional sphere of the

[36] The inquiry is reported in the Ombudsman's Annual Report for 1997, Decision 303/97/PD, also available through the Ombudsman's website (n 29 above). For a positive evaluation of the inquiry, see P Bonnor, 'The European Ombudsman: a novel source of soft law in the European Union' (2000) 25 ELRev 39, 50; for a critical one, see R Rawlings, 'Engaged élites—citizen action and institutional attitudes in Commission enforcement' (2000) 6(1) ELJ 4. For a reply to Rawlings, see P Bonnor, 'Institutional attitudes in context: a comment of Rawlings' "Engaged elites—citizen action and institutional attitudes in commission enforcement"' (2001) 7(1) ELJ 114.

[37] See the Foreword to the Ombudsman's Annual Report for 1998, and article in the European Voice, 20 December 2001–9 January 2002, 'Watchdog calls for complaints code of practice'.

[38] See Parliament Resolution of 16 June 2000 on the 16th Annual Report from the Commission on Monitoring the Application of Community Law, Parliament document number A5-0132/2000, available through the Parliament's website (n 34 above).

[39] Jacob Söderman, 'Medborgaren og grundavtalets väktare' (2001) 3 Europarättslig Tidskrift 285. The article is based on a speech given to the European Law Conference, Stockholm, 10–12 June 2001, 'The citizen, the rule of law and openness', available on the European Ombudsman's website.

Community to becoming matters of everyday administration.[40] Given that the Ombudsman was given the status of an observer in the Convention established by the Laeken Declaration to discuss the future of the Union, he is well placed to promote these proposals.

The Ombudsman's proposals provide an opportunity, which should be welcomed, to reflect on infringement proceedings in terms and categories of good administration. Here are some questions. Should the Commission continue to accept indiscriminately all complaints lodged? Should complainants enjoy better procedural safeguards than is presently the case? Should minor infringements not be pursued? Is it important that all Member States are pursued from time to time? Should the Commission be enabled to transfer complaints to national remedial fora, closer to the facts and the complainant, where such are available? Should confidentiality in principle be upheld?

Whether the Ombudsman's proposals will prosper, fully or partly, remains to be seen. An important factor is what Member States will perceive their interest to be. They may prefer the status quo. It may also be that in a Union with ever more Member States, they consider it to be in their overall interest to have transparent enforcement procedures. They may also have a more direct interest of their own. The case law leaves the impression that national administrations may find that there is room for improvement, in terms of good administration, in the Commission's procedures.[41] The Court of Justice has also expressed views that appear related to concerns of good administration.[42]

---

[40] The changing perception is perhaps also reflected in the debate on judicial reform. One view is that Art 226 cases should go to the 'administrative' Court, ie the Court of First Instance, while another one is that they should stay with the 'constitutional' Court, ie the Court of Justice, see respectively A Arnull, 'Judicial architecture or judicial folly? The challenge facing the European Union' (1999) 24 ELRev 516, 518 and J Dewost in his address to the FIDE Congress 2000, available at http://www.fidelaw.org/.

[41] See for instance the submissions in Case C-359/97 *Commission v United Kingdom* [2000] ECR I-6355, para 22–27 and Case C-317/92 *Commission v Germany* [1994] ECR I-2039, para 2. See also AJ Gil Ibáñez, *El control y la ejecución del Derecho Comunitario* (1998) 231–235.

[42] Case C-422/92 *Commission v Germany* [1995] ECR I-1097, para 17. The case concerned in essence minor infringements. The Court referred to the views expressed by AG Jacobs who stated in para 79 of his Opinion that: 'The Commission should in my view be encouraged to launch proceedings of this kind only after a careful assessment of its priorities, with a view to making the best use of the limited resources of the Court, the Member States and the Commission itself.'

Conclusions

Transparency as a quest for good administration is likely to maintain its topicality for some time. On the other hand, as public access becomes an integral part of daily life in the institutions, it will cease to spark off emotive legal debate and perhaps become the subject of dry commentaries on how the rules work in detail, ie public access will find the place where it belongs. That would constitute a true victory for transparency.

Will transparency make the Union more accountable and legitimate? In my view transparency is a necessary, but in itself insufficient, condition for bringing about that result. Whether transparency will make citizens embrace the Union more warmly is a different question. However, those who claim to be alienated from the European construction will have a heavier burden of proof to discharge in a transparent Union.

6

Enhanced Cooperation or Flexibility in the Post-Nice Era

John A Usher

Flexibility and enhanced cooperation after Nice

The Treaty of Amsterdam introduced general provisions on what it termed 'closer cooperation', which might briefly be summarized as involving Member States being authorized by the EU as a whole to make use of the institutions, procedures and mechanisms laid down by the Treaties to go further than the generality of the Member States. One of the major reforms effected by the Treaty of Nice is to amend those provisions so as to make their use much more of a practical possibility; in the process, the concept of closer cooperation has been renamed 'enhanced cooperation'. However, the general provisions introduced by the Treaty of Amsterdam have not yet been used, so one is tempted to ask why they have been revised. While this may in itself possibly be regarded as a justification for their amendment, it may be suggested that, quite apart from the fact that there was only a period of 18 months between the entry into force of the Treaty of Amsterdam and the negotiation of the Treaty of Nice, these provisions were and are intended to find their vocation in the context of an enlarged EU.

Whatever may be the reasons for the subsequent failure to use these provisions, their revision or replacement was one of the substantive items on the agenda of the IGC which culminated in the Treaty of Nice. The Nice text does make a number of important changes, and the extent to which they may make it more likely that the closer cooperation provisions will be used in practice will be considered later in this chapter. On the other hand, it will be seen that there had already been, and continues to be, a growing number of examples of the use of other forms of flexibility.

While under the Amsterdam version the detailed rules governing the use of closer cooperation in the context of the EC Treaty were set out in Article 11 EC, the Nice Treaty transfers all the detailed conditions relating to the use of enhanced cooperation to Article 43 TEU.

It may be observed at the outset that, while the Amsterdam provisions required the participation of a majority of the Member States, the Nice Treaty substitutes the figure of eight Member States, which is currently a majority, but would be less than a third of the members of an EU of 27. On the other hand, bearing in mind that the figure of 700 seats for the maximum size of the European Parliament introduced by the Treaty of Amsterdam[1] was raised to 732 seats by the Treaty of Nice, it remains to be seen whether this figure will be left untouched by future amendments.

So far as the substantive conditions are concerned, the continuing requirement that closer cooperation should not concern areas which fall within the exclusive competence of the Community raises exactly the same question as arises in the context of subsidiarity under Article 5. Putting it very briefly, the common commercial policy[2] and common fisheries policy[3] have been held to be areas of exclusive Community competence, and it may be suggested that monetary policy has become so in the third stage of Economic and Monetary Union so far as the participants are concerned.[4] On the other hand, it would appear that in other areas of activity, Community competence only becomes exclusive once complete or comprehensive Community legislation has been enacted, even in the area of the common agricultural policy.[5] However, the list in the revised Article 43 TEU will no longer include the requirement set out in the current article 11(1)(b) that closer cooperation should not affect Community 'policies'. Taken literally, this would appear to preclude closer cooperation in the area of the common agricultural policy and in other areas where the Community is required to have a common policy, such as transport.[6] If, however, it is not meant literally, and means that closer cooperation should not be used in areas already subject to Community rules, it adds little to the requirement that it should not be used in areas which fall within the

[1] As Art 189 EC.

[2] Opinion 1/75 [1975] ECR 1355.

[3] Case 804/79 *Commission v UK* [1981] ECR 1045.

[4] By virtue of Art 4(1) EC, there is a single monetary policy at the single currency stage, and under Art 105(2) it is the task of the ESCB to define and implement this monetary policy.

[5] Case 222/82 *Apple and Pear Development Council* [1983] ECR 4083. See Usher, *EC Agricultural Law* (2nd edn, 2002) ch 7.

[6] Art 170 EC.

exclusive competence of the Community—which perhaps explains why it is not in the Nice text.

It may be suggested that problems may arise, however, from the requirement in the current Article 11(1)(e) EC, reproduced in the Nice text of Article 43(f) EU, that closer cooperation should not distort conditions of competition. Historically the use of Article 94 (and subsequently Article 95) EC to enact legislation in areas such as environmental protection or consumer protection was often claimed to be justified on the grounds that differences in national legislation amounted to distortions of competition[7]—yet the result of closer cooperation would appear to be that some Member States will have legislation which differs from that of other Member States. Even before the Amsterdam Treaty, that had already clearly been the result of the Maastricht Social Protocol. However, the view that any differences in national legislation amount to distortions of competition has now been limited by the judgment of the Court in *Germany v European Parliament and Council*[8] in relation to the tobacco advertising directive.[9] The Court there stated that a measure adopted on the basis of Article 95 'must genuinely have as its object the improvement of the conditions for the establishment and functioning of the internal market' and that 'if a mere finding of disparities between national rules and of the abstract risk of obstacles to the exercise of fundamental freedoms or of distortions of competition liable to result therefrom were sufficient to justify the choice of [Article 95] as a legal basis, judicial review of compliance with the proper legal basis might be rendered nugatory'. The Court then went on to assert that in order to justify legislation under Article 95, the distortion of competition must be 'appreciable'. It may therefore be argued from this that, conversely, the differences in legislation resulting from closer cooperation would only breach Article 11 (and the new Article 43 EU) if they in turn were 'appreciable'.

On the other hand, it may be observed that the requirement in Article 11 EC that the proposed cooperation should not concern the citizenship of the Union or discriminate between nationals of Member States is not included in the provisions retained by the Treaty of Nice and transferred by that Treaty to the general provisions of the TEU. This reflects reality, if one might say so: it is already the case that those who travel to a Member State

---

[7] See eg the recitals to Council Dir 85/374 on liability for defective products [1985] OJ L210/29.

[8] Case C-376/98 [2000] ECR I-8419.

[9] EP and Council Dir 98/43 [1998] OJ L213/9.

which participates in Title IV of Part Three of the EC Treaty[10] from a Member State which does not are treated differently from those who travel from another participating State.

Procedurally, the most important change resulting from the Treaty of Nice is that a veto on proposed enhanced cooperation will no longer be possible under Article 40a TEU or Article 11 EC (though the assent of the European Parliament is required if it is a co-decision matter). In the terms of the new Article 40a EU, Member States which intend to establish enhanced cooperation between themselves under Article 40 (with the aim of enabling the Union to develop more rapidly into an area of freedom, security and justice) are to address a request to the Commission, which may submit a proposal to the Council to that effect. Those Member States may then submit an initiative to the Council designed to obtain authorization for the enhanced cooperation concerned. Under Article 40a(2) this authorization may be granted by the Council, acting by a qualified majority, on a proposal from the Commission or on the initiative of at least eight Member States, and after consulting the European Parliament. A member of the Council may request that the matter be referred to the European Council, but once it has been raised before the European Council, the Council may act 'in accordance with the first subparagraph of this paragraph', ie by qualified majority, unlike the present requirement for unanimity if the matter is referred to the European Council.

In the context of the EC Treaty, the revised Article 11 provides that Member States which intend to establish enhanced cooperation between themselves in one of the areas referred to in that Treaty shall address a request to the Commission, which may submit a proposal to the Council to that effect. Authorization to establish such enhanced cooperation may again be granted, in compliance with Articles 43–45 TEU, by the Council, acting by a qualified majority on a proposal from the Commission and after consulting the European Parliament. However, when enhanced cooperation relates to an area covered by the co-decision procedure under Article 251, the *assent* of the European Parliament will be required. As under the EU procedure, a member of the Council may request that the matter be referred to the European Council,[11] but after that matter has been raised before the European Council, the Council may again act by qualified majority.

---

[10] On visas, asylum and immigration, and other matters which will be discussed later in this chapter.

[11] It may be wondered whether this should, as in the current Art 11, be a reference to the Council meeting in the composition of Heads of State or Government.

The Nice Treaty also extends enhanced cooperation to implementation of a joint action or common position under the second pillar in the context of the common foreign and security policy by virtue of a new Article 27b TEU, but subject to a possible veto under Articles 27c and 23(2). Under the new Article 27b TEU, such enhanced cooperation must be aimed at safeguarding the values and serving the interests of the Union as a whole by asserting its identity as a coherent force on the international scene. In particular, it must respect:

(i)   the principles, objectives, general guidelines and consistency of the common foreign and security policy and the decisions taken within the framework of that policy;

(ii) the powers of the European Community; and

(iii) consistency between all the Union's policies and its external activities.

Article 27b makes it clear that enhanced cooperation pursuant to this Title must relate to implementation of a joint action or a common position, and that it must not relate to matters having military or defence implications. The procedure is, however, subtly different from the first and third pillars: under Article 27c, Member States which intend to establish enhanced cooperation between themselves under Article 27b must address a request to the Council to that effect. The request is to be forwarded to the Commission and to the European Parliament *for information* (emphasis added). The Commission is to give its opinion particularly on whether the enhanced cooperation proposed is consistent with Union policies. Authorization is, however, to be granted by the Council, acting in accordance with the second and third subparagraphs of Article 23(2), under which, if a member of the Council declares that, for important and stated reasons of national policy, it intends to oppose the adoption of a decision taken by qualified majority, a vote shall not be taken; rather the Council may, acting by a qualified majority, request that the matter be referred to the European Council for decision by unanimity; compliance with Articles 43–45 TEU is in any event required. Thus enhanced cooperation is extended by the Treaty of Nice to the second pillar subject to procedural rules similar to those which currently allow closer cooperation under the first and third pillars to be blocked by a dissentient State, but enhanced cooperation under the first and third pillars will no longer be subject to such a possibility of veto—and may well, therefore, become a much more practical proposition.

Closer cooperation under the Treaty of Amsterdam

Although the Amsterdam provisions have not been used as such, even if they have given rise to an extensive literature, it should nevertheless be remembered that under the terms of the Amsterdam Treaty itself there are situations where those provisions are deemed to have been used: under Article 1 of the Protocol Integrating the Schengen acquis into the Framework of the European Union, the signatories to the Schengen agreements are 'authorised to establish closer cooperation among themselves' within the scope of those agreements and related provisions; furthermore, under Article 5 of that Protocol, where either Ireland or the United Kingdom or both have not notified the President of the Council in writing within a reasonable period that they wish to take part, 'the authorisation referred to in Article 11 of the Treaty establishing the European Community or Article 40 of the Treaty on European Union[12] shall be deemed to have been granted to the Member States referred to in Article 1 and to Ireland or the United Kingdom where either of them wishes to take part in the areas of cooperation in question'. However, it is here provided that the Council is to decide on the request with the unanimity of its members referred to in Article 1 (ie those participating in Schengen) and of the representative of the Government of the State concerned. This procedure was used, for example, in Council Decision 2000/365,[13] concerning the request of the UK to take part in some of the provisions of the Schengen acquis, as a result of which the UK participates in most of the Schengen arrangements apart from those relating to the crossing of frontiers and hot pursuit across frontiers.

Types of flexibility

One of the most striking features of the experience of flexibility so far has been the scope for 'à la carte' and voluntary flexibility, even though it may be suggested that just two major basic patterns of flexibility may be observed in the EU context. The first is typified by closer cooperation as such; this pattern was pioneered by the Maastricht Social Protocol, which may be construed as a grant of permission by the Community as a whole to the

---

[12] Art 40 TEU sets the general framework for closer cooperation, and Art 11 EC applies the concept in the context of the EC.

[13] [2000] OJ L131/43.

participant States to use Community institutions, mechanisms and legislation. Following the incorporation of its provisions into the main body of the EC Treaty by the Amsterdam Treaty, the Social Protocol has become a matter of history; it remains to be seen whether this will also prove to be a development followed in other areas.

The second basic model is where certain Member States are given authorization to opt out of obligations or areas of activity binding on the generality of Member States. This is most obvious in the context of Economic and Monetary Union,[14] where differentiation arises not just from the special treatment accorded to the UK and Denmark in the Protocols relating to those countries, but also from the fact that it was appreciated that not all Member States would meet the rather strict criteria for economic convergence laid down as the precondition for participation in the monetary union; such States are referred to as 'Member States with a derogation'.[15] The pattern of the opt-out is also followed in the context of Title IV of Part Three of the EC Treaty on free movement of persons, asylum and immigration, introduced by the Treaty of Amsterdam. Under the Protocol on the position of the United Kingdom and Ireland, the United Kingdom and Ireland are not to take part in the adoption by the Council of proposed measures pursuant to this Title of the EC Treaty, and none of the provisions of the Title, no measure adopted pursuant to the Title, no provision of any international agreement concluded by the Community pursuant to that Title, and no decision of the Court of Justice interpreting any such provision or measure is to be binding upon or applicable in the United Kingdom or Ireland. In the case of Denmark, there are similar provisions in a separate Protocol about non-participation in the legislative process and non-application of the relevant provisions.

Besides these formal models, however, the Amsterdam Treaty also introduced areas of purely voluntary participation in areas of activity. The clearest example is in relation to references for preliminary rulings under the Third Pillar of the Treaty on European Union. Here, Article 35 TEU establishes a jurisdiction which is purely voluntary so far as the Member States are concerned: the Court only has jurisdiction to the extent that a Member State declares that it accepts that jurisdiction, and each Member State may determine whether the power to make a reference is to be made available to all courts or limited to courts of final appeal. Furthermore, a

---

[14] See Usher, 'Economic and Monetary Union—a model for flexibility?' (1998) 1 CYELS 39.
[15] Art 122 EC.

Declaration attached to the Amsterdam Treaty states that the Conference notes that Member States may, when making a declaration, reserve the right to make provisions in their national law to the effect that a court of final appeal will be required to refer that matter to the Court of Justice.

It would appear that,[16] when this provision entered into force on 1 May 1999, of those Member Sates which had accepted the jurisdiction of the Court, Spain had limited the power to make references to courts or tribunals against whose decisions there is no judicial remedy under national law, but that the rest made it available to any court or tribunal. Belgium, Germany, Spain, Italy, Luxembourg, the Netherlands and Austria reserved the right to make provisions in their national law to the effect that, where a question is raised in a case pending before any court or tribunal of that State against whose decisions there is no judicial remedy under national law, that court or tribunal will be required to refer that matter to the European Court, a pattern also followed by France when it made its declaration on 14 March 2000.[17] On the other hand, the jurisdiction of the Court has not been accepted by Denmark, Ireland or the United Kingdom.

It is of course inherent in the concept of closer or enhanced cooperation itself that it is open to all Member States and that it allows them to become parties to the cooperation at any time,[18] and this is reflected in the deemed use of the closer cooperation procedure in the Schengen Protocol: as mentioned above, under Article 4 of that Protocol, Ireland and the United Kingdom, which are not bound by the Schengen acquis, may at any time request to take part in some or all of the provisions of this acquis.

Voluntary participation is also possible, and has been invoked, in the context of the apparent opt-outs. Under Article 3 of the Protocol on the position of the United Kingdom and Ireland in relation to Title IV of Part Three of the EC Treaty on visas, asylum and immigration, the United Kingdom or Ireland may notify the President of the Council in writing, within three months after a proposal or initiative has been presented to the Council under this Title, that it wishes to take part in the adoption and application of any such proposed measure. By virtue of Article 4 the United Kingdom or Ireland may at any time after the adoption of a measure by the Council under this Title notify its intention to the Council and to the

---

[16] See [1999] OJ C120/24.
[17] See http://www.legifrance.gouv.fr/html/frame_jo.html.
[18] Art 43(g) TEU.

Commission that it wishes to accept such measure. Thus, although they are made under Title IV, the UK and Ireland are parties to a whole series of measures in the area of judicial cooperation, perhaps the most important being Council Regulation 44/2001 on jurisdiction and the recognition and enforcement of judgments in civil and commercial matters[19] (which replaces the Brussels Convention). There are also, however, examples of the UK and Ireland acting separately: the UK participates in Council Directive 2001/40 on the mutual recognition of decisions on the expulsion of third country nationals,[20] though Ireland does not.

Be that as it may, Ireland may notify the President of the Council in writing that it no longer wishes to be covered by the terms of the Protocol, in which case the normal Treaty provisions will apply to Ireland—though there is no such possibility for the United Kingdom.

However, the Danish Protocol[21] does not exclude Denmark from measures determining the third countries whose nationals must be in possession of a visa when crossing the external borders of the Member States, or measures relating to a uniform format for visas. On the other hand, Denmark has not agreed to opt in to any other measures in this area as a matter of Community law; rather, as a participant in the Schengen Agreement, it is stated that Denmark shall decide within a period of six months after the Council has decided on a proposal or initiative to build upon the Schengen acquis under the provisions of this Title of the EC Treaty, whether it will implement this decision in its national law. If it decides to do so, this decision will create an obligation 'under international law' between Denmark and the other Member States concerned. Nevertheless, like Ireland, Denmark may, in accordance with its constitutional requirements, inform other Member States that it no longer wishes to avail itself of all or part of its Protocol.

The inability of Denmark to opt in on an ad hoc basis to other measures enacted under Title IV creates problems which will be considered in the next section of this chapter. It may, however, be observed that voluntary participation is not unknown even in the area of Economic and Monetary Union. This became apparent in the context of the application, on the eve of the move to Economic and Monetary Union, of the convergence criteria set out in Article 122 EC. Two of these criteria relate to the exchange rate mechanism of the European Monetary System, membership of which is and always was voluntary; it was for each Member State to decide whether to join

---

[19] [2001] OJ L12/1.   [20] [2001] OJ L149/34.   [21] Art 4.

the exchange rate mechanism[22] under the original version, and under the current version participation in the exchange rate mechanism is voluntary for the Member States outside the euro area, although 'Member States with a derogation can be expected to join the mechanism'.[23] The relevant convergence criteria in effect require the observance of the normal fluctuation margins provided for by the exchange rate mechanism (ERM) of the European Monetary System (EMS), for at least two years.

This gave rise to particular issues in relation to Finland, Italy and Sweden. Italy was one of the original participants in the ERM of the EMS, but like the United Kingdom, it found itself having to leave the system in September 1992, and did not rejoin until November 1996, less than two years before the assessment was made. Nevertheless, in its Report,[24] the Commission stated that 'although the lira has participated in the ERM only since November 1996, it has not experienced severe tensions during the review period and has thus ... displayed sufficient stability in the last two years'. Finland, which only joined the Community in 1995, entered the ERM in October 1996, and in its Report[25] the Commission used wording virtually identical to that used in relation to Italy.

However, Sweden, which also joined the Community in 1995, had not participated at all in the ERM, and was known politically not to wish to participate in stage three of EMU, but did not have the benefit (if such it be) of a special protocol like the UK or Denmark. There is no mention of this last point in the Commission's Report, which instead observes that the Swedish crown had never participated in the ERM, and that during the relevant two years it had fluctuated against the ERM currencies, 'reflecting, among other things, the absence of an exchange rate target', and the formal Council Decision[26] uses very similar wording. Both then conclude that Sweden did not fulfil the third convergence criterion. The conclusion may therefore be drawn that while this criterion has not been interpreted literally, a Member State which does not participate at all in the ERM will not be regarded as meeting the criterion, at least if it has suffered currency fluctuation (which is highly likely to be the case). The practical consequence therefore may be said to be that to the extent that membership of the ERM

---

[22] Art 3 of the European Council Resolution of 5 December 1978 (EC Bulletin 1978 No 12 Point 1.1.11).
[23] European Council Resolution of 16 June 1997, para 1.6.
[24] Para 1.3.7.
[25] Para 1.3.12.
[26] Council Dec 98/317 [1998] OJ L139/30.

was and is voluntary, participation in the third stage of Economic and Monetary Union was and is also voluntary, even if no new Member States are offered the special treatment given to the UK and Denmark.

Substantive issues

Although the provisions on closer cooperation may not have been used as such, the areas of differentiated integration which do exist provide many illustrations of the legal issues which may arise in practice. Indeed, one consequence of the entry into force of the Treaty of Amsterdam, in particular the new Title IV of Part Three of the EC Treaty, has been that certain provisions which used to apply to all Member States on the same legal basis no longer do so. Certain aspects of visa policy previously fell within the EC Treaty by virtue of the former Article 100c of EC, which was binding on all the Member States, and by virtue of which a common visa list was enacted in Council Regulation 574/1999.[27] Under the Amsterdam Title on visas, asylum and immigration, Article 100c has been repealed and replaced by provisions (notably Article 62) which in principle are not binding automatically on the UK, Ireland, and Denmark. This raises interesting questions as to the future status of the common visa list, particularly if it should be amended by those Member States participating in the new Title. A solution is, however, specifically envisaged in the case of Denmark: while, in principle, Articles 1 and 2 of the Danish Protocol provide that measures under Title IV shall not be Community law so far as Denmark is concerned, Article 4 of that Protocol declares that these articles 'shall not apply to measures determining the third countries whose nationals must be in possession of a visa when crossing the external borders of the Member States, or measures relating to a uniform format for visas.' The problem has in fact now arisen in practice for the UK and Ireland. Council Regulation 574/1999,[28] adopted under the old Article 100c and therefore binding on all Member States, has now been replaced by Council Regulation 539/2001[29] listing the third countries whose nationals must be in possession of a visa when crossing the external frontiers. The UK and Ireland did not participate in the enactment of the 2001 legislation, and it is declared in the recitals that 'the provisions of this Regulation apply neither to Ireland nor to the United Kingdom'. However, since it is Article 7 of Regulation 539/2001 that repeals

---

[27] [1999] OJ L72/2.   [28] [1999] OJ L72/2.   [29] [2001] OJ L81/1.

Regulation 574/1999, and Regulation 539/2001 does not apply to the United Kingdom or Ireland, the question then arises as to whether Regulation 574/1999 is still in force so far as the UK and Ireland are concerned.

In a number of instances, the choice has been expressly made that the old rules will remain in force for a Member State which does not participate in the new ones. Thus under the Schengen Protocol, it is provided in Article 3 that in so far as parts of the Schengen acquis are determined to have a legal basis in Title IV of the EC Treaty, 'Denmark shall maintain the same rights and obligations in relation to the other signatories to the Schengen agreements, as before the said determination'. A similar approach has been followed in the context of the replacement of the 1968 Brussels Convention on Jurisdiction and Judgments by Council Regulation 44/2001 on jurisdiction and the recognition and enforcement of judgments in civil and commercial matters[30] adopted under Title IV[31] which, despite its heading, relates to areas including judicial cooperation in civil matters as well as visas, asylum and immigration. While the UK and Ireland were able to 'opt in' to this Regulation, this was not legally possible for Denmark, given the absence of an opt-in clause in its Protocol, and it is asserted in the recitals[32] that the Brussels Convention remains in force between Denmark and the Member States which are bound by the Regulation.

Further problems have arisen however where the legislation adopted under Title IV is new and does not replace existing measures binding on other Member States, such as Council Regulation 1346/2000 on insolvency proceedings.[33] Technically, the insolvency Regulation replaced a Convention opened for signature at the end of 1995, but which never came into force because of the UK's failure to sign within the deadline.[34] The recitals record that the UK and Ireland took part in the adoption of the Regulation,[35] but also that Denmark 'is not participating in the adoption of this Regulation, and is therefore not bound by it nor subject to its application'. Similarly, although Council Regulation 1347/2000 on recognition and enforcement of judgments in matrimonial matters and matters of parental responsibility,[36] and Council Regulation 1348/2000 on the service in Member States of judicial and extra-

---

[30] [2001] OJ L12/1.
[31] Arts 61(c) and 67(1) EC.
[32] Para 23.
[33] [2000] OJ L160/1.
[34] See P Stone, *Civil Jurisdiction and Judgments in Europe* (1998) 10.
[35] Para 32.
[36] [2000] OJ L160/19.

judicial documents in civil or commercial matters[37] replaced conventions opened for signature in 1998 and 1997 under the former Article K3(2)(c) TEU, the recitals to both Regulations[38] state that they do not apply to Denmark.

A very clear example of the wide scope of Title IV and therefore of the wide scope of the opt-outs from Title IV may be found in Council Regulation 290/2001 extending the programme of incentives and exchanges for legal practitioners in the area of civil law,[39] the 'Grotius' programme. This, it may be suggested, is far removed from the sensitive areas of asylum, visas and immigration, but it was adopted under Article 61(c), as a measure in the field of judicial cooperation in civil matters, and Article 67(1), both of which fall within Title IV. Although the UK and Ireland opted in, it is recorded[40] that Denmark was neither participating in nor bound by the Regulation.

Extending 'group' legislation to the whole Community

The question therefore has arisen as to whether and how Community legislation binding only on some Member States may be extended to others where there is no possibility of opt in to the legislation as such. A practical example may be seen in the provisions governing the operation of TARGET (Trans-European Automated Real-Time Gross Settlement European Transfer System), the payments system for the euro. While the fear that the 'outs' would be excluded has proved to be unfounded, the price of permitting them to use it is a complex legal framework. This framework is based on a combination of an ECB Guideline[41] adopted by the Governing Council of the ECB addressed to and binding upon the national central banks of the euro-zone, and the TARGET Agreement between the ECB and the national central banks of the Member States which have not adopted the euro but which wish to connect to TARGET. Effectively the Agreement incorporates the provisions of the Guideline, which can only apply as such within the euro-zone, to apply its terms outside the euro-zone.[42] On the other hand, a contract between central banks is hardly an appropriate

---

[37] [2000] OJ L160/37.

[38] Para 25 in the matrimonial Regulation, para 18 in the service Regulation.

[39] [2001] OJ L43/1.

[40] Para 13 of the recitals.

[41] Similar in legal nature to an EC directive; see J-V Louis, 'A legal and institutional approach for building a Monetary Union' (1998) CMLRev 33, 54. The consolidated text of the TARGET Guideline may be found in ECB Guideline 2001/3 [2001] OJ L140/72.

[42] ECB Third Progress Report on the TARGET project, November 1998, 18.

method of extending the territorial scope of, for example, legislation under Title IV, which leaves questions as to whether there could be an agreement between the Community (comprising in this context the Member States participating in an area of enhanced cooperation) and one of its Member States, or between the participating and non-participating Member States, incorporating the terms of the legislation.

However, there may be a simpler solution within the framework of Community law. It may respectfully be suggested that there is a long history of using general powers to legislate on matters which fall outside the scope of the specific Treaty provisions, and that the real question is that of knowing where to draw the line between circumvention and filling a gap. Article 308 provides that if action by the Community should prove necessary to attain, in the course of the operation of the common market, one of the objectives of the Community and the Treaty has not provided the necessary powers, the Council shall, acting unanimously on a proposal from the Commission and after consulting the Parliament, take the appropriate measures. A notable example of its use has arisen from the way the Treaty provisions on Economic and Monetary Union were drafted: Article 123(4) EC, allowing measures to be taken for the introduction of the single currency, can, on its express terms, only be used by the Member States without a derogation, that is, the participants in economic and monetary union, and Council Regulation 1338/2001[43] laying down measures necessary for the protection of the euro against counterfeiting was enacted under this provision. It was obviously desirable, however, that such measures should apply throughout the Community, and so Council Regulation 1339/2001 has been enacted under Article 308 to apply the substantive provisions of Regulation 1338/2001 to the Member States which are not in the euro-zone. It may be suggested that there could hardly be a more obvious example of using a general provision to circumvent the limits of the specific provision, so as to ensure that the same rules can be applied both to the 'ins' and to the 'outs'.

The future use of enhanced cooperation

While the closer cooperation provisions of the Treaty of Amsterdam may never have been used as such, it has been observed that the Nice amendments remove the major procedural barrier of a possible veto in the context

---

[43] [2001] OJ L181/6.

of the EC Treaty, and of police and judicial cooperation under the third pillar. It may be suggested, therefore, that it is realistic to expect use to be made of these provisions, and in the short term, this may well be in conjunction with the existing areas of differentiated integration, in relation to economic and monetary union and in relation to Title IV of the EC Treaty on visas, asylum and immigration.

It does not take too much imagination to anticipate that the twelve Member States participating in economic and monetary union might wish to make use of general Treaty provisions such as Article 93 on taxation, or the catch-all Article 308 discussed above, to enact legislation binding only on them. Mathematically, it may be observed that the twelve States participating in economic and monetary union total 70 votes between them, which is many more than the number required for a qualified majority (62), and the three 'outs' together have only 17 votes, which is not only insufficient to block a decision but is also far below the threshold required (23–25 votes) to trigger the 'Ioannina compromise' to delay a decision.[44] This calculation will remain valid after the entry into force of the Nice Treaty in a Community with its current composition: using the figures in Article 3 of the Nice Protocol on the enlargement of the Union, the 'ins' would have 191 votes, many more than the 169 needed for a qualified majority. However, after enlargement, the 'ins' might well require the support of some of the 'outs' in order to be authorized to participate in enhanced cooperation, depending on how many new States join, and on how many of those are able to participate in EMU in the short term.

Similarly it may be envisaged that the Member States participating in Title IV might wish to use, for example, Article 308 to adopt legislation related to but not envisaged by the provisions of that Title. Again, in the current composition of the Community, the participants constitute a qualified majority by themselves, with 71 votes under the present figures and 194 votes under the Nice formula. However, here enlargement would continue this trend: in a scenario where opt-outs are not likely to be given and no criteria have to be fulfilled on order to participate. Enlargement will simply increase the number of participants in Title IV, and the non-participants will become proportionately a smaller and smaller minority.

The question also arises, at least in theory,[45] as to whether, after enlargement, it would be possible for the existing Member States to use enhanced

---

[44] See Usher, *EC Institutions and Legislation* (1998) 23–25.

[45] It is in no way intended to suggest that this is what is likely to happen.

cooperation to continue to enact legislation binding only on them. In this context, if the full enlargement envisaged in the Nice Declaration on the enlargement of the EU were to take place, the existing Member States would not constitute a qualified majority, having only 237 of the 258 votes required; they would therefore require the support of some of the new Member States. If however, for the sake of argument, enlargement were to take place without Romania and Bulgaria in the first wave, then applying the figure of 73.4 per cent mentioned in the further Declaration on the Qualified Majority Threshold and the Number of Votes for a Blocking Minority in an Enlarged Union to the 321 votes available, a qualified majority would (if rounded up) be 236 votes, which could be achieved by the existing Members on their own. A smaller enlargement would more clearly leave the existing Member States able to use enhanced cooperation on their own.

It may be hoped that an enlarged Community will continued to develop a common acquis—and indeed to the extent that the 'core' is governed by comprehensive Community legislation it has become de facto a matter of exclusive Community competence, and therefore not subject to enhanced cooperation.[46] The reality however is that there are already two major areas where there is differentiated integration, EMU and Title IV of the EC Treaty, and it may be suggested that the Nice provisions on enhanced cooperation may well turn out to have considerable practical utility. Furthermore, they could be relevant to two of the issues raised in the Laeken Declaration,[47] competence and legitimacy. On the question of competence, it has been suggested[48] that enhanced cooperation could be a method of resolving the problem of different national perceptions of the scope of Community competence: those States which felt a matter fell outside Community competence would simply not participate in it. So far as legitimacy is concerned, from a national perspective, the existing areas of differentiated integration show that enhanced cooperation may be a mechanism by which Member States which feel that their public opinion is against participation in a particular area of Union activity can refrain from that activity, while remaining full members of the Union and allowing other Member States to pursue further integration. This however begs the issue of whether legitimacy should be sought at regional, national or Union level—and the experience of Title IV shows that unexpected practical problems can arise.

[46] See n 5 above.

[47] 15 December 2001 (SN 273/01).

[48] Yiannos Tolias, 'The scope of the Community's competence in the light of Article 308 EC— is flexibility the answer?', doctoral thesis submitted at the University of Edinburgh, June 2001.

7

Legitimacy, Accountability, and Delegation in the European Union

*Anand Menon and Stephen Weatherill**

Introduction

The EU has altered profoundly in recent years. Its geographical and functional expansion, coupled with the increasing scope of delegation to the European institutions, has raised a number of issues concerning its relationship with its member states. Questions such as the proper reach of the Union's activities, the appropriate relationship between Union and State competences and how the Union should be subjected to effective systems of supervision all, directly or indirectly, question the proper location of accountability for the exercise of the increasing list of competences delegated by the Member States to the European level. 'Legitimacy' is a well-worn catchphrase within such debates.

It may appear paradoxical that the readiness of the Member States to participate in revision of the Treaties that confers enhanced competence on the Community/Union should generate anxieties about their control over the trajectory of the process. But in fact it is no paradox; rather it is a sign of the peculiar dynamics of the interplay between the multiple levels of authority that characterize the modern governance of Europe. In 2004 a new intergovernmental conference will be convened at which, according to the dictates of the Nice Treaty, there will be a 'deeper and wider debate about the future development of the European Union', underpinned by a recognition of 'the need to improve and to monitor the democratic legitimacy and transparency of the Union and its institutions, to bring them closer to the citizens of the Member States'. The increasing role of the EU as a source of

* Anand Menon gratefully acknowledges the support of British Academy Small Grant SG–31906.

decision-making and the associated reduced autonomy of unilateral action permitted of the Member States, in other words, have generated an instinct-ive anxiety to examine anew the legitimate foundations of the system.

This chapter considers the question of legitimacy in the European Union from a theoretical perspective. It discusses the degree to which the require-ments of delegation to the two appointed supranational bodies—the Euro-pean Court and the European Commission—conflict with a desire to enhance legitimacy and accountability in the European Union. In particular, by drawing on a distinction made in the literature between input and output legitimacy in the EU, we argue that attempts to reinforce the former pose a substantial danger to the maintenance of the latter by impeding the ability of these institutions to carry out their tasks effectively. The EC system, and to a much lesser extent that of the wider non-EC EU system, depends on the existence of an effective Court and Commission.

Our defence of the legitimacy of delegation at the European level is not, however, merely an argument based on efficiency. The notion of legitimacy can be further disaggregated into that emanating from the Member States (central or regional) and also that emanating from the European level. The debate about legitimacy and accountability has too often been imprisoned by assumptions about the correctness of one over the other (usually, though not exclusively, the former over the latter), with the consequence that debate has been conducted at cross-purposes. In contrast, we argue for an appreciation of the functions of *both* state (including sub-state) *and* European institutions in meeting the challenge of securing legitimacy. In this context we claim, without wishing away the issue of accountability, that delegation can be seen of itself to contain a legitimating factor which is not merely rooted in the economic advantages of integration or even more broadly the problem-solving capacity of the Union, but which also possesses a political dimension. This involves appreciation of the nature of EC law as a means to embed within national political and administrative systems legally enforce-able obligations to respect the interests of actors whose voice is excluded or muffled (de jure or de facto) within the national political process. The Court and the Commission achieve this in different ways, but as a general propos-ition it is a perspective that points to the need to grasp that 'improving' the legitimation of the Union through institutional reform may not only imperil its output legitimation; it may also be based on assumptions about the viability of orthodox systems of input legitimacy which are unwarranted.

Thus not only output legitimacy, but also input legitimacy, that secured both by State and the European-level institutions, should be emphasized, and the values of each appreciated as a *combination* approach that reflects the broader challenges of transnational governance. In so far as improvements to one may damage another, it must be asked whether the costs outweigh the benefits, but under a framework that insists on a sceptical rooting-out of assumptions that one should, as a matter of principle, prevail over another. This approach connects to the normative reading of supranationalism that treats it as directed at 'taming' but neither eliminating nor replacing the Member States. This argues for a reading of delegation in the EU context that emphasizes not only output legitimacy, but also the descriptive and normative force of an approach based on a recognition of the multiple layers of authority that exist in Europe as a means to ensure a sufficiently broad understanding of what is at stake in assessing legitimacy and accountability in (and not simply of) the European Union.

Legitimacy and the European Union

Fritz Scharpf has drawn a distinction between input and output legitimacy in assessing the European Union.[1] Democratic self-determination, he insists, requires that choices made by the given political system be driven by the authentic preferences of citizens. This suggests a chain of account-ability linking those governing to those governed. It is input legitimation, or government by the people. But democratic self-determination also demands that those exercising political power are able to achieve a high degree of effectiveness in meeting the expectations of the governed. The democratic process is, for Scharpf, an 'empty ritual' without such delivery—output legitimacy, or government for the people. Scharpf argues vigorously and persuasively that although the Union is regularly and (to some extent) justifiably criticized for deficiencies in input legitimacy, too little attention is paid to the inadequacies of states when judged from the standpoint of output legitimacy. This tends to breed an inflated assumption of the claim of states to legitimacy. Scharpf's key point is that in at least some policy areas it may be possible to conceive of the EU as capable of legitimation by reference to its output, even if input legitimation is lacking.

In a similar vein, Giandomenico Majone famously describes the EU as a 'regulatory State', drawing attention to the remarkable gulf between the Union's (and especially the Community's) extensive rule-making capacity

---

[1] F Scharpf, 'Economic integration, democracy and the welfare state' (1997) 4 JEPP 18; *Governing in Europe: Effective and Democratic?* (1999).

and its negligible administrative infrastructure.[2] Policy-implementation is heavily reliant on the Member States' own legal and administrative agencies. Majone draws normative conclusions. He finds a ready legitimation of the EU through its outputs provided that its activities are confined to securing efficient outcomes. This suggests a temptingly clean-cut model with which to define the proper limits of regulatory activity 'above' the State. It makes the important claim that legitimation may require assessment in different ways in different policy sectors.

The insights of Scharpf and Majone carry great weight in guiding our understanding of the problems associated with the growth of regulatory activity 'above' the State. They are especially valuable in emphasizing the value that is properly attached to output legitimacy. This is especially important in the light of the effect that membership of the EU exerts in confining policy options available to Member States while not recreating equal opportunities for rule-making at transnational level. Under such arrangements, orthodox assumptions about securing input legitimacy for decisions by public bodies are undermined. A response based on reversion to unilateral, bilateral or ad hoc multilateral state action will be confronted by limitations in achieving effective problem solving. A response based on re-creating State structures at transnational level, in order to relocate sites of input legitimacy, raises all manner of awkward problems associated with the disinclination of citizens simply to shift their sense of allegiance. As Fritz Scharpf puts it:

Given the historical, linguistic, cultural, ethnic and institutional diversity of its member states, there is no question that the Union is very far from having achieved the 'thick' collective identity that we have come to take for granted in national democracies—and in its absence, institutional reforms will not greatly increase the input-oriented legitimacy of decisions taken by majority rule.[3]

Consequently, input legitimacy must be seen as one important element in assessing the legitimacy of the European Union, but it should be assessed in combination with an unavoidable appreciation of the virtues of output legitimacy. It is in the very nature of the Union that it invites such nuanced examination. And it is therefore quite proper to identify a road to legitimacy paved by the ability of the Union to deliver responses to problems that would be insoluble or even simply less effectively solved by individual states.

[2] G. Majone, *Regulating Europe* (1996).
[3] F Scharpf, *Governing in Europe: Effective and Democratic?* (1999) 9.

Delegation and the European Union

Thus, assumptions that a higher level of input legitimacy is required to provide a satisfying justification for delegation to supranational institutions, most prominently the Court and the Commission, are flawed in so far as they neglect the damage that this may inflict on output legitimacy. This is especially the case given that the Member States chose to delegate powers to the supranational institutions precisely in order that they be able effectively to carry out tasks that the Member States acting in isolation from each other could not accomplish.

All things being equal, states eschew delegation in order to reduce the political risks associated with a loss of formal decision-making control. Yet there are several reasons why states may opt to delegate. When interactions are repeated, states' time horizons are long, and the utility of cooperation is high, such arrangements can represent rational solutions to problems requiring cooperation.[4] Delegation is a means of solving problems of incomplete contracting and ensuring compliance by principals. Delegation also provides a means of achieving credible policy commitments that may not be possible in its absence.[5] As Moravcsik puts it: '... the decision to delegate ... signals the willingness of national governments to accept an increased political risk of being ... overruled on any individual issue in exchange for more efficient collective decision-making on average'.[6]

In other words, the explanation for this delegation is rooted in the need for actors that operate (to some extent) independently of state interests and which are therefore able to promote a form of 'Community interest' that is (relatively) undistorted by local preferences. This observation plainly begs a great many questions, but is accurate enough at the general level in explaining the need for institutions that each Member State had a confident expectation would ensure the EU bargain was adhered to in reciprocal manner across the whole territory of the Community (later the Union). The autonomy of the institutions is, of course, qualified on several levels.[7]

---

[4] G Garrett, 'International cooperation and institutional choice: the European Community's internal market' (1992) 46 International Organization 533.

[5] M Pollack, 'Delegation, agency and agenda setting in the European Community' (1997) 1 International Organization 51.

[6] A Moravcsik, 'Preferences and power in the European Community: a liberal intergovernmentalist approach' (1993) JCMS 509.

[7] On the Court and the Commission respectively, see A Stone Sweet and J Caporaso, 'From free trade to supranational polity: the European Court and integration' and M Pollack, 'The engines of integration? Supranational autonomy and influence in the European Union'

The important issue for our purposes is that of the relationship between delegation and legitimacy. In setting up delegated agents within the EC, Member States self-consciously took the decision to create institutions constitutionally separated from national legitimation processes. Moreover, by creating the Commission and the Court of Justice as appointed institutions they deliberately omitted to provide them with any direct input legitimacy of their own. Finally, the lack of accountability of the Court and Commission is striking even in comparison to many delegated agents in domestic political settings: the role and functioning of these (including the Bundesbank) can generally be changed by normal legislation; such change within the European Union, however, would require unanimous consent from the 15 Member States—an extremely high hurdle.

Given this, it is easy to understand the widespread criticism of the illegitimacy and lack of accountability of both institutions that has become an increasingly prominent feature of the rhetoric of national political leaders when talking about the EU. Interestingly, that rhetoric has come more and more to mirror the criticisms made by some of the practice of delegation within the United States. Students of the European Union will recognize the sentiment underpinning Low's acerbic criticism of Congress over twenty years ago: '...the practice of delegation itself can hardly be criticized. The practice becomes pathological and criticisable, at the point where it comes to be considered as a good thing in itself, flowing to administrators without guides, checks and safeguards'.[8]

The literature on delegation pays relatively little attention to the issue of legitimacy.[9] Partly, this is because it was derived from, and continues to be applied to, settings where legitimacy is not an issue—notably the relationship between shareholders and managers, or that between employers and employees. Partly, too, scholars who employ the concepts associated with delegation tend, implicitly at least, to base their work upon the assumption that the principal is vested with some form of legitimate authority, and that

---

in W Sandholtz and A Stone Sweet (eds), *European Integration and Supranational Governance* (1998) chs 4 and 8.

[8] TJ Lowi, *The End of Liberalism: The Second Republic of the United States* (1979) 93–4.

[9] For surveys of this literature, see R Elgie and E Jones, 'Agents, principals and the studies of institutions: constructing a principal-centered account of delegation', University of Nottingham, Working Documents in the Study of European Governance, no 5, December 2000; TJ Doleys, 'Member States and the European Commission: theoretical insights from the new economics of organization' (2000) JEPP 532; H Kassim and A Menon, 'Rethinking the application of principal-agent models to the EU: Member States and the European Commission' (2002) JEPP (forthcoming).

the agent can only be deemed to be acting legitimately if its preferences do not diverge from those of the principal.[10] If this assumption is accepted, then it makes sense to argue that the delegated agents such as supranational institutions should be closely monitored, and that the maintenance of legitimacy requires the reinforcement of mechanisms for democratic control such as scrutiny by legitimate national institutions such as national parliaments.

However, as Elgie and Jones argue, most accounts of delegation are myopic, in that they are agent-centric. In other words, they focus on the dangers inherent in the possibility of agency drift and on potential institutional remedies to this problem. In the case of the European Union, however, delegation was rooted in a need to prevent 'principal drift'. In the context of the European Union, where ambiguity is a necessary part of securing agreement between 15 Member States, and where changes of government can mean that even states that initially strongly supported the terms of delegation may turn against them at a later date (the problem of time inconsistency), principal drift represents a real problem. Consequently, ensuring the effectiveness of the EU requires institutional solutions other than those associated with agency-centred accounts. Most notably, in order to retain effectiveness, and hence output efficiency, it is logical to think in terms of insulating the supranational institutions from Member State control.[11] It is only through their independence that the supranational institutions are in a position to promote any Community interest, or to ensure reciprocal respect for the EU bargain. Thus, quite apart from the problems inherent in seeking input legitimacy in a system not characterized by a strong sense of collective self, the logic of delegation in the EU militates strongly against institutional reforms aimed at securing enhanced input legitimacy for the Commission and the Court.

The relative and continued autonomy of the Commission and Court can be justified by more than simple arguments about output legitimacy. Too much of the case for input legitimacy is based on assumptions that legitimation by the states or by systems at European level that resemble those found in the states is the appropriate method for stabilizing the Union. This is to concede far too much to states or state-like creatures as effective and legitimate actors. The very process of delegation to autonomous institutions has a political dimension that is 'democratic' in a manner that reflects the

---

[10] R Elgie and E Jones (n 9 above).   [11] ibid.

growth of a transnational economy underpinned not by a transnational state but rather by a transnational 'process' that rubs away the rough, unrepresentative and (in market terms) illegitimate pretensions of the Member States. It is to this that we now turn.

Delegation, the European market and the 'democratic surplus'

Market-building is the most spectacular success delivered by the process of delegation to the supranational institutions. The Member States have (largely) secured the achievement of an integrated market covering the territory of the Union. This is attributable partly to the performance of the European Court and its allies in the national courts in vigorously applying the relevant Treaty provisions governing, most prominently, free movement and competition policy. Partly, too, it is down to the Commission proposing the legislative initiatives for adoption by the Council (and latterly the Parliament) that have put in place the 're-regulatory' legislative framework for integration. The realization of a more efficient market for Europe offers itself as a factor of output legitimation that can be taken as a justification for an apparent absence of orthodox input legitimacy enjoyed by the key supranational decision-makers (beyond the simple fact of their establishment by the Member States in the first place).

It should not be assumed that delegation and its (in detail, unforeseen) institutional consequences is solely susceptible to legitimation on the basis of output efficiency conceived as effective problem-solving exemplified most vividly by the building of an integrated market. Market-building also deserves recognition for the way in which it causes adjustment to national political processes. This is of importance in constructing a fuller picture of EU legitimacy. This approach insists on the democratic aspects of supranationalism; it depicts EC law as a correction to national political processes that are unaligned with the range of interests that are affected by their decisions.

Maduro has observed that 'national polities have a twofold deficit: on the one hand, they do not control many decision-making processes which impact on those polities but take place outside their borders; on the other hand, national polities exclude from participation and representation many interests which are affected by its decisions'.[12] In short, national-level decision-making assumes what does not exist—a stable set of consumers of those decisions, whose preferences will be fully satisfied by the national polity and who are not joined by other 'external' affected parties. European law works in such a way as to correct these malfunctions. The effective problem-solving aspect of collective action is plain and widely acknowledged in a way that the exclusionary effect of national decision-making is not. This demands an excursion into EC trade law.

The most intriguing case law arising under the Treaty provisions governing free movement of goods and services concerns situations in which a trader based in one state finds access to the market of another state (the 'host state') impeded by public measures which on their face do not discriminate on the basis of origin, but rather simply differ from the rules applied in the home state. The constitutional collision between home state and host state control needs to be managed in a more sophisticated manner than the selection of an absolute rule at either end of the spectrum. A rule of absolute host state control, depriving traders of any right to operate in new markets without adapting themselves fully to local market conditions, would subvert the very notion of competitive market restructuring and the realization of economies of scale. A rule of absolute home state control, stripping away any role for regulation of economic activities on their territories by public bodies in so far as the relevant commercial party is based in another Member State and acting in conformity with the rules applicable there, finds no support in the Treaty. Such a model of ferocious inter-state regulatory competition is opposed by the presence of provisions such as Articles 30 and 55 EC and is more generally inconsistent with the very existence in the Treaty of a power to harmonize divergent national laws, a process which is itself required to take into account interests other than simple market-opening.[13] Consequently the framework idea of a split in competence between the home state and the host state has come to play a vigorous role in the shaping of the Treaty provisions governing free movement of goods and services. It has formed the basis for the European Court's jurisprudence which has converted the Treaty rules into a subtle, flexible and intrusive set of instruments for advancing market integration

---

[12] M Poiares Maduro, 'Europe and the constitution: what if this is as good as it gets?' in J Weiler and M Wind (eds), *Rethinking European Constitutionalism* (forthcoming); also available via http://www.qub.ac.uk/ies/onlinepapers/const.html

[13] See in particular Art 95(3) EC; in different vein, Art 95(4) EC et seq; and more generally the Treaty's *Querschnittsklausel*, Arts 6, 152(1), 153(2) EC.

while seeking to take account of legitimate national interests in regulatory protection.

This is famously the domain of *Cassis de Dijon*.[14] The problem was inter-state regulatory diversity; the effect was the exclusion from the German market of a product lawfully made and marketed in France. The Court, invited to interpret the meaning of Article 28 in such circumstances, provided an enduring formula according to which to assess whether Germany, as the host state, may prevent a product conforming to the rules of the home state, *in casu* France, from reaching its domestic market. A complex judgment, combining genuflections towards the principle of host state control with the imposition of significant threshold requirements on its permissible application in a manner that would exclude imports, asserted in essence that home state control applies as a form of (judicially applied) non-absolute principle of mutual recognition. It prevails in the absence of a sufficiently compelling basis for host state control.

According to the *Cassis* ruling, dual regulation of a product or service will occur only in the limited circumstances in which the host state is able to justify its rules in terms of the public interest. Economically, the result should be the release of wider consumer choice and intensified competition as products and services originating in other Member States but previously suppressed on export markets by local measures of market regulation become more readily available. This shift from (national) public regulation to private autonomy in the market is central to expectations of properly-functioning common markets to which the objectives of the EC Treaty are attached.

But there is a richer basis for assessing this case law rather than the purely economic perspective that would treat the output as legitimate in so far as it generates market efficiencies in Europe. *Cassis de Dijon* and many of its subsequent applications illustrate the confrontation between the development of European market integration and the deadwood of centuries of regulatory tradition in all the Member States. The Court's formula stands for the need to place the regulatory autonomy of the Member States under a control exercised by EC trade law, and to insist that a justification recognized by EC law be shown for public intervention in the market. That the state's political processes have (at some time in the past) generated such a law is not of itself enough to legitimate it. Regulatory choices have to be assessed in the light of their impact on wider processes of integration. One might, of course, object to the values

---

[14] Case 120/78 *Rewe Zentrale v Bundesmonopolverwaltung für Branntwein* [1979] ECR 649.

that the Court attaches to particular interests when it makes these decisions;[15] and/or one might doubt whether, say, trade integration and the interest in, for example, maintaining press diversity[16] or a viable public health care system[17] can truly be weighed on the same scale; and/or one might question whether a judicial forum is the appropriate place to make such choices. As a general observation, however, the case law offers the Court the opportunity to weed out unrepresentative and outdated manifestations of national-level decision-making that are hostile to and inappropriate in an integrating European market of the type to which the Member States have committed themselves under the EC Treaty.

Appreciation of the constitutional dimension is of fundamental importance to a full grasp of the nature of the process of adjudication under the law of free movement.[18] Host state control typically involves the exclusion of out-of-state trading interests from the rule-making process and the neglect of in-state consumer interests. That is, the connection between competence to regulate and responsibility to those affected is inadequately captured by a model which rests on assumptions of (host) state control in a European market that transcends the state. So the free movement case law 'forces' host states to justify their choices in the light of the impact on affected constituencies who are not otherwise (adequately) represented in domestic local political processes but who, most vividly in the case of traders with a direct commercial stake in achieving European market re-structuring, are able to rely on EC law in litigation before national courts in order to jolt national regulatory tradition. Accordingly one could persuasively characterize many of the free movement cases as representing the European Court's attempts to employ EC trade law to feed in out-of-state trading interests and in-state consumer interests to (national) systems for producing regulations which are otherwise

---

[15] See S Weatherill, 'Recent case law concerning the free movement of goods: mapping the frontiers of market deregulation' (1999) 36 CMLRev 51; M Poiares Maduro, 'Striking the elusive balance between economic freedom and social rights in the EU' in P Alston (ed), *The EU and Human Rights* (1999) 449. For critical assessment of this case law see eg C MacMaolain, 'Free movement of foodstuffs, quality requirements and consumer protection: have the Court and Commission both got it wrong?' (2001) 26 ELRev 413.

[16] Case C-368/95 *Vereinigte Familiapress Zeitungsverlags- und vertriebs GmbH v Heinrich Bauer Verlag* [1997] ECR I-3689.

[17] Case C-120/95 *Decker* [1998] ECR I- 1831; see T Hervey, 'Social solidarity: a buttress against internal market law? in J Shaw (ed), *Social Law and Policy in an Evolving European Union* (2001) 31; E Szyszczak, 'Free trade as a fundamental value in the European Union' in K Economides, L Betten, J Bridge, A Tettenborn and V Shrubsall (eds), *Fundamental Values* (2000) 159.

[18] See in particular the groundbreaking work of M Poiares Maduro, *We, The Court* (1998).

over-representative of the interest group comprising in-state traders. The rules, successfully challenged in cases such as *Cassis de Dijon* and many of that ilk, reflected national protection of local suppliers which was not at all advantageous to local consumers or traders based in other Member States; they were thus politically as well as economically protectionist. The application of the rules of free movement served to correct the malfunction of national political processes that were not attuned to the opportunities presented by the broader sweep of market integration in Europe.

In this sense, EC trade law, by imposing on national political processes an obligation to respect the interests of 'foreign' actors, reflects and seeks to address the problems caused by the gap between the growth of a European market and the absence of European political institutions equipped with a general regulatory competence.[19] The home state/host state model for distributing competences in the construction and management of the internal market under primary EC law is, at one level, an exercise in deregulation but, in addition, it asserts unexpectedly direct intervention in orthodox assumptions about responsibility and affected constituencies in national political decision-making. This is significant in that it asserts that this apparent triumph of market over state has a political dimension. It is not simply a case of output legitimation based on the delivery of an efficiently functioning, competitive cross-border market for Europe, while those concerned with input legitimacy can only look on anxiously, aware that national political processes have been blocked from intervening in markets in a wide range of circumstances and that European political processes are not designed to fill this gap in public intervention. Rather, it asserts the democratic potential of supranational law in curing the deficiencies of state-level decisions taken in a transnational economy. It points to a rich notion of transnational—perhaps postnational—governance, which limits the state while not seeking to replace it with a bigger state.

A model that regards EC trade law in the light of this legitimating potential can also be fashioned in examining the pattern of harmonization legislation. In circumstances where restrictive trading rules are shown to be justified according to the *Cassis de Dijon* formula, the responsibility for market-making shifts from Court to legislature. The classic response to lawful regulatory diversity is to introduce harmonized rules that accommodate the perceived need for public intervention in the market, but to do so in

---

[19]   An absence forcibly confirmed by the Court in case C-376/98 *Germany v Parliament and Council* [2000] ECR I-8419 (Tobacco Advertising).

a uniform manner, at European level. The EC sets the framework for trade while also assuming the responsibility for setting a 're-regulatory' standard. There is much to be said about the bargains that are struck in the determination of the content of the re-regulatory regime; and much to be said, too, about the extent to which uniformity is a feasible or desirable goal.[20] However, for present purposes the particular interest lies in the constitutional dimension of re-regulation as a device for securing integrated markets. 'Indirect rule' refers to the pattern according to which rule-making is located at transnational level but the overwhelming majority of implementation and enforcement activity is allocated to and embedded within established national structures of law and administration.[21] It is a powerful model in that it harnesses established national legal and bureaucratic systems to the fulfilment of the Community's mission, allowing the Community to operate as a remarkably lean administration judged by the size of its own staff and direct expenditure, while also tending to sweeten the potentially alienating 'foreign' flavour of EC rules by embedding them within everyday local practice. In this sense the European Community's primary modus operandi is not at all to replace national political processes but rather to require adaptation of existing national systems in order to induce recognition of the salience of un- or under-represented interests that are associated with the process of market integration and deeper inter-state co-ordination. There is a (developing) European market, but there is to be no replacement European State. The gap is bridged by widening the horizons of political, administrative and legal actors within the Member States. Just as the qualified home state/ host state model developed by the Court in its *Cassis de Dijon* formula can persuasively be taken as a method for subjecting national political processes that under-represent interests in market integration to a control that reflects the affected constituencies, so too the 're-regulatory bargain' under secondary legislation can be approached in a similar fashion. Interests that over time have prompted regulation of the market in host states have not been entirely swept aside (though this may sometimes occur); rather, the fact that their expression collided with the process of European market building has caused them to be absorbed into the EC legal order and, under this model of vertical re-distribution of competence, it is now necessary to look (albeit not necessarily

---

[20] The literature on flexibility in its many guises is vast and increasing: see G de Búrca and J Scott (eds), *Constitutional Change in the EU: From Uniformity to Flexibility?* (2000) for a collection of essays and copious bibliographic references.

[21] T Daintith (ed), *Implementing EC Law in the UK: Structures for Indirect Rule* (1995).

exclusively) to Community level—the governing Directive—for the location of the protective rule.

Consider a trader in home state X supplying consumers in host state Y. Interested parties in the host state no longer expect enforcement by 'their' authorities, those of state Y. Rather home state X, implementing the Directive under the model of 'indirect rule' foreseen by Articles 10 and 249 EC, is responsible. So home state X has, via the EC's 're-regulation', become obliged to work as a law enforcement agency on behalf of consumers in host state Y. A home state acts on behalf of all Community citizens not simply its own.[22] *National* agencies, anchored to a political chain of state-focused responsibility and accountability, become responsible for the enforcement of *Community* rules governing the European market. This model of home state enforcement on behalf of parties in the host state runs directly counter to the basics of national-level representative democracy. Especially (but not only) where the traders based in the home state are politically influential and where damage done by failure to police compliance with EC rules would largely be felt by citizens in host States, there are incentives for home states to adopt a lax approach to the enforcement of the 're-regulatory bargain'. The domestic political mandate is not at all tied to the interests of out-of-state consumers. The EC intervention is based on the construction of a European market but associated rule-enforcement is tied to the reality of state systems which are apt to generate decisions (about law enforcement as well as law making) that reflect the interests able directly to influence state political processes; and those are narrower than those envisaged at EC level as affected by market-building achieved by the adoption of secondary legislation. This calls for active supervision of the application of the EC rules; litigation plays a very important function, and the Commission is actively seeking to build wider structures of horizontal and vertical administrative cooperation that will minimize the scope for (deliberate or unwitting)[23] defection.[24] The inclusion of an insistence on improving the application of EC rules at national level in the Commission's White Paper on Governance, published in the summer of 2001, confirms that this is no

---

[22]   This is made explicit in recital 22 to Dir 2000/31, [2000] OJ L178/1.

[23]   On the breadth of reasons for non-compliance, see P Van den Bossche, 'In search of remedies for non-compliance: the experience of the EC' (1996) 3 MJ 371.

[24]   For more detail see K Mortelmans, 'The common market, the internal market and the single market, what's in a market?' (1998) 35 CMLRev 101; S Weatherill, 'New strategies for managing the EC's internal market' (2000) 53 CLP 595; KA Armstrong, 'Governance and the single European market' in P Craig and G de Búrca, *The Evolution of EU Law* (1999) 745.

mere technical matter.[25] It goes to the heart of sustaining a viable system for governing the Union built on horizontal and vertical cooperation between actors at different levels rather than on any desire to make a state at European level. Thus integration can itself be treated not simply as legitim- ate for its economic gains but also as a fundamentally democratic process, which helps to bridge the gap between states and European markets in a manner that does not create a need to re-instate the state at European level.

European trade law limits the exercise of public power in order to protect the individual. What is remarkable is the breaking of the bond between state and citizen. European trade law empowers a category of individuals whose interests are recognized by EC trade law and then imposed on the state process which would normally recognize only a narrower constituency. So the national political community's place as the dominant reference point is challenged. That is, European market-building is reflected not in European state-building but in making national systems more European. It is a system of governance that tolerates a disconnection between the map of political unity and economic unity, partly because attempts to achieve congruence are doomed to failure because the economic map can never be static, but, more positively, because there are imaginative methods for addressing that apparent gulf, which in fact demonstrate that the quest for good and accountable governance can be successfully achieved without being backed into a corner and forced to choose between states in Europe or a European State.[26]

Criticism of the EU as lacking the democratic credentials that are char- acteristic of a state is not to take as given that which is contested. It is to take as given that which is denied. The EU is not a state nor is it to become one. The very combination of European institutional and constitutional archi- tecture alongside those of the Member States itself secures a broader sense of democracy—a democracy which ensures the reflection and representa- tion of interests outside a context which is dependent on and limited by state systems. The EU does not challenge the existence of states but rather it seeks to establish structures that restrain their corruptive capacity to inflict harm.[27] The EU both empowers states (collectively) and limits them. This

---

[25] COM (2001) 428 final 25–26. Similarly, Green Paper on EU Consumer Protection, COM (2001) 531 final 16–19.

[26] This, of course, is not simply an issue for the European Community; cf B Rosamond, 'Discourses of globalization and the social construction of European identities' (1999) 6 JEPP 652.

[27] eg N MacCormick, *Questioning Sovereignty* (1999); JHH Weiler, *The Constitution of Europe* (1999).

is not simply a matter of output legitimacy founded on economic success. It insists also on the virtues of the supranational method in securing that state power is exercised in a manner that reflects the 'Community interest'—those whose interests are not reflected in the normally assumed process of decision-making of a State. It treats the Union as 'a political arena designed not to replace the political arena of the nation-state but rather to supplement it in very necessary, albeit complementary, ways'.[28] This then is transnational democracy and transnational governance, and it is important because it argues that a perspective which embraces the EU as legitimated by its outputs must also take account of the democratic contribution of its law which surpasses issues of input legitimacy contributed either at state level or at European level. In fact, it is a method for accepting that legitimation comes both from state and European level but that, in addition, the very process of integration, by confining state choices while not assuming their replacement at European level, changes the balance between public and private power.

Central to this analysis is the assertion that arguments about legitimacy that assume either state-level legitimacy or European-level legitimacy as the necessary and appropriate basis for assessing the European Union are doubly flawed—they assume one or the other instead of accepting the contributions of both, and they tend to assume input legitimacy as a sufficient basis. The European Union is a divided power system involving 'a progressive constitution of legitimate institutions and powers at the European level, which are complementary to the national constitutions and designed to meet the challenges of an evolving global society'.[29] Our analysis points towards the growth of a coherent constitutional and institutional architecture for Europe, albeit that different sources must be drawn on to make real this vision—the key being not to suppose that one source has any necessary superiority (measured in any sense) over another.

Viewing the issue of legitimacy in this way possesses the particular attraction that it frees us from the trap that treats the increase in private economic power in supra-state domains as a basis for shifting extra public

---

[28] D Curtin, 'Postnational democracy: the European Union in search of a political philosophy' (Inaugural Lecture, Universiteit Utrecht, 1997) 5; cf J Shaw, 'Postnational constitutionalism in the European Union' (1999) 6 JEPP 579; N Reich, 'Union citizenship—metaphor or source of rights' (2001) 7 ELJ 4.

[29] I Pernice, 'Multi-level constitutionalism and the Treaty of Amsterdam: European constitution-making revisited' (1999) 36 CMLRev 703; see also M Horeth, 'No way out for the beast? The unsolved legitimacy problem of European governance' (1999) 6 JEPP 249; P Craig, 'Constitutions, constitutionalism, and the European Union' (2001) 7 ELJ 125.

power to that same level, which in turn draws demands for greater institutional accountability to that level, which is in turn vulnerable to the criticism that it impoverishes the domestic sphere. It also serves as a means for releasing the study of the European Union from another unhelpful 'either/or' model, that which assumes its valid comparator is either an international organization or a state; the international relations versus comparative government dichotomy. Certainly it is useful to employ a comparative method to study the EU and to debate the relative merits of approaches from either sub-discipline in terms of explaining its development or functioning. But this should not blind us to the fact that the European Union represents a unique and novel experiment, and in order to chart possible future courses of development for such an institution, we should not be hamstrung by our reliance on concepts and institutional designs intended for other types of institutional structure at other times.

Conclusions

This chapter has sought to expose some of the limitations of models that respond to the tensions injected by the EU's geographical and functional expansion by insisting on greater input legitimacy. We urge for greater attention to the damage that can thereby be done to output legitimacy. We argue in addition that delegation can be legitimated by a broader notion than merely economic efficiency, though this in itself is not insignificant. The 'problem with states' is not merely that they may be incapable of effective problem-solving. The rise of transnational economies also tends to accentuate the extent to which state decisions may be driven by the orthodox pressures of national-level representative democracy; and yet may impose costs on actors who are intimately affected by those decisions, yet who are not represented or only inadequately represented in the state's political processes. The juxtaposition of state political decision-making and burgeoning transnational economic activity allows or even induces states to externalize costs and a method is required for reducing, if not eliminating, the ability of the state to take decisions which are neglectful of costs imposed on parties who are not able to gain (adequate) access to the (domestic) market for votes. A supranational legal order is capable of achieving this, and exploration of its legitimacy should encompass respect for this capacity.

Assessing problems of legitimacy by extending emphasis on European-level governance can *always* be criticized for its illegitimacy by those who assume the pre-eminence of national-level political structures. It is the specious but primitively compelling 'loss of sovereignty' argument, but such debates cannot sensibly be conducted pending liberation from (frequently unwitting) preconceptions about sites of legitimacy. So solutions must be pragmatic, incremental and cautious. They must identify the different strands of legitimacy and be aware that tweaking one tweaks all. A starting point might have been that output legitimacy is a Union strength while input legitimacy is a state strength, but in fact the interconnections are decidedly more sophisticated than such a model will allow. The least ambitious case made by this paper is that it is wrong to make assumptions about which element to privilege. The more ambitious, and as yet relatively tentative, claim is that we can have it all—provided that all elements are cherished and treated as mutually reinforcing aspects of a broad and multi-level conception of European constitutionalism.[30] That is, a legitimacy test insisting on both input and output legitimacy may be failed both by states and the EU, though in respect of different criteria and/or by different degrees, but taken together, the combination passes. In so far as this represents the essence of transnational governance, it should be seen as a necessarily dynamic and creative process.

There is not the space here to draw out fully the implications of this analysis. One important, though by no means the only, such issue concerns the appropriate scope of EU action. Both Majone and Scharpf argue that the EU should remain somewhat restricted in scope because of the necessary 'strong' (input) legitimation that must underpin many areas of public policy and which the EC lacks.[31] Such preferences should be expressed, if at all, only by Member States. Yet at a time when the EU is embarking on its experiment with a single currency, such arguments seem curiously anachronistic. It may well be that the Union is confronted with the stark choice between, on the one hand, risking its potential to deliver effective outputs by controlling monetary policy in the euro zone without an effective fiscal policy to redress regional disparities and, on the other, venturing into larger scale redistributive policies that surpass its capacity to muster input legit-

---

[30]   Similarly Maduro in Weiler and Wind (n 12 above).

[31]   Scharpf talks of the need for EU policies to satisfy the conditions of low visibility and being conflict minimizing, whilst Majone insists on the need for the Union to steer clear of redistributive policies. See F Scharpf, *Governing in Europe: Effective and Democratic?* (1999) 21–25; G Majone, *Regulating Europe* (1996).

imacy. There are no easy solutions to such dilemmas. The most that we can hope to have achieved here is to suggest that by looking at the structure of the multi-level European constitutional system as a whole, rather than performing misleading 'legitimacy tests' based on standards developed for nation states upon the EU alone, we may have suggested a more appropriate and effective way of beginning the task of thinking about the legitimacy of the Union.

8

The Judicial Architecture of the European Union after Nice

*Laurence W Gormley**

Introduction

That the present judicial architecture of the European Union demonstrates not inconsiderable weaknesses seems now to be widely accepted, although, despite the opportunity which the 2000 IGC offered for root and branch reform of the system, the result in the Treaty of Nice has been to provide some patchwork repairs and a makeover by a team which, on the basis of this offering, would never be allowed its own television programme. In other words, to adapt John Major's famous phrase, this Treaty is several courses short of a banquet. This is particularly disappointing as it is becoming increasingly apparent that despite the construction of the cathedral-like edifice of the Union at Maastricht on the foundations of the European Communities, and the mere jobbing builder's work at Amsterdam,[1] the system is still unable to cope with the demands of litigants for speedy dispute resolution and for effective judicial protection of legitimate interests. Nevertheless, repairers and make-over teams have their value.

This chapter sets out to examine the changes for which the Treaty of Nice provides, and to assess the state of the European Union's central judicial architecture in the light of those changes and in view of the degree to which

---

* This chapter was prepared while I was Visiting Fellow of Sidney Sussex College, Cambridge and of CELS in the Faculty of Law at Cambridge, and finished while I was Visiting Professor at the Faculty of Law of the University of Leuven in Belgium. I acknowledge my gratitude to those institutions for their gracious hospitality.
[1] See LW Gormley, 'Reflections on the architecture of the European Union after the Treaty of Amsterdam' in D O'Keeffe and P Twomey (eds), *Legal Issues of the Amsterdam Treaty* (1999) 57.

they fail to respond to desires expressed in various documents presented to the IGC.

Restructuring the Court

'Court of Justice' remains a name with a variable significance. The Court is at once a single institution of the Communities[2] and composed of two bodies: the Court of Justice itself and the Court of First Instance, or CFI. The Treaty of Nice leaves this arrangement unchanged, but makes a subtle change in the relationship between the two component parts of the institution. The CFI will no longer be merely an attachment to the Court of Justice, but will become a body in its own right.[3] The close linkage is maintained by the retention of the requirement that the CFI's Rules of Procedure be established in agreement with the Court of Justice.[4] The obligation to 'ensure that in the interpretation and application of this Treaty the law is observed' will also be imposed specifically on the CFI, not only, as at present, on the Court of Justice.[5] This obligation applies to each court within its own jurisdiction.[6] This clarifies and corresponds to the requirements of the second sentence of Article 7(1) EC as regards the Court as an institution, and is also appropriate in view of the change that the Treaty of Nice will make possible regarding references for a preliminary ruling.[7] The opportunity has also been taken to upgrade the qualification for membership of the CFI, from 'the ability required for appointment to judicial office' to 'the ability required for appointment to high judicial office'. The perceived increase in status of the CFI is further indicated by the possibility for judicial panels to be attached to it in order to exercise, in certain specific areas, the judicial competence laid down in the Treaty.[8] The CFI will, when the judicial panels are established, become, in the areas concerned, a court which has appellate jurisdiction in relation to decisions of those panels. In

---

[2] Art 7(1) EC.

[3] This is the effect of repealing the existing Arts 225 EC and 140a EAEC.

[4] The new Arts 224 EC and 140 EAEC, 5th para in each case take over the existing Arts 225(4) EC and 140(4) EAEC, although, as noted below, the Council's approval will be by qualified majority instead of the present requirement of unanimity.

[5] See the new Arts 220 EC and 136 EAEC, 1st para in each case.

[6] ibid.

[7] This is dealt with below.

[8] See the new Arts 220 EC and 136 EAEC, 2nd para in each case.

most instances this will be the final determination, although it will be possible for the Court of Justice to review the matter in exceptional cases.[9]

The change in how the composition of the Court of Justice itself is expressed—one judge per Member State—in effect means no immediate change, while preserving the present principle in a manner that avoids constant changes in numbers on accession.[10] It is a clear response to suggestions that the number of judges should be limited, recognizing that just no Member State is going to wish to give up a seat on the Court. Account has, however, been taken of the difficulties posed by a Court composed of some 25 judges. This has been a constant dilemma in the Court's papers on reform proposals.[11] On the one hand, there is the danger of crossing the boundary line between a collegiate court and a deliberative assembly; on the other hand, there is the legitimacy of the institution that flows from the principle of every Member State being represented. Thus, whereas at present the default position under Articles 221 EC and 137 EAEC is that the Court sits in plenary session, save where it is provided that it shall sit in Chambers of three, five, or seven judges, the default position once the Treaty of Nice enters into force will be the reverse: the Court will sit in Chambers or in a Grand Chamber, but may under certain circumstances sit as a full court.[12] The composition of chambers will also change, so that they will only consist of three or five judges.[13] The Grand Chamber will consist of 11 judges, presided over by the President of the Court; the other members will be the presidents of the chambers of five judges and other judges appointed in accordance with conditions which will be laid down in the rules of procedure. Decisions of a Grand Chamber will require at least nine judges to be sitting. Unlike in the case of the European Court of Human Rights, where a Grand Chamber under Article 43 ECHR effectively re-hears a case decided by a Chamber, the Grand Chamber has no appellate function but will sit at the request of a Member State or Community institution that is party to the proceedings in question.[14] In effect the

[9] The working of this system is discussed below.

[10] The present Arts 221 EC and 137 EAEC fix the number of judges at 15 and permit the Council, at the Court's request, inter alia to increase the number of judges. If accession means an even number of Member States, an additional judge can be provided for (as has happened in the past).

[11] See eg *Report of the Court of Justice on certain aspects of the application of the Treaty on European Union* (Luxembourg, May 1995), point 16.

[12] See the new Art 221 EC.

[13] See the new Statute of the Court (henceforth 'new Statute'), Art 16.

[14] At present Member States or Community institutions that are party to proceedings may request that the Court sit in plenary session: Art 221 EC, 3rd para.

Grand Chamber is a compromise between the present defunct seven-judge chambers (which the Court decided on 25 January 1995 would in fact sit as five-judge chambers)[15] and the plenary session. The status of the presidents of the five-judge chambers will be enhanced by their election for a three-year term, with the possibility of re-election once.[16]

At present a full court is formed by 15, 13 or (the minimum) 11 judges, although in practice the full court usually comprises 13 judges. The Nice amendments will, with the present number of Member States, leave that unchanged, but the minimum number of 11 will remain, even if there are 23 or 25 judges. Clearly it is more likely that a full court would be convened with more judges than the minimum, in case of illness or even death, but the prospect does arise of a case being decided by a full court that is not composed of a majority of the judges. No doubt sensible practice will prevail to reduce the likelihood of this occurring. The Court will have to sit as a full court when hearing a request from the European Parliament to dismiss the Ombudsman;[17] or an application by the Council or Commission to compulsorily retire a member of the Commission or deprive him or her of the right to a pension or other benefits in its stead;[18] or a similar application by the Court of Auditors in respect of one of its members.[19] The Court, sitting in a Chamber or Grand Chamber may, where it considers that a case before it is of exceptional importance, and after having heard the Advocate General, decide to refer the case to the full Court.[20] This mirrors the existing practice under Article 95(3) of the Rules of Procedure, which permits a Chamber at any time to refer a case to the full Court.[21] The practice of referral is also expressly provided for in Article 30 ECHR.[22]

The function of Advocate General will undergo a quiet and subtle change as a result of the drafting of the new Articles 222 EC and 138 EAEC, and the final paragraph of Article 20 of the new Statute. Thus the Advocate General will present 'reasoned submissions on cases which, in accordance with the Statute of the Court of Justice, require his involvement'. This heralds a step

---

[15] [1995] OJ C54/2

[16] New Statute, Art 16, 1st para.

[17] Under Arts 195(2) EC or 107d(2) EAEC; new Statute, Art 16, 4th para.

[18] Arts 216 EC or 129 EAEC and 213(2) EC or 126(2) EAEC, final para., respectively; new Statute, Art 16, 4th para.

[19] Art 247(7) EC or 160b(7) EAEC; new Statute, Art 16, 4th para.

[20] New Statute, Art 16, final para.

[21] As to examples of this occurring, see PJG Kapteyn and P VerLoren van Themaat (ed LW Gormley), *Introduction to the Law of the European Communities* (3rd edn, 1998) 253 (note 402).

[22] In this case for relinquishment by a Chamber to the Grand Chamber.

back from the universal role of the Advocate General, as the Court will be able to decide, after hearing him or her, to determine a case without a submission from the Advocate General, where it considers that the case raises no new point of law. The reason for this is clearly to expedite the proceedings and promote a more summary treatment of repetitious cases. It would always have been possible for an Opinion to say simply that this case raises a point of law on which the Court has already pronounced (referring to the judgment(s)) and proposing a decision accordingly. Indeed the Court has disposed of repetitious references clearly and briefly in the past.[23] The amount of work saved, though, will be relatively small: drafting a brief opinion and translating it; but consideration by the Advocate General will still be necessary for him to give a view on whether an opinion is necessary. More worrying, though, is the result that the system that there should be an opinion (however brief) in every case is set aside: it is to be hoped that decisions to dispense with an opinion will be taken only sparingly.

As a result of the new Article 229a EC, the Council may, acting unanimously on a proposal from the Commission, and after consulting the European Parliament, adopt provisions conferring specific jurisdiction on the Court of Justice in disputes relating to the application of Community acts which create Community intellectual property rights. Those jurisdiction provisions will be recommended to the Member States for adoption in accordance with their respective constitutional requirements.

Two important changes relating to the framework governing the operation of the Court of Justice will be introduced by the Treaty of Nice. The first relates to the Statute of the Court, the second to the Rules of Procedure.

---

[23] eg Case 168/86 *Procureur Général v Rousseau* [1987] ECR 995, 1002: 'Consideration of this case has not disclosed any new points not already raised in Case 355/85. In those circumstances, it is sufficient to refer to the grounds of the judgment in that case, a copy of which is attached to this judgment.' AG Slynn (at 999) said 'It is to be noted that the Court's judgment in *Cognet* was supplied to the referring court which, however, maintained its request for a preliminary ruling. Since (as I said in my Opinion of 12 December 1985, in Joined Cases 271 to 274/84 and 6 and 7/85 *Procureur de la République v Chiron*) under Community law and procedure in such a situation it is open to the national court to withdraw a reference, it is to be hoped, in those Member States where it cannot apparently be done at present, that a way may be found for national law and procedure to make a withdrawal possible when no new issue arises, when no new arguments are advanced and where the Court's answer can only be the same.' In Case 95/84 *Boriello v Darras & Tostain* [1986] ECR 2253 the Court noted that 'Consideration of the present case has revealed nothing that was not already known to the Court in Case 229/83. In those circumstances it is sufficient to refer to the grounds of the judgment of 10 January 1985, a copy of which shall be annexed to the present judgment.' See also Rules of Procedure, Art 104(3), permitting disposal of cases by reasoned order.

The Statute is integrally replaced,[24] and various technical points are moved from the body of the EC and EAEC Treaties themselves to the new Statute (which is a Protocol attached to those Treaties). As at present, the new Statute may be amended by the Council, acting unanimously at the request of the Court of Justice and after consulting the European Parliament and the Commission. What is new is that such a request may in future also emanate from the Commission, in which case the Court is consulted along with the European Parliament. A further novelty is that only Title I of the new Statute (Judges and Advocates General) will be protected from amendment in either of these ways; at present the power of amendment may be exercised only in respect of Title III (procedure). Thus matters of organization, the provisions relating to the CFI, and the Final Provisions, will become, along with procedure, matters in which the right of initiative of amendment is shared between the Court of Justice itself and the Commission (in addition to the Member States' rights collectively as Masters of the Treaty during an IGC). This amounts to a strengthening of the Commission's position. While the phrase 'at the request of the Commission' differs from the more usual 'on a proposal from the Commission,' the drafting appears simply designed to indicate parity of the right of initiative. Although the Court's suggestion that it should be able to adopt its own Rules of Procedure was not accepted, the Court's alternative suggestion that the Court's Rules of Procedure should be approved by the Council, acting by qualified majority,[25] rather than by unanimity as at present,[26] was taken on board. The same rule will apply to the Rules of Procedure of the CFI.[27]

In relation to the CFI, the notion of one judge per Member State has been transformed from holy writ to a minimum requirement,[28] with the precise number to be fixed by the new Statute.[29] While the office of Advocate General is envisaged in the CFI,[30] as yet no steps have been taken to provide for the specific appointment of Advocates General other than in the present *ad hoc* form of a judge acting as Advocate General.

---

[24] Art 7 of the Treaty of Nice replaces the statutes annexed to the EC and the EAEC Treaties.

[25] The new Arts 223 EC and 139 EAEC, last para in each case.

[26] Arts 245 EC and 160 EAEC, 3rd para in each case.

[27] The present Arts 225(4) EC and 140(4) EAEC will be replaced by the new Arts 224 EC and 140 EAEC, 5th para in each case. As at present, those Rules will be drawn up in agreement with the Court of Justice.

[28] The new Arts 224 EC and 140 EAEC, 1st para in each case.

[29] The new Statute, Art 48 sets the number at 15, which is still conveniently one per Member State.

[30] The new Arts 224 EC and 140 EAEC, 1st para in each case.

Expanding the centralized Community judiciary

An expansion of the centralized Community judiciary is envisaged by the new Articles 225a EC and 140b EAEC, which will permit the Council, acting unanimously either on a proposal from the Commission and after consulting the European Parliament and the Court of Justice, or at the request of the Court of Justice and after consulting the European Parliament and the Commission, to create judicial panels to deal at first instance with certain classes of action or proceeding in specific areas. The decision establishing a judicial panel will deal with the extent of its jurisdiction and its organization. Decisions of judicial panels would be open to appeal to the CFI only on points of law, unless the decision establishing the judicial panel in question provided for an appeal to that Court also on matters of fact. The criterion for appointment of persons whose independence is beyond doubt by the Council, acting unanimously, will be 'the ability required for appointment to judicial office'. The Rules of Procedure of the judicial panels will have to be established by them in agreement with the Court of Justice, and they will require the approval of the Council, acting by qualified majority. The provisions of Treaty relating to the Court of Justice and of the new Statute will apply to the judicial panels, unless the decision establishing a panel otherwise so provides.[31] The Treaty is silent as to the areas in which judicial panels may be established, but staff cases spring particularly to mind, as do cases relating to the application of the Customs Code and to customs classification; social security and the working of the various common organizations of agricultural markets, as well as industrial and commercial property. These are all specialist areas in which a considerable lightening of the workload of both present elements of the centralized Community judiciary could be achieved. It may be that the existing Boards of Appeal at the Office for Harmonization in the Internal Market (Trade Marks and Designs) (OHIM) could be upgraded to become judicial panels. The judicial panels will be attached to the CFI by virtue of the second paragraphs of the new Articles 220 EC and 136 EAEC.

Allocating jurisdiction

The amendments to be introduced by the Treaty of Nice will facilitate further developments in the allocation of jurisdiction between the Court of

---

[31] This is obviously particularly important in relation to matters such as the oath, and the immunity and removal of members of judicial panels.

Justice and the CFI. The new Article 225 EC[32] clarifies and in principle expands at Treaty level the scope of the CFI's jurisdiction. Thus the new article will confer general jurisdiction on the CFI in relation to actions for annulment;[33] actions for failure to act;[34] actions for damages;[35] staff cases;[36] and arbitration clauses in Community contracts.[37] However, those actions under these provisions which are assigned to the Court of Justice itself or to judicial panels are exceptions to this rule. The actions which will be assigned to the Court of Justice are those brought by Member States, by the Community institutions and by the ECB.[38] At the present this is principally a change of emphasis: general jurisdiction over a wide range of actions is conferred subject to exceptions, rather than specific jurisdiction being carved out of that of the Court of Justice. Significantly, infringement proceedings still remain the exclusive reserve of the Court of Justice itself, which is certainly a missed opportunity, particularly in relation to the more ritual infringements. Given that the jurisdiction of judicial panels will be laid down by the instruments which establish them,[39] the new Statute contains no provisions on this matter.

That the reallocation of jurisdiction between the Court of Justice and the CFI is likely to develop further is apparent from Declaration 12 adopted by the IGC on the signature of the Final Act of the Treaty of Nice. This called on the Court of Justice and the Commission to give overall consideration as soon as possible to this point, in particular as regards direct actions, and to submit suitable proposals as soon as the Treaty of Nice enters into force. In the meantime, the Court of Justice has submitted a Working Document[40] in which it proposes that as far as the direct actions mentioned in the new Articles 225(1) EC and 140a(1) EAEC are concerned, the only actions in respect of which the CFI should not have jurisdiction at first instance would be actions for annulment or failure to act brought by a Member State, a

[32] And the new Art 140a EAEC.
[33] Under Arts 230 EC and 146 EAEC.
[34] Under Arts 232 EC and 148 EAEC.
[35] Under Arts 235 EC and 151 EAEC.
[36] Under Arts 236 EC and 152 EAEC.
[37] Under Arts 238 EC and 153 EAEC.
[38] New Statute, Art 51.
[39] The new Arts 225a EC and 140b EAEC, 2nd para in each case.
[40] See http://curia.eu.int/en/txts/intergov/sn_4716.htm. The Court of Justice has also proposed deleting the present second sentence in new Statute, Art 54, 3rd para in order that the CFI could decline jurisdiction in favour of the Court of Justice in connected cases (such as an action against a basic Council regulation and an action against the implementing Commission regulation).

Community institution or the ECB against either the European Parliament or the Council, or both of them, and those actions brought by a Community institution against the ECB or the Commission, or by the ECB against the Commission. This proposal has so far met with mixed reactions from various delegations within the Council.[41] An allocation of jurisdiction which seeks to keep so-called constitutional issues within the jurisdiction of the Court of Justice itself without causing a reversal of the previous transfers of jurisdiction is recognized as being difficult, hence the choice of actors as the criteria by the Court. On this, as on other matters, further changes will most likely be made when and if the Treaty of Nice enters into force, or shortly thereafter.

The appellate function of the CFI in relation to decisions of judicial panels, once they are established, will in principle be final, as it is clear that review of such judgments of the CFI is meant to be exceptional: only 'where there is a serious risk of the unity or consistency of Community law being affected' may the matter be raised before the Court of Justice.[42] It becomes clear from Article 62 of the new Statute that raising the matter before the Court of Justice is not done by way of appeal; it is not the parties but the First Advocate General who takes the initiative in the matter. While there would appear to be as yet no formal bar to a party requesting the First Advocate General to propose that the Court of Justice review the judgment, the decision whether or not to propose review is clearly a matter for the First Advocate General. Accordingly, it is submitted that the First Advocate General would not be obliged to react in any way to such a request, and nor would his or her decision be open to challenge. His or her discretion is thus unfettered, and an argument may be made that it is appropriate that the parties should not seek to influence the Advocate General. If that view prevails, it may be necessary to adapt the Rules of Procedure to prohibit applications or other communications by the parties to the First Advocate General. On the other hand, it would seem strange if the views of the parties were to be unable to be considered by the First Advocate General, or even by the Court. If the First Advocate General wishes to bring the judgment of the CFI before the Court of Justice, he or she must make the proposal for review within one month of delivery of the decision by the CFI. The Court of Justice will then have one month from the date of the proposal to decide whether or not the decision should be reviewed. That does not, of course,

---

[41]   The Court's Working Paper is also available as Council Document 10790/01 (1 October 2001). See (by mid-February 2002) Council Documents 14596/01 (Germany); 14697/01 (Austria); 14703/01 (France); 15501/01 (United Kingdom); 5305/02 (Italy).

[42]   The new Arts 225(2) EC and 140a(2) EAEC.

mean that the review process has to be completed within one month: it merely means that the Court of Justice must decide within that period whether to subject the decision of the CFI to review. This procedure has a mixed pedigree, with elements reminiscent of various national procedures: review in the interest of the law; an Attorney General's reference or reference from a review commission, and leave to appeal. Clearly, the Statute and/or the Rules of Procedure will have to determine what role, if any, the parties would play in such a review, and what the effects of review will be.[43] It is particularly interesting that the initiation of review is a two-stage process: the First Advocate General must be convinced that review is desirable, then the Court of Justice itself. The decision of the Court whether or not to review the matter is, logically, not open to challenge. The Statute is silent on whether review will be by a Chamber or a Grand Chamber, or even by a full court. It is submitted that review by at least a Grand Chamber would be appropriate.

A further major development is the possibility of the new Statute conferring jurisdiction on the CFI to deal with references for preliminary rulings in specific areas.[44] However, where that court feels that the instant case 'requires a decision of principle likely to affect the unity or consistency of Community law', it may refer the case to the Court of Justice for a ruling. As with judgments of the CFI on appeals against decisions of judicial panels, there is the possibility for review of preliminary rulings given by the CFI 'where there is a serious risk of the unity or consistency of Community law being affected'. The conditions are the same as those outlined above in relation to review of judgments on appeal against decisions of judicial panels. Clearly, though, considerable care will be necessary, as review by the Court of Justice will, if not expedited, simply add substantially to the already considerable time which it takes to reply to the national court which made the reference. It may be here that the Court of Justice will have to treat the discussion of whether to review as in effect a substantive determination. However, this may be taking the bend too tightly for the vehicle of Community justice.

Unsurprisingly, in view of the questions about review which are as yet unresolved, Declaration 13 adopted by the IGC on the signature of the Final Act of the Treaty of Nice recognizes that particular aspects of the review by the Court of Justice under the new Articles 225(2) and (3) EC are so essential

---

[43]   This is clearly recognized by Declaration 13, as to which, see below.

[44]   The new Arts 225(3) EC and 140a(3) EAEC.

as to need definition in the new Statute, namely the role of the parties in proceedings before the Court of Justice, in order to safeguard their rights; the effect of the review procedure on the enforceability of the decision of the CFI, and the effect of the decision of the Court of Justice on the dispute between the parties. Declaration 14 calls on the Council to ensure that the operation of the procedure for appeals against decisions of judicial panels and their review by the Court of Justice, and of preliminary rulings and their reference to or review by the Court of Justice, should be evaluated no later than three years after the entry into force of the Treaty of Nice.

Admissibility and political suspension

Potentially perhaps the most important change from a political point of view, as well as a significant development from a legal point of view, is the conferral of privileged status on the European Parliament in actions for annulment of Community acts.[45] At present the Parliament is a semi-privileged applicant: it has to show that it is protecting its prerogatives in order to be admissible. Once the Treaty of Nice enters into force, this restriction will no longer apply. Where this is likely to be most significant is in relation to challenging delegated legislation adopted by the Commission. Although the Commission nowadays keeps the European Parliament informed of implementing legislation based on acts which were adopted under the co-decision procedure,[46] the possibility of challenging inter alia implementing legislation represents a real improvement. It is to be regretted that the opportunity was not taken to improve the standing requirements for individual litigants or public interest groups.[47]

The other clearly politically important aspect to the Court's jurisdiction in the Nice amendments is that, in relation to the provisions of the new Article 7 TEU, its role is confined to the purely procedural aspects of the process of coping with a serious and persistent breach of the principles of liberty, democracy, respect for human rights and fundamental freedoms and the rule of law set out in Article 6(1) TEU. The Member States were, understandably in view of time constraints and the sensitive nature of the

---

[45]   The new Arts 230 EC and 146 EAEC, 2nd para. The 3rd para is consequently amended to remove the Parliament from the category of semi-privileged applicants.

[46]   Since the *Modus Vivendi* on this issue, [1996] OJ C102/1.

[47]   See LW Gormley, 'Public interest litigation in Community law' (2001) 7 EPL 51.

evaluations, unwilling to allow the Court to review the substantive determinations made by the political process in this area.

Assessment of the effects of the Treaty of Nice on the judicial architecture of the European Union

The above outline of the significant amendments affecting the judicial architecture of the European Union demonstrates that the emphasis has in effect been on shifting the workload and making some basic decisions about representation in the Court of Justice. Yet much more will have to be done before the effects of this Treaty will translate themselves into more effective and even efficient judicial decision-making, both of which are fundamental to the Union's legitimacy. The Treaty of Nice leaves much yet to be agreed and implemented. Moreover, it does nothing to tackle the inherent weaknesses of much of Community dispute resolution. There is no attempt to streamline infringement procedures, for example, by permitting interim measures to be obtained at an earlier phase than at present,[48] so as to afford speedy relief without waiting for the administrative phase to be played out with delaying tactics. Nor is there a clear framework for summary judgments to be given where it is clear that there is no defence—Member States can insist on two rounds of written pleadings defending the indefensible. The possibility of dispensing with the Advocate General's Opinion offers only minimal gains in terms of time. The Due Report[49] argued that the most helpful reform would be to permit the Commission to adopt a decision establishing the infringement, that could be challenged if a Member State really disagreed.[50] This would be without prejudice to the penalty powers of the Court under Article 228(2) EC, which would in this case be for non-compliance with an (unchallenged) decision or a judgment of the Court in response to a challenge to a decision. In the event, this plea has fallen on deaf ears. At the very least, the Due Report's recommendation for a swift and simplified procedure in open and shut cases should have been taken more clearly on board.

Similarly, the very welcome improvement in the standing rights of the European Parliament throws into stark focus just how privileged the

---

[48] Interim measures are obtainable only once an action is pending before the Court of Justice.

[49] *Report by the Working Party on the Future of the European Communities' Judicial System* presented to the Commission, January 2000: http://europa.eu.int/comm/dgs/legal_service/docs/due_en.pdf/, 26.

[50] cf Art 88 ECSC.

privileged litigants are. The openness of an administration to challenge by individuals is a good indicator (although obviously not the only one) of the transparency of the regime and its degree of accountability. It is high time that the unduly restrictive interpretation by the Court of the words 'direct and individual concern' was revisited or that Article 230 EC was further revised to make it clear that Community law has come of age. It is noteworthy that the other Community procedures—such as the procedure against failure to act—are also in need of streamlining and clarification.

The difficulty of deciding what issues are of a constitutional or quasi-constitutional nature and really should stay with the Court of Justice, and what are less serious has already been noted above. The Due Report recommended a test based on the urgency and importance of the question, so that the Court of Justice would sit at first and last instance to hear only those actions for which a rapid judgment is essential to avoid serious problems in the proper functioning of the Community institutions.[51] The only weakness with this otherwise excellent idea is that sometimes major issues of principle manifest themselves in normally unremarkable contexts. Drawing distinctions according to the actors involved (privileged Community institutions; semi-privileged Community institutions or other bodies; Member States, those given special standing under Community instruments or case law, and all others) pays no attention to the seriousness of the issue and perpetuates the impression of multi-track access to justice which does not enhance the coherence, transparency and accountability of the Community system.

That said, the potential importance of the CFI will increase significantly once the further measures envisaged are actually adopted. In keeping with the desire to prepare the Community institutions for enlargement, the way is paved for an increase in the number of members of the CFI. This will certainly be necessary in view of the inevitable increase in its workload. The decision to maintain the principle of one judge per Member State at the Court of Justice should help to develop the confidence of the new Member States and retain that particularly of the existing smaller Member States in the face of the envisaged renunciation of the principle of at least one member of the Commission per Member State.[52] Apart from these points, little in the judicial aspects of the Treaty of Nice consciously equips the centralized Community judiciary to prepare for the challenges of enlargement as such. Nothing has come of suggestions for regional Community courts, which is probably just as well for the coherence of Community law.

---

[51] Due Report, 25.

[52] Treaty of Nice, Protocol on enlargement of the European Union, Art 4(2).

In fact many further improvements can still be made at the level of the Statute or the Rules of Procedure: a clearer mechanism for filtering of all appeals from the CFI to the Court of Justice; shortening the written procedure, perhaps compensated by giving advocates longer time during the hearing; examining whether it really is necessary to allow interventions quite so generously; and looking at translation issues and budgets.[53]

Conclusions

Overall, the impression must be that the jobbing builders' work begun with the Treaty of Amsterdam has been continued in the Treaty of Nice. Yet this is hardly a surprise. The European Union is still in the throes of infancy, even if the Communities are perhaps resembling difficult teenagers in puberty. Neither the judicial architecture of the Union and the Communities, nor the architecture of the edifice as a whole appears to be anything like mature; indeed, it may be that far from having built a full-scale cathedral at Maastricht, the edifice which the builders have constructed so far is in fact a developing one. This may disappoint, but disappointment and surprise in fact under-estimate the enormity of the project. Cathedrals, like Rome, were not built in a day, and represent the collective creative achievement of generations of talents. Final shape and form are as elusive after the Treaty of Nice as they were before it, an impression which is inevitable as the Member States seek to cope with the consequences of further enlargement. Depending on the activities of the Constitutional Convention and the ratification process of the Treaty of Nice, as well as on the outcome of the 2004 IGC, the Treaty of Nice may well be perceived as an essential phase in the development of the Union, and that repairing cracks, inserting expansion joints, and shock absorbers are as essential to the overall success of the project as the development of grand designs and leaps in technological achievement, even if the latter are more remembered. The make-over team certainly does not deserve its own show, and it has certainly failed to meet the real needs of Community citizens and others for a more efficient judicial system, but it may well be that step-by-step progress offers an opportunity for consolidation, evaluation of results, and prepares the way for more dramatic and visible reforms in due course.

---

[53] See the *Report on Translation at the Court of Justice* http://curia.eu.int/en/txts/others/trad.pdf/.

9

On the Legitimacy and Democratic Accountability of the European Central Bank: Legal Arrangements and Practical Experiences

Fabian Amtenbrink

Introduction

Despite the fact that, both with the Treaty of Amsterdam and more recently the Treaty of Nice, an effort was made to address the frequently illustrated 'democratic deficit' and the somewhat weak legitimacy of the EU, these complex issues are far from resolved. Indeed, they may also find their roots in an area of Community law that has remained outside the limelight of discussions on institutional reform, that is the provisions on EMU and in particular the European System of Central Banks (ESCB) and the European Central Bank (ECB) introduced by the Treaty on European Union. In fact, a full understanding of the issue in a wider context of *all* Community bodies also requires a critical review of the legitimacy and democratic accountability of the ECB, which is charged with the *independent* conduct of monetary policy for the economic area of 12 Member States.

Various authors have questioned the legal framework of the ESCB and the ECB, which undoubtedly concentrates on ensuring the independence of the system, rather than introducing a democratically accountable monetary policy authority.[1] The more recent criticism of the approach to the conduct of monetary policy in the Eurozone, as well as the debate in the United

---

[1] LW Gormley and J de Haan, 'The democratic deficit of the European Central Bank' (1996) 21 ELRev 95; R Smits, *The European Central Bank: Institutional Aspects* (1997); F Amtenbrink, *The Democratic Accountability of Central Banks—A Comparative Study of the European Central Bank* (1999).

Kingdom on future membership of EMU, underline that this debate is far from obsolete.

Rather than revisit all facets of the well-known case for the democratic accountability of the ECB,[2] the present contribution will highlight the ways in which the democratic accountability of the ECB has developed since becoming the single monetary policy authority in the Eurozone. Three main elements may be singled out in this context, including the approach to monetary policy objectives of the ECB, its communication strategy vis-à-vis the financial markets and the public at large, and its regular contacts with the European Parliament. All of these elements refer to the transparency of the ECB. Indeed, information may be considered as the key to evaluating the performance of a central bank and thus, to democratic accountability. Information requires transparency because where a central bank does not conduct monetary policy in an open manner, information on the performance of the bank is difficult to acquire.

The monetary policy objective—the Governing Council left to its own devices

Generally, in order to be able to judge the performance of a central bank and thus, to hold it accountable, a yardstick is required in order to measure effectively the fulfilment of the tasks of the bank. In the context of monetary policy such a yardstick should exist in the form of a single or primary and quantified monetary policy objective, that is, what the central bank aims at achieving with regard to monetary policy. To this end, the legal basis of a central bank should state the objective(s) of monetary policy. Moreover, the monetary policy objective should also be clearly defined.[3] A prominent example of a clear prescription of objectives can be found in the legal basis of the Reserve Bank of New Zealand, which defines price stability as its primary objective. Moreover, the governor of the bank has to agree with the government on a tight target range for inflation in a so-called Policy Target Agreement (PTA).[4] Politicians decide on the rate of inflation they consider to be acceptable *ex ante*. The electorate can then decide—also on the basis of

---

[2] Amtenbrink (n 1 above).

[3] CE Walsh, 'Optimal contracts for central bankers' (1995) 48 American Economic Review 150.

[4] The current PTA of December 1999 sets a target range for inflation of between 0% and 3%.

realized inflation rates—whether they agree with these policy choices. The recent Bank of England Act 1998 also introduced legal arrangements under which the monetary policy objective is determined in the legal basis of the bank, while the government defines or quantifies this objective.[5]

The legal basis of the ECB is not unproblematic in this respect, as the first sentence of Article 105 (1) EC refers simply to price stability as the primary objective of the ECB.[6] As a subordinated (secondary) objective, the ECB has to support the general economic policies in the Communities. The EC Treaty falls short of providing a well-defined monetary policy objective, the fulfilment of which could become subject to review. In fact, it is up to the ECB and its Governing Council, which is in principle charged with taking all monetary policy decisions, to quantify this objective. Consequently, the ECB is not only independent in implementing, but to some extent also in formulating monetary policy.

The ECB has adopted what it calls a 'qualified definition' of price stability, referring to a year-on-year increase in the Harmonized Index for Consumer Prices (HICP) for the Euro-area of below two per cent. At the same time the ECB emphasizes that a persistent fall in the price level would not be consistent with the goal of price stability.[7] In achieving this objective and in contrast to many other central banks the ECB has chosen what is commonly referred to as a two-pillar approach, as it monitors both the growth rate of a broad monetary aggregate (M3) and the developments and the risks to price stability in the Eurozone in order to determine its monetary policy strategy.[8] The economic wisdom of the self-chosen two-pillar approach has been viewed critically, not least because it remains unclear to what extent the ECB de facto prioritizes one pillar over the other.[9]

Members of the European Parliament's Committee on Economic and Monetary Affairs have confronted the ECB repeatedly with the fact that the monetary aggregate was above the four and a half per cent reference value set by the ECB at the time and wondered whether this would not

---

[5] Sections 11 and 12 of the Bank of England Act 1998.

[6] Article 2, ESCB and ECB Statute.

[7] Arguably this is a reference to deflation as also being inconsistent with price stability. WH Buiter, 'Alice in Euroland' (1999) 37 JCMS 181, 189.

[8] ECB, 'The two pillars of the ECB's monetary policy strategy' (November 2000) Monthly Bulletin.

[9] D Gros, 'The ECB's unsettling opaqueness' (May 2001) Briefing Paper for the EP Monetary Committee; L Bini-Smaghi and D Gros, *Open Issues in European Central Banking* (2000), 159; J de Haan and F Amtenbrink, 'A non-transparent European Central Bank? Who is to blame?' (2001) Working Paper, University of Groningen.

undermine its validity. The reply given by the president of the ECB during one hearing in April 1999 was revealing, as he tried to downplay the importance of the reference value by describing it as 'Something we look at in the first place and then make a judgement on the actual figure for the monetary policy aggregate, the difference between it and the reference value chosen and to what extent we should interpret that as giving rise to fears for inflation or deflation'.[10]

In the opinion of the bank the first pillar of the self-proclaimed monetary policy strategy of the ECB should not be taken as a benchmark to judge the bank's abilities for economic forecasts either. Asked during the same hearing whether this part of the strategy was not a lot of words for what effectively amounted to an inflation target, the president of the ECB emphasized that it is '...explicitly not an inflation target'.[11]

What is more, some comments of the president of the ECB before the European Parliament leave the impression that the primary objective is interpreted in a way which effectively excludes the observance of the secondary objective as foreseen in Article 105 EC. Indeed, during the April 1999 hearing, the president of the ECB stated:

... the European Central Bank shall contribute to the general goals of the European Community in terms of promoting growth and employment as far as the primary aim of price stability is not being endangered. But then it is our strong belief that the best contribution that monetary policy can make precisely to that end is to create and maintain price stability... I would warn against the reasoning that now that we have achieved price stability with a certain level of interest rates, we should change track and focus on other things, in the interest of the economic policy in general. Our aim is not only to have price stability, but also to maintain it.[12]

During another hearing the president of the ECB emphasized: 'There is only one criterion on which the ECB... will be and should be judged, and that is whether it delivers what it is instituted for, namely price stability... That is the only judgement, the only criterion on which the ECB should be judged.'[13] This reasoning, which the president of the ECB has been repeating with the persistence of a prayer wheel, leaves an observer of events with the somewhat puzzling question under what (economic) conditions the secondary objective of the ECB prescribed by primary Community

[10]   Transcript of hearing of 19 April 1999.
[11]   ibid.
[12]   ibid.
[13]   Transcript of hearing of 29 November 1999.

law will indeed be followed. The single-minded focus of the ECB on price stability has been criticized foremost by the democratically elected MEPs, to whom issues such as unemployment are at least as important as price stability.[14] For the time being the ECB seems to understand its role as limited to demanding economic reforms rather than actively supporting the economic policy with the instruments at its disposal.[15]

What becomes clear from this is that, left to its own devices, a central bank, and the ECB for that matter, applies its own interpretations of what monetary objectives amount to, thereby applying its own economic belief. In principle a system would be desirable in which elected politicians, such as the Council in the composition of the Member States participating in the ESCB, set a target or target range which the ECB would have to meet when implementing the objective of price stability. While the ECB cannot be blamed for the current arrangements under the EC Treaty, it remains a fact that under the current arrangements much depends upon the ECB and the monetary strategy it chooses.

The communication policy—the ECB at its best?

Arguably even the soundest conduct of monetary policy by a central bank is only of limited value if the bank is not communicating its strategy sufficiently to the general public. Indeed, such communication is in the interest of a central bank itself, since it enhances the effectiveness and credibility of monetary policy as the general public and even more so the financial markets (better) understand the banks' approach to monetary policy.[16] Moreover, as has already been observed, information must also form the basis of any meaningful accountability. To this end, in addition to regular central bank bulletins or reports, first of all a central bank should be obliged to publish monetary policy reports at regular intervals. These reports should include details of the bank's past performance and future plans for monetary policy in accordance with the statutory monetary objective. This may be considered even more important where a clear monetary objective is missing because in such a case the central bank can only be judged on the basis of its own statements and any forecasts it may include. Secondly, on the

---

[14] ibid.

[15] Transcript of hearing of 20 March 2000.

[16] IMF, 'Supporting Document to the Code of Good Practices on Transparency in Monetary and Financial Policies' (2000).

basis of these reports, the central bank should be obliged to explain publicly to what extent it has been able to reach the monetary objective(s).

Another important—albeit controversial—element of this communication process is that the legal basis of a central bank should provide for the publication of the minutes of meetings and/or the (reasoned) decisions of the monetary policy board of the bank. Generally, the publication of such minutes is viewed controversially, as many economists argue that the publication of any details of the deliberations during these meetings—including, for example, the different views expressed during the discussions and the voting behaviour of the members of the monetary policy board—would obstruct the effective operation of a central bank and possibly subject central bank officials to political pressure. However, the legal arrangements under the new Bank of England Act 1998 highlight how the publication of such minutes can be achieved without compromising the objectives of the bank. It provides for the publication of the minutes of the newly established Monetary Policy Committee, while at the same time ensuring the efficiency of the decisions taken in the Committee by excluding certain market-sensitive decisions from publication for a pre-determined period of time.[17]

In the first three years of operation the ECB has come under considerable criticism with regard to its communication strategy. Despite the fact that it publishes monthly bulletins and holds press conferences after every second meeting of the Governing Council,[18] explaining its decisions on monetary policy, the financial markets and indeed the public at large seem to have only a limited understanding of the monetary policy strategy of the ECB. This perceived lack of transparency appears at odds with more recent comparative studies, which put the ECB near the top of the transparency scale, only bypassed by the Bank of England.[19] Rather than the quantity of information, the quality and clarity of information provided by the ECB may be at the roots of the communication challenge it faces. While the legal basis of the ECB foresees the publication of reports on the activities of the ESCB on at least a quarterly basis, it does not define in any more detail whether and to what extent they have to include particularities on past performance and projections on the future development of monetary policy and/or self-proclaimed intermediary targets for monetary policy.[20] In practice the

[17] Bank of England Act 1998, s 15 (3): 6 weeks.
[18] Generally, the Governing Council meets twice a month.
[19] D Gros and L Bini-Smaghi, *Is the European Central Bank Sufficiently Accountable and Transparent?* (2001); thereafter J de Haan and F Amtenbrink (n 9 above).

Governing Council has decided to publish monthly bulletins, which include, among other things, an overview of the economic developments in the Eurozone and of the monetary policy decisions of the Governing Council of the ECB. However, the monthly bulletins fall short of providing the reader with any details on the future development of monetary policy or forecasts. As one observer has put it: 'The ECB bulletin is solid, but lacks imagination.'[21]

Indeed, the ECB has persistently rejected the publication of inflation forecasts. When asked by an MEP on one of many occasions whether the ECB could in the future publish such forecasts, the president of the ECB replied:

We will never make isolated inflation forecasts. What we will make—and we have to—is a comprehensive set of expectations about the behaviour of various economic variables, inflation being one of them ... There will also come a moment—it is too early but I personally have no doubt that there will come a moment—when we will also like many other institutions publish our forecasts but I explicitly say forecasts, the multiple, and inflation being one of them, but in such a way that they will never become self-fulfilling prophecies. If we have them in an adequately reliable way, if relationships, which we use, have reached the degree of stability... then we will give them.[22]

It seems that the ECB is reluctant to give out any forecasts as long as it is not convinced that they will be more or less met. Yet, this is precisely the reason why it should not be left to a central bank to decide whether and when it makes its economic and monetary assessments in the form of forecasts subject to external review. Left with this freedom, the bank is likely to ensure that, if at all, it will only publish such forecasts if it is convinced that this will not damage its reputation. It may be due to this lack of forecasts that MEPs in the past have repeatedly asked the president of the ECB to comment on the inflation forecasts by the European Commission in order to gain a better understanding of the ECB's own expectations in this area.[23]

---

[20] Article 15.1 ESCB and ECB Statute. See also Financial Times, 'European Central Bank: transparency, targets and trust' (30 October 1998).

[21] D Gros, 'Improvement of the democratic accountability process' (April 1999) Briefing Paper for the Committee on Economic and Monetary Affairs of the European Parliament, with concrete suggestions for improvements.

[22] Transcript of the hearing of 19 April 1999.

[23] For example transcript of hearing of 29 November 1999.

In a recent development the ECB has started to publish so-called staff economic projections on inflation[24] with a two-year horizon twice a year in the June and December issue of the monthly bulletin.[25] Interestingly, this seems to be the result of direct pressure from the European Parliament's Committee on Economic and Monetary Affairs, which managed to persuade the president of the ECB into pledging to publish such projections. Yet, by referring to 'projections' rather than 'forecasts' the ECB makes it quite clear that it does not want these internal estimations to be considered inflation forecasts. Indeed, already the ECB seems to have returned to its well-known position of rejecting the publication of such inflation forecasts, emphasising that '... the projections do not represent the ultimate synthesis of the Governing Council's assessment of the euro area inflationary outlook'.[26] The president of the ECB went as far as stating that '[T]he Governing Council is neither responsible for the contents of these projections, nor should its performance be judged against them'.[27]

Even though the Governing Council of the ECB keeps minutes of its deliberations, the legal basis of the ECB does not contain any provisions on the publication of minutes of the meetings of the Governing Council.[28] In fact, some interpret the legal basis of the Bank as excluding publication, as Article 10.4 ESCB and ECB Statute states that the '... proceedings of the meetings shall be confidential. The Governing Council of the ECB may decide to publish the results of its deliberations'. It becomes obvious from the rules of procedure of the ECB that the Bank has interpreted this provision as meaning that the proceedings of the decision-making bodies of the ECB and any committee or group established by them are confidential, while the Governing Council may authorize the president of the ECB to make public (only) the outcome of their deliberations.[29]

Moreover, access to the minutes of the meetings of the Governing Board of the ECB or other (market-) sensitive information on the basis on the ECB's rules on public access to documents would certainly also be refused.

---

[24]   This includes the growth rate of real GDP and its components and for HICP inflation.

[25]   WF Duisenberg, Opening Statement before the Committee on Economic and Monetary Affairs of the European Parliament (23 November 2000).

[26]   O Issing, 'The euro area and the single monetary policy' (2001) Oesterreichische Nationalbank, working paper 44, 17.

[27]   n 22 above.

[28]   Such minutes are kept according to Article 5.2, Rules of Procedure ECB, as amended on 22 April 1999 [1999] OJ L 125/38, and are approved by the members of the Governing Council at the following meeting.

[29]   Art 23 Rules of Procedure ECB.

Generally, according to Article 23.2 of the Rules of Procedure of the ECB, all documents drawn up by the ECB are confidential unless the Governing Council decides otherwise. The decision of the ECB of 3 November 1998, which governs public access to documentation and the activities of the ECB,[30] excludes such access where this could 'undermine the protection of the public interest, in particular public security, international relations, *monetary and exchange rate stability…*' and other factors.[31] However, it is questionable whether access to the minutes could be refused indefinitely, as their contents arguably lose their market-sensitivity at some stage.

Despite numerous requests by MEPs, the ECB until now has rejected any moves towards the publication of minutes, referring to the need for secrecy for effective monetary policy decisions, the collective responsibility of the Governing Council, which arguably excludes making public the view of individual members, and the potential threat of outside pressure on members.[32]

When asked by MEPs to provide details on the views and opinions taken by individual members during the meetings of the Governing Council on specific issues, the president of the ECB usually withdraws to general observations without providing any real details. ECB officials frequently point towards the press conferences following every second regular meeting of the Governing Council as a means of making public the main pros and cons which have been discussed in the Governing Council and to state the conclusions which the Governing Council has drawn from them. In the view of the president of the ECB: '…the only thing effectively which we [the Governing Council] are not doing is giving names of people and their vote.'[33] It is doubtful however whether indications of general considerations are enough in order to hold the ECB adequately accountable for its performance. Rather, the current approach adds further to speculation about the monetary policy stands of the ECB and leaves outsiders in the position of fortune tellers, who have to put together a complicated puzzle consisting of bits and pieces of information provided by the bank in its publications and public statements, in order to be able assess the work done in the Governing Council.

[30] ECB/1998/12; [1999] OJ L110/30.

[31] ibid, Art 4. Emphasis added.

[32] See transcript of hearings of 18 January and 19 April 1999; O Issing, 'The Eurosystem: transparent and accountable, or "Willem in Euroland"' (1999) 37 JCMS 503, 511.

[33] Transcript of hearing on 19 April 1999. O Issing, ibid.

Doubts may be in place as to whether the legal basis of the ECB actually has to be interpreted to exclude the publication of minutes, as the equivocal provision may only exclude public access to the meetings of the Governing Council.[34] Moreover, the arguments presented against the publication of minutes are not entirely convincing. The Bank of England Act 1998 demonstrates how arrangements can be put in place to ensure that market-sensitive information is not published before the implementation of the monetary policy decision. Moreover, the mere fact that the legal basis of the ECB refers to the Governing Council as a whole rather than to its individual members and thus, in the view of some, suggests a collective responsibility, does not invalidate the case for the publication of minutes stating the voting behaviour. Either the decisions have been taken by a consensus—as has been claimed to have been the case in most instances in the past[35]—in which case the minutes would reveal exactly that, or the minutes would reveal what would otherwise be covered, that is that there are differences of opinion with regard to the approach to monetary policy between the current 18 members of the Governing Council, including the members of the Executive Board of the ECB and the national central bank governors. Besides, while the prospect of publicity may bear the danger of national central bank governors paying lip service to their respective constituency, non-disclosure, as Buiter observes, may foster political pressure on the national central bank governors, as the latter can '... avoid having to justify or defend yielding to national or local political pressure'.[36] Moreover, rather than damaging the credibility of the Bank, revealing potential differences in opinions among the members of the Governing Council may not only assist in judging the performance of the ECB with regard to the adequacy of their assessment, but also educates a larger audience in understanding monetary policy as a consequence of judgments based on more or less reliable economic data, rather than as an exact science.[37] What is more, the tendency among ECB officials to make certain—sometimes contradictory—statements on monetary policy may not only result from a lack of strictly enforced confidentiality guidelines, but also the failure to communicate

[34] SCW Eijffinger, 'Should the ECB Governing Council decide to publish its minutes of meetings?' (November 2001) Briefing Paper for the Committee for Economic and Monetary Affairs of the European Parliament; Buiter (n 7 above) 191.

[35] Transcript of hearing of 23 November 2000.

[36] Buiter (n 7 above) 192.

[37] F Amtenbrink and J de Haan, 'The European Central Bank: an independent specialized organization of Community law—a comment' (2002) 40 CMLRev 65, 75.

these (diverse) opinions in any other way.[38] Such conflicting statements on the monetary policy issues have made it difficult at times not only for the financial markets to fully understand the ECB.[39] In a recent move to defuse the non-stop speculation in the financial markets with regard to the monetary policy the ECB has announced that although it meets twice a month, it will consider changes to the interest rate only during one of those meetings.[40]

The president of the European Central Bank before the European Parliament—Humphrey-Hawkins revisited?

The legal basis of a central bank should provide for contacts between the central bank and Parliament on a regular basis. This may not only boost the overall transparency of monetary policy, but also constitute an important precondition for those institutions to evaluate the performance of the bank. The relationship between the central bank and Parliament may be considered as the most important institutional contact for the democratic accountability of the bank. While it is true that the transparent conduct of monetary policy supports Parliament in its decision-making process about the performance of the bank, the institutionalized contacts at the same time support the overall transparency of monetary policy. Parliament has the opportunity to review the performance of the central bank with regard to monetary policy on a regular basis, while the central bank at the same time can explain and justify its conduct. These contacts should take place not only on a regular basis, but should also be provided for in the legal basis of the bank. The US Federal Reserve System is a good example for such legal requirements. The well-known Humphrey-Hawkins Procedure ensures that officials of the US Federal Reserve, including the President, have to appear before the Senate and House of Representatives Banking Committees twice a year.[41] Over the years these hearings have gained publicity and

---

[38]   See however section 3.4, ECB Code of Conduct on the contact of ECB officials with the media, [2001] OJ C76/12. This tendency has also been criticized by MEPs, for example during the November 1999 hearing.

[39]   Examples of conflicting statements are compiled in SCW Eijffinger (n 34 above) Table 1.

[40]   As to the rationale behind such a move see C Wyplosz, 'The ECB communication strategy' (December 2001), Briefing Paper for the Committee on Economic and Monetary Affairs of the European Parliament.

[41]   Federal Reserve Act s 2A (1).

today can be described as one of the cornerstones of the democratic accountability of the US Federal Reserve.[42] At the same time these hearings highlight that the value of this exercise for holding the bank effectively accountable for its performance depends both on the questions asked by the members of Congress and the answers provided by the chairman of the US Federal Reserve. As the rather famous remark by Greenspan goes: 'If I say something which you understand fully in this regard, I probably made a mistake.'[43]

Apart from the yearly presentation of an annual report of the activities of the ESCB by the president of the ECB, the European Parliament can ask the members of the Executive Board to appear before the Committee on Economic and Monetary Affairs. Yet, the EC Treaty cannot be interpreted in this respect to amount to a legal obligation for the ECB. And while the president of the ECB and the other members of the Executive Board may have every reason to explain monetary policy to a broader audience, it may be considered to create a psychological difference whether they are re-quired under the law to appear or whether they do so on their own initiative. To be sure, it is unlikely that an incident similar to that in France, where a similarly vague provision applies for the Banque de France, could also occur on the European level. In October 1997, after the Banque de France had raised interest rates, it was 'summoned' to appear before the Finance Committee of Parliament. The governor only appeared after the committee rephrased its request into an invitation, leaving Parliament in the odd position of a petitioner.

Despite the weak reference in the EC Treaty, a practice has grown up whereby the president of the ECB appears before the European Parliament on a quarterly basis. This regular so-called monetary dialogue was estab-lished on the initiative of the European Parliament, whose rules of proced-ure provide for the president of the ECB to be invited to attend the meetings of the committee at least four times a year to make a statement and answer questions.[44] Moreover, the Rules of Procedure state that MEPs may invite the President, Vice President or other members of the Executive Board to attend additional meetings.[45] This practice even surpasses the obligations of the US Federal Reserve under the Humphrey-Hawkins Procedure. It is thus hardly surprising that the president of the ECB has stressed this feature of

[42] F Amtenbrink (n 1 above) 287.
[43] Recorded during the US Senate Banking Committee hearing of 20 June 1995.
[44] Art 40.3, Rules of Procedure EP 1999.
[45] ibid, Art 40.4.

accountability of the ECB, as he knows '... of no central bank in the world which has such intensive contacts with the Parliament of the region it represents as the ECB...'.[46] Yet, while the ECB publicly emphasizes the close and intensive contacts with the European Parliament, it seems that at least in some quarters within the ECB the magnitude of these contacts has sometimes been underestimated in the past. Some MEPs were rather astonished when reading the first annual report of the ECB to find that the European Parliament had only been listed in the section under the heading 'Cooperation with other institutions', which in the first place mentions the representation of the ECB in international institutions like the OECD and the IMF. The Annual Report then states that: '[I]n the European context the close cooperation already existing with the other institutions of the European Union has been further consolidated, in particular with the European Parliament, the EU Council, the Euro-11 group, the European Commission and the Monetary Committee.'[47] Apart from the fact that the enumeration is somewhat misleading, as not all of the bodies mentioned constitute institutions in the sense of Article 7 EC, this unfortunate description of the contacts with the European Parliament may suggest that the ECB does not necessarily give preference to the contacts with the European Parliament as compared to other Community bodies.

The hearings usually start with an opening statement by the President of the ECB, which basically covers the current economic developments and prospects. The opening statement is also used to explain the motives behind the actual monetary policy decisions taken by the Governing Council since the last hearing.[48] This is followed by a question-and-answer session, which usually covers a number of different topics, including the monetary policy concepts and strategy, how the ECB contributes to growth and employment, the international dimension of the euro and issues relating to the democratic accountability and transparency of the ECB. Moreover, a practice has been established whereby the different political groups within the European Parliament will ask questions in order. The MEPs participating in these hearings put much effort into ensuring that the hearings amount to more than just a promotional event for the president of the ECB, as critical questions both on issues of monetary policy and democratic accountability and transparency prevail over words of praise. This may not least be due to

[46] Transcript of hearing of 18 January 1999.

[47] ECB, *Annual Report 1998* (1999) 11.

[48] See, eg, WF Duisenberg, Opening statement before the Committee on Economic and Monetary Affairs of the European Parliament (19 April 1999).

the fact that the European Parliament engages outside experts in the field of economic and monetary matters, which provide the MEPs with so-called briefing papers containing detailed analyses in the areas of responsibility of the ECB and moreover also analyse the public statements of the bank and its officials. Indeed, in their questions to the President of the ECB, MEPs frequently pick up observations and suggestions made in such reports, which are not only available to the ECB, but also to the public at large.[49]

The hearings over the past three years illustrate that MEPs take much interest in the monetary policy strategy of the ECB and its decisions with regard to monetary policy. Interestingly, already, like the members of Congress in the Humphrey-Hawkins Procedure, the MEPs focus on the issues of inflation, but also deflation and the question of how the ECB can contribute to economic development with regard to growth and employment, and it is in this context that the strict interpretation applied by the ECB with regard to its primary monetary objective is bound to clash with the preferences of the elected representatives in the European Parliament. In this context, the President of the ECB has not only been confronted with conflicting statements and arguably bad judgments on the part of the ECB, but also repeatedly with the fact that the ECB in the past has not been able to deliver its own definition of price stability of below two per cent. Moreover, in the past MEPs have expressed their concern about the weak external value of the euro and the consequences this could have on the European economy. With regard to the democratic accountability and transparency of the ECB, the lack of minutes, as well as the style of language used by the ECB in its publications, but also in its presentations to the European Parliament has been criticized for being too complicated.[50] Apart from these issues, which regularly re-emerge, MEPs also address current issues, such as in the past the introduction of the euro, the remaining costs in case of cross-border payments or the enlargement of the EU.

Not only have the MEPs already started to learn how to perform their role, the President of the ECB also plays the questions-and-answers game well. His reactions to questions range from in-depth answers, circumventing certain questions or simply ignoring them, to sometimes rebuffing questions in an almost authoritarian manner. From time to time this approach by the ECB triggers sarcastic comments, as one MEP recently began his question by pointing out, in a supposedly apologetic tone: 'Forgive me President but I

---

[49] See http://www.europarl.eu.int/comparl/econ/emu/default_en.htm/.
[50] Transcript of hearing of 18 January 1999.

have a bad cold so I am both deaf and dumb which makes me the ideal interlocutor for the president of the Central Bank perhaps.'[51]

Despite these encouraging developments in the relationship between the European Parliament and the ECB, there is certainly room for improvement in the role of the European Parliament. One important aspect in the relationship between the European Parliament and the ECB, which is easily forgotten, is that the EC Treaty does not require the national central bank presidents participating in the Governing Council to appear before the European Parliament at all. Put differently, more than half of the members of the monetary policy board of the ECB cannot even be asked to appear before the European Parliament to explain their conduct. Whether this role of the European Parliament will be properly performed by the national parliaments is questionable, since even in countries with regular appearances of central bank officials before Parliament it seems difficult to imagine that an individual central bank governor, representing only one of 18 members in the Governing Council (the other six members make up the Executive Board of the ECB) would be held accountable for the conduct of the Governing Council as a whole.[52] It would be desirable to introduce an arrangement in the legal basis where both the members of the Executive Board and the national central bank governors are required to appear before the European Parliament upon request of the latter. The circumstance that the national central bank governors are appointed on the national level cannot be brought forward against holding them accountable before the European Parliament because they have to be considered as ECB rather than national central bank officials to the extent to which they fulfil ESCB-related tasks and participate in the Governing Council of the ECB. Moreover, the EC Treaty itself puts them on an equal footing with the members of the Executive Board of the ECB with regard to the conditions of dismissal and the right to appeal to the Court of Justice in case of dismissal.

Moreover, under the current legal set-up the European Parliament—alongside the Governing Council of the ECB—only has to be consulted on the appointments of the members of the Executive Board of the ECB.[53] Within the European Parliament the Committee on Economic and Monetary Affairs handles the proposal. Yet, while the plenary session of the European Parliament may, on the basis of the recommendation of its

---

[51] Transcript of hearing of 20 March 2000.

[52] F Amtenbrink, 'The European Central Bank—democratically accountable or unrestrained?' (1999) NJB 72.

[53] Art 112(2)b EC.

standing committee, choose to reject a candidate, the vote is not binding for the Council. Thus, in effect the European Parliament can only delay the appointment procedure. Despite these apparent limitations of the power of the European Parliament, it could nevertheless play an important factor in the forming of public opinion on the candidates. Whether this will actually one day amount to a 'virtual right of veto'[54] remains to be seen. What can be observed already is that the public hearings, which took place during the first appointment of the members of the Executive Board, gave an indication that the European Parliament is willing to make the most of its limited role.

Conclusions

Ending on a positive note, while the current arrangements with regard to the different aspects of democratic accountability have been reviewed rather critically throughout this contribution, it also has to be acknowledged that despite the limited obligations under the EC Treaty the ECB has made considerable efforts to become a transparent central bank, thereby enhancing democratic accountability. Yet, the fact remains that it is up to the ECB to decide on the means and extent to which it provides this transparency. As a result, the ECB appears to be very transparent on paper, whereas the financial markets and also the MEPs seem to have considerable difficulties understanding the monetary policy strategy of the ECB. It may certainly take more than three years to establish faith in a new central bank with a new monetary policy strategy. At the same time, under the current legal arrangements, it will take more than just fine-tuning on the part of the ECB to improve its approach to explaining what it does.

All things considered, the ECB also has to be given credit for the constructive way in which it has interpreted its obligation under the EC Treaty to appear before the European Parliament. By appearing four times a year, the ECB once more does more than it would be legally required to do. It can already be concluded that the European Parliament takes the role which it has been assigned under the Maastricht Treaty very seriously. Indeed, it may understand this role as a welcome opportunity to show once more that it is a fully-grown parliament which is willing to take on more substantial responsibilities in the constitutional structure of the European Union.

[54] In this direction F Jacobs, R Corbett and M Shackleton, *The European Parliament* (3rd edn, 1995), 250–251.

To be sure, some of the well-documented more structural weaknesses of the EC Treaty with regard to the democratic accountability of the ECB and in particular the lack of any concrete legal instruments to hold the ECB accountable (ie. to punish the ECB in case of bad performance) could only be overcome by changing primary Community law itself, the prospect of which remains remote.[55] While there is much to be said in favour of the view that central banks have to have a certain degree of independence in order to fulfil effectively the tasks with which they have been charged by the democratically elected legislator free from political influence or even pressure, this cannot invalidate the argument for democratic accountability of central banks in an open and democratic society. The legitimacy of any institution charged with executive tasks is directly dependent upon the degree to which it is accountable to democratically elected institutions. This is even more the case where such an institution has autonomous law making powers. In the words of Benschop: 'A legitimate European Union has to become more accountable to its citizens. That is a task for the institutions in Brussels, and for the national governments. We need maximum transparency. Show what we do, what choices we stand for, which directions we take.'[56]

---

[55] Such instruments may range from override-mechanisms, the dismissal of central bank officials to ultimately changing the legal basis. See references in n 1 above.

[56] D Benschop, 'Preparing Europe for change' (5 November 2001), speech given by the Dutch State-Secretary for Foreign Affairs during the 2nd British–Dutch Apeldoorn Conference in Edinburgh.

Part II

Constitutionalism and the Future of Europe

The future of Europe is the subject of increasingly intense reflection throughout the Union. One suggestion, mentioned in the Laeken Declaration, is that its accountability and legitimacy would be enhanced if it were equipped with some form of constitutional text, gathering together the fundamental values and organizing principles on which it is based, thereby making them more accessible to the citizen. However, endowing the Union with a formal constitution might be seen as liable to transform its very nature into something for which there is little or no societal support. Moreover, the process of drawing up such a document would be fraught with difficulty.

Whether or not the Union is equipped with such a text, one question of a constitutional nature which needs to be addressed in any serious audit of the Union's accountability and legitimacy is whether the division of jurisdiction between the Union and the Member States should be clarified. This is one of the issues identified in the Nice and Laeken Declarations on the future of the Union. It might be argued that the accountability and legitimacy of the Union would be increased if there were a formal catalogue of the Union's powers, so that citizens could more easily see what it could—and could not—do. Some take the view, however, that such a catalogue might result in an undesirable repatriation of powers from the Union to the Member States and reduce the Union's capacity to respond to changing circumstances.

Few would deny that the democratic credentials of the Union and its Member States are an essential facet of its claim to accountability and legitimacy. Indeed, the principle of democracy is identified in Article 6 TEU as one on which the Union is founded. However, the nature of democracy in the European Union and its legal order remains obscure.

Moreover, although a mechanism exists for suspending the rights of a Member State which commits a serious and persistent breach of one of the principles referred to in Article 6, that mechanism may in practice be hard to invoke. There is in addition an apparent disparity between the extent to which the Union itself respects democratic principles and the degree to which it expects Member States and candidate countries to do so.

Another essential plank of the Union's accountability and legitimacy is the extent to which it is based on the rule of law. That is the result of a remarkable synergy between the authors of the Treaties and the Community Courts. Indeed, like democracy, the rule of law has, since Amsterdam, been included among the select list of principles on which the Union is said to be founded. None the less, the precise meaning of the rule of law in this context is elusive. Moreover, on any view there remain some important respects in which it is only imperfectly observed. It needs to be strengthened if the Union's accountability and legitimacy are to be reinforced.

10

Developing a Constitution for the Union

Frank Vibert

Introduction

At the Laeken European Council in December 2001 the EU formally launched a debate about 'The future of Europe' and agreed on a wide-ranging agenda for the next intergovernmental conference (IGC) to be held in 2004. The IGC will mark a new departure for governments in the EU because, for the first time, the focus of an IGC will centre on the constitutional character of the Union rather than on new functional objectives such as the single market, the single currency or enlargement. These earlier, functionally oriented IGCs certainly had constitutional consequences for the Member States. But now there is a clear change in emphasis. Governments are preparing for negotiations on procedures and institutions without attaching the discussion to some major new policy departure. What is more, the Laeken Declaration cautiously raises the question whether the simplification and reorganization of the Union's Treaties 'might not lead in the long run to the adoption of a constitutional text in the Union'. There is widespread support within the Convention for aiming at the text of a 'constitutional treaty'.

Although the Laeken Declaration tables a wide-ranging set of questions for the next IGC, the core of the agenda continues to centre on four items agreed earlier by the European Council in Nice in December 2000. This chapter therefore starts by identifying the constitutional rationale behind these items and then goes on to discuss the very different views that lie beneath them. These differences of view are illustrative of the divergences underlying the broader agenda. The chapter suggests that when there are such differences of view, a constitution can be approached either by trying to reach agreement on general principles, leaving institutional and procedural specifics to emerge with experience and practice or, conversely, institutional and procedural specifics can be agreed leaving general principles to emerge. The United States illustrates the first approach. The EU is trying the second approach.

This chapter argues that it will be very difficult for the EU to reconcile disagreements on institutional and procedural specifics in the absence of an agreement on general principles. Developing such a set of principles goes well beyond the simplification and reorganization of existing treaties. The prospects for constitutional advance in the 2004 IGC thus look highly uncertain and a definitive constitutional settlement is likely to take much longer and require a different approach.

The 2004 IGC and the shift towards constitutionalism

The treaty changes agreed at the conclusion of the last IGC at Nice at the end of 2000 were of a limited nature to do with the so-called 'left-overs' from the previous agreement at Amsterdam. At the same time the European Council agreed at Nice on a declaration identifying four topics for the agenda for the next IGC in 2004. This agenda has now been broadened in the Laeken Declaration adopted by the European Council in December 2001, but the four items remain at the centre of the wider agenda. These are:

(1) the establishment of a more precise and transparent demarcation of powers between the EU and the Member States;
(2) the status of the Charter of Fundamental Rights;
(3) the simplification of the Treaties; and
(4) the role of national parliaments in the EU.

Laeken has broadened the context for the examination of these questions, adding questions on the better definition of the Union's legislative instruments to the questions relating to the division of powers and placing the examination of the role of national parliaments within the general question of how to improve the democratic legitimacy of Union action and the efficiency of Union institutions. It is in relation to the issue of the treatment of the Charter of Fundamental Rights and the simplification of the Treaties

that the Laeken Declaration raises the question of the adoption of a constitutional text 'in the long run'.

There is a clear constitutional rationale behind the core agenda items
which potentially could help the Union achieve its goal of moving towards 'a
constitutional text'.

Checks and balances and the division of competences

The desire to achieve a clearer demarcation of powers between the EU and
the Member States can be linked in a straightforward way to the need felt by
certain governments for a more intelligible system of checks and balances on
the powers of the EU. Enough governments now seem to feel that the
existing principle of the attribution of powers does not seem to have set
adequate or understandable limits to what can be done under the Treaties.
In addition, the procedural doctrine of subsidiarity does not seem to halt a
centralizing dynamic and it appears to be felt that the principle can be better
upheld with the assistance of a clearer division of competences.

Clarifying responsibility for rights

The status of the EU's Charter of Fundamental Rights, agreed at Nice by
joint proclamation of the Council, Parliament and Commission, was left
unclear.[1] Some see incorporation as the decisive instrument for converting
the Treaties into a constitution. This is disputed by those who follow the
Court in regarding the Treaty base as already possessing the character of a
constitution. It is also somewhat unhistorical. It is worth remembering that
the American Bill of Rights was not part of the original design of the
American constitution but added through amendment.

Governments possibly see the issue in rather simpler terms, namely that
the time has come to review how rights should be reflected in Europe's
Treaties and to sort out where different sorts of claims about rights should
be recognized—'recognized' in the sense of legislated on and adjudicated.[2]
In this context there is a long-standing question about the relationship
between the development of rights jurisdiction under the EU Treaties and
the European Convention on Human Rights of the Council of Europe. The
need to clarify arrangements has been given added urgency by the events of
11 September and in particular by the subsequent spate of new framework

[1] See chapter by Jacobs in this volume.
[2] See chapter by McBride in this volume.

decisions under the police and judicial cooperation pillar of the Treaties which has drawn new attention to the need to protect civil liberties. There is also no doubting the background worry that democracy and the rule of law is of historically recent origin for a majority of countries in an enlarged union.

Treaty simplification and intelligibility

The Laeken Declaration brackets the questions relating to the treatment of rights together with questions relating to the simplification of the Treaties and the possible preparation of a 'basic' treaty. There is a clear recognition that the present Treaty base is unintelligible. As a result of their inaccessibility the Treaties do nothing to foster a sense of European citizenship or sense of participation in Europe's political processes or popular identification with Europe's system of government. The exercise of simplification is intended to go well beyond the renumbering exercise and the removal of redundant provisions carried out in the Amsterdam treaty revisions and is cautiously labelled 'towards a constitution'.[3]

The role of national parliaments and the 'democratic deficit'

The 2004 IGC will examine fourthly the role of national parliaments in the European institutional architecture within a broader set of institutional concerns relating to the so-called 'democratic deficit'. Political theorists have tended to argue that scaling up the size of a political system does not by itself lead to a democratic deficit. If powers go up from the Member State to the larger unit of the Union there may be a loss of traditional means of democratic control at the level of the Member State, but there can, in theory, be offsetting gains. The democratic gains can occur through new forms of democratic control at the Union level and at the level below the Member State—in other words through increased powers for the regions.[4]

This calculation of a net democratic gain or net lack of democratic loss does not seem to be working. At the EU level, governments seem to have gained discretionary authority and the European Parliament is not seen as truly representative. While there has been decentralization in a number of Member States, others, notably Germany, feel that their regional governments have lost powers. Even if regional gains in some Member States

---

[3] See further chapter by Dyrberg in this volume.
[4] RA Dahl and ER Tufte, *Size and Democracy* (1973).

outweigh losses in others, the important point for the regions is that a strong voice within the Member State does not convert into a strong voice for regional governments in the Union. A desire to look at the role of national parliaments is therefore one way of responding to perceptions that there is some kind of democratic redress required in order to better balance out democratic losses with democratic gains. The Laeken Declaration widens this concern about democratic legitimacy beyond the role of national parliaments to include questions relating to the Commission, the Council and the European Parliament itself.

The differences of view

Beneath the surface of the agreement on the core agenda items lie some profound disagreements on what the underlying problems are and how to remedy them. It is these underlying divisions that will make it difficult for governments to make progress on the Union's constitutional agenda in 2004 and later IGCs, without agreement on general principles and some over-arching constitutional concept. The scope for divisive debate can be illustrated in respect of each of the central agenda items.

Treaty simplification

At first sight the least controversial item on the agenda is Treaty simplification. No one suggests that the current Treaty base is easily understood. Yet even Treaty simplification will prove controversial.[5] Some see it as possible to make the Treaties intelligible by a process of reduction—in other words to be approached mainly by the extraction of a basic text from the existing Treaty text. Others see the exercise as about trying to identify for public opinion what the fundamentals of the Union really are. This would involve departing quite substantially from the current Treaty base in order to reflect unwritten practice, key judgments of the Court of Justice and the current realities of institutional roles. Others see it as about trying to respond to the sense that the public does not participate in Europe's system of government. This goes beyond mere Treaty simplification so as to include the other reforms needed to induce a sense of participation. These therefore represent

---

[5] See further chapter by Dyrberg in this volume.

very different views about the objectives of simplification and have very different implications.

The shortcomings of the reductionist approach have been demonstrated by the exercise undertaken by the Robert Schuman Centre.[6] The extraction of items of constitutional importance from the existing Treaty base still leaves too much unstated or unclear. Yet attempts to introduce clarity would involve importing into the simplified Treaty base major elements from outside, for example to clarify the role of the institutions.

Clarifying competences

Similar differences of approach exist in relation to the push for a clearer distribution of competences. Some see the exercise as just to clarify the existing attribution of powers in the Treaty base; others however, see it as an opportunity to reconsider the existing attribution.[7] Still others see it as part of a broader procedural question about how to deal with the centralizing tendencies of systems of distributed powers and the different ways of approaching attribution. There is a further division about justiciability. The German government may be looking for clearer divisions of power that are legally binding. Yet Tony Blair insists that the division of competences should provide political guidelines rather than justiciable demarcations.

The treatment of rights

The question of whether or not to incorporate the Charter of Fundamental Rights will also be contentious. For some, incorporation is essential so as to ensure that a system of law such as EU law is embedded within constitutional norms that ensure that it is a just system of law. 'Just' in this context means that the law must respect not only standards of procedural justice but also notions of substantive justice.[8] The incorporation of rights can also be seen as providing a way of unifying the legal structure for Europe because they provide a set of norms to which all can subscribe and which are common to different legal systems in Europe.

---

[6] For the text and a discussion of this approach, see K Feus (ed), *A Simplified Treaty for the European Union?* (2001).

[7] See chapter by de Búrca and de Witte in this volume.

[8] See chapter by Arnull in this volume.

However, others are concerned about the way responsibility for rights conveys authority in a political system. While traditionally, rights are seen as a defence against authority, at the same time they also confer authority on whoever is to enforce or interpret them.[9] In modern political systems the language of rights is used extensively as the main way to talk about political principles and thus an extensive list of rights, or list of fundamental rights from which a further extensive list of derived rights can be extracted, means that there is a correspondingly expansive conveyance of authority. This leads to questioning whether incorporation of the Charter of Fundamental Rights is compatible with a decentralized attribution of powers.

National parliaments

One of the areas for the most extensive differences of opinion and approach lies behind the desire to look again at the role of national parliaments. In recent years the European Parliament has increased its powers through the IGC process and, as a result of the 'co-decision' procedure, can block or substantially amend legislation approved by the Council of Ministers in ways that far surpass the means of many national parliaments to amend or block the legislation proposed by their governments in their national setting. The essential reason for this difference in legislative power is that in the national setting the composition of a parliament reflects the electorate's choice of parties for government. If the parties forming a government fail to support it on important votes in the parliament the government will lose office. By contrast, the Council of Ministers (sometimes referred to as the 'co-legislator' in EU processes) does not depend on party support in the European Parliament for office and the composition of the European Parliament does not reflect the choice of the electorate of a government for the Union. The European Parliament can amend or block legislation without bringing down the Council. In other words in Member States there is typically a fusion of powers between parliament and government while the EU has evolved a system of separation of powers.

The acquisition of powers by the European Parliament has not stopped criticism of its role. In particular, low voter turnout in the last elections has been seen as undermining its claim to be representative—a claim that is already viewed as weak in the absence of a public opinion and political parties that cross the Union.[10] There is therefore a case

[9] C Tilly (ed), *The Formation of States in Western Europe* (1985).

[10] For a recent discussion see H Wallace and AR Young, *Participation and Policy Making in the European Union* (1997).

for looking at the relationship of the European Parliament and national parliaments to see whether they can mesh their activities more effectively together.

The umbrella phrase 'democratic deficit' conceals a number of different ways of examining the questions involved. One way of framing the questions is through the lens of 'accountability'. National parliaments are still seen to be the main vehicles for holding ministers or governments to account, and can in the last resort force resignations, while the European Parliament cannot. At the same time national parliaments feel that ministers slip from the grip of their normal methods of accountability, because when ministers go to Brussels they can blame others if their own position or mandate is overruled.

Possible ways of strengthening 'accountability' in the Union range from developing the Commission as the 'government' of the EU with the European Parliament exercising greater control over appointments to the Commission and the performance of Commissioners, to strengthening the role of the European scrutiny committees in national parliaments, and to developing a practice of joint hearings between committees of national parliaments and the European Parliament on upcoming legislation and ministerial attitudes to it.

Among these possibilities, Germany is one Member State that has suggested that the Commission should be developed as the 'government' of the EU—a long-standing ambition of the Commission itself. However, Germany still seems to envisage that the European Council should be in charge of setting the public policy agenda for the Union, and in modern systems of government it is this agenda setting role that is arguably the most important function of 'governments'. Semantics aside, the debate highlights the very awkward position in which the Commission finds itself, squeezed between Council and European Parliament. On the one hand it is very much aware of the role of the European Parliament in bringing down the Santer Commission and thus does not want to position itself too far from it. On the other hand, the Council increasingly drives its policy mandate. If the Commission is seen as unresponsive to the Council it will find itself increasingly by-passed when important decisions have to be taken and the Council confers capital-to-capital or builds up the Council secretariat and the system of special representatives.

A second way of framing the questions involved is through the lens of 'legitimacy'. For some, because the European Parliament is seen to be only weakly 'representative', the need is to strengthen the legitimacy of action by the Union. According to this view, if national parliaments were to be more clearly involved in Union decisions to act, it would help establish in front of public opinion that when the Union acts, it acts with the authority of national parliaments as well as with the authority of Union institutions. This way of framing the question places the emphasis on the potential role of national parliaments in scrutinizing whether legislation is needed or not—in other words, on the operation of subsidiarity and in providing some kind of democratic overview of what former French Prime Minister Lionel Jospin has called 'the state of the Union'. This leads both France and Britain to support some kind of second chamber composed of national parliamentarians that could perform this oversight role.

The European Parliament has reacted defensively to such suggestions because it fears an erosion of its own ability to amend or block legislative and other proposals and it fears it might end up with a diminished role. Turf wars apart, there is a real issue about the cumbersome nature of existing EU legislative procedures. To quieten these fears it would need to be shown that a second chamber could speed up EU processes by pruning out unnecessary legislation rather than necessarily acting to slow things down even more.

A third way of framing the questions focuses on the more pragmatic issue of how to improve the quality of legislation in the EU. The nub of the issue is that in modern societies, markets move very quickly while political processes move slowly. Moreover much of the knowledge needed to ground legislation on a sound knowledge or evidence base is not within parliaments or centralized bureaucracies but is held in the private sector or among experts and expert agencies.

The problem is not unique to the EU but does surface in a very visible form because EU processes are very slow and much of the expertise needed for the European Parliament to play its revising role in a constructive way does not exist among the membership of the European Parliament. The response so far is leading both to a move away from the 'hard law' procedures of the directive and regulation to the soft law procedures of the 'open method of coordination' and to an attempt to reinstate the directive as a general framework instrument. Potential further developments include non-parliamentary techniques, such as a much greater role for performance audit in the EU. But in addition there is the possibility of building up professional staff support for the European Parliament and also the possibility that national parliaments should play a greater role in the substance of legislative formation as well as in the scrutiny of previously enacted measures because they bring to bear better knowledge of conditions and circumstances in their Member State.

In whichever ways the questions are framed, whether through the lens of 'accountability', or 'legitimacy', or the 'quality of legislation', there is a growing awareness that the answers lie in both national parliaments and the European Parliament accepting that they have a joint responsibility in each of these areas. In this very general sense, bicameralism, with or without an actual second chamber of national parliamentarians, is on the agenda. Nor are the remedies confined to parliaments. By including questions relating to each of the institutions as well as to legislative instruments, the Laeken Declaration has ensured that questions of democracy and efficiency in the Union will be looked at through each of the lenses outlined above.

The constitutional approach

While governments have been able to agree on the central items for the 2004 IGC together with a wide-ranging list of surrounding questions, it is clear from the Laeken Declaration that there are very substantial differences of view about the possible answers to the questions raised. In addition there will be other reform discussions proceeding in parallel in coming years. For example, the reform of the CAP is already underway in the context of the new round of WTO trade negotiations agreed in Doha. EU budget reform will also have to be tackled before the end of the current financial framework in 2006 so as to take account of new Member States expected to join from 2004. In addition, the Commission has made proposals on how to improve law-making and regulatory processes in the EU, while at the same time the Council is also making important changes to its own organization and operations. These parallel negotiations could bring important changes to EU practices that do not entail Treaty change. However where Treaty changes are involved they could be introduced into future IGCs when ripe for agreement. What this all adds up to is that there is an extraordinarily extensive range of discussions and negotiations getting underway of constitutional importance. The question is how best to approach the Laeken objective of moving 'towards a constitution for European citizens'.

There are a number of reasons why governments are approaching the framing of 'a constitutional text' very hesitantly and in a long-term perspective. First, the procedure for putting in place a constitution is itself a source of great difficulty. For the 2004 IGC it has been agreed that the agenda will be prepared by a Convention bringing together members of the European Parliament, members of national parliaments, the Commission and representatives of governments. It is unclear how well this procedure (which draws on that followed for drafting the Charter of Fundamental Rights) will work. Constitutional experts suggest that legislatures do not necessarily contain sufficient constitutional expertise and one constitutional expert writing about constitutional conventions suggests that they should not include any institution with a vested interest in the outcome.[11] According to such criteria the Convention is not the right body for drawing up constitutional proposals. For 2004, governments are hedging their bets. The Convention will report to governments prior to the start of the actual negotiations and thus governments will retain the whip hand in deciding how to treat the report of the Convention. It is governments that will decide what to present for national ratification procedures.

Secondly, there is an issue of principle relating to constitutional norms which extends beyond the many specific questions enumerated in the Laeken Declaration. For example, the British government had indicated until recently that it did not want to see an EU constitution and one possible reason was the view that a constitution is a mark of a state and the British government did not wish statehood to be conferred on the EU. While some constitutional lawyers like to discuss constitutional content in terms of statehood, the underlying issue is not statehood as such but, instead, what the necessary content of a constitution comprises—what the necessary descriptive elements are—of institutions and powers—and what the necessary or desirable normative elements are.[12] At one end of this debate are those who would argue that a constitution is about formalizing the basic rules of a political association and, since the forms of political association can be many and various, the content of a constitution can be equally varied. At the other end are those who would argue that a constitution requires both minimum descriptive elements and certain necessary normative elements of both a procedural and substantive nature. If all these

---

[11] J Elster (ed), *Deliberative Democracy* (1998).

[12] The issue of framing constitutional norms in terms of 'statehood' seems particularly active for German constitutional lawyers. See I Pernice, *The European Constitution* (2001).

requirements are met, the character of European political union will be closely analogous to that of a state.[13] Some Member States would prefer to avoid this whole debate.

Thirdly, there are issues not of principle but of sheer pragmatism. The question is whether this is a good moment in the history of the EU to attempt to formalize its most important rules. The British government, and no doubt some others, would prefer the present evolutionary process to continue, with some formalization in selected areas, but without trying to formalize all that is most important. The most compelling reason for this is simply that the EU stands on the verge of a major expansion of its membership and that a lasting formalization of the constitutional rules should await experience of how the enlarged Union works and the experience of the new members themselves.

Against this background of theoretical and practical divisions there are real world advantages in what have been termed 'incompletely theorised' agreements.[14] They are useful when there is agreement on general principles but not agreement on their application and conversely when there is agreement at the level of how to deal with a particular case even if people are not ready to agree on the general principle. Approaching an EU constitution by looking at a list of specific institutional and procedural questions may be seen as taking advantage of one approach to an incompletely theorized agreement. In other words, the hope is that there can be agreement on how to treat specific issues without necessarily having to agree on general constitutional principles. In this sense constitution-making in the EU is in strong contrast with the approach of the American founding fathers who prepared a constitution on the basis of general principles leaving much to evolve in their application.

The need for principles

The overall picture is one where there are good reasons for the Member States to be focusing their attention on explicit constitutional questions. At the same time, governments are moving 'towards a constitution' for the

---

[13] John Rawls, eg, distinguishes between 'procedural democracy' and 'constitutional democracy' and argues that 'A constitutional regime is one in which laws and statutes must be consistent with certain fundamental rights and liberties ... with a bill of rights specifying those freedoms': J Rawls, *Justice as Fairness: A Restatement* (2001) 145.

[14] C Sunstein, *Legal Reasoning and Political Conflict* (1996).

Union very hesitantly for a mixture of reasons of both principle and pragmatism. In particular they are adopting a strategy of trying to reach agreement on a range of specific items, leaving general principles to one side, rather than focusing on general principles and leaving specifics to evolve. The question is whether this strategy is likely to work. There are four main reasons for doubt.

The need to review fundamentals

A first reason to think about general principles is the need to think in greater depth about the fundamentals of the EU. The fact of the matter is that the EU is now almost 50 years old and the setting facing systems of government everywhere has changed out of all recognition. Globalization, the information revolution and the ageing of higher income societies are having an impact on all systems of government. In addition, for Europe the end of the Cold War has brought about the possibility of a genuinely European Union rather than a limited club of western European nations.

Sometimes questions about the fundamental character of the EU are expressed in terms of a conflict between minimalist conceptions built around free trade and what Lionel Jospin has called 'societal' conceptions which build in broader concepts of what Europe is all about. While this is one way of expressing the issue, it can be expressed more neutrally in terms of a basic question about how systems of political choice and systems of market choice are best put together in today's world.[15]

From this broader perspective, a question such as whether to incorporate the Charter of Fundamental Rights in a European constitution should be approached as part of a rethink about how communication takes place in modern systems of political choice and how the use of the language of rights has changed in recent decades.[16] Equally, it seems a mistake to embark on trying to divide competences without thinking about how the functions of modern governments are changing and where the comparative advantage of the EU as a system of government really lies. Similarly if the traditional calculations of political scientists about democracy in large political systems no longer work then we need to think about the possible relevance of other

---

[15] F Vibert, *Europe Simple, Europe Strong* (2001).

[16] In their medieval origin, rights were seen as guides to 'right reason' and this aspect of 'rights talk' needs greater recognition today. See B Tierney, *The Idea of Natural Rights* (1997).

approaches to organization.[17] Some have suggested that network theory is relevant,[18] but the network model is too flawed to apply to models of democratic systems of government. Equally, however, in thinking through the organizational fundamentals that need to underlie institutional and procedural architecture in the modern world the eighteenth century vocabulary of political organization invoked by words such as 'federal' does not take us very far. In supporting the idea of a European constitution, Lionel Jospin has said that it would only be meaningful if it were the result of in-depth reform and not the product of a simple redrafting of the current Treaties.

The need for a coherent outcome

Secondly, there are reasons to think that answers to institutional specifics will only be coherent if arrived at on the basis of constitutional principle.[19] For example, there is much discussion of whether the Commission should be chosen by the European Parliament rather than by the Council. The choice ultimately hinges on whether the Union should continue to develop a system of separation of powers between Council and Parliament or look to national models of parliamentary fusion. Similarly, articulating any role for national parliaments as guardians of the demarcation of powers in the Union also involves taking a view on the principles of constitutional guardianship and what constitutes in the Union context, as America's founding fathers put it, 'the least dangerous' branch of government. In short, negotiations on institutional specifics, unattached to a set of constitutional principles, are likely to produce an inconsistent and incoherent outcome.

Issue linkage and bargaining

Thirdly, the negotiating context is one where an outside standard is needed in order to judge the range of possible outcomes. Both the institutions represented in the Convention and the Member States negotiating in the IGC are dealing with a Nash bargaining situation (where each participant's bargaining objective is shaped in the light of the bargaining objective of the others). In this kind of bargaining situation a number of different equilibrium

---

[17] Business models are the most obvious source of borrowings. See OE Williamson, *Markets and Hierarchies* (1975) for the attempt to define an efficient organization by bringing together theories of bounded rationality with transactions cost economics.

[18] M Castells, *The Rise of the Network Society* (1996) is probably the best known proponent.

[19] F Vibert, *Europe: A Constitution for the Millennium* (1995).

points are possible—with no guarantee that any will be desirable as measured by an outside normative standard of what a good constitution should consist of.[20] Governments will not be able to evade this broader standard and it would be better to make it explicit.

A different way of looking at the practicalities of the negotiating context is to see it as involving a choice between issue linkage and side payments.[21] Side payments have been prevalent, allegedly, throughout the EU's history. While side payments can be helpful in reaching agreements they do not help transparency or necessarily guarantee right outcomes. Principles would not only help ensure that any issue linkage is constitutionally consistent but would also help identify side payments because they would help anomalies to be detected. Explicit principles would also help make sure that any side payments work in the right direction.

Public opinion and the finalité

A final reason in favour of a more principled approach is that public opinion could look at the overall concept and make their judgment accordingly. Currently it seems as though the public is not enthused by institutional detail and inter-institutional bickering and there is a danger that, in the absence of understandable general principles, the public reaction to the Union's constitutional development will be negative. Of course the public may react negatively also to a general concept and send the governments back to the drawing board but there comes a point when this is a risk that has to be taken. There is a lack of identity with, and a lack of sense of participation in, Europe's system of government at present across Europe that is highly undesirable. In the past it has led governments and EU institutions to seek legitimacy through a never-ending chase after new functional goals rather than confronting the basic issue of how to achieve a sense of democratic participation in a large and distant political space. There is now a chance to get out of this cycle. But this sense of lack of participation in EU processes is not something that can be addressed through what is perceived as incomprehensible institutional in-fighting. It involves a more fundamental review of Union functions, organization and character.

---

[20] B Skyrms, *The Dynamics of Rational Deliberation* (1990) is one of the game theorists who emphasizes the importance of the characteristics of Nash equilibrium.

[21] K Arrow, *Barriers to Conflict Resolution* (1995) identifies issue linkage and side payments as the two main means to resolve conflicts.

Conclusion: the constitutional moment

Ahead of enlargement, the 2004 IGC may not be the moment to formalize all the most important constitutional rules of the Union. Nevertheless it is difficult to see a successful development of the Union in the absence of at least a set of guiding constitutional principles—even if a comprehensive settlement is to be left for later years and subsequent IGCs. Moreover, the prospect of a much larger Union does provide an opportune moment for a stocktaking and review of the fundamentals. The American constitution was agreed at the level of general principles leaving many of the specifics to be worked out in practice. Europe is adopting the opposite tack of trying to agree on a wide agenda of specifics while avoiding general principles. I do not see Europe achieving a successful system of government unless we can get the basic principles right as America's founding fathers were able to do.

11

Drafting a Constitution for Europe: A Case of Too Many Borders?

Sophie Boyron

Introduction

The rapid succession of Treaty negotiations has ignited interest in the adoption of a formal constitution for the European Union. This was reflected in a speech given at the Humboldt University in Berlin on 12 May 2000 by Joschka Fischer, the then German Foreign Minister.[1] Discussion on the merits of adopting a constitution for the Union is often combined with reflection on the appropriateness of the Treaties' amendment procedure and the need to define more clearly the powers and competences of the Union.

If the aim is to adopt a formal Constitution for the European Union, the reorganization of the Treaties, which has been proposed, might not be sufficient to achieve this task;[2] deeper reforms are needed. Furthermore, it will be argued that the type of reforms suggested by many politicians fall short of the momentous constitutional change necessary for the adoption of a European constitution: not only are the institutional solutions often inspired by the politician's national model, but they also concentrate on the main and most visible EU institutions: the European Parliament, the Council, the Commission. This narrows the constitutional reform agenda

---

[1] 'From confederation to federation: thoughts on the finality of European integration'. An English translation of the speech is contained in C Joerges, Y Mény and J HH Weiler (eds), *What Kind of Constitution for What Kind of Polity? Responses to Joschka Fischer* (2000) 19. More recently, Lionel Jospin, Romano Prodi and Chris Patten have made proposals along the same lines.

[2] See *A Basic Treaty for the European Union—A Study of the Reorganisation of the Treaties* (European University Institute/Robert Schuman Centre for Advanced Studies, 15 May 2000) http://www.iue.it/RSC/pdf/Report-Treaties. pdf/.

considerably. It is important, therefore, to start afresh. To do so, an investigation into the various meanings of the term constitution will be conducted first. This will gives us the possibility to determine the fundamental elements that a constitution should contain and to give some directions in drafting a constitution for the European Union. However, a note of warning must be sounded at the start of this enterprise: the investigation into the drafting of such a constitution will take us across many borders, not only territorial but also disciplinary.

Constitutions: from definition to building blocks

A quick survey of constitutional law textbooks reveals that there are a number of acceptable meanings of the term constitution. In most constitutional systems, the question is rarely controversial: there the constitution is included in a clearly labelled document. Still, often in such systems a distinction is made between the formal and substantive constitution;[3] that is, the 'codified' or formal constitution must be read in the light of other sources, such as judicial decisions interpreting its provisions and practices, or conventions developed by the various constitutional actors outside the formal text of the constitution.[4]

In systems where there is no formal constitution, the question of definition is of great importance. Although most constitutional writers favour their own angle of study and infer from it their own definition of the term,[5] it is possible to isolate three different trends: a formal, a descriptive and a functional definition. Each of these addresses, in effect, a different question with regard to the concept. What form does the constitution take?[6] What does the constitution contain?[7] What functions does a constitution

---

[3]   See C Turpin, *British Government and the Constitution: Texts, Cases and Materials* (1999) 3.

[4]   See also on this point C Munro, *Studies in Constitutional Law* (2nd edn, 1999) 3. He does not seem to believe that there is a fundamental difference between 'uncodified' and 'documentary' constitutions.

[5]   See I Loveland, *Constitutional Law: A Critical Introduction* (2000) 2: 'The book does not, however, offer a one sentence "definition" of the constitution, on the grounds that such a task cannot sensibly be performed. Rather, the entire book may be seen as a "definition"'.

[6]   See E Barendt, *An Introduction to Constitutional Law* (1998) 1: 'The constitution of a state is the written document or text which outlines the powers of its parliament, government, courts, and other important national institutions ...'

[7]   See C Turpin, *British Government and the Constitution: Texts, Cases and Materials* (1999) 4: 'An institutional description of the Constitution would include Parliament, the Cabinet and

fulfil?[8] Although all these conceptions deal with one aspect, they are often combined so as to produce a more 'complete' definition of the term.[9] Rather than propose a definition of the term, which might be restrictive, these conceptions will be used to establish a series of questions to be investigated further on.

What functions does a constitution fulfil? Constitutions are generally held to establish and regulate a system of government. However, this general statement is not completely satisfactory: the list of functions can vary considerably from writer to writer[10] and from country to country. To establish the list of functions that a specific constitution needs to fulfil, it is necessary to know the reasons for adopting it in the first place: the vision of society that it was designed to put into place, the fundamental values it aims to protect, and so on.

What form should a constitution take? This should not be reduced to a question of drafting precision or format (ie basic treaty or constitution). The choice of a separate document begs the question as to its place in the hierarchy of norms, its higher legal status (or otherwise) and consequently, its protection and its stability.

What does the constitution contain? From the above analysis, it is possible to establish a list of the fundamental elements that ought to be included in a formal constitution:

- a societal project/fundamental reasons for its adoption;
- a system of government, established and regulated so as to give life to the project by performing the functions and protecting the choices identified in it;
- an enforcement mechanism, to protect the above constitutional settlement (usually in the form of judicial/constitutional control);

the courts, the Queen and her ministers, and such offices as those of the Parliamentary Ombudsman, the Comptroller and Auditor General, and the Director of Public Prosecutions. Of course these institutions and offices are themselves to be explained by reference to rules and practices which constitute them or define their powers and activity'.

[8] See E Barendt, *An Introduction to Constitutional Law* (1998) 2: 'Obviously it is important to have some idea of what a constitution is, what (in most countries) the constitutional text contains, in order to appreciate the distinctive character of constitutional law. But it is also essential to ask another question: what are constitutions for?'

[9] In fact many writers resort to a combination of aspects to provide a definition of the British Constitution.

[10] For instance, some add that constitutions organize the relationship between citizens and the state, but there is no indication as to why such a specific function is included.

- a rule of change, to ensure stability of the same (usually in the form of an amendment procedure).

These fundamental elements ought to constitute the building blocks of a future European constitution.

The search for a European project

As mentioned above, it is not really possible to establish a clear list of what a constitution does in the abstract; the general statement that a constitution creates and controls the institutions necessary to the system of government is singularly uninformative. It is possible to quote a number of generic functions that constitutions often fulfil: they are said to organize the accountability of government, to enshrine a threshold protection of fundamental rights and freedoms, to set up the rules that will define the degree of popular participation in the decision-making process; and so on. However, these assertions are both too vague and unjustified to be helpful when drafting a constitution. Furthermore, if one looks at specific constitutions, the formulation of those functions is clearly dictated by certain choices of principle, choices that could not and should not be transferred straight over to the European constitution. It is, therefore, absolutely necessary to reflect on the reasons for the adoption of a European constitution before deciding on what the European constitution should do and what functions it should fulfil.

In modern constitutions, declarations of rights often (but not always) accompany new constitutions. It is often overlooked, however, that these texts were, and still are, more than simple lists of rights and freedoms. They define the choices a society wants to make for itself. For instance, the French Declaration of 1789 marked the end of absolute monarchy, the prohibition of professional corporations, the recognition that every man has equal rights, and the appearance of the concept of citizenship. To some extent this wider conception has been overlooked in the EU context, as witnessed by the discussions surrounding the new Charter of Fundamental Rights.[11] The recognition and protection of rights and freedoms is a central element when it comes to reflecting on a vision of society, but they should not be recognized on their own. As far as the European Union is concerned, they

[11] The demands of both the German and the Italian Constitutional Courts for better protection of human rights in the Community may have contributed to a narrow construction of the issue.

ought to be part of a wider debate concerning the Union, its project, the relationship with national constitutions and their vision of society and so on. In effect, an opportunity was missed with the drafting of the Charter: although it lists a number of rights and freedoms and tries to tailor these to particular traits and problems of the Union,[12] the Charter is not part of a general reflection on the role and aims of the Union. Not only would this have helped to justify the granting of rights in a legal environment already saturated with rights protection at the national and international levels, but more importantly it would have helped define the role and place that the Union sees for itself.

Before considering the drafting of a constitution for the European Union, it will be necessary to establish the reasons and aims for such a project so as to decide on the following issues:

- The reason(s) for a supra-national constitution. From the beginning, the aims and reasons for creating the Communities were ambiguous. Various roles for the Union have been put forward in recent years: an influential and protective role in view of globalization, an ethical role in its relationship with the developing world and so on. However, these do not seem to justify fully the move towards closer political Union.

- The relationship between the European constitution and international law.

- The relationship between national constitutions and the European constitution. The issue of precedence ought to be resolved by the inclusion of the principle of supremacy of European law in the constitutional text.[13] The statelessness of the Union[14] needs also to be integral to the debate. Should it be acknowledged or even proclaimed? How do state-based constitutions interact with a stateless constitution?

- The recognition and place of the various actors involved at all levels of the Union's system and their respective relationships: Member State governments, citizens/civil society, European institutions, national parliaments, the regional/federal/devolved institutions in the Member States.

---

[12] The issue of information is crucial to the development of the Union and the Charter includes a right to information. However, it could have been better tailored to the demands of the Union.

[13] At present, there is a certain latitude and sometimes tensions at the jurisdictional border but this has not given rise to serious constitutional battles as yet.

[14] See S Weatherill, 'Is constitutional finality feasible or desirable? On the cases for European constitutionalism and a European Constitution' (forthcoming).

- The balance of power between the various institutions and levels of government.
- The role to be played by different cultures in the politically integrated Union. People are worried that a European constitution might signal the end of a rich cultural diversity; it is therefore important for these issues to be clearly addressed by the constitution.

Some have argued that it would be extremely difficult, if not impossible, to capture such a vision and include it in a European constitution: too many of the numerous constituencies participating in the process diverge in their vision of the European Union. There is not one European project but many, often pulling in opposite directions.[15] However, one should neither idealize nor simplify what a constitution really does: it would be mistaken to believe that constitutions always express and implement a clear project arising from a strong political consensus. Constitutions often reflect contradicting trends, which get translated into contradictory institutional arrangements.[16] Adopting a constitution is unlikely to be a panacea, neither is the resulting document likely to settle the question of the European project once and for all. Nevertheless, it would be a significant achievement if the constitution created an appropriate space and structure where different trends and diverging projects could not only be accommodated, but allowed to negotiate their relative influence in an ever-fluctuating balance.

However, these issues are the most difficult ones and might well be decided by default. This would have serious consequences when trying to determine the system of government to be adopted.

The system of government: something old, something new

If a European constitution were to be drafted at this stage, it would be difficult to put forward precise proposals for a specific system of government: the issues listed previously would need to be addressed first. Still, it might be possible to sound a warning and make a constructive proposal on the basis of the present experience.

[15]   See D Wincott, 'Does the European Union pervert democracy? Questions of democracy in new constitutionalist thought on the future of Europe' (1998) 4 ELJ 411, 427.

[16]   For instance, such contradicting trends can be seen in the French Constitution of 1958, whose provisions facilitated many different constitutional readings.

A message from political science relayed by legal theory

With the European Parliament, the Council, the Commission, the Courts and its various decision-making procedures, the European Union has a system of government, albeit a complex one, since the institutional balance and organization varies with the subject matter and the pillar to which it belongs. However, this system has been the subject of mounting criticism and the main bulk of the proposals for reform concentrates on 'improving' it: election of the Commission President, clearer definition of the Union's competences, extension of the co-decision procedure to other areas, simplification of the Treaties, including, among other things, the abolition of the pillar system.[17]

In fact, in the past most changes to the European institutional system have been made with a view to making it more acceptable; still, little appears to have been achieved. According to many political scientists, this arises partly from the fact that European governance does not overlap with the European institutional system (not to use the term government): by simply modifying the institutional arrangements, the power to influence/alter the system is merely 'institution deep' and does not carry into the complex multi-level system of networks from which emerge legislation, implementing measures and negotiated compliance. Unless lawyers are ready to examine and integrate these into their constitutional analysis, they are condemned to represent and regulate the European institutional system in the most superficial manner.[18]

The picture drawn in political science literature is also echoed in the field of legal theory. Some writers have pointed out that legal orders are being 'colonized' by new forms of power;[19] moreover, these forms of power challenge directly the hierarchical and pyramidal representation, which is used generally to depict and explain the functioning of legal orders and which was justified by the existence of sovereign states governing stable territories independently. The change in the forms of power are the result of parallel changes in the world of today, such as globalization, the decrease in the State's political and economic capacity, the rise of powerful private actors. This requires that the pyramidal and hierarchical representation be

[17] In the Laeken Declaration, these issues (and many others) are raised in the form of open questions.

[18] See B Kohler-Koch and R Eising, *The Transformation of Governance in the European Union* (1999) ch 1.

[19] See F Ost and M Van de Kerchove, *De la pyramide au réseau—Pour une théorie dialectique du droit* (forthcoming); I Ramonet, *Géopolitique du chaos* (1999).

abandoned and consequently signals the need for a change of paradigm.[20] The same writers propose that a representation based on the idea of law as network be adopted instead. It emphasizes the relational character of law and distances itself from the idea of hierarchy. It reflects the changing patterns of rule-making and complex inter-institutional relationships that can be found within and between many legal orders. It captures perfectly the evolutions that are being witnessed in the European polity.

Drafting a European constitution: should the multi-level system of governance be constitutionalized?

If a European constitution were to be drafted, it would be desirable that the divide between institutional arrangements and the reality of governance, mentioned above, should be addressed. To achieve this, the existing tension between the two paradigms needs to be understood. In reality, an understanding of law as a network might well be replacing the hierarchical and pyramidal understanding of law. The creation of the European Union's legal order does strike at the very heart of the same hierarchical and pyramidal representation; however, many principles, tools and standards of constitutional law, which are commonly used in the institutional law of the European Union, are the product of the pyramidal representation.[21] In fact, viewed in this light one should be wary of many proposals for reform canvassed recently.

However, a recent and radical proposal would in effect allow for the representation of law as a network to inform the drafting of the future European constitution.[22] Its authors note that political scientists have labelled and repeatedly analysed the Union as a system of multi-level governance where national, regional and European levels of decision-making are interwoven into complex networks;[23] consequently, they suggested that not only should the concept of a multi-level system of governance be central to reflection on the European constitution, but that

[20] Here paradigm is used in the sense explained by T Kuhn, *Structures of Scientific Revolutions* (2nd edn, 1970).

[21] The parliamentary responsibility which has been created between the Commission and the European Parliament is a good example of this.

[22] See TA Borsel and T Risse 'Who is afraid of a European Federation? How to constitutionalise a multi-level Governance system?' in C Joerges, Y Mény and JHH Weiler (n 1 above) 45.

[23] See F Scharpf, 'Community and autonomy: multi-level policy-making in the European Union' (1994) 1 JEPP 219; J Peterson, 'Decision-making in the European Union: towards a framework for analysis' (1995) 2 JEPP 69; G Marks, L Hooghe and K Blank, 'European integration from the 1980s: State-centric v multi-level governance' (1996) 34 JCMS 341.

it should be literally constitutionalized. Although the solution is tempting in its elegance and rationality, it leaves the reader slightly dissatisfied: the analysis is concerned mainly with the relationship between the European Union and the Member States; there is little mention of the sub-national level and, although the existence of policy networks is acknowledged, the analysis does not specify whether the process of constitutionalization should extend to them and, if so, how. Still, the authors followed a valid methodological approach in attempting to move away from solutions based on national constitutional experience and trying to create new conceptual tools to understand and capture the sui generis character of the European Union.

A formal constitution?

Even if a decision were made on only some of the issues canvassed above, the choices should be included in a formal constitution. Similarly, topics which are hotly debated at present, such as the Charter of Fundamental Rights and its legal effect, the possible election of the Commission President, the role of national parliaments, the determination of the European Union's competences, the simplification and consolidation of the Treaties, are more appropriate to a constitutional text than a simple treaty.[24] These are of such importance that they should be granted higher status, for symbolic as well as legal reasons, and receive the protection that would be attached to a formal constitution.

The amendment procedure: dynamism or stability?

A rule of change: re-thinking its foundations

Normally a rule of change enables necessary constitutional evolution while protecting the stability of the constitutional settlement as a whole. In the context of the European Union, unlike most constitutions, stability is not the main object of such a rule; there it needs to facilitate and structure a regular dynamic for change. It is clear from previous developments that the constitution of the European Union is a constitution in constant transition, a constitution where the institutional balance is evolving permanently and

---

[24] These matters are all included in the Laeken Declaration on the future of Europe, 15 December 2001.

where the underlying project of the European Union is shifting rapidly. Therefore, the rule of change should not aim at protecting the stability of the existing arrangements, but should help identify and fashion this dynamic for change.

In search of a new structure

Successive IGCs have been heavily criticized for being undemocratic, cumbersome and inefficient. It is true that the last two IGCs have demonstrated that on controversial matters, agreements are negotiated at the very last moment, often requiring Heads of State or Government to meet for longer than planned.[25] Furthermore, these agreements, brokered in the early hours of the morning, may result in badly drafted provisions.[26] Lastly, although IGCs and their result attract considerable media coverage, the European populations and many other constituencies are excluded from them.[27] Consequently, this process does very little either to enhance the legitimacy of the Union or to structure a regular dynamic for change and reform has often been advocated.

Seen in this light, the resort to a Convention to draft the Charter of Fundamental Rights was not only an attempt to escape the cumbersome IGC process, but also a way of putting a new procedure to the test. It was hoped that the drafting experience of the Charter of Fundamental Rights would be positive and provide an alternative structure to the IGCs. Although the Convention on the Future of Europe, which the European Council decided at Laeken to convene, will not replace the IGC in 2004, its final document will be a starting point for the IGC's negotiations.

The participation of populations: from veto to dialogue

Another difficult question is the involvement of the population(s) in the constitutional process. In fact, three separate questions need to be addressed here:

(1) Should the population(s) be involved at all?
(2) What form should this participation take?
(3) Which populations should be canvassed?

[25] The Nice summit went on for two extra days.

[26] The negotiation of the re-weighting of the votes in Council at Nice is a good example of this. See A Arnull, 'Size matters' (2001) 26 ELRev 1.

[27] The most remarkable exclusions during the 2000 IGC were those of the candidate countries.

It appears from political speeches and academic writings that popular participation is often considered necessary in relation to constitutional change, and that some form of referendum seems to be the inevitable procedural solution. However, governments of the European Union are likely to be particularly hesitant to pursue this solution. Too many referenda have been unsuccessful.[28] Consequently, governments are not confident that the referendum is the appropriate mechanism to secure popular support. Part of the problem lies in the fact that referenda are stuck on the end of the process, suggesting that popular participation comes only as an after-thought and in some Member States only. The 'end of process referendum' might allow sufficient popular participation when amending a national constitution; after all, there are pre-existing national public spaces (with recognized actors) where a national constitutional debate can take place. In the European Union context, however, any mechanism designed to secure popular participation will have to create its own intrinsic structure for facilitating debate, so as to redeem the absence of a European public space. In this latter case, an 'end of process referendum' does not foster participation and debate: it creates no structure and there is little left to debate. It becomes a quasi-coercive instrument to obtain systematic approval. It is not surprising that a referendum has sometimes been turned into a veto.

If a constitution were to be adopted through referendum, it might be advisable to involve the populations at various stages of the drafting process. A solution might reside in a process which would be punctuated by a *series of referenda*: the first could ask the populations whether they support the principle of a European Constitution and whether they approve of the process by which this Constitution is to be negotiated and adopted;[29] the second (if the results to the first one were positive) would ask the population to approve a list of constitutional principles/structures which the authors of the constitution would have to respect and/or integrate in the new constitution;[30] finally, a third referendum would ask the populations to

---

[28] See the Danish 'no' to the ratification of the Maastricht Treaty in 1992 and the Irish rejection of the Nice Treaty in 2001.

[29] It is important to link these two issues. People are more likely to acquiesce in a project if they feel it belongs to them. This point should be remembered when discussions about the process are under way. In this context, the new convention format falls well short of what is desirable.

[30] When deciding on these principles, populations could also participate in identifying them, following the example of many previous constitutions, such as that of South Africa.

approve the final text.[31] This system might secure more popular involvement and support. It would also compel national governments and those responsible for drafting the text to provide a continual flow of information as to the state of the negotiations at any given time and to be attentive to the demands of civil society during the entire process.

Again the definition of population in this context is a difficult one. However, in practical terms, the voting system could be created so as to combine and respect the views of both the population of the Union and the national populations: for instance, the requirement of a double majority would avoid making a difficult choice.

The importance of temporal considerations

The present IGCs are already integrated in a recognized time frame; the date for the next IGC is announced a long time in advance and an agenda, even if only in outline, is made known at the same time;[32] the procedure itself includes a number of steps which provide a clear time frame during which the agenda is finalized: first, Member States agree to an agenda during European Council summits and a specific negotiation process is often put into place.[33] Then follows the preparatory period during which Parliament,[34] Commission[35] and Presidency draft and adopt documents setting their positions and preferences before the long IGC process starts. The drafting of these instruments is important not only for each institution to determine and test its demands and negotiating strategies well in advance but also to allow, after many comparisons and assessments, for an adjustment of the respective positions in view of the decisions and proposals made by other actors. For instance, while the political responsibility for the Nice negotiations rested with the General Affairs Council, the basic work of preparation was done by a group of government representatives, which closely resembled the Reflection Group established for the 1996 IGC and

[31] Such a heavy process should be used to produce a relatively final constitution; it would not be possible to resort to such a process on a regular basis.

[32] Lately, it has become customary to announce the next IGC as the previous one draws to a close.

[33] The Helsinki European Council (10–11 December 1999) agreed the issues to be covered by the 2000 IGC. It also dealt with the formal process that the negotiations would follow.

[34] See the resolution containing the European Parliament's proposals for the IGC, 13 April 2000, A5-0086/2000.

[35] Opinion of 26 January 2000, 'Adapting the institutions to make a success of enlargement', COM (2000) 34.

which met twice monthly. Thus prepared, the issues were then examined by the General Affairs Council. Furthermore, the two European Councils of Feira and Biarritz outlined the progress achieved so far and tried to broker agreement in relation to difficult topics, such as the weighing of votes. This creates a flexible time frame, during which specific solutions emerge and are put to the test.[36] In fact, while many provisions and changes are agreed to in effect long before the conclusion of the IGC,[37] other subjects need the meeting of Heads of State or Government for final agreement. In that case, the date of their meeting fixes the ultimate deadline.[38]

As emphasized above, the process of change ought to be understood and reintegrated in a time frame, and this is even more relevant beyond the strict IGC procedure. A reflection concerning the concept of time might help to address a number of other concerns as well. Every constitution is at the core of a permanent dynamic for change, for which there is more or less demand; no constitution is ever static. This is all the more true of the European Union and this creates a problem in itself. New institutions or new mechanisms are rarely introduced in their full and final version in one single amendment; on the contrary, their powers are increased, the procedures simplified during later IGCs. In short, new provisions are far from perfect creations at the time of their introduction. For instance, the co-decision procedure introduced at Maastricht was rightly criticized for its complexity and the limited range of matters it actually covered. However, the procedure as amended at Amsterdam is much more acceptable. Nonetheless, this drawn out 'creative process' tends to engender criticisms.[39] Controlling the development of the project by establishing an agenda with stages and targets and integrating it to the amendment process would take away this impression of failure. It would also allow aims of each legal creation to be determined more precisely. For instance, the Charter of Fundamental Rights proclaimed at Nice was criticized because of the refusal of Member States to give it legal effect. However, the decision is not final and will be revisited during the next IGC. Furthermore, by announcing this so early, various political and institutional actors can take a position on

---

[36] Similar ideas, concepts and solutions are often discussed in these documents.

[37] The provisions of the Treaty of Nice concerning the Union's judicial architecture were decided long before the Nice summit.

[38] Many have argued that, because of the need to achieve a result, too many compromises are made and too many provisions are watered down. Although this is a serious drawback to such negotiations, it might nonetheless represent the starting point for a later IGC.

[39] See F Dehousse, 'Rediscovering functionalism' in C Joerges, Y Mény and JHH Weiler (n 1 above), 195.

the issue and organize their campaigns accordingly. For instance, the attitudes of the Court of Justice and national courts will be paramount when deciding on this issue;[40] the legal landscape is likely to be different in 2004.

When time or historical data are used in legal analysis, they are often represented and expressed as a linear continuum,[41] whereas philosophers,[42] historians,[43] psychologists, and even scientists draw a very different picture. Their approach is instructive, since many tend to regard European integration as a linear process.[44] For instance, politicians and sometimes commentators seem to be obsessed with the idea that the integration process should never appear to pause or stop.[45] Furthermore if the idea of ever-progressing linear integration were to be abandoned as being unfit to represent what happens in the integration process, new horizons might be opened concerning the process of change itself. The amendment process would need to be altered so as to allow for the expression of pauses in the integration process: for instance, there is no way to deal with the situation which arises when a Member State's electorate finds fault with a freshly negotiated treaty. This is viewed pejoratively and presented as disrupting the linear integration process.

In search of a method of constitutional/treaty change?

The process of constitutional change is often hampered by myths and traditions. Also, as in any area of legal reform, legal transplants or experiences from other systems are frequently advocated and resorted to in order to deal with a specific issue.[46] Furthermore, the European Union system is

---

[40]   See for instance, Case C-173/99 *BECTU*, judgment of 26 June 2001.

[41]   See P Hébraud, 'Obervations du temps dans le droit civil' in *Etudes offertes à Pierre Kayser* (1979) Vol 2, 1.

[42]   See G Bachelard, *La dialectique de la durée* (1989).

[43]   See P Veyne, *Comment on écrit l'histoire* (1996).

[44]   See J Shaw, 'Constitutionalism and flexibility in the EU: developing a relational approach' in G de Búrca and J Scott (eds), *Constitutional Change in the EU: From Uniformity to Flexibility?* (2000) 346: 'In other words, postnationalism is not about a linear movement towards a more "integrated" Europe in the conventional sense so often used by the so-called "integration-through-law" movement, but involves a reflexive critique of institutions, legal forms and identity formations beyond statist limits'. Also M la Torre, 'Legal pluralism as evolutionary achievement of Community law' (1999) 12 Ratio Juris 182.

[45]   See Fischer's speech (n 1 above, 20) where he says that we cannot even afford to pause.

[46]   This is all the more true in that there are 15 national constitutional experiences to choose from and which compete for 'European endorsement'.

dogged by numerous myths and inaccurate representations.[47] These have had an impact on successive amendments of the Treaties and could influence the drafting of the future constitution.[48] In effect the discussions and solutions regarding the democratic deficit feed this mythical construct: many amendments have tended to increase the powers of the European Parliament but this has not resulted in a marked change of attitude nor in a serious reduction of the democratic deficit. This is not to say that the democratic deficit is not a serious problem; it is simply argued here that a popular representation of the EU has driven the amendment process to the detriment of a more appropriate and relevant solution for the European Union. Consequently, in order to deal with all these problems, it is advisable to have a strong method of constitutional change.

In the Union, constitutional change often takes place over a long period of time and is clearly incremental; as a result, it is possible to assess and rectify the procedure, principle or institution, as new Treaty negotiations get under way.[49] Furthermore, the process has been a real success in relation to specific provisions: the co-decision procedure was the subject of an in-depth empirical assessment by the three institutions involved. Statistics were collated and the specific practices surrounding the procedure were identified and analysed. As a result, a series of amendments based directly on those findings were proposed and agreed to at Amsterdam. This experience should be encouraged and systematized. Not only would it help in attenuating the tendency that has been mentioned above, but it would also allow for a more independent framework of reference and standards.

When it comes to the original and creative moment, there seems to be no method at all. New procedures, new institutions or principles seem to appear in the constitutional debate without any previous research on their impact and possible effect on the present arrangements. For instance, the resort to 'a Convention' to draft the Charter of Fundamental Rights was decided quite rapidly without much examination as to the benefits of such a format and whether it was the best possible option. This is all the more important since new mechanisms, institutions or principles, once adopted, are difficult to discard. Rarely has an innovation been rejected or abandoned. The process for identifying and assessing new ideas needs to be more

---

[47] See for instance Fischer's speech: '…it is viewed as a bureaucratic affair run by a faceless, soulless Eurocracy in Brussels—at best boring, at worst dangerous' (n 1 above, 19).

[48] See the list of issues contained in the Laeken Declaration that the 2004 IGC is supposed to tackle.

[49] However, this might create serious problems in setting the agenda.

systematic. This would help the emergence of appropriate tools, well adapted to the specificity of the European Union system.

Upholding the constitution: flexible judicial protection

Once established, the rules and principles in a constitution need to be protected and their enforcement ensured. Normally, constitutions entrust this function to a judicial body, such as a constitutional or supreme court. In the system of the European Union, various remedies organized by the Treaties empower the Commission, the European Courts and the national courts to ensure that the Treaties are respected. In fact, the Court of Justice and the national courts have, over the years, entered into a complex and sometimes difficult dialogue, which has resulted in an optimization of the methods of control and enforcement already in place.

It might be useful to analyse this relationship in more depth. Such a study might assist reflection on inter-institutional and multi-level dialogue, which would be extremely useful in view of previous analyses. The types of dialogue between European Courts and national courts, the structures allowing it, the constraints over it and the various resulting outcomes, ought to be examined. It could form the basis of a further study aimed at recognizing, facilitating and structuring similar relationships between other institutional groupings across various levels of governance.

The Laeken process: a constitution for the people, without the people

At Laeken, the decision was taken that a Convention be convened so as to prepare the way for the 2004 IGC. It is hoped that it will strengthen the legitimacy and the efficiency of the process. In effect, the composition of the Convention is relatively well balanced and includes delegations from the candidate countries.[50] Furthermore, it is headed by three very influential politicians. However, the role of the Convention is relatively limited: 'it will be a starting point for the discussions in the IGC'. In fact, the content of

[50] They can take part in the proceedings but cannot stop the emergence of a consensus among Member States.

the document it will produce is likely to determine its degree of influence during the IGC negotiations: if it adopts clear recommendations by consensus[51] on the major issues that are canvassed in the Laeken Declaration, then it will be difficult and illogical for the IGC to ignore the document. As it is, the Convention has already decided to adopt all recommendations by consensus, but this might put a serious strain on its proceedings, especially since it has one year to produce the document.

The peoples of Europe will have very limited access to the Convention, except via a so-called Forum of organizations representing civil society, which will receive regular information on the Convention's proceedings and may be heard or consulted on specific topics. Considering the type of issues that the IGC is supposed to be discussing, better popular participation should have been organized. Nonetheless, if the IGC adopts a treaty/constitution which deals with the issues listed at Laeken, many Member States will have to revise their constitutions before adopting it. At that stage, there will be plenty of opportunity for popular opinion to be voiced.

---

[51] The Laeken Declaration specifies that the final document produced by the Convention may either list different options (indicating the degree of support) or make recommendations when consensus is reached. The Convention decided at the outset to produce recommendations on the basis of consensus.

12

The Delimitation of Powers Between the EU and its Member States

Gráinne de Búrca and Bruno de Witte

The competence question in the European constitutional debate

The exact division of powers and competences at EU level has, to date, been left to be determined rather fluidly, by a mixture of action and initiative on the part of the relevant EU institutions, which can be challenged during the political process or ultimately before the Court of Justice in the event of opposition. Because so many of the Treaty provisions which confer power—and in particular some of the earlier and original provisions of the Community Treaties—are broadly defined and do not specify what the relationship with national powers in that field should be, this kind of gradual and fluid process has perhaps been unsurprising. It is particularly noteworthy that the Court of Justice has contented itself with incidental interventions,[1] something which can be explained in part but not entirely by reference to the paucity of suitable opportunities presented to the Court through litigation. In particular, the Court of Justice has conspicuously never attempted to delineate a complete doctrine of the division of powers between the EC and the Member States, even while it has been quite forceful and doctrinally comprehensive in related fields of European constitutional law, such as that of the role and duties of national courts in the enforcement of EC law, or the protection of fundamental rights.

---

[1] The most notable case in recent years has been the Tobacco Advertising ruling, Case C-376/98 *Germany v European Parliament and Council* [2000] ECR I-8419, and there has been only a handful of decisions over the years which deal in some way with the 'division of competence' issue.

This does not mean that there is currently a total lack of coherence in the allocation of powers between the EU and its Member States. With respect to the 'first pillar', the fundamental rule on the allocation of powers (sometimes known as the principle of attributed powers or competences) is clearly expressed by Article 5 EC, namely that the European Community can act only within the fields and for the purposes mentioned in the Treaty. The powers of the European Union, acting under the second and third pillars, are not subject to Article 5 EC, nor to any similar express provision in the EU Treaty,[2] but it is quite obvious that the same rule of enumerated powers is implicitly applicable there—it corresponds, in fact, to the general rule that the powers of an international organization are only those that are either enumerated in its founding instrument or are implied by these express powers. The specific powers of the EC and of the EU are then mentioned and delimited in the many individual 'legal basis' articles to be found across the Treaties. In fact, these specific powers are defined in much more detail than is usually the case for the constitutional delimitation of powers in a federal state. In this sense, the vertical delimitation of powers is arguably accomplished with greater clarity and precision within the European Union's founding instruments than in the constitutions of most federal states. Notwithstanding this fact, and not least in part because of the powerful differences of popular and political opinion over the nature of the EU and the extent to which it can be compared with other genuinely federal systems, the question of reform of the present system of delimitation of powers has found its way to the top of the EU's constitutional agenda.

One of the four key questions to be addressed in the post-Nice process is, according to the English text of the Declaration on the Future of the Union attached to the Treaty of Nice, 'how to establish and monitor a more precise delimitation of powers between the European Union and the Member States, reflecting the principle of subsidiarity'. Of these four specific themes, the question of powers or competences[3] was that

---

[2] A Dashwood 'States in the European Union' (1998) 23 ELRev 201, 210 has explained this difference by reference to the fact that Member State autonomy remains strong under these pillars, so that demarcation of competences is less important (although we note that this is a feature which may well be changing).

[3] We use the terms 'powers' and 'competences' interchangeably. A provisional version of the Nice Declaration (document SN 5333/00) used the word 'competencies' instead of 'powers'. The French version of the Declaration uses the term *compétences* and the German version *Zuständigkeiten*, but *compétences* was ultimately translated into English as 'powers'. The relationship between the two English terms in the context of EU law thus remains rather confused, whereas in French and other languages, a clear distinction is drawn between the *compétences* of the EC/EU as an organization, and the *pouvoirs* of its individual

which was developed in greatest detail in the Laeken Declaration one year later.[4]

We propose to begin by outlining the main elements of the unfolding debate on competences, in the context of the adoption of the Declarations of Nice and Laeken. In particular, the concerns out of which the call to establish a more precise delimitation of powers was born should be examined, since these are likely to inform the kinds of concrete proposals that are being made.[5] Various commentators and political actors have articulated a desire for greater clarity, for more transparency and certainty about where responsibility lies. Thus, one fairly widely shared aim is to be able to see more clearly and more readily *qui fait quoi*, that is, which level(s) of government may be responsible for which kinds of policy action. Apart from this somewhat general and unfocused concern, a number of observations can be made about the current stage of the debate.

First, the emphasis is primarily on clarifying what currently exists rather than redrawing the boundaries, although this emphasis is not uncontested. For some, the call for clearer delimitation of competences reflects a political wish to reverse part of the process of integration to date, in 'returning' powers which the EC/EU has hitherto exercised, to the state or sub-state level. However, the dominant wish (certainly outside Germany and the eurosceptic wing of the British political classes) is not so much to remove definitively some of the European Union's existing powers or to reduce its policy role, but rather to *clarify* its role, the scope of its powers and the conditions for their exercise. Although certain comments and proposals which have already been made, in particular by actors from the German *Länder*, indicate a desire for the renationalization of particular EC powers, this paper proceeds on the basis that there is a broad political consensus in favour of greater *precision* and greater *clarification* in the division of powers (which necessarily entails some degree of change), rather than in favour of making very substantial amendments to the existing policy competences of the EC and EU. This seems to be the approach adopted in the Laeken Declaration.

Secondly, the political misgivings about the present delimitation of powers (expressed most prominently by the German *Länder*) focus often

institutions: see V Constantinesco, *Compétences et pouvoirs dans les Communautés européennes* (1974).

[4] Laeken Declaration on the Future of the European Union, Annex I to the Conclusions of the Laeken European Council, 14–15 December 2001, SN 300/1/01 REV 1.

[5] For a survey of the competence debate and of the reform proposals made so far, see I Pernice, 'Rethinking the methods of dividing and controlling the competencies of the Union' in European Commission, *Europe 2004. Le grand débat* (2001) 96, 102.

on a limited number of specific EC Treaty articles, more particularly on Articles 95 and 308. These are the only two articles mentioned explicitly in the Laeken Declaration, which contains the following question: 'Should Articles 95 and 308 of the treaty be reviewed for this purpose in the light of the "acquis jurisprudentiel"?' These last two words—a terminological creation of the Laeken summit—may refer to the fact that the Court of Justice has found the use or proposed use of precisely these articles to be *ultra vires* in two important rulings, Opinion 2/94 on EC accession to the European Convention of Human Rights, and the judgment on the legality of the Tobacco Advertising Directive.[6] These are two legal bases which (positively) allow the European Community to 'react to fresh challenges' but also (negatively) allow for the 'creeping expansion' of EC competences to the detriment of the Member States.[7] If a consensus could be found on a reformulation of these two articles, it would help significantly to defuse some of the political misgivings about the present system of division of competences.

Thirdly, the focus is clearly on the delimitation of the internal legislative powers of the European Community, although this must be situated within a wider picture. The division of powers between the EC/EU and its Member States as regards administrative (or executive) powers, budgetary and fiscal powers, and judicial powers could equally well be examined. Further, the division of powers in the field of external relations is also highly relevant, and greater clarity could certainly be achieved in this field.[8]

Fourthly, reform of the delimitation of powers is apparently intended to encompass the intergovernmental pillars of the European Union as well as the Community pillar. The competences section of the Laeken Declaration systematically refers to the 'Union' rather than to the 'Community'.[9] Moreover, some of the specific questions contained in that section address division of powers questions relating to the second and third pillars, alongside the more numerous questions referring to the EC pillar.[10] Added pressure

[6] Case C-376/98 (n 1 above) and Opinion 2/94 [1996] ECR I-1759.

[7] The phrases between inverted commas are quoted from the Laeken Declaration (at 22) which expressly refers to Arts 95 and 308.

[8] The definition of the EC's common commercial policy is made almost incomprehensible by the Nice Treaty amendments to Art 133 EC. See HG Krenzler and C Pitschas, 'Progress or stagnation? The common commercial policy after Nice' (2001) EFA Rev 291.

[9] This supports our observation at n 2 above, that the salience of the 'attributed competence' question may be growing in relation to the second and third pillars, even if it was not previously considered to be an issue of concern outside the first pillar.

[10] Laeken Declaration (at 22): 'How, for example, should a more coherent common foreign policy and defence policy be developed? Should the Petersberg tasks be updated? Do we want to adopt a more integrated approach to police and criminal law cooperation?'

to adopt a cross-pillar approach to the question of division of powers may stem from the Treaty reorganization project which was also included in the post-Nice agenda and in the Laeken Declaration.[11] If the EC and EU Treaties were to be merged, and if a distinction were to be made between a (merged) basic treaty and the other, less foundational treaty provisions, then the general principles governing the system of competences would clearly have to cover all the areas of European Union policy. This would obviously not prevent the competences currently falling within the more intergovernmental domains of the second and third pillars from being defined or delimited in distinct ways, but certainly the issue of Community competences could no longer be considered in isolation.

Fifthly, the emphasis of the political debate, this time around, is on the *existence* of powers rather than on their exercise.[12] The principle of subsidiarity is not contested but its potential to clarify relations between the EU and its Member States appears to be seen as marginal. However, although the language of subsidiarity seems less central to the competences debate than hitherto, the issue of allocation of power remains fundamentally linked to the issue of the forms, institutional mechanisms and decision-making processes for the exercise of such power. The question of the allocation of powers to the EU cannot be framed as a yes-or-no question, since on any operational understanding it is crucially linked to the forms or instruments that can be used for developing EU policies, and to the institutional and decision-making processes for the exercise of those powers.

Sixthly, the Nice Declaration mentioned two different but complementary reforms: new provisions on the demarcation of powers between the EU and the Member States, but also new procedural devices for 'monitoring' respect for this allocation of powers. Some may well conclude that a 'more precise delimitation' is impossible to achieve, but that a better monitoring of the existing system of allocation of powers is possible; whereas others may believe a more precise delimitation is possible, but that there is no need to create new monitoring mechanisms. Finally, it may be the case that a better system for monitoring the *exercise* of existing powers would assist in clarifying the boundaries of those powers, and hence in clarifying the allocation of

---

[11] Laeken Declaration (at 23–24): 'Towards a Constitution for European citizens'.

[12] Contrast the views expressed in the paper published by the European Policy Centre: 'Beyond the delimitation of competences: implementing subsidiarity', *The Europe We Need*, Working Paper, 25 September 2001.

powers themselves.[13] In any case, the intention is clearly to think out some new forms of institutional design that would help to ensure observance of the division of powers chosen. Various options have been proposed in the literature.[14] The monitoring function could be entrusted to a new judicial organ that could be composed, at least in part, of members drawn from the national supreme or constitutional courts. Some years ago, Joseph Weiler proposed the creation of a special European Constitutional Council for deciding division of powers issues.[15] More recently, German politicians have advocated the creation of a European 'Competence Court'.[16] Alternatively, the monitoring of the delimitation of powers could be entrusted to a newly created *political* organ. Ingolf Pernice proposed setting up an advisory 'subsidiarity committee' composed of members of the national parliaments, to be consulted in the course of the EU legislative process.[17] A more radical version of this would be to set up a second house of the European Parliament, composed of national MPs, whose main task would be to exercise political control over the delimitation of powers.[18]

We will not attempt, within the constraints of this brief contribution, to develop all of the issues mentioned above. Our comments will focus on three questions only: the proposed establishment of a new list or categories of competences; the proposal to rephrase or delete some controversial 'legal

[13] The more thorough than usual attempt of the Court of Justice in the recent Tobacco Advertising case to clarify the scope and limits of the internal market regulatory power in Art 95 EC can, for example, be seen both as an endeavour to monitor the exercise of power by the EU institutions but also to delimit the boundaries of that power.

[14] For a survey of these monitoring proposals, see F Mayer, 'Die drei Dimensionen der europäischen Kompetenzdebatte' (2001) 61 Zeitschrift für ausländisches öffentliches Recht und Völkerrecht 577, 601.

[15] J Weiler, 'The European Union belongs to its citizens: three immodest proposals' (1997) 22 ELRev 150, 155.

[16] U Goll and M Kenntner, 'Brauchen wir ein europäisches Kompetenzgericht?' (2002) Europäische Zeitschrift für Wirtschaftsrecht 101 (the first author is Minister of Justice of the *Land* Baden-Württemberg).

[17] I Pernice, 'Kompetenzabgrenzung im europäischen Verfassungsverbund' (2000) Juristen Zeitung 866, 876; I Pernice (n 5 above) 112–113. This suggestion brings together the idea of enhancing the role of national parliaments (another major item on the post-Nice agenda) with that of establishing a better system for monitoring the delimitation of powers.

[18] See Tony Blair's Warsaw speech to the Polish Stock Exchange, 9 November 2000. A version of this idea was repeated, more recently, in a joint paper issued by Blair and the Polish Prime Minister, Leszek Miller, on 2 November 2001, and again in a speech in the Hague on 21 February 2002 by the UK's Foreign Minister Jack Straw. Straw also added the alternative option of entrusting this task to the 'European Scrutiny Committees from Parliaments across the EU, meeting collectively', see http://www.fco.gov.uk/news/newstext.asp?5508 (for the Blair/Miller speech) and http://www.fco.gov.uk/news/speechtext.asp?5926 (for the Straw speech).

basis' articles; and the proposal to develop or introduce new institutional forms and mechanisms for the exercise of EU powers. In doing so, we will adopt the characteristic style of the Laeken Declaration and provide the title of each of the three sections with a question mark.

Lists of competences or categories of powers?

The text of the Nice Declaration does not suggest that a *Kompetenzkatalog* should be drawn up in accordance with the wishes expressed by the German *Länder* last year. Indeed, the impetus for such a catalogue appears to arise mainly from the German debate and is not widely supported.

One pragmatic reason for this may be the realization that the vast majority of policy areas are currently the subject of shared powers between the EU and the Member States. Only a very small list of powers can be said to belong exclusively to the EC/EU, and a relatively small (and rarely articulated) list of powers can be said to belong exclusively to the Member States. An increasingly wide spectrum of policy competence is shared, and this reality rather seems to defeat one of the purposes of the *Kompetenzkatalog*, which would be to prevent the encroachment by one level of government on the protected powers of the other. While it is more contentious to declare that the Member States possess very few exclusive powers than it is to say the same of the EU, it is nonetheless increasingly true. Further, the exclusive powers of the States can no longer be described generally in terms of broad policy areas or sectors. For example, it cannot be said that the Member States retain exclusive competence in the field of criminal law and policy, or of family law and policy, since these are clearly areas with which many specific provisions and policies of EC and EU law intersect. While certain aspects of these general policy areas, such as, for example, prison rules, or the substantive terms of national divorce laws, clearly fall to be decided by the Member States alone and are barely touched by EU law, it is increasingly difficult to identify and isolate areas of exclusive EC or national competence without descending into this kind of detail.

The degree of detail and specificity which would be required to ensure an accurate *Kompetenzkatalog* for the EU would thus arguably undermine another of its purported aims, which is that of ensuring greater clarity, transparency and 'citizen-friendliness' in the description of the respective powers of the different levels of government. Further, it is not clear that a list of these defined areas would address the stronger constitutional concerns which seem to underpin the desire for a catalogue, namely to protect national and subnational competences in these protected areas and to prevent intrusion by the EU institutions.

One possible route that could be taken in the current constitutional debate, instead of drafting a complete *Kompetenzkatalog* covering all policy areas, would be to expand the list of specific 'reserved domains' for Member States or the list of 'excluded domains' for the EU. This is currently done in a partial way in the Treaty in relation to particular types of measure within specific policy sectors such as the prohibition on harmonizing measures in the fields of health, culture and education.[19] Otherwise, there are currently few domains specifically listed as being reserved to the Member States, apart from the standard public policy, security and health exceptions to a range of EC rules. However, an attempt might be made to define and articulate more precisely those policy sectors or domains in which the Member States decisively do not wish the EU to have any role, although the fact that this has not as yet been done may indicate that there is little agreement amongst the states as to what these might be.

Another route would be to try to present a systematic view of the existing categories of EU competences, and in that way to bring a greater degree of clarity to the existing, admittedly rather complex system. In order to provide a preliminary typology, some of the principal categories are set out below.

Exclusive EU powers

The notion that certain powers would belong exclusively to the European Community was introduced in EC law by the case law of the Court of Justice. In a small number of cases, the Court specified that a certain power of the EC was exclusive so that the Member States were no longer allowed to adopt separate legislative measures or to conclude separate treaties with third countries; in other cases, it held that a certain power was non-exclusive, so that the existence of an EC policy did not prevent the Member States from acting, so long as their action was consistent with this Community policy. But the Court of Justice never proposed a general doctrine on this matter, nor did it ever indicate an exhaustive list of exclusive powers.

The distinction made its first formal appearance in the text of the EC Treaty at Maastricht, when Article 3b (now 5) EC specified that the

---

[19] See eg Arts 149(4), 150(4), 151(5) and 152(4) EC.

principle of subsidiarity applies in areas 'which do not fall within the exclusive competence' of the Community. The article does not specify those areas, and there has been considerable speculation on this point in the legal literature ever since. The debate over the meaning of 'exclusive' Community competence has been lively but entirely inconclusive,[20] and the Amsterdam protocol on subsidiarity and proportionality has not provided any clarification on this issue.

Nonetheless, it is best to assume that only very few European Community powers are exclusive: the two areas identified by the Court of Justice, namely common commercial policy in the sense of Article 133 (in its pre-Nice version)[21] and the policy for the protection of the biological resources of the sea, should probably now be joined by monetary policy (at least for the countries participating in the single currency). It has also occasionally been claimed, mainly by the Commission,[22] that the establishment and functioning of the internal market is an exclusive EC power, but this qualification is rather misleading. This is a broad functional power which, by definition, belongs to the EC institutions and not to the Member States (and only in this sense can it be said to belong exclusively to the EC), but it is also a power which invariably covers many policy areas in which the Member States have retained an autonomous and even a primary capacity to legislate. Thus the concrete policy content of an internal market measure can rarely if ever be said to fall within the scope of exclusive EC powers. Further, the Commission regularly invokes the principle of subsidiarity in the explanatory memoranda to legislative proposals in the internal market field, which suggests that it does not seek to claim that they fall within the Community's exclusive competence, and the Court has also engaged with subsidiarity arguments in relation to legislative measures adopted under Article 95.[23]

Therefore, on this point, the next IGC could usefully clarify matters by expressly listing which policy areas fall within the EC's exclusive competence. On a narrow view, the category of exclusive powers would comprise only international trade as defined in Article 133 EC (pre-Nice version) and

---

[20]   See more generally G de Búrca, 'Reappraising subsidiarity's significance after Amsterdam', *Harvard Jean Monnet Working Paper 7/1999*, http://www.jeanmonnetprogram.org (with further references to the literature on this debate).

[21]   The text of Art 133 EC as amended by the Nice Treaty includes within the scope of that article certain new powers which the drafters of the Treaty took pains to define as shared between the EC and its Member States, unlike the traditional trade-in-goods core of Art 133.

[22]   See also the Opinion of AG Fennelly in the Tobacco Advertising case (n 1 above) para 142.

[23]   See Case C-377/98 *Netherlands v Parliament and Council*, judgment of 9 October 2001.

the protection of the biological resources of the sea. It would be for the IGC to decide whether or not *monetary policy* and *international trade in services*, or other areas, should be added to the list. In any case, the advantage of inserting a paragraph of this kind in the Treaty would be to clarify the fact that the list of exclusive EC powers is extremely limited.

Shared powers

The vast bulk of EC powers are law-making powers which are 'non-exclusive', but there is no clear agreement on how to define these in more positive terms. The term 'shared powers' (*compétences partagées*) is often used, as is the term 'concurrent powers' (*compétences concurrentes*). Similar terms are used in the constitutional law of federal and regional states, although they may describe different legal realities.[24]

Armin von Bogdandy and Jürgen Bast have recently proposed a distinction, within the existing system of EC powers, between *concurrent powers* and *parallel powers*.[25] The main difference seems to be that concurrent powers can gradually be used by the EC in such an exhaustive way that, eventually, no room is left for autonomous law-making by the Member States, whereas parallel powers are characterized by the fact that separate action by the EU and the Member States with respect to the same subject matter always remains possible. Our impression is that this distinction, although theoretically valid, is of limited practical importance, and that both types of powers can be included, for the sake of clarity, within a broader category of shared powers. In all areas falling within this broad category, the exercise of EC powers does not exclude the continuing exercise of law-making powers by the Member States, but makes it subject to respect for the principle of the primacy of EC law. In some cases, it is true, the EC has enacted such a wide-ranging system of norms that little autonomy is left to the Member States. An example of this is the field of agriculture. Nonetheless, national law-

---

[24] For a comparative constitutional typology, see J Ziller 'L'Etat composé et son avenir en France' (2001) 103 Revue politique et parlementaire, No 1009/1010, 151, 154. The conceptual pitfalls of seeking to draw lessons for the EU from a comparison of national constitutional systems are evident. In German constitutional law, for example, a distinction is made between concurrent and framework federal powers in Arts 74 and 75 of the Grundgesetz respectively, while the new text of Art 117 of the Italian Constitution introduces the concept of *materie di legislazione concorrente*, yet defines these in a way which corresponds substantively to the German notion of 'framework' rather than 'concurrent' powers.

[25] A von Bogdandy and J Bast, 'Die Vertikale Kompetenzordnung der europäischen Union' (2001) europäische Grundrechte Zeitschrift 441, 447; an English version of this article is forthcoming in (2002) 39 CMLRev.

making capacity continues to exist even in this area, and is precluded only to the extent that it conflicts with specific norms of EC law. On this basis, agricultural policy can equally be listed among the shared powers of the EC alongside areas such as environmental policy, where Member State room for manoeuvre is much larger.

Complementary powers

The concept of complementary powers (*compétences complémentaires; Ergän-zungskompetenzen*) is proposed by the German *Länder* as one of the main categories of future EU powers.[26] Although the term is not widely used in the EC law literature,[27] this type of power effectively exists in the EC Treaty, mainly with regard to the newer policy fields added by the Treaty of Maastricht. For instance, Article 149 on education states: 'The Community shall contribute to the development of quality education by encouraging cooperation between Member States and, if necessary, by supporting and supplementing their action…'. Similar phrasing is used to define the EC's role in the fields of vocational training, culture and health, and indeed its role in these areas is often precisely supportive: providing funding, supporting particular programmes etc. The Community's competences in the fields of economic policy and employment policy (the latter added by the Amsterdam Treaty) have been phrased somewhat differently and indeed probably deliberately pointed to a different set of policy goals. In these crucial though highly sensitive policy areas, the emphasis is on coordinating Member State activities rather than simply supporting their activities. Yet both support and coordination, in their different ways, can be listed under the heading of 'complementary powers'. What distinguishes these various areas of EC policy is that the power to adopt binding laws is essentially left in the hands of the Member States or their regions, and European intervention takes a different and often softer form. This is sometimes made explicit in the text of the EC Treaty. As mentioned above, the Community is permitted to take incentive measures in the field of education excluding any harmonization of national laws and regulations.[28]

---

[26] W Clement, *Europa gestalten—nicht verwalten. Die Kompetenzordnung der europäischen Union nach Nizza* (Berlin, Humboldt University, 12 February 2001), point IX (the English translation of this speech uses the term 'supplementary' rather than 'complementary'). Clement is currently prime minister of the *Länd* Nordrhein-Westfalen.

[27] But see H Bribosia, 'Subsidiarité et répartition des compétences entre la Communauté et ses Etats membres' (1992) Revue du marché unique européen 165, 183.

[28] See n 19 above.

Thus, what exists already within the EC system of competences is a kind of sub-category of shared (in our terms, complementary) powers, in which the primacy of the Member States' role is emphasized by the use of certain typical clauses. Again, if the current debate aims at clarification rather than radical reform, it would be useful to spell this out in the general introductory part of the Treaty. As with exclusive powers, the actual listing of policy areas fitting within this category is currently contestable and would be a matter for political debate. It is questionable, for instance, whether health still fits in this category. Since the Treaty of Amsterdam, certain aspects of health policy have been brought within the category of shared law-making powers of the EC (see Article 152(4)(a) and (b) EC), and the political evolution since Amsterdam gives further support for the view that health should no longer be considered as a merely complementary power of the EC. Nevertheless, it may be worthwhile attempting to list the complementary powers of the EC so as to distinguish them from other shared powers such as environmental or consumer policy, where there is less protection for the continued policy autonomy of the Member States.

A new Treaty article on categories of EC powers?

Consequently, our conclusion is that a mild reform of the Treaty text so as to codify the categories of EU powers along the lines suggested could indeed contribute towards clarifying the competence question. In a somewhat different context, Stephen Weatherill has argued that: 'recognition of the modern reality of shared competence... is capable of providing a means of correcting the misleading impression of an over-ambitious Community that is liable to damage national and local identity.'[29] The fact that EC powers are usually shared, and that some of them are merely complementary, is often ignored or misunderstood in political and media commentary on the European Union. Therefore, the existing legal situation could be usefully clarified by adding a new provision in the (basic) Treaty immediately after the current Article 5 EC. This new provision would confirm that, as a general rule, powers are shared between the EU and its Member States, and it would define the legal relationship between both levels of government in the field of shared powers. Such a new 'Article 5a' could be formulated as follows:

1. The European Community has exclusive powers in relation to international trade in goods and for the protection of marine biological resources [and for X

---

[29] S Weatherill, *Law and Integration in the European Union* (1995) 290.

or Y]. The Member States may act in these fields only when authorized or required to do so by the European Community.

2. The European Community has complementary powers in the fields of culture, education, vocational training, health, employment, economic policy and industrial policy [and X or Y]. The Member States retain their law-making powers in these fields. The European Community's role is to coordinate or to support Member State policies in these fields, in accordance with the principles of subsidiarity and proportionality.

3. In all other policy areas covered by this Treaty, the European Community and the Member States have shared law-making powers. The European Community exercises its powers in accordance with the principles of subsidiarity and proportionality. The Member States exercise their powers within the limits set by the other provisions of this Treaty and by secondary Community law.

The inclusion of this or a similarly worded Article in the Treaty would have the advantage of signalling clearly that shared powers are the norm, both at the present time and for the future. This view would be reinforced, rather than weakened, by the fact that no list of shared powers is given. The Article would also signal the continuing prevalence of Member State responsibility in a broad range of socially significant policy areas, while refraining from conveying the misleading message that the Member States have preserved, or could preserve, exclusive control over certain policy areas.

Reformulation or deletion of the functional competences?

The Laeken Declaration expressly asks whether Article 95 and Article 308 ought to be reviewed, in light of the twin challenges of preventing the 'creeping expansion of competences' from encroaching on national and regional powers, and yet allowing the EU to 'continue to be able to react to fresh challenges and developments and…to explore new policy areas'. One kind of reform would be to reduce the substantive scope of either or both Articles. There is no constitutional obstacle to a repatriation of powers.[30] If the Member States were to decide that powers which they had transferred to the EC in an earlier Treaty should now be returned to the States by means of a Treaty amendment, they have the power to do so.

---

[30] For a 'pre-Nice' discussion of the legal and political issues surrounding the transfer of EC powers back to the states, see D Obradovic, 'Repatriation of powers in the European Community' (1997) 34 CMLRev 59.

Both these Treaty articles contain functional competences. Whereas many other powers of the EC are defined in terms of a particular sector, which often serves as the heading for a distinct title or chapter in the treaty (such as agriculture, transport, environment, education), these powers are not so defined. Instead they are defined in terms of a cross-sectoral policy objective to be achieved which is, essentially, the establishment and functioning of the internal market. Particular legal bases are provided for each of the four freedoms and for the various aspects of competition policy which also comprise the internal market. The functional character of these powers implies that measures based on them will often impinge on policy fields that have not, as such, been entrusted to the EC or in which the Treaty gives the EC only a minor role. There are very many examples of this phenomenon in the legislative practice of the European Community. To illustrate but a few:

- In 1993, the EC adopted a directive on the return of works of art illegally removed from the territory of a Member State. This was an internal market measure, based on Article 100a (now 95), although it directly affects what many Member States define as cultural policy, for which the EC did not have a specific sectoral competence.
- The EC has adopted a number of directives on the recognition of diplomas. These are measures facilitating the free movement of professionals in the European Union, and are legally justified as such, but they also have a noticeable impact on the exercise of Member States' education policies.

Because of their particular nature, the functional powers have caused the greatest amount of political controversy and seem to be, more than any others, at the root of the demand for a 'more precise delimitation'. However, precisely because of their functional nature, such a more precise delimitation may also be more difficult to achieve. On the other hand, it may be exactly in the field of these functionally defined and hence potentially expansive powers that closer attention to monitoring their exercise could be paid. This need not necessarily be done only by strengthened ex-post judicial review, but could also be addressed by building in better institutional safeguards and by attempting to ensure that concerns such as those enunciated in the Amsterdam protocol on subsidiarity and proportionality are taken more seriously by the Commission and the Council, as well as by their committees and working groups. A commitment to considering systematically the impact of the exercise of these functionally defined powers on other reserved or protected Member State powers, whether in the field of health, education, culture or another, would be highly desirable. As the Amsterdam protocol demonstrates, however, the existence of guidelines at present seems to be insufficient to discipline the European institutions, and it may be that a specific commitment of the kind suggested above should be included within the definition of the functional powers themselves, and not only in a general subsidiarity-type provision or protocol.

The case of Article 95 EC

Article 95 EC permits the Community to adopt by qualified majority 'measures for the approximation of the provisions laid down by law, regulation or administrative action in Member States which have as their object the establishment and functioning of the internal market'. It was extensively used during the years following the Single European Act during the most intensive period of internal market construction and regulation. Since much of the core single market programme has been completed, however, this provision has been used in other less technical and more contentious areas, leading to a number of notable challenges such as those in the Tobacco Advertising and the Biotechnology cases.[31]

One limit to the use of Article 95 EC, however, is that its object must be the harmonization of national laws, which means that it cannot be used to do things which Member States cannot do separately (because of their limited territorial jurisdiction), like creating a new European form of intellectual property or a new Europe-wide company form.[32]

The text of Article 95 EC could be clarified somewhat by incorporating into it the two purposes for which, according to the case law of the Court of Justice, the European Community may act under that article. These purposes are the elimination of distortions of competition and the elimination of barriers to inter-state trade. In addition, a requirement could be added that the recitals of EC measures based on Article 95 should specifically indicate how the content of the measure is justified in terms of one of these two purposes.[33] The weak control thus far exercised by the Court of Justice in the somewhat similar context of considering whether the legislator has

---

[31] See Cases C-376/98 (n 1 above) and C-377/98 (n 23 above).

[32] Dashwood (n 2 above) 209. See Case C-377/98 (n 23 above) para 24.

[33] This procedural requirement is proposed by K Lenaerts, 'La Déclaration de Laeken: premier jalon d'une Constitution européenne?' (2002) 10 Journal des Tribunaux—Droit européen 29, 34.

addressed the question of the compliance of a legislative measure with the subsidiarity principle, in particular since the Court has not specifically required this to be demonstrated with any degree of evidentiary rigour in the recitals, suggests that it would be advisable to write a clear and express requirement of this kind into the text of Article 95 EC of the Treaty.

In order to clarify matters further, a separate paragraph on the nature of EC harmonization powers in the field of the internal market could be added. If the Treaty were to include a definition of shared powers, as suggested in the previous section, a separate paragraph could be included stating explicitly that internal market powers are shared powers and that, therefore, the EC must exercise these powers in accordance with the principles of subsidiarity and proportionality.

The case of Article 308 EC

Article 308 EC allows the European Community to adopt measures necessary for attaining the objectives of the Treaty, where no other, more specific powers can be used. It has thus served as a residual power to fill a particular kind of gap in the system of enumerated powers. The German Constitutional Court, in its *Maastricht* judgment, called it a 'competence extension provision' (*Kompetenzerweiterungsvorschrift*).[34] The Court of Justice has however insisted that this Article 'cannot serve as a basis for widening the scope of Community powers beyond the general framework created by the provisions of the Treaty as a whole'.[35] Despite these reassuring (and late appearing) words, there has been widespread concern, in particular amongst the *Länder*, that this article was used by the Council as a basis for the surreptitious erosion of Member State powers.[36] Various proposals for reform of Article 308 EC, which has long been viewed with suspicion by those calling for a clearer delimitation of Community competences and in particular by the German *Länder*, have been made before and during recent intergovernmental conferences. This question has now been placed explicitly on the post-Nice and post-Laeken agenda on future reform of the Union.

[34] For an English language translation of the judgment see [1994] 1 CMLR 57.
[35] Opinion 2/94 (n 6 above) para 30.
[36] For analyses of the use of Art 308 EC at different stages in the Community's history, see J Weiler 'The transformation of Europe' (1991) 100 Yale Law Journal 2403 and more recently M Bungenberg, *Artikel 235 EGV nach Maastricht: die Auswirkungen der Einheitlichen europäischen Akte und des Vertrages über die europäische Union auf die Handlungsbefugnis des Artikel 235 EGV (Artikel 308 EGV nF)* (1999).

A deletion of this Article would constitute a major constitutional change. It has served as the legal basis for about 700 EC legal acts so far. The argument often made is that Article 308 EC may have been useful in earlier stages of the European integration process, but that the EU is now an 'adult' organization with a large number of express powers, so that a residual power of this kind is no longer needed. A related and more pointed argument is that the disadvantages, in terms of the erosion of Member State powers, now outweigh the advantages, in terms of flexibility, of this provision.

These arguments can be questioned. Long-standing practice over the years demonstrates that, however precisely EC powers are sought to be defined in the Treaty, circumstances always arise in which all Member State governments seek to use Article 308 EC in order to address an issue of common concern for which the Treaty does not give the necessary powers. The value of a flexible clause like Article 308 EC was underlined by two related political events in the early 1990s: the reunification of Germany, and the changes in Central and Eastern Europe. In both cases, action by the EC was considered to be legally or politically necessary, but the existing Treaty system did not provide for adequate means of action. The Member States and the EC institutions were very willing to resort to what was then Article 235 EC in order to take swift action. A similar situation occurred with the third phase of Economic and Monetary Union. Despite the very detailed nature of the Maastricht Treaty provisions on EMU, there was no express legal basis for the introduction of the euro in the absence of a Council decision stating which Member States were to adopt the common currency; hence, the Euro Regulation (No 1103/97) had to be based, without any discord, on Article 235.

In the course of the last IGC, the Portuguese Presidency circulated a note in which it identified three areas of Community policy for which Article 308 EC was repeatedly used in the last decade and even after the Amsterdam Treaty: the establishment of Community agencies, non-trade cooperation with non-developing third states, and energy.[37] The Presidency therefore suggested the creation of a specific legal basis in the EC Treaty for all three areas, but agreement was reached on only one of the three. The Treaty of Nice will thus introduce a new Article 181a EC providing an express power to adopt 'economic, financial

---

[37] CONFER 4711/00 of 22 February 2000: http://db.consilium.eu.int/cig/default.as-p?lang=en/.

and technical cooperation measures with third countries'.[38] For the two other subjects identified, Article 308 EC will presumably continue to be used in the future. However, even if the Treaty of Nice had created an express legal basis for these matters also, it is very likely that Article 308 EC would again prove very useful for some other, as yet unidentified, purpose on which all States would readily agree, and yet which would not necessarily bring about the kind of fundamental constitutional or institutional change prohibited by the Court of Justice in Opinion 2/94. Article 308 EC has proved a useful tool throughout the EC's history. As we have argued, its usefulness has not necessarily diminished with the growth of express EC competences, and it can be responsibly used in a way which does not endeavour to amend the Treaty surreptitiously. In our view, its deletion would constitute a significant loss.

A less drastic option would be to reconsider its present formulation, either by tightening the substantive conditions for its use, for example by excluding the possibility of its exercise in a way which would impinge on aspects of specific Member State powers which are reserved or protected under other Treaty provisions. Secondly, new procedural requirements could be added, such as the assent of the European Parliament,[39] or some form of consultation of national parliaments.[40] In the context of this suggestion, however, it is worth noting that measures based on Article 308 EC have sometimes been rather urgent.

If Article 308 EC is to be modified, the deletion of the words 'in the operation of the common market' should also be considered.[41] They are the remnant of a time when, under the original Treaty of Rome, the powers of

---

[38] The text of Art 181a adds, in rather a puzzling way, that the EC can only take such action 'within its sphere of competence'. It is not clear to what extent the EC's powers are limited by the addition of these words.

[39] This was already suggested by 'some members' of the Reflection Group set up prior to the 1996 IGC; see para 125 of the Reflection Group's report. The European Parliament unsurprisingly supports such a reform.

[40] The degree of involvement of national parliaments in such matters is currently regulated in accordance with different national rules. Thus the European affairs committee of the Danish parliament takes a particularly critical look at EC proposals based on Art 308 EC, as do the Select Committees of the United Kingdom's House of Commons and House of Lords. The German law on the Cooperation of the Federation and the *Länder* in Matters Concerning the EU contains a special clause concerning draft EC measures based on Art 308 EC. For an English-language translation of this clause, see J Kokott, 'Federal States in federal Europe: the German *Länder* and problems of European integration' (1997) EPL 607, 629.

[41] For an argument to the contrary, see A Dashwood, 'The limits of European Community powers' (1996) 21 ELRev 113.

the EEC were essentially restricted to establishing and regulating the operation of the common market. Today, however, Article 308 EC is far more often used in situations which have only a very tenuous link with the operation of the common market, and these words have arguably now become unduly restrictive.[42] While this proposal would appear to liberalize the conditions for the use of Article 308 EC, contrary to the concerns expressed by the German *Länder*, it does not necessarily mean that other substantive and procedural conditions, such as those suggested in the previous paragraph, could or should not be added. However, what it does indicate is that a restriction on the exercise of a residual power which was drafted at the time the EEC was largely only a common market and not the more integrated social and political entity which it now is, may be inappropriate to the reality of today's EU.

New constraints of form or new policy options?

As we have argued in the introductory section to this chapter, the post-Nice mandate calling for a more precise delimitation and monitoring of powers cannot be addressed only by considering the actual existence and formal allocation of power in particular fields to the EU. Just as important, or in our view perhaps even more important, are the nature, scope and form of each type of power, and the institutional processes for both the exercise and the review of those powers.

We have set out above the various kinds of powers held by the EC and EU and categorized them according to whether they are exclusive, shared, or complementary to Member State powers, and to whether they incorporate particular kinds of limitation. Another way of delimiting the powers of the EU vis-à-vis the Member States however would be to specify what form particular powers should take, for example whether framework measures or soft law instruments should be used. While this could be said to relate more to the regulation of the exercise of powers rather than to the delimitation of the powers themselves, this distinction is a conceptual one which is not always of substantive significance. Further, when powers are defined and allocated according to a particular form or subject to particular procedural conditions, this will often also serve better to delimit the division of powers in question.

---

[42] For some recent Art 308 EC proposals, see COM(2000)898 on the funding of European political parties, and COM(2001)569 on freezing suspected terrorist assets.

There have always been examples in the EC Treaty of injunctions addressed to the institutions to exercise their powers (in a certain manner), and also prohibitions against acting in a certain manner. Several legal bases, such as Article 94 (ex 100) EC, specified that the EC could act only by means of a directive, and therefore not by means of a regulation. This distinction was evidently meaningful to the drafters of the Treaty of Rome, since directives seemed intended to leave more discretion in implementation to the Member States, even if it has become less meaningful today, in view of the normative density and enhanced direct enforceability of directives. Another limitation as to the available type of legal instrument is contained in Article 293 (ex 220) EC, which states that the Member States may, in certain fields, conclude international conventions among themselves, to be separately ratified by their parliaments. However, in the practice of the institutions and the Member States since 1957, this article was not interpreted as limiting the possibility for the use of other EC instruments to deal with the matters listed therein, provided that these matters came within the scope of another legal basis in the EC Treaty. Today, and particularly since the Treaty of Amsterdam included a specific Community competence to deal with civil law in Article 65 EC, the role of Article 293 has sharply declined. However, the optional use of the instrument of a convention between Member States—which, as a more traditional instrument of international law, may be thought to preserve greater domestic autonomy and control over European policy than other instruments—has been revived, and is quite frequently used in the context of the third pillar.[43]

These examples show that the formal or instrumental delimitation of EU competences is a longstanding and familiar EC legal device. More recently, since the Maastricht and Amsterdam Treaties in particular, there has been more frequent use of the related but broader device of delimiting EU competences by circumscribing the kind of policy action which can be undertaken, or by providing only for very soft forms of law. Consider, for example, the two different kinds of complementary EU power which we identified above, namely supplementary powers and coordinating powers. Article 149 EC as enacted by the Treaty of Amsterdam provides an instance of the first of these, in accordance with which the Community is permitted to adopt incentive measures in the field of education 'excluding any har-

---

[43] B de Witte, 'Chameleonic Member States: differentiation by means of partial and parallel international agreements' in B de Witte, D Hanf and E Vos (eds), *The Many Faces of Differentiation in EU Law* (2001) 231, 248–251.

monisation of the laws and regulations of the Member States'.[44] These provisions do not imply that entire policy areas fall outside the sphere of EC powers, but they prescribe more modestly that certain means of intervention in certain areas are excluded.[45] They do not require, or proscribe, the use of a particular legal instrument, but they prohibit a particular degree of policy intensity, namely the harmonization of national laws.

An important example of the second of the two kinds of complementary EU power can be seen in a somewhat different and increasingly prevalent form of policy-instrumental delimitation which has become known, since the Lisbon European Council of 2000, as the open method of coordination (OMC). This policy approach, which was first adopted in the Maastricht Treaty for the purpose of coordinating national macro-economic policies, was applied in a somewhat different manner to employment policy by the Treaty of Amsterdam. Since the Lisbon summit popularized this soft policy approach under the name of OMC, it has been applied to a growing number of policy areas, including social exclusion, education and pensions, and has been proposed in a number of others where the possibility of adopting harder and stronger legal measures already exists, such as immigration and asylum policy. The emphasis within those policy areas to which the OMC is applied is not so much on prescribing the use of a particular kind of soft legal instrument as it is on the detailed formulation of a soft and quite elaborate decision-making and implementation process. It is a strategy which leaves a considerable amount of policy autonomy to the Member States, and which blends the setting of guidelines (involving the input of a range of existing and new institutional actors) at EU level with the elaboration of Member State action plans at national level in an iterative process which is intended to bring about greater coordination as well as learning in these policy fields.[46]

Apart from describing and classifying these existing categories of complementary EU power, as we have suggested above, the current constitutional reform could also lead to a more detailed specification of the form that EU measures may take. Thus, if an action programme, recommendation or other

---

[44] See for other such provisions n 19 above.

[45] The effect of these 'no harmonisation clauses' is to be extended to the field of external trade by the new text of Art 133(6) EC as amended by the Nice Treaty.

[46] See further chapter by Sycszczak in this volume; J Scott and D Trubek, 'Mind the gap: law and new approaches to governance in Europe' (2002) ELJ (forthcoming) and O Gerstenberg, 'The new Europe: part of the problem—or part of the solution to the problem?' (2002) 22 OJLS 563.

form of soft law is mandated in a particular area, for example, the autonomy of the Member States in that area will be hindered less than if more formally binding or directly effective obligations can be adopted. Similarly, it could be specified that in a given policy area, only framework measures should be taken at the Community level, or that the open method of coordination should be applied. On the other hand, it should be acknowledged that there is a real risk involved in the inscription of such formal constraints on Community policy-making into the text of the Treaties. There is a danger that they could impose a straitjacket which might inordinately hinder the EU's ability to 'react to fresh challenges'. While the process of retrospective constitutionalization of spontaneous legal and policy innovations is a distinguished one in EC and EU history, we should nonetheless acknowledge the risk of rigidity and ossification inherent in this strategy.

Conclusion

To sum up the observations and suggestions made in this chapter, we have argued that the adoption of a *Kompetenzkatalog* would not be a desirable step for the EU. An examination of the concerns underlying the 'delimitation of powers' debate suggests to us that many of these could be addressed without radical changes being made. We would advocate the clarification and articulation of the Community's exclusive powers, and a listing of the broad categories of powers, including what we have described as a sub-category (within the category of shared powers) of complementary powers. Some of the 'troublesome' functional powers (Articles 95 and 308 EC) could be slightly amended by appropriate additions to the text of the Treaty, but we have argued that their deletion would be an unnecessary and disproportionate step in relation to the nature of the concerns raised by their exercise. Finally, we have discussed the constraints of form inherent in the structure of some of the existing complementary competences—the supplementary and the coordinating powers in particular. We have suggested that while these have proved to be useful mechanisms for permitting the Member States to achieve a degree of Europeanization of important and interdependent policy fields without losing significant domestic control over these areas, one of the risks of trying to turn some of these facilitative mechanisms into formal Treaty-based constraints on EU action may be that their very advantages of flexibility, responsiveness and adaptability may be lost.

13

The EU and Democracy—Lawful and Legitimate Intervention in the Domestic Affairs of States?

Nanette Neuwahl and Steven Wheatley *

Introduction

This chapter examines the nature of democracy in the European Union and its legal order. Much of the current discussion about the EU and democracy is concerned with the institutions of the EC/EU itself, rather than with its impact on the democratic systems of Member States and third countries. This chapter considers the expediency of procedures whereby democratic principles can be enforced against States within the framework of the EU. Particular attention is paid to the sanctions imposed by the 14 EU Member States against Austria throughout 2000, and the 'enforcement' of democratic principles by the EU in its relations with those States applying for membership of the Union. Finally, attention is drawn to possible areas of reform.

The principles of democracy

A democratic regime is one in which political power is based on the will of the people, and which provides all citizens with the opportunity to participate equally in the political life of the state. There is no universal legal

* The authors would like to thank Fiona Beveridge, University of Liverpool, Haluk Kabaalioglu, Chairman of Turkish Universities Association in EC Studies (TUNEACS) and Allan Rosas, Principal Legal Adviser, European Commission Legal Service, for their comments. The views expressed, and any errors, remain, of course, the responsibility of the authors.

obligation to introduce democracy.[1] Any repudiation of the democratically
expressed will of the population of a State will constitute a serious violation
of the internal aspect of that people's right to self-determination.[2] The road
to democracy, then, is one-way. This is recognized in Europe where the
States and international organizations have made it clear that democracy is
the only legitimate form of government.[3] The point is made clear for
Member States of the EU in the Treaty on European Union: 'The Union
is founded on the principles of liberty, democracy, respect for human rights
and fundamental freedoms, and the rule of law, principles which are
common to the Member States'.[4] Further, one of the objectives of the
European Union's Common Foreign and Security Policy is 'to develop
and consolidate democracy and the rule of law, and respect for human rights
and fundamental freedoms'.[5]

The requirements of democratic government may be achieved through a
variety of mechanisms and institutions. Democracy, in the words of the UN
Secretary General, is 'not a model to be copied but a goal to be attained'.[6] To
associate democracy with particular institutions is to 'elevate a means into
an end, [and] to confuse an instrument with its purpose'.[7] Democracy is
defined primarily by reference to its underlying principles (namely, popular
sovereignty and political equality), and only secondarily in terms of the
institutions which embody them. A democratic State is one in which political power is based on the will of the people, and in which all citizens have
the opportunity to participate in the political life.[8] From these requirements
a number of characteristics of democracy follow—and these will be
common to all democratic regimes.

Free and fair elections

Democratic legitimacy depends upon the will of the people to their
being governed by those in power. It is impossible to conceive of a demo-

---

[1]   See, on this point, G Fox and B Roth (eds), *Democratic Governance and International Law*
(2000) passim.

[2]   Warsaw Declaration: Towards a Community of Democracies (2000) 39 ILM 1306.

[3]   S Wheatley, 'Democracy in international law: a European perspective' (2002) 51 ICLQ
225, 234–235.

[4]   Art 6 (1) TEU.

[5]   Art 11 TEU. See also Art 177 EC.

[6]   UN Secretary General, 'Support by the United Nations system of the efforts of
Governments to promote and consolidate new or restored democracies', UN Doc A/52/
513, 21 October 1997, para 27.

[7]   D Beetham, *Democracy and Human Rights* (1999) 3.

[8]   J Crawford, *Democracy in International Law* (1994) 4.

cratic State which did not seek to ascertain that will through free and fair elections. The requirement of electoral legitimacy is contained in the Universal Declaration on Human Rights;[9] in the Universal Declaration on Democracy;[10] in the Warsaw Declaration: Towards a Community of Democracies;[11] in the work of the Organization for Security and Cooperation in Europe (OSCE);[12] and that of the UN Commission on Human Rights.[13] Moreover, it is specifically required by both the International Covenant on Civil and Political Rights,[14] and the European Convention on Human Rights.[15] No particular electoral system need be introduced,[16] although the international instruments make clear that all must provide for regular elections, which are free and fair, with universal and equal suffrage, open to multiple parties, conducted by secret ballot, monitored by independent electoral authorities, and free of fraud and intimidation.

The purpose of elections is to ensure that the will of the people is the basis of the authority of government. Elections guarantee every citizen the right to participate in a system of collective decision-making that ultimately determines policy, leadership, and authority.[17] As a minimum, there must be free and fair elections for the legislative branch of government,[18] which should possess the requisite powers to legislate, and the means to hold the executive to account.[19] The composition of the legislature(s) represents the clearest manifestation of the will of the people. Consequently, it is important that their members, which will normally number many hundreds, as far as

---

[9] See Art 21(3), Universal Declaration on Human Rights: GA Resolution 217A (III).

[10] Inter-Parliamentary Union's Universal Declaration on Democracy (adopted without a vote by the Inter-Parliamentary Council at its 161st session (Cairo, 16 September 1997)), para 12: (2000) 1 Netherlands Quarterly of Human Rights 127. The IPU, established in 1889, is the world organization of parliaments of sovereign States. Over a hundred national parliaments are currently members: http://www.ipu.org/.

[11] Warsaw Declaration (n 2 above).

[12] See CSCE Charter of Paris for a New Europe (1991) 30 ILM 190, and Document of the Copenhagen Meeting of the Conference on the Human Dimension of the CSCE, (1990) 29 ILM 1318, para 6.

[13] See UN Commission on Human Rights, 'Promoting and consolidating democracy', UN Doc E/CN.4/RES/2000/47, adopted 25 April 2000, preamble and para 1(d).

[14] Art 25 ICCPR (1966).

[15] Art 3 of the First Protocol, of the European Convention on Human Rights (1952) (P1-3, ECHR).

[16] *Case of Mathieu-Mohin and Clerfayt* Series A No 113, (1987) 10 EHRR 1 para 54.

[17] J Waldron, *Law and Disagreement* (1999) 233.

[18] G Nodia, 'Nationalism and democracy' in L Diamond and M Plattner (eds), *Nationalism, Ethnic Conflict and Democracy* (1994) 3, 5.

[19] Universal Declaration on Democracy (n 10 above) para 11.

possible, represent the diversity of the society,[20] reflecting what the Canadian Supreme Court has called 'the diversity of [the] social mosaic'.[21]

The right to seek to influence decisions and to be heard

In addition to the periodic right to participate in elections, citizens enjoy, without distinction, an ongoing general right to participate in, and seek to influence the outcomes of, decision-making processes. A democratic government is obliged to listen and take into account the representations made to it on particular issues. All voices must be heard and listened to, particularly those of persons likely to be affected by particular policies and decisions.[22] The importance of participation is highlighted by the United Nations Commission on Human Rights: democracy requires that 'the widest participation in the democratic dialogue by all sectors and actors of society must be promoted in order to come to agreements on appropriate solutions to the social, economic and cultural problems of a society.'[23]

The governing majority cannot justify indifference to minority views by reference to its democratic mandate to govern according to its policies and ideologies. In a democracy the views of a majority cannot always prevail: 'a balance must be achieved which ensures the fair and proper treatment of minorities and avoids any abuse of a dominant position'.[24] There is no real democracy if certain sections of the population are not able to participate in the democratic processes.[25] Having regard to the interests of minorities involves more than listening to their interests and opinions, it requires that they be taken into account when decisions are reached.

---

[20] See also UN Commission on Human Rights, 'Ways and means of overcoming obstacles to the establishment of a democratic society and requirements for the maintenance of democracy', adopted 7 March 1995, UN Doc E/CN.4/RES/1995/60, preamble.

[21] [1991] 2 SCR Reference re Prov Electoral Boundaries (Sask) 158.

[22] S Marks, *The Riddle of all Constitutions* (2000) 60.

[23] UN Commission on Human Rights, 'Ways and means of overcoming obstacles to the establishment of a democratic society' (n 20 above) preamble.

[24] *Chassagnou and others v France*, Reports of Judgments and Decisions 1999-III, (2000) 29 EHRR 615, para 112.

[25] See OSCE Report on the Linguistic Rights of Persons Belonging to National Minorities in the OSCE Area: http://www.osce.org/inst/hcnm/index.html/ See further N Neuwahl, 'The more the merrier? Hungarian and Romany minorities in Slovakia' (2000) 22 Liverpool Law Review 21, 27.

Politics in a democracy

Democratic government requires institutional structures within which the will of the people may be discerned through political dialogue and debate. Politics is not, however, an individual occupation. Individuals participate in the political processes through political parties and pressure groups.[26] Political parties are of central importance as they provide organizational structures through which individuals can both seek to gain political office, and participate effectively in political debate.[27] The UN Human Rights Committee has made clear that the right of citizens to vote presupposes a right to stand for election as members of a political party.[28] This ensures that the electorate has a free choice of candidates, allowing them to choose between a plurality of political ideas.[29] Individuals must enjoy the freedom to establish political parties, and those organizations should be provided with the necessary legal guarantees to enable them to compete with each other on a basis of equality.[30] The rights of political parties are guaranteed by the effective application of the human rights to free association and expression,[31] with the European Court of Human Rights making clear that it will be difficult for the State to justify restrictions on their activities.[32]

Equally important to the right of freedom of association is that of expression. Democracy, according to the European Court of Human Rights, 'thrives on freedom of expression'.[33] Indeed, the German Federal

---

[26] Legitimate political activity includes the freedom to debate public affairs, to hold peaceful demonstrations and meetings, to criticize and oppose, to publish political material, and to advertise political ideas: see General Comment 25 (57), adopted by the Human Rights Committee: UN Doc CCPR/C/21/Rev1/Add7 (1996) para 26.

[27] *United Communist Party of Turkey and Others v Turkey* Reports of Judgments and Decisions 1998-I, (1998) 26 EHRR 121 para 44. See also Art 191 EC, as amended by the Nice Treaty; 'Progress review and recommendations', adopted by the Third International Conference of the New or Restored Democracies on Democracy and Development held at Bucharest 2–4 Sept. 1997, in which 80 States participated (UN Doc A/52/334, 11 September 1997).

[28] General Comment 25 (n 26 above) para 12.

[29] ibid, para 15.

[30] Copenhagen Document (n 12 above) para 7.6.

[31] Although not expressly mentioned in Art 11 ECHR on the right to freedom of association, the European Court of Human Rights has confirmed that, as a form of association essential to the proper functioning of democracy, political parties fall within its scope: *United Communist Party of Turkey and others v Turkey* Reports of Judgments and Decisions 1998-I, (1998) 26 EHRR 121 para 25.

[32] ibid, para 46.

[33] *Socialist Party and others v Turkey* Reports of Judgments and Decisions 1998-III, (1998) 27 EHRR 51 para 45.

Constitutional Court has argued that the essence of democracy is the continuous free debate between opposing social forces, interests and ideas. Through this, political goals become clarified, and a public opinion emerges which forms the beginnings of political intentions.[34] Informed participation in political debate is then an essential component of democratic government; without it 'a true democracy cannot grow and prosper'.[35] Although freedom of political debate is important for all citizens, the European Court of Human Rights has recognized that it is particularly important for political parties. Political parties and their active members, represent their electorate, draw attention to their preoccupations and defend their interests.[36] Interference with their freedom of expression calls, in the words of the Court, 'for the closest scrutiny', particularly when the politician is a member of an opposition party.[37] The same point has been made about elected representatives.[38]

Freedom of political expression applies not only to ideas that are favourably received, but also those that offend, shock or disturb: 'such are the demands of that pluralism, tolerance and broadmindedness without which there is no "democratic society" '.[39] There must be open debate, with citizens able to express their ideas, including unpopular ones, free from government interference.[40] There can be no justification for hindering a political group solely because it seeks to debate contentious issues or propose solutions to difficult problems.[41] This requirement applies not only against the State, but also against other political parties and activists. Democracy requires a right to be free from intimidation, which is not defined solely by reference to acts of, or threats of, physical violence. In Austria, the systematic use of libel

---

[34] *Brunner v European Union Treaty* (German Federal Constitutional Court) [1994] 1 CMLR 57 para 41.

[35] UN Secretary-General, 'Support by the United Nations system of the efforts of Governments to promote and consolidate new or restored democracies', UN Doc A/53/554, 20 October 1998, para 25.

[36] *Socialist Party and Others v Turkey* Reports of Judgments and Decisions 1998-III, (1998) 27 EHRR 51 para 41.

[37] *Incal v Turkey* Reports of Judgments and Decisions 1998-IV, (1998) 29 EHRR 449 para 46.

[38] *Jerusalem v Austria*, judgment of 27 February 2001 paras 36 and 40.

[39] *Ahmed and others v United Kingdom* Reports of Judgments and Decisions 1998-VI, (2000) 29 EHRR 1 para 55.

[40] G Klosko, *Democratic Procedures and Liberal Consensus* (2000) 43.

[41] *Socialist Party and Others v Turkey* Reports of Judgments and Decisions 1998-III, (1998) 27 EHRR 51 para 45. Also, *United Communist Party of Turkey and Others v Turkey* Reports of Judgments and Decisions 1998-I, (1998) 26 EHRR 121 para 57.

procedures by members of the *Freiheits Partei Österreich* to suppress criticism (especially after they formed part of the federal Austrian government) can be characterized as a form of intimidation.[42] A democratic system of government requires that a diverse range of political projects be proposed and debated.[43] There is little scope for restrictions on this political debate on issues of public interest.[44] As the European Court of Human Rights made clear in *Socialist Party and Others v Turkey:*

[The] fact that...a political programme is considered incompatible with the current principles and structures...does not make it incompatible with the rules of democracy. It is of the essence of democracy to allow diverse political programmes to be proposed and debated, even those that call into question the way a State is currently organised, *provided that they do not harm democracy itself.*[45]

The only limits on the rights to freedom of political expression and association are then those that seek to protect democracy and the democratic system. Thus a political party may campaign for a change in the law on two conditions: (1) the means used to that end must in every respect be legal and democratic; (2) the change proposed must itself be compatible with fundamental democratic principles.[46] These limitations may seek to protect the cardinal principles of democracy: popular sovereignty,[47] and political equality. Thus the State may proscribe political parties which adopt 'an ambiguous stance with regard to the use of force to gain power and retain it'.[48] Further, it may limit the rights of parties that seek to promote hatred between the different groups of society. Democracy can be intolerant of intolerance of the

---

[42] M Ahtisaari, J Frowein and M Oreja, 'Report on the Austrian Government's Commitment to the Common European Values, in Particular Concerning the Rights of Minorities, Refugees and Immigrants, and the Evolution of the Political Nature of the FPÖ' (The Wise Men Report) (2001) 40 ILM 101, para 103.

[43] *Case of Freedom and Democracy Party* Reports of Judgments and Decisions 1999-VIII, para 41.

[44] *Wingrove v United Kingdom* Reports of Judgments and Decisions 1996-V, (1996) 24 EHRR 1 para 58.

[45] *Socialist Party and others v Turkey* Reports of Judgments and Decisions 1998-III, (1998) 27 EHRR 51 para 47 (emphasis added).

[46] *Refah Partisi and others v Turkey,* judgment of 31 July 2001, (2002) 35 EHRR 3, para 47.

[47] See *Ahmed and others v United Kingdom* Reports of Judgments and Decisions 1998-VI, (2000) 29 EHRR 1 para 54; *Baskaya and Okçuoglu v Turkey,* Reports of Judgments and Decisions 1999-IV, (2001) 31 EHRR 10 para 62; *Incal v Turkey* Reports of Judgments and Decisions 1998-IV, (1998) 29 EHRR 449 para 58; see also *Sener v Turkey,* judgment 18 July 2000, para 45.

[48] *Refah Partisi and others v Turkey,* judgment of 31 July 2001, (2002) 35 EHRR 3, para 81.

equal value of all within the political community.[49] The Strasbourg authorities have repeatedly found inadmissible complaints from neo-Nazi organizations regarding limits on their freedom of expression. Such limitations are
justified by reference to the prohibition on the abuse of rights contained in
Article 17 of the European Convention on Human Rights.[50]

Enforcement in the framework of the EU

In Article 6(1) TEU 'democracy' is raised to a basic principle of European
Union law. This section deals with the enforcement of that principle as
against EU Member States, and in relation to those States applying for
membership of the Union. The European Union continually stresses democracy in dialogue with third countries in démarches in the framework
of the Common Foreign and Security Policy, and democracy, together
with human rights, is the subject of countless initiatives and support measures in third countries,[51] and also of conditions in bilateral trade agreements.[52]

Accession strategy

Article 49 TEU, introduced by the Treaty of Amsterdam, provides that any
European State which respects the principles set out in Article 6(1) may

[49] Support for this position may be found in a number of international human rights
instruments. See, inter alia, Art 20(2), ICCPR (1966); 'The incompatibility between democracy and racism', UN Commission on Human Rights, UN Doc E/CN.4/RES/2000/40,
preamble; International Convention on the Elimination of All Forms of Racial Discrimination (1966), Art 4; GA Resolution 55/82, 'Measures to be taken against racial discrimination
or ethnic exclusiveness and xenophobia, including, in particular, neo-Nazism', adopted 26
February 2001, UN Doc A/RES/55/82, para 3.
[50] See, eg, *Glimmerveen and Hagenbeek v the Netherlands* App. Nos. 8384/78 and 8406/78
(1979) 18 DR 187.
[51] See Communication from the Commission to the Council and the EP on the European
Union's Role in Promoting Human Rights and Democratisation in Third Countries, COM
(2001) 252 final, Brussels 8 May 2001: http://europa.eu.int/comm/external_relations/
human_rights/doc/com01_252_en.pdf/. See, also, 'Report on the Implementation of the
European Initiative for Human Rights and Democracy in 2000', SEC (2001) 803, Brussels,
22 May 2001. European Commission, 'Report from the Commission on Measures Intended
to Promote Observance of Human Rights and Democratic Principles in External Relations
for 1996–1999', COM (2001) 726, Brussels, 4 November 2000. Further, European Commission, 'European Initiative for Democracy and Human Rights, Macro Projects Compendium
2001': http://europa.eu.int/comm/europeaid/reports/compendium2001macro.pdf/.
[52] European Commission, 'The Inclusion of Respect for Democratic Principles and
Human Rights in Agreements Between the Community and Third Countries', COM (95) final.

apply to become a member of the Union. Democracy is thus made a precondition and a legal criterion for accession, if not explicitly for continuation of membership. Democracy has been introduced as a general condition for accession negotiations since its articulation in the 'Copenhagen criteria'. The European Council established in June 1993 that EU membership required that the candidate country had achieved stability of institutions guaranteeing democracy, the rule of law, human rights and respect for and protection of minorities.[53]

Compliance with these Copenhagen criteria is assessed on an annual basis.[54] The Annual Reports on Turkey are always used to remind the country of the need for improvement in matters of human rights and democracy.[55] As regards Slovakia, the European Commission recommended deferring early accession negotiations on the grounds that democracy was not fully guaranteed in that country, a point largely evidenced by the treatment of minorities under the Meciar regime.[56] Thus, whereas a State's obligation to protect and promote the identity of its minority groups is not an explicit condition of EU membership,[57] those aspects that come under the ambit of democracy are. As Slovakia failed to fulfil the democracy test, it was excluded from the first wave of applicants agreed at the Luxembourg Council.[58]

The introduction of Article 49 TEU is not merely a reaffirmation of the EU's support for democratic forms of government, it is also the entrenchment of that policy into a legal commitment to be applied in the accession process. It follows that national parliaments are required to prevent acces-

[53] Conclusions of the Presidency, Copenhagen European Council, June 1993.

[54] European Commission, DG Enlargement, Strategy Paper, Regular Reports from the Commission on Progress towards Accession by each of the candidate countries, 8 November 2000: http://europa.eu.int/comm/enlargement/report_11_00/index.htm/.

[55] On Turkey's progress towards accession, see: http://europa.eu.int/comm/enlargement/turkey/index.htm/.

[56] Bull EC Suppl 9/97, 19–20.

[57] cf Art 6(1) taken together with Art 49 TEU. On minority protection within the European Union see, inter alia, M Estebanez, 'The protection of national or ethnic, religious and linguistic minorities' in N Neuwahl and A Rosas (eds), *The European Union and Human Rights* (1994) 135; G Toggenburg, 'A rough orientation through a delicate relationship: the European Union's endeavours for (its) minorities' (2000) 4 EIoP no 16, http://eiop.or.at/eiop/texte/2000-016a.htm/; B de Witte, 'The European Community and its minorities' in C Brölmann (ed), *Peoples and Minorities in International Law* (1993) 167. On EU activity for the protection of minorities external to the Union, see G Pentassuglis, 'The EU and the protection of minorities: the case of Eastern Europe' (2001) 12 EJIL 3.

[58] 2000 Regular Report on Slovakia's Progress towards Accession, 8 November 2000: http://europa.eu.int/comm/enlargement/slovakia/index.htm/.

sion by a State acting in breach of the principles on which the Union is based. Whether they always do so is open to question. The confusion over Cyprus demonstrates that policy-makers sometimes gloss over the issue of the fulfilment of the criterion.

'Repressive' action

In Amsterdam a 'repressive' procedure was introduced into the TEU with the applications by former communist States of Central and Eastern Europe in mind.[59] Recognizing the scale of the impending political and economic transformations, it was realized that premature enlargement could undermine the stability of the Union itself.[60] The provisions were supplemented in Nice by an 'early warning system'.[61] Article 7 TEU sets out a procedure for the Council to determine the existence of a serious and persistent breach by a Member State of the principles on which the European Union is founded—as per Article 6(1) TEU. One of these principles is democracy. Article 7 TEU, and Article 309 EC, thus constitute a legally binding agreement as to the nature of the government within Member States of the EU. Violation of this principle raises the possibility of the introduction of significant sanctions against the State concerned, although these will probably not extend to termination of membership.[62] European integration is about people, not just about governments. The integration process is irreversible. In the absence of express provisions to the contrary, once a State is a member of the Union, it is permanently in.[63] Blocking of diplomatic

[59] The term repressive is used here in contrast to the 'preventive action' which may be taken against prospective Member States before accession.

[60] J Gower, 'The Charter of Fundamental Rights and EU enlargement: consolidating democracy or imposing new hurdles?' in Federal Trust (ed), *The EU Charter of Fundamental Rights, Text and Commentaries* (2000) 225, 228.

[61] The Treaty of Nice introduced a new para 1 to Art 7 TEU: 'On a reasoned proposal by one third of the Member States, by the European Parliament or by the Commission, the Council, acting by a majority of four-fifths of its members after obtaining the assent of European Parliament, may determine that there is a clear risk of a serious breach by a Member State of the principles mentioned in Art 6(1), and address appropriate recommendations to that State. Before making such a determination, the Council shall hear the Member State in question and, acting in accordance with the same procedure, may call on independent persons to submit within a reasonable time limit a report on the situation in the Member State in question'.

[62] A Verhoeven, 'How democratic need European Union members be? Some thoughts after Amsterdam' (1998) 23 ELRev 217, 223. Cf authors cited there.

[63] Theoretically it would be possible to make the maintenance of democracy an explicit requirement in the new acts of accession, yet this would in effect create a two-speed Europe which may not be expedient.

relations and suspension of rights are, however, among the possibilities. The Council, acting by a qualified majority (disregarding the vote of the Member State in question), may suspend certain of the rights deriving from the application of the EU Treaty to the Member State in question (Article 7(2) TEU). It is explicitly provided that this may include the voting rights of the representatives of the government of the Member State in the Council.[64] Article 309 EC regulates action that can be taken in the field of the EC Treaty in a virtually identical way. This was necessary because, by virtue of Article 47 TEU, provisions of the Treaty on European Union do not affect the EC Treaty unless explicitly provided for.

None of the above-mentioned procedures has ever been used. It remains the case that the main avenue for securing democracy rights in EU Member States will be through national courts and by application to the European Court of Human Rights in Strasbourg.[65] The Court of Justice of the European Communities can also be called upon where it can be argued that the application of EC law is affected by a breach of a fundamental principle of law common to the legal systems of the Member States.[66] As a result, many issues of democracy will be solved without the need for the application of sanctions under Articles 7 TEU and 309 EC.

In determining a violation of the obligations that follow from a commitment to democratic government, the elections aspect is relatively straightforward. It is more difficult to ascertain when the other aspects of democratic government (freedom of political activity and debate, and right to participate in the decision-making processes) have been breached, and when they have been breached to a sufficient degree to occasion a violation of an international obligation. In the EU, only the most serious and persistent breaches are internationalized. For 'non-serious' breaches of democratic obligations, States must rely on their right to take action under general

---

[64] When taking the decision, the Council is, however, always obliged to 'take into account' the possible consequences of a suspension on the rights and obligations of natural and legal persons.

[65] eg *Case of Matthews v the United Kingdom*, Reports of Judgments and Decisions 1999-I, (1999) 28 EHRR 361, on the failure by the United Kingdom to organize European elections in Gibraltar.

[66] See, inter alia, N Reich, 'A European Constitution for citizens: reflections on the rethinking of Union and Community law' (1997) 3 ELJ 129; B de Witte, 'Community law and national constitutional values' (1991) 1 LIEI 1; B de Witte, 'The past and future role of the European Court of Justice in the protection of human rights' in P Alston (ed), *The European Union and Human Rights* (2000) 859. For Court of Justice case law on the principle of democracy, see eg Case 138/79 *Roquette Frères v Council* [1980] ECR 3333; and Case C-300/89, *Commission v Council* (Titanium Dioxide) [1991] ECR I-2867.

international law. The form and structures of government are normally only a matter for the State concerned.[67] Only where States (as in Southern Rhodesia and South Africa) introduced racist minority rule has the international community traditionally considered the nature of the regime problematic.[68] International law does not, though, preclude States from agreeing an exception to the principle of non-interference, as in the Statute of the Council of Europe,[69] which provides for the expulsion of a Member in case of serious breaches of agreed principles including the rule of law and human rights. In the absence of internationally agreed norms, States do not have any legitimate interest in the internal political system of another State, and the imposition of any sanctions to encourage reform would be both illegitimate and unlawful. Where sanctions are introduced they must be within the limits of proportionality,[70] and it may be doubted whether the sanctions by the 14 against Austria, which were high profile and lasted many months, fulfilled this requirement.

But does the existence of Article 7 TEU and 309 EC not preclude EU Member States from undertaking individual or collective action against another Member State in cases of breach of obligations relating to the nature of the democratic government in that State—as in case of the sanctions imposed against Austria by the 14 Member States?[71] We think not. If this were the case, the clauses might well be redundant in practice, as the mechanism provided for might be debilitated by disagreement over what constitutes a serious and persistent breach by a Member State, as opposed to a minor and occasional infringement. There is no objective way of establishing, for instance, whether a practice of racial discrimination in local elections amounts to a serious breach attributable to a Member State. These are significant questions at a time when right-wing political parties are enjoying a resurgence in their electoral fortunes in many EU states. Moreover, the EU

[67] See the *Nicaragua* case (Merits) ICJ Rep 1986 14, para 261.

[68] This position has changed in recent years: see, generally, G Fox and B Roth (eds), *Democratic Governance and International Law* (2000).

[69] See Arts 8, 3 and 1 of the Statute of the Council of Europe.

[70] Proportionality presupposes that a peaceful settlement was attempted first, and in case of failure, that sanctions should be proportionate to the breach and do not go further (or last longer) than what is required to remedy the situation.

[71] The sanctions which Austria's 14 EU partners applied following the inclusion of the FPÖ in the Government consisted of the suspension of bilateral official contacts at the political level; the reception of Austrian Ambassadors in EU capitals only on a technical level; and the withholding of support for Austrian candidates for positions in international organizations. See M Merlingen, C Mudde and U Sedelmeier, 'The right and the righteous? European norms, domestic politics and the sanctions against Austria' (2001) 39 JCMS 59.

system may be paralysed by disagreement among the Member States both about the severity of the offence, and the type of reaction the situation calls for. Further, if the adoption of the EU mechanisms precluded the exercise of other rights under general international law, it might leave Member States without the possibility of a rapid response to particularly heinous offences.

The inter-state obligations of Member States of the European Union do not solely arise out of membership of the EU. Obligations under general and European international law when breached give rise to a right to impose sanctions in accordance with those legal regimes. There is no evidence from the adoption of the agreed procedures in the TEU that the Member States were prepared to agree on the internationalization of a principle only to relinquish the right to assess compliance with it, as this would defeat the purpose of the provisions. This is no small matter for the EU. It is not merely a question of intervention for the sake of democracy. It is the EU integration process itself that is at stake. In the advanced state of integration the EU has reached, instability within one country can have a detrimental effect on the functioning of the system as a whole. Furthermore, there is no encompassing judicial mechanism for supervising action or non-action by the Council in relation to the enforcement of democratic principles.[72] Therefore, there is no guarantee of the rule of law, at least, no guarantee of legal certainty or equity. This should be taken as an indication that when regulating enforcement of the Union's foundations, there was no attempt at regulating this area comprehensively. Consequently, the better view seems to be that action by Member States, or a number of them, under international law is not precluded by the existence of a common procedure. In EU law, therefore, there are more substantive than procedural restrictions.

The exception to this general position is the circumstance in which the proposed countermeasure is incompatible with EC law. It is well established that EC law overrides national law, and it is generally assumed that EC law cannot be affected by agreements reached between some of the Member States. As a result, rights of Member States arising under the EC Treaty can only be affected by virtue of the procedure under Article 309 EC.[73] Further,

---

[72] The jurisdiction of the Court of Justice is triggered if the EC Treaty is affected. See Art 46 TEU, and Arts 309, 230 and 234 EC. Cf A Arnull, *The European Union and its Court of Justice* (1999) 218.

[73] Sanctions by the EC against Third States are regulated primarily by Arts 297 and 301 EC. See further M Hofstötter, 'Suspension of rights by international organizations—the European Union, the European Communities and other international organizations' in V Kronenberger (ed), *The European Union and the International Legal Order: Discord or Harmony*

it is unclear whether the rights of citizens can ever be affected,[74] but this is a matter that can be brought before a court. In spite of these restrictions, Member States and institutions like the European Parliament can in practice create a lot of problems for an offending Member State, rendering difficult or impossible its participation in various EC agencies and bodies until it ceases to offend.

Enhancing legitimacy

Compliance with internationally accepted standards on democracy is normally an issue for domestic courts, with some oversight by the European Court of Human Rights. However, in some instances this may not suffice. Judicial disputes centre on isolated cases of individual rights. The judicial process may not be capable of identifying or preventing a deterioration of the democratic climate in the country. The case of Austria reawakened Europe to the possibility of undemocratic political parties achieving power through the democratic process. That said, the 'Austrian' sanctions cannot be seen in isolation from the process of European integration. They were meant to discourage hate against foreigners in general, which is contrary to the idea of European integration, and needed to be countered to safeguard the enlargement project. But it is not only Austria that encounters these problems. The European Commission against Racism and Intolerance of the Council of Europe has released a damning report on the situation in Germany, determining that the 'existing legal framework and policy measures have not proven to be sufficient to effectively deal with or solve these problems'.[75] The German Government pointed out that Germany 'observed the rule of law',[76] and its Federal Minister for the Interior, Otto Schily, threatened to suspend German subsidies to the Council of Europe.[77] The reaction of the other EU Member States to this? None.

(2001) 23; P Koutrakos, *Trade, Foreign Policy & Defence in EU Constitutional Law* (2001) chs 3 and 7. See also Alston (ed) (n 66 above) chs 18, 20, 21 and 22.

[74] See para 2 of Art 309 EC and Art 7 TEU.

[75] ECRI, Second Report on Germany adopted 15 December 2000, CRI 2001/36, released Strasbourg 3 July 2001, executive summary: http://www.ecri.coe.int/en/08/01/13/CBC%202%20Germany.pdf/.

[76] ibid, annex to the report.

[77] D Henning, 'Council of Europe finds 'general climate' fostering racism in Germany', World Socialist Website, 21 July 200: http://www.wsws.org/articles/2001/jul2001/euro-

Inconsistency of application of legal sanctions does not impact on the legality of their use, but it can lead to questions as to their legitimacy. Follesdal, who distinguishes between legally, socially and normatively legitimate laws and authorities,[78] points out that in order to be effective rules need not only to be lawful, but also observed and accepted, that is considered justified, within society. The high profile sanctions imposed against Austria were not considered legitimate by the Austrian people, and were said to have fuelled nationalism.[79]

Perhaps the greatest irony of the Austrian affair was the imposition of sanctions in response to the constitution of an unwelcome, but democratically elected, government by a profoundly undemocratic process. Austria was put 'on trial' by the 14 and found 'guilty' without charges being detailed, and without right of defence or requirements of proof. A report into the issue recommended for the future the introduction of preventive and monitoring mechanisms in Article 7 TEU.[80] The Nice amendments in part address these concerns; but as long as any intervention by the EU is not perceived as legitimate, the outlook of proposals for more monitoring mechanisms is uncertain.

There are other aspects to the legitimacy problem as well. According to one commentator,[81] the Haider phenomenon was simply an example of big business interests exploiting democracy by recruiting the votes of less educated people with catchy slogans. Paradoxically it was again business interests (in central and east European markets) that led to the counter-reaction. On this account, it almost seems as if governments are not really in charge. Meanwhile, the Wise Men Report reveals that the international measures were misunderstood as being directed against the Austrian citizen.[82]

To enhance democracy and democratic legitimacy in the EU, the cultivation of a European civil society is key. Not only does this address a relapse into nationalism, it fits in with a more general demand to democratize international governance, which needs—like national government—to be

---

j21.shtml. It is not known whether there is any connection with the subsequent praise by the Council of Europe Deputy Secretary General of Germany's policies against foreigners.

[78] A Follesdal, 'Democracy, legitimacy and majority rule in the European Union' in M Nentwich and A Weale (eds), *Political Theory and the European Union: Legitimacy, Constitutional Choice and Citizenship* (1998) 34, 36.

[79] The Wise Men Report n 42 above, para 116.

[80] ibid, para 117.

[81] P Schwarz, 'The European Union's sanctions against Austria', World Socialist Website, 22 February 2000: http://www.wsws.org/articles/2000/feb2000/haid-f22.shtml/.

[82] n 79 above, para 116.

made accountable to standards of democracy, legitimacy and the rule of law. Finally, there is clearly a connection between domestic and international legitimacy. Reasonable measures are sometimes required to show that the EU takes democracy as seriously on the home front as in its external policies. The EU observatory on racism and xenophobia could play a useful role here,[83] and the scope of the European Initiative for Human Rights and Democracy could be expanded. In this way internal and external policy could be made more consistent.

[83] C Gearty, 'The internal and the external "other" in the Union legal order: racism, religious intolerance and xenophobia in Europe' in Alston (ed) (n 66 above) 327.

14

The Rule of Law in the European Union

Anthony Arnull[*]

What is the rule of law?

In the aftermath of the Second World War, the rule of law occupied a prominent place in international efforts to safeguard human rights and maintain peace and security. Like human rights, however, the rule of law was not mentioned in the original European Community Treaties. The omission was not rectified until Maastricht, when the term appeared in the preamble to the Treaty on European Union and new provisions on a common foreign and security policy[1] and development cooperation.[2] Since then, the concept has assumed an increasing profile in the affairs of the Union. In June 1993, the Copenhagen European Council included the rule of law among the criteria which the candidate countries of Central and Eastern Europe would have to meet before accession. At Amsterdam, the rule of law was specified as one of the principles on which the Union was to be regarded as founded.[3] The Treaty on European Union was amended to restrict the right to apply for membership of the Union to European States which respect those principles.[4] Moreover, a serious and persistent breach of such a principle by a Member State might henceforward lead to the suspension of its rights.[5]

So there is no doubt that the notion of the rule of law has come to occupy an important place in the scale of values underlying the Union and that it

---

[*] I am grateful to Alan Bogg, Sophie Boyron, Gordon Woodman and Michael Zwanzger for their advice on some of the issues discussed in this chapter.
[1] Art J.1(2) (now 11(1)) TEU.
[2] Art 130u(2) (now 177(2)) EC.
[3] See Art 6(1) TEU.
[4] See Art 49 TEU.
[5] See Art 7 TEU, amended at Nice.

has considerable political resonance. What is less clear is what it means in a Union context, any attempt at a formal definition having been eschewed. The way the rule of law or allied concepts, such as *l'Etat de droit* or *Rechtsstaatlichkeit*,[6] are understood in a national setting cannot be determinative, as this will be conditioned by a particular legal or historical context and may vary from State to State. As with so many other concepts which have counterparts in the national legal systems, an autonomous Union concept of the rule of law needs to be identified. For this purpose, it is helpful to turn to the works of legal and political theorists. They are generally[7] (though not universally)[8] agreed on the utility of the concept of the rule of law and on its basic elements, though there is a lively debate about how far it extends.

A useful starting point is FA Hayek's widely quoted definition of the concept. Contrasting it with arbitrary government, Hayek wrote of the rule of law:[9] 'Stripped of all technicalities this means that government in all its actions is bound by rules fixed and announced beforehand—rules which make it possible to foresee with fair certainty how the authority will use its coercive powers in given circumstances, and to plan one's individual affairs on the basis of this knowledge.' That definition has a number of implications,[10] of which the following are some of the more important. If particular laws are to be an effective guide to action, they must be publicized, reasonably clear and prospective rather than retrospective in effect. Some degree of vagueness in the law is admittedly inevitable and may even be desirable.[11] That does not mean that the law can never constitute an adequate guide, as long as there is a commitment on the part of those responsible for formulating the law to minimizing unnecessary vagueness. There must in addition be an independent and impartial judiciary with responsibility for resolving disputes over precisely what the law requires and providing effective remedies where the law is breached. The judiciary must respect the rules of

---

[6] Those are the terms used in the French and German versions respectively of Art 6(1) TEU.

[7] See R Dworkin, *A Matter of Principle* (1985) 11; P Craig, 'Formal and substantive conceptions of the rule of law: an analytical framework' [1997] PL 467, 487.

[8] For a sceptical view of the notion's value, see RM Unger, *Law in Modern Society* (1976) 176–181 and 192–223.

[9] *The Road to Serfdom* (1944) 54. Cf AV Dicey, *Introduction to the Study of the Law of the Constitution* (10th edn, 1959) Part II. For a concise modern assessment of Dicey's views, see J Jowell, 'The rule of law today' in J Jowell and D Oliver (eds), *The Changing Constitution* (4th edn, 2000) 3.

[10] See J Raz, *The Authority of Law* (1979) ch 11, 214–219; LL Fuller, *The Morality of Law* (1969) 39; B Beinart, 'The rule of law' (1962) Acta Juridica 99.

[11] See TAO Endicott, 'The impossibility of the rule of law' (1999) 19 OJLS 1.

natural justice and be accessible to those who claim that their rights have been infringed. Controversies must be decided timeously and according to rational and reasonably predictable principles. Judgments and the reasoning on which they are based must be made public so that they can guide future conduct and be the subject of critical scrutiny.

The various elements of the rule of law may sometimes be difficult to reconcile. For example, it may only be possible for fully reasoned judgments to be given within a reasonable time if access to the courts is to some extent restricted. Moreover, the rule of law may conflict with other values which society regards as important.[12] But a community which observes the rule of law will take seriously the extent to which it is achieved and strive to avoid anything which might tend to undermine it. It is therefore evident that the Union has high expectations of its Member States and the candidate countries. To what extent, though, does the Union itself, and in particular its Court of Justice, respect the rule of law? That is the principal question adumbrated in this chapter.

The rule of law under the Union Treaties

Although references to the rule of law only started to appear in the Union Treaties relatively recently, the concept has always been implicit in the legal system of the Union.[13] That system was conceived as one in which specially established institutions would be endowed with powers to lay down binding rules affecting the Member States and their citizens. Each institution was to act within the limits of the powers conferred on it. This principle of conferred or attributed powers required an appropriate system of legal remedies to be put in place, so that the precise limits of the institutions' powers could be determined in cases of doubt. More particularly, the system had to ensure that rules laid down by the institutions when acting within their powers were applied and that, when an institution acted outside its powers, it was appropriately sanctioned. It would have been out of keeping with the legal traditions of the six original Member States for institutions enjoying such far-reaching powers to have escaped judicial control.[14] It was therefore envisaged from the outset that the institutional structure of the

---

[12] Raz (n 10 above) 228. Endicott (n 11 above) 5–6 gives the example of national security.

[13] See W Hallstein, *Europe in the Making* (1972) 30–37.

[14] See Lord Mackenzie Stuart, *The European Communities and the Rule of Law* (1977) 6–14.

Community (as it then was) would include a Court of Justice with the express duty to ensure observance of 'the law'. Each of the three original Treaties equipped the Court with far-reaching powers to enable it to discharge that duty. Particularly noteworthy was the so-called preliminary rulings procedure, under which national courts were enabled to ask the Court of Justice for guidance on the effect of the Treaties on cases they were called upon to decide.

However, the structure put in place by the Treaties, though innovative, was incomplete. What effect might Community law produce if invoked in the national courts? What would happen if it conflicted with a rule of national law? What if breach by a Member State of a Community rule caused loss to an individual? The answers to these questions are now well known. In the famous *Van Gend en Loos* case decided in 1963,[15] the Court held that an article of the EEC Treaty conferred rights on individuals which national courts were bound to uphold, a quality that has become known as direct effect. The following year, the Court made it clear that directly effective provisions of Community law took precedence over inconsistent provisions of national law.[16] More recently the Court held that there is 'inherent in the system' of the EC Treaty a principle rendering liable in damages States which breach Community law and thereby cause loss to individuals.[17]

Reactions to the role played by the Court

These cases underlined the importance of the preliminary rulings procedure in consolidating the rule of law in the Community, each being referred to the Court of Justice by a national court. Like any court, the Court of Justice can only deal with issues it is called upon to decide. The preliminary rulings procedure ensured that it was confronted with a range of fundamental questions about the characteristics of the Community system which it might not otherwise have had the chance to address. Of course, for the preliminary rulings procedure to achieve its objective of ensuring the uniform application of Community law, properly interpreted, it is necessary for the national courts to play their part by making references in appropriate

---

[15] Case 26/62 [1963] ECR 1.
[16] See Case 6/64 *Costa v ENEL* [1964] ECR 585.
[17] Joined Cases C-6/90 and C-9/90 *Francovich and Others* [1991] ECR I-5357.

cases and applying loyally the rulings delivered by the Court of Justice. Although there has been the occasional hiccup, on the whole the national courts have complied remarkably conscientiously with the duties imposed on them by the preliminary rulings procedure.[18] Indeed, the volume of references has now reached such a level that methods are being sought to reduce the burden they impose on the Court of Justice.

That the national courts have played a full part in making the preliminary rulings procedure work perhaps partly reflects the broadly favourable reaction the Court's early case law encountered among academic lawyers in countries where judges traditionally attach considerable weight to the writings of scholars. A sign that this academic consensus was breaking down came with the publication in 1986 of Hjalte Rasmussen's book, *On Law and Policy in the European Court of Justice*, where it was argued that excessive recourse to policy considerations of its own was threatening to undermine the Court's authority and legitimacy. During the period preceding the IGC which led to the Treaty of Amsterdam, the Court was also subject to a wave of criticism, particularly in the United Kingdom and Germany, for allegedly overstepping the limits of the judicial function.[19]

If the Court were widely perceived as having routinely exceeded its authority, the consequences for the legitimacy of the Union would be serious in at least two senses. For the institution charged with policing compliance with the principle of conferred powers to disregard the limits on its own powers would rightly be considered unconscionable. Moreover, many of the Court's decisions, to which critics like Rasmussen object, appear to have had the effect of strengthening the rule of law. If those decisions were found to be illegitimate, the rule of law in the Union would turn out to be built on sand. One test of the legitimacy of its case law is the effect on the Court of successive amendments to the Treaties. To what extent do these reflect unhappiness on the part of the Member States with the role it has played?

The first major change to the judicial system of the Communities came with the Single European Act, which made provision for a Court of First Instance (CFI) to be attached to the Court of Justice. The CFI was a response to two related concerns: the increasing difficulty the Court was experiencing in coping with its growing workload and the need to reinforce

---

[18] See KJ Alter, *Establishing the Supremacy of European Law* (2001) chs 2–4; JHH Weiler, *The Constitution of Europe* (1999) 32–33; AM Arnull, *The European Union and its Court of Justice* (1999) 559–561.

[19] See PJG Kapteyn, 'The Court of Justice after Amsterdam: taking stock' in T Heukels, N Blokker and M Brus (eds), *The European Union after Amsterdam* (1998) 139, 140.

judicial scrutiny of factual matters. It was to have jurisdiction in a limited range of cases laid down by the Council and its decisions were to be subject to a right of appeal to the Court of Justice on points of law. This important reform, designed to enable the Court to perform its functions more effectively, reflected continued confidence in the Court on the part of the Member States. Moreover, by giving the Court the last word on questions of law, the Member States ensured that the approach of the CFI would be modelled on that of the Court itself.

The Maastricht Treaty was more ambivalent. The Court was part of the so-called Community method which was to apply in only a very attenuated form under the second and third pillars of the Union which that Treaty created. Accordingly, all the new provisions on foreign and security policy and practically all those on justice and home affairs were excluded from its jurisdiction. Moreover, protocols were agreed with the objective of limiting the potential effect of the Court's case law on pensions, abortion and the acquisition of property in Denmark. On the other hand, the Treaty endorsed the Court's case law on fundamental rights and the status of the European Parliament in annulment proceedings. It also granted the Court important new powers, including the power to impose financial penalties on Member States found to have breached their Treaty obligations and to hear actions against the European Central Bank and national central banks. In addition, a limitation previously imposed on the categories of case which could be transferred to the CFI was removed.

The Treaty of Amsterdam was less ambivalent in the support it reflected for the Court, although it too contained provisions which represented a response to the Court's case law. The most prominent was designed to reverse a controversial decision[20] which appeared to rule out so-called positive or affirmative action in the field of equal treatment for men and women. Others were evidently intended to reduce opportunities for creativity exploited by the Court when interpreting similar provisions in the past.[21] More significant in the present context were new provisions giving the Court jurisdiction over the new Title IV of Part Three of the EC Treaty, entitled 'Visas, asylum, immigration and other policies related to free movement of persons', and Title VI of the Treaty on European Union, the third pillar, renamed 'Provisions on police and judicial cooperation in criminal matters'. It is true that the Court's powers in relation to both Titles

---

[20] Case C-450/93 *Kalanke v Bremen* [1995] ECR I-3051.
[21] See eg Art 13 EC; Art 34(2)(b) and (c) TEU.

are more limited than those it normally enjoys under the EC Treaty. However, to the extent that the two Titles deal with matters which previously fell within the scope of the Treaties at all, they were covered by the Maastricht version of Title VI, which made very little provision for the involvement of the Court. Notwithstanding their undoubted defects (an issue considered further below), the provisions introduced at Amsterdam should therefore be regarded as having strengthened rather than weakened the rule of law. It was suggested by the Commission at the 2000 IGC that the Court's jurisdiction under Title IV of Part Three of the EC Treaty should be aligned with its jurisdiction under the rest of that Treaty. That sensible suggestion was not taken up by the Member States, but it is likely to gather momentum over the coming years. More generally, it is striking that none of the suggestions made in the run-up to Amsterdam for curbing the role of the Court was acted on by the Member States.

The focus at Nice was on reforming the Union's judicial system to enable the two Courts to cope with their workload, which shows no signs of diminishing. Thus, the Council is to have extensive powers to alter the so-called judicial architecture of the Union. In addition, the Court will be given limited jurisdiction over the procedure for suspending the rights of Member States who fail to respect founding principles of the Union. On the other hand, the Member States were not willing to allow the Court to amend its Rules of Procedure without seeking the approval of the Council, although the Council will be able to grant its approval by qualified majority vote rather than, as previously, only by unanimity.[22]

The cumulative effect of successive changes to the Treaties has therefore been to strengthen the central role originally envisaged for the Court.[23] While the Member States have perfectly properly retained control over the architecture of the system, they have only rarely reacted by way of Treaty change to developments in the case law. Sometimes the case law has been endorsed, as with the Maastricht provisions on fundamental rights and the status of the European Parliament in annulment proceedings. Where amendments to the Treaties have seemed to reflect dissatisfaction with developments in the case law, this has not been on the fundamental principles of the system but on limited, sometimes technical, points: affirmative action, pensions, abortion, the right to own property in Denmark.

---

[22] See chapter by Gormley in this volume; AM Arnull, 'Modernising the Community Courts' (2000) 3 CYELS 37.

[23] cf Alter (n 18 above) ch 5.

Certainty and foreseeability in the case law of the Court

If the Member States have not shown any general dissatisfaction with the way in which the Court has built on the foundations laid by the original Treaties, might it not still be said that the Court's readiness to fill gaps in the Treaties has undermined certainty and foreseeability, important elements of the rule of law? That question is related to the Court's approach to the interpretation of written provisions of Community law, an approach in which not only the wording but also the spirit and general scheme of the measure in question are treated as important.

At its most basic level, the rule of law requires the law to be binding.[24] That requirement lay behind the Court's case law on direct effect, primacy and State liability in damages. That case law may not in every respect have been anticipated by the Member States and in that sense be said to have run counter to the principle of certainty. But for individuals it promoted certainty by enabling them to rely on the commitments given by the Member States when they signed the Treaties and on the provisions of duly enacted Community legislation.

The Treaties were of course silent on the questions of direct effect, primacy and State liability, so the Court's case law may also be said to have increased certainty by removing doubt. The situation is somewhat different where a Treaty provision appears to resolve a question in a particular way but is interpreted in another sense by the Court. An example is the case law on the status of the European Parliament in annulment proceedings under the EC Treaty, decided at a time when the relevant article[25] did not refer to the Parliament. The Court decided that annulment proceedings could be brought against measures adopted by the Parliament which were intended to have legal effects vis-à-vis third parties. It observed: 'the European Economic Community is a Community based on the rule of law, inasmuch as neither its Member States nor its institutions can avoid a review of the question whether the measures adopted by them are in conformity with the basic constitutional charter, the Treaty.'[26] The Court later decided that the Parliament could bring annulment proceedings against the Council or the Commission where the purpose of the proceedings was to protect the Parliament's prerogatives.[27] Those decisions caused

---

[24]   Raz (n 10 above) 212; Beinart (n 10 above) 121.

[25]   Art 173 (now 230) EC.

[26]   See Case 294/83 *Les Verts v European Parliament* [1986] ECR 1339, para 23.

[27]   See Case C-70/88 *Parliament v Council* ('Chernobyl') [1990] ECR I-2041.

some surprise and have been criticized as inconsistent with the language of the Treaty and motivated by a desire on the part of the Court to extend its own powers.[28] Both, however, were firmly grounded on rule of law considerations, namely the need to prevent acts of the Parliament which had legal effects from escaping judicial review and to give the Parliament a remedy where its own prerogatives were infringed by other institutions. All that may fairly be said is that they illustrate the difficulties which can arise in reconciling different components of the rule of law.

As for the Court's general approach to interpretation, some of the principles it applies directly reflect rule of law considerations.[29] Thus, Community acts are presumed not to be retrospective, a presumption which the Court treats as particularly difficult to rebut in the field of criminal law. Where an act is intended to operate retrospectively, the Court will strike it down unless retrospective effect is necessary to achieve its objectives and the legitimate expectations of those affected by it are respected. The Court has even on occasion limited the effect on the past of its own judgments,[30] notwithstanding the general principle that the judgments of a court interpreting a legal rule establish its effect since the moment it entered into force. It is undoubtedly true that the Court attaches less weight than some national courts to the language of the provision in question, but there are two reasons why the language cannot always be treated as decisive. The first is that the broad and general terms in which many Community provisions are drafted makes a literal approach to their interpretation futile. The second is that Community law is multi-lingual and all the language versions are equally authentic. This poses problems of interpretation which do not arise to anything like the same degree in any national system.

So it was inevitable that the Court would make extensive use of the so-called teleological and contextual approaches to interpretation. Those approaches are facilitated by the inclusion in the Treaties and Community acts of statements of the reasons on which they are based, but there is undoubtedly a price to pay in terms of certainty and predictability. Given the need for Union law to be expressed in a language which is understood by the citizens of all the Member States, that price has to be paid. It does,

---

[28] See Sir Patrick Neill, 'The European Court of Justice: a case study in judicial activism' (1995) European Policy Forum, 27–29.

[29] See further Arnull (n 18 above) ch 14. Cf TC Hartley, *Constitutional Problems of the European Union* (1999) chs 2 and 4.

[30] This was done for the first time in Case 43/75 *Defrenne v SABENA* [1976] ECR 455.

however, require constant vigilance to ensure that the drafting of Union legislation is of the highest possible quality, a standard which is not always met.[31]

A balance sheet

Notwithstanding what has been said so far, there remain several respects in which observance of the rule of law in the Union remains imperfect. One of the most pressing concerns the question of access to the Courts. Article 47 of the EU Charter of Fundamental Rights provides: 'Everyone whose rights and freedoms guaranteed by the law of the Union are violated has the right to an effective remedy before a tribunal...' That provision was cited by the CFI in *max.mobil v Commission,*[32] a competition case where judicial review was described as 'one of the general principles that are observed in a State governed by the rule of law and are common to the constitutional traditions of the Member States...'

Among the main remedies for which the EC Treaty provides is the action for annulment, which enables unlawful acts of the Community institutions to be quashed. That remedy can only be invoked by individuals and businesses if they can satisfy demanding rules on standing. For many years, those rules were interpreted very strictly by both the Court and the CFI. The result was that many annulment actions brought by private applicants were dismissed as inadmissible without examination of their merits. The remedy became wholly inadequate to protect the rights of such applicants and to ensure that the institutions acted within their powers.

If the Community Courts were concerned about the effect of relaxing the standing rules on the number of cases brought, they might have been assuaged by the Treaty of Nice, which offered the prospect of new arrangements to help them cope with their workload. The post-Nice process of reflection on the future of the Union also highlighted the need for it to be made more accountable. It was against that background that in 2002 important moves were made with a view to securing a judicial relaxation of

---

[31] See further Declaration No 39 adopted at Amsterdam; C Timmermans, 'How can one improve the quality of Community legislation?' (1997) 34 CMLRev 1229. Cf the Interinstitutional Agreement of 28 November 2001 on a more structured use of the recasting technique for legal acts, [2002] OJ C77/1.

[32] Case T-54/99, judgment of 30 January 2002, para 57. Cf para 48.

the standing rules in annulment actions brought by private applicants.[33] However, it its judgment of 25 July 2002 in *Unión de Pequeños Agricultores v Council*, the Court of Justice reaffirmed its existing case law, observing that any reform of the system currently in force would require an amendment to the EC Treaty. Such an amendment must be considered essential if the rule of law in the Union is to be properly secured.

The position under Titles V and VI of the TEU is even less satisfactory. The need for stronger judicial scrutiny of the Union's activities under those Titles was underlined by the Union's response to the events of 11 September 2001. On 27 December 2001, the Council adopted two common positions, both based on Article 15 (which is in Title V) and Article 34 (which is in Title VI) of the TEU. One of them[34] imposes obligations on the Member States while the other[35] contains a definition of 'terrorist act'[36] and identifies individuals and groups suspected of involvement in such acts. Neither is subject to review by the Court of Justice or apparently by any other court. Is this important? After all, common positions merely define 'the approach of the Union to a particular matter' and the requirements of the rule of law are perhaps met if measures giving effect to common positions are subject to judicial review. The definition of 'terrorist act' set out in the second of the two common positions referred to above, for example, applies to a regulation on combating terrorism.[37] Although adopted under the EC Treaty, that regulation is not based on any of the provisions of Title IV of Part Three. It is therefore fully subject to the judicial remedies for which that Treaty provides. If a common position were implemented by measures of Union law which were not subject to all the judicial remedies laid down in the EC Treaty, as would be the case if this were done under Title IV of Part Three of that Treaty or Title VI of the TEU, the position would be less satisfactory. The same would be so if it were implemented by national measures, for the extent to which the common position could be challenged would then depend on national law. Some Member States might not allow such implementing measures to be challenged. Those that did might not apply the

---

[33] See AG Jacobs in Case C-50/00 P *Unión de Pequeños Agricultores v Council*, Opinion of 21 March 2002; Case T-177/01 *Jégo-Quéré v Commission*, judgment of 3 May 2002. For a review of earlier case law, see AM Arnull, 'Private applicants and the action for annulment since *Codorniu*' (2001) 38 CMLRev 7.

[34] Common Position 2001/930/CFSP on combating terrorism, [2001] OJ L344/90.

[35] Common Position 2001/931/CFSP on the application of specific measures to combat terrorism, [2001] OJ L344/93.

[36] ibid, Art 1(3).

[37] Reg 2580/2001 of 27 December 2001, [2001] OJ L344/70.

same principles. This is hardly conducive to the level of certainty which the rule of law requires.

Opportunities to challenge the Framework Decision on the European arrest warrant,[38] based on Title VI of the TEU, are equally limited. The gist is that 'when a judicial authority of a Member State requests the surrender of a person, either because he has been convicted of an offence or because he is being prosecuted, its decision must be recognised and executed automatically throughout the Union.'[39] This mechanism will replace extradition between Member States.

The rule of law requires that a requested person should be able to challenge both the compatibility of a European arrest warrant with the Framework Decision and the very validity of the Framework Decision itself. The national courts can be expected to deal with the first issue and will need to comply with the European Convention on Human Rights in doing so. If they need guidance on the interpretation of the Framework Decision, it may be possible for them to ask the Court of Justice for a preliminary ruling (see below). The Court of Justice will not itself be able to review national measures concerning law and order or internal security, but a referring court will have to apply the preliminary ruling on the interpretation of the Framework Decision to the facts of the case. It is less clear how a requested person will be able to contest the validity of the Framework Decision. Individuals will not be able to challenge the Framework Decision directly before the Community Courts.[40] Again, this may not matter: framework decisions are binding on the Member States as to the result to be achieved, but leave to the national authorities the choice of form and methods. They do not produce direct effect.[41] So the rule of law is perhaps adequately protected if the requested person can challenge the validity of the Framework Decision before the courts of either the issuing or the executing Member State. Whether this will be possible seems to depend on the effect of Article 35 TEU.

Article 35(1) TEU confers on the Court of Justice jurisdiction to give preliminary rulings on (among other things) the validity and interpretation

[38] Adopted by the Council on 13 June 2002. The text had not been published at the time of writing. The discussion that follows is based on the proposal presented by the Commission, COM (2001) 522 final, 25 September 2001.

[39] ibid 5.

[40] Only a Member State or the Commission may ask the Court of Justice to review the legality of framework decisions: Art 35(6) TEU. Even if individuals could bring proceedings under that provision, it is unlikely that they would be regarded as having standing to challenge the Framework Decision on the European arrest warrant.

[41] See Art 34(2)(b) TEU.

of framework decisions. However, Member States do not have to accept the Court's jurisdiction.[42] If a Member State declines to do so, it is not clear whether its national courts could declare a framework decision invalid. Even if they purported to do so, their decisions might not be followed elsewhere in the Union. If a Member State does accept the Court's jurisdiction, it may *either* extend the right to refer to all its national courts *or* confine that right to top courts whose decisions cannot be challenged.[43] If it opts for the former, it seems clear that it will be possible for the validity of a framework decision to be raised in its national courts. If it opts for the latter, it seems equally clear that it will be possible for this to be done before its top courts, but less clear whether the same is true of proceedings before its lower courts. So the question whether the validity of the Framework Decision can be reviewed may depend on the exercise of discretion by the Member States. Alternatively there is a risk that the Framework Decision will be declared invalid in some Member States but not in others, because the decision is taken by a national court which has no power to make a reference to the Court of Justice. Both outcomes seem inimical to the rule of law. Similar issues are raised by the Framework Decision on combating terrorism, also based on Title VI TEU, which is intended to approximate the laws of the Member States regarding terrorist offences.[44]

Two further issues might usefully be tackled if the rule of law in the Union is to be consolidated.[45] One concerns the independence of its judiciary.[46] This has two aspects. The first is the way in which members of the Community Courts are appointed, the second the extent to which they are open to outside pressure while in office. The present system, under which members are appointed by common accord of the Governments of the Member States, is defective on both counts. Leaving appointments solely in the hands of the Member States does not sufficiently distance the exercise from the domestic political process. Members' relatively short terms of office mean they may be influenced by a wish to ensure that their mandate is renewed. Although the Courts give collegiate judgments, signed by all the judges taking part in a case, this is only a partial safeguard and does not protect Advocates General. It is unimportant whether any appointments

---

[42] See Art 35(2) TEU.

[43] See Art 35(3) TEU.

[44] Council Framework Decision 2002/475/JHA of 13 June 2002, [2002] OJ L164/3.

[45] See further FG Jacobs, 'Human rights in the European Union: the role of the Court of Justice' (2001) 26 ELRev 331, 339; chapter by Hillion in this volume.

[46] See J Wouters, 'Institutional and constitutional challenges for the European Union—some reflections in the light of the Treaty of Nice' (2001) 26 ELRev 342, 345.

have actually been influenced by political considerations, for here perception and potential are what counts. There is a strong case for placing appointments to the Courts in the hands of an independent commission and for extending the term of office to life or a non-renewable term which is significantly longer than the present six-year term.[47]

The other concerns the way in which the Courts communicate the rationale for their decisions to the parties and to society at large. The Courts now explain in greater detail than previously their reasoning, in particular the effect of their decisions on previous case law.[48] However, practice remains far from perfect. In a case decided in 2000,[49] a full Court of eleven Judges appeared to modify a fundamental principle of the law relating to the Community's liability in damages. The case was an appeal from a decision of a three-Judge chamber of the CFI.[50] The parties, the CFI and the Court's Advocate General had approached it on the basis that the principle in question remained valid. In its judgment, the Court did not refer to the voluminous case law[51] in which that principle had been applied. The case seems inconsistent with the rule of law on several counts. First, the case was decided on the basis of a principle which was not that which was understood to apply at the time the material facts occurred. Secondly, the parties were deprived of the right to be heard on the merits or otherwise of the principle which the Court chose to apply. Thirdly, the Court failed to acknowledge the departure its decision represented from the law as it was previously understood. These defects were only partly cured by the fact that the preferred line did not seem to affect the outcome of the case, the Court concluding by dismissing the appeal.

The limits of the rule of law

The basic elements of the rule of law are purely technical: they are concerned with the form, rather than the content, of the law and with the

---

[47] See T Koopmans, 'The future of the Court of Justice of the European Communities' (1991) 11 YEL 15. Cf Alter (n 18 above) 199–200, who discounts the possibility that appointment and reappointment might be used to influence the Court, but mentions three cases where this is said to have occurred.

[48] See further Arnull (n 18 above) ch 15.

[49] Case C-352/98 P *Laboratoires Pharmaceutiques Bergaderm and Goupil v Commission*, judgment of 4 July 2000. Cf Case T-177/01 *Jégo-Quéré v Commission* (n 33 above).

[50] Case T-199/96 [1998] ECR II-2805.

[51] Beginning with Case 5/71 *Zuckerfabrik Schöppenstedt v Council* [1971] ECR 975.

mechanics of the legal system. Some writers maintain that the notion does not extend any further than this. As Dworkin explains,[52] 'Those who have this conception of the rule of law do care about the content of the rules in the rule book, but they say that this is a matter of substantive justice, and that substantive justice is an independent ideal, in no sense part of the ideal of the rule of law.' On this view, 'the rule of law is just one of the virtues which a legal system may possess and by which it is to be judged.'[53] However, the notion is sometimes used in a wider sense to embrace aspects of the law's substantive content, often implying something about the rights of the individual.[54] Although the formal conception of the rule of law makes certain ethical assumptions about individual dignity and autonomy,[55] advocates of the substantive conception seek to go further and bring under the umbrella of the rule of law a series of more specific moral and political rights and duties. It is in broadly this sense that the German concept of the *Rechtstaat*[56] and the French concept of *l'Etat de droit*[57] are understood. This was reflected in a speech on the future of the enlarged Europe given by the then French Prime Minister, Mr Lionel Jospin, on 28 May 2001.[58] Having referred to the importance of '*l'Etat de droit*' in Europe, he added that Europe was the only political entity in which the death penalty no longer existed. It was, he said, the land where respect for the individual was at its zenith.

The dividing-line between the formal and the substantive conception of the rule of law can be difficult to draw, not least because some of the technical elements of the rule of law are regarded as fundamental rights.[59] However, there are risks in reversing the process by including in the rule of

---

[52]   Dworkin (n 7 above) 11.

[53]   Raz (n 10 above) 211.

[54]   See eg Dworkin (n 7 above) ch 1; TRS Allan, *Law, Liberty, and Justice* (1993) ch 2; TRS Allan, *Constitutional Justice* (2001); Sir John Laws, 'Judicial review and the meaning of law' in C Forsyth (ed), *Judicial Review and the Constitution* (2000) 173, 183–185; Jowell (n 9 above); Lord Steyn in *R v Home Secretary, ex parte Pierson* [1998] AC 539, 591. Cf D Dyzenhaus, 'Form and substance in the rule of law: a democratic justification for judicial review?' in Forsyth (ed), *Judicial Review and the Constitution* (2000) 141. For a general discussion of so-called formal and substantive conceptions of the rule of law, see Craig (n 7 above).

[55]   See Allan, *Law, Liberty, and Justice* (1993) 34; J Raz, *Ethics in the Public Domain* (1994) ch 17.

[56]   See G Robbers, *An Introduction to German Law* (1998) 60–62; DP Kommers, *The Constitutional Jurisprudence of the Federal Republic of Germany* (1997) 36–37; cf N MacCormick, *Questioning Sovereignty* (1999) 44–48.

[57]   See D Chagnollaud and J-L Quermonne, *Le gouvernement de la France sous la Ve République* (1996) ch VII; J Bell, *French Constitutional Law* (1992) ch 2.

[58]   http://www.premier-ministre.gouv.fr/fr/p.cfm?ref=249271/. An English text was published in *Europe* on 30 May 2001.

[59]   See eg Arts 20 and 47–50 of the Charter of Fundamental Rights; Arts 6, 7 and 13 ECHR.

law rights which go beyond the form of the law and the mechanics of the legal system. One is that advocates of specific moral and political values, whatever they may be, may be led to invoke the rule of law in order to avoid articulating the rationale for such values. The resulting loss of transparency may undermine the accountability of policy-makers and the legitimacy of the decision-making process. Moreover, the rhetorical force of the rule of law may ultimately be weakened, even when used in a formal sense, for people may come to associate it with nothing more than a particular set of policy preferences. These are likely to be more controversial than the general ethical assumptions underlying the formal conception of the principle.

In the context of the Union, the formal conception enables the rule of law to be given a meaning which is distinct from, though complementary to, that of the other principles on which the Union is said to be founded: liberty, democracy and respect for human rights and fundamental freedoms. The rule of law should not be regarded as a high-sounding but indeterminate addition to that list but as a particular set of requirements about the form of the law and the mechanics of the legal systems of the Union and its Member States.[60] The formal conception of the concept is consistent with Article 11(1) TEU, which sets out the objectives of the common foreign and security policy, and Article 177(2) EC, on Community policy in the sphere of development cooperation,[61] both of which seem to refer to the rule of law as a distinct value. It is reflected in the Commission's 1997 reports on the extent to which the candidate countries of Central and Eastern Europe satisfied the Copenhagen criteria.[62] These dealt with the structure and functioning of the judiciary separately from human rights and the protection of minorities, an approach followed in subsequent reports.

As for the death penalty, its abolition in peacetime is required by Protocol No 6 to the European Convention on Human Rights. That Protocol has been ratified by all the Member States of the EU and it would be incompatible

---

[60] Raz (n 10 above) 211, cautions against confusing the rule of law with, among other things, democracy, human rights and respect for the dignity of man. On the shift in the emphasis of liberal lawyers from the rule of law to a bill of rights in apartheid South Africa, see M Chanock, 'A post-Calvinist catechism or a post-Communist manifesto? Intersecting narratives in the South African bill of rights debate' in P Alston (ed), *Promoting Human Rights Through Bills of Rights* (1999) 392, 397.

[61] See B Simma, JB Aschenbrenner and C Schulte, 'Human rights considerations in the development co-operation activities of the EC' in P Alston (ed), *The EU and Human Rights* (1999) 571, especially 601–603.

[62] Bulletin of the EU, Supplements 6–15/97.

with the rule of law for any of them to disregard it.[63] But as long as the requirements of due process are met, a legal system which applies the death penalty may conform to the rule of law, although we may object to it on other grounds.

[63] Protocol No 13, which has not yet entered into force, will abolish the death penalty in all circumstances. The death penalty is also prohibited by Art 2(2) of the EU Charter of Fundamental Rights, but it is not clear whether the Charter has any legal effect and the extent to which it applies to the Member States is in any event limited. See chapter by Jacobs in this volume.

Part III

Fundamental Rights and Social Rights

The place of the individual in a political system is fundamental to its accountability and legitimacy. The Union and its institutions are subject to the case law of the Court of Justice on the protection of fundamental rights and to the Union's Charter of Fundamental Rights, solemnly proclaimed at Nice in December 2000. Both draw heavily on the European Convention on Human Rights, to which all the Member States are party. The Union itself has not (yet) acceded to the Convention, but is required by the Maastricht Treaty to respect its requirements. Does this complex framework ensure an appropriate level of protection for fundamental rights in the Union? Should the Charter's status be elevated from that of a proclamation to something that is formally binding? What is the proper relationship between the Union and the European Convention on Human Rights?

Chapter III of the Charter contains an important set of provisions on equality, which in many respects reflect pre-existing provisions of the EC Treaty. Prominent among those provisions is Article 13. Introduced at Amsterdam, that provision authorizes the Council, within the limits of the Community's powers, 'to combat discrimination based on sex, racial or ethnic origin, religion or belief, disability, age or sexual orientation'. In 2000, the Council adopted two directives under Article 13 which raise delicate questions about how best to protect the basic social values to which the Union is committed and on which its accountability and legitimacy in part depend.

An underlying issue here is the need to strike a proper balance between protecting individual rights and the demands of economic competitiveness. In a Union context, this means reconciling the European social model, where the costs of high levels of social protection are borne more readily, and Anglo-Saxon capitalism, where there is greater willingness to entrust the fate of individuals to the market. The way the Union deals with the tension between these two conceptions of the place of the individual in society will have profound implications for its accountability and legitimacy.

15

Protecting Fundamental Rights in Europe: A Legal Analysis

Jeremy McBride

Introduction

There can hardly be room for complacency about the protection of human rights within Europe when they are currently imperilled by factors such as economic dislocation, internal strife, natural disasters, racism, terrorism and transition to democracy. There must, therefore, be a continuing concern about the adequacy of the mechanisms available to protect them. However, at present the main threat comes more from states than from the various entities operating at the international and supranational levels, of which the European Union is the most important. Moreover this threat exists as much in those states currently within the Union as in those who are candidates for membership and those who are not even at that stage. The scale of the incursions on rights and freedoms may vary amongst these three categories of states but it is apparent from the cases coming before the European Court of Human Rights that almost all of them have significant deficiencies in their laws and practices.[1] These deficiencies stem not only from the various sources of difficulty already mentioned but also from the continuing failure to address problems of a longstanding character.[2] Although the human rights problems that are posed by the Union and other entities at the supranational and international levels may not be particularly serious at present,[3] concern about the adequacy of protection against these

---

[1] The whole picture is never evident from such cases but they are a good indicator of major problems.

[2] Unduly long judicial proceedings in Italy being the most notable example.

[3] Human rights can, however, be affected by various enforcement powers, the content of legislative measures and staffing practices.

entities is bound to increase as their competence—notably the Union's enhanced home affairs and security role—and willingness to intervene within states grows and as the limitations of existing safeguards become clearer.[4]

In seeking to meet the concern since the end of the Second World War for more effective protection of human rights—a vital element in the legitimacy and accountability of entities at all levels—numerous proclamations of rights have been adopted. Indeed Europe in both its narrow and wider senses[5] might well be regarded as having been overwhelmed with such proclamations but the efficacy of what is actually being achieved by them is certainly mixed. Shortcomings in this regard can be attributed to a number of considerations. First, not all proclamations can be regarded as complete legal instruments as they do not constitute a basis for obtaining a conclusive determination of specific claims. This failing can be an inherent characteristic of a proclamation but it can also be a matter of the institutions and processes provided to handle disputes. Secondly, proclamations can engender confusion as to the nature of the commitment being undertaken and thus impede their effective realization. This is partly because of apparent differences in the formulation being used but also because of the inappropriateness of the language used for the entities to which particular provisions are supposed to apply. Thirdly, there is scope for doubting the reliability of the appraisal made as to actual compliance with the obligations being undertaken. This is of particular concern where the appraisal is being performed by institutions other than courts but problems can also arise from different competences to make the appraisal, insufficient power to act and inadequate resources to meet the demand for a remedy. The overall consequence is that the assurance apparently afforded by the various proclamations is not entirely reliable. These issues not only determine the context within which the European Union's Charter of Fundamental Rights has been adopted but they are also relevant to any consideration of the contribution which it can be expected to make towards improved human rights protection. They are, therefore, examined further in the succeeding sections of this chapter.

---

[4] An egregious example of the latter can be seen in the unsuccessful challenge to the NATO bombing of Former Yugoslavia in *Bankovic v Belgium et al*, admissibility decision of 19 December 2001.

[5] Apart from the Union of 15 States, there is the Council of Europe with 44 States and the Organization for Cooperation and Security in Europe with 55 States.

The legal character of proclamations

A contrast is often made between approaches to the protection of human rights involving the adoption of specific measures and the use of constitutional guarantees. The former approach was the one pursued exclusively by the United Kingdom until the enactment of the Human Rights Act 1998 and it had until now also been a characteristic of the Union, since, notwithstanding the judicial development of general principles, the most significant protection lay in specific provisions in the Treaties, regulations and directives.[6] On the other hand reliance on general statements of rights in constitutional provisions has long found favour in most continental European countries and it is also an approach that has been followed in an array of texts adopted at the regional and international level.

In reality the two approaches are more often complementary than alternatives, since constitutional guarantees generally need to be underpinned by implementing measures, but the contrast between them is generally made with a view to suggesting that reliance on general statements is misguided. The root of such a perception is invariably to be found in the observation of Dicey—a noted nineteenth century British constitutional writer—that 'most foreign[7] constitution makers have begun with declarations of rights'.[8] This was not, of course, a tribute and his antipathy to this approach, which shaped thinking in the United Kingdom for far longer than was appropriate, is evident in his further observation that:

> [this] course of action has more often than not been forced upon them by the stress of circumstances, and by the consideration that to lay down general principles of law is the proper and natural function of legislators. But any knowledge of history suffices to show that foreign constitutionalists have, while occupied in defining rights, given insufficient attention to the absolute necessity for the provision of adequate remedies by which the rights they proclaimed might be enforced.[9]

Whether this is an apposite comment in respect of the EU Charter of Fundamental Rights—which is not supposed to be legally binding—remains to be seen but it is certainly not an accurate reflection of the present position in most European States (whether within or outside the Union), since their constitutional guarantees can generally be secured through the

---

[6] See Part C in P Alston (ed), *The EU and Human Rights* (1999).
[7] ie, continental or, as many people in England say, European.
[8] AV Dicey, *Introduction to the Study of the Law of the Constitution* (10th edn, 1959) 198.
[9] ibid.

courts. Nor is it a reflection of the position under the European Convention on Human Rights, which has made an important contribution over the last fifty years to preventing many serious violations of human rights from occurring or, where they have, in ensuring that a suitable remedy for them is then provided.[10] The Convention emulates constitutional guarantees in not only being legally binding but also in providing for recourse to a court which can conclusively determine whether or not an aspect of a country's law or practice breaches a particular right or freedom and thereby create an obligation to remedy the situation.

The enforceability of the European Convention is, however, still very much the exception at the regional and international level; the human rights movement during the post-Second World War era has been marked more often by proclamations of rights which are either without legal force or whose legal force—in the sense of being able conclusively to determine disputes by reference to them—is somewhat uncertain, showing that Dicey's observation is as much applicable to twentieth and perhaps twenty-first century international actors as nineteenth century constitution-makers. The most famous of these proclamations is undoubtedly the Universal Declaration of Human Rights. However, as this instrument has demonstrated, it does not follow that something cannot be influential even though it is not legally binding. Thus, although the Declaration has come to acquire some legal force—either through elements becoming customary international law or being seen as an authentic interpretation of the United Nations Charter—this is much less significant than the way in which it has come to shape the human rights debate and captured the popular imagination, constantly being invoked where injustice is perceived to have occurred.[11]

The non-legal approach to assuring human rights has also been significant in a specifically European context, namely, through the Conference and later Organization on Cooperation and Security in Europe (OSCE). The human dimension or human rights provisions in the Helsinki Final Act were in an explicitly non-legally binding instrument but their influence on the subsequent political process was substantial—providing a basis for arguments that particular action should be taken or that certain measures contrary to human rights should not be continued.[12] This undoubtedly

---

[10]   See DJ Harris, M O'Boyle and C Warbrick, *Law of the European Convention on Human Rights* (1995).

[11]   See G Alfredsson and A Eide (eds), *The Universal Declaration of Human Rights* (1999).

[12]   See A Bloed, *The Conference on Security and Cooperation in Europe* (1993).

contributed to a more favourable environment for human rights protection prior to the fall of the Berlin Wall[13] and this has continued afterwards with a succession of further non-binding proclamations such as the Copenhagen Document, the Charter of Paris for a New Europe and the Moscow Document.[14] The subsequent operations of the OSCE—given legitimacy more by these and other proclamations than other formally binding instruments—have played an important part in improving the human rights situation in candidate states for the European Union, although the focus is now much more on the non-candidate states in South Eastern Europe and in Central Asia.

There are, in addition to the Universal Declaration and the OSCE documents, many other proclamations of a non-legal character at the European and international level. These can be found, for example, in resolutions of the General Assembly of the United Nations and recommendations of the Committee of Ministers of the Council of Europe,[15] to say nothing of the general comments and recommendations adopted by the United Nations human rights treaty bodies and sundry sets of principles that have been proclaimed by non-governmental organizations and gatherings here and there of international experts.[16] Such soft law has generally been helpful in shaping our understanding of what is entailed by particular rights and thus assisting in the interpretation of explicitly legal obligations; the meaning of degrading treatment has, for example, been established in part by consideration of the Standard Minimum Rules for the Treatment of Prisoners, which were approved by the Economic and Social Council of the United Nations.[17]

There has, however, also been a significant trend within Europe towards the adoption of instruments which are formally binding under international law but which fail to provide any means of conclusively determining whether or not the obligations thereby created have been fulfilled. This is certainly regrettable given that the key to the European Convention's

---

[13] Even if the motives may have been mixed.

[14] Adopted in June 1990, November 1990 and July 1992.

[15] eg the Declaration on the Rights of Persons Belonging to National or Ethnic, Religious and Linguistic Minorities, GA Res 47/135 of 18 December 1992.

[16] eg the Limburg Principles on the Implementation of the International Covenant on Economic, Social and Cultural Rights (1987) 9 HRQ 121.

[17] By resolutions 663 C (XXIV) of 31 July 1957 and 2076 (LXII) of 13 May 1977. A regional equivalent was adopted by the Council of Europe as the European Prison Rules in 1977. On soft law generally, see J Toman, 'Quasi-legal standards and guidelines for protecting human rights' in H Hannum (ed), *Guide to International Practice* (2nd edn, 1992).

impact has been the right of individual petition which—contrary to the trend—has been strengthened by the adoption of Protocol 11, whereby this procedure ceased to be an optional feature and individual applicants were formally recognized as parties in proceedings before the Strasbourg Court. Such a feature is, for example, absent from the European Convention's counterpart in economic and social rights, the European Social Charter. This certainly establishes legal obligations—albeit with some flexibility as to the ones which have to be accepted—but implementation by states parties is merely to be supervised by a Committee of Experts, which can adopt conclusions on reports submitted by states themselves; and these conclusions may eventually reach the Committee of Ministers which is then able, by a two-thirds majority, to make any necessary recommendations for action.[18] Although this long-winded process may still have contributed in some way to the improvement in the implementation of social and economic rights, the low-key nature of the process has made its actual impact difficult to assess.[19] Some modification has been effected by an additional protocol providing for a system of collective complaints which enables various non-governmental organizations—not the victim but bodies with special competence—to complain about the non-implementation of particular organizations. The supervising committee can make this assessment of the complaint but it is still left to the Committee of Ministers, by a two-thirds vote, to make recommendations which it has so far done in only three cases.[20] Nevertheless this is still a step towards adjudication, which is nowhere in sight for another potentially significant human rights proclamation, the Framework Convention on National Minorities. This sets certain standards whose implementation is to be monitored through the examination of periodic reports by an advisory committee, which is supposed to assist the Committee of Ministers in evaluating the adequacy of the measures taken to give effect to the principles in the Convention. This device was the approach preferred to the alternative canvassed of incorporating provisions on minority rights into an additional protocol to the European Convention; in other words the less legal approach was preferred. Supervising mechanisms without the capacity to make authoritative rulings are also to be found in the European Charter for Regional or Minority Languages and the Convention for the Protection of Individuals with regard to the Automatic Processing of Personal Data.

---

[18] The conclusions have to pass through a sub-committee of the Governmental Committee of the Council of Europe.

[19] D Harris and J Darcy, *The European Social Charter* (2nd edn, 2001).

[20] Complaints 6, 7 and 10.

Concern about the repercussions of legal force for human rights has also led to a reluctance to expand the scope of the European Convention, as seen clearly in the case of minority rights, but also in respect of the continuing difficulty in getting more specific guarantees on the rights of detainees and administrative justice.[21] It can also be seen in the long battle to remedy the most serious deficiency in the European Convention through the adoption of an equal protection provision and the fact that so far Georgia and Cyprus are the only European States prepared to ratify the resulting Protocol 12.

The EU Charter does not even reflect this trend for weaker legal protection and is more like the Universal Declaration, in proclaiming rights without itself being the formal basis for the obligation to respect them. As such it is not entirely without legal consequence since, as an articulation of the law—albeit somewhat inchoate—that is supposed to govern the activities of the Union, it has the potential to shape adjudication by courts. In this regard, although not adding to what is already there in terms of legal status, the Charter might be seen as providing a more extensive listing than that found in the European Convention, the instrument most relied upon by the European Court of Justice and to which compliance is now enjoined.[22] However, in the absence of any new cause of action, the Charter is likely to be only a negative instrument, influencing restraints on action by the institutions, rather than something that requires more positive measures to be taken. Indeed concern about the latter possibility has been a factor in the opposition to the adoption of a legally binding instrument by the European Union.[23] The failure to add anything may ultimately prove to be a source of grave disillusionment, notwithstanding the initial delight with the rainbow of rights produced by the Charter's prism-like effect. The fact that the Charter's provisions are not legally binding does not, of course, mean that they will not be implemented nor that, like the Universal Declaration, they will not ultimately lead to instruments with more legal force; but their lack of clear priority is remarkable for something created by an entity generally noted for the legal efficacy of its measures. It may, of course, be that the Court of Justice will find some way of giving the Charter legal force but this

---

[21] The latter is required to expand the applicability of Art 6, which is limited to the determination of criminal liability and private law rights.

[22] Art 6(2) TEU.

[23] The purposive approach to the interpretation of the European Convention, (discussed further in the following section) has disclosed many more obligations than its drafters might originally have imagined.

is likely to entail a convoluted legal analysis that can hardly be an appropriate basis for a rights guarantee.

Certainty in the commitments made

As Dicey's observation illustrated, the general common law perspective of constitutional/international rights guarantees was that they were full of broad generalities and were thus not the business of lawyers.[24] This is an approach which has been abandoned, with more and more common law jurisdictions adopting Bills of Rights and similar instruments—the United Kingdom being among the more recent converts—and the growing volume of case law in the courts demonstrates that lawyers can do something useful with rights guarantees, if not in every case. This is, of course, merely an echo of what has already been achieved in proceedings under the European Convention.[25] The provisions in the latter have not proved unduly problematic to interpret and apply because, despite being broadly-framed, they use straightforward language and identify the relevant considerations for judging the acceptability of limitations on rights.[26] Yet it is evident that there are other international instruments which do create unnecessary uncertainty as to what is protected and a notable example is the Framework Convention on National Minorities. This is meant to be the principal European standard on minority rights, yet it does not actually address the key issue of what is meant to be a national minority, leaving unclear who is meant to be the beneficiary of its provisions. The reluctance to set some parameters for such a fundamental concept is in marked contrast to the specification in the European Charter for Regional or Minority Languages that traditional minorities— its beneficiaries and potentially just as elusive a concept as 'national minority'—be linked to a particular territory in the country concerned and do not include migrants. The uncertainty of the legal obligations in the Framework Convention is increased by the fact that, apart from the clear right in Article 3 to choose whether or not to belong to a minority, the provisions are collectively characterized by Article 19 as 'principles', from which rights and freedoms are supposed to be derived

---

[24] This was not, however, the view taken in the United States.

[25] As well as in many national jurisdictions.

[26] This is not to minimize the difficulties that there can be in defining the scope of a State's margin of appreciation when working out the appropriate balance: see Harris, O'Boyle and Warbrick (n 10 above) 290–93.

and thus the actual commitments are lacking in specificity. The formulation used can thus undermine the potential value of an instrument. This is certainly an issue where scrutiny of the Charter's provisions would be appropriate before acceding to pressure for it to be transformed into law and a number of potential problems in this regard can be seen.

As it stands the Charter is clearly meant to be a declaratory instrument, underlined by the preambular reference to securing greater visibility for rights and by Article 52(2)'s confirmation that those rights based on Community Treaties or the Treaty on European Union shall be exercised under the conditions and within the limits defined by them. However, although such provisions might be understandable in the present context, their retention would not be desirable in a legally binding instrument, particularly one that is meant to have some kind of constitutional status, since the scope for dynamic and purposive interpretation—a vital feature for a constitutional style instrument such as the European Convention—will be very uncertain. Although the present provisions do not seem as draconian as the clauses found in many Commonwealth constitutions that preserved existing (colonial) law notwithstanding any conflict with their rights guarantees, and thereby limited the priority accorded to the provisions in the latter, they are still likely to inhibit the reasoned creativity which is the lifeblood of such guarantees.

The Charter provisions are shaped in particular by the European Convention but are not identical to them. There is nothing wrong with that since national provisions in many European countries rely both upon treaties in addition to the European Convention and their own constitutional guarantees which are formulated in different ways from the former; the United Kingdom is unusual in its reliance solely on the European Convention as a constitutional guarantee of rights. Nevertheless greater consistency in the terminology used and the interpretative approach followed might be appropriate for instruments such as the Charter and the Convention, which are both of a pan-European character. There is certainly an attempt to secure consistency in the latter respect in Article 52(3) of the Charter, which provides that the meaning and sense of provisions derived from the European Convention shall be the same as those laid down by the Convention. However, unlike the Human Rights Act 1998,[27] the reference to the significance of the all-important case law of the Strasbourg Court is only a preambular one and there is no specific requirement for this actually to be

---

[27] s 2(1).

taken into account. Moreover there is no indication as to what might be the consequence for achieving a consistent interpretation given that other provisions in the Charter appear to indicate possibly different priorities from the Convention. Thus there is an overarching guarantee of dignity in Article 1, which may give the Charter a more modern flavour, but this might be at the expense of the principle of non-discrimination in the Convention.[28] As for consistency in the terminology being used, there was a deliberate element of reformulation and updating of the provisions but this is not in itself significant from a legal viewpoint. More important is the fact that there are areas where the language used is much vaguer, such as in respect of life and forced labour.[29] However, there are also areas where the provisions are more elaborate, notably the specific guarantees on the integrity of the person and on personal data in Articles 4 and 8 which are treated separately from the prohibition on torture and inhuman and degrading treatment and the right to respect for private and family life in Articles 4 and 7, which otherwise broadly follow Articles 3 and 8 ECHR respectively. Both of these are certainly matters on which there is already substantial case law by the Strasbourg Court, and it remains to be seen whether the articulation of specific elements of the rights concerned might stifle the further development which is likely to occur in this case law. The elaboration can also be confusing: Article 17(2) states that intellectual property 'shall be protected', connoting a positive obligation but at the same time implying that the guarantee of other property interests might be restricted to limiting expropriation and regulation, despite the recognition of more extensive obligations by the Strasbourg Court.[30] Furthermore the reformulation appears to foreclose the possibility of a right of access to official information being derived from the freedom of expression guarantee since there is a specific provision on access to documents in Article 42. However, the latter is restricted to those of the Parliament, Council and Commission and this is likely to be useful in arguing that allowing access to official documents is not a matter which Member States are expected to observe and possibly to confirm the limited institutional applicability of the Charter

---

[28] Established by Art 14 and an extensive case law rendering arbitrary treatment unacceptable. This principle is also of fundamental importance in other international instruments, such as the International Covenant on Civil and Political Rights, the International Convention on the Elimination of All Forms of Racial Discrimination and the Convention on the Elimination of All Forms of Discrimination against Women.

[29] Arts 2 and 5.

[30] See *Raimondo v Italy*, judgment of 22 February 1994. It should also be noted that the Strasbourg Court interprets 'possessions' to cover all forms of property interests.

discussed further below.[31] There is also a potentially misleading use of language in respect of another international instrument: Article 18 provides that the right to asylum is to be granted with due regard to the Geneva Convention but that treaty does not create such a right of asylum but only a duty of *non-refoulement* and whether more is intended is obscured by the manner of this reference to it. However, this specific reference to an international obligation of Member States of the Union in addition to the Convention serves to underline the complete absence of any link between the Charter's provisions on social rights and the European Social Charter which all of them have also ratified.[32]

Other areas of difficulty concern the application of the provisions, both as regards beneficiaries and those whose behaviour is being controlled. As regards the former, the Charter retains the formulation of the Convention that most provisions apply to 'Everyone' and the only context in which rights are limited to European citizens is in the fifth chapter dealing with voting, accountability, movement and diplomatic and consular protection. The absence of any reference in other provisions, including social rights, to citizenship of the Union should ensure that this is not a prerequisite for the protection to be afforded. Indeed such an inclusive approach would be essential to prevent international guarantees from being infringed[33] and it is an improvement on some constitutional guarantees in Europe that are restricted to citizens. With regard to those bound by the Charter, Article 51 is very specific about it being applicable primarily to the institutions and bodies of the Union and only to the Member States when they are implementing Union law. However, this concentration on the exercise of power by the latter and, despite the many references to policies, the stipulation that the Charter does not establish any new power or task for the Community or the Union[34] is likely to reinforce the perception of this instrument as no more than a constraint on the exercise of power. This narrow approach is in marked contrast to the more rights-based approach of international guarantees: the fundamental duty for states under Article

[31] For an analysis of the drafting process, see P Drzemczewski, 'The Council of Europe's position with respect to the EU Charter of Fundamental Rights' (2001) 22 HRLJ 14.

[32] Although not all the protocols or the 1996 Revised European Social Charter. The non-binding character of the EU Charter forecloses for the moment debate over the justiciability of the social and economic rights which it includes, but this may be less problematic than is often imagined.

[33] Rights, whether for citizens or non-citizens, do not have to be guaranteed at the constitutional level.

[34] Art 51(2).

1 ECHR is to secure to everyone within their jurisdiction the rights and freedoms set out in the treaty. In other words it is the rights and freedoms that are the priority and it is up to the state to find the means and, as is increasingly evident in Strasbourg case law, this can involve positive measures such as the duty to investigate deaths.[35] Not only does the formulation adopted in the Charter give little scope for meeting these requirements, but the lack of powers point in Article 51(2) also appears to run counter to the statement in Article 52(2) that the meaning and scope of certain provisions is the same as those derived from the European Convention. This is also likely to have an impact on the potential for the Charter's provisions to have a horizontal effect, a concomitant of the positive obligations involved in rights as private actions can encroach upon them.[36] The present status of the Charter would, of course, preclude it from being an independent source of such obligations but the character of these provisions could also have an adverse influence on the way existing sources of power within the Union are interpreted. This could, of course, be welcomed by some states but could equally result in significant voids in the actual realization of rights and freedoms.

Assessing and achieving compliance

Assessment of the adequacy of compliance with standards undoubtedly suffers where the decision-making is of a political/administrative rather than a judicial character.[37] This can be a consequence of a focus on a general situation rather than an individual case, the absence of an open and adversarial procedure before a conclusion is reached, and the potential for the latter to be influenced by considerations other than the applicable rules, as well as undue optimism about what has been achieved or what certain measures might be expected to achieve.[38] Certainly standards appear sometimes to have been relaxed when taking decisions on the admission or continued membership of states to the Council of Europe—matters for which compliance with human rights norms is of particular importance—

---

[35] *Kaya v Turkey,* judgment of 19 February 1998.

[36] See *A v United Kingdom,* judgment of 23 September 1998, concerning ill-treatment of a child by his step-father.

[37] The expert bodies making recommendations under the European Social Charter and the Framework Convention are in the latter camp but they do not have the final say.

[38] This is not to suggest that judges are never influenced by such considerations.

and when the Committee of Ministers supervises the execution of the Strasbourg Court's judgments.[39] There is undoubtedly a risk of this fate befalling the Charter, given that its essentially non-legal status will allow more scope for appraisal of compliance by non-judicial actors such as the Commission, Council and Parliament. This may be more likely where human rights are relevant to dealings outside the Union than with respect to actions affecting persons within it, since the latter will at least be able to rely on their pre-existing rights under the law. However, even in that context there can be no authoritative judicial ruling on the issue of compliance with the Charter itself.

Another potential problem regarding assessment of compliance with obligations arises when there is no certain path towards conclusive resolution of conflicts between the different actors involved in this task, even though they are supposed to be applying identical or substantially similar provisions. Already there have been different conclusions reached as to the interpretation of provisions in the European Convention by the two European Courts[40] but this is not so problematic where there is no overlapping jurisdictional responsibility; the Convention is currently binding on Union entities as a matter of Union rather than international law. However, the position is less clear cut where action by Member States is involved; while the Strasbourg Court seems to be abandoning its self-denying ordinance that this cannot give rise to responsibility under the Convention,[41] there is no guarantee that the Court of Justice would not regard a response to such a finding as incompatible with a Member State's obligations within the Union. Moreover, even if the Strasbourg Court cannot at present make rulings as to the compatibility of action by Union entities with the Convention, it might seem strange to European citizens affected by this that the same provision is applied in different ways by two regional courts. It may, of course, be that the effect of the provision in Article 52(2) discussed in the preceding section will be to preclude, rather than mitigate, the possibility of such divergence occurring. But this seems unlikely given the continued failure of the courts in countries bound by the Convention to reach the same conclusion as the

[39] Discretion exists because of the limited nature of these judgments; see below. However, there is now less willingness to accept assurances of effective reform when repeated violations of the same character occur.

[40] See D Spielmann, 'Human rights case law in the Strasbourg and Luxembourg Courts: conflicts, inconsistencies, and complementarities' in Alston (n 6 above) 757.

[41] See *Van de Hurk v The Netherlands*, judgment of 19 April 1994 and *Matthews v United Kingdom*, judgment of 18 February 1999.

Strasbourg Court on the application of its provisions, even where there is guidance to be derived from existing case law. It is also possible that unambiguous legal force for the Charter would lead to human rights problems within the Union sphere being satisfactorily resolved at that level, with any divergent interpretation that emerges being seen to be of no consequence. However, this seems improbable given the inability of courts other than the Court of Justice to satisfy litigants that they have correctly applied rights guaranteed by either their constitutions or the Convention. In the longer term, there will thus be a need to take seriously the need for a more integrated human rights order within Europe, with the primacy being afforded to the Strasbourg Court and the Convention might seem to be the most straightforward solution.[42]

Although the Strasbourg Court is better placed than many other institutions supervising compliance with the international and regional human rights obligations applicable to European states, in that its rulings are binding and it can award compensation, those rulings have no automatic effect on the legal orders to which they apply[43] and there are also other remedies that might be more usefully awarded.[44] There is undoubtedly some scope for rectifying these shortcomings,[45] as well as for extending such a mandate to other areas of human rights,[46] but it is evident that an international tribunal's role is essentially one of last resort and that it cannot match the authority and power that can be wielded by national courts. However, as is evident from the overburdened Strasbourg Court, national measures implementing the European Convention are currently inadequate and a greater focus on remedying this deficiency would be a more efficient use of existing, limited resources than any further expansion of the capacity of the Court, for which sufficient extra funding is in any event unlikely to be available. In this regard the United Kingdom's Human Rights Act 1998 is a potentially useful response to these problems. The character of the Charter means that it cannot meet the need, insofar as this exists, for

[42] See HC Krüger and J Polakiewicz, 'Proposals for a coherent human rights protection system in Europe' (2001) 22 HRLJ 1. However, this does not address similar concerns about other internationally guaranteed rights not included in the Convention.

[43] Although some do permit reliance on them in their courts.

[44] Such as a requirement that proceedings be re-opened and specific administrative measures be taken.

[45] Such as identifying, though not ordering, the appropriate remedy; see 'Report of the Evaluation Group to the Committee of Ministers on the European Court of Human Rights' (2001) EG 1 para 49.

[46] Notably economic and social rights.

a comparable response within the Union framework, but increased visibility for the rights listed makes it unlikely that the sort of situation Dicey found in much of Europe in the nineteenth century will be unduly tolerated there in the present one.

Conclusion

Proclamations can be empty gestures but they can also make a significant contribution to the effective protection of rights. Whether they do so ultimately depends on the framework within which they are placed. Their capacity to inspire and regulate the behaviour of public bodies ought not to be underestimated, but individuals are likely to enjoy greater security if they are not only legally binding but are also well-crafted, with their implementation being subject to independent judicial appraisal. The Charter does not fulfil all these requirements but, like the Universal Declaration, it may serve as a staging post to something that does do so. Moreover, in contrast to the United Nations, the Union has the advantage of having already in place a court with compulsory jurisdiction to provide an authoritative appraisal of compliance with the rights proclaimed,[47] whether or not that court is then subject to the overall scrutiny of the Strasbourg Court so as to achieve an appropriate institutional order.

[47] The two International Covenants (Civil and Political and Economic, Social and Cultural) are legally binding but supervised by bodies whose appraisal is not unquestionably authoritative. Emphasis on the importance of courts does not mean that other mechanisms are not also essential for human rights protection.

16

The EU Charter of Fundamental Rights

*FG Jacobs**

Introduction

In this chapter I am asked to consider the Charter not only in a technical legal perspective but in the broader context of the debate on the legitimacy and accountability of the European Union. That context seems a particularly appropriate one, because the Charter's significance may prove to be greater in that context than in terms of its immediate legal effects. If the Charter is examined in a narrower legal perspective in terms of its content, its scope and its status, it might seem to have relatively little significance. It would, however, be unwise to prejudge the impact of the Charter even in that perspective. In any event, it will be useful to recall the main features of the Charter.

First, as regards its legal status, as is well known it is not—at least not yet—legally binding. Although formally adopted at Nice in December 2000 by the Union's political institutions, the European Council decided, on that occasion, not to take a decision on its legal status. Nor is it intended to create new rights, but rather to give, as it was put, greater visibility—a higher profile—to existing rights. But of course new formulations may have some impact on the substance of the rights.

Second, as regards its scope, it is not a Charter for the Member States, but rather for the EU institutions:[1] this point becomes clear only towards the end of the Charter, in Chapter VII, 'General provisions'. Article 51(1) in that Chapter states: 'The provisions of this Charter are addressed to the institutions and bodies of the Union ... and', it adds, 'to the Member States only

---

* This chapter was completed in January 2002.

[1] It is noteworthy that the Charter is an EU Charter, rather than an EC Charter, and refers to the institutions of the European Union, as does the Treaty of Nice (see for example the preamble and Art 1(4)).

when they are implementing Union law.'[2] The addition 'to the Member States only when they are implementing Union law' is interesting insofar as it circumscribes by a precise formula the scope of Member States' responsibility in a way which reflects their existing responsibility under Community law. Indeed it reflects what is in my view a correct approach, even though the case law of the Court of Justice can be read as going further than that. But the term 'addressed to' is also significant in itself: perhaps the provisions do not 'apply to' the institutions and the Member States, because the Charter is not binding; but its provisions are addressed to them, and so can perhaps be expected to have some effect.

Third, as regards its content, the Charter essentially includes three categories of rights: first, a catalogue of the classic civil and political rights, principally but not exclusively concerned with liberty of the person; secondly, certain fundamental (and perhaps some rather less fundamental?) social and economic rights; and thirdly, under the heading 'Citizens' rights', the fundamental rights granted by the Community Treaties to citizens of the EU (ie nationals of the Member States): for example, the freedom of movement and of residence for EU citizens. Although the rights are traditional, the Charter sets them out using a novel structure; the rights contained in the Charter are ordered under six heads: dignity, freedoms, equality, solidarity, citizenship and justice.

The need for the Charter

I would suggest as a first point that the Charter is a response to a long-standing concern. The concern (expressed both in political circles and by certain national courts, notably the German Constitutional Court) was that the EC, and later the EU, had no instrument setting out what were to be regarded as fundamental rights. Almost every legal system in the modern world has such an instrument, or catalogue, to use a Germanism. It is often contained in the constitution. Certainly anyone drawing up a constitution today would include a bill of rights. It is true that until recently the UK had no such formal instrument—the Bill of Rights of 1689 being an instrument of a different kind. But of course it had—and has—no written constitution. It did however, when drawing up constitutions on the independence of its

---

[2] 'Union law' is used in the Charter to include 'Community law'; the same practice is used in the present chapter.

former colonies, incorporate the European Convention on Human Rights. And it finally incorporated the Convention in UK law when it enacted the Human Rights Act 1998.

Before then human rights were protected in English law by the common law. And the position was similar in EC law in that respect for fundamental rights was the creation of case law. The Court of Justice developed a substantial body of law, derived, in the absence of Treaty provisions, from the constitutions and laws of the Member States, and taking account also—indeed giving special significance to—the European Convention on Human Rights. This case law of the Court was ultimately incorporated into the Community Treaties by the Maastricht Treaty, which provided in what is now Article 6 of the Treaty on European Union:

(1) The Union is founded on the principles of liberty, democracy, respect for human rights and fundamental freedoms, and the rule of law, principles which are common to the Member States.
(2) The Union shall respect fundamental rights, as guaranteed by the European Convention [on Human Rights] and as they result from the constitutional traditions common to the Member States...

However, this formulation, while it symbolized the Union's attachment to respect for fundamental rights, did not meet concerns about the absence of a catalogue or code. It leaves open the question: which rights, apart from those guaranteed by the European Convention on Human Rights? The reference to 'the constitutional traditions common to the Member States' is not, it must be admitted, a model of precision. Moreover, most fundamental rights are also subject to certain limitations, on certain specified grounds: how are these to be assessed and applied? So it may have seemed useful for the EU to have a catalogue.

There is perhaps a further reason why the Charter would be useful. In the past, fundamental rights issues were of rather limited scope in Community law. Typically, what may have been at issue was whether a Community regulation interfered unduly with the right to property or the right to carry on a professional activity or a business. More recently, as will be seen shortly, a wider range of issues has begun to come before the Court. Some classic rights have been invoked in new forms; and some rather newer rights have been accepted as fundamental. So the concern for a catalogue—and an up-to-date catalogue—was perhaps more fully justified.

That concern was not limited to a need for a justiciable system to be applied within the EU's own legal order: in its external relations with the rest of the world, human rights were of an increasingly high profile. Not surprisingly: human rights have been one of the predominant themes over the past half-century in international law and in international relations generally. As regards the EU, let me take two recent examples.

First, there is the current process of enlargement of the EU. As amended by the Treaty of Amsterdam, Article 49 TEU provides that any European state *which respects the principles set out in Article 6(1)* may apply to become a member of the Union. Respect for human rights and observance of the rule of law are naturally in the forefront of the enlargement process; claims are being made by the EU of the applicant countries, whose standards are under scrutiny on this as on other matters—the development of a market economy, protection of the environment, a properly functioning administrative and judicial system.

Secondly, human rights clauses were now being systematically included in treaties between the EU and third states. In its foreign policy the EU was regularly making representations on human rights matters to other countries, from China to the US. Yet the EU lacked its own point of reference. And where it sought to insist that third countries which wished to deal with the EU should have an effective Bill of Rights, its efforts were perhaps less successful if it could not point to one of its own. So it was not only from the point of view of internal legal methodology that an EU bill of rights began to seem attractive. That external perspective is important when we consider the doubts that might be raised about the need for a Charter as an internal legal instrument or even the criticisms that can be advanced by lawyers of the content and form of the Charter as an internal legal instrument.

A question which inevitably arises in considering the need for the Charter is the significance of the European Convention on Human Rights. Politically, however, it had to be accepted that the way for EU accession to the Convention seemed, for the time being, closed—a point to which I shall return below.

On the substance, there were perhaps two main conflicting considerations, each carrying great weight. On the one hand, it was important that the Convention should not be 'upstaged'. On the other hand, there was felt to be a need for the EU to have its own catalogue, updated and adapted to its needs.

In the result, the picture is complex. Some of the Convention rights are taken over, but re-formulated, which may cause confusion. However, the position is clearly set out in Article 52 of the Charter, 'Scope of guaranteed rights', which provides in paragraph 3:

Insofar as this Charter contains rights which correspond to rights guaranteed by the Convention . . . , the meaning and scope of those rights shall be the same as those laid down by the said Convention. This provision shall not prevent Union law providing more extensive protection.

Moreover Article 53, 'Level of protection', provides

Nothing in this Charter shall be interpreted as restricting or adversely affecting human rights and fundamental freedoms as recognised, in their respective fields of application, by Union law and international law and by international agreements to which the Union, the Community or all the Member States are party, including the European Convention [on Human Rights], and by the Member States' constitutions.

Moreover, as has been seen, in many respects the Charter goes beyond the Convention.

It may also be asked how relevant many of the fundamental rights in the Charter are to the activities of the Union. It seems to me, however, that they are indeed relevant. Let me take first the classic civil and political rights. At first sight it might seem that the most fundamental rights proclaimed by the Charter— human dignity in Article 1, or the right to life and the prohibition of the death penalty in Article 2—have little to do with the EU institutions. That is not so. Already in the short life of the Charter a serious allegation has been made by a Member State that a major piece of Community legislation (the biotechnology directive on the patenting of products of human origin) violates human dignity.[3] Even though the Charter is not itself binding, there can be no doubt that respect for human dignity is a fundamental right protected by Community law. Human dignity is not in terms recognized by the European Convention on Human Rights, although the prohibition of 'degrading treatment' has in certain contexts been held to protect human dignity. That illustrates what seems to me, as a 'user', a significant value of the Charter, within certain limits: it not only provides a convenient point of reference, serving to identify what rights are fundamental; it also serves to give them a clear and up-to-date formulation, and, in relation to those rights which are not absolute, to set out, very succinctly, the permissible limitations.

The right to life and the prohibition of the death penalty have not yet come before the Court, although the right to life might have been regarded as in issue some years ago in the well-known case from the Republic of

---

[3] Case C-377/98 *Netherlands v Parliament and Council*, judgment of 9 October 2001.

Ireland concerning abortion services.[4] The practice of abortion raises the extremely sensitive question of the point at which the right to life begins, and whether it confers protection on the unborn foetus. In the event the Court was able to resolve the case without addressing the issue.

Again, however, we should not confine our assessment of the Charter to the judicial perspective: the right to life and the prohibition of the death penalty have long been invoked by the EU on the political level; thus the EU has regularly made representations, with which applicant states have associated themselves, protesting against certain applications of the death penalty, notably in the United States. And current moves towards a common approach to extradition may reflect the position now taken in Europe that extradition will be refused where it is liable to lead to the death penalty.

When we come to the social and economic rights contained in the Charter (and grouped under the head 'solidarity'), the position is perhaps more controversial. There have often been questions about whether such rights should be protected by the same instruments as civil and political rights. In their nature such rights often seem different in kind, requiring positive intervention by the state, rather than protecting the individual against the state—although this may be an over-simplification. From a lawyer's perspective, social and economic rights do seem rights of a different kind from civil and political rights, not always legally enforceable, and perhaps not always justiciable at all. In human rights instruments, the mechanism to secure their respect is often, as in the 1961 European Social Charter of the Council of Europe, a reporting mechanism, under which states are asked to make periodic reports, which are then examined by a committee of independent experts. It is noteworthy also that under that Charter, Member States may select a menu of rights to which they commit themselves, a procedure which suggests that acceptance reflects the policy orientation of particular governments at particular periods, or may depend on the level of social and economic development, and which may cast doubt on the universal and fundamental character of the rights in question. Similarly the Community Charter of the Fundamental Social Rights of Workers was initially accepted only by 11 of the then 12 Member States of the EU, not by the then Conservative Government of the UK.

Nonetheless the social and economic rights contained in the Charter must be recognized as more than pious aspirations. They are based in part on the European Social Charter and on the Community Charter which I have

---

[4] Case C-159/90 *Grogan and Others* [1991] ECR I-4685.

mentioned, and also on Community social legislation; thus the text of Article 32 of the Charter (prohibition of child labour and protection of young people at work) has its origins in Article 7 of the European Social Charter, points 20–23 of the Community Charter, and a 1994 Community directive on the protection of young people at work. The effect of the Charter here may be to encourage the Court to take a broad view of the rights already recognized by existing instruments, in view of the endorsement given by the Charter to their fundamental status. Difficulties might, however, arise where the rights in question have not previously been given explicit recognition. Can such rights be regarded as falling within the constitutional traditions of the Member States and as having legal force as an expression of those traditions? Can inclusion in the Charter in itself give them legal effect?

The position is perhaps more straightforward with the third category of rights: those included under the head 'Citizens' rights', namely the fundamental rights granted by the Community Treaties to citizens of the EU. Here the Court is, if I may put it in this way, on familiar territory: it knows these rights and has some experience in applying them; it recognizes their fundamental character and imposes a relatively narrow construction on their limitation clauses. The Charter itself also provides a measure of reassurance: according to Article 52(2), rights which are based on the EC Treaty or the EU Treaty are to be exercised 'under the conditions and within the limits defined by those Treaties'. This has been taken to mean, surely correctly, that the Charter is merely a neutral confirmation of those rights, without any widening or reduction of their scope.[5]

This brief overview gives some idea of what the Charter is, in the sense of what it contains. We may now look more generally at its effects: to start with, its legal significance.

The legal significance of the Charter

It has been suggested that some legal significance should be attached to the constitution of the body which drew up the Charter, and to the original way in which it proceeded. It was drawn up by a body consisting of members of the European Parliament and of national Parliaments, and representatives of the Heads of State or Government of the EU Member States and of the

---

[5] See K Lenaerts and E De Smijter, 'A "Bill of Rights" for the European Union' (2001) 38 CMLRev 273, 282.

president of the European Commission. In contrast to the traditional methods of diplomacy followed by intergovernmental conferences for amending the Treaties, the body (which decided to call itself 'Convention', echoing both French and US history,[6] but perhaps causing unnecessary confusion with the European Convention on Human Rights) followed a very open procedure, receiving representation from a wide range of sources and publicizing its working papers. (It received more than 1000 documents, emanating from more than 200 sources.) The IGC did not incorporate the Charter into the Treaties or include a reference to it in Article 6(2) EU. Instead, on 7 December 2000, the Charter was solemnly proclaimed by the European Parliament, the Council and the Commission. Moreover the Parliament and the Commission appear to have accepted that they are bound by it.

A first question which arises is whether the Charter is binding internally on the institutions which proclaimed it, or in any event on the institutions which have accepted its binding effect. Some have gone further and have suggested that the effect of solemn proclamation of the Charter by the institutions which have legislative powers may be not very different from that of insertion of the Charter into the Treaties.[7] But the fact remains that the Charter was not given formal legal effect, and moreover that the European Council formally reserved the question at Nice, deciding instead that 'the European Council, at its meeting at Laeken/Brussels in December 2001, will agree on a declaration containing appropriate initiatives for the continuation of [the debate about the future development of the EU]. The process should address, inter alia…the status of the Charter of Fundamental Rights of the European Union proclaimed in Nice'.

Since the Convention did not receive any instructions as to the legal status of the Charter it was to draft, it decided to draw it up in a form in which it could become legally binding and enforceable. No doubt that was the correct approach, since any other approach would have precluded the possibility of a subsequent political decision to incorporate the Charter in the Treaties or otherwise give it legal effect.

That background may help to explain the degree of caution hitherto shown by the Court of Justice in abstaining in its judgments from reference

---

[6] Including the 'Constitutional Convention' which in 1787 adopted the Constitution of the USA.

[7] eg Lenaerts and De Smijter (n 5 above) 298–9.

to the Charter. And although the Advocates General have invoked the Charter in several cases, they have done so in various ways which do not necessarily imply recognition of any legal force.

Thus Advocate General Mischo does so in his opinion in *D and Sweden v Council*,[8] a staff case concerning, among other things, an alleged discrimination on the basis of sexual orientation. He notes as a confirmation of his reasoning that the difference between marriage, on the one hand, and a partnership between persons of the same sex, on the other hand, is recognized by the Charter.[9]

Particular mention may be made of *BECTU*,[10] a case from the UK concerning the right to paid annual leave. Advocate General Tizzano notes that, in the Community context, the Heads of State enshrined that right in paragraph 8 of the Community Charter of the Fundamental Social Rights of Workers. He continues:

Even more significant, it seems to me, is the fact that that right is now solemnly upheld in the Charter of Fundamental Rights of the European Union, published on 7 December 2000 by the European Parliament, the Council and the Commission after approval by the Heads of State and Government of the Member States, often on the basis of an express and specific mandate from the national Parliaments.[11]

He then adds:

Admittedly... the Charter of Fundamental Rights of the European Union has not been recognised as having genuine legislative scope in the strict sense. In other words, formally, it is not in itself binding. However, without wishing to participate here in the wide-ranging debate now going on as to the effects which, in other forms and by other means, the Charter may nevertheless produce, the fact remains that it includes statements which appear in large measure to reaffirm rights which are enshrined in other instruments... I think therefore that, in proceedings concerned with the nature and scope of a fundamental right, the relevant statements of the Charter cannot be ignored; in particular, we cannot ignore its clear purpose of serving, where its provisions so allow, as a substantive point of reference for all those involved—Member States, institutions, natural and legal persons—in the Community context. Accordingly, I consider that the Charter provides us with the most reliable and definitive confirmation of the fact that the right to paid annual leave constitutes a fundamental right.[12]

---

[8] Joined Cases C-122/99 P and C-125/99 P [2001] ECR I-4319.

[9] At para 97.

[10] Case C-173/99 [2001] ECR 4881.

[11] At para 26.

[12] At paras 27 and 28.

So far there is no judgment or order by the Court of Justice referring to the Charter. However the Court of First Instance relied upon it in the *max.mobil* case.[13] Here the Court held that, to the extent that the Commission is required to undertake a diligent and impartial examination of complaints that Member States have infringed the competition rules, the fulfilment of that obligation must be amenable to judicial review. The Court of First Instance stated:[14]

Such judicial review is also one of the general principles that are observed in a State governed by the rule of law and are common to the constitutional traditions of the Member States, as is confirmed by Article 47 of the Charter of Fundamental Rights, under which any person whose rights guaranteed by the law of the Union are violated has the right to an effective remedy before a tribunal.

Independently of the use which the Courts may make of the Charter, it seems likely to be increasingly invoked, cited, and used as a point of reference in legal and political discourse generally. That leads to a consideration of the broader impact of the Charter.

The development of a fundamental rights 'culture'

The Charter may contribute to the development of a more rights-oriented system, both legally and more generally.

Legally, the Community Treaties are not conceived as a rights-based system: they are largely framed in terms of obligations of Member States and powers of the institutions. Discourse in legal argument tends to reflect that emphasis: individual rights emerge only as a reflex, and although economic rights are stressed by the Court's approach, fundamental rights tend to have a secondary role. Thus for example, in a case on supply of services, the emphasis is characteristically on reviewing restrictions in the light of the internal market, and on the need for effectiveness, uniformity, etc.; a claim to, say, freedom of expression will tend to emerge as a subsidiary argument and be dealt with more summarily. The Charter may lead to a greater emphasis on freedom of expression and other fundamental rights.

On a broader front, and independently of any legally binding effect which it may have on the political institutions, the Charter may reinforce in the

---

[13] Case T-54/99, judgment of 30 January 2002.   [14] At para 57 of the judgment.

minds of administrators and legislators the rights of the individual and the need to respect them. It may also carry a more powerful message to the public at large.

The wider significance of the Charter drafting process

In assessing the broader impact of the Charter, especially in enhancing the legitimacy of the EU, we should not lose sight of the significance of the unprecedented process by which the Charter was generated: the Charter body composed of a combination of government representatives, Parliamentarians, and experts; its proceedings given much publicity; its deliberations fed by inputs from the public and from interested non-governmental organizations.

The Charter process appears to have been particularly successful in that the substance of the text adopted by the Convention, notwithstanding inevitable criticism, met with a large measure of approval, and the text was not amended in any respect before its endorsement by the political institutions.

The process provides a striking contrast with the customary process of inter-governmental negotiations, which are characteristically conducted in secret, by methods sometimes compared with horse-trading (although it is no longer obvious why horse-traders should be treated so invidiously); moreover they are often apparently dominated by laborious negotiations on matters of lesser importance but of particular sensitivity to certain Governments while issues of greater public interest are given little attention.

It is above all significant that the Charter process has been recognized as a precedent to be followed with a far wider remit in advance of the next IGC. The Laeken Declaration on the Future of the European Union, adopted by the European Council at Laeken, Belgium in December 2001, states:

In order to pave the way for the next IGC as broadly and openly as possible, the European Council has decided to convene a Convention composed of the main parties involved in the debate on the future of the Union ... It will be the task of that Convention to consider the key issues arising for the Union's future development and try to identify the various possible responses.

The European Council also agreed to establish a Forum which would contribute to the work of the Convention and engage in dialogue with it:

In order for the debate to be broadly based and involve all citizens, a Forum will be opened for organisations representing civil society (the social partners, the business world, NGOs, academia, etc.). It will take the form of a structured network of organisations receiving regular information on the Convention's proceedings. Their contributions will serve as input into the debate.

Most appropriately, one of the issues for the Convention (which as appears from the above is not limited to the 'Nice left-overs' but has the broadest remit) is likely to be the status to be given to the Charter itself. Although that question is not specifically assigned to the Convention, the Laeken Declaration states, under the head 'Towards a Constitution for European citizens', that 'Thought would also have to be given to whether the Charter of Fundamental Rights should be included in the basic treaties and to whether the European Community should accede to the European Convention on Human Rights'.

While the final decisions will of course be taken by the IGC, the improvement in the Union's constitution-making process can only be welcomed, and is a direct result of the Charter process.

The future of the Charter

While it is not possible to predict how the role of the Charter will evolve, two lines of possible evolution can be mentioned. First, the use of the Charter before the Community Courts is likely to develop: it will no doubt be increasingly invoked by litigants and may be increasingly cited by the Courts, even without any formal change in its legal status. Secondly, consideration by the new Convention may lead to formal developments in the next IGC; the Charter might, for example, be given formal recognition in the preamble to the new Treaty, given some constitutional or other status, or embodied in some form in the substance of the Treaty (for example in the current Article 6(2) TEU).

More far-reaching questions may also arise: at present, as we have seen, it is addressed to the institutions of the EU and to the Member States where they implement EU law. Should its scope be enlarged to encompass the Member States in all respects? That seems both unnecessary and undesirable. Respect for fundamental rights in areas within the competence of the Member States can and should be left to their national courts and to the European Court of Human Rights. To confer an additional layer of jurisdiction on the Court of Justice is unnecessary, and would both overload the Court itself and weaken the Convention system.

However, if the jurisdictional difficulties could be overcome, it is perhaps not impossible that respect for the Charter might become, for Member States, an EU obligation. Indeed there is already, as we have seen, an implicit obligation under Article 6(1) TEU for Member States to respect human rights and fundamental freedoms, since such respect is said to be one of the principles on which the Union is founded; and the Council may take action under Article 7 where there is a serious and persistent breach by a Member State of principles mentioned in Article 6(1)—or, under the Treaty of Nice, where there is a clear risk of a serious breach of those principles.

So there is already a clear EU competence in relation to Member States' human rights obligations and this could be extended to the Charter. Perhaps, however, such obligations should not be brought within the Community judicial system but should remain on the political level. Indeed the European Parliament has stated that it intends to review annually the observance by Member States of the Charter rights and freedoms.

On the political level, the Charter could become a benchmark for evaluating the conduct of Member States.

Other desirable improvements in judicial protection

Independently of the Charter, there may be a need for improvements in judicial protection of the rights of individuals within the EU. The need for such improvements is indeed highlighted by the adoption of the Charter.

In this field there is already, of course, a substantial body of case law which the Court of Justice has developed over the years. One of the basic principles which the Court has developed is that of effective judicial protection. The Court has stressed, in particular, the obligation of national courts to ensure the effective protection of Community rights (rights which are not limited to 'fundamental rights'), and that line of case law has had remarkable, almost revolutionary implications for national law and national remedies as has been demonstrated in recent years in such cases as *Factortame*[15] and *Francovich*.[16] But the principle of effective judicial protection also applies to the

---

[15] Joined Cases C-46/93 and C-48/93 *Brasserie du Pêcheur and Factortame* [1996] ECR I-1029.

[16] Joined Cases C-6/90 and C-9/90 *Francovich and Others* [1991] ECR I-5357.

Community Courts themselves. Three significant improvements may be mentioned.

First, access for individuals to challenge Community measures before the Community judicature could be improved. The restrictive test of standing for individuals, adopted many years ago in the *Plaumann* case,[17] and largely although not wholly followed since, is very widely criticized, and is perhaps particularly inappropriate since the establishment of the Court of First Instance with a particular responsibility for improving the judicial protection of individual interests. Moreover the right of access to a court with jurisdiction to grant a remedy is now widely recognized as a fundamental right; it would be paradoxical in the age of the Charter for that right not to be recognized in the Union's own judicial system. It may be possible for that development to be achieved by an evolution of the Court's case law, without the need for Treaty amendment.

Secondly, if fundamental rights are indeed to be fully protected in the Union's judicial system, there may be a need to extend judicial protection more widely, particularly as the Union's powers are extended and new bodies with, for example, police powers and investigative powers are set up. It is significant that Article 51(1) of the Charter, cited above, states that the provisions of the Charter are addressed to the institutions *and bodies* of the Union. At present, the Court's jurisdiction extends to the institutions, but not to such bodies. There may be a need therefore for Treaty amendment to ensure that any exercise of power which may involve infringement of fundamental rights by any Union institution or other Union body is subject to effective judicial review. Again, the principle of effective judicial protection requires no less than this.

This leads to a third urgent need for reform. While it could be said, under the original EEC Treaty as interpreted by the Court of Justice, that (subject to the limitations on direct access for individuals) all Community acts were subject to judicial review and that there was a complete system of remedies, there is now, after the Maastricht three-pillar structure and the further complexities introduced by the Amsterdam Treaty, an almost grotesque patchwork in the judicial system, such that there is even controversy whether in certain areas the Court has jurisdiction or not. What is required is that the existing jurisdictional morass should be replaced by a clear and intelligible system in which the exercise of all Union powers is again subject to judicial review and the provision of effective remedies.

[17] Case 25/62 [1963] ECR 95.

All these improvements seem desirable, or even necessary, if the European Union is to develop as a coherent and comprehensible entity, and should perhaps be among the first matters for consideration if steps are taken to improve the legitimacy and accountability of the EU.

Accession to the European Convention on Human Rights

The accession of the EC to the European Convention on Human Rights is, as mentioned, included on the agenda by the Laeken Declaration. Community accession to the Convention is an issue which has been debated for more than twenty years, and there are of course strong arguments on both sides of the debate. Here it may be sufficient to make two points.

First, the existence of the Charter, even if it were to be given formal legal or even constitutional recognition, does not of itself provide any legal or other argument against accession. The Charter—although it may have been conceived in part as a short-term alternative to accession—can coexist with the Convention. That would reflect the position in the Member States. Thus the Member States (all of whom are parties to the Convention) have their own Bills of Rights which operate side by side both with the incorporation of the Convention in national law (in those states where it is so incorporated) and with their participation in the Convention system, including their acceptance of the jurisdiction of the European Court of Human Rights.

Secondly, so far as the Court of Justice is concerned, the fact that it ruled in 1996[18] that accession was incompatible with the Treaty as it then stood should not, I am sure, be taken to mean that, beyond the formal objection which it raised at the time, the Court is opposed to the principle of accession by the Community or by the Union. (Indeed, the President and other members of the Court have expressed themselves personally in favour of accession.) In any event, even if the objection raised by the Court were still valid today, it could be overcome, if the political will were present, by an appropriate Treaty amendment. The fact is that at the time of the Court's Opinion there were also strong political objections by Member States. Even today, the objections may still be political rather than legal. The political objections today seem mainly to lie in the idea that accession would increase the Community's (or Union's) powers. But this is partly a matter of perspective. For others, accession might be seen rather as limiting those powers, by

[18] Opinion 2/94 [1996] ECR I-1759.

subjecting their exercise to additional and external scrutiny for compliance with the principle of respect for human rights.

Conclusion

While one of the reasons for the Charter may have been the desire for a greater degree of legitimacy, and indeed popular support, for the European Union, it remains to be seen how far that will be the result. It could even be thought that the adoption of a Charter of fundamental rights which could not be enforced might have the opposite effect. Much may depend on what recognition is given to the Charter, and whether it is accompanied by other measures both to improve the judicial protection of the individual and to connect the individual more effectively with the Union's institutions.

17

The Principle of Non-Discrimination in the Post-Nice Era

Evelyn Ellis

The anti-discrimination directives adopted in 2000

The subject-matter of this chapter is the two anti-discrimination directives which were adopted in 2000.[1] Together these instruments forbid discrimination on the grounds of race, religion, age, disability and sexual orientation. Being directives, they will have full binding force throughout the Union once their implementation periods have expired, but they require legislation to be passed by the Member States to incorporate their provisions into the national legal systems.[2] After this has happened, the instruments will govern both the public and the private sectors.[3]

Although these two directives were enacted before the Nice Conference took place, the underlying theme of a likely future expansion of the Union to include states in Central and Eastern Europe provided the backdrop, and even to some extent the raison d'être, for the adoption of the new measures. There was a clear desire which was expressed by the representatives of the

---

[1] Council Directive 2000/43 of 29 June 2000 implementing the principle of equal treatment between persons irrespective of racial or ethnic origin [2000] OJ L180/22; Council Directive 2000/78 of 27 November 2000 establishing a general framework for equal treatment in employment and occupation [2000] OJ L303/46. See also M Bell, 'Article 13 EC: the European Commission's anti-discrimination proposals' (2000) 29 ILJ 79.

[2] See Art 249 EC.

[3] Exceptionally, even an unimplemented directive can be enforced against the State or one of its organs provided that its implementation period has expired and that its provisions are sufficiently precise to be enforced judicially as they stand. See Case 148/78 *Pubblico Ministero v Ratti* [1979] ECR 1629, Case 152/84 *Marshall v Southampton and South-West Hampshire Area Health Authority* [1986] ECR 723, Case C-91/92 *Faccini Dori v Recreb* [1994] ECR I-3325, and Case C-188/89 *Foster v British Gas plc* [1990] ECR I-3313.

Member States during the legislative process, as well as by the Commission and the European Parliament, to set a civilized minimum standard for the protection of vulnerable groups against discrimination.

The significance of the directives

The enactment of these directives marks an extremely important moment in the history of the EU's activities in the area of social policy. The prohibition of discrimination on the ground of nationality, at least if that nationality is that of one of the Member States, has been a part of the Community's law since the outset.[4] The evolution of its laws on sex discrimination, although this might well come as a surprise to the drafters of the original Treaty of Rome were they alive today, continues apace and is well accepted.[5]

However, the enactment of law forbidding discrimination on the grounds of race, religion, disability, age and sexual orientation represents a huge new step. The outlawing of discrimination on the ground of nationality is an essential aspect of a developed common market, where the free mobility of persons is as important as the free mobility of goods; it is a fundamental aspect of the underlying philosophy. The same is probably true of the rules forbidding sex discrimination; although the European Court of Justice has always ascribed a more humanitarian function to it,[6] it should not be forgotten that what actually inspired the equal pay provision was the commercial impulse not to penalize those states which already respected the principle.[7] Notwithstanding that the legislation and the Court have now gone much further than this crude basic in protecting workers from sex discrimination, there nonetheless remains an essential economic kernel to much of this law.

However, when it comes to law forbidding discrimination on other, wider grounds, the EU is stepping far more overtly into the arena of social policy.

---

[4] See Arts 12 and 39 EC.

[5] See Art 141 EC, the Equal Pay Directive (Dir 75/117, [1975] OJ L45/19), the Equal Treatment Directive (Dir 76/207 [1976] OJ L39/40), the Social Security Directive (Dir 79/7 [1979] OJ L6/24), the Occupational Social Security Directive (Dir 86/378 [1986] OJ L225/40), the Directive on the Self-Employed (Dir 86/613 [1986] OJ L359/56), the Pregnancy Directive (Dir 92/85 [1992] OJ L 348/1), the Directive on Parental Leave (Dir 96/34 [1996] OJ L145/4), the Directive on Part-Time Work (Dir 97/81 [1998] OJ L14/9), and the Burden of Proof Directive (Dir 97/80 [1998] OJ L14/6).

[6] Its original statement to this effect is to be found in Case 43/75 *Defrenne v Sabena* [1976] ECR 455, 471–472.

[7] J Forman, 'The equal pay principle under Community law' (1982) 1 LIEI 17.

Admittedly, the new rules are bound to have some economic impact. Nevertheless, the rationale for enacting them lies preponderantly in the concepts of fairness, autonomy, human dignity and respect for human rights, the creation of a better society in which the quality of people's lives will be improved. The importance of this development in the law is therefore not confined to the new substantive rights which it will give to those within its scope. It is also a clear signal that the EU is shifting the political goalposts. It appears that today it regards itself as a legitimate legislator for the protection of the welfare of its citizens in situations which go well beyond those with merely economic consequences for the single market.

The background to the directives

A new Article 13 was added to the Treaty of Rome by the Treaty of Amsterdam in 1997. It provides:

Without prejudice to the other provisions of this Treaty and within the limits of the powers conferred by it upon the Community, the Council, acting unanimously on a proposal from the Commission and after consulting the European Parliament, may take appropriate action to combat discrimination based on sex, racial or ethnic origin, religion or belief, disability, age or sexual orientation.

This was an important addition to the Treaty because there is no inherent power to legislate vested in the EU;[8] it is unlike the UK's national Parliament at Westminster, which of course possesses at least a theoretical power to pass legislation on any subject. The enactment of an authority such as Article 13 was therefore necessary before any work could be done by the Union in the wider fields of discrimination; it also represented a statement of political intent.

The catalyst for its inclusion was undoubtedly a general fear about racism within the EU. In addition to fears resulting from the rise to power of the Freedom Party in Austria in 1999/2000 and the emergence of extreme right-wing groups in Germany and other places, there was a perception among the Member States that some of the aspiring entrant states in central and eastern Europe posed serious problems in relation to racial, ethnic and religious tolerance, especially as far as the Roma were concerned. The

---

[8] The EU's most general mandate for legislation is contained in Art 308 EC.

Commission and the Member States took the view that it was vital to ensure that the 'acquis communautaire' contained strong anti-discrimination legislation in good time before those states became members of the Union.

The breadth of the intended ban on discrimination was, however, a matter of debate. In the run-up to the Inter-Governmental Conference of 1996, all the Member States apart from the UK had expressed a desire for an extension to the Treaty to cover legislation prohibiting race discrimination. A number were also in favour of outlawing discrimination on the ground of religion. The UK's Conservative administration, which held office until 1997, alone maintained that EU legislation in these areas was inappropriate; invoking the principle of subsidiarity, it argued that such matters were better left to individual Member States and that legislation should be tailored to their specific circumstances. Interestingly enough, no other Member State shared this view about anti-discrimination legislation and, the UK apart, there was a consensus that action at EU level could achieve results which could not be achieved by the Member States acting alone. The UK's attitude changed only with the election of the Labour government in 1997, which was keen to be seen to be playing a more positive role in the EU legislative process. The UK's change of heart in 1997 made it possible for the Council to reach the unanimous agreement needed to insert the new Article 13 into the Treaty. There was, however, little general agreement at the outset about the inclusion of prohibited grounds other than race and religion. Credit for the final form of the Article, embracing as it does also disability, age and sexual orientation, is largely due to the influence of the Irish Presidency of the Council in the second half of 1996.[9]

Given the important influence of racial discrimination on the evolution of Article 13, it might perhaps have been expected that race would have been afforded some sort of exalted status by the Member States. No form of hierarchy is however created by Article 13. Conversely, the Article does not mandate identical legislative treatment for each of the prohibited categories which it enumerates. The way is therefore left open for umbrella-like legislation extending to all the listed forms of discrimination; or for specific legislation dealing with each individual area; or, indeed, for a combination of these approaches. The fact that the Commission chose to deal with race in one instrument and with all the other prohibited classes in another single

---

[9] Irish law at this time contained the most sophisticated provisions on discrimination in the Community. The Employment Equality Act 1998 prohibits discrimination on grounds of gender, marital status, family status, sexual orientation, religious belief, age, disability, race and membership of the travelling community.

instrument is significant because it manifests more than a hint of political realism. The Commission was aware that there existed more enthusiasm for banning some types of discrimination than others and it was keen to go as far as it could to exploit the opportunity offered by Article 13.

The content of the directives

The Race Directive

The Race Directive contains a long preamble, stressing the commitment of the EU to the protection of fundamental human rights and the particular concern being felt at the present time about racism[10] and xenophobia. Many of its paragraphs expressly foreshadow substantive articles of the Directive itself. In strictly legal terms, the most significant part of the preamble is Recital 13 which states that the directive is intended to apply to third country nationals, though not to discrimination on the ground of nationality itself; it adds that the Directive is without prejudice to provisions governing the entry and residence of third country nationals and their access to employment and occupation.

Also of particular note are the subsequent two recitals. Recital 14 reminds all concerned that the Community should, in accordance with Article 3(2) of the EC Treaty, aim to eliminate inequalities and promote sex equality, 'especially since women are often the victims of multiple discrimination'. Recital 15 makes implicit reference to the sensitivity of recording racial origin in some parts of the EU and states that indirect discrimination may be established by any means 'including on the basis of statistical evidence'.

Article 1 of the Directive explains that its purpose is 'to lay down a framework for combating discrimination on the grounds of racial or ethnic origin, with a view to putting into effect in the Member States the principle of equal treatment'.

Article 2 states that there must be no direct or indirect discrimination based on racial or ethnic origin. For the first time in EU law, the directive defines direct discrimination. In doing so, it draws heavily on the wording of section 1(1)(a) of the UK's Race Relations Act 1976: 'direct discrimination shall be taken to occur where one person is treated less favourably than

---

[10] Recital 6 of the Preamble states: 'The European Union rejects theories which attempt to determine the existence of separate human races. The use of the term "racial origin" in this Directive does not imply an acceptance of such theories'.

another is, has been or would be treated in a comparable situation on grounds of racial or ethnic origin'.[11] An important feature of this drafting, therefore, is that direct discrimination on racial or ethnic grounds does not require the existence of an actual comparator and that mere hypothetical comparison is sufficient to discharge the legislative standard. Indirect discrimination is a concept which is today broadly familiar to the legal world; it acknowledges that behaviour can produce a discriminatory impact even though it is not explicitly predicated upon a prohibited classification; thus, it has long been accepted, for example, that a practice which excludes part-time workers indirectly discriminates against women since the overwhelming majority of part-timers in the EU are female.[12] In its definition of indirect discrimination, the Directive attempts a difficult compromise; it seeks a broader application than that of the pre-existing sex discrimination legislation, which required actual damage to have occurred to the victim,[13] but yet it tries to stop short of penalizing all behaviour with the potential for an adverse racial or ethnic impact, since the latter result would be oppressive to employers and other respondents. The desire to protect against contingent as well as existing harm sprang partly from the principle that it is preferable to prevent damage than to compensate for it and also from the distaste in some Member States for the collection of racial and ethnic data which has already been referred to.[14] Article 2(2)(b) therefore states:

Indirect discrimination shall be taken to occur where an apparently neutral provision, criterion or practice would put persons of a racial or ethnic origin at a particular disadvantage compared with other persons, unless that provision criterion or practice is objectively justified by a legitimate aim and the means of achieving that aim are appropriate and necessary.

---

[11] Art 2(2)(a) of the Directive.

[12] See eg Case 96/80 *Jenkins v Kingsgate Ltd* [1981] ECR 911 and Case 170/84 *Bilka-Kaufhaus GmbH v Weber Von Hartz* [1986] ECR 1607.

[13] Art 2 of the Burden of Proof Directive defines indirect discrimination for the purposes of sex discrimination law as 'where an apparently neutral provision, criterion or practice disadvantages a substantially higher proportion of the members of one sex unless that provision, criterion or practice is appropriate and necessary and can be justified by objective factors unrelated to sex'. However, this definition will be aligned with that contained in the Race Directive when the changes to the Equal Treatment Directive agreed by the Conciliation Committee in May 2002 come into effect. Art 2(1)(a) of the amended directive defines indirect sex discrimination as occurring 'Where an apparently neutral provision, criterion or practice *would put* persons of one sex at a particular disadvantage...' (emphasis added).

[14] The new definition is also based upon that adopted by the Court of Justice in relation to discrimination on the ground of nationality against migrant workers; see Case C-237/94 *O'Flynn v Adjudication Officer* [1996] ECR I-2617.

Article 2(3) of the Directive expressly includes harassment as a pro-hibited form of discrimination. Harassment is defined as unwanted conduct related to racial or ethnic origin which 'takes place with the purpose or effect of violating the dignity of a person and of creating an intimidating, hostile, degrading, humiliating or offensive environment'. Article 2(4) also outlaws the giving of instructions to discriminate.

The scope of the Race Directive is articulated in Article 3 and is much wider than that of the parallel sex discrimination legislation, which at present only covers the world of economic work. The Race Directive not only applies to all aspects of employment, self-employment, occupation and vocational training, but it also extends to social protection including social security and healthcare, social advantages, education, and access to and supply of goods and services which are available to the public including housing. Considerable doubt surrounds the meaning of 'social advantages'. The Commission in its Explanatory Memorandum referred to the meaning of social advantages arrived at by the Court of Justice in relation to the free movement of workers, in other words, benefits of an economic or cultural nature granted either by public authorities or private organizations;[15] it said that the same meaning was intended to be applied here, so that the directive might cover such matters as concessionary travel on public transport, reduced prices for cultural or other events and subsidized meals in schools for children from low income families.[16] The meaning of 'goods and ser-vices' in this context will also require further elaboration by the Court of Justice. Healthcare and housing are not prima facie within the scope of the Treaty and therefore their inclusion within the scope of the Directive is not apparently authorized by Article 13; however, these matters might be covered where another Community right, perhaps freedom of movement, was in question. Thus a victim might, for example, complain about racial discrimination over healthcare where he or she had migrated to another Community country in search of a job. As presaged by the Preamble, Article 3(2) provides that the instrument does not apply to immigration; this exception is expressed in terms which are broad enough to extend beyond a mere decision not to admit such persons into a Member State or to deport them since the paragraph excludes 'any treatment which arises from the legal status of the third-country nationals and stateless persons concerned'.

Article 4 contains an exception for 'genuine and determining occupa-tional requirements' which is largely modelled on the provision contained

---

[15] See Reg 1612/68 on the free movement of workers, [1968] OJ L257/2, Art 7(2).
[16] See eg Case 32/75 *Cristini v SNCF* [1975] ECR 1085.

in section 5 of the UK's Race Relations Act 1976. Thus, a difference in treatment which is based on a characteristic related to racial or ethnic origin is excused where, by reason of the nature of the particular occupational activities concerned or of the context in which they are carried out, such a characteristic constitutes a genuine and determining occupational requirement, provided that the objective is legitimate and the requirement is proportionate. The Directive does not therefore, for example, render it unlawful for a director to choose a black man to play the part of Othello. Although there is obviously scope for argument at the margins of this provision, it is essentially a non-controversial part of the instrument.

The same cannot be said of Article 5 which permits positive action. This states: 'With a view to ensuring full equality in practice, the principle of equal treatment shall not prevent any Member State from maintaining or adopting specific measures to prevent or compensate for disadvantages linked to racial or ethnic origin'. This provision seems to have been particularly badly affected by the lottery of the Commission's drafting process. It is not an accurate reproduction of either the equivalent provision in the Equal Treatment Directive or of Article 141(4) of the EC Treaty. The Equal Treatment Directive refers in Article 2(4) to 'measures to promote equal opportunities for men and women, in particular by removing existing inequalities which affect women's opportunities', and Article 141(4) permits the Member States to maintain or adopt measures 'providing for specific advantages in order to make it easier for the under-represented sex to pursue a vocational activity or to prevent or compensate for disadvantages in professional careers'. It is unclear whether the departure in the new Directive from the wording of these other provisions is intended to be of significance nor, if it is so intended, what that significance is. Furthermore, the case law of the Court of Justice on the equivalent sex discrimination provisions is notoriously inscrutable,[17] which itself is probably evidence of the deep political and philosophical tensions which surround the whole matter of positive action. In particular, it is not known whether any measure of reverse discrimination is intended to be permitted and, if it is, within what limits. In the view of the present writer, because of the legitimate scope for a wide diversity of views on the role of positive action, this is an area where it is unacceptable to leave the resolution of the meaning of the law entirely in judicial hands.

The remaining articles of the Race Directive are less controversial. Article 6 permits the Member States to legislate in terms which are more

---

[17] See Case C-450/93 *Kalanke v Bremen* [1995] ECR I-3051, Case C-409/95 *Marschall v Land Nordrhein-Westfalen* [1997] ECR I-6363 and Case C-158/97 *Badeck* [2001] 2 CMLR 6.

favourable to the equality principle than the directive demands. They are not, however, permitted to use the directive to reduce their existing levels of protection against discrimination. Article 7 requires 'judicial and/or administrative procedures' for the victims of discrimination, though it is doubtful whether a mere administrative process would satisfy the judicial standard for the protection of fundamental human rights. Article 7 also provides that representative actions must be available to the victims of discrimination. The article is to be read together with Article 15 which mandates sanctions for unlawful discrimination which are 'effective, proportionate and dissuasive' and which may comprise the payment of compensation to the victim.

Article 8 reflects the rule established both by decisions of the Court of Justice[18] and by the Burden of Proof Directive[19] to the effect that the proof of a prima facie case casts the burden of disproof onto the respondent.

Article 9 outlaws victimization in broad terms: 'Member States shall introduce into their national legal systems such measures as are necessary to protect individuals from any adverse treatment or adverse consequence as a reaction to a complaint or to proceedings aimed at enforcing compliance with the principle of equal treatment'.

Of the remaining articles, the other two of particular note are Article 13, which requires the establishment of an independent body or bodies for the promotion of the equality principle, along the lines of the British Commission for Racial Equality, and Article 16 which contains a compliance date of July 2003.

The Framework Directive [20]

The 'Framework' Directive is a somewhat misleading title for this instrument, suggesting as it does that the Directive is merely the precursor to more detailed legislation and is not itself sufficiently precise to admit of direct enforcement before national courts. However, it is a useful shorthand name which saves making reference to all the grounds of discrimination which are dealt with by the instrument.

Its Preamble expresses many of the same aspirations to equality and respect for human rights as found in the Race Directive. The Directive opens with the statement that it is intended 'to lay down a general frame-

---

[18] See Case C-127/92 *Enderby v Frenchay Health Authority* [1993] ECR I-5535.
[19] See n 13.
[20] See P Skidmore, 'EC Framework Directive on equal treatment in employment: towards a comprehensive Community anti-discrimination policy?' (2001) 30 ILJ 126.

work for combating discrimination on the grounds of religion or belief, disability, age or sexual orientation as regards employment and occupation'.[21] Two things are immediately obvious from this formulation: the material scope of the instrument is considerably more limited than that of the Race Directive (being confined entirely to the sphere of work) and there is more room for the role of the courts, particularly the Court of Justice, in interpreting this instrument; this is because terms such as 'religion or belief', 'disability' and 'sexual orientation' are much more open to debate than the expressions 'race or ethnic origin' which have come to have a reasonably widespread common meaning. Jews and Muslims fairly clearly have a religion or belief, but what about the Moonies or the Etherealist Society? Are hay fever sufferers and anorexics disabled? Does a paedophile have a distinct sexual orientation? There are very many as-yet unanswered questions about the types of discrimination outlawed by this instrument and it will probably be years before a body of case law is established.

In similar terms to those used in the Race Directive, Article 2(2) of the Framework Directive forbids both direct and indirect discrimination. However, indirect discrimination against the disabled can be exonerated where an employer has provided reasonable accommodation for the disabled person.

Also in common with the Race Directive, there are provisions on harassment,[22] instructions to discriminate,[23] positive action,[24] remedies[25] and victimization,[26] although unlike the Race Directive there is no requirement on the Member States to set up national bodies such as the Equality Commissions.

The Framework Directive is, however, essentially a much more controversial piece of legislation than the Race Directive. This is reflected in a number of its provisions, some of which emerged at a very late stage in the legislative process. Five in particular of these provisions merit further attention. The first is Article 2(5) which provides that the Directive is to be 'without prejudice to measures laid down by national law which, in a democratic society, are necessary for public security, for the maintenance of public order and the prevention of criminal offences, the protection of health, and for the protection of the rights and freedoms of others'. This provision was intended to protect against paedophilia and other sexual offences, but its wording is wider than would be necessary to achieve this

---

[21] Art 1 of the Framework Directive.   [22] Art 2(3).
[23] Art 2(4).   [24] Art 7.   [25] Arts 9 and 17.   [26] Art 11.

objective. Also of note is Article 3(4) which provides that the directive does not have to be applied to discrimination on the grounds of age or disability in relation to the armed forces. This is a blanket defence, covering all jobs in the armed forces, even desk jobs for which youth and complete physical health would not appear essential.

In relation to genuine occupational requirements, the directive contains a bizarre exception for a measure of discrimination by religious organizations. Article 4(2) provides:

Member States may maintain national legislation in force at the date of adoption of this Directive or provide for future legislation incorporating national practices existing at the date of adoption of this Directive pursuant to which, in the case of occupational activities within churches and other public or private organisations the ethos of which is based on religion or belief, a difference of treatment based on a person's religion or belief shall not constitute discrimination where, by reason of the nature of these activities or of the context in which they are carried out, a person's religion or belief constitute a genuine, legitimate and justified occupational requirement, having regard to the organisation's ethos. This difference of treatment shall be implemented taking account of Member States' constitutional provisions and principles, as well as the general principles of Community law, and should not justify discrimination on another ground.

Provided that its provisions are otherwise complied with, this Directive shall thus not prejudice the right of churches and other public or private organizations, the ethos of which is based on religion or belief, acting in conformity with national constitutions and laws, to require individuals working for them to act in good faith and with loyalty to the organization's ethos.

The convoluted nature of this provision testifies to the real tension which exists between the right not to be discriminated against and the right of individuals to religious freedom. This area has caused a huge political outcry and there is undoubtedly great strength of feeling on the subject. For instance, in the House of Lords debate on this instrument, Lord Vinson said: '[B]ehind this particular directive lies the eternal argument between liberty and equality. The fact remains that liberté and egalité are inherently irreconcilable';[27] Lord Laing claimed that the Directive neutered 'those of us who hold strong religious beliefs and wish to stand up for them';[28] and Lady Young called the Directive 'another nail in the coffin of the whole Judeo Christian basis of our society'.[29] Whilst few would deny the right of the

[27] HL Hansard, 30 June 2000, Col 1216.
[28] ibid, Col 1220.
[29] ibid, Col 1189.

Church of England to demand that its ministers subscribe to the teachings of the Anglican Church, the position is not so clear where, for example, the tenets of a particular religion prohibit homosexuality.[30]

The fourth problematic provision in the Directive is Article 6, which states:

Notwithstanding Article 2(2), Member States may provide that differences of treatment on grounds of age shall not constitute discrimination, if, within the context of national law, they are objectively and reasonably justified by a legitimate aim, including legitimate employment policy, labour market and vocational training objectives, and if the means of achieving that aim are appropriate and necessary.

Age discrimination is another notoriously difficult area in which to achieve a sensible legislative balance. On the one hand, with a growing elderly population across Europe, there is clearly an incentive to protect the employment of older people.[31] Yet, on the other hand, it is important to be able to preserve job opportunities for young people and there are also numerous situations in which an employer might legitimately wish to employ a younger person. Article 6 is so broadly phrased that it appears to erode most of the right not to be discriminated against on the ground of age. Again, only time and the decisions of the courts will tell how effective this Article actually proves to be.

The fifth oddity in the framework directive is to be found in Article 15. Introduced into the instrument at the eleventh hour, this Article permits discrimination in recruitment to the police force in Northern Ireland (to permit the Patten reforms) and also in relation to the employment of teachers in Northern Ireland schools. Much could be said about this remarkable Article. It was certainly subjected to little or no public debate. It is curious in that it is entirely confined to Northern Ireland; not only does this appear to concretize the difficulties of that province, but it also fails to

---

[30]   The minutes of evidence taken before the House of Lords Select Committee on the EU on 15 November 2000 record Tessa Jowell MP (the responsible UK minister) as stating: 'The provisions in 4(2)(a) really deal with identity and make clear that religious institutions could not refuse to employ somebody simply because of their sexual orientation. However, and this is where Article 4(2)(b) comes into play, if that person's behaviour was so at variance with the values and beliefs of the organisation then they could be held to be acting in a way that was incompatible with the organisation's ethos, but that would be a question of conduct rather than a question of identity'.

[31]   For a compelling argument in favour of this point of view, see A Lester, 'Age discrimination in equality' (2001) 100 Equal Opportunities Review 36.

recognize the potential for similar problems to arise in other parts of the EU. Amusingly, however, the speed and stealth with which this provision was enacted may well prove to be its undoing: even though the Northern Ireland police service and teaching profession may be excepted from the scope of the framework directive, they may well still be covered by the Race Direct- ive. Being a Protestant or a Catholic in Northern Ireland is probably a matter of ethnicity as well as religion, so discrimination on these grounds is probably caught by the earlier directive!

National legislation to implement the Framework Directive must be in force by December 2003, apart from in the cases of age and disability where the period is extended to 2006.[32]

The role of democracy

Both directives were considered by sub-committee F of the House of Lords Select Committee on the EU and reservations were expressed about each.[33] Nevertheless, notwithstanding the Committee's view that amendments were needed to the draft race directive, political agreement on the race directive was reached at the Council meeting held on 6 June 2000; agree- ment on a final text was subsequently arrived at on 29 June. The House of Lords scrutiny reserve was overridden by the government and in the House of Commons, where similar reservations had been expressed, the whipping system ensured that all the Labour members of the Select Committee bar one accepted the draft race directive without reserve and the way was therefore clear for the government to assent to it.

Despite this flouting of the process of parliamentary scrutiny, it is strongly arguable that the government acted wisely. There was a feeling of genuine urgency in the Member States and in the EU institutions about the need for race discrimination legislation before the accession of new coun- tries to the Union. The Portuguese Presidency had made it clear that it was anxious to get the race legislation onto the statute book and the UK government clearly felt that this was an opportunity not to be missed. It certainly did not want to become politically isolated over an issue such as this. Another important factor was undoubtedly also that the UK leads the

---

[32] Art 18 of the Framework Directive.

[33] *EU Proposals to Combat Discrimination* House of Lords Select Committee on the EU, Session 1999–2000, 9th Report, HL Paper 68.

way in this type of legislation; after the enactment of the Race Relations (Amendment) Act 2000, the directive requires little if any further response from the UK, whereas this is not true of many Member States who have sparse legislative provision dealing with racial discrimination. In addition, there was anecdotal evidence to suggest that UK citizens from racial and ethnic minorities suffer discrimination in other Member States of the EU so that the UK had everything to gain and nothing to lose from the passage of the race directive.

The same political imperatives were not evident in the case of the Framework Directive. Political agreement on this instrument was reached in October 2000, which caused a much more substantial protest in the UK Parliament than had been voiced in relation to the race directive. This was largely because the final version of the instrument had never been shown to Parliament or to its Select Committees. The Commission had wasted everybody's time and resources by producing an out-of-date text and the British government only received the accurate English text one day before the Council meeting. In these circumstances, the scrutiny process was effectively undermined. The Minister concerned, Tessa Jowell, made some literally midnight concessions which had never been publicly discussed and whose wisdom may yet be challenged. In addition to undermining the domestic Parliamentary process, it is also arguable that the European Parliament's role was side-tracked as well, since it was not consulted on the substance of what was ultimately enacted; this of course gives rise to the possibility that the instrument is legally invalid.

The indecent haste with which the French Presidency forced the Framework Directive through the Council also gave a powerful bargaining hand to each of the Member States. Because of the text of the enabling Article 13, the Directive required the unanimous support of all the Member States. This probably enabled the British minister to rail-road the other members of the Council into accepting the provisions in relation to Northern Ireland.

Problems posed by the new legislation

Despite the welcome content of the new Directives, some serious problems are to be anticipated in their wake. The first concerns the element of discretion entrusted to the Court of Justice in relation to the meaning of key terms. The establishment of clear definitions is certain to prove expensive for employees and employers, as well as costly of the Court's scarce time. There is also the risk that uncertainty about its application will bring the new legislation into disrepute and earn it the resentment of employers.

Secondly, the relationship between the new legislation and the existing EU sex discrimination legislation requires the urgent attention of the EU's legislature. A rift between the two bodies of law will be logically indefensible and also practically unfortunate in cases of multiple discrimination, for example, where a black woman complains of discrimination.

Thirdly, the relationship between the Directives and the Charter of Fundamental Rights[34] may in time require to be articulated by the Court of Justice. Although the Charter at present has no legal effect, it contains several provisions whose content mirrors but is not identical to that of the Directives.[35]

Finally, the Directives can be criticized for their essentially old-fashioned design. Both concentrate on retrospective fault-finding, create an adversarial approach and centre on the role played by individual claims. In short, they are based on what is sometimes dubbed the '1970s British model'. Yet experience, particularly in Northern Ireland, shows that, to be effective, legislation needs to be inclusive and to stimulate employers and others to take active steps to widen participation. It would therefore have been preferable for the new Directives to include more positive features, in particular, a duty for public authorities to promote equality of opportunity and a system of monitoring to promote fairer participation. Nevertheless, the legislation should help to enhance the legitimacy of the EU in terms of social and economic protection and the creation of a fairer and more civilized society.

[34] [2000] OJ C364/01.

[35] See in particular Art 7 on respect for private and family life; Art 10 on freedom of thought, conscience and religion; Art 11 on freedom of expression, Art 20 on equality before the law; Art 21 on non-discrimination; Art 23 on equality between men and women; Art 25 on the rights of the elderly; and Art 26 on the integration of persons with disabilities.

18

Protecting Fundamental Rights and Social Rights: An Economic Analysis

Lothar Funk

The Charter of Fundamental Rights and the European social model

At the Nice Summit in December 2000 it became clear that previously vague ideas about the finality of the integration process require more exact definition. However, political debate about the future of Europe, and particularly the division of work between the European, national and regional levels, has been dominated by two extreme alternatives. Minimalist nation-statists favour a reduction of political integration and its replacement by an extended free trade zone. Maximalist federalists push for 'ever closer union' and a federation of European states supported by a constitutional agreement with clearly defined jurisdictions and democratic legitimation and monitoring in a union of peoples rather than of states.[1] In this chapter I consider further alternatives. In addition to statism, a constitutionalist alternative to maximalist federalism, based on economic analysis, is considered. Moreover, recent developments suggest that new forms of governance are emerging in Europe.[2] These may add further options between 'federalism' and 'statism'.

In this chapter these alternatives are assessed through an economic analysis of the EU Charter of Fundamental Rights.[3] The role of such

---

[1] J Janning, 'A Europe without borders. Policies of managing change' (International Bertelsmann Forum, 19–20 January 2001, 6–8).

[2] Discussed in the chapters by Szyszcak and Wincott in this volume.

[3] C McCrudden, 'The future of the EU Charter of Fundamental Rights' (New York University School of Law, 2001, 10). See further the chapters by McBride and Jacobs in this volume. On the important question of whether the Charter has horizontal repercussions binding private companies and citizens, as most of the social rights of the Charter suggest, see

analysis is to assess the efficiency and legitimacy of the Charter, including the questions of whether it should be binding at a supranational level. At the heart of this debate is whether the Charter can and should fulfil an integrationist function and whether it is important to save the goals of the 'European social model'. In particular the positive rights to protection and entitlements mirror the European Union's goal of social cohesion, which may refer to the idea of not alienating European workers from the process of integration. Therefore, the debate about the future of the Charter is bound up with the broader debate on the European social model.

Among others, the European Commissioner for Social Affairs, Anna Diamantopoulou talks in a positive sense about common principles of a European social model which 'ensures a healthy balance between economic growth and social cohesion'.[4] From this perspective the European social model is not based on economic efficiency alone. It tries to strike a balance between social spending and social protection on the one hand and competitiveness and economic efficiency on the other. Moreover, these two elements form a triangular relationship with a third, a high employment rate in the context of an increasingly globalized economic system (see Figure 18.1). Facing persistently high EU unemployment, the crucial future task in terms of economic policy according to the Commission of the European Communities will be 'modernising the European social model and investing in people ... to retain the European social values of solidarity

Figure 18.1. The European Commission's triangle of economic policies

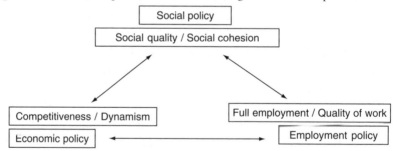

T von Danwitz, 'The EU Charter of Fundamental Rights' (2001) 2 Internationale Politik—Transatlantic Edition 23, 26.

[4]   In 'The European social model: promoting economic and social progress' (address to the International Conference on Achieving Balanced Economic and Social Growth, 19 March 2001).

and justice while improving economic performance'.[5] Such an agenda sets out to ensure economic success in terms of employment and economic growth without giving up the common principles of the European social model. These include rather extensive basic social security cover for all citizens[6] and a relatively egalitarian wage and income distribution compared to the United States.[7]

Several questions immediately arise when thinking about this triangle: What is the appropriate relationship between rights and employment, and between rights and competitiveness, as well as between rights and social policies in general? Are solidarity and equality rights foundational of economic success, or a drag on it? Strong adherents to the idea of a European social model generally support a (legally enforceable) charter of rights. The espousal of equality and solidarity rights can be regarded as a move by those who oppose the development of a more free-market 'US-model' of economic growth and development. For those who believe that a trade-off between competitiveness and social protection is inevitable, the Charter symbolizes a re-balancing of the Community towards social protection and against free market forces. A compromise between these two competing points of view is the aspiration of the Charter to shape the social character of Europe by establishing minimum standards. The political idea of the current declaration is that such an approach protects the competences of the Member States, for on the whole it leads to regulations below the average level.

However, from an economic perspective, regulations which aim to reduce inequality or to increase efficiency by imposing minimum standards often have unwanted side-effects resulting in a 'tyranny of good intentions': lower efficiency or a rising inequality or both. An example is possibly very generous mandatory safety expenditures resulting from Article 31. This would equalize earnings by removing dangerous jobs, but could cause unemployment. The maximum hours mandate could be another example of a definitely bad policy from an economic perspective. It reduces efficiency because the parties know best what hours suit them, and increases inequality because only unskilled workers will in general have their hours

---

[5] Commission, *Communication from the Commission to the Council, the European Parliament, the Economic and Social Committee and the Committee of the Regions*, 28 June 2000, 6. Figure 18.1 is also drawn from this source.

[6] KH Paqué, 'Structural unemployment in Europe: a bird's-eye view' in JT Addison and PJJ Welfens (eds), *Labor Markets and Social Security. Wage Costs, Social Security Financing and Labor Market Reforms in Europe* (1998) 17, 37.

[7] According to Anna Diamantopoulou (n 4 above) 3, the US shows 'the results of not having adequate social policies'.

restricted, whereas managerial workers and the self-employed are effect-ively excluded.[8] Finally, the recently controversially discussed European Commission's draft directive on temporary agency workers demands that agency workers would have the same pay and conditions as an equivalent permanent employee in the user company after six weeks. This is indirectly justified by commissioner Anna Diamantopoulou with the principle of non-discrimination which is also part of the Charter: 'We cannot agree with the political concept that employers can benefit from the flexibility of staff and at the same time pay them less'.[9] Such a proposal is, however, anti-competitive and would most likely destroy jobs beneficial to both employees and em-ployers. It is doubtful whether this kind of legislation should be imposed on members of the European Union and why a legally binding Charter should increase the likelihood of successfully implementing a 'one-size-fits-all' legislation when national laws can easily cope with such problems and prevent exploitation. Due to the contrasting views presented and the pos-sible trade-offs of the current and even more of a future legally binding Charter, the question arises: 'what would economists put into the Charter of Fundamental Rights?'

How to legitimize a charter of fundamental rights at the EU level: an economic evaluation

Two myths prevail concerning the Charter of Fundamental Rights. Federal-ists normally regard its role as legitimacy-increasing, whereas nation-statists complain that the Charter is a further milestone towards an EU superstate. They may also argue that it diminishes efficiency. However, a third option also exists. From a 'constitutional economics' perspective it might be appro-priate to limit the content of the Charter to a classic defence of the rights of citizens against the state and only include social rights to minimum stand-ards if they are acceptable to all countries.

To avoid unwanted economic side-effects, the legitimacy-increasing role of the Charter emphasized by federalists needs to be rather limited. Leaving aside the rhetorical effect, from an economic perspective a binding

---

[8] JT Addison, CR Barrett and WS Siebert, 'The economics of labour market regulation' in JT Addison and WS Siebert (eds), *Labour Markets in Europe* (1997) 62, 76–79; G Stull, 'The difficulties of imposing labour standards' http://econserv2.bess.tcd.i.e./SER/1998/Essay17.htm/ (1998) 2–3.

[9] Quoted from The Guardian, 21 March 2002.

European Charter of Fundamental Rights would not appear to produce any qualitative leap in legal terms—unless, of course, one were secretly striving for a direct or indirect transfer of the sovereignty still in the hands of the Member States in the Union. Such a transfer of the sovereignty is currently not to be expected and if it were, the side-effects of implementing inefficient 'one-size-fits-all' economic policies at the supranational level would rather increase than reduce the current problems of the European Union.

On the other hand, a Charter of Fundamental Rights is not necessarily a milestone towards an EU superstate as nation-statists contend. An economically optimal Charter in which the level of rights represents only a lowest-common-denominator compromise will be 'ineffective' when markets operate efficiently. It will not, for example, result in legally binding wage floors above the market clearing level. Indeed, it would not be marred by unintended economic side-effects at all. Moreover, a Charter can be economically favourable when it leads to an increase in efficiency as well as less inequality.[10] The current Charter is, however, probably economically damaging even though it is non-binding due to the strategy of the Commission. Its pragmatic approach is that 'institutions that will have proclaimed the Charter will have committed themselves to respecting it'.[11] Even if the Charter is only a political declaration it is likely to have legal effects, as the European Court of Justice is likely to take it into account in its decisions. Past experience suggests that this may pose economic dangers,[12] but they are not as strong as the risks inherent in a legally binding Charter with more ambitious social rights.

We therefore need to wave farewell to the naive, simplistic points of view prevalent in much of superficial political debate. What is needed instead is an evaluation of the reasonable content of such a Charter against the background of deeper issues like the European social model underlying

---

[10] See S Deakin, 'Social rights and the market' in U Mückenberger (ed), *Manifesto Social Europe* (2001) 17, 33–35; JT Addison and WS Siebert, *Regulating European Labour Markets: More Costs than Benefits* (1999).

[11] A Wiener, 'The constitutional significance of the charter of fundamental rights' (2001) 18 German Law Journal 7, available on http://www.germanlawjournal.com/print.php?id=113/.

[12] According to U Roth and V Thomas, 'Europe on the path to a common social policy' (2000) 34 Inter Nationes Basis-Info 13, the Judges of the European Court of Justice 'have frequently set social policy signals, most of which have resulted in a strengthening of workers' rights'. It has also been claimed that, whereas the Court 'has been quite effective in striking down laws of the Member States that are anti-competitive they have never ruled against a significant centralising regulation or directive of the Council of Ministers': see N Barry, *Competitive Federalism: The Case of the European Union* (The Centre for the New Europe, 2001) 9.

the debate about the future of the Charter. Nobel Prize-winning US econo-mist James Buchanan founded normative constitutional economics (also known as constitutional political economy). It is an ideal tool to analyse these questions. 'Constitutional economics starts with the assumption that politicians try to maximize their own individual utility—like everybody else'.[13] The constitutional level of rule choice is distinguished from the post-constitutional level of strategic choice within rules. This distinction is at the heart of constitutional economics. The Charter of Fundamental Rights concerns rule choice, so constitutional economics appears to be the most appropriate form of analysis for it. In other words, what to include as well as who should be responsible for designing a desirable and therefore legitimate Charter is a problem of choosing the 'rules of the game' under which the citizens of a polity may wish to live.

The 'European Union's institutions are exercising powers which either were delegated by the governments of the Member States or were usurped by the Commission and the European Court of Justice through far-reaching interpretation of Treaty provisions'.[14] Therefore, an analysis of the legitim-acy of the Charter of Fundamental Rights should rest on its ability to help to close the legitimacy gap of the European Union. In particular, analysis of 'output' and 'input' legitimacy could discover how legitimate a binding Charter would be. Regarding the EU as an appropriate level can be justified for three reasons:[15]

(1) 'Member states agree to formulating a common policy because joint problem-solving provides added value. In terms of policy performance, the EU is, from a systematic point of view, not inferior to domestic policies; the process may be more cumbersome and the compromise agreed upon not as close to the median voter as it may be in a national setting. Yet, despite this, the policy is expected to be more effective'. In other words: 'The test of EU action is its capacity to *add value*, where the EU can help tackle problems that would otherwise overcome national governments, and where it can make a constructive contribution, then it

[13] S Voigt, 'What constitution for Europe? The constitutional question from the point of view of (positive) constitutional economics' in T Bruha, JJ Hesse and C Nowak (eds), *Welche Verfassung für Europa?* (2001) 41, 49.
[14] M Höreth, 'The European Commission's White Paper on Governance: a tool-kit for closing the legitimacy gap of EU policy-making?' (2001 Centre for European Integration Studies, 22).
[15] B Kohler-Koch, 'The Commission White Paper and the improvement of European governance' (New York University School of Law, 2001, 12–13).

should act. Where it cannot add value, it should keep out of the way. This is a stronger version of the subsidiarity thesis: Europe is a political response to globalization, not another layer of government trying to solve local problems'.[16]

(2) 'Despite public debate on the Union's democratic deficit, there is still a widespread belief that the EU is the appropriate level for coping with quite a number of political issues and that—in principle—the institutions are apt to do it'.[17]

(3) The orthodox reading that the EU lacks legitimacy because it neither has a demos nor a European state is outdated. In order to function, an EU with nation states not just as a transitory but as a permanent type of polity does not need citizens with a predominant European identity in order to be as legitimate as the state. 'This EU polity is both: a compound and a unitary system... The ("imagined") political community is still the nation. The Union will be based on a "political society" with national, though "Europeanised", identities'.[18]

Let us start with the assumption that the third proposition is or will be accepted by the current members and the new entrants because otherwise it would not make sense to be an EU member. Traditionally, the EU's legitimacy is mainly based on output legitimacy, in other words on the efficiency and effectiveness of European problem-solving ability. The question then is what kind of Charter can enhance the problem-solving capacity and ability of European governance thereby strengthening the output dimension of Union legitimacy?

Constitutional political economy supplies an important criterion of what should be included in such a Charter which may be seen as a vehicle for constitution making. Government should have no role in policy choice, other than implementing the (near) unanimously selected alternative from the set of choices.

Those who expect to gain from a policy change must find a way to compensate, and credibly commit to making that compensation, to secure the consent of nearly all the affected parties. It will still be true that the gains to gainers must exceed the losses to losers, but the surplus in gains must be distributed, rather than taken from

---

[16] D Miliband, 'Perspectives on European integration—a British view' (Max Planck Institute for the Study of Societies, 2002, 2).

[17] Kohler-Koch (n 15 above) 12.

[18] ibid 13.

the losers. The compensation could be in the form of side payments on the issue question, or it could be concessions in another policy area...[19]

From an economic point of view the inevitable result of this criterion must be that 'policy-makers should strive for minimum standards, but only ones that are acceptable to all countries',[20] that is, the criterion of unanimity needs to be observed. One important reason why it appears economically optimal to choose the lowest common denominator is simply the still undecided struggle among alternative schools in economic policy matters. In the words of James K Galbraith: 'The notion that mainstream economics has somehow demonstrated, as opposed to having merely asserted, the triumph over the Keynesian view is quite wrong'.[21] Therefore, one has to take into account at least the two main post-war economic approaches. Fundamentally, they are based on two opposite views.

The first view is what has been called regulated or managed capitalism. It shows a rather strong bias towards state-led regulation and an 'enabling' role of the government, for example as a facilitator of collaboration amongst powerful groups in order to sustain social peace. Whereas adherents of the alternative neoliberal economics school support 'one best way' for all economies based on general microeconomic and macroeconomic principles and very limited interference with markets, proponents of the existence of a welfare optimal regulated capitalism do not accept the wholesale importation of one model: 'Our challenge today is to modernise the variety of models of the social market economy that exist in Europe, based on their own strengths, traditions, and histories, not to try and harmonize them into a single model'.[22] In terms of macroeconomic policy, they normally support some kind of Keynesian demand management, blaming a tight monetary and fiscal policy for persistently high unemployment in the European Union.[23] The role of and instruments for effective microeconomic policy will differ across countries because varieties of capitalism differ, without either being

---

[19] MC Munger, *Analyzing Policy. Choices, Conflicts and Practices* (2000) 358.
[20] Centre for Economic Policy Research, 'Social Europe' http://www.cepr.org/pubs/eep/articles/socialeu.htm/at 2.
[21] JK Galbraith, 'A contribution to the state of economics in France and the world' (2001) Post-Autistic Economics Newsletter 4.
[22] Miliband (n 16 above) 5.
[23] R Schobben ' "New Governance" in the European Union: a cross-disciplinary comparison' (2000) 10 Regional and Federal Studies 35, 38–39; D Soskice, B Hancké, G Trumbull and A Wren, 'Wage bargaining, labour markets and macroeconomic performance in Germany and the Netherlands' in L Delsen and E de Jong (eds), *The German and Dutch Economies. Who Follows Whom?* (1998) 39, 42.

obviously superior in the medium-term.[24] Corporate governance, labour relations and government institutions interact in highly specific ways and it may be illusory to design a 'one best way', for example, for the European Union based on benchmarking. Textbook deregulation appears as a dangerous obsession and is most likely welfare decreasing for a coordinated market economy like Germany. 'The Anglo-Saxon deregulatory road is, for all practical purposes, a dangerous one, since it would upset the system of careful microeconomic balances at the heart of German companies that are central to German export success. It severs the ties between the skilled workers (and probably the engineers as well) and the companies—in short the German high-quality incremental innovation strategy.'[25] This school of thought generally supports social policy at the European level due to social dumping or unfair competition problems. According to Addison 'the basic point of the argument is this: if Member States do have different policies, effective coordination to prevent a race to the bottom cannot be left to the market, and some form of pan-European regulation setting minimum standards is necessary. Absent this, so the argument runs, bad policies will simply drive out good ones'.[26]

Neoliberalism has been the mainstream economic position for at least 25 years. It accepts only limited intervention by the state. Fiscal policy should concentrate on allocation, not stabilization during economic downturns. Monetary policy should keep inflation low rather than being aimed at full employment. Incomes policy has little effect on inflation but can cause micro damage. There is no long-run trade-off between inflation and unemployment. As a result monetary policy can be depoliticized and put in the hands of central bankers. The underlying microeconomic principle is efficiency, not equity. More precisely, (neoliberal) economists are concerned whenever possible with 'Pareto efficiency', which exists when no one can be made better off without someone being made worse off. The 'Pareto principle' is the belief that ('Pareto') improvements that make at least one individual better off without making anyone worse off should be instituted.

However, most single economic policy options do adversely affect some individuals. In other words, they are not Pareto-improvements in the strict

---

[24] T Gries, 'Soziales Marktmodell Europa versus liberales Marktmodell Amerika' (2001) 8 Wirtschaftsdienst 462.

[25] Soskice, Hancké, Trumbull and Wren (n 23 above) 50–51; L Funk, 'The "Storm before the Calm" thesis re-examined' in J Leonhard and L Funk (eds), *Ten Years of German Unification: Transfer, Transformation, Incorporation?* (2002) 183.

[26] JT Addison, 'Is Community social policy beneficial, irrelevant, or harmful to the labour market performance of the European Union?' (University of Potsdam, 2000, 7).

sense because some people could find themselves worse off after they have been implemented. We therefore need an alternative mechanism for deciding whether to implement a particular policy. Very often the Kaldor-Hicks criterion is used. This criterion is based on cost-benefit analysis and requires the gainers and the losers from a policy change to be identified. Neoliberals usually accept the following rule, which goes beyond the 'Pareto principle': If gains to gainers exceed losses to losers, implement the policy change, whether or not gainers actually compensate losers. So laws which set minimum wages or which otherwise establish legally binding wage floors above the market clearing level need to be changed without necessarily compensating the workers whose wages fall, because the economy will then rise to higher gross domestic product. This rise results from increasing demand for labour that allows the less able workers to get access to the labour market.

Furthermore, in this view a case can be made against the supranational coordination of social policies and regulatory frameworks that would result from a binding Charter of Fundamental Rights including social rights. These rights would lead to higher than market-clearing wage costs, at least in some countries. Even though it can be shown in a game theoretical context that cooperation between agents of economic policy improves overall efficiency, neoliberals see the problem as more complicated:

Requiring policy coordination blurs the lines of responsibility of policy agents; asking for coordination may allow agents to shift their responsibility to someone else as a scapegoat. Therefore, there should be a clear policy assignment in the sense that the leading responsibilities of the policy agents should be clearly defined.[27]

Additionally, empirical research seems to support the notion 'that some groups (typically youth and older workers) are adversely impacted by employment protection'.[28] In sum and only slightly sharpened, the neoliberal view about microeconomic and macroeconomic policy is almost the exact opposite of the regulated capitalism position, as Figure 18.2 shows.

Such strong scientific differences over economic regulatory policy hardly make it possible to find a consensus on a Charter of Fundamental Rights, especially for countries which are very heterogeneous, for example in levels of real income. This makes the result of the Nice summit unsurprising: the Charter as a non-binding solemn proclamation, including many vague

---

[27] H Siebert, 'The assignment problem' in SK Berninghaus and M Braulke (eds), *Beiträge zur Mikro- und Makroökonomik* (2001) 439, 444.

[28] Addison (n 26 above) 10.

Figure 18.2. Opposing views of alternative economic schools on reforms in continental Europe

Economic Schools / Reform in field of	Regulated Capitalism	Neoliberal Economics
Macroeconomic institutions	Urgently required	Basically OK
Microeconomic institutions	Basically OK	Urgently required

articles with a(n almost) 'lowest common denominator' character. Taking into account persistent differences in the evaluation of economic policy proposals and the unavoidable package deals at intergovernmental conferences, this result is probably also the best one could expect from a practical constitutional political economy perspective. The present compromise allows a 'better-than-nothing' evaluation from adherents to regulated capitalism and a 'the-worst-has-been-avoided' statement by proponents of neoliberalism. Nonetheless, medium-term dangers due to possibly inappropriate directives by the Commission and decisions of the Court need to be kept in mind. After 'its proclamation, the EP, the Commission and some Advocate Generals have made it clear that they will act as if the Charter were a binding document'.[29]

However, in contrast to the contentions of adherents of regulated capitalism, both neoliberal and constitutional economics approaches demonstrate that times of increased competition among states due to globalization do not necessarily lead to a wild-west capitalism. As Vanberg argues, it is

not obvious at all why it should pose a threat to protectionist provisions that reflect common citizenship interests, that is, provisions that are desirable for all members of the jurisdiction because they make it a more attractive constitutional niche for all

---

[29] EO Eriksen, 'Democratic or technocratic governance?' (New York University School of Law, 2001, 13–14).

of them. If there exist generally advantageous protectionist provisions, provisions that are indeed in the common interest of the constituency as a whole, they should be able to evolve and to be maintained in a regime of free choice among jurisdictions.[30]

Democracy and constitutionalism

Growing public debate on the Union's democratic deficit apparently makes the EU's future legitimacy depend increasingly on democratic participation and institutionalized mechanisms to sanction unwanted behaviour. For example, on 23 February 2002 The Independent answered the question 'How can we make the EU more democratically accountable?' by arguing 'This must mean more power for the directly elected element of the EU's present constitution, the European Parliament'. But increasing the effectiveness and efficiency of EU policy is still at least as important for the legitimacy of the Union as diminishing the democratic deficit. Potentially, the two can conflict:

There is a natural tendency to judge the democratic credentials of EU institutions against the tried and tested methods of national democracy. Hence talk of the democratic deficit. But what people want above all from the EU is *delivery*, while legitimacy is essential democracy is a bonus; the real source of discontent in Europe today concerns the effectiveness of EU actions. That is why I emphasize the delivery deficit.[31]

For structural reasons democratic mechanisms cannot cope with the delivery deficit alone. Economists generally recognize that the most important delivery deficit of the European Union is *competitive*, and would also apply to a more democratized European Union of rationally ignorant voters. Such voters have no rational interests in controlling politicians effectively. It would be more costly than beneficial for them individually. This is already a problem at the national level, but it is even more pervasive at the European level which is much less transparent. As a result, elected politicians have no strong interest in effectively promoting an efficient free market. Its long-run advantages are thinly spread while new regulations and subsidies visibly

---

[30] V Vanberg, 'Constitutional order and economic evolution: competitive and protectionist interests in democratic society' in R Mudambi, P Navarra and G Sovvrio (eds), *Rules and Reason. Perspectives on Constitutional Political Economy* (2001) 33, 52.
[31] Miliband (n 16 above) 4.

protect certain groups without hurting others strongly in the short term. However, such policies are damaging to the growth and employment of the European economy in the medium and long term. As its effects are asymmetrical, enlargement could make this problem worse: 'The benefits are long-term and widely spread, but the costs are more immediate and concentrated on a few sectors and regions. The losers are readily identifiable and vocal, while the gainers are the quiet (and often unknowing) majority'.[32] It is thus somewhat misleading to argue that the main problem of the European Union is a 'democratic deficit' due to too many unelected bodies in the system. A solution which calls only for 'more democracy' is unlikely to solve the delivery problem in a satisfying way.[33]

Nonetheless it is generally true that 'output legitimacy has to be supplemented by input legitimacy'.[34] According to political science, this needs to involve equal and effective participation and institutionalized accountability to ensure reliability, that is a commitment to binding agreements on the part of decision-makers. But what does this mean in terms of the constitutional political economy approach? According to this school 'justice should emerge naturally from a constitutional process'.[35] Input legitimacy, therefore, should approach in its ideal form consensual agreement. It should not be discriminatory because participants promote separable interests in society, but should be 'constitutional' by effectively advancing the interests of all citizens.

Thus, ordinary politics deals with the crafting of rules where opposition may be significant, and may change frequently over time, so that the rules themselves must be easily changeable...Rules determined within the confines of ordinary politics can be changed quite easily.[36]

In other words, if controversy exists over which policy better increases efficiency, then output legitimacy should be part of ordinary politics, that is, it should be normally majoritarian and non-consensual. 'However, constitutional politics deals with long-lasting rules conceived in the interest of all elements of society so that, ideally, opposition is non-existent'.[37]

---

[32] H Grabbe, 'Translating Ireland' (4 July 2001 The Wall Street Journal Europe).

[33] Barry (n 12 above) 13–17.

[34] Kohler-Koch (n 15 above) 8.

[35] R Mudambi, P Navarra and G Sobbrio, 'Constitutional issues in modern democracies' in R Mudambi, P Navarra and G Sobbrio (eds), *Rules and Reason. Perspectives on Constitutional Political Economy* (2001) 1.

[36] ibid 2–3.

[37] ibid 3.

How can the implementation of long-lasting rules be achieved in practice? The basic idea is that 'contractors' should examine rules from behind a 'veil of ignorance' or 'uncertainty' with regard to their own interests in future periods.

Since future self-interest is either unknown or uncertain, criteria of fairness may replace those of advantage. In this framework, agreement may emerge by a process in which the person who advances an argument in support of one particular rule must invoke criteria that take on elements of general or public interest. The question of legitimisation, therefore, requires that the constitutional structure remain categorically distinct from the operation of ordinary politics.[38]

This conception of generating (input) legitimacy in a social order uses the veil of ignorance or uncertainty to prevent particular interests from backing a constitution which favours their own position. Instead it facilitates agreement on rules that define a 'social contract' based on a list of permanent or quasi-permanent parameters for social interaction. Such interaction takes place over a whole sequence of periods to achieve optimally the common good for all members of society.

How can such a contractarian proposal best be operationalized to generate an EU Charter of Fundamental Rights? Can it be written in a way that it effectively advances the interests of *all* citizens? Solving the problem of input legitimacy requires the identification of the process and actors by which a Charter could be written as a provisional constitutional treaty (or part of it) for Europe which has desirable consequences from a constitutional political economy perspective. The convention-method is in general a proper way to increase input legitimacy, but the devil is in the details. At least two conditions should be fulfilled:[39]

First, the rules of living together have to be created in a one-off participatory process of discussion, analysis, persuasion, and mutual agreement, which we may call a constitutional convention. Secondly, the convention should not include (a majority of) persons whose long-run political careers depend on the result of the convention's decisions, because it would be clearly rational for these persons to write the constitutional rules to maximize their long-term career prospects. Rather it is important to elect a separate group of people to the constitutional convention. As Mueller has put it:

---

[38]   Mudambi, Navarra and Sobbrio (n 35 above).

[39]   ibid; Mueller, 'On writing a constitution' in R Mudambi, P Navarra and G Sobbrio (eds), *Rules and Reason. Perspectives on Constitutonal Political Economy* (2001) 9; R Vaubel, 'Der Hochmut der Institutionen' (1 March 2002) Rheinischer Merkur.

... it is better to elect a separate group of people to the constitutional convention than to have the constitutional convention formed by those elected to serve in the parliament. The rational voter realizes that a different set of issues is to be decided at a constitutional convention, and thus that a different type of person should be chosen to participate. Given the one-shot nature of the convention, the voter knows that, once elected, her representative will be free to vote as he pleases at the convention. The citizen wants, therefore, to elect persons noted for their integrity as well as their honesty and judgement—qualities not always found in those who choose politics for a career.... If the constitutional convention is properly constituted, the citizen *knows* that he has been fairly represented. He can observe and consider the arguments on all sides of the issue as it is deba-ted;... The citizen knows, and presumably accepts, that the original constitution was ratified by a substantial majority and that any changes in it require the same majority...[40]

The first condition was fulfilled in the process of generating the Charter. But critics of the Charter argue that the Convention (like the later one estab-lished in Laeken on a future constitution) failed the second condition. Roland Vaubel argues that the majority of members of such a Convention should not have a strong interest in a centralized EU state. Too many members of the convention were members of the European Parliament (16), representatives of the Commission (1) or representatives of national governments/the European Council (15).[41] Only a minority of the Conven-tion was composed of representatives of national Parliaments (30/62). They meet the test of subsidiarity, being more likely to argue that laws should be passed by the level of government closest to the citizen and that the competences of the EU should be clearly described and limited.

In sum, the Convention of the Charter ran at least some risk of legitimiza-tion and strengthening of actually illegitimate power positions because the composition of the membership was not optimal. The less than optimal composition of the Convention from a contractarian perspective also dem-onstrates that the Charter is used as

part of a symbolic policy that works according to the logic of strategic intervention, ie top-down action that seeks to convince the 'other' (citizen) of a given goal. If this strategic intervention is not turned around to a more open-ended approach of discursive interaction which does not only aspire to broaden input but which is also

[40] Mueller (n 39 above) 24 and 26.
[41] Vaubel (n 39 above). See also P Zimmermann-Steinhart, 'Der Konvent: die neue Methode?' (2002) 51 Gesellschaft-Wirtschaft-Politik 65, 67; R Vaubel, *Europa-Chauvinismus. Der Hochmut der Institutionen* (2001) 126–134 and 190–200.

prepared to listen and perhaps adapt previous policy positions accordingly, the constitutional significance of the Charter is likely to produce unintended consequences such as 'fuelling anti-EU-feelings' similar to previous cases of symbolic policymaking in the EU.[42]

Vaubel argues that a legitimate constitutional treaty for Europe (including the Charter) should neither be prepared by an intergovernmental conference nor by a constitutional Convention composed of representatives of institutions that support a more centralized European Union.[43] Instead, a constitutional political economy perspective suggests that an inter-parliamentary conference consisting of members of national parliaments might secure legitimacy. As the national parliaments will decide whether to accept the final constitutional treaty, they should be able to correct the current personnel of the constitutional Convention on the Future of Europe.

Figure 18.3 summarizes the legitimacy analysis. It clarifies fundamental differences between federalist and 'constitutional economics' perspectives on the Charter. Both approaches face dilemmas. Whereas the federalist perspective is probably politically viable in the short and medium term, its economic results are not desirable because of the disregard of potential unwanted side-effects. Costly new regulations may improve the situation of some, but create 'outsiders' who bear the costs (the opposite rhetoric of proponents of regulation notwithstanding). The constitutional political economy approach could bolster output as well as input legitimacy, but it faces a dilemma of political viability. Its implementation may be problematic as those currently holding power would probably see it reduced in the future. Solutions to current problems of democracy and legitimacy[44] based on simple reforms like strengthening the Commission and Parliament[45] are neither promising nor available. Hence we are likely to have to live with compromises or hope for lucky circumstances. However, one alternative means of (partly) closing the European legitimacy gap may exist, as we shall see.

[42] Wiener (n 11 above) 9.

[43] Vaubel (n 39 above).

[44] K Hughes, 'Is this Europe's Philadelphia?' (28 February 2002 Wall Street Journal Europe).

[45] H-E Scharrer, 'Single market or national industrial policies?' (2002) 37 Intereconomics 66.

Figure 18.3. Competing approaches on increasing the legitimacy of the European Union

Approach / Features	Federalist Perspective	Constitutional Economics Perspective
Goals	Creation of European identity	Output and input legitimacy
Shape of basic rights at the European level	Not too narrow; effective in practice	Minimum standards, but only ones that are acceptable to all countries; ineffective when markets operate efficiently
Main actors	Commission, Council, Courts	Nations: they should be given more power
Problems	Creation or persistence of outsiders because of unintended consequences of interference with market	Approach rather difficult to implement, because powerful vested interest groups undermine it

Conclusions

Social rights are not always unambiguously positive: they are helpful if they seek to remedy market failures and protect the disadvantaged members of society from the consequences of their economic weaknesses. But sometimes, perversely, social rights protect better off groups. A legally binding Charter in the European Union is likely to be economically damaging unless it is limited to minimum standards that are acceptable to all countries. The level of rights granted by the Charter should represent only a lowest common denominator compromise from an economic perspective. It should give priority to individual liberty rights.[46]

The highly divergent expectations and concepts that various states bring to this project mean there is an inherent potential for conflict. This may occur not only in the field of social rights[47] in very different economic and institutional environments[48] but also 'recent studies on rights policy in the wider Europe have demonstrated that, far from a European convergence in the area of rights policy, divergence is predominant'.[49] The integration process could surely do without the difficulties that would doubtless arise if the Charter were made binding—or worse if this endeavour were to fail. From an economic perspective, the opportunity costs of the time used to bargain the final content of such a Charter might be high (distracting attention from (more) important issues). If the purpose of the exercise is more transparency through simplification of the legal framework, it might make more sense to agree an uncontroversial list of duties and limits of the European Union including fundamental rights.

Softer methods such as the 'open coordination' approach—a form of peer pressure and benchmarking—may avoid the problems of the minimalist and maximalist alternatives.[50] This method appears to be tailor-made for a hybrid like the EU, with both federal and intergovernmental features. It is based on 'intensive transgovernmentalism'[51] and avoids the pitfalls of the traditional one-size-fits-all 'Community method' which appears out of date partly due to enlargement. In certain areas, like pension and employment policy, 'the lack of legitimacy' resulting from the use of the Community method 'could blow the Union apart'.[52] The duty to force through EU policies might break governments or lead to violent protests (see Figure 18.4 for a comparison of both approaches). Especially in important areas touching domestic economic governance and national electoral credibility:

[46] 'A good constitution' (28 February 2002 The Wall Street Journal Europe).

[47] F Bosvieux, 'A business perspective on the EU Charter' in K Feus (ed), *An EU Charter of Fundamental Rights. Text and Commentaries* (2001) 147.

[48] On the strong legal differences between British and German labour markets, see M Allen, 'Die Rechte der Arbeitnehmer in Deutschland und dem Vereinigten Königreich' (2002) 55 ifo Schnelldienst 19.

[49] Wiener (n 11 above) 7.

[50] See also the chapters by Szyszczak and Wincott in this volume.

[51] H Wallace, 'Experiments in European governance' in M Jachtenfuchs and M Knodt (eds), *Regieren in Internationalen Institutionen* (2002) 255.

[52] F Scharpf, 'European governance: common concerns vs the challenge of diversity' in M Jachtenfuchs and M Knodt (eds), *Regieren in Internationalen Institutionen* (2002) 271, 276.

Figure 18.4. Alternative approaches: traditional Community versus intensive transgovernmentalism

Approach Features	Traditional Community	Intensive Transgovernmentalism
Targets	'Ever closer union'	Chances for all: present and new members
Methods	Extensive delegation, hard rule-making and common programmes in more and more areas	Soft experimental methods; open method of coordination
Main actors	Commission, Council, Courts	Nations: they should be given more power
Problems	Legitimacy, efficiency and accountability rather low	Diversity rises, but on net very likely less problems

a new variant form of policy cooperation may be emerging, which seems to leave the formal locus of political responsibility and legitimacy with the Member States. This methodology invents informal instruments and soft tools which have the potential advantages, first, of flexible adaptation that avoid the rigidities of the traditional 'Community method' and, second, of a differently constructed version of subsidiarity. If this turned out to be a sustainable methodology, it could also provide a form of 'incremental constitutionalism', without the contested bargaining of intergovernmental conferences and attendant national ratification hurdles.[53]

[53] Wallace (n 51 above) 266–267.

Part IV

New Governance and the European Union

One of the European Union's foundations is the rule of law. Although by no means perfect, Community law provides a remarkably secure basis for a wide range of policies. It represents an extraordinary historical achievement, without which the legislation establishing the internal market and giving effect to many of the Community's policies, being based on the traditional 'Community method', might well have proved ineffective. However, while that method is particularly appropriate for attaining regulatory objectives and protecting individual rights, there are some forms of policy to which it is less well suited.

The relationship between the Union and its Member States involves a constant (re)balancing of powers and concerns. Given the continuing attachment of the peoples of Europe to their welfare states, social and regional redistribution play a substantial role in securing legitimacy for government across Europe. The search for an advantageous equilibrium between European market integration and regional and social policies continues. To achieve the right balance, a 'new governance' agenda has emerged. Beginning in the 1990s with the European Employment Strategy, this approach has been based on new forms of cooperation between the Member States, involving soft rules and such techniques as target setting, benchmarking and policy transfer. Although quite distinct from the role it plays in the 'Community method', the Commission plays a vital part in these new processes. The new approach was consolidated at Lisbon in 2000 where it came to be known as the 'open method of co-ordination' (OMC). In this context EMU deserves particularly close attention. The completion of monetary union has both intensified the potential tension between economic integration and social and regional objectives and created a need for increased coordination between member governments, particularly on questions of the conduct of fiscal policy and structural economic modernization. The relationship between the Community method and new forms of governance, especially the OMC, is likely to be a central feature of the debate about the future of Europe.

19

Social Policy in the Post-Nice Era

Erika Szyszczak

Social policy after Nice

The Treaty of Nice gives the impression that, after the momentous changes to social policy in the Maastricht and Amsterdam Treaties, the Member States had run out of ideas and ambition for any further development of social policy in the Community. The only Treaty amendments to social policy are to be found in Article 13 EC, where a new sub paragraph, Article 13(2), was added, allowing the Member States to adopt incentive measures; and the addition of a new indent to Article 137 EC, which allows the Community to support and complement the activities of the Member States in the area of 'the modernization of social protection schemes...'[1] Linked to the latter amendment, a new Article 144 EC allows for the creation of a Social Protection Committee.[2] These small, ad hoc, unconnected and seemingly innocuous and uncontested Treaty changes have a significance much greater than may be realized.

Of greater visible significance for social policy was the Nice European Council's adoption of the Commission's Social Policy Agenda (SPA).[3] This document appears as a series of policy aspirations lacking a legislative backbone. This was not the original intention of the Member States. The European Employment Strategy (EES) which had evolved since 1997 had

---

[1] Art 137(k) EC. The Council may only '...adopt measures designed to encourage cooperation between Member States through initiatives aimed at improving knowledge, developing exchanges of information and best practices, promoting innovative approaches and evaluating experiences excluding any harmonization of the laws and regulations of the Member States'.

[2] The Committee was already established by a Council Decision of 29 June 2000, [2000] OJ L172/26.

[3] COM(2000) 379 final.

focused attention on the *quantity* of employment at the expense of the *quality* of employment. The Lisbon Summit of March 2000 proposed to correct this imbalance by adding a *quality* dimension to the over-arching objective of the EU of achieving a dynamic and competitive society.[4] The SPA claimed to create a new social paradigm for the Community. Of importance in the SPA is the reliance on a form of governance, the open method of coordination, which is to be used alongside the conventional policy-making and decision-making processes in the EU.

By the time of the Nice Council Meeting of December 2000 the open method of coordination had generated a new dynamic in the development of social policy in the EU. It had created new law-making processes resulting in flexible forms of law and regulation. Additionally it had introduced new political actors working within the existing multi-tiered structures of EU governance, creating new sites of organization and cooperation and legitimizing a role for the EU in an area previously resistant to Community intervention.[5] As a result a broad area of social policy, ranging from industrial relations, labour and social law to social protection schemes had been Europeanized.

Another important dimension to the development of the quality of social policy post-Nice is the adoption of the solemn proclamation of a Charter of Fundamental Rights for the EU.[6] The new Charter not only consolidates a number of European fundamental social rights but also introduces some new ones. While the legal status of the Charter remains to be resolved at the next IGC in 2004, the influence of a fundamental rights dimension to social policy has already been felt.

Post-Nice a new social policy paradigm is emerging whereby what were previously perceived of as separate, competing and seemingly irreconcilable issues have been brought together to create complementary policies. The most discernible attribute of the new social policy paradigm is the fluidity it has created between a number of disparate, sometimes competing themes of EU policy to create a new form of social policy. Within the new paradigm is an attempt at a reconciliation of the perceived and actual

[4] 'The Union has today set itself a new strategic goal for the next decade: to become the most competitive and dynamic knowledge-based economy in the world, capable of sustaining economic growth with more and more better jobs and greater social cohesion.' Lisbon European Council, Presidency Conclusions, paras 5–7, 23–24 March 2000: http://www.portugal.ue-2000.pt/uk/docmne-main02.htm/.

[5] E Szyszczak, 'The new paradigm for social policy: a virtuous circle?' (2001) 38 CMLRev 1125.

[6] [2000] OJ C364/1. See chapter by Jacobs in this volume.

tension between a number of countervailing and contradictory issues in the EU: the competition between the economic aims of the Internal Market and the political, social and citizenship ideals of the emerging EU polity; the use of macro-economic planning and micro-economic implementation of policy; moves towards greater acknowledgment of fundamental social rights alongside moves away from creating centralized directly effective Community law rights to de-centralized minimum standards.

Linked together, these outcomes of the 2000 IGC and Nice European Council of December 2000 make a contribution to the ongoing process of creating a new social policy paradigm for the Community which is characterized by new political actors and the development of new tools and techniques of governance. This chapter will address the distinctive characteristics of the new social policy paradigm from the perspectives of accountability and legitimacy by examining the new forms of governance utilized in the open method of coordination as it is being developed in the field of social policy.

The open method of coordination

At the Lisbon Summit in March 2000, the European Council agreed that the open method of coordination would be a major factor in realizing the ambitious goals of the Summit which should define the shape of Europe for the next decade. An analysis of how the open method of coordination has worked in practice provides a useful analytical tool for the analysis of new processes of governance which are emerging in the EU; how such processes measure up to the post-Maastricht ideals of decreasing the democratic deficit of the EU, increasing accountability, transparency and openness; and, the role of such processes in creating a new constitutional order for the emerging post-national polity to which the constitution builders aspire for the European Union.

The open method of coordination was used in relation to economic and monetary union (EMU) and in an experimental form in the Essen Employment Strategy. These pre-cursors were quite different forms of coordination revealing the breadth of flexibility the open method of coordination can bring to EU governance. Under EMU coordination of economic policies was a Treaty obligation involving a set of common objectives to ensure sustained convergence and economic performance amongst the Member States. This was not a loose ideal but was clarified by the convergence criteria also set out in the Treaty and the incentive of qualifying for the second stage of EMU. The Stability and Growth Pact of 1997 took away the Member States' autonomy even further. Not only are the Member States accountable under a multilateral surveillance programme, monetary sovereignty has been lost to a concept of pooled sovereignty in terms of overall fiscal balances and accountability to peer review and susceptibility to sanctions. The Broad Economic Guidelines of the Member States and the Community set out the recommendations for the EU as well as individual Member States but, as we saw with the case of Ireland in 2001, the sanctions for non-compliance—or disagreement—with the recommendations boil down to peer pressure as well as the political and economic power wielded by financial markets.

In contrast the Essen employment strategy using the open method of coordination developed outside the Treaty structure through European Council meetings. Although the Conclusions of successive Council meetings after Essen reinforced the Essen aims and objectives, the lack of an institutional framework facilitating peer pressure, incentives and sanctions explains the comparative failure of the employment strategy. De la Porte, Pochet and Room go further, arguing that the comparative success of the EMU over the Essen strategy can also be attributable to German monetary hegemony which held together the coordination of monetary and fiscal cooperation.[7] In contrast there was no hegemony of ideas for tackling the labour market and the Essen strategy floundered as a result of a lack of leadership and disagreement over the correct way to regulate labour markets.[8] At the Amsterdam IGC in 1997, the Member States agreed to institutionalize a process for the coordination of a European labour market strategy, borrowing the institutional design of multilateral surveillance, benchmarking and peer group review from the EMU design. The Employment Chapter contained in Articles 125–130 EC established new processes mirroring the institutional design and processes of EMU. A difference between the EMU process of coordination and the employment process is the lack of incentives and sanctions in the latter. The Member States took advantage of the political climate which accepted the fast-track implementation of the new Employment Chapter at the special 'Jobs Summit' in Luxembourg in November 1997 establishing the EES (which became

[7] C De La Porte, P Pochet, and G Room, 'Social benchmarking and EU governance' (2001) 11 JESP 291.

[8] E Szyszczak, 'The evolving European Employment Strategy' in J Shaw (ed), *Social Law and Policy in an Evolving European Union* (2000) 197.

known as the Luxembourg Process), introducing other coordinating processes in the Cologne and Cardiff Processes.

The term 'open method of coordination' was coined at the Lisbon Summit in 2000 in order not only to name but also to capture and institutionalize the Luxembourg, Cardiff and Cologne Processes, and the Broad Guidelines of the Economic Policies of the Member States and of the Community. The first three Processes have emerged and evolved from European Council Meetings and are usually categorized as pragmatic responses to the integration demands of EMU. Each Process is named after the European Council meeting where it was adopted. This is an important signifier, legitimating the Process in the same way recent Treaties—Maastricht, Amsterdam, Nice—have received their nomenclature. At the Lisbon Summit of March 2000 the Member States not only endorsed these Processes but underlined their confidence in them, by declaring that they were sufficient and that no new Processes would be necessary to realize the aims of the Lisbon Summit.

The purpose of these Processes is two-fold: to deliver policy outcomes and to create *processes* to achieve the policy outcomes. From a definitional point of view the Commission and the European Council have been vague as to what the open method of coordination is. The Commission Communication on the Social Policy Agenda presented in June 2000 describes it as: 'establishing guidelines, setting benchmarks, concrete targets and a monitoring system to evaluate progress via a peer group review'.[9] In contrast the European Council Conclusions of Santa Maria da Feira in June 2000 describe it as merely improving coordination between the various Council formations and ensuring close cooperation between the Council Presidency and the Commission under the overall guidance of the European Council. As we shall discover, the word 'open' may mean the *method* of the process and the *lack of closure* to the process.

A new form of governance?

Legitimacy

The Luxembourg Process uses a combination of techniques, inter alia, participation in the implementation of policy-making, benchmarking, exchange of best practice and information, peer review and cooperation and

[9] See n 3 above, 9.

coordination within a widely meshed and multi-level interactive framework in order to achieve its aims.

While the Luxembourg Process has a Treaty base in Title VIII, the Commission has used soft law documents to build a consensus amongst the Member States, as well as other political actors, most notably the social partners, on the need to achieve a better mix of economic and social policies and the need to see unemployment as a common problem of the EU. Legitimacy for the Process was achieved by a Resolution made at the Amsterdam IGC in 1997, which fast-tracked the Employment Chapter into operation. The procedures were realized by a special Jobs Summit held in Luxembourg in November 1997. From this the Luxembourg Process gathered its own spectacular momentum, legitimating its role as a governance process.

Accountability, benchmarking and peer review

The Luxembourg Process is organized around the four central pillars of Employability, Entrepreneurship, Adaptability and Equal Opportunities between Men and Women (with sex equality mainstreamed through all of the pillars). The Commission proposes a set of Guidelines to implement the objectives of the four pillars. These Guidelines have evolved over time. There are 18 Guidelines with a new idea introduced into the 2001 Guidelines of Horizontal Guidelines.[10] In addition to specific objectives and targets, the Guidelines also carry a number of diffused messages on the respective roles of the actors in the process, the new balances to be struck between new and traditional policies of the Member States, the need for modernization of workplace practices, the need for a new balance between individual and collective, public and private, responsibility for employment and unemployment.

The Council may endorse or alter the Guidelines. The legitimacy of the Guidelines has not been questioned and the Council moved from implementing the Guidelines through a Resolution to a Decision in 2001. The Guidelines form the benchmarks for the peer review. The Member States implement the Guidelines through National Action Plans (NAPs). The NAPs are submitted to the Commission where they are reviewed by the Commission, the Employment Committee and other Member States. The NAPs are not very detailed and often are distilled statements of domestic policy which are already being implemented. Tensions have arisen

---

[10] Council Decision of 19 January 2001 on Guidelines for Member States' Employment Policies for the Year 2001 [2001] OJ L22/18.

in that, while the EU has created processes for achieving a consensus on the benchmarks, the Member States retain the autonomy to implement the benchmarks. Where the achievement of a benchmark may involve complex structural economic changes at the national level, the EU processes have little coercive reach.

An important aspect of the open method of coordination is that it is seen as an iterative process; at the Lisbon Summit it was described as 'a learning process for all'. Yet, in reality the formal processes for exchange of best practice are institutionally limited out of practical necessity. Peer review processes also reveal a 'softly softly' approach, which is necessary to build up trust between the Member States. In the Luxembourg Process peer group review is implemented by each Member State making a formal presentation of their NAP for 20 minutes. Then two other Member States review the NAP for 15 minutes. There is a brief discussion between the Member States for 10 minutes and then the Member State, under scrutiny, is allowed a reply for 10 minutes. This process of peer review takes place over a period of two days leaving very little time for in depth discussion. In 1999 the Commission initiated a complementary process of sharing best practice. This involves a Member State volunteering to present an aspect of its employment policy which it considers to be best practice. The Commission organizes a conference where delegates from some, or all, of the Member States can discuss the best practice.

Following the peer review of the NAPs, a Joint Employment Report is prepared between the Commission and Council. From the conclusions drawn from the Joint Report the Commission proposes Recommendations which are endorsed but can be modified by the Council. The Recommendations tend to be vague and quite general in nature and the Commission has responded to requests from the Member States to reduce their number. A weakness of the process is the lack of sanctions available to the Commission and the Member States if one Member State disagrees with, or refuses to implement, the Commission's Recommendations.

Legitimizing Community competence in the area of modernizing social protection

What is remarkable about the Luxembourg Process is the way the policy of modernizing social protection has been brought within the remit of the EES and within Community competence as a result of the Treaty of Nice. National systems of social protection have lost their independent dynamic and have been mainstreamed into the employment policy of the EU, making them subservient to the economic aims of the EU.

Historical analysis shows how this occurred through a pattern of consensus-building utilizing soft law. In 1992 the Council passed two Recommendations recognizing the need for a convergence strategy for national social protection systems as a consequence of the monetary integration project.[11] These were followed by two Commission Communications in 1995[12] and 1997.[13] In these the Commission argues that the Member States face common challenges and common concerns. Thus a common understanding and a regulatory space for the EU is created in order to orchestrate the modernization of social protection. The fears of the Member States are also raised. The 'European social model' is perceived to be under threat if the modernization of social protection is not addressed at EU level fora. The Commission takes it upon itself to indicate routes along which the modernization of social protection can be pursued. After an initial policy of convergence, social protection is to be mainstreamed into the Luxembourg Process. The same strategy used in the EES is deployed for the modernization of social protection. The Commission acts as a conduit, reinforcing cooperation between the main actors. We see the use of EU and national level fora, the creation and legitimization of a 'European Social Model' by attributing it with a socio-political identity, the use of central pillars around which the new model can be constructed, the search for common indicators, the use of two-yearly NAPs, the use of EU-coordinated institutional arrangements and new political actors including the new Social Protection Committee now integrated into the EC Treaty.

While the Treaty of Nice stresses that social protection is still within the Member States' competence, the Luxembourg Process has brought about a discernible shift in the balance between the Member States' autonomy and EU goals. As the example of EMU has shown, the peer pressure to find solutions acceptable to the EU integration project may be used to legitimize

---

[11] Council Recommendation 92/442/EC on the convergence of social policy objectives [1992] OJ L245/49; Council Recommendation 92/441/EC on common criteria concerning sufficient resources and social assistance [1992] OJ L245/46.

[12] EC Commission, The Future of Social Protection: Framework for a European Debate COM (95) 466.

[13] EC Commission, Modernising and Improving Social Protection in the European Union COM (97) 102.

change and make politically sensitive changes to national policy. The EES, now containing a modernization of social protection programme, has been firmly linked to the Lisbon economic strategy. Thus the open method of coordination has been a useful tool which is able to penetrate an area hitherto jealously guarded as being within Member State competence and to legitimize EU competence.

Benchmarking and peer review are the central methodological tools of the open method of co-ordination in the area of social policy. In the Luxembourg Process, the Commission has chosen a number of indicators to measure the labour market performance of the Member States inter se and the labour market performance of the EU against that of the US and Japan. One criticism of the Luxembourg Process is that it goes beyond the remit of the original Employment Chapter introduced at the Amsterdam IGC and its findings have been used to create league tables which are used in peer pressure.

Benchmarking is an important methodological tool in the Modernization of Social Protection programme post-Nice. The Commission sees benchmarking as instrument to promote change and to mobilize all actors to move in this direction.[14] But benchmarking in the area of social protection is not a policy tool which is easily transferable. First of all, social protection schemes have developed across the fifteen Member States within different economic, fiscal and political contexts. There is no common definition of what constitutes a social protection scheme, although it has now been suggested that, for the purposes of EU integration, such schemes must embrace statutory, occupational and fiscal schemes in all the Member States,[15] as well as taxation and other fiscal advantages created through the use of transfers. Another pressing obstacle, linked to the entrenched differences between the national social protection schemes is the lack of comparative statistical data upon which benchmarking is reliant.[16] Finally, as De la Porte et al point out, in direct contrast to EMU the modernization of social protection project 'lacks a hegemony capable of enforcing a single vision of social objectives'.[17] The direction in the post-Nice era of social policy is through the

[14] ibid.
[15] J Berghmann, 'Social protection in the European Union' in A Bosco and M Hutsebaut (eds), *Social Protection in Europe. Facing up to Changes and Challenges* (1997) 17.
[16] There is a scheme called ESSPROS (European System of Integrated Social Protection Statistics) but this lacks the common indicators necessary to be of sufficient use for benchmarking purposes: EC Commission, Report from the Commission, Social Protection in Europe in 1999 COM (2000) 163 final.
[17] See De La Porte, Pochet and Room, n 7 above, 297.

evaluation of the efficiency of *public* policies fraught with the awareness of the difficulties of extrapolating out in a vacuum policies relating to social protection independently of the historic, cultural, economic national context in which social protection schemes evolved at the national level and the necessity for democratic approval for changes to such fundamental structures.

The legitimacy and accountability of new political actors

One of the purposes of the new form of governance implemented through the open method of coordination is to create and endorse consensus building, not only between the Member States, but also between the various political actors within the multi-tiered structures of governance of the EU. The aim is to involve all the stakeholders, the new civil society, in the new Europe, in policy formation, decision-making and implementation of the new social policy.[18] Given the multiplicity of different structures and actors, it can be argued that the open method of coordination creates new forms of governance rather than one particular kind of governance structure. This creates problems for the EU of how to manage the decentralizing tendencies inherent in policy and decision-making.

In the Luxembourg Process, the formation of the NAPs varies from Member State to Member State. Customary and legal rights to consultation, participation and legal redress (where exclusion from, or disagreement with, the process occurs) will depend upon the local institutional and legal culture. The crucial new actors are the social partners, who have replaced the European Parliament as the representative stakeholder in social matters in both Titles VIII and XI of the EC Treaty. The role of the social partners in decision-making has been enhanced since the 1980s, but also the increase in the amount of soft regulation of industrial relations, for example, joint opinions, declarations, resolutions, codes of conduct and guidelines, has contributed to the Europeanization of industrial relations within Europe.[19]

The Luxembourg Process, as outlined in Title VIII of the EC Treaty, did not envisage an important role for the social partners and they are not mentioned in the same institutional sense as the role set out for them in

---

[18] See this use of a wider section of civil society in policy formation and implementation in the recent Art 13 EC directives, discussed by Ellis in this volume.

[19] EC Commission, *Industrial Relations in Europe* 2000 (OOPEC, Brussels, 2000).

Title XI of the EC Treaty. Yet the social partners have played a crucial role in implementing the EES in the Employment Guidelines, through sectoral agreements and through the use of Title VIII by creating Framework Agreements implemented through Directives.[20]

In the Employment Guidelines the social partners are given specific roles. The Guidelines for the year 2001 reveal that this is an evolutionary process whereby new roles have been created. The social partners are 'invited' to be responsible for the reporting on actions within their autonomous remit in accordance with the overall objectives of the Guidelines, creating what the Commission argues is a new synergy between the national and the EU level. Thus the social partners have become part of the élite in decision-making and policy implementation in EU governance techniques, raising similar questions about the legitimacy and representativity of the social partners which have already been raised under Title XI.[21] In the modernization of social protection programme the issue is more acute. The establishment of High Level Groups, exchanges of best practice and information between national civil servants and EU officials currently lacks transparency and accountability.

The creation of new configurations of actors raises questions about transparency and the accountability of those who hold power in the EU. It also raises legal issues about how the stakeholders can protect their rights, which are evolving through custom and practice in the new processes of governance. Leaving aside the justiciability of the acts which emerge from the processes, the Community law concept of locus standi gives inadequate protection to the stakeholders in the new Europe. A useful way forward in recognizing the emergent legal interests could be by drawing parallels with the rise of third party claims and recognition of limited rights, especially those of competitors, in the competition sphere where the Court of Justice has shown a willingness to protect certain kinds of economic interests. Community public law has not yet reached sufficient maturity to identify the kind of legal rights to representation and participation which need protecting in the open method of co-ordination and has little to say on how they should be protected. The underlying premise seems to be that the EU is still an embryonic and fragile system and that lawyers and the courts should stay out of the polycentric decision-making structures. Given the multiplicity of interests at stake, law and legal claims are not always seen as

---

[20] eg Dir 97/81/EC [1997] OJ L14/9; Dir 99/70/EC [1999] OJ L175/43.
[21] Case T-135/96 *UEAPME v Council* [1998] ECR II-2335.

the most useful way of regulating such relationships. These new forms of governance are thus at odds with the lawyer's tendency to want to see linear progression in the evolution of a political system and maturity in the evolution of rights in the legal system based upon the rule of law.[22]

Lawyers will also need to re-think the relationship between public power and private power. Inherent within the new social policy paradigm in the post-Nice era is the turn to the market to deliver what were previously perceived of as public goods and services. Fundamental questions arise as to whether public services can survive in the competitive markets of the Lisbon economic agenda, the role for the State in providing public services under competitive conditions and a plethora of issues about the accountability of private power in the market.[23] Conversely the shift towards the market and the private provision of public services also raises the question of how far the law can and should extend the privileges normally ascribed to public power to private power which is being asked to assume the delivery of public goods and services in competitive markets.

Future governance of the EU

The open method of coordination has been accepted as a new mode of governance for the EU in the post-Lisbon agenda. It might be argued that it is merely a re-working of old processes of governance, for example the use of intergovernmentalism, the battle for supremacy and competence between the Member States, the Community and its institutions or part of the new governance culture which embraces aspects of 'opt-outs' and 'opt ins', subsidiarity, flexibility and a post-regulatory approach which allows for variation, generous margins of discretion and a preference for voluntary cooperation instead of detailed, centralized and inflexible rules. The open method of coordination exists outside the processes of institutional and constitutional reform of the EU. While this may be acceptable for political expediency it raises a number of problems for the issues of legitimacy and accountability which are the focus of this book. From a legal perspective a major problem inherent within the open method of coordination is the absence of closure in the process. This is seen in the ideas of coordination,

---

[22] See chapter by Arnull in this volume.

[23] A Amato, *Antitrust and the Bounds of Power: The Dilemma of Liberal Democracy in the History of the Market* (1997).

which, in new areas impervious to the harmonizing and convergence processes of the integration project in the past, must start with simple forms of dialogue exchange. There are some successes of the open method of coordination which result in legal forms and it may be that it is a necessary first step to establishing the ground for enhanced cooperation: a preliminary political process which cannot be easily articulated in legal form. There is also a lack of closure manifested in the absence of sanctions for non-compliance with the processes.

Another legitimacy issue raised by the open method of coordination is the effect it has on the existing institutional balance of the EU. This balance is now a central and delicate concern in the constitutional review of the EU in the light of the future enlargement process. A simple explanation of the role of the open method of coordination in the post-Nice era is to categorize it as the dominance of Member State competence in the EU, traditionally located in the rise of the power of the European Council. This power is not easily captured in the institutional framework, and the successive amendments to that framework. Arguments have been made that, through the changes to governance techniques, the traditional institutions of the EU, particularly the Commission, have ceded political power to the European Council and the Member States.[24] Certainly there are changes to the inter-institutional dynamics of the EU as a result of the open method of coordination. The European Parliament does not have a formal role in the process and the attempts by the Committee of the Regions to have a role recognized as a formal tier of governance in the EU are also affected by the open method of coordination. The Commission has in fact proved to be a durable institution in the evolution of the open method of coordination and its political role could be cited as an example of the Commission's enduring capacity to augment its power. Not content to be merely a facilitator or conduit of policy, the Commission has used the open method of coordination to perform the roles of initiator and transformer of policy through the use of soft law, the preparatory documents for European Council meetings and the follow-up to Summits. All these forms of policy transference have had a crucial role in consensus building since the Lisbon Summit of March 2000. The Commission has stressed that it has a central role to play in providing the stability, the anchor and the collective history and memory of the EU against the rotating Presidencies and changes in national political power.

---

[24]   D Hodson and I Maher, 'The open method as a new mode of governance: the case of soft law economic policy coordination' (2001) 39 JCMS 16.

Although the resignation of the Santer Commission threw the institution into crisis and soul-searching, it also provided the political opportunity for the new President, Romano Prodi, to adapt the Commission to react to the spill-over effects of EMU which demanded, inter alia, the abolition of the vertical segregation of policies within the Commission Directorates-General and the move towards addressing the coordination and interaction of different economic policies.

In order to legitimize the use of the open method of coordination it has sometimes been classified as a dynamic form of subsidiarity: 'cooperative subsidiarity' or 'horizontal subsidiarity' are different terms used to capture the multi-level involvement of sub-EU actors and institutions. The open method of coordination can be viewed as an aspect of what de Búrca[25] calls the cultural framework of decision-making post-Maastricht and can be assessed as part of an evolutionary form of governance. But the conventional understanding of subsidiarity is that it defines the *level* of power which is most appropriate for each sphere of action and in particular is related to the principle of proximity: decisions should be taken as closely as possible to the area affected. In contrast, the open method of coordination does something else. It is both an iterative and interactive process. It recognizes the inter-relationship and inter-dependence between different spheres of economic and social policy as well as promoting the interaction between different levels of power and spheres of action in the multilevel governance structures of the EU. Another feature of the open method of coordination, distancing it from the label of subsidiarity, is that it is a widely meshed process, in principle embracing all stakeholders in consultation, implementation and decision-making. In subtle ways it can transfer competence away from the national level to European processes. Social policy shows that it is a useful tool in the Europeanization of a number of policy areas previously inhabited by national interests, be they displayed in forms of private or public power. Within the area of social policy all the relevant actors, from the EU to the local level, must now articulate their strategy and actions within the multi-level logic of the Lisbon agenda.

While an acceptable legal definition of the open method of coordination may continue to elude the written constitutional framework of the EU, it has received an unprecedented level of political acceptance in the area of social

---

[25] G de Búrca, 'Reappraising subsidiarity's significance after Amsterdam' (Harvard Jean Monnet Working Paper 7/99).

policy. The open method of coordination is a practical, pragmatic and principled response to the post-Maastricht legitimacy crisis in the EU, while providing much needed legitimacy for EU action in a wide area of social policy. Through the use of National Action Plans the EU is able to orchestrate a process of vertical decentralization. The legitimacy for EU intervention is seen to come from the national level, through democratic national procedures. Although the Employment Guidelines set the agenda, policy is portrayed as being formed at the national level with the EU merely facilitating cooperation between the Member States and the various sub-national, regional and transnational actors. The open method of coordination goes further. It creates new forms of élites with power to influence and implement decision-making in the EU. While the open method of coordination has been used by the Commission as an example of improving transparency and deepening democratic participation in decision-making in the EU,[26] the experience of social policy post-Nice reveals that it can lead to new forms of opaque decision-making particularly by the social partners, representatives of civil society and civil servants. Arguably good governance requires public discussion of the role and form of social policy in the EU, public discussion and scrutiny of the choice of indicators used in the governance process of benchmarking and the creation of fora where policy can be challenged. The absence of closure in the open method of coordination does not allow this to occur easily.

The open method of coordination may be legitimized as a form of negative integration. It allows for flexibility in policy making and is part of the maturation of the legal process in that monitoring of national policies, peer pressure, the coordination of policies, common indicators can be seen not only as a form of policy transfer but as part of the process of eliminating differences between the Member States which are barriers to integration. But the open method of coordination appears opaque, using complex but informal institutional frameworks emphasizing processes rather than outcomes. What we have seen is that the open method of coordination plays an important role in agenda setting leading towards new forms of positive integration. The Employment Guidelines have assumed a normative identity with clear policy choices infused throughout. Scharpf has argued that while negative integration can be legitimated by reference to the EC Treaty, positive integration can only be legitimated by an institutional infrastructure embracing principles of democratic accountability and a collective

---

[26] European Governance: A White Paper COM (2001) 428.

identity.[27] In this respect the open method of coordination could be legitimated by the use of the revised Title XI of the EC Treaty where the aims of the EES could be implemented in legal form. To date this route has been under-used.

An important feature of the open method of coordination is that it respects diversity. Since 1997 it has developed its own logic in the field of social policy and can be legitimized politically as a child of its time. It represents a political compromise between the logic of pure integration and the logic of simple cooperation: 'a third way' of European governance. Ferrera, Hemerijk and Rhodes have described the open method of coordination as suspended somewhere between harmonization, the heavy top-down governance mechanism deemed unworkable in the enlarged EU, and the principle of mutual recognition developed from *Cassis de Dijon* and employed in the Internal Market regulatory package where the resulting regulatory competition is deemed too much of a risk.[28] The problems engendered by European integration are too complex to be handled by simple international agreement but a new model of governance is necessary for the prospect of an enlarged Union in the 21st century. In showing its utility in bringing politically sensitive areas such as social policy within Community competence, the open method of coordination may find a role for resolving other sensitive areas such as the coordination of immigration or taxation issues. The process of constitutional reform in the EU continues to be experimental. The open method of coordination reveals that new modes of governance can be tried out and fine-tuned without involving a systemic change in governance. If it works, the process of European integration moves on. If it does not work the EU can revert back to traditional ways of governance without the agony of an IGC and the revision and ratification of a new Treaty.

[27] F Scharpf, *Games Real Actors Play* (1997), ch 9.
[28] M Femera, A Hemerijk and M Rhodes, *The Future of Social Europe: Recasting Work and Welfare in the New Economy* (2001).

20

EMU and Enlargement: Twin Threats to European Regional Cohesion?

Ronald L Martin

Introduction

There can be little doubt that the European Union is entering an historic phase in its evolution. Over the next decade or so, two major developments are set to transform the economic landscape of the EU. First, the formal introduction of a single currency union—the Eurozone—on 1 January 2002 marked a major step in the economic integration (or 'deepening') process in the EU. Covering 12 of the 15 Member States, some 300 million EU citizens, this formative move towards full economic and monetary union (EMU) is the culmination of an idea that dates back thirty years to the Werner Plan of 1970.[1] Money is one of the most tangible symbols of nationhood, of a nation's territorial integrity, sovereignty, and history, and by abandoning their own currencies for the euro, the twelve members of the Eurozone are shedding not only part of their cultural identity but a considerable element of their economic autonomy. By ceding national interest rate and exchange rate policy to the European Central Bank, the Eurozone states have committed themselves to a single 'one-size-fits-all' monetary policy. The argument is that the benefits of monetary integration—greater economic efficiency, higher economic growth, and the creation of a reserve currency

---

[1] The 12 members of the single currency (Eurozone) are: Austria, Belgium, Finland, France, Germany, Greece, Ireland, Italy, Luxembourg, the Netherlands, Portugal, and Spain. Britain, Denmark and Sweden remain, for the moment, outside the formal Eurozone. For a discussion of the Werner Plan, see G Magnifico, *European Monetary Unification* (1973). A useful summary of the evolution of the various stages of EMU since the Werner Plan can be found in C Dent, *The European Economy* (1997).

to rival the US dollar—will more than outweigh the loss of national monetary independence.

Second, following on the heels of this historic development, an ambitious programme is taking shape for a further major enlargement (or 'widening') of the EU. Negotiations are under way with 12 additional candidate countries, mainly the central and eastern European countries (CEECs) that, if successful, could eventually almost double the membership of the EU and increase its population to 500 million.[2] Membership of the EU is seen by these states as offering major opportunities for economic development and modernization. For the EU, eastwards enlargement is welcomed not only for its contribution to political stability across Europe, but also for the economic gains it will bring in terms of an expanded market and new possibilities for investment and growth.

These twin developments also pose several challenges, however, not least for another key policy goal of the EU, namely the pursuit of economic and social cohesion. According to the European Commission, the goal of 'cohesion'

seeks to combine a system of economic organisation based on market forces, freedom of opportunity and enterprise with a commitment to the values of internal solidarity and mutual support which ensures open access for all members of society to services of general benefit and protection.[3]

As formulated in Article 158 (ex 130a) EC, the notion of cohesion is set in terms of 'harmonious development' with a specific geographical dimension: 'reducing disparities between the levels of development of the various regions and the backwardness of the least favoured regions'.[4] So far as the geographical dimension is concerned, according to the Commission's 1993 White Paper on this theme, the reduction of disparities between Member States and regions is held to mean convergence of basic incomes through higher GDP growth, of competitiveness, and of employment.[5] The Commission is at pains to point out that regional convergence should be achieved

---

[2] The applicant states are: Bulgaria, Czech Republic, Estonia, Hungary, Latvia, Lithuania, Poland, Romania, Slovakia, Slovenia, Cyprus and Malta. Negotiations have yet to get underway with Turkey, as a possible thirteenth applicant. The first phase of this enlargement—involving ten of the applicant states—is planned for 2004.

[3] Commission of the European Communites, *First Report on Social Cohesion* (1996) 13.

[4] Commission of the European Communities, *Unity, Solidarity, Diversity for Europe, its People and its Territory: Second Report on Economic and Social Cohesion* (2000) 13.

[5] Commission of the European Communities, *Growth, Competitiveness and Employment: The Challenges and Ways Forward into the 21st Century* (1993).

by increasing the competitiveness, growth and structural modernization of the lagging and less prosperous regions (ie, 'positive convergence'), not by reducing the growth or employment of the more prosperous areas of the Union (ie, 'negative convergence'). Seen in these terms, regional cohesion—the convergence of regional incomes and welfare—is essential to the legitimacy of EMU as a political goal.

My argument in this chapter is that, together, the introduction of the single currency zone, as the latest step on the road to full EMU, and further large-scale enlargement could seriously frustrate this pursuit of regional cohesion or convergence. Of course, at this stage, discussions about the regional impacts of monetary union and enlargement are necessarily speculative, since the euro has only just been introduced and eastwards enlargement has yet to occur. But neither recent trends in regional disparities across the EU nor theoretical arguments about the regional consequences of EMU provide grounds for believing that regional adjustments to these two historic events will be straightforward or painless. While the European Commission is certainly not unaware of the potential problems,[6] their potential scale and implications have not been sufficiently acknowledged. It is far from clear that regional cohesion will improve (regional disparities will narrow), even over the medium to long term, and there is a real possibility that regional divergence could occur. At the very least, the strains on the Structural and Cohesion Funds could be considerable if regional disparities are to be contained and reduced. Yet further, there may well be an increasing need for—but probably equally strong public resistance to—the surrender of Member States' fiscal powers to a single, centralized fiscal stabilization system within the Eurozone as the logical counterpart to the common currency and a single monetary policy.

Recent trends in regional cohesion: the story so far

Looking at relatively simple indices of regional socio-economic welfare, the European Commission has tended to the view that regional disparities in the EU have been narrowing over the past quarter-century, in other words

[6] See eg Commission of the European Communities, *The Single Market Review: Regional Growth and Convergence* (1997); Commission of the European Communities, *First Report on Economic and Social Cohesion* (1996); Commission of the European Communities, *Unity, Solidarity, Diversity for Europe, its People and its Territory: Second Report on Economic and Social Cohesion* (2001).

that there has been regional convergence and thus increasing regional cohesion.[7] However, the situation is not as straightforward or clear-cut as the European Commission seems to believe. In fact, numerous studies have examined the regional convergence issue in the EU, and the findings admit of various interpretations: much depends on the index of regional economic performance that is examined, the statistical technique employed to measure convergence, and the time period over which the analysis is conducted. While many studies find some evidence for convergence, some commentators argue that no significant convergence has occurred at all, and some that perhaps there has even been some divergence.[8]

Attention has mainly focused on two concepts or measures of regional convergence in the EU. The first of these (so-called growth regression or β-convergence) is based on the idea (derived from the neoclassical theory of economic growth) that if regional convergence ('catch-up') is to occur, those regions with the lowest initial per capita incomes should show the highest growth rates of per capita incomes over time, and vice versa. The statistical estimate of this inverse relationship (β) between initial levels of regional per capita incomes and their subsequent growth gives the 'speed' of convergence. A group of regions is said to be characterized by so-called σ-convergence if the dispersion (variance or standard deviation) of their relative per capita incomes tends to decline over time.[9]

If regions converge towards a common per capita income, *absolute* convergence is said to occur; in this case the dispersion (variance) of regional per capita incomes would tend to zero. If, because of enduring structural, technological and institutional differences across regions, regional per capita incomes converge, not to some common value, but to different long-run relativities, then *conditional* β-convergence is said to occur, and

---

[7] Commission of the European Communities, *Sixth Periodic Report on the Social and Economic Situation and Development of the Regions of the European Union* (1999); Commission of the European Communities, *Unity, Solidarity, Diversity for Europe, its People and its Territory: Second Report on Economic and Social Cohesion* (2001).

[8] For surveys of these studies, see, for example, H Armstrong and R Vickerman (eds), *Convergence and Divergence among European Regions* (1995); R Martin and P Sunley, 'Slow convergence? New endogenous growth theory and regional development' (1998) 74 Economic Geography 201; K Button and E Pentecost, *Regional Economic Performance within the European Union* (1999); R Martin, 'EMU versus the regions? Regional convergence and divergence in Euroland' (2001) 1 Journal of Economic Geography 51.

[9] The concept of σ-convergence is closely related to β-convergence, although the correspondence is not exact. Technically, the degree of correspondence will depend on how closely the growth regression fits the data statistically (ie, on the size and variance of the error terms in the regression).

in this case the dispersion of regional incomes would decline towards some non-zero long-run value. If the relationship between initial regional per capita incomes and their growth over time is positive, this indicates regional divergence (and increasing dispersion of regional incomes).

Estimates of β-convergence for the EU regions over the period from the mid-1970s to the late 1990s have rarely exceeded −0.02, and are often much lower than this. A value of −0.02 indicates a rate of convergence of about two per cent per annum.[10] This is turn implies that it would take about 35 years for an initial regional disparity in per capita incomes to be halved. When this type of analysis has been carried out for separate sub-periods, it appears that the rate of convergence slowed appreciably after the mid-1980s, to around −0.01, which implies a regional disparity 'half-life' of around 70 years. Such values hardly suggest rapid convergence. And to compound matters, the growth regression approach has itself been shown to exaggerate the degree of convergence.[11]

Evidence of the overall slow rate of regional convergence, and the apparent change in the movement of regional disparities in the late 1980s is shown in Figure 20.1. This plots the regional dispersion of absolute per capita output (in 1985 constant prices) over the 1975–1999 period both for the 15 EU Member States and for the NUTS2–level regions across the EU-15 (excluding East Germany).[12] The coefficient of variation is used rather than standard deviation, since it adjusts for trends in the mean level of per capita output, and thus provides a more accurate indicator of relative inequalities over time.[13] This suggests that while there was some convergence from 1975 up to the late 1980s, this has since been followed by a

[10] Since the growth regression is typically estimated in logarithmic form, the regression coefficient, β, gives the speed of convergence as an annual rate.

[11] See for example, D Quah, 'Galton's Fallacy and tests of the convergence hypothesis' (1993) 95 Scandinavian Journal of Economics 427.

[12] The NUTS territorial units classification system employed by the EU is defined at four levels—NUTS0 are the nation states, NUTS1 are standard regions, NUTS2 are subregions, counties or provinces, and NUTS3 are local districts. Most official EU discussions of regional issues tend to use NUTS2 and NUTS3. Below the level of nation states, NUTS units do not necessarily represent functional economic or labour market areas.

[13] There is in fact an interesting issue here. The standard deviation and coefficient of variation need not move closely together over time. This relates to the basic question of how we measure regional disparities as absolute differentials about the EU average, or as relativities (ratios of the EU average). If for example, regional per capita incomes all increased by the same absolute amount, regional differentials would remain the same but regional relativities would narrow (converge). Conversely if regional incomes all increased by the same proportion, regional differentials would widen but regional relativities would remain constant.

Figure 20.1. Dispersion (Coefficient of Variation) of GDP per head across the EU-15 Member States and NUTS2 Regions, 1975–1999 (1985 Prices)

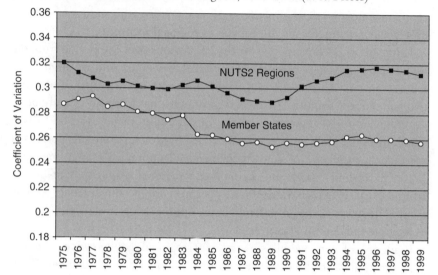

corresponding degree of divergence, especially over the first half of the 1990s, leaving the net position at the end of that decade little changed from that in the mid-1970s.

Other studies have examined regional employment evolutions across the EU, rather than regional output or incomes. Thus if the year-on-year cumulative employment growth patterns of EU regions are examined for the past two decades or so, these show a marked divergence in almost all Member States, with the fastest job growth almost invariably occurring in the more prosperous regions.[14] Such divergent regional employment growth helps to explain the steady rise in regional unemployment disparities over the same period,[15] and the corresponding high degree of persistence in regional unemployment rate rankings across the EU that have been noted by some observers.[16]

[14] R Martin and P Tyler, 'Regional employment evolutions in the European Union: a preliminary analysis' (2000) 34 Regional Studies 601.
[15] Commission of the European Communities, *Unity, Solidarity, Diversity for Europe, its People and its Territory: Second Report on Economic and Social Cohesion,* Vol 2 (2001) 20.
[16] That is to say, the geographical pattern of unemployment across the EU displays a high degree of similarity (correlation) through time (regions with high unemployment tend to remain so for long periods, and likewise for regions with low unemployment rates). This is in contrast to the situation in the US, where the map of unemployment can change quite markedly from one year to the next: see M Baddeley, RL Martin and P Tyler, 'European

In sum, the evidence for regional convergence is mixed, and even at best (in the case of regional incomes) convergence has been slow. Furthermore, it is difficult to discern any significant favourable 'integration' or 'regional policy' effects on regional convergence over the 1980s or 1990s, in particular the major increase in the Structural Funds after 1986 and the impact of the Single Market. Admittedly, testing for such effects is notoriously difficult. For one thing, it is unclear just how long it takes for regions to adjust to such developments. Patterns and processes of regional development—in both leading and lagging regions—are often characterized by a high degree of 'path dependence' or persistence. For another, it is far from easy to construct a valid counterfactual position—of what would have happened in the absence of moves towards economic integration and the strengthening of regional policy—against which to compare actual regional outcomes. Furthermore, economic and political circumstances have themselves been changing dramatically, and with them the nature of the 'regional problem' itself, irrespective of EU integration and regional policy intervention. Like other parts of the advanced capitalist world, the EU Member States have been undergoing a profound economic re-orientation, spearheaded particularly by globalization and a major wave of technological innovation (based especially around information technologies). To isolate the impact of policy developments from these ongoing systemic processes is exceedingly difficult.

What recent trends in regional convergence do suggest, however, is that regional cohesion—in the sense of regional convergence—operates very slowly, and that the effects of any major shocks that increase regional economic disparities across the EU are likely to be long-lasting.

Regional cohesion and the euro: is the EU an optimum currency area?

The introduction of the single currency zone is just one such shock. The underlying idea of an optimum currency area (OCA) is that in order to reduce the costs and maximize the benefits of monetary unification, there should be a reasonable degree of economic homogeneity amongst the countries making up the currency area. Since monetary union entails the surrender of individual national autonomy and accountability over ex-

regional unemployment disparities: convergence or persistence?' (1998) 5 European Urban and Regional Studies 195.

change rate and other monetary policies, the homogeneity condition ensures that member countries are equally affected by external economic shocks, and that none are unduly destabilized by the imposition of centralized currency area policies regarding the exchange rate, interest rate and so on. Hence the emphasis on the 'national convergence criteria' as a condition of membership of the Eurozone set up by the Maastricht Treaty.

However, although national monetary convergence criteria are obviously important, equally so are sub-national, ie, regional and local, aspects of the European monetary integration process. There are two main issues here. First, regional economic convergence is just as relevant as national monetary convergence to the success of the Eurozone. And, second, EMU will have significant implications for the individual regions of Member States. Some commentators take a very pessimistic view on this latter point:

In the debate on the Euro, very little attention is paid to differences in the levels of income and unemployment across the regions of Europe, and whether a single currency is likely to narrow or exacerbate these differences. This is an important issue because existing regional inequalities already pose a threat to the cohesion of the European Union. There is a very real possibility that the single currency, without an effective regional policy will worsen these disparities.[17]

For Thirlwall, the outcome appears quite clear. Monetary union in Europe will cause economic divergence amongst the regions and this in turn could well threaten to undermine the whole single currency programme.[18]

The reasoning behind this pessimistic view is that the regions making up the twelve Member State Eurozone do not in fact constitute an OCA. As Magnifico pointed out some time ago, in a highly prescient but curiously neglected discussion of the regional dimensions of EMU, optimum currency area theory raises a number of key issues for regional development.[19] The basic problem is that the more the regions making up a common currency area differ in competitiveness, productivity, prosperity, economic structure, and trade specialization, the more they will differ in their responses to economic shocks arising from shifts in demand, technology, competition, central monetary policy, and so on: regional shocks will be asymmetric or idiosyncratic. Since, by definition, the regions of a currency union are unable to counter shocks by resorting to devaluation or interest rate

---

[17] AP Thirlwall, 'European unity could flounder on regional neglect' 31 January 2000, Guardian 23.

[18] AP Thirlwall, *The Euro and Regional Divergence in Europe* (2000).

[19] G Magnifico, *European Monetary Unification* (1973).

changes, they must rely on other forms of adjustment if differential regional shocks are not to widen or exacerbate regional economic disparities.

Thus, with a single fixed exchange rate across a currency area, a high degree of factor mobility (both between sectors within regions, and between regions) is necessary if spatially asymmetric demand, technology and monetary shocks are not to result in major regional imbalances in economic growth and development. Where factor mobility between the regions, say North and South, of a monetary union is low, and other mechanisms of inter-regional stabilization—such as a high degree of wage flexibility—are absent or weak, a relative shift of demand from the products of the North to those of the South will cause unemployment in the North and inflation in the South. Unemployment in the North could be prevented by expanding the money supply or reducing interest rates, but this likely to generate inflation in the fully employed South. Conversely, attempts to control inflation in the South would be at the cost of more unemployment in the North. If geographical mobility of labour and capital is low, or uneven, across regions, then inter-regional equilibration will not occur. Put simply, the more that regions differ in 'unemployment proneness' and 'propensity to inflation', and the lower is the inter-regional mobility of labour and capital, the less they constitute an OCA, and arguably should not join a single currency and common exchange rate.

Regional cohesion, then, can be argued to be of paramount significance for the success of the Eurozone. The greater the degree of regional economic balance, the easier it will be to manage the Eurozone interest rate and exchange rate without generating unwanted regionally disparate impacts on jobs and inflation; and by the same token the less will be the pressure for unwanted monetary policy changes arising from region-specific unemployment or inflation problems. Thirlwall's complaint, however, is precisely that there is in fact too much regional imbalance across the Eurozone for it to function optimally as a common currency area. As Magnifico argued, a possible implication for the EU is that the regions that best meet the conditions of an OCA may well not form a contiguous geographical entity that is congruent with the territorial boundaries of the constituent Member States. Rather, Magnifico postulated, one might imagine an arrangement in which only the core regions of Member States (with similar high levels of growth, prosperity and incomes) meet the conditions required by an OCA, leaving the remaining (less prosperous and peripheral) regions linked to, but outside, the common currency area. Politically, of course, such a configuration would hardly be feasible.

In any case, even within individual nation states—national single currency spaces—regions differ in economic structure, trade specialization, and so on. In this sense, an individual nation state might not constitute an OCA. The counter argument is that inter-regional factor mobility will be greater within a nation state than between nation states. In the EU, for example, linguistic and cultural barriers are likely to continue to limit the geographical movement of labour between member countries. In addition, individual nation states also have their own unified fiscal systems, so that differential regional shocks will set off compensating automatic inter-regional fiscal flows (via the national tax-benefit system) that help prevent the widening of regional economic disparities and thus serve to maintain regional socio-economic cohesion. Indeed, a common fiscal system can be argued to be the logical counterpart to a single currency, and an integral component of an OCA. Such a centralized fiscal system seems a long way off indeed in the Eurozone, not least because it would entail a massive transfer of sovereignty and autonomy from the Member States to central EU authorities. This means that the main brunt of fiscal transfers to Eurozone regions adversely hit by demand, supply or technology shocks will be borne by the internal tax-benefit flows and regional policy spending within Member States, assisted by allocations from the EU Structural Funds.

According to Thirlwall, however, the problem is not just that the existing scale of regional imbalance across the EU makes the creation of the Eurozone questionable, it is also that progressive EMU and the single currency will in turn exacerbate regional disparities. The European Commission appears to take a somewhat different view. The premise underlying the Commission's discussions of regional cohesion seems to be that formation of the Eurozone should stimulate regional convergence since a single currency improves the movement of capital, labour and knowledge between regions, opens up new market opportunities, facilitates trade, and thereby promotes economic growth and job creation in all areas of the Eurozone. It is recognized that convergence will not occur overnight, so that lagging and economically depressed regions need some assistance in adjusting to the economic changes and opportunities generated by the process of EMU. But the European Commision's view does seem to be strongly influenced by what conventional neoclassical growth theory would predict (see Table 20.1 below).

Other theoretical perspectives lead to different predictions. For example, as Paul Krugman and others have argued, factor mobility may in

Table 20.1. Competing theoretical perspectives on the impact of EMU on regional cohesion

Theory	Main Mechanisms	Predicted Regional Outcomes
Neoclassical Growth Theory	EMU facilitates greater competition, trade, and greater mobility of capital, labour and technology, thereby promoting diminishing returns to factors of production and equalization of factor returns across regions	Convergent regional growth paths to common equilibrium per capita income
Increasing Returns Theory	EMU facilitates greater competition, trade, and factor flows, which permit increasing returns to scale and specialization	Increasing regional specialization and hence region-specific shocks, which in the presence of factor mobility lead to regional agglomeration and divergent growth paths
Endogenous Growth Theory	Accumulation of skills, knowledge and technology assumed localized, with both tending to concentrate in areas with pre-existing advantages.	Limited regional convergence (to different long run equilibrium levels of per capita income), or even divergence

fact intensify rather than reduce regional disparities in economic growth.[20] Using new ideas from the economics of increasing returns, this alternative perspective holds that factor mobility can lead to cumulative growth advan-

[20] P Krugman, 'The lessons of Massachussetts for EMU' in F Torres and F Giavazzi (eds), *Adjustment and Growth in the European Monetary Union* (1993) 241.

tages in the more prosperous regions—attracted by the economies of agglomeration in such areas—rather than to a reduction in unemployment and a revival of growth in depressed regions. This process could be compounded in the case of the EU, these authors go on to suggest, because increasing EMU could intensify regional economic specialization—through market size, comparative advantage and trade effects—thereby increasing the likelihood of asymmetric and idiosyncratic regional shocks. If these set off large inter-regional factor flows, the result could be regional divergence rather than regional convergence, as growth concentrates in the prosperous regions; at the very least, the prospects for regional convergence are likely to be much reduced.

A not- dissimilar outcome is predicted by some versions of so-called new endogenous growth theory. In this instance, labour flows out of economically depressed regions are argued to be selective, biased towards the more skilled and enterprising workers. This implies a progressive build up of skilled human capital in the more prosperous regions. At the same time, endogenous growth theory stresses the relative immobility—the slow or limited spillover—of technological innovation between regions. If technological innovation emanates primarily from the more prosperous regions (because of the presence there of highly skilled and better educated labour, and more enterprising human capital formation), it may reinforce the growth dynamic there, attracting yet further inflows of labour and capital, thereby generating regional economic divergence. Thus, in contrast to the standard neoclassical assumption that factor flows reduce regional economic disparities and restore regional equilibrium, in the agglomeration models based on increasing returns theory and the new economics of endogenous growth, regional disparities need not narrow and could well widen.

As mentioned earlier, it will obviously be some time before sufficient empirical evidence is available to test these competing scenarios in the EU case. For this reason, some observers have suggested using the regional development experience of an existing, comparably-sized continental economic and monetary union as a guide to what to expect in the EU. The United States, a long-time monetary union, is usually taken as the exemplar. Thus a number of American scholars have argued that the US shows how a continent-sized single market and currency union works in practice, and that as Europe moves progressively towards the sort of integrated economic and financial space which has long been in existence in the US, the processes and paths of regional development in the EU are likely to become increasingly similar to those in the US.[21] Indeed, the European Commission itself regularly uses the US as a yardstick in its discussions of regional economic development and disparities in the EU.[22]

But to use the economic geography of the US as a predictor of the regional impact of integration and enlargement in the EU is highly problematic. European capitalism remains distinctly different from the US in terms of political, institutional and cultural embeddedness;[23] labour mobility, which plays a key role as a regional adjustment mechanism in the US, is never likely to be as high in the EU; as argued above, there seems little prospect, even over the medium term, that the EU will establish a centralized, Union-wide system of inter-regional automatic fiscal stabilizers of the sort found in the US;[24] and the considerable differences in the nature, size and operation of regional economies between the US and EU make direct comparison difficult and potentially misleading.[25]

The challenge of enlargement for regional cohesion

The planned eastwards enlargement of the EU will represent no less a shock to the regional system of the Union than the formation of the Eurozone. At a stroke, enlargement to include all 12 current applicant entrants will double the per capita income gaps between countries and regions. The average GDP per head of the new applicant states is less than 50 per cent of that in the existing EU-15 (see Figure 20.2). Thus enlargement will lower the average per capita income across the EU considerably. On current data,

[21] eg, O Blanchard and L Katz, 'Regional evolutions' (1992) 1 Brookings Papers in Economic Activity 159; T Bayoumi and B Eichengreen, 'Shocking aspects of European monetary integration' in F Torres and F Giavazzi (eds) *Adjustment and Growth in the European Monetary Union* (1993) 193.

[22] Commission of the European Communities, *Unity, Solidarity, Diversity for Europe, its People and its Territory: Second Report on Economic and Social Cohesion*, Vol 1 (2001).

[23] For discussions of this issue, see, eg, S Berger and R Dore, *National Diversity and Global Capitalism* (1996); J R Hollingsworth and R Boyer, *Contemporary Capitalism: The Embeddedness of Institutions* (1997); P Hall and D Soskice, *Varieties of Capitalism: Institutional Foundations of Comparative Advantage* (2001).

[24] It has been estimated, eg, that in the US as much as one third of a negative demand shock in a state is cushioned by automatic inter-state transfers operating though the Federal tax and fiscal system: see X Sala-i-Martin and J Sachs, 'Fiscal federalism and optimum currency areas: evidence for Europe from the United States' (Working Paper 3855, National Bureau of Economic Research, Cambridge MA 1991).

[25] See R Martin, 'EMU versus the regions? Convergence and divergence in Euroland' (2001) 1 Journal of Economic Geography 51.

Figure 20.2. GDP per Head (PPS) Across EU Member and Applicant States, 1999
EU-26 = 100 (Excludes Malta)

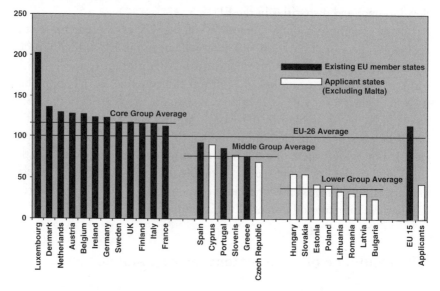

none of the new Member States will have average per capita incomes that
exceed the new (lower) EU-27 mean. In fact, at this national level, enlargement will produce a three-tiered EU. The most prosperous group of
Member States will consist of a 'core' of 12 leading countries (the existing
EU-15 minus Spain, Portugal and Greece), all with average per capita
incomes around 20 per cent above the new EU-27 average. This is followed
by a middle group of seven states (Spain, Portugal, Greece, together with
Cyprus, Malta, Slovenia and the Czech Republic), with average per capita
incomes around 80 per cent (actually between 68 per cent and 95 per cent)
of the EU-27 figure. The real change compared to the Union of today,
however, would be the existence of a third group of Member States, comprising the eight remaining candidate countries, where average income per
head is only around 40 per cent of the EU-27 mean.

At the regional scale, enlargement does not increase the overall degree of
disparity (between regional extremes) that significantly (see Figure 20.3), but
it does increase the number of regions with low per capita incomes dramatically.[26] This will threaten regional cohesion in three ways. First, the

---

[26] M Dunford and A Smith, 'Catching up or falling behind? Economic performance and
the trajectories of economic development in an enlarged Europe' (2001) Economic Geography (forthcoming).

Figure 20.3. Regional Extremes in GDP per Head (PPS) 1998 (Excludes Malta)

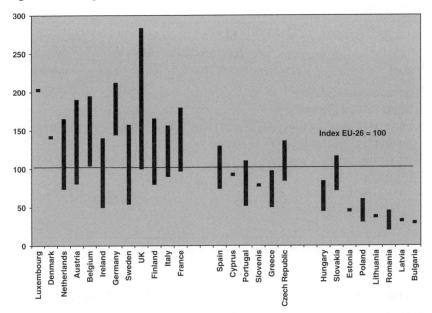

number of regions with average incomes below 75 per cent of the EU average—the threshold at which regions become eligible for Objective 1 Structural Fund assistance—will rise. If the present EU-15 average per capita GDP is used as the base, the number of such regions would jump from 46 to 97. Even if the new lower EU-27 average per capita GDP figure is used, the number still rises markedly from 46 to 70. Put another way, with enlargement, the population living in low income regions will grow from 71 million to 174 million. This would represent an increase from 19 per cent of the population in the present EU-15 to 36 per cent of that in the EU-27 if the EU-15 average GDP per capita index is used as the base, or to 26 per cent if the new, lower EU-27 average income is used. Thus, either way, the *extent* of regional inequality in the EU will increase substantially.

Second, in addition, enlargement will also increase the *intensity* of regional disparity. Per capita GDP in the lagging regions of the EU-15 averages 68 per cent of the EU-15 mean. In the lagging regions in the applicant states, it averages around 37 per cent of the EU-15 mean. Thus the two groups of regions together would have a GDP per head of less than half of the present EU-15 average.[27] But because the statistical effect of

---

[27] These calculations are those made by the European Commission.

Table 20.2. The Implications of Enlargement for Low Income Regions in the EU

Index Used	EU-15 EU-15 as index base	EU-26 EU-15 as index base	EU-26 EU-26 as index base
Number of regions falling below 75% of average	46	97	70
Population in those regions (millions)	71	174	125
Population as proportion of EU total	19%	36%	26%
Average GDP per head (PPS) of regions falling below 75%	66	48	46

Source: Eurostat (Regional Policy Directorate-General). EU-26 is used instead of EU-27 because of lack of data on Malta.

enlargement will be to reduce the EU average GDP per head by an estimated 18–20 per cent, on current values some 27 or so regions in the EU-15, containing around 50 million inhabitants, will be raised above 75 per cent of the EU-27 average income. Obviously, in an absolute sense, nothing will have changed to the incomes and levels of socio-economic welfare in these regions. Their sudden relative improvement will simply be a statistical product of the addition to the Union of several regions with even lower per capita incomes: poor regions are not suddenly made rich by adding yet poorer regions.

The European Commission itself acknowledges that if enlargement goes ahead as planned, the challenge to regional cohesion in the EU-27 could be said to be 'twice as widespread and twice as large as at present'.[28] It is, furthermore, a challenge that is likely to persist for some considerable time. If the rate of regional convergence in the applicant countries were to be similar to that estimated across the EU-15 over the past decade or so (see above), it would take at least two generations for the increased regional income gap created by enlargement to be halved. Some—inclining to the predictions of neoclassical growth theory—have argued that the applicant countries have considerable growth potential precisely because their low cost and unproductive industries offer considerable opportunities for new

[28] Commission of the European Communities, *Unity, Solidarity, Diversity for Europe, its People and its Territory: Second Report on Economic and Social Cohesion*, Vol 1 (2001) 9.

investment, and incomes could grow much faster than has been typical across the EU-15 in recent years. Against this view, however, one can point to the run-down industries, poor infrastructures, backward agriculture, lack of skilled labour and outmoded institutions in the CEECs as major obstacles to their rapid development. It seems likely that, because of their pre-existing endogenous advantages, economic activity and wealth creation will continue to agglomerate in the 'core' regions of the EU-15, and that economic catch–up in the poor regions throughout most of the enlargement countries will be slow and limited. Convergence towards the EU level of GDP in these regions will require nothing short of a dramatic change in their underlying structural conditions (in terms of capital of all kinds and different labour force skills). The inevitable industrial rationalization and restructuring that will take place is bound to have highly disruptive effects on the labour markets in many of the regions of the enlargement states, and is likely to put severe upward pressure on regional unemployment and poverty.

Herein lies the third threat to regional cohesion. Enlargement will pose a major challenge to the structural and regional policies of the EU. Since their creation, the Structural Funds and the Cohesion Funds have represented the main instruments of social, economic and regional cohesion policy. They are aimed at strengthening the structural factors which determine the competitiveness, and thereby the growth potential, of the less advantaged regions. Structural support for Objective 1 regions lies at the heart of this programme. According to the European Commission, the impact of the Structural Funds on the Objective 1 regions has been positive, contributing to an improvement in the relative per capita incomes of these areas. However, they seem to have had little or no impact on improving the labour productivity and unemployment performance of the Objective 1 regions, and some authors have argued that they may not be adequate to prevent geographical polarization of growth and prosperity within the new Eurozone.[29]

With enlargement, intense strains will be put on the Structural and other regional funds and their allocation: how will the Structural Funds accommodate enlargement? Whereas Structural Fund expenditures increased over the two programming periods, 1988–1993 and 1994–1999, they are due to decline in the period 2000–2006 from just over €350 billion to just over €300 billion, or from 0.45 per cent of EU GDP to 0.30 per cent. There is

[29] P Braunerhjelm, R Faini, V Norman, F Rauner and P Seabright, 'Integration and the regions of Europe: how the right policies can prevent polarisation' *Monitoring European Integration*, (2000) 10 Centre for Economic Performance, M Boldrin and F Canova, 'Inequality and convergence: considering European regional policies', ibid.

to be continued support for the EU-15, but at the same time funds are being ring-fenced for the CEEC accession states. The implication is that there will have to be a re-allocation away from many presently assisted areas in the EU-15 to the poor regions in the enlargement states. As was noted above, perhaps as many as 50 poorer regions in the EU-15 will rise above the 75 per cent income threshold, and many such areas could cease to be eligible for EU support. In other words, there will be fewer 'old' EU regions supported, even though they will remain economically depressed.

The crucial issue here, therefore, is how best to withdraw support from these current Objective 1 regions. An abrupt end would have a highly detrimental impact on clients and projects in progress. An extended tapering of support over some reasonable time horizon would obviously be preferable, but even this could have wider negative effects on the invest-ment and development climate within such regions. Given that the re-sources dedicated to the Structural Funds are likely to remain pegged or even reduced beyond 2006, there will almost certainly be several unhappy regions within the old EU-15. The need for development support in these regions will not suddenly have disappeared, but they will cease to figure within the regional cohesion policies of the EU.

What is clear is that a major rethink of structural policy will be called for beyond 2006, not just to accommodate enlargement itself but also to respond to the new types of cohesion problems presented in the CEECs, and the impact of withdrawal of aid from many existing cohesion regions. The European Commission itself has posed ten key questions for public debate on the future of cohesion policy.[30] The fundamental question is what the role of cohesion policy should be in an enlarged Union of nearly 30 Member States, containing within itself an 'inner' monetary union, in a context of

---

[30] See Commission of the European Communities, *Unity, Solidarity, Diversity for Europe, its People and its Territory: Second Report on Economic and Social Cohesion*, Vol 1 (2001) xxxix. The questions are as follows:

  (i) What will be the role of cohesion policy in an enlarged Union of nearly 30 Member States in a context of rapid economic and social change? How is it possible to further economic convergence and preserve the European model of society?

 (ii) How should Community policies be made more coherent? How should the contribu-tion of other Community policies to the pursuit of cohesion be improved?

(iii) How should cohesion policy be modified in preparation for an unprecedented expan-sion of the Union? Should cohesion policy also address territorial cohesion in order to take better account of the major spatial imbalances in the Union?

(iv) How can cohesion policy be focused on measures which have a high Community value added?

rapid economic, technological and social change. How will it be possible to further regional convergence under these conditions?

Conclusion

At issue, essentially, are two basic questions. Is the EU an optimum currency area? And is there an optimum size of the EU? While some discussion and debate has surrounded the former, the latter has attracted much less attention, and indeed seems not to have figured in the official discussions about enlargement. With both, the issue of regional cohesion assumes key importance. Monetary union prevents resort to national monetary policies and therefore increases the exposure of regions—and especially the less prosperous regions—of the Eurozone to economic shocks. Simultaneously, the stability clauses associated with the creation of the single currency drastically reduce the autonomy of member countries in the field of fiscal policy. The implication is that the pursuit of regional cohesion will put additional strains on the Structural Funds.

At the same time, enlargement will expand the scale of regional disparities in the EU. Not only will the entry of the central and eastern European countries widen considerably the nature of regional problems within the EU, enlargement will raise a corresponding challenge for the policy process itself. The sheer diversity of economic, social and institutional conditions across the enlarged Union will necessitate a rethink of the Structural Funds and their operation. In the context of a likely limit to additional Structural Fund spending, of changes in the EU voting balance consequential on enlarged membership, and of the tensions arising from the loss of Structural Fund assistance by many current Objective 1 regions, the redesign of the Funds could be a contentious process. Regional cohesion is crucially important for the success and legitimacy of EMU and enlargement, but is itself threatened by each.

(v) What should be the priorities to bring about balanced and sustainable territorial development in the Union?

(vi) How should the economic convergence of lagging regions of the Union be encouraged?

(vii) What kind of Community intervention is required for other regions?

(viii) What methods should be used to determine the division of funds between Member States and between regions?

(ix) What principles should govern the implementation of Community intervention?

(x) What should be the response to increased needs with regard to the economic, social and territorial dimensions of cohesion?

21

EMU and the Lisbon Goals in an Enlarged European Union

Andy W Mullineux and Cillian Ryan

Introduction

One of the challenges facing the EU is the rate at which it can undertake new initiatives while ensuring that previous experiments have been successfully completed. Thus, the Union is still in the process of ensuring compliance with the principles of the single market, while undertaking one of the greatest currency experiments in modern history, and simultaneously looking to the East and planning for its future expansion. Thus the expansion agreed at Nice is taking place within the context of a developing internal European economy with a new currency seeking legitimacy and strength. Externally the Union is facing an increasingly globalized world economy where the main world currencies are jockeying for position in a renewed debate over rate fixing, currency boards and adoption of common currencies. Indeed Robert Mundell, a Nobel Prize-winning economist and strong supporter of EMU, has recently advocated the adoption of a new world currency at a variety of forums.[1]

The problems associated with currency values, or more importantly the misalignment of a currency's value, are amply demonstrated by the consequences for the UK manufacturing sector of sterling's excessive strength in the early 1980s. It is also arguable that the depth of the current US recession may be in part a result of overvaluation of the dollar compared with both the yen and the euro. Thus cross rates between the euro, the US dollar and the

---

[1] See for example the Nobel debate between Milton Friedman and Robert Mundell http://www.nationalpost.com/features/duel/index.html/(2001), or 'Nobel Prize Winner Proposes New Currency–"intor"':http://english.peopledaily.com.cn/200110/20/eng20011020_82798.html/(2001) or report on http://www.ceps.be/Events/111401.htm/.

yen may need to be managed more effectively in future since, self evidently, all three currencies cannot be strong at the same time.

This chapter is concerned with the EU's 'output legitimacy'. Clearly the economic performance of the Union is central to this aspect of legitimacy. The creation of the euro raises the stakes here, as any failure of the new currency would seriously dent the legitimacy of the Union, while its success is partly contingent on Europe's economic performance. Thus the importance of the Union's strategy for enhancing Europe's economy, as set out at the Lisbon Summit in 2000, grows. While a broadly plausible model was set out at Lisbon, its implementation is by no means guaranteed. Equally the general economic performance of the Union and the vitality of the euro will depend on good management of enlargement, so that its economic opportunities can be exploited, while pitfalls are avoided. But the euro cannot be judged only on the European stage. Its international or global impact and performance may be more important. Whether prompted by general economic pressures or a process of competition between currencies partly triggered by the euro itself (and particularly reactions to the euro by those managing the dollar) a single global currency may be in the making. If this is the case, then the real test for the euro may be whether it can position itself to become the (main) global currency. For this to occur, Europe's economy must become the most vital in the world. If it can be achieved new economic opportunities that should enhance the Union's 'output legitimacy' would be created.

To address these issues this chapter is organized as follows. The first section considers the relationship between the strength of an economy and the strength of its currency, concentrating on the dollar and the euro. In the second section, the benefits of having fewer currencies are explored. In the third section, the Lisbon goals are enumerated and the prospects for their achievement are briefly explored. The fourth section then considers the likely impact on the strength of the euro of the proposed post-Nice enlargement (and participation in the Eurozone by the UK, Sweden and Denmark). Deliberations about the likely outcome of the currency competition are presented in the concluding section.

Economic strength and the euro

The background to the post-Nice European economy is a commitment undertaken at the Lisbon Summit in March 2000 to make the EU 'the most competitive and dynamic knowledge based economy in the world, capable of sustainable economic growth with more and better jobs and greater social cohesion, by 2010'. By focusing on this ambitious goal, the Lisbon summit implicitly recognized the vital linkage between currency strength and economic strength. In a world where we continue to have multiple currencies, the success or otherwise of a currency will depend not just on its acceptability within its geographic boundaries, but also on its perceived worth, outside those boundaries, both as a means of payment and a store of value. Indeed, we have many examples, even among candidate EU entrants, where past poor economic performance has resulted in a lack of acceptability of their currency outside their borders, leading to the parallel circulation within the country of an international currency (usually US dollars or Deutschmarks). While we would never envision that the euro will hit such an extreme, any currency uncertainty imposes additional costs on trades internationally and reduces the incentive both for domestic and inward investment.

Thus, the stronger the Euroland or Eurozone economy, the better is its record of dynamic growth; and the brighter its prospects, the stronger will be its currency internationally. Conversely, the stronger the perception of its currency internationally, the greater the confidence there will be in the success of the Euroland economy and the brighter will be its prospects of dynamic growth. In that sense, the future of the euro experiment is intrinsically bound up with the achievement of the Lisbon goals. Only by ensuring that Euroland succeeds economically can we hope to ensure that the euro enjoys widespread acceptability as a world currency for trade and investment purposes. There are, of course, costs associated with the overvaluation of a currency.

But given the size of Euroland, why should we be concerned particularly about the role of the euro outside the Euroland? The growing trend towards the globalization of the world economy as a result of the past GATT initiatives and the more recent and continuing WTO rounds—in particular, GATS and capital market liberalization, trade related aspects of intellectual property rights (TRIPS), and trade related investment measures (TRIMS)—mean the Union is likely to face a greater degree of competition in the international marketplace. While EMU seems set to generate further internal trade, globalization is likely to mean that external trade will continue to grow in importance. This matters for the euro, because besides competitiveness, the currency of trade itself may be important with regard to the sourcing and volume of trade, and as we discuss below, economic prosperity. Furthermore, as globalization progresses, smaller countries are beginning to reappraise the value of their own currency and trading dependence and to look to the anchor currencies (or some basket of them) as an alternative.

Costs and benefits of fewer currencies: the economic case

What is the optimum number of currencies in the world? Robert Mundell, the Nobel Laureate, is reported to have said that the optimum number of currencies is like the optimum number of gods—an odd number less than three. Mundell's economic analysis was based on the notion of an optimum currency area. This is a region, country or group of countries which is subject to relatively similar external economic shocks and where capital and, perhaps more importantly, labour is able to flow relatively freely within the relevant area in response to internal sectoral shocks. The idea is that the area is able to handle internal economic disequilibria through internal markets and perhaps (regional) fiscal policy, without recourse to monetary policy, which can then be reserved to respond in a coordinated way to common external shocks, for example a sharp change in oil prices. The benefits which flow from the common-currency area is the reduction in transactions costs and risk associated with trading in different currencies throughout the area. The resultant growth in trade denominated in the common currency not only raises economic welfare in itself, but it may also allow certain industries, restricted by the size of their home market, to grow to an optimum size, thereby achieving better scale efficiency. Hence costs of production will be lowered and productivity increased with the result that companies enjoy cheaper goods and producers become more competitive in the global market.

Obviously, the constituents of the area will not all be identical, and it is unlikely that the area's ability to respond to internal shocks will be perfect, so prospective member governments must conduct a cost-benefit analysis on the gains from increased area trade and scale efficiency versus the loss of monetary independence and thus the ability to adopt customized responses to external stocks. It should be noted, however, that true independence in interest rate setting depends on a willingness to let the country's key exchange rates (ie against the US dollar, and the euro and the yen) float freely. As noted earlier, this can have adverse consequences if long periods of overvaluation have to be tolerated, as in the UK in the 1980s.

So what are the appropriate optimal currency areas in the world today? The instinctive response to this question is perhaps the set of existing currency areas. After all, if we observe that most currency areas are synonymous with the nation state then they must have emerged from some optimization process. However, recently Alesina and Barro have challenged the notion that this 'optimum currency' area is typically the nation state and suggest instead that monetary policy is a public good best provided at supranational level.[2] What is required is an appropriate analysis of the benefits associated with reduced transactions costs, increased trade and specialization, compared with the cost of foregone monetary independence. In particular they suggest that most of the smaller nations could benefit by allying themselves with one or other of the anchor currencies. At the extreme end of the spectrum there are those who argue that monetary policy is so ineffective anyway at smoothing output fluctuations that its loss is negligible and, logically, we ought to move to Mundell's optimum number of currencies, that odd number less than three. It is worth noting that neither the UK nor Italy, with their 'North-South divides', nor Germany, especially post-unification, appears to be any more of an optimum currency area, in which a 'one size' interest rate policy fits all, than the EU at large! Further while the recent travails in Argentina might caution against the immutable fixing of exchange rates (against the dollar in this case), arguably the source of Argentina's current problems has probably more to do with their poor fiscal discipline than any fundamental monetary problems. If, however, the logical consequence of this evolving discussion is a move towards a small number of currencies or perhaps even a single world currency, what currencies will be in pole position in a decade (or several decades) to assume this mantle, and does it matter?

So what evidence do we have on costs and benefits? Research into the value of fixed-rate regimes (such as the old ERM) has tended to yield ambiguous results and at best it suggests only small output and welfare gains. The argument seems to be that the uncertainty associated with the stability of fixed-rate regimes does not lead to a significant reduction in risk premia and interest-rate spreads, and hence the opportunity to respond to real economic shocks offered by a flexible regime is more valuable.[3] Recent research by Rose, however, suggests that the gains from implementing a

---

[2] A Alesina and RJ Barro, 'Currency unions' (2002) Quarterly Journal of Economics (forthcoming).

[3] V Arora and O Jeanne, 'Integration and the exchange rate regime: some lessons from Canada' (IMF Policy Discussion paper 01/1).

single currency (as opposed to a fixed currency regime) are significantly larger than previously believed, and ought to facilitate greater and stronger economic growth.[4] He estimates that the volume of trade, as a consequence of a single currency is likely to grow 25 times more than that due to a fixed-currency mechanism alone. In other words the real economic gains accrue from a common currency rather than a fixed-rate regime. Again Argentina, with its 'hard fix' to the US dollar using a currency board would appear to bear this out. Rose's estimates were that trade would grow by a factor of two to three, an extremely large number compared with standard predictions of trade growth due to traditional trade-liberalization agreements such as the previous GATT rounds.

But why are these gains likely to be so high? Traditionally, economists (including Mundell) have argued that optimum currency areas ought to involve similar economies with similar cyclical fluctuations and at a similar stage of development. This was to allow the monetary authority to react to an external shock in a way that suited all members equally. If countries are at dissimilar points in the cycle, then a counter-argument is that international trade is in itself a cycle-smoothing mechanism. It allows domestic surplus production to be sold overseas during times of depressed consumer demand or production booms and greater imports at times of depressed domestic production or during consumer or investment booms. According to this argument, expansionist monetary policy during a domestic recession for example, will result in a depreciation of the currency, and perhaps provide a short-run palliative. However, such discretionary intervention ultimately results in a greater overall level of exchange rate uncertainty, thus reducing the underlying volume of the very trade and foreign investment required to yield smoother output cycles. Hence what Rose appears to be identifying is a significant rise in welfare-enhancing, internal trade growth as a result of the adoption of a common currency.

The recognition of this possibility has led to some discussion about 'dollar-ization' in both Canada and Mexico. It lay behind the initial adoption of the dollar currency board in Argentina and the decision of a variety of smaller Asian and African states to tie their currencies either to the dollar or to the currency of a former colonial master (in most cases now the euro). The interest in the use of domestic or anchor currencies by states is likely to increase as globalization itself progresses and formal and informal currency

---

[4] A Rose, 'One money, one market: estimating the effect of common currency on trade' (2000) 30 Economic Policy: A European Policy Forum 7.

unions or areas may emerge. The euro has already been adopted by numerous countries outside the official Eurozone, including countries formerly pegged to the Deutschmark (eg Estonia) or using the African French Franc.

So, on the basis of current evidence, which currency or currencies are likely to emerge as the leading contenders to be the key currencies for trade and investment (and indeed government and central bank reserves)? Clearly, a strong currency of a large trading country is more likely to encourage invoicing in that currency and hence will tend to promote trade sourced in that currency. This will give it an edge as an anchor for a currency area. Hence globalization inherently involves currency competition and, in particular, competition between the US dollar and the euro, and to a lesser extent the yen.

In their paper, Alesina and Barro suggested that currently Central American countries and Mexico should tie to the dollar, but that South American countries, due to their higher volume of trade with Europe, ought to consider a dollar/euro basket. Whether Argentina opts to do this or to revert to a dollar standard following its current fiscally inspired depreciation crisis remains to be seen, though there is no doubt that its real appreciation relative to Brazil was also a contributory factor. Alesina and Barro also suggest that many African and Eastern European countries are candidates for the euro, but that the yen, with the possible exception of Indonesia, does not currently look like a good prospect for an anchor currency. However, the immediate possibility of this sort of currency initiative does not look promising, especially in the light of Argentina's recent abandonment of its dollar currency board, and significant movement on this front is likely to lie well into the future.

It should be noted that the issuer of a currency used widely for commerce and as a reserve currency outside the issuing area gains considerable 'seigniorage'. The gain to EU coffers from the fact the European Central Bank prints money at only a nominal cost and this money is ultimately used by EU citizens to buy real goods from abroad provides an example. The gain is equal to the portion of this money that foreigners hold or otherwise use without using it to buy EU goods. This represents 'seigniorage' or an economic gain to the EU akin to that enjoyed by a forger of domestic currency. Thus, whichever currency emerges as the dominant currency of trade is set to enjoy considerable economic benefits. Obviously if we were ultimately to move to a single world currency one obstacle to be overcome would be an agreement on the distribution of the 'seigniorage' accrued from the issuance of this world currency by the world central bank. Just as the EU preferred to invent the euro and establish the European Central Bank, rather than adopt the Deutschmark and the Bundesbank, so 'the world' is likely to prefer to establish a new currency and central bank, rather than see the US dollar/Federal Reserve or the euro/ECB take on the role. Similarly, just as the EU wanted to share the 'seigniorage' benefits amongst its members, rather than see it accrue to Germany via the Bundesbank, so 'the world' would perhaps like to see the 'seigniorage' used, by the World Bank for example, to fund anti-poverty and development programmes. The big difference is that the EU is a democratic entity whilst 'the world' may have no choice but to accept the '*Legomoney*', if you will excuse the pun, of the US dollar or the euro as the currency of world trade.

Given the significant gains to the EU economy of being the principal anchor currency, we need to consider what the likely state of the competing currencies will be in a decade or so. In particular, what is the likelihood that the Lisbon goals are obtainable (given the policies adopted) and what is likely to be the effect of the post-Nice expansion of the EU on the strength of the euro; and how are these two sets of policies likely to affect the prospects of the euro as a serious rival to the US dollar as the main currency of trade denomination and strategic reserves.

What were the Lisbon targets and how is Euroland doing?

The EU is a much more mixed economy in terms of state intervention and involvement in production than the US. Acknowledging this fact, the Lisbon European Council agreed a set of targets on policy actions by the Commission, Member States and the European Parliament. It hoped these targets would facilitate its goal of making the EU 'the most competitive and dynamic knowledge based economy in the world by 2010'. They amount to a set of 'Third-Way' policies to foster economic growth and include, *inter alia*:

- government promotion of e-commerce;
- mapping of R&D Centres of Excellence;
- the establishment of an Innovation Scorecard to promote best practice;
- liberalization of telecoms, utilities, particularly in the energy sector, and transport;
- business start-up league tables (with an emphasis on highlighting good practice in reducing costs and facilitating ease of establishment);
- a European charter for small manufacturing enterprises; and

- an employment action plan, including the setting of educational and human capital goals, and modernizing social protection.

Associated with each of these broad areas was a list of specific objectives for year one. In its 2001 Review of the Internal Market Strategy the Commission acknowledged that even in the first flurry of enthusiasm associated with the project, only 8 of the 12 priority actions were completed and only 20 (56 per cent) of the 36 wider target actions.[5] In addition to this lack-lustre performance, the economic environment facing the EU has worsened considerably compared with the state of the international economy at the time of the Lisbon summit. With oil prices reaching a peak in the autumn of 2000, the collapse of the information and communication technology (ICT) sector, a fall in world economic growth to 2 per cent and an even more dramatic decline in world trade growth from 11 per cent to 1 per cent in 2001, EU growth has fallen from 3.85 per cent in 2000 to 1.7 per cent in 2001. The period has also seen a halt to the secular decline in unemployment since the mid-1990s and unemployment is expected to start rising again in 2002. All this was before the events of 11 September 2001, when some indicators had been suggesting that the recession in the US might be bottoming out, and the US is not now expected to emerge from recession until later in 2002.

Another goal of Lisbon, EMU and the 'single financial market' is the establishment of efficient EU capital markets, an area in which most EU countries, other than the UK, has lagged behind the US. Despite poor levels of banking competition (and indeed service) in some regions, there is a belief that US industry and commerce enjoys a competitive edge as a result of the efficiency of its capital markets, the most advanced in the world, because these markets give it access to cheaper and more appropriate financing. Could Europe have spawned and fostered the rapid growth of Intel and Microsoft?

The introduction of the euro on 1 January 1999 kick-started the development of the euro denominated 'junk (below 'investment grade') bond' market. The initial rapid growth has been inhibited, however, by the subsequent global economic slowdown. There has also been significant consolidation of stock and futures and options exchanges, but yet more consolidation appears to be needed. As the 2001 Ecofin-commissioned Lamfalussy Report on the regulation of EU securities markets makes

---

[5] Commission of the European Communities, Working Together to Maintain Momentum: 2001 Review of the Internal Market Strategy (COM (2001) 198 final).

clear, flexibility is needed to remove regulatory impediments to the more rapid development of EU capital markets. The Committee's proposals[6] involve establishing a quasi-independent body with the power to make rapid decisions. The European Parliament is concerned about the implied lack of control that it will have over the body. Naturally, given the pre-eminence of the City as a financial centre, the UK is particularly keen to see progress made in this area.

Achieving the Lisbon goals implicitly entails doing better than the US, ie becoming more competitive than the US by raising productivity levels and cutting costs, rather than relying on the euro's depreciation against the dollar.

Rather than focusing on new measures to achieve the EU goals of being the world leader by 2010, Member States are currently more worried about the short-term economic environment. Furthermore, the need to maintain confidence in the euro has to some extent limited the scope for action on the part of the ECB, who have only cut their interest rates three times during 2001, compared with 11 cuts by US authorities. Nevertheless, there are reasons to believe that this downturn may have served the EU better than the US in the long-run race to be number one in 2010. The US had far greater exposure to the ICT downturn than Europe, its consumers have significantly higher levels of indebtedness, and its current account is in greater deficit. The launch of euro notes and coins on 1 January 2002 is likely to create an energizing focus, as well as providing possibilities for greater internal trading. Together with the internal-market initiative (even if everyone has not wholeheartedly responded as Lisbon directed) these changes provide grounds for optimism that internal-EU growth may allow it to steal a march on the US over the next three years.

Price comparability across the EU should force cost cutting by producers and contain price increases. The surge in US productivity growth that occurred in the second half of the 1990s is very real. Unusually, US productivity has continued to grow significantly, albeit at a slower pace, during the slowdown and the recession that started on 1 March 2001. Following adjustments to official statistics, it is now clear that US product-ivity growth in the late 1990s was overestimated somewhat, but no similar technology-driven surge in productivity has been achieved in the EU, or Japan for that matter. Hence, since the Lisbon Summit, the EU has actually

---

[6] See A Lamfalussy, 'Reflections on the regulation of European securities markets' (SUERF Study No 14, October 2001).

been falling behind the US in the competitiveness stakes and is probably continuing to do so.

In speculating about the future of the EU, and the possible effects of enlargement on its position in the world by 2010, we need to consider likely developments in its key competitor economies, Japan and the US. Japan and the yen are in a very poor state and do not pose an immediate threat. It is hard to see any progress until the seemingly intractable banking-sector bad-debt problem is resolved. Alesina and Barro did not find the yen to be advantageous as an anchor currency except in the case of Indonesia. Thus for our purposes, the primary competition is likely to be from the US.

Indeed, as noted, the main Lisbon target is essentially to catch up with, and overtake, the US in a decade or so. Not only does this require the EU to overhaul the massive productivity lead that the US has built up, but it must do so with higher tax levels. The European model of capitalist democracy derives legitimacy from a welfare system that is more comprehensive and costly than that of the US model. US taxes are generally lower, and have been further reduced by the Bush administration. Further, by opting out of the Kyoto convention, because of the burden it would have placed on US producers, the Bush administration believes it has further increased US competitiveness relative to the participating countries, including Japan and the EU member states. However, Baldwin and Krugman[7] argue that, rather than seeing a race to the bottom in tax competition and government-service provision, industry is more likely to be attracted to the region where workers (and thus consumers) most want to live. Thus, it may well be that Europe's higher investment in health and welfare and environmental protection will pay dividends in terms of long-term economic growth, ie that the European model will prevail. If Baldwin and Krugman are right, then the European Lisbon goals will be achieved; the euro will strengthen against the dollar, and perhaps even replace it as a world currency!

What about the effect of candidate countries on EU and euro strength?

Will EU enlargement weaken or strengthen the euro? Most economic indicators in the enlargement candidate countries suggest that they are

[7] R Baldwin and P Krugman 'Agglomeration, integration and tax harmonization' (CEPR Discussion Papers No 2630, November 2001).

below the EU averages in all the key areas. For example, if we use existing market exchange rates, per capita income ranges from only 50 per cent of the EU average in Slovenia to a mere 7 per cent in Bulgaria.[8] Even allowing for the fact that the official exchange rate is probably undervalued in these candidate countries (due to historical reasons and on-going fragility) alternative estimates of per capita income range from 70 per cent of the EU average in Slovenia to 23 per cent in Bulgaria.[9] Furthermore, the economies of the candidates differ substantially in composition from current members. They are likely to experience higher growth rates in the immediate future, higher inflation (or more correctly, higher prices for local non-trades goods such as land and services) and to be susceptible to different kinds of economic shocks. These shocks will be difficult to accommodate if they were to join the euro in the near term. After all, since the combined GDP of the candidate's only amounts to 6–7 per cent of euro area GDP, their concerns are likely to be dominated by the needs of the current members. However, these 'problems' are likely to persist for some time. Even if accession candidates were to join the euro before the end of the decade it could be argued that the fragile state of their economies and financial systems will weaken the currency, and therefore jeopardize Europe's hope of being the world leader by 2010.

However, currency markets look to the future. Arguably the current apparent weakness of the euro against the dollar (and the UK pound sterling) arises because the currency markets have already accounted for these factors. There may also be some fear that the EU may use inappropriate conversion rates (as the Bundesbank did with the East German mark for political reasons) that have also been factored into the current market perception of the euro. However, these candidates have already experienced strong economic growth in recent years. Their current performance on many Maastricht criteria indicators are superior to those enjoyed by the 'Club Med' group of entrants. This might argue for early admission of the first group of countries to Euroland (with immediate ERM II on accession and full membership by 2005). If this occurs, at appropriate rates, and without major difficulties, then many of the markets' fears about even the

---

[8] Source: European Commission, Directorate-General for Economic and Financial Affairs ('Enlargement Argumentaire', No 5, September 2001).

[9] Using purchasing power parity exchange rates which effectively values currencies by comparing what each will buy in terms of real goods in their own country, rather what their current market value will allow them to buy in the other.

less-prepared countries may be alleviated and we will see a substantial strengthening of the euro.

As the euro is already a major factor in the candidate countries, the discussion above may be somewhat academic. The Deutschmark/euro circulates as a parallel currency and some currencies are tied to the euro by various exchange rate arrangements. Bulgaria and Estonia operate currency boards (fixed peg to the euro/Deutschmark), and Hungary, Cyprus and Malta all target the euro via some (less rigid) exchange rate mechanism. The Czech Republic, Poland, the Slovak Republic, Slovenia and Romania all operate floating bands with inflation targeting (and thus with 50–60 per cent of their trade with the EU they are already shadowing the euro to some extent). Only Lithuania has a fixed peg to the US dollar, although dollars also rival euro/Deutschmarks as parallel currencies in some candidate countries. Hence the euro is already extending its tentacles eastward, and this growth in usage as a trading currency can only strengthen its position with or without ERM membership by the candidate countries.

It should also be remembered that the UK, Sweden and Denmark have yet to join the Eurozone. The UK is a large country and if it continues to perform well, despite consumer debt much closer to US levels than the rest of the EU, then its participation may well counteract or even offset any tendency for Eurozone participation by new EU entrants to weaken the euro. Sweden and Denmark are also relatively strong economies and their entry, possibly jointly with sterling, to Euroland will reinforce any strengthening tendency. If all EU Member States adopt the euro the economic mass of the EU will be much larger then the US.

We have already suggested that size itself may matter. With a bigger area, a bigger population, and hence a bigger total number of both internal and external trades, sheer magnitude may lead to a switch from dollar to euro invoicing and an increased holding by central banks of euro reserves. The US may build on NAFTA by extending at the free trade area southwards and using it as a basis for forming a (perhaps new) dollar union, possibly managed by an American Central Bank in place of the US Federal Reserve. Unless this happens, on balance we tend to argue that the euro will strengthen.

Conclusions

Recent events in Argentina notwithstanding, there are already signs that the dollar area itself may expand. There has been murmuring both within

Mexico and Canada concerning the possibility of 'dollar-izing', and, if anything, the Argentinian crisis may encourage Mexico to tie themselves more closely to the dollar. Ecuador adopted a fixed rate in 2001. Argentina, following a period of adjustment to depreciation may well be tempted to opt similarly for permanent currency union, though there are some suggestions from both within the IMF and Alesina and Barro that Argentina ought to peg to a euro/dollar basket.

So where will currency competition be carried out? Within Russia and eastern Europe there has already been a competition of sorts between domestic currencies, the dollar and the Deutschmark, which is likely to intensify with the introduction of the euro. In the Far East, the yen will remain a potent competitor and euro penetration at the expense of the dollar is likely to be marginal, at least in the medium term. In any of these markets, the more successful the euro and the economic performance on which it is based, the greater its penetration is likely to be.

What of the longer-term effect? One of the most intriguing scenarios might be the implication of a successful euro for a return to Keynes' proposals following World War II, and thus the possibility of creating a single world currency. While large regionally separated and multi-sectored countries such as the US, Canada and perhaps India and Australia (but not really Russia and China due to low monetization of trade generally prior to communism) have existed with a single currency for some time,[10] EMU marks the first time that such a disparate set of states have given up the discretionary monetary policy in such an irrevocable fashion. Many economists predict that this will turn out not to have any particularly deleterious effects. Regional inflation (or more correctly the change in relative prices of regionally non-tradable goods such as housing, land and service sector labour) may be relatively modest. In these conditions, the long-standing debate about the usefulness or otherwise of discretionary monetary policy might be resolved. If this proves to be the case, a successful euro may strengthen the case for the adoption of a single, world money. The impact of such a development on the legitimacy of the Union will rest on the choice of currency to play that global role. Will it be the euro, the US dollar, or a new currency issued by the yet to be established World Central Bank?

---

[10]   Though some states and provinces only joined currency unions at a much later date.

22

The Governance White Paper, the Commission and the Search for Legitimacy

*Daniel Wincott**

Introduction

If their rhetoric is anything to go by, Europe's political leaders believe that the EU faces a crisis of legitimacy. Discussion of bringing Europe 'closer' to its citizens is regular fare when they gather to discuss the future. It is widely agreed that the popular 'permissive consensus' on which the European Community was based for its first thirty years has ended. As many Europeans now seem actively hostile to the Union as are enthusiastic about it. For many others, EU issues simply fall outside the core of their social and political concerns. Political leaders in the Member States and at the European level sense a threat from the increasing evidence of disconnection and some hostility about the EU among the peoples of Europe, which exists alongside enduring elements of enthusiasm. Legitimacy questions hover around the (now more or less permanent) IGC process. However, each IGC ends not with a bang, but with a whimper, as expectations that the 'big issues' would be addressed are disappointed, often being deferred to yet another IGC. Yet these perceived problems have not prevented the Union from continuing to deepen (for example through monetary union) or to widen (the on-going issue of eastern enlargement).

The challenge of legitimacy is typically addressed in at least two ways, which need not be mutually exclusive. Legitimacy might be improved if the peoples of Europe were better served by and/or more fully involved in the

* I would like to acknowledge the support of ESRC Grant L 213252043 for the research on which this chapter is based.

Union. The relationship between these two factors—the involvement of people in the Union and the manner in which it serves their interests—is a crucial matter for debate. Fritz Scharpf's influential formulation contrasts 'input' legitimacy, based on the identity and concerned with appropriate forms of involvement, with 'output' legitimacy, based on interests and rooted in efficient and effective policy.[1] Several recent EU 'projects', such as The Charter of Fundamental Rights, the White Paper on European Governance and the Constitutional Convention, have sought to address one or both of these issues. Typically, these projects have not used conventional EU methods of political organization, instead seeking to view the legitimacy issue from an unusual perspective. Sometimes the purpose may have been to move away from traditional 'interest-based' EU politics to generate a more detached and long-term view—a kind of 'constitutional perspective' if you like—on legitimacy. On other occasions the idea may have been to draw new groups into the EU 'circle'.

This chapter focuses on the Commission's main contribution to these debates 'European Governance: A White Paper', published in July 2001.[2] Unusually, this document considers both the 'inputs'—patterns of participation and involvement—and the 'outputs'—modes of governance—in the EU. As with the Charter of Fundamental Rights, the White Paper aspires to generate new forms of public participation in Euro-politics. Indeed, in early drafts the Governance team positioned the White Paper as an attempt to *democratize* the EU. Moreover, the first of the White Paper's four sections making substantive proposals for change concentrates on 'better involvement'. Of course, the ambition of the White Paper is quite different, and its scope in one sense much narrower than that of the other projects. The White Paper seeks to make changes largely within the existing Treaty framework of the Union,[3] while 'constitutional' changes usually would be expected to lead to reforms of the Treaty. The question of whether the Charter will lead to Treaty change has not yet been answered finally and the creation of a formal constitutional document would certainly require a revision of the European Union Treaty. Moreover, the White Paper is a Commission document, setting out that institution's official vision of the future of Europe.

---

[1] F Scharpf, *Governing in Europe: Effective and Democratic?* (1999).

[2] Commission, 'European Governance: A White Paper', COM (2001) 428, 25 July 2001.

[3] The principle that the White Paper would make suggestions only within the existing Treaty framework was weakened in the final stages of its drafting. This change was connected to a re-positioning of the White Paper as a 'building block' for the Future of Europe debate rather than a definitive document.

As with the Charter of Fundamental Rights, from which the Governance Team drew some inspiration, the process of drafting the White Paper was unusual. The small 'Governance Team' took the principle responsibility for this work. It was led by Jerome Vignon, former head of the Forward Studies Unit, was supported by 12 'inter-service' working groups, which were designed to cut across traditional lines of authority within the Commission. Both the core team and the working groups consulted widely with academics, governmental bodies (including local and regional governments) and civil society. A number of open discussion 'fora' were organized on particular themes. In other words, the drafting process sought to provide a model for the sort of 'involvement' that the White Paper advocated.

Its proposals on 'better involvement' cannot be read in isolation from the rest of the White Paper. In the end, I argue, the White Paper can be read in two ways. It seems torn between returning to an historic image of the Community method and looking forward to a new approach to EU governance.[4] On one reading the White Paper appears to set out a vision of a new balance between different policy instruments, and between formal policies and less formal means of achieving Union objectives. This approach is compatible with a vision of the Union has having already achieved the broad framework for European *integration*, or at least most of the necessary and possible tasks of integration. The tasks of managing the Union may require a new, more differentiated approach. The White Paper can also be read as a robust defence of the traditional Community method, and particularly of the Commission's role within it . Many of the proposals in the White Paper re-centre the Union around the Commission. In some areas it is appropriate for the Commission to play a central role, in others it may not be.

EU legitimacy: inputs and outputs, substance and form

Scharpf's argument is that the prospects for the EU to gain 'input' legitimacy are poor, as there is little likelihood of a European identity developing. Thus EU legitimacy must be based largely on its outputs. Of course, the output approach does not necessarily eliminate any role for wider involvement in the EU, but it places involvement in an adjunct rather than a primary position, perhaps widening the range of policy options considered.

---

[4] D Wincott 'Looking forward or harking back? The Commission and the reform of governance in the EU' (2001) 39 JCMS 897.

The key dilemma for Scharpf concerns the relationship between economic and social outputs. EU legitimacy is potentially enhanced by its contribution to the economic success of Europe, he argues, but may be eroded by a perception that it threatens national traditions of social welfare provision.

The relationship between the economic and social sources of legitimacy begs a question about the clarity of the distinction between 'input' and 'output' legitimacy. While useful for purposes of argument and analysis, this distinction can be pushed too far. The deep issue concerns the relationship between 'inputs' and 'outputs'. However 'efficiently' achieved, an inappropriate outcome will not enhance legitimacy. Who is to decide what constitutes an appropriate, or indeed an efficient outcome? For some analysts these issues are relatively clear-cut. Those who depict the EU as a 'regulatory state' suggest that the EU is and/or should be concerned with economic efficiency pursued through regulatory policies rather than social equality and redistribution.[6] This focus on efficient economic outputs at the European level reflects the limited nature of European identity, making it an inappropriate basis for social policies, which require a deeper solidarity. Traditionally, such theorists have focused on the dynamism of the Commission, although recently they have become increasingly concerned about the efficiency of EU regulation.[7] The proposed solution is to insulate the regulatory process further from popular influence.

The Liberal Intergovernmentalist (LI) theory starts from the opposite explanatory premise, attributing the dynamism of the Union to choices made by Member States, not the creativity of the Commission. Yet the LI position on issues of legitimacy is strikingly reminiscent of the regulatory theorists, at least as this position was developed initially. Moravcsik remains more optimistic about the current format of the Union than Majone.[8] However, for both scholars any attempt to democratize the EU is not merely unlikely to help, but could actually harm the Union.

Scharpf, Majone and Moravcsik agree that there is little scope for the EU level itself to acquire 'input' legitimacy. Moravcsik suggests that the identity 'inputs' into EU policies are relatively stable, and appropriately channelled through Member States. He seems unperturbed by the objection that it is difficult to hold the Member States (or more accurately agents of national executives) to account in their 'European' activities. Moravcsik's confidence

---

[5] Scharpf (n 1 above).

[6] G Majone, 'Europe's "democratic deficit": the question of standards' (1998) 4 ELJ 5.

[7] G Majone, 'The credibility crisis of Community regulation' (2000) 38 JCMS 273.

[8] A Moravcsik, 'If it ain't broke, don't fix it!' (Newsweek International, 4 March 2002).

is, perhaps, due to his view of the Union as essentially intergovernmental. He also seems to regard States not as fragmented but relatively coherent, and essentially legitimate themselves. Apparently Scharpf argues that input legitimacy is unlikely to sustain the Union, but recognizes that concerns about social welfare at the national level may undercut the substantive legitimacy of the EU, an issue largely ignored by Moravcsik. Majone argues that the EU should be judged on the efficiency of its outputs, implying that a general agreement can be found on the appropriate criteria for such a judgment. His view of the nature of identity in Europe may be more nuanced. He sometimes seems to suggest that Europeans have developed more market-oriented values, which manifest themselves at both European and national levels.

If all these distinguished analysts agree that the EU is unlikely to benefit from strong 'input' legitimacy, why, then, is so much rhetoric developed around, and effort expended upon, widening involvement in the EU? Sharpf recognizes that EU legitimacy is closely bound up with the legitimacy of its Member States. For this reason, Majone's strict separation of EU efficiency policy from national welfare provision is unsustainable. Moreover, the complex politics and policy of the EU has never focused solely on efficiency, to the exclusion of redistribution. Equally, however, output legitimacy cannot be wholly separated from the character of the inputs into European politics. The EU does provide a framework within which some groups are able to make claims that would have gone unrecognized at the national level, perhaps contributing to the development of a European element in their identities[9] (albeit perhaps of a secondary sort).

The complex character of the Union stains the credibility of Moravcsik's claim that the Union is transparent with a clear separation of powers. Indeed, a strong case can be made that the Union's historic dynamism has not been based on any particular participants in its development (whether Majone's Commission or Moravcsik's Member States), but instead in the fusion of national and European elements across the various institutions of the Union.[10] Giving both Member State and European actors a stake in most policy and 'constitutional' issues has blurred the lines between institutions, but allowed each to feel confident of having an input into the incremental process of EU development. Dynamic though it may be, such 'blurring' is at the expense of the readability of the process from outside the elite groups involved. It is at this 'blurring' that the White Paper takes aim.

[9]   As Menon and Weatherill argue in this volume.
[10]   W Wessels, 'Nice results: the millennium IGC in the EU's evolution' (2001) 39 JCMS 192.

The White Paper

Why 'governance'?

'Governance' is a notoriously slippery concept, but does suggest a certain modesty about the capacity of 'government'. The White Paper offers the following definition: '"Governance" means rules, processes and behaviour that affect the way in which powers are exercised at European level, particularly as regards openness, participation, accountability, effectiveness and coherence'.[11] A 'traditional' view of government suggests that (sovereign) political power is capable of achieving its purposes in a relatively unproblematic manner. Thus, for example, traditional views of 'regulation' suggest that when public authorities set out rules they will generally achieve their objectives, whatever they might be. Equally, 'welfare states' can achieve their purposes if policy is properly designed and political will is sufficiently strong. From a 'governance' perspective, however, the emphasis is typically placed on the interaction between the 'regulator' and 'regulatee', between those 'governing' and the 'governed'. In the case of the European Union, and especially the Commission, a shift to a 'governance' framework might unsettle some conventional images of a power struggle between member governments and European institutions. By adopting the language of 'governance' the Commission might seem to be finally dispelling the idea that it saw itself as a 'European *Government* in waiting'. In this context, the aspiration of attempting to improve the effectiveness of the Union within the scope and limits of its existing framework (both modest and demanding) might seem appropriate.

In addition, however, one major thrust of the White Paper is to return the major institutions to their core tasks, as set out in the Treaty. In this context, the use of the existing framework might become a source of strength for the Commission in driving forward their 'White Paper' arguments. The message here is that the institutions have moved a fair distance away from their core roles. Instead of each institution having a relatively clear and readable purpose, each has become increasingly entwined with the other institutions. The White Paper focuses on the undesirable consequences of this institutional fusion,[12] without paying a great deal of attention to the reasons why it developed. Unless the causes of institutional entanglement can be diag-

---

[11] Commission (n 2 above) 8. It may be worth noting that this definition is offered in a footnote.

[12] Wessels (n 10 above).

nosed, the reasons for eliminating it will remain confused and the prospects for doing so will be remote. Moreover, at least partly because the objectives of the Union are much broader than those of the Communities, there has been a proliferation of decision-making processes. An additional and related development is that the 'core tasks' of the institutions have become much more diffuse. It is striking that the White Paper lacks any significant discussion of the wider tasks of the Union. Its authors sometimes seem nostalgic, dreaming wistfully of an older, simpler world.

The concept of governance, then, represents a novel and seemingly modest starting point for the Commission to make an intervention in the debates about the future of Europe. While the text of the White Paper shows some evidence of this new modesty, it also strikes another note. Written in a period of some anxiety within the Commission, the White Paper is by turns modest and assertive about its own future role. In some particular proposals, for example those on regulatory agencies, the mixture of these two elements is deeply problematic.

Scope and form of the White Paper

The White Paper is divided into four major sections:

I Why Reform European Governance?
II Principles of Good Governance
III Proposals for Change and
IV From Governance to the Future of Europe.

The second section identifies five 'Principles of Good Governance' as cross cutting themes 'important for establishing more democratic governance'.[13] These principles are *openness, participation, accountability, effectiveness and coherence.* The core of the White Paper is set out in the third section, which is itself divided into four parts, dealing in turn with

i. better involvement,
ii. better policies, regulation and delivery,
iii. the EU's contribution to global governance, and
iv. refocused policies and institutions.

For present purposes the brief section on global governance is of relatively little interest, although it may reveal a certain concern with defending and expanding the Commission's role as the international voice of the Union.

---

[13] Commission (n 2 above) 10.

The other three sections are all much more important, but the balance between the section on 'better policies, regulation and delivery' and that on 'refocused policies and institutions' is key to understanding the significance of the first section on 'involvement'.

The structure of the White Paper may represent a significant rhetorical strategy on the part of the Commission. There are clear differences between issues of consultation, participation and involvement; the international role of the Union; and its policy profile and institutional structure each requiring separate consideration. It is much less obvious that improving policy (regulation and delivery) can or should be distinguished from refocusing policy (and institutions). On closer inspection the section on better policy sets out a new range of ways of addressing the objectives of the Union, ranging well beyond traditional legislation. As such it appears to de-centre traditional approaches to EU policy making, embodied in the 'Community method'. Important questions are raised in this discussion about how we decide whether legislation of any sort is appropriate and the range of alternative means of achieving Union objectives, including self-regulation, co-regulation, independent regulatory agencies, the greater use of contracts in policy delivery and the 'Open Method of Coordination' (OMC).[14] This stress on a variety of modes of governance contrasts sharply with the discussion of refocusing policies and institutions—and especially with the final section of the White Paper—where the emphasis is firmly on the Community method, giving the impression that the other modes of governance discussed are second best.

'Better policy, regulation and delivery'

The range of proposals included in the discussion of improving policy, regulation and delivery appears to suggest that the traditional 'Community method' would become only one of a range of possible techniques for attaining the purposes of the Union. Thus, for example, the OMC may represent an alternative to the Community method, centred on the European Council and based on the sharing of information and processes of policy learning rather formally binding rules. The Commission has an essential role in the OMC, which is sometimes overlooked, co-ordinating the cooperation and drafting joint reports based on national submissions.

---

[14]   See D Wincott, 'Beyond social regulation? Social policy at Lisbon: new instruments or a new agenda?' (2003) Public Administration (forthcoming) and chapter by Szyszczak in this volume.

Important though this role may be, it is a quite different role to that the Commission plays within the Community method.

Equally, advocates of powerful independent European regulatory agencies (IRAs) depict these bodies as an alternative to the Community method, based on the separation of the setting of policy objectives from their implementation. Their purpose is to create efficient mechanisms for regulation by insulating the agencies from popular influence to an even greater extent than the Commission and related methods of policy making and implementation in the Union. The fear of advocates of IRAs is that the Commission is becoming too politicized to carry out its regulatory functions adequately. Indeed, some theorists of Union 'regulation' see it as a system in crisis. So far from seeking the solution to this crisis in a democratization of EU regulation, they look to create regulatory agencies with clear mandates that are fully independent of both national control and the Commission. To the extent that this vision of the potential role of IRAs is persuasive, the implications for the Commission could be significant. The Commission might lose a number of its most authoritative functions, including the enforcement of policies in areas such as competition, the environment, food safety and perhaps some related aspects of agriculture. Alternatively the Commission itself might become a 'super' IRA, concentrating on implementation and losing its role in the initiation of policy. Either way, the changes would not simply strip away some of the existing powers of the Commission, they would also alter the balance of power among the various EU institutions. It is by no means clear that each deepening of the overall supranational character of the Union necessarily enhances the authority and power of all supranational institutions. For example, while monetary union has clearly enhanced the supranational character of the Union, its impact on the power and authority of the Commission is not (yet) obvious. The development of new forms of inter- and trans-governmental policy coordination around the European Central Bank may, inter alia, mark a shift of power between the Member States and the Commission.

In the context of analysing the potential contribution of IRAs in the EU context, the White Paper's discussion of expert advice merits a mention. The location of the discussion of expert involvement in Union policy-making in the section on improving policy, not that on improving involvement, may be significant. It might signal that the authors of the White Paper regard experts as part efficient policy-making, rather than its 'social foundation'. Although the case for IRAs does not necessarily rest mainly on their expertise, the logic of de-politicizing expertise and seeking the 'best' scientific inputs into policy is congruent with that for agency independence.

Even drawing attention to the choice about whether to legislate or 'make policy' at all might change the dynamics of EU rule-making significantly. The implication is that previously, the focus of attention of the political institutions of the Union was more on developing the scope of policy and not enough on ensuring its effectiveness. Whereas previously the Union might have been accused of emphasizing the making of new policy more than effectiveness of existing rules, two proposals in this section of the White Paper could point in a new direction. First, strong emphasis is placed on the overall coherence of Union policies. Making Union rules serve some over-arching purpose more explicitly will not be easy. It would certainly involve reining in the instincts of individual Directorates-General to develop new rules to attain their particular objectives, in the name of ensuring that all rules aggregate to a consistent whole. There may be some tension between the White Paper's emphasis on policy coherence and the use of increasingly diverse methods for achieving the objectives of the European Union. The establishment of IRAs, in particular, might exacerbate problems of policy coordination as the various agencies sought to defend their independence. At the very least, at their creation such agencies would have to be given clear mandates that were both mutually consistent and that cut with the grain of the wider purposes of the Union.

Second, the emphasis on policy delivery again suggests that a smaller volume of effectively implemented rules and policies would now be preferred to the continuous development of new policy, and associated establishment of new areas of Community competence. Such an approach might go some way to meeting the substantial 'implementation gap'.[15] Taken together with the suggestion that legislation should be developed only if it can be shown that it will actually help to meet specified objectives, all this suggests that policies should be better focused (ironically the term used in the subsequent discussion of policies and institutions) on these overarching objectives.

As well as discussing alternatives to it, the section on improving policy, regulation and delivery also proposes changes to the Community method. These changes generally point in the direction of enhancing or perhaps re-establishing the independence of the Commission itself within the processes

---

[15]   D Dimitrakopoulos and J Richardson, 'Implementing EU public policy' in J Richardson (ed), *European Union: Power and Policy-Making* (2nd edn, 2001) 335.

of legislation and implementation. The general idea is that legislation should be pitched at a more general or abstract level, providing a framework for implementation, rather than becoming embroiled in the detail. These changes would allow the overall purpose of legislation to be stated more clearly. As a corollary, the Commission would play a greater discretionary role in the implementation of detailed policy provisions. This is not simply a vision for future legislation, it also has implications for the existing body of rules. The White Paper proposes an extensive simplification of the body of EU law. These proposals might also make it easier for the Commission to monitor national implementation of EU policies, although here the White Paper mainly signals the Commission's intent to monitor implementation and enforcement more closely, but in more or less the same ways that it already plays this role.

All in all, the proposals of the White Paper to improve policies, regulation and delivery might be read as a manifesto for the governance of a 'mature' European Union. Essentially, they seem to suggest that the Union has already achieved its basic shape and scope and that a range of different techniques might be appropriate to manage and implement its future agenda. At first sight, this section of the White Paper appears to suggest that the Commission's role might vary significantly in different areas of Union policy. It might usually play a smaller part in those policy areas that will now fall outside the traditional Community method (such as those using the OMC and IRAs), but an enhanced one in those areas that remain within it. On this vision, increasing the involvement of actors and groups historically marginalized within the Union might feed in to some modes of governance (say the use of contracts in policy delivery, or co-regulation), but be less appropriate in others (IRAs). Enhancing involvement might also change the balance between the various governance modes, increasing the use of some, but decreasing the use of others. Separating out these different 'modes' of Union action will influence the power of the Commission, perhaps weakening it capacity to act as a 'motor of integration' deeply involved in all areas of Union activity. Its ability to use areas in which it has established authority to gain leverage in other areas would decline. In a Union that has already achieved maturity, this might be regarded as a virtue.

Yet, even within this section of the White Paper, there are good reasons for questioning this interpretation. The first concerns the overarching objective or mission of the Union, of which the White Paper makes great play. Of course, a clear consensus on the ultimate purposes of a polity is an extremely demanding criterion of maturity (for which nation states could we make such a claim?[16]). Nevertheless, the White Paper itself places considerable emphasis on the identification of a clear overall mission for the Union and such a mission is also necessary if more detailed policies are to be made more coherent. The key question is, can such a mission be identified, and what might it be? It would, surely, have to go beyond and perhaps replace the established formula of the 'ever closer union of the peoples of Europe'. It is not clear that a consensus can be achieved on these questions.

The second question is crucial. If the Union is to make greater use of a wider range of methods in achieving its objectives, who will make the choice between them, and how will it be made? These issues are given added significance due to the White Paper's emphasis on policy coherence. The White Paper does not explicitly discuss the issue of who would choose between the different methods. On the face of it we might expect that the Commission itself would be central to these decisions, given its historic role as initiator of policy. Moreover, for decisions about whether or not to legislate, about when to choose co-regulation, or tripartite contracts as a method of policy delivery, it seems obvious that the Commission would play a key role, and perhaps even the central one. This might even be true in relation to the issue of when to create an IRA, given that several possible agencies might involve parts of the Commission being 'hived off'.

However, if we are standing on the cusp of a new form of governance, in which the Community method is only one of several 'modes', the argument based on the Commission's traditional power of initiation within that method is of less relevance. This point becomes particularly clear when considering the OMC. The fact that the European Council, not the Commission holds the whip hand in it is almost a defining characteristic of the OMC. By including this method within the range of new modes of governance, the White Paper raises the stakes on the issues of policy coherence, coordination and choice between these 'modes'. It is extremely unlikely that the European Council will grant the Commission the right to decide when the OMC would be used. Instead, some process involving the Commission and the European Council in selecting between modes of governance, in the light of expert advice would need to be designed. It is a serious oversight of the White Paper that no clear proposals are made on this issue.

---

[16] The analogy here is far from perfect. To the extent that the EU is their deliberate creation, the Member States ought to be able to provide an explanation of its purpose, at least at a general level.

Turning from the question of *who* decides between governance modes, to *how* such decisions are made, the White Paper is more explicit. Its discussion of alternative modes of governance typically includes a set of conditions in which an alternative to the Community method could be used. Indeed, the fact that these modes are effectively presented as alternatives to the Community method begins to tell a story. Although in principle the White Paper sets out a case for several important alternative modes to be used, a close reading of its provisions, for example on the OMC and IRAs, tells quite a different story. In relation to IRAs, for example, the circumstances in which the White Paper envisages that an agency could be created are so restrictive that they effectively undermine the case for creating such an agency in the first place.[17] Indeed, the criteria set out could have been written in order to rule out the creation of a Competition Agency, independent of the Commission. The White Paper seeks explicitly to prevent the use of the OMC when action under the Community method is 'possible', but also stipulates that it should be used only to achieve defined Treaty objectives. Unless we believe that where it can be used the Community method will always be the best means of achieving Union objectives, the first of these criteria is hardly consistent with the White Paper's commitment to choosing the most appropriate method of so doing, based on evidence.

The issue of who will coordinate across different governance modes, and the re-reading of the discussion of these alternative modes it provoked, together suggest that rather than diversifying the means by which the Union should move towards its goals, the White Paper might have another agenda. This suspicion is deepened when we turn to its section on refocusing policies and institutions.

Refocusing policies and institutions

This fourth part of the third section of the White Paper is the most forcefully argued. The fact that it considers policy issues initially appears strange. Why should it consider policy issues separately from the earlier discussion (and separated by a brief discussion of the global dimension)? In fact, this discussion could have been presented together with the analysis of policy coherence, particularly across the traditional hierarchies of Union policy-making. Indeed, it is in this section that brief allusion is made to the importance of coordination of policy objectives across institutions.[18] Much

---

[17] Wincott (n 4 above).   [18] Commission (n 2 above) 29.

of the discussion of policy here is concerned with clearly setting and stating medium and longer term policy objectives and priorities, with statements of how the Commission intends to play this role in the future.

However, the thrust of this section of the White Paper starts to become clear towards the end of its discussion of policy. Here the White Paper asserts a central role of the Commission itself. While the European Council retains a considerable role in shaping the strategic direction for the Union, the Commission is seen as shaping the Council's agenda. The strong implication is that the Commission's customary role of initiating policy should extend across the full range of Union activities discussed in the White Paper. In this context it is worth noting that the White Paper does not touch on topics related to justice, home affairs, foreign or security policy to any great extent. Its focus seems to be on policies connected to the European Community aspect of the Union. Even within its apparent frame of reference, however, the centrality of the Commission in initiation is open to question, most clearly in relation to the OMC, but potentially across a number of the new modes of governance.

The basic thrust of the White Paper's reflections on Europe's institutions is to re-assert the distinctions between them and to refocus each on its 'core' role. This discussion includes sharp criticism of some of these institutions. The Council of Ministers comes in for particular opprobrium for its failure to coordinate across its various formations. More particularly, the General Affairs Council is chastised for the failure of its political leadership, both at European level and between this and the national level. As a consequence the Council is no longer capable of arbitrating between sectoral interests and the European Council is inappropriately drawn in to detailed policy debates. It is not clear how far the Council's failure is a matter of inadequate political will or a structural change in the character of the Union. In a resonant phrase, the White Paper suggests that the 'Union has moved from a diplomatic to a democratic process'[19] implying that the General Affairs Council is no longer the appropriate forum to coordinate the Council. Instead, it suggests a body is required that can 'coordinate *all* aspects of EU policy both in the Council and at home'.[20] Any such body would require immense political prestige. Although the White Paper makes no suggestion about the institutional formula necessary to achieve such coordination, it seems to rule out the use of the European Council in this role.

---

[19] Commission (n 2 above) 29.   [20] ibid.

The White Paper discusses how the role of the Commission itself should be refocused, making much more detailed suggestions than those set out for any other institution. However, criticism of the Commission itself is notably absent from the White Paper, particularly in comparison to the treatment meted out to the Council of Ministers. Are we to believe that the problem of sectoralization of policy-making in the Union is only the fault of the Council? Is the Commission itself wholly free of these faults? A further major change to the role of the Commission as it is currently practised appears right at the end of this section. It provides one of the most striking suggestions in the whole of the substantive discussion of the White Paper. In two short paragraphs it proposes the whole system of committees that have grown up around and between the Union's main institutions be swept away, in order to 'make decision-making simpler, faster and easier to understand'.[21] The effect of such a change would be to free the Commission from a series of mechanisms by which national governments and their representatives have become embroiled in the execution of Union policies.

By separating out the various institutions more strictly, the sort of 'fused' policy-making that is somewhat characteristic of the Union at the moment would become impossible. In effect, various 'modes' of EU policy-making and European institutions combine, re-combine and merge in the complex formation that is the EU. Arguably this 'fusion' has occurred because each of the states and institutions wishes to protect its stake in policy-making at each stage of the process. According to some analysts it is a source of dynamism in the integration process. What, from a policy perspective appears to be a lack of clarity and an inability to attribute responsibility for policy, from an integration perspective may represent the creation of a collective responsibility and will. However, in a mature polity, the effective management of policy should, perhaps, become more important than the continual expansion of its scope. Rather than having every actor somewhat involved in all aspects of policy, different actors would play more central roles in the various modes of governance, with some actors or institutions playing little or no role in any particular mode. Equally, however, the Commission's traditional role as a motor of integration would no longer be relevant. The balance between different actors and concerns would be reflected in the mix of modes of governance, rather than in the complex and opaque mix of actors and institutions within more traditional modes. If the role of each institution was more clearly defined and different modes of EU

---

[21] Commission (n 2 above) 31.

policy were specified more clearly, both as to their form and the legitimate scope of their application, confidence in the overall balance of the Union would depend on the mix of governance modes and the means by which choices were made between them in any given case. However, the overall tenor of the discussion in this section points in a different direction.

Participation and the 'Future of Europe'

The concluding section of the White Paper looks forward to the debate on the Future of Europe. While it does summarize much of the earlier discussion, it does so in a way that goes well beyond that material, and significantly alters its meaning and significance. The key claim in this section is that the proposals in the White Paper 'lead in one direction: a *reinvigoration of the Community method*'.[22] This, then, is the somewhat surprising conclusion of a document whose purpose was to explore new modes of governance. It is, as Kenneth Armstrong has commented, 'like *déjà vu* all over again'.[23] The emphasis on the Community method places it once again at the heart of Union policy-making. Moreover, placed in this position, the reinvigoration of the Community method essentially enhances the Commission's own role within it, by clearing out the various actors and interests that have gradually become entangled in it. Such a strategy might be plausible if the Community method was conceived as one governance mode among equals, as it were, where other actors and institutions could play their full role in other modes, assuming a trustworthy mechanism for maintaining balance between them could be found. It is less plausible if the Community method is to remain the core mode of Union governance.

This conclusion casts much of the earlier discussion in a rather different light. For example, the qualifications that hedge around the discussions of the OMC and IRAs appear to marginalize them in comparison with this emphasis on the Community method. More importantly, it places the discussion of the White Paper's proposals for 'better involvement' in a particular perspective. This section appears especially important to the White Paper's ambition to address the alienation and disenchantment that Europeans feel about the Union's work. The range of other proposals in the White Paper is designed to make the Union more efficient, effective and appropriate to its task. Each seeks to improve some aspect of the output of

---

[22] Commission (n 2 above) 34, emphasis in the original.
[23] KA Armstrong, 'The White Paper and the rediscovery of civil society' (2001) 14 EUSA Review 6.

the Union. However, none of these proposals addresses how the objectives of the Union are set. The White Paper's substantive policy proposals, starting with issues of improving involvement in Union processes, might be cause for optimism on this count. And indeed, the White Paper states that 'civil society plays an important role in giving voice to the concerns of citizens'.[24] The White Paper's discussion of improving involvement ranges over issues of decentralization—reaching out to regional and local authorities—as well as civil society. In principle decentralization and civil society might have been considered together fruitfully. Effective responsiveness to and involvement of the sub-national level is much more likely if government and non-governmental actors were treated in an integrated manner. However, the Commission faced a basic structural difficulty in considering these two strands together. It has much greater scope to engage with civil society, while engagement with local and regional authorities would be mediated by national government to a much greater extent. In effect, the White Paper was largely restricted to recommending that national governments reconsider the manner in which local and regional authorities are involved in the EU.

Yet if the White Paper seems to hold out a promise of getting citizens involved in setting Union priorities, this idea, arguably always somewhat idealistic, is quickly dispelled. The White Paper quickly turns from seeing it as a source of priorities for the Union, to depicting it as a resource for the Union. First civil society is seen as a means of delivering services that meet people's needs. Second, 'better involvement' is depicted as providing 'a chance to get citizens involved *in achieving the Union's objectives*'[25] rather than the other way round. Finally, the White Paper is somewhat unclear about the scope to be granted to civil society as a means of channelling 'feedback, criticism and protests', first suggesting that this is legitimate and valuable before going on to argue that 'participation is not about institutionalising protest'.[26] Particularly in relation to civil society, but also with respect to local and regional authorities, the White Paper is largely concerned with structuring the manner in which a wider set of actors becomes involved in the Union. Many of these proposals are substantively unobjectionable, such as the application of standards of good governance to civil society organizations before allowing them into EU processes. However, given the emphasis on using civil society to achieve Union objectives, the

---

[24] Commission (n 2 above) 14.   [25] Commission (n 2 above) 15.   [26] ibid.

suspicion remains that the White Paper privileges a desire to domesticate civil society over a concern to serve it.

Placed in the perspective of the discussion of the refocusing of the institutions and the reinvigoration of the Community method, this suspicion strengthens. The proposals to improve 'involvement' largely assume that the Commission will be the principal interlocutor for civil society and the key agency involved in the structuring of these relations. Civil society becomes a potential resource bolstering the position of a strengthened Commission within an enhanced Community method. The claim made by Governance Working Group IIa that partnership arrangements 'obviously constitute an incentive for the NGO community to organize themselves in pan-European structures'[27] gives an indication of the nature of this agenda. By contrast, proposals to enhance the role of local and regional authorities are likely to complicate national processes of European policy-making.

The appropriate form and extent of public participation in European governance will vary between different modes of governance, yet there is no discussion in the White Paper of the relationship between modes of governance and forms of participation. Indeed, the assumption appears to be that the proposals in 'better involvement' will improve all governance modes. But this is hardly the case; indeed, sometimes the logic of other proposals is quite the opposite. For example, proposals for IRAs are largely based on the exclusion of the public from direct participation in policy-making. The purpose of this method of structuring policy is to free policy decisions from the immediate demands of the public and of politicians, so that they can serve longer-term objectives. As it has operated so far, the OMC has been largely a sphere of elite, governmental activity. However, it may create some scope for wider involvement in the future. Other modes of governance, such as co-regulation and contract based policy delivery probably create more scope for wider involvement in EU governance.

If, in the end, the White Paper centres its proposals on a reinvigorated Community method, with an enhanced executive role for the Commission, the key question becomes 'what is the appropriate form of public participation within this method?' We have seen that scholars from Moravcsik to Majone argue forcefully that there is little or no legitimate role for direct 'democratic' participation even here.[28] Channelling further participation through the Commission risks politicizing it to the extent that it would no

---

[27]   See Armstrong (n 23 above) 7 for a discussion.
[28]   Moravcsik (n 7 above), Majone (n 5 above).

longer be able to play its key role as an honest broker between the Member States.

Conclusion

The Commission's White Paper on European governance is an original and thought-provoking exercise. The basis for a novel approach to European governance is contained within it. By disentangling the various European institutions from one another and separating out different modes of governance for various purposes, the White Paper provides a model for the governance of a mature Union that is worthy of rather more widespread and generous discussion than it received initially. Turning our main attention from integration to governance does not mean that integration is wholly halted. Instead, new forms and dimensions of identity may be developing around Europe, perhaps providing a basis for novel forms of input to or involvement with the EU. Rather than depicting the EU as a pure model of some sort (for example of a regulatory state) the governance agenda suggests that the mixed character of the Union should be reflected in the variety of governance modes, rather than the fusion of its various elements. Thus, agencies could handle some aspects of market regulation, while issues of social policy could be addressed through the OMC.

Within such a vision, the Community method would still play a significant role. The case for enhanced executive autonomy for the Commission within this method is powerful. Moreover, if significant powers were 'hived off' to independent regulatory agencies, then the case against the Commission having its own direct channels and structures of communication with civil society is weakened. Indeed, if new forms and dimensions of European identity are developing, then the case for new forms of European level 'input' from society would be strengthened.

However, this interesting vision of the future of the Union is largely obscured by the internal Commission politics of the White Paper. Time and again the potential impact of important proposals is undercut by a concern to defend and enhance the Commission's own institutional prerogatives. Both IRAs and the OMC are limited in this way. Despite sharp criticism of other institutions, not a single criticism is made of the Commission for acting outside its core mission. The justification for the Commission's role in city and town 'twinning' or partnership, for example, hardly compares to its current roles in the internal market, gender equality or competition. How much more credible would the White Paper have been if the Commission had led by example, suggesting areas in which it might withdraw from 'non-core' activities. Equally, the White Paper does not consider the ways in which the implementation of some of its own proposals might shift the boundaries of the core tasks for each institution. Finally, in a model of the EU based on 'mixed modes of governance', the choice between these modes becomes politically crucial. The White Paper leaves the impression that such choice will be made primarily by the Commission, largely ignoring the reasons for the 'fusion' of EU institutions and the growth of the role of the European Council. For a mixed system of governance to work effectively, the concerns of both supranational institutions and Member States will have to be taken into account at this crucial stage.

Effective political leadership is necessary if current concerns about the legitimacy of the EU are to be addressed in a satisfactory manner. Although the White Paper raises many interesting ideas, in the end, these ideas are somewhat obscured behind the institutional self-interest of the Commission. The spectacle of this institution jealously guarding its own institutional prerogatives will hinder, not help the Union in its search for legitimacy.

Part V

Enlargement and the Movement of People

The enlargement of the Union to include many countries of Central and Eastern Europe will banish forever the image of the Union as a rich man's club. It offers the prospect of reuniting the continent in conditions of stability, democracy and prosperity. But it will bring into the Union a new constituency with new expectations, governments and people whose experiences since the end of the Second World War have been profoundly different to those of the Union of 15. A properly functioning Union will need to respond to the expectations of the people of the new Member States if they are to regard it as legitimate. Their views will be coloured by the way the accession process has been conducted and the terms on which they are allowed to accede. Moreover, if enlargement damages stability and prosperity in the West, the legitimacy of the Union in older Member States may be undermined.

23

Enlargement of the European Union: A Legal Analysis

Christophe Hillion*

Introduction

In Nice, the European Council reaffirmed 'the historic significance of the European Union enlargement process and the political priority which it attaches to the success of that process'. Enlargement has been an important catalyst in bringing the legitimacy of the European Union to the fore. While furthering the *European* dimension of the integration process, and thus making it more legitimate, enlargement to 20 or more countries from central, eastern and south-east Europe[1] also raises fears as regards its potential impact on the Union's achievements and future, both in substantive and institutional terms. It has thus been approached with a great deal of caution, sometimes even with genuine reluctance by several Member States.[2]

Enlargements have always tended to be perceived as a threat of dilution, or even dislocation, of the integration process. Concerns to preserve the existing dynamic, principles and rules of integration have consequently led to the establishment and strengthening of admission conditions well beyond

---

* The author wishes to thank Graham Avery, Michael Dougan, Geoffrey Edwards, Christophe Humpe and Anne Myrjord for their helpful comments. Any remaining mistakes are the author's responsibility only.

[1] Bulgaria, the Czech Republic, Estonia, Hungary, Latvia, Lithuania, Poland, Romania, Slovakia and Slovenia (referred to collectively as the 'Central and Eastern European Countries' or CEECs) have, together with Cyprus, Malta and Turkey, applied for membership. They could be followed by other countries from the former Yugoslavia, Moldova, Ukraine, and possibly Russia.

[2] A Mayhew, *Recreating Europe* (1998) 27; H Ojanen 'Enlargement: a permanent threat for the EU and a policy problem for Finland?' (2001) Northern Dimensions 24; G Burghardt and F Cameron, 'The enlargement of the European Union' (1997) 2 EFA Rev 7, 21.

the vague and open provisions of the Treaty. Indeed, because of its magnitude and its specificity, the current enlargement has also stimulated the creation of numerous instruments to secure the best possible preparation of candidates for membership.

The enlargement process should also be evaluated in terms of its legitimacy: not only is it bound to colour relations between 'old' and 'new' Member States after their accession, but the Union's dealings with the outside world, in this case the candidate countries, also help to shape its very identity. From a legal point of view, analysing the legitimacy of the enlargement is intrinsically linked to the role of the rule of law, defined in a broad sense:[3] to what extent is it based on predictable procedures and clearly defined rules?

In the present contribution, the issue of legitimacy is addressed by focusing on the way the EU defines and monitors the terms of the accession process. This implies drawing lessons from previous enlargements as well as analysing the specificity of the current one. The aim is to show that the latter, although guided by existing accession principles, has sparked the development of legal and, most notably, quasi-legal conditions, instruments and practices. In that sense, it looks much more institutionalized than previous ones, having the effect of raising the candidates' expectation to enter once the standards are met. In practice however, the development of accession conditions has not made the process more predictable. Established on the basis of Treaty provisions, such conditions have been designed, particularly by the European Council, outside the usual Treaty (EU and EC) procedures and regularly adjusted as enlargement gained pace. Whilst such a 'permanent adaptation'[4] has provided the Union with substantial leeway to monitor the process closely, it has also generated an increasing feeling of uncertainty and discomfort for the candidates as to the terms of their accession to the EU.

This chapter focuses on two elements that illustrate this uncertainty: the accession criteria as they have been revisited, and the so-called 'pre-accession strategy' which was specifically set up to prepare the candidates for accession. For reasons of space and because they are still under way at the time of writing, accession negotiations will be referred to only to the extent that they are useful for the analysis.[5]

---

[3] See chapter by Arnull in this volume.

[4] M Maresceau, 'The EU pre-accession strategies: a political and legal analysis' in M Maresceau and E Lannon (eds) *The EU's Enlargement and Mediterranean Strategies* (2001) 3; K Inglis, 'The Europe Agreements compared in the light of their pre-accession reorientation' (2000) 37 CMLRev 1173, 1175.

[5] On negotiations, Maresceau (n 4 above) 7; P Nicolaides, S Raja Boean, F Bollen and P Pezaros, *A Guide to the Enlargement of the European Union (II)* (1999) 46–59.

The general conditions of accession

Treaty provisions

In its Preamble, the EC Treaty expressly provides that the Member States '[call] upon the other peoples of Europe who share their ideal to join in their efforts'. The accession procedure and principles are set out in Article 49 TEU, which encapsulates consecutive revisions of the original Article 237 EEC.[6] Changes have been made as regards the procedure of accession, which now involves the European Parliament;[7] the Article has also been altered to accommodate the evolving nature of the Community itself.[8] It was only with the Amsterdam Treaty, however, that the accession *conditions* were expressly revisited. Hitherto, the sole Treaty requirement was that a state must be *European* to be eligible for membership.

Any European State... 'Europeanness' was included in the Treaty from the outset and, although somewhat equivocal, may be regarded as fundamental in the body of accession principles. Surprisingly, one had to wait until 1992 for the term 'European' to be thoroughly considered.[9] Having blessed the starting of accession negotiations with Austria, Finland, Norway and Sweden, the Maastricht European Council of December 1991 asked the Commission to envisage the implications of other European States' accession to the Union. The Commission presented its report at the 1992 Lisbon European Council, in a fundamentally changed geopolitical context.[10] Having recalled that 'the Community ha[d] never been a closed club and

---

[6] The specific procedures to accede to the ECSC and Euratom are set out in Art 98 ECSC and 205 EAEC, respectively.

[7] Art 8 SEA modified Art 237(1) EEC: the Council acts unanimously after consulting the Commission and 'after receiving the assent of the European Parliament, which shall act by an absolute majority of its component members'. It is worth noting that the European Parliament's assent is not required in the context of the Euratom Treaty.

[8] At Maastricht, Art 237 EEC was turned into Art O TEU. As a mechanical consequence of the structural change introduced by the Treaty, Art O(2) provided that 'the conditions of admission and the adjustments to the *Treaties on which the Union is founded* which such admission entails shall be the subject of an agreement between the Member States and the applicant State' (emphasis added). In other words, new Member States accede to the Union as a whole, ie encompassing 'the European Communities, supplemented by the policies and forms of cooperation established by [the TEU]' (Art 1(3) TEU).

[9] Morocco's informal application was diplomatically silenced by the Council of Ministers. It was considered that Morocco was not a 'European State' without the latter concept being defined.

[10] 'Europe and the challenge of enlargement', Supplement 3/92, Bulletin of the EC 1992, 11.

[could not] refuse the historic challenge to assume the continental responsibilities and contribute to the development of a political and economic order for the whole of Europe', it proposed an open definition of 'European':

It combines geographical, historical and cultural elements which all contribute to the European identity. The shared experience of proximity, ideas, values and historical interaction cannot be condensed into a simple formula, and is subject to review by each succeeding generation...it is neither possible nor opportune to establish now the frontiers of the European Union whose contours will be shaped over many years to come.[11]

Thus, the Commission refrained from giving a clear and definitive limit to the enlargement process. By emphasising the 'continental responsibilities' of the Union, it rather foresaw the latter's further expansion.

...which respects the principles of Article 6(1) TEU.   A candidate has to respect liberty, democracy, respect for human rights and fundamental freedoms, and the rule of law, for its application to be considered. The introduction of this condition into the Treaty illustrates the growing importance of the political commitment entailed by EU membership, although like various other conditions of enlargement it is not entirely new.[12]

The conditions of admission and the adjustments to the Treaties shall be the subject of an agreement between the Member States and the applicant state.   In 1978, the Court was asked to give a preliminary ruling on these conditions.[13] It considered that Article 237 EEC (now 49 TEU) laid down:

a precise procedure encompassed within well-defined limits for the admission of new Member States, during which the conditions of accession are to be drawn up by the authorities indicated in the article itself. *Thus the legal conditions for such accession remain to be defined in the context of that procedure without it being possible to determine the content judicially in advance.* (emphasis added)

It concluded that it could not, in proceedings pursuant to Article 177 (now 234) EC, 'give a ruling on the *form or subject matter of the conditions which might be adopted*' (emphasis added).[14]

---

[11] Supplement 3/92, Bulletin of the EC 1992, 11.
[12] F Capotorti, M Hilf, FG Jacobs and J-P Jacqué, *The European Union Treaty* (1986) 34.
[13] Case 93/78 *Mattheus v Doego* [1978] ECR 2203.
[14] Paras 7–9 of the judgment.

Thus, whilst the *procedure* is clear, the substantive *conditions of admission* cannot be determined in advance. Being subject to negotiation, such conditions are deemed to be uncertain until they are enshrined in the Accession Treaty. The Court did not want to limit the discretion of the Member States, as negotiating parties.

It seems however that negotiation has actually played a reduced role. In practice, candidates always have had to adapt to and accept the Union's requirements. As Marc Maresceau pointed out, '[o]n the whole, in accession negotiations, there is little substance to be "negotiated" since a candidate wants to join something which exists'.[15] Indeed, the origin and development of key accession conditions are not so much the result of negotiations; nor is it the outcome of a law making procedure defined in the Treaty. They rather result from the Member States and Commission's creativity.

Elaboration of accession conditions

Based on concerns related to specific candidate states, conditions have been established and elaborated in a piecemeal and incremental manner. A brief overview on how they have appeared will provide the backdrop against which the conduct of the current enlargement process can be evaluated.

Adopting the acquis. Although not mentioned in Article 49 TEU, one of the key accession principles is the acceding state's obligation to adopt the broadly defined Community/Union's rules and objectives, often referred to as the *acquis communautaire*.[16] A landmark in the establishment of this principle was the Hague Conference of the Heads of State or Government of December 1969[17] whose purpose was inter alia to envisage the conditions of admission of Denmark, Ireland, Norway and the United Kingdom. There, the six Member States gave their blessing to the Community's enlargement 'insofar as the applicant states accept the Treaties and their political aims, the decisions taken since the entry into force of the Treaties and the options adopted in the sphere of development'.[18] The Commission, in its formal

---

[15] Maresceau (n 4 above).

[16] The concept of acquis communautaire was first mentioned in the initial Commission Opinion on the accession of Denmark, Ireland, Norway and the UK to the Communities; Supplement 9/10, Bulletin of the EEC 1969. On this concept, see C Delcourt, 'The *acquis communautaire*: has the concept had its day?' (2001) 38 CMLRev 829.

[17] C Preston, 'Obstacles to EU enlargement: the classical method and the prospects for a wider Europe' (1995) 33 JCMS 451, 452.

[18] Bulletin of the EEC 1/1970, 16.

Opinion on the four applications, followed a similar line,[19] also echoed in the Preamble of the 1972 Accession Treaty concluded by the Member States and the applicant countries.[20] The Parties were 'determined, *in the spirit of the Treaties*, to construct an ever closer union among the peoples of Europe *on the foundation already laid*' (emphasis added).[21]

This initial approach was confirmed in subsequent enlargements.[22] It is always the candidate's duty to approximate its legislation to make it compatible with that of the EC/EU. Moreover, rather than by changing existing rules, problems of adjustment have been solved through the establishment of transitional measures,[23] which have to be interpreted strictly.[24]

In other words, the understanding of the 'conditions of admission and the adjustments to the Treaties' to be negotiated by the Parties, has been strict, even restrictive. Only in exceptional cases has 'adjustment' been envisaged as a re-negotiation of the acquis with the applicant state.[25] The scope for negotiation has been minimal and essentially of a technical nature. Indeed, because enlargement tends to stimulate Member States' reflex of preservation and continuity, it is also an occasion for the latter to re-affirm what the Community/Union foundations are, or as the case may be, even an opportunity to expose principles which have not always been clearly displayed before, like the economic and political accession criteria.

---

[19] Commission Opinion of 19 January 1972 on the accession of Denmark, Ireland, Norway and the UK [1972] OJ L73/3.

[20] See also the Opening Statement of the President of the Council of Ministers at the opening of negotiations in Luxembourg in June 1970, cited in C O'Neil, *Britain's Entry into the European Community* (2000) 425.

[21] Second indent, Preamble of the Accession Treaty [1972] OJ L73/5.

[22] The Commission reaffirmed the same principle in its opinions on the Greek, Portuguese and Spanish applications ([1979] OJ L 291/3 and [1985] OJ L 302/3); the respective Preambles of the Accession Treaties repeated the provisions contained in the previous Accession Treaty ([1979] OJ L 291/9 and [1985] OJ L 302/9); see P Dagtoglou, 'The southern enlargement of the European Community' (1984) 21 CMLRev 149. Austria, Finland and Sweden's accessions were also subject to the same condition: see D Booß and J Forman, 'Enlargement: legal and procedural aspects' (1995) 32 CMLRev 95, 100–101, Preston (n 17 above) 453.

[23] Principle established by the Council of Ministers; see Fourth General Report on the Activities of the Communities, 1970, 260.

[24] Case 231/78 *Commission v UK* [1979] ECR 1459. Booß and Forman (n 22 above) 101.

[25] On the political, legal and practical rationale of this interpretation, see J-P Puissochet, *L'Elargissement des Communautés Européennes* (1974) 19–20. It is worth noting that Art 2 TEU requires that the acquis be maintained in full. On rare revisions of Community policies in the context of accession negotiations, one may mention Protocol No 6 to the last Accession Treaty on the creation of new 'objective 6' of the regional policy; one could also mention the development of the EC fisheries policy through the Accession Treaty with the UK.

The political and economic conditions of accession. Following the UK's application for membership, French President de Gaulle declared in a famous press conference of January 1963, that Britain was not ready to accede because, inter alia, of its economic situation, deemed to be an obstacle to its participation in the Common Market. Britain's economic and monetary situation was again invoked to postpone the negotiations the Wilson Government had tried to resume in 1967. According to the Council of Ministers: 'one Member State considered that the re-establishment of the British economy must be completed before Great Britain's request can be considered'.[26]

This economic condition also played a substantial role in the following enlargements to Greece, Portugal and Spain.[27] In addition, given those countries' recent emergence from dictatorships, the Member States also insisted on the fulfilment of political criteria that had not been an issue in the first enlargement. The Copenhagen European Council of April 1978 declared that: 'respect for and maintenance of representative democracy and human rights in each Member State are essential elements of membership in the European Communities'.[28]

Enlargements to Greece, Portugal and Spain were clearly subject to this political requirement, though not expressed in the respective Accession Treaties.[29] Unsurprisingly, it did not have the same significance for Austria's, Finland's and Sweden's accession. However, both political and economic conditions have made a remarkable comeback in the context of the present enlargement process.[30]

The conditions of the current enlargement

The legitimacy of the current enlargement process rests in part on the extent to which the conditions of accession are defined and applied in a predictable manner. It is argued that the aforementioned conditions have been elaborated, strengthened, and sometimes applied in a different way,

[26] Puissochet (n 25 above) 16; C Preston, *Enlargement and Integration in the European Union* (1997) 31.

[27] Dagtoglou (n 22 above) 152–153.

[28] Declaration on Democracy, Copenhagen European Council, Bulletin of the EC 3/78, 6. It followed the 'Common Declaration on Fundamental Rights' signed in April 1977 by the Presidents of the EP, Commission and Council respectively; Bulletin of the EC 3–1977, 5.

[29] [1979] OJ L 291/3 and [1985] OJ L 302/3.

[30] It was indeed in this context that the political condition was included in Art 49 TEU.

while new conditions have been added, notably during the process. Such a revision may have produced more detailed and sophisticated accession criteria, a necessity given—to use the Commission's terminology—the 'nature and number of candidates'. Nevertheless, it has paradoxically made enlargement appear more uncertain, especially from the candidates' point of view; particularly because enlargement has also become subject to an obligation to be met by the Union itself.

Candidates' obligations

A milestone in the current enlargement process is the formal recognition by the 1993 Copenhagen European Council that: 'the Associated Countries in Central and Eastern Europe that so desire shall become members of the European Union. Accession will take place as soon as an associated country is able to assume the obligations of membership by satisfying the economic and political conditions required.'

The European Council thereby recognized that the accession of the countries of Central and Eastern Europe to the EU was a common objective.[31] At the same time, it set out a list of accession conditions, the 'Copenhagen criteria', on the basis of which the candidate country had to ensure:

- the stability of institutions guaranteeing democracy, the rule of law, human rights and respect for and protection of minorities;
- the existence of a functioning market economy as well as the capacity to cope with competitive pressure and market forces within the Union;
- the ability to take on the obligations of membership including adherence to the aims of political, economic and monetary union.

The substance of the Copenhagen criteria was not entirely new,[32] yet they made the accession conditions appear more institutionalized than in previous enlargements; also their application has been stricter while, paradoxically, they entail at the same time evolving obligations.

Further institutionalized conditions.   In being set out by the European Council, the conditions have been given further political authority. One could even argue that, drafted in such a prescriptive way, they have become legal-

---

[31]   M Maresceau, 'From Europe Agreements to accession negotiations' in G Venturini (ed) *Europa di Domani* (2002); Mayhew (n 2 above) 23–29.
[32]   See the section on 'The conditions of the current enlargement', above.

like requirements.[33] By declaring that 'accession will take place as soon as an associated country is able to assume the *obligations of membership by satisfying the economic and political conditions required*' (emphasis added), the European Council actually supplements the general conditions of Article 49 TEU, thereby giving a quasi-constitutional nature to the Copenhagen criteria. The fact that they are also relied upon in the assessment of the applications of other associated countries tends to confirm such a nature.[34]

Stricter application. Being more institutionalized, the accession criteria also seem to be applied more strictly than in previous enlargements. For the first time, the acquis has to be adopted as a whole *before* accession.[35] The current approach therefore contrasts with the enlargement to Greece, Spain and Portugal: the Commission recommended 'a measure of flexibility in the management of transitional periods' used for the new members' legal adaptation. It was felt that 'the strict lines of the first Accession Treaty [could] be the opposite of what [was] intended: instead of guaranteeing orderly integration of the acceding countries into the Community system, the enlarged Community [could] seize up or the new members... [could] find it impossible to honour their obligations.'[36] In the present situation, the approach has changed as legal adaptation is essentially a pre-accession process.

Such a requirement is all the more remarkable in that not only is the acquis continuously adjusted as integration deepens,[37] but also none of the opt-outs granted to current members is available to the candidates. Hence accession implies inter alia the adoption of the Schengen acquis and the acquis on Economic and Monetary Union.[38] In addition, the

---

[33] See also the section on 'The Accession Partnership', below.

[34] Turkey's application is also subject to the Copenhagen criteria. It is likely that the countries from the former Yugoslavia, which are 'potential candidates' (Feira European Council, 2000) will also have to observe these criteria.

[35] Agenda 2000 (COM(1997)2000) 69–70 and the speech of Enlargement Commissioner Verheugen before the European Parliament on 4 September 2001, DN:SPEECH/01/363.

[36] 'The transitional period and the institutional implications of enlargement', Bulletin EC, Supplement 2/78, 6. In another Communication on 'the Problems of Enlargement' presented at the Copenhagen European Council of December 1982, the Commission noted that 'differentiated application of Community measures and instruments in the applicant countries' could be increasingly used throughout the transition period. It added that 'in general... possibilities for differentiation compatible with the treaties already exist[ed]'; Bulletin of the EC, Supplement 8/83, 7.

[37] Agenda 2000 (n 35 above) 49.

[38] Commission Strategy Paper 2001 http://europa.eu.int/comm/enlargement/report2001/3.

definition of the acquis to be adopted is far from being clear, as it includes not only 'hard-law' legislation but also additional principles established by the Court or practices developed by the institutions.[39] The introduction of the EU Charter of Fundamental Rights in the enlargement's glossary is interesting from that point of view.[40]

Evolving obligations.   The development of the Union partly explains the continuous adjustment of accession obligations. But the latter's moving character is also due to the development by the European Council of the criteria themselves. For instance, in the aftermath of Copenhagen, the Madrid European Council considered that in order to ensure effective implementation of the acquis before entry, applicant countries should also create the conditions for their integration through the *adjustment of their administrative and judicial structures.* The subsequent European Councils confirmed and elaborated this additional institutional requirement.[41] Indeed, the 2001 Commission Strategy Paper, upheld by the Laeken European Council of December 2001,[42] shows how important administrative and judicial adjustment has become as a candidate's pre-accession obligation.[43]

[39] H Grabbe 'A partnership for accession? The implications of EU conditionality for Central and East European applicants', RSC Working Paper 12/99, 6–7; Delcourt (n 16 above).

[40] In its 2001 Strategy Paper, the Commission referred to the Charter ([2000] OJ C 364/1) as an instrument which 'emphasizes' the political principles which have to be observed by the candidate countries, ie the Copenhagen political criteria and the principles of Art 6 TEU. It could be argued that this reference indicated that the candidates are expected to take the Charter into account.

[41] eg the Feira, Nice and Göteborg European Councils.

[42] Having underlined that progress in the negotiations is based on convincing progress in adopting, implementing and enforcing the acquis, the Strategy Paper establishes an Action Plan for administrative and judicial capacity whereby the Commission 'will increase support for institution building and monitor closely the fulfilment of undertakings made in the negotiations'. See also pt 9 of the Conclusions of the Laeken European Council.

[43] The consequence of that obligation is strong pressure for reform which, although positive in principle, might have side effects. Particularly, it has often implied the establishment of extraordinary internal procedures for adopting legislation. Slovenia, for instance, has established a single reading procedure while the normal procedure provides for three readings within the Parliament. Poland and Hungary have also set up accelerated parliamentary debates. This looks like a paradox in view of the Copenhagen rule-of-law requirement. Indeed, the current Polish political situation could suggest that the resulting pressure might also benefit euro-scepticism and extremist parties; Rzeczpospolita, 25 September 2001; Financial Times, 11 January 2002.

The Helsinki European Council also elaborated the political criteria. It 'urge[d] the candidate countries to make every effort to resolve any outstanding border disputes and other related issues. Failing this they should within a reasonable time bring the dispute to the International Court of Justice.' The Conclusions also state that the European Council will review the situation relating to any outstanding disputes, in particular concerning the repercussions on the accession process at the latest by the end of 2004.[44]

All in all, the candidates' obligations as set out in Copenhagen have been further adapted, making accession increasingly look like a moving target. This flexibility is also noticeable in the changing role of the criteria.

The initial approach adopted by the EU was that the Copenhagen political and economic criteria had to be fulfilled if the candidate was to start negotiations, that is for it to be considered admissible. This approach was established at the Luxembourg European Council in 1997,[45] following the Commission's Opinion included in Agenda 2000. The Opinion suggested that although progress had still to be made in a number of applicant states, only Slovakia did not satisfy the Copenhagen political criteria, a 'necessary but insufficient condition for opening negotiations'.[46] As to the fulfilment of the economic criteria, which was assessed in a more prospective way, Hungary and Poland came 'closest to meeting them, while the Czech Republic and Slovenia [were] not far behind'. It was also felt that Estonia, while meeting the first criterion, would need to make progress to meet the second. Considering that the Czech Republic, Estonia, Hungary, Poland and Slovenia could be in a position to satisfy all the conditions of membership in the medium term, the Commission recommended that negotiations should start only with these five candidates as well as with Cyprus ('5+1'). The Luxembourg European Council upheld the Commission's analysis and negotiations actually started in March 1998 with the 5+1.

The Luxembourg Conclusions seemed to indicate that a country aspiring to accede to the EU could be eligible without being admissible.[47] One

[44] Arguably from a legal point of view, a new condition relating to nuclear safety was added in Helsinki following the Commission's 1999 regular report. For comments, see *Le processus d'élargissement de l'Union européenne à la veille du Conseil européen d'Helsinki* (1999) Assemblée Nationale, Rapport d'Information no 1995, 33.

[45] It was confirmed by the 1999 Cologne European Council, pt 59 of the Conclusions.

[46] Agenda 2000 (n 35 above) 49.

[47] It is noteworthy that a country's aspirations have to be officially acknowledged, which was not the case for Ukraine and Moldova. The European Conference established by the Luxembourg European Council was designed to bring together Member States and European states aspiring to become members. Moldova and Ukraine's applications to take part

interpretation of the role of the conditions in relation to the status of potential Member States could then be that a country is eligible when it satisfies the constitutional requirement, that is, the country is European. It becomes admissible when the Copenhagen political and economic criteria are fulfilled (or close to being fulfilled in the case of the latter). The Accession negotiations may then begin. Admission takes place after the negotiation process when the Accession Treaty is finally signed and ratified by the Member States and the acceding state.[48]

The EU approach changed at Helsinki in 1999. With the Kosovo crisis in the background, the European Council moved on to a more inclusive approach, in view of the progress made by the applicants to meet the criteria. Negotiations were then launched with all the candidates from Central and Eastern Europe as well as with Malta, after the change of government. Turkey, however, was still found to have failed the admissibility test, on the grounds that it did not meet the political criteria, albeit applied more softly in the case of the other CEECs, particularly when it comes to the respect of minorities.[49] It nevertheless remained eligible, despite the fact that the political condition was 'constitutionalized' by being inserted in Article 49 TEU.

In spite of being more institutionalized and apparently applied more strictly, the accession criteria cannot be considered as enhancing the certainty of the EU enlargement process. When analysed from a 'hard-law' perspective, non-Treaty-based accession rules have essentially been determined and further interpreted on a unilateral basis by the European Council, and as such do not possess a legally binding effect. Nevertheless, the mutation of the accession conditions into more tangible legal benchmarks in combination with the increasing institutionalization of the process through the European Council's role, raises the level of expectation of 'complying' applicants. Although their observance does not confer on the candidates a right to accede, the criteria's embryonic constitutional character increasingly commit the Union, at least in principle.

---

were turned down, indicating that they were not considered as 'aspiring'. Since then the situation has changed. The Göteborg European Council of June 2001 declared that '[w]ith a view to strengthening the Union's partnership with Ukraine and Moldova', they will be invited to join the Conference. They were invited, along with Russia, to the European Conference of October 2001 but they could not take part in most of the discussions.

[48] On these subtle semantic choices, see Maresceau (n 4 above) 5–6.
[49] ibid 18.

Obligations of the EU

The Copenhagen European Council considered that enlargement should be subject not only to the applicant states' fulfilment of the above-mentioned conditions, but also to 'the Union's capacity to absorb new members, while maintaining the momentum of European integration in the general interest of both the Union and the candidate countries'. Although the Member States initially agreed to proceed with a limited enlargement on the basis of the Amsterdam Treaty,[50] the 1997 Luxembourg European Council later considered that an additional IGC would nevertheless be necessary for any enlargement to take place.

Institutional reforms have always been part of the discussions in the context of previous enlargements,[51] yet they never constituted a *conditio sine qua non*. The magnitude of the current expansion partly explains the EU change of attitude. On the other hand, it has made the process even less predictable. As underlined by P Holmes et al, 'in reality, the CEECs are implicitly being required to take on obligations in advance of accession negotiations, while the EU side is absolved from matching commitments.'[52] The Union, through its Member States, acts both as judge and party as enlargement depends not only on its own assessment whether the candidate satisfies the criteria, but also on whether it considers itself able to open up.

To conclude, the development of the accession conditions and their application can be seen as a continuous process, in which both the contents of the criteria and their role are subject to change, resulting in reduced predictability for the candidates. This tendency has been accentuated in the current enlargement, not least because of instruments adopted in the pre-accession phase. It emphasizes the Union's concern to make enlargement as manageable as possible.

---

[50] Art 2, Amsterdam Protocol on Enlargement.

[51] Memorandum submitted by the Commission to the Hague Conference of 1969, cited in Puissochet (n 25 above) 17. In its Opinion on Austria's application, the Commission considered that 'enlargement... will entail, *when the time comes*, institutional adjustments *according to the nature and number of accessions*' (emphasis added) (Bulletin of the EC, Supplement 4/92, 5).

[52] P Holmes, U Sedelmeier, A Smith, E Smith, H Wallace, A Young, 'The European Union and Central and Eastern Europe: pre-accession strategies', SEI Working Paper No 15, 1.

The 'pre-accession strategy': monitoring the way candidates meet the accession criteria

The specificity of the Union's approach towards the current enlargement stems in particular from the establishment and development of a sophisticated pre-membership phase: the so-called 'pre-accession strategy'.[53] Never before has the Community applied such a policy to candidates.[54] It has been elaborated through various steps, in consideration of the development of the applicants' situation, whereas its consistency seems to have been envisaged *a posteriori*. Among the various elements of the pre-accession strategy, three instruments deserve particular attention: the Europe Agreements, the White Paper 'on the preparation of the associated countries for integration into the internal market', and the Accession Partnership.

Europe Agreements

In the history of enlargement, association agreements have often played an important role in the candidates' preparation for accession.[55] The Europe Agreements, although association agreements, were initially conceived by the Community as an alternative to accession.[56] Such agreements were concluded in 1991 with Hungary, Poland, (then) Czechoslovakia; and were later signed with Bulgaria and Romania, the three Baltic States and Slovenia. They constituted a special advanced form of association aimed at accompanying the economic and political transition of the CEECs. In this respect, an assistance programme ('PHARE') was also established to provide for the financial means to support the CEECs' transition.

The Copenhagen European Council radically changed the political objective of the Europe Agreements by linking them to accession.[57] Together with a number of instruments unilaterally designed by the EU, the Europe Agreements became part of the 'pre-accession strategy' launched by the Essen European Council in 1994, to monitor closely the accession

[53] M Maresceau 'On association, partnership, pre-accession and accession' in M Maresceau (ed), *Enlarging the European Union* (1997) 3.

[54] The Commission had envisaged a pre-accession strategy for Greece which was rejected by the Member States.

[55] eg Greece and several EFTA countries.

[56] See COM (90) 278; Inglis (n 4 above) 1173.

[57] Yet they were not renegotiated, partly because the CEECs felt that it would be another trick to delay the accession process; Maresceau (n 53 above).

preparation of the candidate countries. Indeed, these new instruments have subtly modified the associated countries' obligations under the Europe Agreements, which nonetheless remain the legal basis of their relations with the Community and its Member States.[58] In particular, they have strengthened and elaborated the associated countries' obligation to approximate their legislation. Two measures are of particular interest from this point of view: the White Paper, and the Accession Partnership.

The White Paper

The Commission's White Paper[59] was established as a guide which highlights some of the EC legislation the candidates are expected to adopt with a view to entering the internal market.[60] Later approved by the Cannes European Council of June 1995, it has played a critical role in between the EU and the CEECs relation. Deprived of any legally binding effect, the document is 'not part of the negotiations for accession and does not prejudge any aspect of such negotiations, including possible transitional arrangements',[61] yet in real terms, its impact has been remarkable for two particular reasons.

First of all, the White Paper defines the scope of approximation of law in a much more detailed manner than envisaged in the Europe Agreements. Whilst each agreement states that the major precondition for the associated country's economic integration into the Community is the approximation of its existing and future legislation to that of the Community, it requires that each associated country ensure 'that [its] *future* legislation is compatible with Community legislation *as far as possible*' (emphasis added).[62] The White Paper goes further as it sets out what should be approximated as regards internal market legislation in 23 sectors. Indeed, without establishing any timetable, it nonetheless suggests concrete approximation scenarios in its Annex.[63]

---

[58] As confirmed by various decisions of the Court of Justice concerning the Europe Agreements: see, inter alia, judgments of 27 September 2001 in Cases C-63/99 *Gloszczuk*; C-235/99 *Kondova*; C-257/99 *Barkoci and Malik* and judgment of 20 November 2001 in Case C-268/99 *Jany.*

[59] COM(95) 163 final and its Annex, COM(95) 163 final/2.

[60] M-A Gaudissart and A Sinnaeve, 'The role of the White Paper' in Maresceau (n 53 above) 41.

[61] Pt 1.8, Preamble, WP.

[62] eg Art 67 EA Hungary. Art 68 EA outlines several areas where approximation should take place.

[63] Part 3 of the Annex.

Secondly, it is by reference to this White Paper, although implicitly, that the Commission gave its initial Opinions on each of the candidates' preparedness for membership. When the Madrid European Council asked for these opinions to be ready by the end of the 1996 IGC, the Commission sent a questionnaire to each of the applicants to check their progress in adopting the acquis, as particularly highlighted in the White Paper. Looking at the answers thus provided, one sees the impact that the White Paper had on the candidates' approximation process.[64] At several points, Agenda 2000 underlined the importance of the White Paper as a 'benchmark' and the usefulness of the replies as 'a starting point' for preparing the Opinions. It also indicated that 'further progress in implementing the measures indicated in the [White Paper] will remain both an essential method of preparation and an approximate yardstick for the applicants' degree of preparedness'.[65]

Although the candidates were in principle free not to follow the White Paper, ignoring it would have been detrimental to their endeavour to accede.[66] Thus, despite its non-legally binding value, and its incomplete character,[67] the White Paper has had an influence on the rights and duties of the CEECs vis-à-vis the EU, as originally defined in the Europe Agreements. Emphasizing the importance of 'soft-law' in the enlargement process, the impact of the White Paper also highlights the Commission's control on the candidates' preparation for accession. This control has since been consolidated thanks to the establishment of the Accession Partnership.

The Accession Partnership

Introduced in Agenda 2000, the Accession Partnership was conceived as the key element of the 'enhanced pre-accession strategy'. It is a unilateral instrument proposed by the Commission and adopted by the Council in the form of a regulation based on Article 308 EC.[68] Its purpose has essentially been to make sure that the PHARE assistance, now included in a new 'pre-accession assistance', is directed specifically towards the candidates' needs in their preparation for membership, as envisaged and monitored by

---

[64] In the Polish Government's 'Replies' to the Commission's questionnaire, one reads that 'the Polish commitment to adapting its legislation both *existing* and future to the acquis is demonstrated [inter alia by] the implementation in Polish law of normative legal acts recommended in the European Commission's White Paper...' (emphasis added); Introduction part 26.

[65] Agenda 2000 (n 35 above) 48.

[66] Gaudissart and Sinnaeve (n 60 above) 46.

[67] ibid 67–68.

[68] Council Regulation 622/98 [1998] OJ L 85/1.

the Commission. Based on the Council Regulation, further individual Accession Partnerships have regularly been adopted, as Council Decisions addressed to the candidates.[69] Each decision sets out for each candidate a list of priorities covering, beyond the initial objectives of the Europe Agreements, all the Union's acquis on which its financial and administrative resources should be focused.

More specifically, the Accession Partnership introduces further *conditionality* on the allocation of financial assistance and ultimately on accession itself.[70] Both have become subject to the achievement of the specific Accession Partnership objectives defined by the Commission, in 'consultation' with the candidates. This achievement is assessed on a regular basis, also by the Commission. When it is felt that the applicant does not comply with the commitments contained in the Europe Agreement, 'and/or when progress towards fulfilment of the Copenhagen criteria is insufficient', the Accession Partnership empowers the Council, on the basis of a Commission proposal, to take any appropriate measures with regard to any pre-accession assistance granted.[71]

Like the White Paper, the Accession Partnerships therefore elaborate the candidates' obligation to approximate their legislation beyond what the Europe Agreements require with a view to meeting the Copenhagen criteria. Moreover, by setting out priorities and objectives in the form of Council decisions addressed to the candidates, and by establishing, in the form of a regulation, a control procedure combined with a system of sanctions, the Accession Partnerships strengthen the quasi-legal/soft law nature of the Copenhagen criteria. Being part of secondary legislation, the former actually makes the latter look like primary law.

Finally, the Accession Partnerships also strengthen the Union's control on the candidates' preparation for membership, and more globally on their societal transformation.[72] Incidentally, the EU position becomes ever stronger in the context of accession negotiations. On the basis of the Accession Partnership, the Council's power to sanction the candidate country—via a reduction or suspension of pre-accession funds geared to help its

---

[69] The first individual Accession Partnerships were adopted after Reg 622/98 in 1998, the second in 1999 following the Commission's regular progress report on the candidates' preparation. Updated Accession Partnerships were proposed by the Commission in 2001.

[70] For a comprehensive analysis of the Accession Partnership, see Grabbe (n 39 above) 13–18.

[71] Art 4, Reg 622/98.

[72] P-C Müller-Graff, 'The legal framework for the enlargement of the internal market to Central and Eastern Europe' (1999) 6 MJ 192.

accession—while the latter is negotiating with the Member States, renders accession negotiations more illusionary than suggested above. This '*mise sous tutelle*', consolidated by the recent 'Action Plan on administrative and judicial capacity'[73] makes enlargement more foreseeable for the Union than pre-dictable for the candidates.

Conclusion

Undoubtedly, the provisions on enlargement form a specific core of prin-ciples which cannot be approached as a traditional field of EU law. Since it involves political negotiations, the enlargement process entails a certain level of uncertainty. At the same time, considering that the Treaty estab-lishes a number of rules, which have been elaborated, further institutional-ized and supplemented by other conditions, one could have assumed these would guarantee a higher level of predictability.

The present enlargement process shows a different picture. What appears to be a meticulously prepared process can also be regarded as a continuous inflation of instruments and references which have made accession rules and their management increasingly complex, particularly for the candidates. Whilst this development corresponds to a legitimate EU concern to pre-serve its acquis, it undermines its image as a rule-of-law-based entity. This is unfortunate considering the extent to which the rule of law has been advocated during the whole pre-accession phase and that it lies at the very heart of the EU's legitimacy.

[73] Strategy Paper 2001 (n 38 above) 18.

24

Legitimacy and Accountability in EU Enlargement: Political Perspectives from the Candidate States

*Brigid Fowler**

From the Hungarian point of view, what Nice means is that ... the door opens to the promised land, in which by then there will be less promise ... [1]

This chapter explores democratic political legitimacy and accountability in EU enlargement, focusing on the candidate countries of central and eastern Europe (CEE).[2] Issues of legitimacy and accountability in enlargement have become more relevant as the process has gathered force since the EU's December 2000 Nice summit. In some respects, Nice represented a major step forward in the enlargement process. It established what was at the time the closest thing to an enlargement timetable the EU had produced, with a 'road map' to the conclusion of accession negotiations for some candidates by the end of 2002, and the specification of the EU's 'hope' for enlargement in 2004. This timetable has become firmer since Nice, with the EU at its December 2001 Laeken summit naming eight CEE states (excluding Bulgaria and Romania) which it expects to be able to join the Union in 2004 (together with Cyprus and Malta). Nice also saw the candidate states featuring for the first time in EU institutional politics, with their own

* For helpful comments and advice during the drafting of this chapter, I would like to thank Claire Gordon, Heather Grabbe, Karen Henderson, Jonathan Lipkin, Sean Hanley, Aleks Szczerbiak and Kasia Wolczuk.
[1] Magyar Hírlap, Budapest, 12 December 2000.
[2] There are ten CEE candidate states: Bulgaria, the Czech Republic, Estonia, Hungary, Latvia, Lithuania, Poland, Romania, Slovakia and Slovenia. This chapter does not consider the remaining two states negotiating accession, Cyprus and Malta. The chapter was completed over New Year 2002.

views on specific institutional questions, and their future Council and European Parliament voting weights laid down in the Nice Treaty.[3]

These developments had important psychological effects, helping to transform enlargement from a distant prospect into an imminent reality. Enlargement politics since Nice have reflected this shift, and this chapter draws its examples from this period. However, Nice did not change the basic nature of the enlargement process. The discussion of legitimacy and accountability in the enlargement process in this chapter falls into five sections. The first shows how institutional mechanisms of democratic legitimation and accountability in enlargement remain in the candidate states on the one hand, and the EU and its Member States on the other. In this institutional context, the second section presents the difficulties represented for the legitimacy of enlargement by levels of public support for the process, in both the EU and the CEE candidates. The third, fourth and fifth sections explore in more detail the ways in which accession is—or is not—legitimated in the CEE states, dividing accession for this purpose into project (the accession goal), process (accession preparations and negotiations) and product (accession treaties and referenda). A key theme is the relationship between EU accession and perceptions in CEE of broader developments since the fall of communism.

Institutional legitimacy and accountability across the EU/candidate state divide

Any attempt to assess legitimacy and accountability in enlargement encounters an immediate difficulty—legitimacy for, and accountability to, whom? Among the various understandings of the concepts of legitimacy and accountability, the common core is that these notions concern the relationship between a given society, and those who have power over it. In democratic systems, the measure adopted by this chapter, there are institutional mechanisms by which a society can hold accountable those in political authority, and contribute to their legitimacy—by expressing consent to their exercise of power, or by making societal values known and thus allowing leaders to respond. EU enlargement is being pursued jointly by EU and CEE leaders

---

[3]   Details of the provisions for the new Member States are given in D Galloway, *The Treaty of Nice and Beyond* (2001) and D Phinnemore, 'The Treaty of Nice, EU enlargement and the implications for Romania' (2001) 1 Romanian Journal of Society and Politics 5.

and is affecting populations in both existing and future Member States—the whole of the EU's post-enlargement society.[4] However, this society will share a set of political institutions only once enlargement has taken place. During the enlargement process, there are separate institutional mechanisms of democratic legitimation and accountability in operation—in the EU on the one hand, and in each candidate state on the other. This means that the leaders pursuing enlargement are accountable to, and must be legitimate for, separate publics.

Institutional mechanisms of democratic legitimation and accountability in the EU are, of course, often seen as inadequate to the nature of the influence the Union now wields (as other contributions to this volume make clear). The strongest such mechanisms continue to operate at national level, with the EU legitimated and its leaders held accountable mostly indirectly, via the participation of Member State governments. In this light, mechanisms of legitimation and accountability in enlargement might be thought to operate more strongly and straightforwardly in the candidate states—their accession is being pursued by individual, democratically elected national governments (which have clearly stated their accession goal), without the complications that come with EU membership. The candidate states' dealings with the EU during accession might then be thought to be adequately legitimated via their national governments, in a model of legitimation proposed for states' involvement with 'ordinary' international organizations.

However, the EU is already having an influence on the candidate states greater than that exercised by other international organizations, and comparable with that which it has on existing members. This is as a result of the accession conditionality developed for the current enlargement.[5] Although they have had no input into its development, the candidate states are required to implement the EU's body of law (the acquis communautaire) before they accede to the Union. Because the EU ultimately determines whether candidates will join, in political terms too it wields decisive power over their capacity to achieve their accession goal, and all that accompanies it—but only national governments can be held accountable by CEE publics

---

[4] Lack of space precludes discussion of the implications of enlargement for CEE states which are not prospective EU members.

[5] See chapter by Hillion in this volume and, on conditionality and other EU pre-accession policies, also A Mayhew, *Recreating Europe* (1998); H Grabbe, 'A partnership for accession? The implications of EU conditionality for the Central and East European applicants' (1999) European University Institute, Robert Schuman Centre Working Paper 99/12; and M Baun, *A Wider Europe. The Process and Politics of European Union Enlargement* (2000).

for accession outcomes. Given the scope of the EU's influence over the candidate states, but their lack of access even to the (unsatisfactory) mechanisms of democratic legitimation and accountability that come with membership, they seem to face a double deficit.[6] Of course, the timelag before new members gain access to the EU's mechanisms of legitimation and accountability is unavoidable, since the right to participate in EU institutions is precisely what is gained only on accession.

The tough entry terms set by current EU leaders spring from the fact that these leaders remain most directly accountable to their own national populations. It is of course politically and normatively justifiable for EU leaders to seek to protect the gains which Union membership has brought their societies. For candidate state leaders, however, the fact that the most direct mechanisms of democratic legitimation and accountability operate at national level is more problematic. Given the strength of the influence wielded by the EU before enlargement, there is a mismatch in the candidate states between their national mechanisms of legitimation and accountability, and the location of legal and political power. The timelag before the creation of political institutions shared across the EU/candidate state divide is similarly problematic primarily for the candidates. Member State populations will feel the effects of enlargement mostly after it occurs, whereas the current candidates will have seen their institutions, policies and politics profoundly affected by the Union before they become its members. The difficulty for candidate state leaders, as we shall see, is that their capacity to respond to their own populations is limited by the requirement to fulfil preferences arising from the legitimation and accountability needs of current EU leaders. For example, CEE refusals to implement elements of the acquis until the moment of accession can be seen as attempts to reduce the disjuncture between sources of legal authority and institutions of democratic accountability; but such moves are criticized by the EU as obstacles to membership.[7]

Absent all but the most tenuous institutionalized links between candidate state populations and the EU, there are two political mechanisms which might help to bridge the gap. They build a concern for the views of popula-

---

[6] This discussion draws on Beetham and Lord's presentation of arguments about forms of legitimacy as applied to the EU: D Beetham and C Lord, *Legitimacy and the European Union* (1998) 1–22.

[7] CEE élites have, however, also sometimes widened the mismatch between the enlargement process and their domestic mechanisms of accountability, by seeking to shuffle all responsibility for perceived enlargement delay onto the EU. The EU is equally disingenuous when it claims that the timing of enlargement will be determined only by the candidates' 'readiness'—which the EU judges.

tions on the other side of the EU/candidate state divide into the enlargement process, and might therefore operate to reduce its legitimacy deficit.

First, political élites may be conscious that their actions during the enlargement process will impact on the views about the Union held by its post-enlargement society as a whole. This society will include populations with which post-enlargement EU leaders may previously have had no institutional links of legitimacy or accountability. Inasmuch as any EU leader wants the EU as a whole to be seen as legitimate, s/he may thus feel constrained to take the views of such societies into account before they become partners in the Union.

Secondly, before enlargement can take place, the approval of the European Parliament must be secured and the accession treaties must be ratified by the parliaments of each new member and all existing members. Most of the CEE candidates also plan to hold accession referenda (to be discussed below). The ratification of accession treaties, especially by referenda, will offer a form of legitimation to all those involved in their negotiation, on the EU and candidate state side alike. Any leader sincerely promoting enlargement to his or her own national audience must hope that the policy is not rejected elsewhere. All leaders involved in the negotiation of the treaties thus have an interest in ensuring that the accession terms will win the support of all other states.

However, this does not override national leaders' need to remain legitimate in the eyes of their own public, to which they remain most directly accountable. It may be European in content, but even ratification is ultimately national in form, since leaders' prime responsibility is to get the accession treaties through their own parliaments. The most direct institutional mechanisms of legitimation and accountability in enlargement thus remain those linked to national audiences.

Public opinion on either side of the EU/candidate state divide

In this institutional context, Figure 24.1 suggests some of the difficulties now accompanying enlargement, as regards one aspect of the legitimacy issue—public support. From the European Commission's Eurobarometer data for 1991–2001, the figure presents various measures of support for EU membership (line 1) and enlargement (lines 2–4) among the existing EU population, and of support for membership among the CEE-10 (lines 5–6). There are discontinuities in the data for both groups. In particular, a question on general CEE-10 support for membership was asked only in 1991–1992 and 2001, with a question on accession referenda voting intentions being asked instead in 1995–1997 and as well in 2001.[8] There was no Eurobarometer polling in the CEE-10 at all in 1998–2000. To plug this gap somewhat, line 6 also shows the response to the referendum question in a Taylor Nelson Sofres (TNS) survey taken in 2000 on a sample size similar to that used in Eurobarometer.[9] To cope with the fact that non-Member State polling has sometimes included Cyprus, Malta, Turkey and non-candidate CEE states into weighted averages, the CEE-10 figures shown in Figure 24.1 are unweighted averages for the ten states being considered here.

Line 1 can be taken as a rough indicator of the decline in the EU's legitimacy for its existing population. Against this background, lines 2–4 point to the enlargement dilemma facing EU leaders—on these indicators, enlarging the EU to CEE appears unlikely to repair the legitimacy problems it faces among its existing population, and may exacerbate them.[10] Support among the EU population for enlargement in general rose above 50 per cent only in the immediate aftermath of the 11 September 2001 terrorist attacks in the United States; average support for the accession of the ten named CEE candidate states has only briefly exceeded 40 per cent; and the proportion of the EU population regarding enlargement as a priority has never topped 30 per cent.

Even as the enlargement process has gathered force (indeed, as a consequence of its newly advanced stage), the period since Nice has seen public reservations reflected increasingly openly in the stances of some EU leaders. France—where public support for enlargement is among the lowest—has shown signs of reluctance, and some in Austria, Germany and Italy have floated the prospect of vetoing the process.[11] Most prominently in terms of its impact on the enlargement negotiations, the EU cited public fears about labour migration in Austria and Germany to justify its refusal to open its

---

[8] The most continuous Eurobarometer dataset for the CEE-10 is for a question on the EU's image, positive or negative, but this seems an inadequate proxy for views on actual membership.

[9] The comparability of the Eurobarometer and TNS polling is further suggested by the 58% figure for a CEE-10 referendum 'yes' produced by a second TNS poll taken in autumn 2001. This is close to the 60% shown in Figure 24.1 on the basis of the Eurobarometer poll taken around the same time. The 2001 TNS survey is available from http://www.tnsofres.com/freereport.cfm.

[10] cf chapter by Martin in this volume.

[11] Leaving aside Greece's threatened veto if the Cyprus issue is not resolved to its satisfaction.

Figure 24.1. Support for EU membership and enlargement in the EU-15 and CEE-10, 1991–2001 (%)

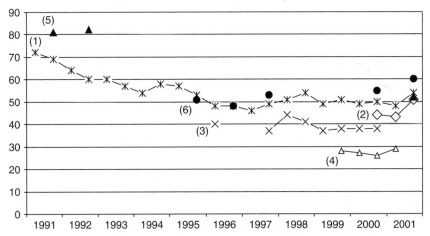

−✕− (1) EU-15 support for own membership (membership 'good thing')

−◇− (2) EU-15 support for enlargement in general (agree with statement 'the EU should be enlarged')

−✕− (3) Average of EU-15 support for the accession of the 10 individual CEEC candidate states (in favour of country X joining)

−△− (4) Average in EU-15 regarding enlargement as a priority policy for the EU

−▲− (5) CEE-10 support for own membership in general (1991 8 states only)

−●− (6) CEE-10 'yes' in accession referendum

Sources: For the EU-15 (EU-12 1991–1994), Eurobarometers 35–56 (1991–2001); for the CEE-10, Central and Eastern Eurobarometers 2–8 (1991–1997), Taylor Nelson Sofres EU Accession Opinion Survey 1 (2000) and Applicant Countries Eurobarometer 1 (2001). Eurobarometer surveys are published by the European Commission Directorate-General for Press and Communication and many are available via http://europa.eu.int/comm/dg10/epo. The 2000 Taylor Nelson Sofres poll is accessible via the website of the participating Polish institution, OBOP, at http://www.obop.com.pl/homeframe_eng.htm. The data are plotted against the dates of fieldwork (spring and autumn each year), not publication.

labour market fully to the new Member States immediately on enlargement. These public worries were acknowledged to have overridden the fact that the likelihood of large-scale migration is low.[12]

The new Member States might be thought to be a source from which the enlarged EU could boost its legitimacy. A queue of 13 (formally acknow-

---

[12] See, eg, the comments of Commission President Prodi and Enlargement Commissioner Verheugen in Prague, RFE/RL Newsline, 6 April 2001.

ledged) states wishing to join suggests that the Union is seen as having considerable value. As regards public opinion, the pro-membership camp in CEE retains a clear majority over the anti-, and public support for membership is usually seen as being higher than in the existing EU.[13] However, line 5 in Figure 24.1 highlights the dramatic fall in support for membership among the CEE-10 since the early 1990s, such that the difference between CEE-10 and EU-15 levels of support has almost disappeared. Against over 80 per cent in the early 1990s, support for membership in the CEE-10 stood at 52 per cent in autumn 2001.

The autumn 2001 figures, showing support for membership among the CEE-10 marginally lower than among the EU-15, may represent the one-off impact in the EU of the September terrorist attacks in the United States. However, the data for the CEE-10 accord with other evidence that figures for clear supporters of EU membership in general (line 5) are systematically lower than those for intended referenda 'yes' voters (line 6). Many of those who do not know whether they support membership, or are doubtful or unenthusiastic about it, appear nevertheless to expect to endorse it. While the referendum-based measure has often been used as the indicator of support for membership in CEE, the measure of support for membership in general is that which is comparable with figures for support for membership among the EU-15. On this basis, support for membership in the CEE-10 may well have been close to or even below that measured for the EU-15 since the mid-1990s, hovering around or perhaps below the 50 per cent mark.

The CEE-10 figures would probably be higher if they were weighted. Eurobarometer usually announces weighted figures, and it is weighted measures which will impact on the announced level of overall support for EU membership in the enlarged Union. However, weighted figures privilege the large CEE states: Poland, where levels of support were very high for much of the 1990s (but have fallen to unexceptional levels since 1998–99); and Romania, which will not join the EU in its next enlargement.[14] Given these considerations, it is difficult to see—on the basis of current figures—

---

[13] Although always with large variations between countries. In the first Applicant Countries Eurobarometer (ACE) taken in October 2001, the range was from 80% (Romania) to 33% (Estonia and Latvia). This chapter aims to help explain changes in levels of CEE-10 support for membership. The range of absolute levels within which support moves in any state is also shaped by national contexts that cannot be discussed here for reasons of space.

[14] The October 2001 ACE also included Turkey—another large state with high levels of public support for membership. The weighted average of support for membership in all 13 applicants announced by Eurobarometer was 59%, against 52% for the unweighted CEE-10 figure shown in Figure 24.1.

that enlargement to the eight CEE states in prospect (plus Cyprus and Malta) is likely to bring a major boost to the EU's overall public support. Of course, public opinion may shift under the impact of the final stages of the enlargement process;[15] and public support is only one element in the legitimacy equation.

Just as in the EU, in the candidate states the period since Nice has seen some increasingly prominent manifestations of unease about enlargement. Most notably, in Poland's September 2001 parliamentary elections, a party explicitly opposing EU membership won representation for the first time, with 8 per cent of the vote; another force setting conditions which effectively exclude membership (the Self-Defence party of agrarian populist leader Andrzej Lepper) scored 10 per cent, and two further parties with reservations about accession garnered 18 per cent between them. Across the CEE-10, mass opinion increasingly resembles the 'permissive consensus' identified in the EU, rather than enthusiasm; membership is increasingly being revealed as an elite project. Just as in the EU, the fact that leaders are accountable most directly at national level is thus coming to represent a difficulty for some CEE politicians pursuing enlargement, with mass pressures sometimes narrowing their room for manoeuvre in dealings with the EU. The increasingly elitist nature of EU membership in CEE was presumably not the form of convergence envisaged by EU leaders in designing the accession process.

How is EU membership legitimated in the CEE-10, and why has it lost in support in recent years? The discussion which follows, of accession as project, process and product, fleshes out some of the points already made. The focus will be on legitimacy rather than accountability, with more emphasis on language, perceptions and expectations than formal institutions.[16]

Accession as project: the post-communist connection

The main argument for the legitimacy of EU membership in CEE is that membership is intimately connected with the entire project of post-

---

[15] For example, EU public opinion about enlargement might improve given that Bulgaria and Romania are set to be excluded, since there has consistently been high public resistance to their accession.

[16] In particular, the discussion here about perceived relationships in CEE between EU accession and broader post-communist change is separate from the debate about whether EU accession is actually helpful to post-communist transformation.

communist transformation. After the end of communist rule, CEE leaders very quickly formulated the wish to join the then European Community. The CEE states wished to become stable and secure democracies; wealthy, 'modern' and 'European'; and with a voice in the world and greater control over their own destinies. It was felt that they could achieve such aims only by becoming EU members. This argument for membership combines two types of legitimacy claim: the system performance type (membership will help to deliver democracy, security, wealth and influence) and the identity/values type ('we are European'). The perceived link between EU membership and the rejection of communism has produced consensus on the accession goal among all mainstream CEE parties. Mirroring those in the EU who argue that the CEE states' wish to join gives the EU the right to set tough conditions, the strongest supporters of accession in CEE argue that the legitimacy of the membership goal overrides the discomforts of the accession process.

In their rhetoric, both EU and CEE political élites have sought to keep the linkage between EU accession and post-communist transformation as tight as possible. For both, the connection offers a means of legitimizing enlargement, since the development of stable and wealthier democracies in CEE is in the interests of all. Invoking the mutual benefits that will flow from successful post-communist transformation is a means for leaders to build legitimacy across the EU/candidate state divide, as discussed above.

For CEE leaders, the legitimation linkage between EU membership and post-communist change also works the other way: the claim that domestic reforms are needed for accession is used frequently as a means of seeking to justify them. This rhetorical tactic relies on the existence of high levels of support for membership. Indeed, CEE political élites sometimes seek to use the EU goal as a prop for reforms which are generated primarily domestic-ally and are, at best, only indirectly related to accession.

In the countries closest to accession, this kind of language comes increas-ingly as competing pro-membership élites seek to link membership with their particular domestic appeals and projects—their understandings of the meanings of post-communist change. In Hungary, for example, liberals see EU membership as anchoring the free market economics, tolerance, rule of law and small, politically neutral state they fear may not be fully secure at home. The Hungarian Socialist Party, the main communist successor or-ganization, sees membership as part of the technocratic 'modernization' it has long been seeking to deliver, and as promoting higher wages and greater social and workers' rights. Meanwhile, the moderate right envisages mem-bership affirming Hungarian national (and often Christian) identity in a

community that protects cultural diversity. The legitimacy of EU membership can be boosted by such efforts to link it to positive domestic projects. In
CEE, however, where popular knowledge is limited about what is truly
required for accession, the way in which all mainstream political élites so
routinely invoke the EU goal may also threaten to surround it with cynicism.

There are at least two further difficulties with the attempt to hold post-
communist change and EU accession together in the public mind as a means
of legitimizing membership. First, where there has been tangible positive
change, CEE élites are most likely to claim responsibility themselves, rather
than credit the EU. Second, and most importantly, post-communist change
has in any case mostly been painful and disillusioning for CEE populations.
Where CEE publics perceive a general association between preparations for
EU membership and what has been taking place since 1989–90, the EU
accession goal tends to suffer. The evidence is that in most cases, such an
association exists—for many, accession is seen as offering more of what they
are already getting, and from the same people.[17] In socio-economic terms,
for example, the strongest supporters of EU membership are the 'winners' of
transition and those most satisfied with, and supportive of, liberal democratic politics and free market economics. The least enthusiastic about EU
membership are the 'losers' of transition and those least impressed with the
operation of democratic politics and market economics since 1989–90.[18]
Over time, support for EU membership tends to move in tandem with

[17] Where high support for membership has survived, as in Romania, it may partly be
because accession remains so distant that it is seen as promising something different from
existing post-communist experience. The perception of accession as élitist, and as promising
more of what populations are already getting from their governments, has been fuelled
because preparations primarily involve national executives, with little sub-national or civil
society involvement. See M Bessenyey Williams, 'Exporting the democratic deficit. Hungary's experience with EU integration' (2001) 48 Problems of Post-Communism 27; H
Grabbe, 'How does Europeanization affect CEE governance? Conditionality, diffusion and
diversity' (2001) 8 JEPP 1013 and J Hughes, G Sasse and C Gordon, 'Saying "maybe" to the
"return to Europe": élites and the political space for euroscepticism in Central and Eastern
Europe' (revised version of a paper presented at the Seventh Biennial ECSA Convention,
Madison, Wisconsin, 31 May–2 June 2001).

[18] Socio-economic bases of support for accession are analysed with Eurobarometer data
in R Cichowski, 'Western dreams, Eastern realities. Support for the European Union in
Central and Eastern Europe' (2000) 33 Comparative Political Studies 1243; and J Štebe,
'Support for the European Union from a comparative perspective: stability and change in the
period of transition' (2001) 2 Central European Political Science Review 92. C Haerpfer
presents similar analysis using New Democracies Barometer data in 'Public opinion on
European Union enlargement' (2001) Centre for the Study of Public Policy, University of
Strathclyde, Studies in Public Policy No 343. Local data for Poland and Slovakia respectively
are presented in A Szczerbiak, 'Polish public opinion: explaining declining support for EU

general indicators of post-communist opinion, such as support for systemic reforms, approval of a market economy, or, sometimes, government approval ratings. Even when an unpopular reform or phenomenon is not seen as a direct consequence of the EU membership drive, its effects are likely to be mediated via these general indicators into an indirect impact on support for accession. EU accession may lose out via this process of 'discontent displacement'[19] even by being seen simply as another change, by populations tired of the permanent revolutions in which they have been engaged since 1989–90. The link with post-communist change, potentially the strongest source of legitimacy for EU membership in CEE, is thus also its greatest vulnerability. And CEE élites who seek to rely on the legitimacy of the EU goal to aid domestic reforms risk undermining support for the goal itself.

Accession as process: negotiations and conditionality

For the candidate states engaged in it the longest, the accession process has helped to prise apart the linkage between post-communist transformation and EU membership. This has allowed a different form of de-legitimation of EU membership to occur, in which accession loses out in its own right, not because of wider post-communist developments. In this context, it is worth noting that Cichowski and Haerpfer[20] both identify weaker-than-average correlations between attitudes to the EU and general socio-economic/ attitudinal variables in Poland, where public debate about the specific merits and demerits of EU membership has been the most vibrant in CEE.

Those who acquire doubts about membership primarily because of the accession process do not necessarily reject broad post-communist goals, but see membership as inimical to them—at least on the terms on offer. This is analogous to the position of those in the EU who agree that the CEE states should become stable and more prosperous democracies, and even that the EU should help, but do not concur that this can be done only by granting membership. However, for CEE leaders who are pursuing membership, the

membership' (2001) 39 JCMS 105, and K Henderson, 'Euroscepticism or europhobia: opposition attitudes to the EU in the Slovak Republic' (2001) Sussex European Institute, University of Sussex, Working Paper No 50.

[19] G Pridham, 'EU accession and domestic politics: policy consensus and interactive dynamics in Central and Eastern Europe' (2001) 1 Perspectives on European Politics and Society 49, 55.

[20] See n 18 above.

need to fulfil EU preferences constrains their ability to make a better fit between domestic post-communist aspirations and accession terms.

The accession process impacts most strongly on CEE views where it reinforces impressions about membership deriving from general post-communist experiences. Apart from those associated with socio-economic phenomena, the most important such perception is probably that the CEE states remain marginalized, weak and overly subject to foreign institutions and interests. This view has important political as well as economic elements.

Both elements of the accession process—meeting entry conditions, and negotiating entry terms—have contributed to its independent impact in CEE. Conditionality inherently challenges the notion that post-communist reforms and preparation for EU membership are synonymous, since it implies that the reforms in question might not otherwise be implemented. CEE elites similarly drive a wedge between accession and domestic reforms when they invoke the EU goal, not domestic considerations, as the prime motivation for any measure.

A particular set of difficulties of this type surrounds the use of the notions of 'Europe' and 'European' in enlargement discourse. Both EU and CEE leaders elide the Union with 'Europe', as a means of seeking to legitimize it. This encourages CEE leaders, especially in front of EU audiences, to argue for their countries' accession in cultural/identity terms ('we have always been European'). However, this argument implies that one can be European without being a member of the EU. Equally, if joining the Union were conditional only on 'being European' in historical or cultural terms, the CEE states would have been able to join before now.[21] Thus some CEE leaders have on occasion acknowledged that EU accession is not about 'being European', but rather hard economic bargaining. In his 1998 data, Haerpfer found the strongest correlations between supporting EU membership and 'feeling European' in states that had not begun an accession process or had progressed least far in it. The link was weaker in the Czech Republic, Poland and Slovenia, suggesting that some populations which had experienced more intense engagement with the EU were also more willing to view membership as distinct from 'being European'.[22]

The use of 'European' claims to try to legitimize measures intended to aid EU accession is also problematic because the acquis communautaire faces

---

[21] The EU's appropriation of 'Europeanness' also affects the views of the Union held by those who view themselves as 'European' but are not being considered for membership—in Ukraine, for example.

[22] See n 18 above.

competition for the 'European' mantle from alternative sources of 'Europeanness'. One such source is the Council of Europe, which often sets standards or makes recommendations broader in scope even than the acquis. A second source is the EU Member States themselves. In policy areas where the acquis does not extend, or does so only with general provisions, or where accession conditionality leaves room for interpretation, CEE policy-makers can cite any practice or institution employed by an existing EU Member State and claim that it is 'European'. For example, Hungarian supporters of elected regional government—which is not a requirement of EU membership—argued that the Council of Europe's European Charter of Regional Self-Government, which does call for elected regional authorities, should be taken as the measure of 'Europeanness' in this field. In response, supporters of a government-dominated administrative regional tier cited Ireland and Portugal to argue that it was perfectly possible to be 'European' without elected regional government.[23]

These kinds of arguments undermine claims that EU accession requirements necessarily coincide with other post-communist objectives, revealing the requirements as purely the responsibility of the Union. Where they conflict with what are felt to be legitimate aspirations of post-communist transformation, a number of specific aspects of the acquis are by now arousing concern in CEE and helping to cast doubt over the EU membership goal. There is no scope here to discuss such worries in detail, but they include, for example, those surrounding foreign ownership of land and property, allowed by the free movement of capital; or the erection of new barriers to cross-border relationships at the EU's new frontiers, as a result of the Schengen regime.[24]

Principled objections to the loss of sovereignty flowing from EU membership have featured less heavily in unease about membership in CEE than

[23] This paragraph draws on studies I have conducted of Hungarian policy-making under 'European' influences in two areas, regional reform and minority rights. See B Fowler, 'Fuzzing citizenship, nationalising political space: a framework for interpreting the Hungarian "status law" as a new form of kin-state policy in Central and Eastern Europe' (2002) Sussex European Institute, University of Sussex, One Europe or Several? Programme Working Paper 40/02; and 'Hungary: patterns of political conflict over territorial-administrative reform' (2002) 12 Regional and Federal Studies 15. On diversity as a challenge to EU conditionality, see also Grabbe (n 17 above).

[24] Mayhew provides an overview of candidate state difficulties with aspects of the acquis in his account of the accession negotiations; 'Enlargement of the European Union: an analysis of the negotiations with the Central and Eastern European candidate states' (2000) Sussex European Institute, University of Sussex, Working Paper No 39.

in the EU, although they are gaining prominence. Where such worries have arisen, it is often in connection with the perception that the EU seeks to dominate the accession states, and impose only its own interests on them. Closely related is the impression that the EU does not really want new CEE members, and fails to take their aspirations and needs seriously. Instead, the EU's attitude to the CEE candidates is often felt to be patronizing and distant. This is a case of an impression building up since the start of the post-communist period, and reinforced by the accession process.[25] The tougher conditionality employed in the current enlargement compared to earlier ones, for example, removes the legitimacy that comes from precedent, and suggests to candidates that they are viewed as less competent and trust-worthy than any previous applicants. The fact that current conditionality is more extensive than the acquis makes the candidates also feel the victims of double standards.

In CEE, this perceived EU attitude is often felt to result not just from the politics of enlargement, but from longstanding historical prejudices about the region. As one illustration of the sensitivities involved, Böröcz identified a 'sense of alienness' in the Commission's attitude to Hungary from the fact that official Commission documents in Hungarian failed to reproduce correctly an accented letter also found in French.[26] Against a history of peripheralization and oppression in CEE, these impressions of the EU conflict with the sense that the post-communist experience should at least involve being treated with equal respect.

In terms of the legitimation of membership, the sense that the EU has a negative attitude towards the CEE candidates is problematic, first, because it conflicts with official EU rhetoric welcoming enlargement. This under-mines the credibility of the EU and its leaders, and thus their attempts and those of their CEE counterparts to legitimize EU membership in CEE. The view that the EU might not actually admit the CEE states was a consideration advanced, for example, in support of the 'Manifesto of Euro-realism' adopted in April 2001 by the Civic Democratic Party of former Czech Premier Klaus, which canvassed the prospect of the Czech Republic remaining outside the Union. At mass level, there is some correlation between lower overall support for membership in a state and a higher share of the population viewing the EU as the primary beneficiary of their relationship.

---

[25] Particularly those aspects of the process discussed by Hillion in this volume.

[26] J Böröcz, 'The fox and the raven: the European Union and Hungary renegotiate the margins of "Europe"' (2000) 42 Comparative Studies in Society and History 847, 860.

Second, concerns about EU domination create dilemmas for CEE leaders as they pursue accession. One response is to portray the inequities experienced by candidates as flowing inevitably from their status, and as not persisting beyond accession. According to this approach, which is broadly that adopted by Hungary, the discomforts of the accession process are best ended by achieving membership as soon as possible, even if the accession terms have to be less than ideal.

The alternative response is to try to enhance candidates' relative standing before accession, thereby proving to doubtful publics that dealings with the EU need not be humiliating. This strategy may be pursued by holding out for more favourable entry terms, for example. It is in this context that the rejection of 'second-class membership'—encapsulated in the CEE states' prospective lack of equal access to EU labour markets and agricultural subsidies—has become a prominent CEE theme. Poland has probably tried hardest among the candidate states to assert its interests against those of the EU.

However, this second approach can threaten the membership goal altogether, domestically and in terms of interaction with the EU. The wish to join the Union only from a position of strength leads some CEE politicians to set conditions that effectively make accession impossible in the foreseeable future. This is the position of Poland's Lepper, for example, or of Hungary's extreme nationalist István Csurka, who argues that Hungary will only be strong enough to achieve a fully equal membership in 20–25 years.[27] A slower accession process, giving the candidates more time to prepare and strengthen their economies, would find some mass support.[28] However, it is politically impossible for mainstream CEE political leaders to suggest any delay, for fear that any signs of misgivings about membership in the candidates would strengthen those in the EU who oppose enlargement altogether. For the same reason, CEE élites have been wary of highlighting disaffection about membership among their publics, including possible difficulties in accession referenda, as a means of trying to win concessions from the EU. Now that enlargement seems set to go ahead in 2004, however,

[27] Hungarian Radio interview, 11 December 2001, in BBC Monitoring Global Newsline, 12 December 2001.

[28] In the October 2001 ACE, the ranking of populations from those seeing the pace of their accession process as too slow, to those viewing it as about right, to those seeing it as almost too fast, resembled strongly the ranking of populations most to least supportive of membership. See also the data in A Szczerbiak (n 18 above) and the Central European Opinion Research Group Joint Omnibus Surveys taken in September 2000 and March 2001, available via http://www.ceorg-europe.org/.

simply holding out for better entry terms risks failing to complete negotiations in time.

Accession as product: treaties and referenda

The vast majority of the CEE candidates plan to hold referenda on their EU accession. Most states which expect to complete negotiations at the end of 2002 apparently plan to put their accession treaties to voters in the course of 2003, before acceding to the Union. It is not yet clear whether referenda will be held before or after parliamentary ratification of the treaties by the candidates.

CEE plans to hold accession referenda mostly reflect the preferences of political parties, not a constitutional obligation. Despite the relative lack of discussion of formal sovereignty-related questions, CEE élites most likely feel that referenda are warranted by the special nature and implications of any decision to join the EU.[29] The CEE states may also be following the example set by the EFTA states in the mid-1990s.

In the Union, recent EU-related referenda have seen the mobilization of anti-integration opinion which is not represented in normal parliamentary elections or by the major parties. Given the consensus on accession among mainstream parties, this is one scenario for the referenda in CEE. The anti-accession vote might snowball into a general rejection of post-communist élites and developments, picking up support from those with no specific opinion on the EU.

However, this would probably require a lead from anti-EU political élites. Under normal circumstances, those most alienated from post-communist developments are probably those least likely to vote in the accession referenda at all. In addition, a 'no' to accession would seem to require much stronger feelings than 'no' votes in the EU that do not jeopardize membership. On current indicators, the CEE plebiscites seem likely to deliver clear 'yes' results. The 2001 ACE figures give an average of 60 per cent of the voting-age population in the CEE-10 who would approve accession, and 77 per cent among those intending to vote. This kind of result will endow membership with an important form of legitimacy.

However, the value of the vote will be reduced by low turnout.[30] Indeed, turnout could fall from current indicators if the non-voting camp is swelled

[29] The Czech Republic and Poland did not hold referenda on NATO accession but will on the EU.

by those who currently expect to vote 'yes' but are doubtful about membership, or reject a particular aspect of the accession process and decide to trust others to produce a 'yes' result. On the other hand, if these kinds of voters do vote 'yes', it will be particularly difficult to interpret the vote as an unqualified endorsement of membership. In addition, low participation could become a serious problem for some states which have a 50 per cent turnout requirement for valid referenda—principally Poland.[31]

Conclusion

EU enlargement to CEE is a joint project of the Union and the candidate states. It will affect both sets of populations and is declared to be in the interests of all. This chapter has explored the challenges to democratic legitimacy and accountability which arise because the key institutional mechanisms of legitimation and accountability for leaders pursuing enlargement remain at the national level. This produces a set of interlocking dilemmas which represent the more serious problem for the candidate states. Seeking to protect the benefits which EU membership has brought to their populations, and thereby also the increasingly fragile legitimacy of the EU, existing EU members are controlling entry to the Union fiercely. This reduces the extent to which CEE leaders can be responsible for outcomes in the enlargement process, but only they are accountable to CEE populations. The dominance of the EU in enlargement reduces the legitimacy of accession in CEE, both in itself and by impacting on the new members' entry terms. The legitimacy of the accession goal is already vulnerable in the CEE states because of its felt connection to negative post-communist phenomena. Seeking to bolster the legitimacy of accession, CEE leaders may attempt to reduce EU dominance, narrow the mismatch between sources of power and institutions of legitimation and accountability ahead of accession, and increase the fit between CEE aspirations and membership terms. However, this strategy tends to threaten the accession goal itself.

---

[30] Hungary's NATO accession referendum yielded an 85% 'yes' vote on a 49% turnout.
[31] Other states with such a requirement include Slovakia and Slovenia. On the referenda, see J Hughes, G Sasse and C Gordon (n 17 above) and, for the Polish case, A Szczerbiak (n 18 above).

25

Free Movement of Persons in the European Union: The Legal Framework

Julian Lonbay

Introduction

At the special meeting in Tampere in October 1999 the Member States discussed the creation of an area of freedom, security and justice in the European Union.[1] The aims were ambitious and involved developing a comprehensive approach to migration, including approximating rules on the admission and residence of third country nationals who should be treated fairly and with equality vis-à-vis European citizens. The policy was also to take into account the needs of neighbouring countries. Additionally Member States were to try to create a common European asylum system. These vaulting ambitions were not present in the 1950s when the European Communities began their life, but have gradually evolved and been implemented using a variety of legal instruments. This chapter cannot deal with all the policy issues in this area; however it will outline the legal framework created to achieve this massive undertaking and point out some of the major weaknesses in its structure in the light of a number of the proposals currently on the table in order to achieve the an area of freedom, security and justice in the European Union.

Types of legal order

The Treaty of Rome 1957, as much amended, is a creature of public international law; the initial validity and authority of the Treaty stems

---

[1] See Presidency Conclusions, Tampere European Council, 15 and 16 October 1999 http://ue.eu.int/newsroom/LoadDoc.asp?MAX=1&DOC=!!!&BID=76&DID=59122&P = 2017&LANG=1/.

from this fact. International treaties still retain their importance with the European scheme of free movement of persons. There are several reasons for this. First, the whole EC/EU system owes much to this pre-existing international legal order, including the question of personality.[2] Secondly, there are several regional, treaty-based, regimes[3] (mostly now subsumed by EC/EU law) dealing with free movement of persons. There are also general Treaties governing the law on asylum and refugees[4] that bind the Member States. In addition, there is a series of treaties to which the EC and Member States are parties, for example, the EC Association Treaties, some of which deal with the movement of persons,[5] and especially, the EEA Treaty which entered into force on 1 January 1994.[6] Then there are Treaties made by the Member States both outwith the context of the EU's pillars (Dublin Convention on Asylum)[7] and within the context of the pillars of the Maastricht, Amsterdam and Nice Treaties (for example, the EUROPOL Treaty). International law is binding on Member States and on the EU/EC but its effects within the Member States will vary according to their own internal constitutional provisions.

States derive jurisdiction to regulate their internal (domestic) affairs from recognition by international law of their (mostly) territorially related rights. They have power and control, inter alia, over nationality and citizenship.[8] This is a means of controlling the flow of persons across national boundaries.

---

[2] See chapter by Dashwood in this volume.

[3] Nordic Council regimes; Benelux Regime, and the UK–Irish Common Travel Area. See generally J Handoll, *Free Movement of Persons in the EU* (1995).

[4] eg, the Geneva Convention relating to the status of refugees, 1951 (as amended).

[5] eg, the EEC–Turkey Association Agreement [1963] OJ C113/2. See further M Hedemann-Robinson, 'An overview of recent legal developments at Community level in relation to third country nationals resident within the European Union, with particular reference to the case law of the European Court of Justice' (2001) 38 CMLRev 525, 541–558. This agreement does not however grant autonomous mobility rights to Turks, which still depend on a Member State's initial authorization. Nevertheless the EEC Turkey Agreement grants more rights than the Europe Agreements with the Central and Eastern European States, eg [1993] OJ L347/2. These Agreements reserve to the Member States rights regarding immigration.

[6] Agreement creating a European Economic Area [1994] OJ L1/3. The EEA grants extensive rights of mobility and equality to non-EU nationals, unlike most of the Association Agreements. See also the relatively generous agreement with Switzerland: http://www.europa.admin.ch/ba/off/abkommen/e/ab_e_personnes_a.pdf/.

[7] The Dublin Convention determining the State responsible for examining applications for asylum lodged in one of the Member States of the European Communities. See generally N Blake, 'The Dublin Convention and rights of asylum seekers in the European Union' in E Guild and C Harlow (eds), *Implementing Amsterdam: Immigration and Asylum Rights in EC Law* (2001) 95.

[8] Subject to the rules of international law: see the *Nottebohm* case ICJ Rep 1955 4.

It is the complex process of the letting go of this power to the EC and EU decision making processes and the legal convolutions caused by its uneven and slow transfer that this chapter deals with.

European Community law itself has famously created its own new legal order,[9] which has grown through a series of judicially inspired phases—supremacy, direct effect and associated remedies—to its current, more or less unchallenged status as the semi-constitutional law for all the Member States. This law has traditionally sought a uniform outcome in the Member States, and in fact uniformity has been itself one of the justifications for the supremacy of EC law. The post-Nice position on uniformity is challenged especially by the effects of Title IV of Part Three of the EC Treaty, as we shall see.

Also, naturally there are the legal orders of the Member States, in which many national (municipal) laws are still flourishing. These regulate free movement of persons including rules on nationality and immigration, asylum, extradition and until recently for all Member States' border controls and so on. So already one can see that we have three legal orders introduced, each with its own internal hierarchy of norms. In the Community legal order, the Treaties take precedence, followed by the secondary legal norms, such as regulations, directives and decisions. In the national legal orders, there are fifteen modes of distributing powers and competences. The free movement of persons falls under all these categories of law, hence the jungle-like profusion of rules applicable in the area. This chapter now seeks to outline the position of the EC and EU and the Member States in relation to the free movement of persons.

The evolution of the free movement of persons

In the early days of the EEC, the right to freedom of movement was bestowed on those having the nationality of a Member State who were economically active.[10] Non-EU nationals were subject to national rules as regards entry to the State.[11] The EC policy gradually changed to include all

---

[9] Case 26/62 *Van Gend en Loos* [1963] ECR 1.

[10] Art 39 EC talks of workers whereas Arts 43 and 49 EC specifically refer to nationals of Member States. The non-discrimination rule in Art 12 EC refers to nationals of the Member States.

[11] cf Case C-369/90 *Mario Vicente Micheletti v Delegacion del Gobierno en Cantabria* [1992] ECR I-4165; see also Case C-192/99 *R v Manjit Kaur* [2001] ECR I-1237.

nationals of the Member States whether economically active or not, though with conditions imposed on those who were not economically active.[12]

In 1993, the Maastricht Treaty introduced the notion of European citizenship in Article 17 EC. European citizenship complements that of the Member States and is automatically conferred on all their nationals. The Court of Justice has used the notion of European citizenship to extend the rights of such citizens,[13] which in turn has encouraged the legislator to extend the rights of mobility and residence more widely. The Commission has now proposed a complete reform of the rules for the movement and residence rights of EU citizens and their families.[14] The reform will sweep away the existing two Regulations and nine Directives. Those in work will have residence rights by virtue of a simple Declaration whilst those not in work will for four years need to prove sufficient means and sickness insurance; thereafter they will have a guaranteed right of permanent residence. This reform, if adopted, will considerably simplify EC law in this field, as well as extend the rights of EU citizens.

The EC process of liberalizing mobility for those who were economically active was not confined to nationals of the Member States. It extended to non-EU nationals in some cases. For example, the families of Member State nationals exercising the right of free movement were included, whether of Member State nationality or not, by secondary Community law.[15] Conversely some EU nationals, who had not exercised their free movement rights, were denied the benefits of EC law rights, for example, to family reunification.[16]

---

[12] A series of directives in the 1990s extended the rights of movement more widely but conditionally, those moving needing to be self-sufficient and covered by health insurance. See Council Directive 90/364/EEC of 28 June 1990 on the right of residence [1990] OJ L180/26; Council Directive 90/365/EEC of 28 June 1990 on the right of residence for employees and self-employed persons who have ceased their occupational activity [1990] OJ L180/28; Council Directive 93/96/EEC of 29 October 1993 on the right of residence for students [1993] OJ L317/59.

[13] Case C-184/99 *Rudy Grzelczyk v Centre public d'aide sociale d'Ottignies-Louvain-la-Neuve*, judgment of 20 September 2001. The Court of Justice stated at para 31: 'Union citizenship is destined to be the fundamental status of nationals of the Member States, enabling those who find themselves in the same situation to enjoy the same treatment in law irrespective of their nationality, subject to such exceptions as are expressly provided for.'

[14] Proposal for a European Parliament and Council Directive on the right of citizens of the Union and their family members to move and reside freely within the territory of the Member States, COM(2001) 257 final.

[15] Council Regulation 1612/68/EEC of 15 October 1968 on freedom of movement for workers within the Community [1968] OJ L257/2.

[16] Joined Cases 35 to 36/82 *Morson and Jhanjan v Netherlands* [1982] ECR 3723.

One of the main areas of contention has been in relation to non-EU nationals,[17] often referred to as third country nationals, and controls over migration flows. There are about ten million third country nationals in the EU.[18] They do not, in general,[19] have EC mobility rights[20] and were excluded from the equal treatment principle.[21] The mood has now changed and the Charter of Fundamental Rights[22] (Article 20) has an equal protection clause, though, as yet, no formal legal status as law.[23] The Tampere Council clearly wished to elevate the status of third country nationals.[24] In the view of Kees Groenendijk[25] the provision of secure immigration and residence rights with equal status being granted to long term residents who are nationals of third countries[26] would be more effective than strengthened rules on equality of treatment at securing them a sound status within the EU.[27] This aim could be achieved much more easily if internal frontiers were removed, but this achievement has proved elusive.

The removal of the internal borders was largely completed for the free movement of goods by the great push to achieve the single market launched by Lord Cockfield's White Paper in 1985.[28] However, the reinforcement of the external frontiers of the EC, a necessary pre-condition to removing the internal barriers to the free movement of people, involves harmonizing matters such as police controls that were and still are within the compe-

[17] There is an extensive literature on this. See Hedemann-Robinson (n 5 above) 525 (note 1).

[18] Communication from the Commission to the Council and the European Parliament on immigration and asylum policies, COM(94) 23 final.

[19] Except for EEA nationals.

[20] Nor therefore related rights, such as applications of the rules on mutual recognition of diplomas. See Case C-154/93 *Tawil-Albertini* [1994] ECR I-451.

[21] Art 12 EC. See notably the much criticized Case C-351/95 *Kadiman v Freistaat Bayern* [1997] ECR I-2133 which can be contrasted with Case 267/83 *Aissatou Diatta v Land Berlin* [1985] ECR 567.

[22] Charter of Fundamental Rights adopted at the Nice Summit in December 2000. See chapter by Jacobs in this volume.

[23] The European Court of Human Rights ruled in *Berrehab v The Netherlands* Series A No 138, (1989) 11 EHRR 322 that expulsion of a family member could violate Art 8 ECHR, but not that there is a right to family reunification.

[24] Tampere Council Conclusions 1999, CFSP Presidency Statement: Tampere (16/10/1999), Point 18; Press Nr: 200/1/99. http://ue.eu.int/newsroom/LoadDoc.asp?MAX=1&DOC=!!!&BID= 76&DID=59122&GRP=2017&LANG=1/.

[25] K Groenendijk, 'Security of residence and access to free movement for settled third country nationals under Community law' in Guild and Harlow (n 7 above) 240.

[26] eg proposal for a Council Directive concerning the status of third country nationals who are long-term residents, COM(2001) 127 final, [2001] OJ C E 240/79.

[27] See chapter by Ellis in this volume.

[28] Lord Cockfield's White Paper, COM(85) 310.

tence of the Member States. Moreover, the EC also lacked the internal competence to control immigration, asylum and refugee issues. Some Member States were very reluctant to allow the EC competence in these sensitive areas.

The Single European Act (SEA)

The Single European Act, which came into force in 1986, re-defined the common market as the internal market which Article 14 EC explains is '... an area without internal frontiers in which the free movement of goods, persons, services and capital is ensured in accordance with the provisions of this Treaty...'[29] As Article 14 covers the free movement of persons, the Commission's view was that it extended to third country nationals, since otherwise it would be impossible to remove the internal frontiers.[30] At the signing of the SEA, a Declaration to the effect that the Member States retained control of immigration was adopted. They would work together to promote the free movement of persons by cooperating over the entry, movement and residence of nationals of third countries. This suggests that non-EU nationals are not covered by the provisions of the EC Treaty. Thus it would be in accordance with the EC law to disallow entry to a Member State after checking whether the person involved has entry rights. The Court of Justice effectively decided that this was the case in *Wijsenbeek*,[31] holding that the Treaty rules on the internal market and citizenship were not absolute. Until the Member States adopted rules regarding the external borders of the Community, immigration, the grant of visas, asylum and the exchange of information on those questions, automatic rights would not arise. Member States 'retained the right to carry out identity checks at the internal frontiers of the Community, requiring persons to present a valid identity card or passport... in order to be able to establish whether the person concerned is a national of a Member State, thus having the right to move freely within the territory of the Member States, or a national of a non-member country, not having that right'.[32]

The Schengen regime

The reluctance of some Member States, particularly the UK, to create a full internal market for persons had led a small group of Member States to

[29] A Declaration to the SEA indicated that the 1992 deadline should have no legal effects.
[30] SEC (92) 877 fin; cf White Paper on European Social Policy, COM (94) 35.
[31] Case C-378/97 [1999] ECR I-6207.
[32] ibid para 43.

create a separate Treaty regime, the Schengen Treaty which was launched in 1985[33] and was a creature of international law. Ultimately almost all of the Member States and some non-Member States, namely Iceland and Norway, joined the Schengen area system. Its aims were to create the common external border and flanking measures necessary to control movement of persons at the external frontier of the Schengen area (visas, police measures, asylum and so on), thus allowing the dismantling of the internal frontiers. The Schengen system, eventually amounting to several hundred pages of law, gradually grew at the side of Community law along with the number of participating States. Thus there existed in the late 1980s and early 1990s several regimes for the free movement of persons. The EC Treaty permitted Member States to maintain frontier controls over persons. Most of the Member States had joined the Schengen system and pooled their competence in order to create a common external frontier and remove the internal barriers to free movement of people. Some regional arrangements, notably the Common Travel Area between the UK and Ireland, also continued to exist.[34]

The Maastricht Treaty

The Maastricht Treaty, which came into force in 1993, created the pillar structure, allowing intergovernmental action in the field of Justice and Home Affairs under Title VI (Articles K.1 to K.11), including rules on external borders, immigration, residence and employment of third country nationals. There was not a great deal of progress made on these matters largely because of the requirement of unanimity for decision-making. The Maastricht Treaty did however pave the way for increased discussion of the free movement of persons within the EU framework and it became clear that one aim of most of the Member States of the EU was to remove national boundaries. Most Member States are keen to replace them with a common external frontier[35] as is evident from the Conclu-

---

[33] For a brief introduction see J Lonbay, 'Free movement of persons, recognition of qualifications, and working conditions' (1998) 47 ICLQ 224.

[34] Denmark was a member of the Schengen group primarily because the Nordic free movement regime required it.

[35] This has more or less been achieved in relation to goods. See the Single Market Scoreboard: http://europa.eu.int/comm/internal_market/en/update/score/score9en.pdf/.

sions of several European Council meetings, notably at Vienna[36] and Tampere.[37]

The Amsterdam Treaty

The EU now promotes the aim of creating an area of freedom, security and justice. Under the Treaty of Amsterdam the free movement of persons content of the Justice and Home Affairs pillar of the Maastricht Treaty[38] was sent to Title IV of Part Three of the EC Treaty and cooperation in criminal law matters was added to Title VI TEU. Thus the EU Treaty now provides jurisdiction for the many necessary flanking measures, primarily in the criminal law sphere, though Title VI EU allows for unanimity in decision-making and is outwith the relatively strict disciplines of EC deci-sion-making and judicial control.[39] The Amsterdam Treaty also provided procedures[40] to allow the Schengen acquis[41] to be adopted, more or less wholesale, into Community or Union law. The Schengen Protocol has now been used to locate a legal basis[42] for the Schengen measures under EC and EU law.[43]

The main obstacle to the total removal of internal frontiers for persons and the creation of a common external frontier in relation to the movement of persons is that three of the Member States, the UK, Ireland and Denmark,

[36] Vienna Action Plan on Mobility (1998) [1999] OJ C19/1: http://ue.eu.int/ejn/ data/ vol_a/1_Programmes_de_travail_plans_d_action/13844en. html/.

[37] Tampere Council Conclusions 1999, CFSP Presidency Statement: Tampere (16/10/ 1999)—Press Nr: 200/1/99: http://ue.eu.int/newsroom/LoadDoc.asp?MAX=1&DOC-=!!!&BID= 76 & DID= 59122&GRP=2017&LANG=1/; [1999] OJ C19/9.

[38] E Guild, 'The constitutional consequences of law-making in the third pillar of the European Union' in P Craig and C Harlow (eds), *Law-Making in the European Union* (1988) 65.

[39] Art 35 TEU.

[40] Protocol integrating the Schengen acquis into the framework of the European Union. http://europa.eu.int/eur-lex/en/treaties/livre313.html/.

[41] The Schengen acquis can now be seen at [2000] OJ L239/1.

[42] Council Decision 99/435/EC of 20 May 1999 concerning the definition of the Schen-gen acquis for the purpose of determining, in conformity with the relevant provisions of the Treaty establishing the European Community and the Treaty on European Union, the legal basis for each of the provisions or decisions which constitute the acquis [1999] OJ L176/1; Council Decision 1999/436/EC of 20 May 1999 determining, in conformity with the relevant provisions of the Treaty establishing the European Community and the Treaty on European Union, the legal basis for each of the provisions or decisions which constitute the Schengen acquis [1999] OJ L 176/17.

[43] See PJ Kuijper, 'Some legal problems associated with communitarization of policy on visa, asylum, and immigration under the Amsterdam Treaty and incorporation of the Schengen acquis' (2000) 37 CMLRev 345, 346–350.

could not agree to this transfer of competence to the EC. As a result of the compromises reached during the negotiation of the Amsterdam Treaty,[44] some Member States retain their internal competence as regards frontiers and some do not. The Amsterdam Treaty also threatens some steps backwards. For example, the Maastricht Treaty included visa policy as a matter of EC competence (Article 100c). This has now moved to Title IV EC. The old EC measures will be updated[45] and the UK and Ireland will be able to avoid their application, via their Title IV EC opt-out.[46]

The new Title IV internal competences would normally grant the EC external competences in these matters. However all the Member States agreed, in the 'Protocol on External Relations of the Member States with regard to the Crossing of External Borders', that measures dealing with standards and procedures to be followed by Member States in carrying out checks on persons crossing the external frontiers would not affect 'the competence of Member States to regulate and conclude agreements with third countries as long as they respect Community law and other relevant international agreements'. Clearly the UK, Ireland and Denmark retain their competence in all of the Title IV areas (unless they opt in) and will be able to create parallel agreements as necessary, though subject to Article 10 EC, which requires Member States to facilitate the achievement of the Community's tasks.[47]

The Amsterdam Treaty has created a potentially very difficult position for uniformity of EC law as three Protocols[48] allow for a series of exemptions and opt outs allowing a bifurcation of Community law itself within Title IV EC. Article 1 of the United Kingdom's Article 14 Protocol[49] entitles the United Kingdom, notwithstanding Article 14 EC or any other EC or EU law, 'to exercise at its frontiers with other Member States such controls on persons seeking to enter the United Kingdom as it may consider necessary' to verify and determine entry rights of persons coming to the UK. It continues:

[44] D O'Keeffe, 'Can the leopard change its spots? Visas, immigration and asylum following Amsterdam' in D O'Keeffe and P Twomey (eds), *Legal Issues of the Amsterdam Treaty* (1999) 271.

[45] Proposal for a Council Regulation amending Reg 1683/95 laying down a uniform format for visas, COM(2001) 157 final; [2001] OJ C E 180/310.

[46] Denmark's Protocol requires its participation regarding visas but by Art 5 it is excluded as regards residence permits.

[47] The scope of the general provisions of the Treaty such as Art 10 and others are also arguably affected by the opt-outs dealt with below.

[48] See chapter by Monar in this volume.

[49] Protocol on the application of certain aspects of Art 14 (ex 7a) of the Treaty establishing the European Community to the United Kingdom and to Ireland.

Nothing in Article 14 of the Treaty establishing the European Community or in any other provision of that Treaty or of the Treaty on European Union or in any measure adopted under them shall prejudice the right of the United Kingdom to adopt or exercise any such controls...

This Protocol on Article 14 potentially has a wide-ranging impact. The Commission proposals on freedom of third country nationals to provide cross-border services,[50] for example, are formally based on Article 49 EC.[51] This is a 'normal' EC provision which allows the Council to extend the provisions of the Treaty Chapter on services 'to nationals of a third country who provide services and who are established within the Community'. As we have seen, the Protocol on Article 14 reserves to the UK the power to exercise border controls on persons in order to verify rights of entry and regulate entry of those not having entry rights. Can the UK use this Protocol to opt out of a provision emanating from Article 49 EC which forms part of the acquis communautaire? It is trying to do so, arguing that the opt-outs for Article 14 and Title IV EC would otherwise be undermined.[52] Whilst it would seem most undesirable for such a hole to appear in the singularity of the internal market rules, the Treaty amendment created at Amsterdam explicitly allows the UK to maintain its border controls 'notwithstanding Article 14 EC [or] *any other provision of that Treaty...*' (emphasis added). Article 49 is such a provision. According to the interpretative principle of *lex posterior derogat legi priori*, a later law should normally prevail over an earlier law. That of *lex specialis derogat legi generali* means that the more precise law normally takes priority over a general law. Both principles would seem to favour the UK's view that it should be able to control the entry of third country nationals under such a directive, should it be adopted. The draft directive requires Member States to issue an 'EC service provision card' to third country nationals meeting certain conditions who are established[53] in

---

[50] Amended proposal for a Council Directive extending the freedom to provide cross-border services to third country nationals established within the Community, COM (2000) 271 final, [2000] OJ C E 311/197. Another proposal for a Directive of the European Parliament and of the Council on the posting of workers who are third country nationals for the provision of cross-border services (COM(2000) 271 final, [2000] OJ C E 311/187) was sent at the same time.

[51] There is no formal legal basis in Title IV regarding cross-border service provision for third country nationals. This is probably because Member States thought that Art 49 EC was sufficient.

[52] House of Lords Select Committee on the European Union, 'A Community immigration policy' 13th Report, 2001.

[53] Art 1(3) sets out conditions, for example, that the third country national must be established and have been resident for at least 12 months.

their territory. The third country national, armed with the EC service provision card and a valid passport or ID card, has the right to enter all Member States in order to provide a service provided s/he has a statement from the 'service recipient' confirming the provision of the service and indicating the likely duration of the stay.[54] Clearly this would eliminate the UK's 'cast-iron' guarantee on maintaining its own border controls on admission. Article 49 EC gives the EC the power to adopt the Directive by qualified majority vote so the UK cannot formally block the adoption of the Directive. However, once it is adopted, its legal consequences for the UK would be different than for other Member States and the Protocol would appear to allow the UK to regulate and control actual entry of such third country nationals (including refusal of admission) *despite* EC law on its face giving them a cast-iron right of entry to the UK. This is a major challenge to the legal order. How can it tolerate the law meaning two things depending on where litigation arises, and despite very clear wording of such a provision? Litigation is bound to ensue. This situation has been openly permitted to develop as the next Protocol regarding Title IV measures makes clear.

In the Protocol on the position of the United Kingdom and Ireland, Article 2 states that none of the provisions or measures adopted under of Title IV EC 'shall be binding upon or applicable in the United Kingdom or Ireland; and no such provision, measure or decision shall in any way affect the competences, rights and obligations of those States; and no such provision, measure or decision shall in any way affect the acquis communautaire nor form part of Community law as they apply to the United Kingdom or Ireland.'

This Protocol reinforces the bifurcation of Community law. In mitigation both the UK and Ireland have opted in[55] to much of the Schengen acquis that has fleshed out this area of Community law.[56] The UK will participate in asylum, temporary protection, carrier liability, readmission agreements, mutual recognition of expulsion decisions, and judicial cooperation.[57] It

---

[54] See Art 3.

[55] Under the Protocol they can seek to opt in at the proposal stage (Art 3) or after the decision has been adopted (Art 4). See M Hedemann-Robinson, 'The area of freedom, security and justice with regards to the UK, Ireland and Denmark: the "opt-in opt-outs" under the Treaty of Amsterdam' in D O'Keeffe and P Twomey (eds), *Legal Issues of the Amsterdam Treaty* (1999) 289, 294.

[56] In contrast, the new Member States must accept Title IV EC in full.

[57] Council Dec 2000/365/EC concerning the request of the United Kingdom of Great Britain and Northern Ireland to take part in some of the provisions of the Schengen acquis [2000] OJ L131/43.

will not participate in anything that might compromise its internal frontier controls[58] or on admission policy.[59] However where the UK and Ireland have not opted into Schengen measures, mainly in the area of border control measures, then there will be two versions of EC law, both equally valid but utterly different in substance. The version applicable will depend on where the litigation arises. Moreover case precedents of the Court of Justice will not be universally applicable. These factors comprise a big snake in the jungle ready to catch the unwary and dealing a blow to the uniformity principle that underpins much of the legitimacy of the EC legal order.

The Danish opt-out has a similar effect on EC law, though Denmark remains bound by the ex-Schengen rules as a matter of international law. Thus its implementation measures are not subject to EC law principles of direct effect nor to judicial control by the Court of Justice.

Impacts on decision-making

There are important institutional implications created by the system (sic) chosen for the delivery of decisions regarding the free movement of persons. The split between Title VI TEU and Title IV EC as a legal basis has led to significant consequential decision-making differences, Title VI TEU being inter-governmental in nature. Additionally, within Title IV EC, the European Parliament is marginalized, left only with a consultation role.[60] The Commission is forced to share its precious 'right of initiative' with Member States.[61] The Council will, moreover, have to act with unanimity in most cases.[62] There is also, as we have seen, decision-making that allows participation by non-Member States (Norway

---

[58] This policy was considered to be untenable in the longer term by the House of Lords Select Committee on the European Union: 'Schengen and the UK border controls' (1998–1999, 17th Report, HL 37). That view was repeated in the Select Committee's 13th Report on 'A Community immigration policy': n 52 above, paras 127–131.

[59] 13th Report on 'A Community immigration policy' (n 52 above) para 14.

[60] Under the Nice Treaty the possibility of using Art 251 (co-decision) is permitted in some circumstances and a Declaration (No 5) urges the Council to ensure that co-decision applies to most of the Title IV EC matters from May 2004: cf Art 67(2) EC.

[61] Art 67 EC. Member States have not been slow to utilize their new rights of initiative, see eg the French proposal for a directive on mutual recognition of decisions concerning expulsion of third country nationals, [2000] OJ C253/1 (now adopted: [2001] OJ L149/34); Council Regulation 1091/2001 on freedom of movement with a long stay visa [2001] OJ L150/4, which is also based on a French initiative.

[62] Art 67 EC.

and Iceland) whilst actual Member States are excluded. If a measure under Title IV EC is building on Schengen then the UK and Ireland can opt in, Denmark can adopt it ex post and Norway and Iceland (non-Member States) can shape it in the Mixed Committee.[63] If it is a Title IV EC measure not related to Schengen then Norway and Iceland have no role, nor probably does Denmark. The UK and Ireland could still join in under Article 3 of their Protocol.[64]

The Mixed Committee is a creation of the Agreement[65] between Iceland, Norway and the Council[66] which allows Norway and Iceland to meet at Ministerial, senior official and expert levels with the relevant level EC/EU representatives and COREPER (including any relevant working groups) which are discussing Schengen-related matters. In the Mixed Comittee they can make their views known and argue as they wish for amendments to proposals and so on. Thus, Norway and Iceland are involved in helping to draft the measures,[67] but thereafter it is the Council that adopts any decisions.[68] There Norway and Iceland have no right to be present, yet they must comply with the resulting measures, whatever they may be, or the agreement is terminated.

[63] The topics for such decisions can be found in Council Dec 1999/437/EC of 17 May 1999 on certain arrangements for the application of the Agreement concluded by the Council of the European Union and the Republic of Iceland and the Kingdom of Norway concerning the association of those two States with the implementation, application and development of the Schengen acquis [1999] OJ L176/31.

[64] New proposals indicate this legal basis, eg COM (2001) 303 final (Proposal for a Council Directive on minimum standards for giving temporary protection in the event of a mass influx of displaced persons and on measures promoting a balance of efforts between Member States in receiving such persons and bearing the consequences thereof), 24 May 2000, 12; COM (2001) 181 final (Proposal for a Council Directive laying down minimum standards on the reception of applicants for asylum in Member States) 35, [2001] OJ C213/286, to which the UK intends to opt in. See House of Lords Select Committee on the European Union (2001–2002, 8th Report, HL 49), 'Minimum standards of reception conditions for asylum seekers'. See also paras 6–8 of the preamble to Reg 1091/2001 (n 61 above).

[65] Agreement concluded by the Council of the European Union and the Republic of Iceland and the Kingdom of Norway concerning the latter's association with the implementation, application and development of the Schengen acquis–Final Act [1999] OJ L176/36.

[66] Council Decision 1999/439/EC of 17 May 1999 on the conclusion of the Agreement with the Republic of Iceland and the Kingdom of Norway concerning the latters' association with the implementation, application and development of the Schengen acquis [1999] OJ L176/35.

[67] In drawing up proposals, the Commission must informally seek advice from experts of Iceland and Norway in the same way as it seeks advice from experts of the Member States: Art 6, Agreement with Iceland and Norway concerning the Schengen acquis (n 65 above).

[68] ibid, Art 8.

Conclusions

So we see that EC law currently covers non-EU nationals in some matters but gives priority and additional rights of free movement only to EU citizens. A plethora of proposals[69] will, if adopted, greatly improve the rights of non-EU nationals resident in the Member States.[70] We have also seen that the move to deal with the external aspects of free movement of persons and non-nationals in a uniform manner has been blocked, with difficult repercussions for EC law. The resulting division results in two types of valid EC law with no 'health warning' necessarily apparent.[71] The proposed Directive on the right to family reunification[72] includes rights of family reunification for third country nationals, but also for EC nationals who are non-movers.[73] Presumably the Member States could not bear the thought that non-nationals would have greater rights than EU citizens.[74] However, if adopted, it will not necessarily bind the UK and Ireland. Both countries can opt in (Article 3 Protocol). However if they do not this means that UK nationals, for example, will have fewer rights to family reunification than anyone else. It appears that the UK has chosen not to opt in.[75] This is, of course, the choice of the UK, but it is contrary to the non-discrimination

[69] See Communication from the Commission to the Council and the European Parliament—Biannual update of the scoreboard to review progress on the creation of an area of 'freedom, security and justice' in the European Union (second half of 2001) COM(2001) 628 final. This lists 48 pages of proposals in this area.

[70] Notably proposal for a Council Directive on the conditions of entry and residence of third country nationals for the purpose of paid employment and self-employed economic activities, COM(2001) 386 fin, [2001] OJ E C332/ 248, and the proposal for a Council Directive concerning the status of third country nationals who are long-term residents, COM (2001) 127 fin, [2001] OJ E C240/79, which the UK has declared that it will not opt in to. There is in addition the proposal to equalize access to social security rights for third country nationals [1998] OJ C 6/15.

[71] For example the proposed Directive on the cross-border provision of services by third country nationals. See n 50 above.

[72] Amended proposal for a Council Directive on the right to family reunification (presented by the Commission pursuant to Art 250(2) of the EC Treaty), COM(2000)624, [2001] OJ E C62/99. See generally G Brinkmann, 'Family reunion, third country nationals and the Community's new powers' in Guild and Harlow (n 7 above) 241. Brinkmann points out (at 264) that under the proposal the family members have more rights than the third country national who got a job in the first place (see Arts 8 and 12 of the proposal).

[73] Art 4 of the proposal.

[74] Proposal for a Council Directive on the right to family reunification, COM(1999) 638 final 14.

[75] House of Lords Select Committee on the European Union, 13th Report, para 124 (see n 59 above).

clause in the Charter of Fundamental Rights,[76] and it will mean that lawyers will have to beware. In the past EC law on its face might have created exceptions, but there may be no such overt warnings in these new rules. It will purport to be EC law, which in the past would have had a pan-EC writ. No longer. However the preamble of the EC measure will normally indicate to which Member States it applies,[77] though in its text the final article might well still say: 'This Directive is addressed to the Member States', which is somewhat misleading.[78]

The Court of Justice itself has a weakened jurisdiction under Title IV EC.[79] Fewer national courts are granted the right to refer questions regarding EC law relating to Title IV EC and law and order and internal security are excluded explicitly from its purview.[80] It can now, however, offer interpretative rulings at the request of the Council, the Commission or a Member State.[81]

The Commission now recognizes that the EU needs more non-EU labour.[82] This is in part why it is moving ahead rapidly with a relatively large programme of measures on free movement of persons[83] and opening a full debate on immigration policy.[84] Some of the new measures raise complex legal issues of jurisdiction as a result of the compromises made at Amsterdam, and others are simply confusing to the UK and Ireland as the measures are proposed as though all the Member States will adopt them.

---

[76] Art 20: 'Everyone is equal before the law'. The Charter, as yet, has no binding force.

[77] Council Dir 2001/51/EC of 28 June 2001 supplementing the provisions of Art 26 of the Convention implementing the Schengen Agreement of 14 June 1985, [2001] OJ L187/45, which the UK is joining whilst Ireland is not. Council Dec 2002/192/EC of 28 February 2002 concerning Ireland's request to take part in some of the provisions of the Schengen acquis [2002] OJ L64/20 indicates which parts of Schengen Ireland will adhere to.

[78] It is not clear what will be the outcome in the Directive on the provision of cross-border services for third country nationals. Currently there is a stand-off and the preamble contains no such wording, making it an even more dangerous provision. See n 50 above.

[79] Generally see E Guild and S Peers, 'Deference or defiance? The Court of Justice's jurisdiction over immigration and asylum' in Guild and Harlow (n 7 above) 267; S Peers, 'Who's judging the watchmen? The judicial system of the area of freedom, security and justice' (2000) 18 YEL 337.

[80] Art 68 EC.

[81] Art 68(3) EC.

[82] Communication from the Commission to the Council, 'New European labour markets, open to all, with access for all', COM(2001)116 (28 February 2001). See chapter by Dell'Olio in this volume.

[83] See n 69 above.

[84] Communication from the Commission to the Council and the European Parliament on a Community immigration policy, COM(2000) 757 final.

They are not differentiated by subject matter but rather comprise a complex web of interlocking proposals that are not well cross referred.[85] As the House of Lord Select Committee on the European Union has noted, this raises severe problems for the UK. The UK may like some proposals and yet if they are not complete in themselves, or rely on other proposals which it rejects, it makes it very difficult for the UK (and Ireland) to exercise their right to opt in. This could be the price the Commission and other Member States are exacting for their opt-out.

The status of third country nationals is likely to be considerably improved when the proposals currently on the table are adopted. Their social rights and status will be considerably enhanced. However these gains will not be Community-wide. There will continue to be a considerable lack of unity in the rules in this area due to the opt-outs permitted at Amsterdam. This will be to the detriment of the rights of third country nationals and a properly functioning single market for persons. Thus, the Tampere ambitions of equal treatment for third country nationals legally resident in the EU are unlikely to be realized as some Member States have, and are exercising, the legal power to block their achievement. Moreover, as explained, Community law itself is at risk of becoming so complex and difficult to understand and operate that the legal order itself will be threatened. This risk is considerably exacerbated by the limited role given to the Court of Justice in helping national courts to deal with issues arising under Title IV EC (and Title VI TEU). This detracts considerably from the achievements made in this field over the last few years. It might have been better to let the Schengen regime continue.

---

[85] See House of Lords Select Committee on the European Union, 'The legal status of long term residents' (2001–2002, 5th Report, HL 33), para 53.

26

Managing the EU's New External Border

Judy Batt

Introduction

The revolutions of 1989–91 in central and eastern Europe signalled not only the ideological and practical bankruptcy of the communist system, but also the enormous prestige of the idea of 'Europe' among the peoples of this region: a key slogan encapsulating the meaning of the revolutions was the 'return to Europe'. Paradoxically, this demand was asserted with enthusiasm just at a time when the popular legitimacy of the EU among citizens of its Member States appeared to be in decline. The peoples of central and eastern Europe seemed oblivious to the EU's alleged 'democratic deficit', and untroubled by the implications of supra-national integration for their only recently recovered national sovereignty. In part, this could be attributed to naïve euphoria and lack of knowledge and understanding of the practical meaning of 'returning to Europe', in the sense of joining the EU. Nevertheless, the peoples of central and eastern Europe were not to be persuaded by west European attempts to deflect their aspirations for early membership in either the EU or NATO. The arguments for delay were weakened not only by their unmistakable taint of cynical self-interest on the part of some existing Member States, and by the fact that other west European non-Member States such as Austria, Sweden and Finland were now also abandoning neutrality in favour of EU membership. They also betrayed an underlying failure to appreciate the depth and seriousness of the central and eastern Europe's commitment to the European project.

This commitment arises from the specific history and enduring geopolitical predicament of this region, comprising a set of relatively small states, formed out of the collapse of the Habsburg, Russian and Ottoman empires in the early twentieth century, thereafter chronically vulnerable both to external pressure from larger, revisionist and imperialist neighbours to the west and east, and to internal instability due to ethnic divisions and socio-economic backwardness. Throwing off the Soviet yoke and embarking on the 'transition to democracy' did not automatically lead to a stable, durable order in the region. The break-up, in rapid succession, of the Yugoslav, Soviet and Czechoslovak multinational federations, and the widespread reappearance of tensions between national majorities and minorities, all pointed to the danger of fragmentation and conflict. The idea that the enormous task of economic transformation could rapidly and successfully be achieved without full access to the key markets of western Europe was equally unconvincing. Notwithstanding the long-term success of Germany's containment within EU and NATO structures, and the rapid demise of the Soviet/Russian threat after 1991, a pervasive sense of insecurity continued to afflict the region in the face of the multiple challenges of post-communist reconstruction.

In this context, 'Europe' connoted a comprehensive vision linking external security with internal stability: following the model of Franco–German reconciliation, an overarching framework of supra-national integration would provide the conditions for the states of central and eastern Europe to proceed to build for themselves a better way of life in terms of material prosperity, democratic government, and inter-ethnic harmony. The notion that the small, weak and impoverished central and eastern European states could be left to do this by themselves appeared not only unrealistic, but a betrayal of the very purposes that the 'founding fathers' of European integration had intended. After 1989, the division of Europe was supposed to have ended, and the 'hour of Europe' was proclaimed to have arrived. The legitimacy of the EU itself was now bound up with its effective execution of wider responsibilities for the stability and security of the whole continent. For the central and eastern European states, it was self-evident that EU enlargement was the key means to securing those objectives.

This reaffirmation of the core purposes of the EU found much sympathy, particularly among foreign policy élites within the Commission and the Member States, and eventually, by the time of the Copenhagen Council in 1993, the Member States recognized that enlargement could not be denied. Nevertheless problems remained. West European public opinion was far less receptive to grand strategic visions of Europe, and continued to evaluate the EU largely in terms of its success in promoting socio-economic prosperity. While there was much broad sympathy for the central and eastern Europeans' aspirations to EU membership, the first de facto enlargement—German unification—delivered a shock to expectations of continued growth, and had a sobering impact on popular attitudes towards further eastward expansion, as the possible costs began to be taken into account. But the suggestion that enlargement should be restricted only to the more prosperous of the central and eastern European states confirmed the image of the EU as a narrowly self-interested 'rich man's club', unwilling and incapable of rising to the wider challenges of building a new, pan-European order.

This unfortunate tendency was strengthened, moreover, by the fact that, as an inescapable concomitant of deepening EU integration, barriers to entry for new members were continually rising. The distinction between 'insiders' and 'outsiders' was becoming more, not less, salient by the day as the acquis communautaire expanded. If the EU were to enlarge, it would have to be in stages, subject to conditions that would ensure the new Member States were fully compatible and capable of taking on the whole acquis (by now some 80,000 pages long), so as to minimize disruption to the progress of deepening integration. The development of the Single Market and currency union meant that the significance of borders between Member States progressively declined. But the external border would still retain paramount importance in defining and defending the emerging 'Area of Freedom, Security and Justice'. The clear implication was that eastward enlargement would by no means automatically do away with division in Europe, but would replicate it in a new form at some point further to the east—that is, between central and eastern European states themselves. The impact of this on both prospective new Member States and states in central and eastern Europe that would find themselves (temporarily or for the long term) on the 'wrong side' of the new external border raises questions about the promise of enlargement as a means of 'spreading stability' throughout Europe.

The impact of open borders in central and eastern Europe since 1989

It is worth reiterating a general point that is often overlooked by western policy-makers and politicians: the right to hold a passport and to use it to move freely across borders is, from the point of view of most 'ordinary citizens' of central and eastern Europe, probably the most significant positive achievement of the revolutions of 1989–91. Under communism, obtaining a passport involved lengthy, complex and humiliating procedures, including securing testimonials of 'political reliability' from employers and local authorities, and often unpleasant negotiations with the police issuing authorities. Passports had to be surrendered on return from abroad, and the whole process repeated for each projected journey. Separate procedures were applied and different types of documents issued for travel to 'fraternal countries' of the Soviet bloc and to western countries. Surprisingly, for citizens of the more 'liberal', open states like Poland and Hungary, travel to the west could actually be easier than travel into the Soviet Union. This was due in large part to acute Soviet sensitivities about political control in the western border regions of the Soviet Republics of Belarus and Ukraine, extensive territories of which had been annexed from the neighbouring central and eastern European states in the course of World War II. Despite post-war population transfers, ethnic minorities of, for example, Poles, Hungarians and Slovaks could still be found in western Soviet borderland regions, where they lived under constant suspicion of 'disloyalty' to their new Soviet homeland—notwithstanding the fact that their 'mother countries' in central and eastern Europe were now supposedly 'fraternal allies' tightly integrated in the Soviet bloc. Minorities of Belarussians, Lithuanians, Ukrainians (including the Rusyns, an ethnic group forcibly suppressed in the Soviet Union by Stalin and merged into the Ukrainian nation) living as citizens of the central and eastern European states were equally suspect as a conduit for unorthodox ideas into the Soviet Union, and their possibilities of maintaining contacts with family members across the border were tightly circumscribed. Minority language education and culture were at first wholly abolished, then later allowed limited revival only under the closest political surveillance. History teaching, in addition to the standard Marxist–Leninist scheme, was here also heavily charged with the perpetuation of negative ethno-national stereotypes and memories of bitter ethnic conflict before and during World War II, in order to reinforce mutual hostility and thus justify the enforced post-war division. Between non-Soviet states of central and eastern Europe, moreover, lingering territorial insecurities (for example, between the GDR and Poland) and ethnic issues (notably, between Hungary and Romania) often led communist authorities to place obstacles in the way of their citizens' ease of travel. At times of regime crisis, for example in 1956 in Hungary, 1968 in Czechoslovakia and 1980–81 in Poland, 'fraternal' neighbours within the socialist bloc would usually close the borders completely. Cross-border contacts of even the most modest kind were thus seen by the communist authorities as fraught with danger, and only undertaken with no little apprehension by borderland residents themselves.

Opinion polls conducted in the declining years of the communist regime in the more open states like Poland and Hungary regularly indicated that the one thing that most irked ordinary people was their lack of freedom to travel. Indeed, the right to move freely seems to have been at the very heart of central and eastern European citizens' understanding of what it meant to be 'free', and it has retained this place in the post-communist period. After all, since 1989, the experience of 'freedom' in the neo-liberal sense of the free market has been at best a mixed blessing from the point of view of the vast majority of central and eastern European workers and consumers. Disillusion with 'freedom' as realized in practice under the new democratic governments in central and eastern Europe (although not, by and large, with the principle of democracy itself) set in with depressing rapidity after the first free elections. But 'freedom' as the opportunity to travel has expanded greatly, and is widely appreciated. For example, between 1990 and 1997, the numbers crossing Poland's eastern border grew almost three times, from 10.9 million to 29.5 million, nearly 16 million of the latter figure being between Poland and Ukraine. The vast majority of these crossing are made westwards, by Ukrainians travelling to Poland, turning Poland into one of the world's top ten 'tourist destinations' in 1997![1]

In fact, most of this 'tourism' is a cover for massive unregistered economic activity undertaken on a small scale by very large numbers of individuals, crossing the border daily, weekly, or for short-term stays abroad in order to survive, their livelihoods having been decimated by the collapse of the communist system and the subsequent hesitant and inconsistent economic 'transition' in the states formed out of the former Soviet Union. Regions along the former Soviet western border were particularly vulnerable, im-poverished rural areas that had been neglected for years. Cities are few and far between in this region, and those that exist were, by the end of the communist period, in a dilapidated, decaying condition. The transport and communications infrastructure that once linked these regions with western neighbours had been allowed to rot. Many bridges destroyed in the war, for example over the river Bug that forms the Polish–Ukrainian border, were never rebuilt. Yet these regions also remained blighted by their distance from their new capitals in the Soviet republics: as locals in the western Ukrainian region of Transcarpathia (annexed to Soviet Ukraine from

[1] See K Wolczuk and R Wolczuk, *Poland and Ukraine. A Strategic Partnership in a Changing Europe?* (2002).

Czechoslovakia at the end of the war) put it, 'Transcarpathia is as far from Kiev as it is from God!' In the Soviet period, about one-third of the working age population of that region had to leave to find work elsewhere in Ukraine or Russia. After the break-up of the Soviet Union, and especially after the Russian financial collapse of 1998 (which also brought the fragile Ukrainian economy down with it), most of these people transferred their sights westwards to the buoyant Polish and Hungarian economies, where demand for cheap unregistered labour was high, particularly for building sites in the major cities and seasonal work in agriculture.

The opening of the border created huge opportunities for what became known as 'ants'—informal and spontaneous armies of individuals regularly crossing the border with a suitcase or two of goods to trade, exploiting price differentials and filling gaps in poorly-supplied, erratic local markets. A flourishing network of bazaars sprang up in the border regions, and, on the western side, new shopping centres developed to cater for the needs of eastern visitors. The range of goods traded goes well beyond smuggled alcohol and tobacco. Local observations of shopping centres on the Hungarian side of the Hungarian–Romanian border indicate that these provide Romanian customers with daily necessities like sugar and milk. The large quantities purchased also suggest that the customers are often firms rather than individuals.[2] By the second half of the 1990s, more than half of the consumer goods (including foodstuffs, furniture, household goods, home improvement products, clothing and footwear) sold in western Ukraine came from Poland. A study by the UK Department for International Development estimated that informal cross-border trade conducted out of Lviv region in western Ukraine approximately equalled the region's officially-registered trade with Poland. Despite the negative aspects of this, in terms of lost revenue to state treasuries, the benefits of such trade for the border regions and their inhabitants are obvious. It is estimated that about 240,000 people live by bazaar trade across the Polish–Ukrainian border, about three-quarters of whom have no other source of income.[3] For many individuals, occasional trips can help top up incomes that otherwise would fall below subsistence level. For example, in 2000, this author was told that a Transcarpathian schoolteacher could double his or her monthly official salary of about $20 by crossing into Hungary twice with a tank full of petrol to sell on

---

[2] See G Hunya and A Telegdi, 'Hungarian-Romanian cross-border economic cooperation' (*Countdown* project of the Vienna Institute for International Economic Studies (WIIW), 2001). Online at: http://eu-enlargement.org/discuss/default.asp?topic=research/.

[3] See Wolczuk and Wolczuk (n 1 above).

to a Hungarian motorist. On the western side of the border, towns that might otherwise be languishing in peripheral decline are able to sustain above-average growth through cross-border trade, and thus to some extent offset the growing west–east regional disparities that have become evident in central and eastern European states neighbouring the EU. For example, about 30 to 40 per cent of small and medium sized enterprises in the Polish eastern city of Lublin are estimated to survive by commerce with Ukraine, and the total net surplus gained by Poland from this 'grey' trade across the border with Ukraine has been estimated at about $1.5 billion a year.[4]

Burgeoning cross-border traffic has brought new contacts between individuals and ethnic groups, and stimulated a revival not only of minority identities, but also regional identities. Sometimes this has been an uncomfortable process, but potential tensions have been mitigated by growing local appreciation of the practical advantages of the open border. For example, the city of Przemysl in south-eastern Poland, whose large Ukrainian minority population had been forcibly dispersed by the Polish communist authorities after the war, found it hard to come to terms with the new appearance of large numbers of Ukrainian visitors in the 1990s, and the corresponding rise in the use of Ukrainian in public.[5] When the tiny remaining local Ukrainian minority raised demands for restitution of their Greek-Catholic church (transferred to the Catholic Church after the dispersal of the Ukrainians), and for the restoration of the city's long-neglected Ukrainian cemetery (where Ukrainians who had died fighting Poles during the war were buried), this new assertiveness evoked fears among local Poles that the 'Polishness' of the region would be brought into question. But over time, local Poles came to appreciate the economic benefits to be gained from increasing cross-border contact with Ukrainians, as new shops, roads and tourist facilities were built to meet the Ukrainian visitors' needs. The region became an enthusiastic supporter of the Polish government's efforts to develop strong links with Ukraine, and found a new mission for itself as 'Europe's gateway to Ukraine'.

In Transcarpathia, the new opening to the west prompted a revival of the Rusyn identity among the majority Ukrainian population of the region. This

---

[4] House of Lords Select Committee on the EU, 'Enlargement and EU External Frontier Controls' (2000), 16.

[5] See K Wolczuk, 'Polish–Ukrainian borderlands: the case of Lviv and Przemysl' in K Krzystofek and A Sadowski (eds), *Ethnic Borderlands in Europe: Harmony or Conflict?* (2001) 213; M Kisielowska-Lipman, 'Political transition in Poland's eastern borderlands: the "Ethnic Question"' in J Batt and K Wolczuk (eds), *Region, State and Identity in Central and Eastern Europe* (2002).

people had been officially abolished as a national group by Stalin, and were declared Ukrainian. Their Greek-Catholic churches were transferred to the Russian Orthodox ownership. In the late 1980s, alongside the Ukrainian national revival, an attempt was made to revive the Rusyn identity as distinct from Ukrainian, and contacts began to be made with fellow Rusyns in neighbouring Poland, Slovakia and Hungary. The attempt was firmly squelched by the new Ukrainian authorities, fearing separatist tendencies. In the meanwhile, Rusyns have made common cause with Transcarpathia's minorities of Hungarians, Slovaks, Germans, Roma and others in seeking greater administrative decentralization, amounting to a special autonomous status for the region, that, they hope, might enable it to act as Ukraine's 'gateway to Europe'. Given the parlous state of the local economy, this seems, for the present, a forlorn hope. Nevertheless, what is significant is the way in which this newly embraced mission has united a complex multi-ethnic population behind a regional identity centred on openness to the west.[6]

Banat in south-west Romania is another multi-ethnic border region that, like Transcarpathia, has successfully maintained ethnic peace through the transition period.[7] Its population is overwhelmingly Romanian, but they take pride in the region's 'multicultural' and 'central European' heritage, visibly on display in the regional capital of Timisoara, a gem of Habsburg high baroque architecture that styles itself 'Little Vienna'. Relations between the Romanian majority and the local ethnic minorities here are very good. In contrast to Transcarpathia, Banat is economically more advanced than the rest of the state, and thus readier to take advantage of both economic transformation and new opportunities for cross-border economic cooperation. Banaters reject the Romanian nationalism that has dominated politics in Bucharest for much of the post-1989 period, and are dismayed at the ineptitude and corruption of the national political élites, whom they largely blame for Romania's lagging position in EU accession. The shared regional identity has fostered the sense of mission as Romania's 'gateway to Europe', leading the way in economic reform, pluralist democratization and toleration.

The borderland regions between central and eastern Europe and the former Soviet Union have all embraced the idea of 'Euroregions', modelled

---

[6] See J Batt, 'Transcarpathia: peripheral region at the "Centre of Europe"' in Batt and Wolczuk (n 5 above).

[7] See J Batt, 'Reinventing Banat' in Batt and Wolczuk (n 5 above).

on west European practice, as a vital means of developing cross-border economic, political and cultural cooperation. Several of these have been set up, covering the full span of the borders from north to south. They have all, however, faced problems of lack of support from national capitals, lack of resources, inexperienced and inefficient regional administrations within over-centralized states, inadequate transport infrastructure, etc. The Duna-Maros-Koros-Tisza Euroregion, uniting counties in south-east Hungary, south-west Romania and Yugoslav Vojvodina, has also been paralysed by the embargo on Milosevic's Yugoslavia and the 1999 NATO bombing. And yet these Euroregions could provide the framework for stability and prosperity across the EU external border. Flourishing Euroregions could avert the danger of economic impoverishment in the borderlands, with the associated implications of rising criminality, emigration pressures, etc. They could also support the achievements of the borderlands in multi-ethnic coexistence, and help to realise these regions' aspirations to act as 'gateways to Europe' for their more sluggish national hinterlands.

The eastern borderlands have thus achieved much since 1989, largely by their own efforts, often in the face of unhelpful policies and nationalist rhetoric emanating from state capitals, and have managed this, moreover, in an international context of heightened uncertainty when the meanings of borders were being redefined across Europe (German unification; disintegration of USSR, Czechoslovakia, Yugoslavia). The formation of several new states, with uncertain or contested national identities, undefined relations with their neighbours, and of course the wars in Yugoslavia, further added to the sense of insecurity. The sudden opening up of previously closed or tightly restricted borders between the former Soviet Union and the central and eastern European countries offered not only opportunities but challenges to the stability of borderland regions. Yet we find they have managed to establish new bases of internal stability and to promote cross-border contacts 'from below'. The EU's external border and visa regimes are now viewed in the eastern borderlands with dismay.

EU enlargement: the implications of 'Schengen'

With the first wave of EU eastward enlargement expected to take place in 2004, the eastern borders of Poland, Hungary and (assuming it manages to join at the same time) Slovakia will become the new external borders of the EU. The accession Candidates (unlike existing Member States such as the

UK) do not have the right to 'opt out' of the Schengen acquis, which was incorporated into the EU framework at Amsterdam and as such is now a non-negotiable obligation for all future EU members. This acquis is based on the 1985 Schengen Agreement and the 1990 Convention, together with all the decisions and rules adopted thereafter by the Executive Committee of Schengen. The aim is to create an area of free movement within the EU by removing controls at the common borders of the participating states. In compensation, controls are to be strengthened at the external borders, where a Member State neighbours with a non-Member State. Thus while EU-Europe moves towards increasingly 'soft', permeable internal borders, the external border will retain all the traditional functions of a 'hard' state border. It is here that the key functions of customs and immigration control and security are to continue to be carried out. This is accompanied by an array of 'flanking' measures designed to enhance security in the Schengen area, including strict control of the external frontier according to common rules (contained in the Schengen Manual for the External Frontier); the exchange of information on prohibited immigrants, wanted persons, stolen vehicles etc; enhanced police cooperation between participating states; measures promoting judicial cooperation; and movement towards a common visa, asylum and immigration policy.[8]

Implementing this system at the new external frontier after the first wave of enlargement will obviously have an enormous impact, and one that is potentially highly detrimental to the border regions and to the states that find themselves excluded—temporarily or for the indefinite future—from enlargement. What had become, since the fall of communism, a relatively soft border, will once again become hard. The impact is likely to be all the more severe due to the increasing preoccupation of existing Member States with the perceived threats of organized crime, illegal migration, and more recently terrorism emanating from the east, against which even tighter controls are often advocated. The practical as well as the symbolic and psychological significance of this for the peoples of the eastern borderlands and the 'outsider' states could amount to a 'New Iron Curtain'.

The most immediate effect will be the implementation of the EU's common visa regime. Travel between, say, Poland and Ukraine, and Hungary and Yugoslavia, has been visa free, but upon accession, Poland and Hungary will be required to enforce visas. This will unavoidably lead to a dramatic decline in the numbers of individuals travelling in from the

---

[8] See M Anderson and E Bort, *The Frontiers of the European Union* (2001).

neighbouring countries, insofar as the administrative infrastructure to process visa requests at the current level of traffic simply does not exist, and the costs of expanding it to meet demand at this level would be prohibitive for the new Member States. Without a network of new consular posts in the western regions of non-Member States, applicants will have to travel to the state capitals to obtain visas. What this means is not often appreciated by western policy-makers: for example, Kiev is an eighteen-hour train journey from Transcarpathia. Although multiple-entry visas are not ruled out by the common visa regime, these have not hitherto been widely granted. A special regime for residents of border regions could be envisaged, but this would have its own drawbacks: given the likely intense interest of citizens of non-Member States in maintaining their access to western neighbours, any system could be open to abuse, and, moreover, would not necessarily be welcomed by governments of these states, ever anxious about centrifugalism in their western regions.[9]

The border itself will need substantial investment in order to satisfy Schengen standards of efficiency and control. This has been going on for some years with support from EU PHARE technical assistance funds. Much more will be required. It is not impossible that such investment will bring improvements from the point of view of ordinary travellers. There are far too few border crossings in the east, and lengthy delays (at busy times, lasting several days) have long been the norm. Modernized infrastructure and more crossing-points could speed things up, which, together with better training of border guards and customs officials, could reduce the incidence of corruption and arbitrariness frequently reported by travellers.

The question remains, however, whether the costs of attempting to implement the Schengen regime as hitherto operated may not be too high, not only in immediate financial terms, but in terms of the EU's broader strategic objective of 'spreading stability eastwards' by enlargement. The effectiveness of border controls and visas in countering perceived threats of organized crime and illegal migration is widely questioned. Meanwhile, the prospect of the Schengen border has already had an unsettling effect on Polish–Ukrainian relations, shaking the trust that had been carefully built up between the two states in a 'strategic partnership' which sought to overcome painful historical legacies in mutual relations by working together

---

[9] For an imaginative review of possible options for adjusting the visa regime to the realities of the EU's future eastern border, see the report produced for the Stefan Batory Foundation in Warsaw, *The Half-Open Door: the Eastern Border of the Enlarged European Union* (2001).

towards Ukraine's inclusion into European integration. The relationship with Ukraine has become a pivot of Poland's foreign policy, and is recognized as a priority right across the political spectrum. The stability of Ukraine, its independence from Russia and eventual integration into the west are defined as vital national interests in Poland, and Polish élites can be expected to continue to press the case for a more positive and energetic EU commitment to Ukraine after Poland's accession.

The destabilizing ramifications of the Schengen regime for Hungary's relations with its neighbours became obvious in 2001, when the Hungarian parliament passed the so-called 'Status Law', offering ethnic Hungarians in countries that will not join the EU at the same time as Hungary special privileges in Hungary (including access to education, health care and the labour market). The law was justified as a means of persuading Hungarian minorities not to emigrate en masse to Hungary in the face of the imposition of the Schengen border and visa regimes, but it caused a political furore in Romania, Slovakia and Yugoslavia, where it was widely interpreted as institutionalizing ethnic discrimination against their non-Hungarian citizens and as an infringement of international law in extending its remit to the territory of those states.[10]

Potentially even more destabilizing could be the impact of Hungary's implementation of the Schengen regime on its southern border with Yugoslavia. Travel between these two states was fairly easy during the communist period, even though Yugoslavia was not a member of the Soviet bloc. Moreover, Hungary kept the border open all through the decade of war in Yugoslavia and western embargo, making Hungary one of the very few countries to which Yugoslavs continued to have unimpeded access in order to remind themselves what 'normal' life felt like. Despite the ousting of Milosevic in autumn 2000, Yugoslavia's return to a democratic and western-oriented course remains extremely precarious. A considerable amount of popular mistrust, if not outright hostility, to the west, the EU and NATO remains to be overcome. The imposition of the Schengen regime by Hungary upon its accession to the EU cannot fail to be highly damaging, not only to Hungarian–Yugoslav relations, but also to the objectives of the EU's Stability Pact in the Balkans.

---

[10] For a comprehensive analysis of the issues, see B Fowler, 'Fuzzing citizenship, nationalising political space: a framework for interpreting the Hungarian "status law" as a new form of kin-state policy in Central and Eastern Europe' (Sussex European Institute, University of Sussex, One Europe or Several Programme, Working Paper 40/02 2002) and the *Venice Commission Report on the Preferential Treatment of National Minorities by their Kin-States* (2001).

The arrival of the new EU external border and visa regimes could also have a destabilizing effect within the states left out of the first wave of enlargement. It seems likely to disrupt the cross-border economic interdependencies that have build up between border regions over the past decade. While inwards foreign investment may be expected to take advantage of relatively cheap labour and proximity to EU markets, in the short term, many individuals and small firms will face acute economic insecurity. If temporary cross-border commuting for employment and ethnic minorities' access to kin-states to the west become markedly more difficult, then mass emigration seems likely to result, precisely the opposite effect to the aims of EU policy. Border regions, faced with renewed peripheralization, may direct their frustration more aggressively against the policies of state capitals, leading to intensified centre-periphery tensions. The new Member States themselves are likely to face demands for additional support from their eastern regions if cross-border trade and economic cooperation decline significantly. The potential negative impact of EU enlargement on the eastern borderlands also raises questions about the workability of the border and visa regimes themselves in an environment of impoverishment and instability, which would not be conducive to building local 'administrative capacity', fighting corruption and criminalization.

Policy implications for the EU

While some technical fixes may help to smooth the implementation of the Schengen regime at the border, there is little sign of readiness for flexibility on the part of existing Member States. Instead, applicant countries are being asked to implement the Schengen regime in full as a precondition of membership, although it is far from clear what this actually means. In fact, the Schengen Information System was designed to allow for connections to only 18 countries, and an upgraded 'SIS 2' capable of extension to all the prospective new Member States will not be ready until 2005. In practice, accession to the Schengen group of countries has been a two-stage process: applicants have signed up to the terms of membership, but controls on their internal borders with existing members have only been lifted after several years (seven in the case of Italy and Greece) of close monitoring and inspection of their external border regime by the existing members to ensure that it fully satisfies their requirements. Thus while a 'transition period' is possible, so that new Member States could be admitted to the EU before being fully 'Schengen compatible', precisely what would be enough to satisfy the conditions for EU accession remains unclear.[11]

Moreover, this raises the prospect of a protracted period after enlargement during which the new Member States would not be fully incorporated into the operational parts of the Schengen system and controls would be maintained on their internal frontiers with the old Member States. This could provoke political tensions within the enlarged EU, as public opinion in the new Member States would read this as 'second class' membership, and governments of those states might be excluded from a full say in the future development of the Schengen regime in which they have a vital interest.

Moreover, the excessive focus on border controls diverts attention from the need to build cooperative relations with the EU's new eastern neighbours. Effective management of the border depends on relations of trust and partnership between EU Member States and the eastern neighbours, and long-term commitment to work together on shared problems. The framework for building such relations needs to be provided by a more coherent and broadly-conceived strategy on the part of the EU for active engagement with the eastern neighbours, recognising the profound impact of both enlargement and deepening integration on them: a 'proximity policy', as suggested by one of the Commission's working groups preparing the White Paper on Governance:

The Union's proximity policy is not a question of 'external' policy, in the traditional sense, but brings into play most of the 'domestic' policies of the Union, as neighbouring countries either prepare for full membership, or deepen their political and economic integration by taking on different aspects of the Union's policies such as customs union, single market, cooperation in the fight against crime.[12]

Part of such a policy would also include a more realistic immigration policy based on acknowledgement of the mutual benefits to be gained by a properly regulated increase in access to EU labour markets for workers from neighbouring states. Immigration into the EU has been allowed at only about half the US rate of immigration in the past two decades, but demand for labour is clear in many sectors, and has been a major 'pull factor' in stimulating unregulated, illegal immigration, and the highly undesirable phenomenon of organized trafficking in human beings. Attempting to resist

---

[11] See House of Lords Select Committee (n 4 above) 18.
[12] *Policies for an Enlarged Union* (2001) 23.

this simply by tighter border controls only has the effect of driving up the price, and thus the profits, of this criminal trade.[13] While fears of a 'brain drain' out of the poorer eastern neighbours have been articulated, we also need to remember that the experience of temporary work in the west can be a valuable means of transferring know-how that can be applied to the benefit of sender countries when migrant workers return home.

A further component of an enhanced EU proximity policy would be support for socio-economic development in the neighbouring countries, including a strong emphasis on regional development at the border. A coordinated and generously-funded programme for promoting 'Euroregions' along the new external border, possibly under a dedicated Task Force in the Commission, would integrate cross-border components of PHARE and TACIS technical assistance funds and the Stability Pact, and focus the activities of the Directorates General for Enlargement, External Relations, Justice and Home Affairs, Regions, and others. This could be complemented by a more visible, permanent representation of the EU in the borderland regions as a point of direct contact with local authorities and individual citizens, with the dual function of improving communications with them (for example, offering advice and assistance in preparing projects), and enhancing understanding and awareness among EU policy-makers of the conditions and needs of the borderland regions. This might also play a far from insignificant symbolic role, countering the impression that the EU is solely interested in strengthening the exclusionary function of the external border, and signalling appreciation of the aspirations of the border regions to act as 'gateways' to the EU, conduits for the 'Europeanization' of the eastern neighbours.

---

[13] See G Amato and J Batt, *Final Report of the Reflection Group on the Long-Term Implications of EU Enlargement: the Nature of the New Border* (1999), 57.

27

Immigration after Nice: From 'Zero Immigration' to Market Necessity

Fiorella Dell'Olio

Introduction

The idea of building a secure space in Europe has been at the centre of the integration process for decades. Immigration and asylum have been increasingly presented, in particular during the last twenty years, as a danger to both the public order and labour market stability. Immigration, therefore, becomes a security question in that discussions about security within the area of migration are often presented as an inevitable policy response to the problem of public order.[1] According to this view, the perception of a security problem triggers a response, which is to say that evidence of a problem precedes any reaction in terms of policy.[2]

In a democratic regime, the idea of security is partly predicated on the idea of justice. In turn, 'justice' is a complex and contested concept, ranging over such issues as the rule of law, fundamental rights, fairness and questions of (re)distribution. The fair administration of justice is one of the means by which a political system gains legitimacy. The principle of justice therefore must be central in the policy-making process. Since the normative and prescriptive tradition in relation to justice has always been preoccupied with the problem of legitimacy as an empirical and behavioural concept, the EU needs to accommodate the attendant exigencies through its policy-making practices. With respect to immigration and asylum, the effort to

---

[1] V Guiraudon, 'European integration and migration policy: vertical policy-making as venue shopping' (2000) 38 JCMS 251; J Huysmans, 'The European Union and the securitization of migration' (2000) 38 JCMS 751; D Kostakopoulou, 'The "protective Union": change and continuity in migration law and policy in post-Amsterdam Europe' (2000) 38 JCMS 497.

[2] Huysmans (n 1 above) 757.

build a secure space serves this purpose. This is why immigration has been placed within the policy area of justice, freedom, and home affairs. The resolution of the immigration issue can be seen, inter alia, as means by which to increase the legitimacy of the EU. The period after the Nice Summit is decisive, and summit resolutions must be seen to be effective if the conclusions put forward at the Tampere Summit in 1999 are to be more prescriptive than indicative.[3]

After Amsterdam, Tampere and Nice, both official debate and legislative measures on immigration and asylum are shifting away from a 'zero immigration policy' to a more open approach from which the EU could benefit. It is becoming increasingly clear that a 'zero immigration policy' is no longer appropriate for Europe. A joint British, French, and German paper, prepared for the Tampere Summit, concluded that the EU was close to developing minimum standards for the procedure of granting the status of refugee, to guarantee the quality of the decision taken, the rights of asylum seekers and the rapid return of failed asylum seekers.[4] Importantly, the paper also stated that zero immigration and the return of legally resident foreigners must be rejected. Total freedom of residence for foreigners, by the same token, must also be rejected as equally unrealistic.[5] Statements of this kind are, however, never satisfactory for the public and there needs to be a 'just' set of principles that permits the maintenance of an open doors policy for eligible foreign populations, while ensuring that Europe remains a secure space. The question, then, concerns the maintenance of security in a space that allows for some sort of immigration flow.

This essay argues that European policy-making in the field of immigration is not abandoning its focus on security but that the principle of justice is increasingly based on a different rationale in which the logic of the market plays an ever more important role.[6] This means that moving from a 'zero

---

[3] The Schengen effort to harmonize immigration policies moved ahead during the Tampere European Council (15–16 October 1999), where EU leaders agreed on a 10-point plan to crack down on organized crime, create a common procedure and status for refugees, strengthen citizen's access to justice across borders and boost the rights of long-term residents from non-EU countries. See EU Bulletin 10-1999, Justice and Home Affairs Cooperation, 2/8, 3/8.

[4] There nevertheless remain many differences between EU Member States. Germany, eg, does not grant asylum to victims of non-state oppression from organizations such as militias or ethnic groups.

[5] 'EU: Tampere Summit' (1999) 6 Migration News 11.

[6] The chapter deals mainly with the problem of immigration rather than asylum, though immigration and asylum are often treated together at the EU level, and as a consequence the term immigration used in an EU context often refers also to asylum.

immigration policy' to a policy of market necessity also demands the elimination, or at least reduction, of the negative connotations typically attached to the idea of immigration in terms of security to something more positive. The essay considers the EU's new approach towards immigration, the extent to which it provides a basis for increasing legitimacy, and the problems that underlie the new approach.

Demographic and economic context: the short-term strategy

Economic migration into Western Europe has been said to be close to zero since the 1970s.[7] This is because zero immigration policies have thus far allowed for entries based on: (1) humanitarian reasons and (2) family reunion. Many economic migrants, therefore, have been driven either to seek entry through asylum procedures or to enter illegally as a last resort. Given the economic opportunities now available in the EU, however, this analysis seems no longer appropriate. Policy makers have started to recognize that zero immigration policies do not take into consideration labour market needs and thus play into the hands of well-organized traffickers and unscrupulous employers. Europol estimates that hundreds of thousands of migrants are smuggled each year into Europe; many of these are either employed as undeclared workers or suffer dire consequences.[8] This was certainly the case for the 58 illegal Chinese immigrants who suffocated to death in the back of a container lorry at Dover. While procedures are already in place at the EU level to coordinate policies in a number of areas to facilitate the operation of the Single Market, sufficient attention has been given neither to the role of third country nationals in the EU labour market nor to the need for accompanying measures in support of the integration of existing and prospective migrants.

There are demographic trends in the EU that are particularly striking:

(1) decreased population growth; and
(2) a marked rise in the average age of the population.

---

[7] N Hopkinsons, 'Migration into Western Europe' in report based on Wilton Park conference on 'Political refugees and economic migrants from South and East and West European responses' 370 (9–13 September 1991).

[8] Europol, Annual Report 2000 (2001).

Eurostat estimates that between 1975 and 1995 the population of the EU grew from 349 to 372 million people and the proportion of the elderly rose from 13 per cent to 15.4 per cent. Between 1995 and 2025, however, the population will grow more slowly and will then begin to decline. The working age population will also begin to decline within the next 10 years while the over-65 age group will continue to rise and is expected to reach 22.4 per cent of the population.[9]

Across the EU as a whole, net migration is regarded as the principal component of population growth, but the European Commission sees immigration only as a short-term solution to the demographic problem. This is because immigrants tend to adopt the fertility patterns of the host country once settled. Equally, increased immigration will not, of itself, be an effective long-term way to deal with labour market imbalances, including skills shortages, which should be addressed by an overall strategy of structural policies in the field of employment and human resources development.[10]

The labour market is characterized by the insufficient participation of women and elderly people in the work force and by long-term structural unemployment, with marked regional differences. The European Council has often emphasized the problems caused by the underdevelopment of the services sector, especially in the areas of telecommunications and the Internet, and the widening skills gap, especially in information technology where increasing numbers of jobs remain unfilled. Shortages in the traditional low-skilled areas, such as agriculture and tourism, are continuing even where there are high levels of unemployment in spite of the efforts being made to combat these phenomena. These shortages could undermine the EU's competitive position in the global economy. It is estimated, for example, that a shortage of migrants in agriculture and some sectors of industry would have negative consequences.[11] They are exacerbated, moreover, by restrictive policies that target primarily unskilled and semi-skilled immigrants mainly from non-OECD countries, while providing greater scope for highly skilled labourers demanded by western markets.[12]

---

[9] Eurostat, 'Patterns and trends in international migration in Western Europe' (2000).

[10] COM (2000) 757 final, Communication from the Commission to the Council and the European Parliament: on a Community immigration policy.

[11] J Salt, J Clarke, S Schmidt, J Hogarth, P Densham and P Compton, 'Assessment of possible migration pressure and its labour market impact following EU enlargement to Central and Eastern Europe, part 1' (Research Brief No 138, Department for Education and Employment, 1999).

[12] R Miles, *Racism after Race Relations* (1993).

There is a dichotomy between the security discourse and the market discourse. The former typically concerns low-skilled immigrants and is more restrictive in nature, while the latter concerns high-skilled immigrants and is more permissive. Huysmans suggests that 'the regulation and mediation of immigration through the labour market has cultural effects' in that high-skilled labour tends to be more culturally similar to the domestic labour force of the host country while the low-skilled labour force 'tend to be perceived as culturally different'.[13] The link between control and the logic of market necessity is both pervasive and powerful.

Dealing with immigration at the supranational level

The Amsterdam Treaty, which came into force in May 1999, was intended to give the EU considerable powers in the area of immigration. It specifically included immigration and asylum issues in the normal EU law-making field, the so-called 'first pillar' of the European Community.[14] Article 66 EC established that the Council of Ministers 'shall take measures to ensure cooperation' in the areas of immigration and asylum. To facilitate the implementation of this and other measures referred to in Article 66 EC, a new Protocol was agreed at Nice.[15] The Protocol established that 'from May 2004 the Council of Ministers shall act by qualified majority on a proposal from the Commission and after consulting the European Parliament'. The importance of this Protocol, in other words, lay in ensuring cooperation among Member States in immigration and asylum. It also expedites the decision-making process in these areas to a greater extent than is possible when unanimity is required. Article 67 EC also laid the groundwork for the eventual extension of the qualified majority vote to all areas of immigration and asylum. At the moment, however, there are only two areas in which the Council may make decisions by qualified majority vote.[16] These concern:

(1) third countries whose nationals must be in possession of visas when crossing the external borders, and
(2) a uniform format for visas.[17]

[13]   Huysmans (n 1 above) 764.
[14]   See Title IV of Part Three of the EC Treaty (Visas, Asylum, Immigration and Other Policies Related to Free Movement of Persons).
[15]   See Treaty of Nice, Protocol on Art 67 EC.
[16]   See Art 67(3) EC.
[17]   See Art 62(2)(b)(i) and (iii) respectively.

From May 2004, however, the Council may decide unanimously to apply Article 251 EC, which would extend qualified majority voting to all immigration and asylum issues or to any portion thereof.[18] Declaration No 5, also agreed upon at Nice, increases the likelihood of a broad extension of qualified majority voting.

As mentioned earlier, during the Tampere meeting in 1999, EU leaders decided to develop a 'common asylum and immigration policy'. The term 'common' was preferred by the Council of Ministers over the Commission's proposal for a 'single immigration and asylum system'. Whereas the term 'single' was suggestive of a more centralized system in which the Commission played a highly relevant role, the term 'common' was more evocative of inter-governmental cooperation and reserved a significant degree of influence to Member States. 'Cooperation' is indeed a more appropriate term than 'integration' to describe the approach that Member States have taken towards immigration policy.[19]

The European Summit at Tampere was intended to be a major step towards reforms that will bring the EU closer to its citizens. An interesting mechanism born at Tampere, under the initiative of the Commission, was the idea of the 'scoreboard', a monitoring system similar to that used in the context of the Single Market Action Plan. The general aim was to develop an overall framework at the EU level, with common standards and procedures as well as a mechanism for setting objectives and indicative targets, within which Member States would develop and implement national policies. The scoreboard also stresses the need for the development of a common immigration policy under a new framework for cooperation at the Community level, to be coordinated by the Commission. Two basic arguments justifying the cooperative approach emerge from official debates:

(1) individual Member States alone cannot handle the challenges thrown up by increased immigration;
(2) there is 'aggregated value' to be gained by increased coordination between the Member States themselves and between immigration policies and other policies directly linked to Europe's economic and social development.

[18] Art 251 EC describes the co-decision procedure according to which the Council may normally act by qualified majority vote.

[19] COM (2001) 387, Communication from the Commission to the Council and the European Parliament on an open method of coordination for the Community immigration policy.

The scoreboard system follows three basic objectives. First, immigrants need to be seen as playing a positive role in the economy. This means a more selective immigration policy for economic purposes to meet both skilled and unskilled needs. Secondly, the EU must develop efficient management strategies for dealing with migration flows (root-causes) and it must work towards improving conditions in the home countries that contribute most to immigration into the EU. This implies the adoption of a more open and transparent policy with clear rules and procedures that would enable potential economic migrants to make applications in their countries of origin based on reliable information about the criteria on which candidates will be judged in host-countries. Finally, the EU needs to combat illegal immigration and it has to make sure that the country of origin has good readmission policies.[20] This approach is aimed to reduce smuggling and illegal entry.[21] According to Commissioner Vitorino, this last objective is indispensable for the coherent realization of the former two.[22]

The scoreboard constitutes the operational level of a new culture of European cooperation, and recent developments at the international level have boosted the commitments of the EU to take joint action.[23] These commitments were established before the tragic events of 11 September 2001, but they have been taken more seriously after that period. In the last scoreboard in the second half of 2001, it is interesting to note the dramatic change of tone of the Commission, which emphasizes even more forcefully the need to implement the Tampere programme in accordance with the timetable.

Following the events of 11 September, moreover, the European Council has decided to develop an 'Action Plan on the fight against terrorism'. This Plan covers several policy areas, including external, economic/financial, transportation, and Justice and Home Affairs policy. With regard to the latter, a separate plan of action has been developed, covering policy in areas such as judicial cooperation, cooperation between police and intelligence services, the financing of terrorism, border control, and other measures. In an extraordinary JHA Council of 20 September 2001, the 'measures at the

[20] COM (2001) 672 final, Communication from the Commission to the Council and the European Parliament on a common policy on illegal immigration.
[21] 'A single market in crime', The Economist, 16 October 1999.
[22] 'Towards a common immigration policy for the European Union', opening speech by Commissioner Antonio Vitorino for the Conference on 'Migrations: Scenarios for the 21st Century' (Rome, 12 July 2000).
[23] It would be premature at this stage to speculate about the long-term consequences in this context of the events of 11 September 2001.

border' chapter addressed concerns relating to the issue of identity documents, residence permits and visas, and the functioning of the Schengen Information System (SIS).[24] In all, the scoreboard covers 18 different areas in the banner of 'freedom, security and justice', and it is updated every six months.

By comparing the scoreboards, it is possible to monitor the extent to which and pace at which the EU programme in each area has been or is being fulfilled. In general, the scoreboards illustrate that there has been progress, though it is far from satisfactory. The main responsibility for the adoption of policies lies in the hands of Member States and the Council of Ministers. The Council has to decide on Commission proposals and, as mentioned above, many of these decisions will continue to require a unanimous vote at least until 2004. Progress can be seen in the adoption by the Council of Ministers of a package of anti-discrimination measures proposed by the Commission, which also indicates that the struggle against social exclusion has been placed on the European social agenda.[25] Other important legislative proposals on family reunification, admission for employment purposes and assessment of flows into the EU, with regard to demographic changes and the situation of the labour market, nevertheless are still waiting a response from the Council of Ministers.

The decision taken at Amsterdam to move immigration and asylum from the third to the 'first pillar' of the Treaty was in part intended to enable these policy areas to benefit from a more dynamic Community decision-making process, including the involvement of the European Parliament and the Court of Justice. Furthermore, the conclusions that emerged from the Tampere meeting delineated the measures considered essential for building common policies in these related areas. On several occasions, the Commission has expressed concern about delays in accomplishing these commitments. The intention of the 'pillar switch' was to give to these issues a greater sense of urgency and more flexibility, but unfortunately this is not yet the case.

Some positive developments can be reported, but discussions in the Council of Ministers on several draft proposals reveal the familiar phenomenon of one or more Member States being reluctant to contemplate any

[24] See also Antonio Vitorino's speeches 01/467 of 17 October 2001 and 01/608 of 4 December 2001.

[25] Council Directive 2000/43/EC of 29 June 2000 implementing the principle of equal treatment between persons irrespective of race or ethnic origin [2000] OJ L180/22. See chapter by Ellis in this volume.

adjustment in national policy. The problems involved in reaching a common policy thus are still reminiscent of pre-Amsterdam, before immigration and asylum had been moved to the first pillar. In an area such as immigration, where nearly all decisions still require a unanimous vote, there is consequently an almost total absence of effective pressure to encourage intransigent Member States to make essential concessions. The only appreciable pressure has come from the Commission itself, which has invited national governments to reflect carefully on whether they are taking full advantage of the possibilities of the existing Treaties, on how they will use the improvements offered by Nice, and on what institutional and decision-making changes may be needed in future Treaties including the abandonment of the principle of unanimity in areas presently blocked.[26]

How just is the 'Community immigration policy'?

The general picture that emerges is one of a policy-making logic at the EU level in which internal policies (management of migration flows and admission of economic migrants) and external policies (partnerships with third countries) need to develop in a coherent and complementary manner.[27] The question here concerns the legitimacy of such a policy-making logic. The problem of legitimacy within a policy system is linked with many other issues, for example the distribution of resources and equality in terms of opportunity and application of law and justice. A just approach towards immigration has, I argue, to take into consideration all of these issues.

Restrictive and less restrictive approaches towards immigration have been based mainly on three lines of reasoning. First, the idea of state sovereignty is the objection most often advanced against free immigration.[28] Walzer analyses this aspect in *Spheres of Justice* by saying that the state has the legitimate right to restrict entry before other smaller community units begin to appropriate responsibility for doing so themselves.[29] Closure,

---

[26] COM (2001) 628 final, Communication from the Commission to the Council and the European Parliament: biannual update of the scoreboard to review progress on the creation of an area of freedom, security and justice (second half of 2001).

[27] COM (2001) 387 final, Communication from the Commission to the Council and the European Parliament on an open method of coordination for the Community immigration policy. This is also one of the areas covered in the scoreboard.

[28] A Dowty, *Closed Borders: The Contemporary Assault on Freedom of Movement* (1987).

[29] Walzer uses the term 'neighbourhoods', presumably referring to associations of people, whether formal or informal, or local councils within their own jurisdiction.

therefore must be admitted somewhere.[30] Secondly, there is the problem of preserving cultural identities. Restrictions may sometimes be justified because they are necessary to preserve a distinct culture or way of life.[31] Finally, there is the issue of distribution of resources. In western societies, the welfare state establishes principles of distributive justice. According to Freeman, it is the very existence of economic inequalities within the international system that creates a stimulus to migration. As some states can afford much greater expenditure on welfare than others, there is the need to control immigration 'if socially determined privileges are to be maintained'.[32] In this sense, the welfare state establishes principles of distributive justice that depart from free-market principles.[33]

It is clear that these three lines of reasoning on restriction towards immigration are obsolete. As national governments relinquish a large measure of control over immigration to the EU, the idea of state sovereignty that permits closure on moral grounds is no longer acceptable. To this point, however, the EU has simply adopted the state-like approach. In the context of globalization, it is nevertheless immigration that is becoming a moral problem rather than its restriction. By the same token, the defence of cultural distinctiveness, in a multicultural scenario such as the EU, is increasingly anachronistic. Rich states have a moral obligation to transfer resources and adopt measures to reduce drastically the prevailing international economic inequalities. It is the fulfilment of this obligation that would make the difference. Fewer people would want to move, the receiving countries would be less flooded by asylum seekers and immigrants, and those few still wishing to move could be accommodated somewhere.

So far, the EU seems to have approached this problem simply by shifting its approach from a zero immigration policy to the logic of the market. While this approach perhaps responds well to internal labour market exigencies, it fails to address the underlying conditions in countries of origin that encourage migration in the first place. The balance between security and utility within the EU certainly would not stop immigration flows and pressure from

[30] Walzer, *Spheres of Justice* (1983) 31–63.

[31] JH Carens, 'Migration and morality: a liberal egalitarian perspective' in B Barry and RE Goodin (eds), *Free Movement: Ethical Issues in the Transnational Migration of People and Money* (1992) 28.

[32] GP Freeman, 'Migration and the political economy of the welfare state' *Annals of the American Academy of Political and Social Science* (1986), no 485, 51; Z Layton-Henry, 'Citizenship and migrant workers in Western Europe' in U Vogel and M Moran (eds), *The Frontiers of Citizenship* (1991) 107, 112.

[33] ibid.

the outside world. EU experts are debating the capacity of the economic system to absorb immigration from third countries. As shown above, official debates now tend to stress the shrinking size of the EU working population and the potential for a structural crisis in the distribution of wealth that can undermine the EU's competitiveness in the short term. There is, however, another problem to be considered, and this has to do with the readiness of the system to integrate immigrants politically. This will depend largely upon how citizens perceive the social and economic problems posed by immigration. Does the new approach improve this perception?

There is the need to develop a 'just' approach not only towards immigrants and third countries but also towards people within the EU. EU policies towards immigration need to be legitimized not only from outside but also from inside. One of the problems within the EU is that any justice-based approach towards immigration would need to be legitimized by two contrasting points of view: one that seeks restrictions for reasons of security and to preserve the existing system of values within society, and another seeking more open borders for which absolute state control over immigration is difficult to reconcile with a (universal) principle of justice. EU Member States and the Commission thus have the difficult task of pleasing both points of view (not to mention the considerable grey area in between them) in achieving what they call 'greater coherence' of internal and external policies towards immigration. The 'greater coherence' discourse states that, in practice, the EU needs to draw up firm and fair common policies for dealing with immigration and, where possible, these policies need to be based on partnerships with countries of origin.[34]

On the one hand, the internal policy lays the foundation for a justice-based approach that is dictated by market necessity and seeks to assure the public that some immigrants, though clearly not all, are essentially beneficial to the economy. The open approach is 'just', and the coordination of market necessity and security market works only to the extent that security is preserved and guaranteed. This means that the EU, acting like a sovereign state, has the right to impose closure and this imposition is morally defensible.[35] On the other, external policy lays the foundation for a justice-based

[34] See Presidency Conclusions, Tampere European Council, 15–16 October 1999, 3: 'The Union as well as Member States are invited to contribute, within their respective competence under the Treaties, to a greater coherence of internal and external policies of the Union. Partnership with third countries concerned will also be a key element for the success of such a policy, with a view to promoting co-development'.

[35] See Walzer (n 30 above).

approach that aims to improve external conditions within third countries contributing most to immigration into the EU. The EU and third country partnerships should substantially reduce incentives for third country nationals to migrate into the EU.[36] This is what is called the 'remote control policy',[37] which is a way of dealing with the overall pool of prospective migrants. Many believe that it is intended as a mechanism by which to distinguish unwanted migrants from more welcome categories (skilled workers, tourists, business people, contract labourers) before they arrive in the territory of receiving countries.[38] In this case, the restrictive approach would be 'just' only if multilateral or bilateral agreements substantially change the life of people in source countries. Despite numerous commitments and some substantial progress towards improving conditions in source countries, the processes are still very slow. Within the EU, moreover, high tariffs inhibit trade with Africa and Asia in particular without decreasing poverty and starvation in these areas. This is part of a wider debate that calls for the EU to implement reforms, for example in the Common Agricultural Policy.[39]

The EU's approach towards immigration combines inclusive and exclusive elements. There is, however, a structural problem with a policy-making approach such as this. In the first place, this approach is based partly on an idea of distributive justice through which the EU is willing to open its doors only under conditions of market necessity and only if there are sufficient resources available to accommodate an influx of third country nationals. Secondly, this approach is based partly on a vague idea of a redistributive justice centred mainly on the improvement of external conditions without a clear and systematic operation in this direction.

It is highly unlikely that any significant global redistribution of economic resources will be realized in the very short term. Therefore, the policy-making approach that the EU is putting in place cannot develop in a

---

[36] Action plans have been established through partnerships such as ASEM (Asia-Europe Meeting), EMP (Euro-Mediterranean Partnership). Other action plans have been established on the initiative of the High Level Group on Immigration and Asylum.

[37] Guiraudon (n 1 above) 259.

[38] C Joppke, 'Why liberal states accept unwanted migration' (1998) 50 World Politics 266.

[39] P Collier and D Dollar, 'Can the world cut poverty in half? How policy reform and effective aid can meet international development goals' (World Bank, Development Research Group, Policy Research Working Paper 2403, 2000); GJ Borjas, 'Economic research on the determinants of immigration: lessons for the European Union' (World Bank technical paper no 438, Europe and Central Asia Poverty Reduction and Economic Management Series, 1999).

consistent and complementary manner as long as the EU and Member States do not develop an external policy approach which matches the objectives of the internal policy. This is a challenging target for the EU and its failure would mean that 'if we cannot move enough money to where needy people are, then we will have to count on moving as many of the needy people as possible to where the money is'.[40] There is now certainly a greater sense of global responsibility for richer countries than before. This has helped to bring about an expansion of the idea of distributive justice from one limited by national borders to one that transcends national boundaries and assumes a more international scope. Nevertheless, this greater sense of global responsibility is still incompatible with the state-like forms of restrictions adopted by the EU.

The discourse of state sovereignty as the moral underpinning of a restrictive immigration policy has partly been replaced by the more pragmatic discourse of economic utility. The legitimacy of state control is still taken for granted, but states are now more accountable to the international community. The EU is now putting forward a policy that seeks to strike a balance between 'security' and 'utility', and the European Commission Communication on 'a community immigration policy' is indeed based on such an approach.[41] This means that the efficient control of frontiers and firm action against illegal immigration and human trafficking is now balanced by debate about the benefits that immigration can bring. Nevertheless, the approach also provides a legitimate justification for exclusion when either the internal labour market is saturated or when a security threat is present.

There are two final remarks worth making. First, the realization of a policy towards immigration in which there is a balance between security and utility would not be cost-free. There will certainly be short-term costs for settlement policies and integration, though these costs will reinforce the socio-economic contribution of migrants in the long-term and also reduce discrimination and social exclusion. This is an important point for further debate because it would bring the issue of labour immigration into the discussion on the development of economic and social policy and it would provide measures in support of the integration of both existing and prospective immigrants. Secondly, the EU risks being accused once more of inconsistency by 'keeping the door closed and the window open', as Brian

---

[40] RE Goodin, 'If people were money' in Barry and Goodin (eds) (n 31 above) 8.
[41] COM (2000) 757 final (n 10 above).

Barry puts it, 'though both contribute to the objective of combining ventilation with security'.[42]

Conclusion

The central theme of this chapter concerns the formation of a new political paradigm that is emerging in the EU with respect to immigration. Policy-making in the area of immigration is driven less by a zero immigration policy and increasingly by a policy of market necessity. The exigencies of the market provide the basis for a just approach towards immigration and they are shaping the dominant political paradigm used by the EU for balancing 'restriction and permission'. If the world has indeed changed after the tragic events of 11 September 2001, the significance of these events for immigration policy cannot be underestimated, particularly in so far as concerns the issue of security. Although an analysis of the changes wrought by the events of 11 September lies beyond the scope of this essay, it would seem appropriate to mention very briefly some of the consequences. First, an immediate consequence has been the recognition of the need for greater security, both to reassure the public and to address genuine shortcomings that have become obvious only since 11 September. Secondly, the early signals suggest that the crisis could foster improvements in terms of cooperation between Member States.

These consequences, however, would not have much effect on the exigencies of the labour market within the EU for new immigration, and this increases the need to develop a more just and convincing approach towards immigration. By the same token, the opening up of legal admission policies for labour migration from non-EU countries will now require stronger and clearer justification in order to develop an adequate control strategy. There are, nevertheless, strong doubts that the strategy of a controlled approach adopted by the EU and based on a common assessment of the economic and demographic development of the Union, of its capacity for the reception of migrants, and of the situation in the countries of origin is satisfactory in the eyes of the public. A major problem is simply that Member States diverge from each other in many respects. Reception capacity, links to countries

---

[42]   B Barry, 'Quest for consistency: a sceptical view' in Barry and Goodin (eds) (n 31 above) 287. Though this expression is used by Brian Barry in relation to his own view on restrictive policy towards immigration, it also sums up the EU approach in this field.

of origin, the development of integration policies, and the exigencies of domestic labour markets vary widely from one Member State to another and the EU's political and operational agenda for overcoming this impasse is still very vague.

At this juncture, there are still two areas in which it is difficult to gauge the prospects for success of greater emphasis on the logic of market necessity. These areas concern the ability of market logic to foster increased legitimacy in a wider EU, and to contribute to a more positive attitude towards immigration. There are two main questions with which I would like to conclude this essay. First, is the logic of market necessity sufficient to tackle all the problems related to the issue of immigration? Secondly, to what extent is it utopian to believe that an intergovernmental approach is satisfactory and would in the end reflect the relative weight of each Member State, while national representatives seek to maximize domestically aggregated interests in interstate bargaining? The challenges ahead now appear much harder than ever before and immigration is an area in which citizens expect to see positive results. This is something on which politicians should start to think about more seriously, perhaps with a view towards taking advantage of the opportunities now offered at the supranational level.

Concluding Remarks

28

National States, European Union and Changing Dynamics in the Quest for Legitimacy

Daniel Wincott

In these concluding remarks I seek to place issues of legitimacy and accountability in the European Union in a broad panorama of European politics. The argument I sketch here is rooted in a view of Europe's double distinctiveness. First, Europe is the home of the national state, the location in which this political form reached its fullest development.[1] The second distinctive aspect of Europe was the creation of a supranational polity, whose institutions subsequently developed an unparalleled authority. In what seems to be a paradox, this supranationalism was a vital element in the development of Europe's national states.[2] In the early years of the integration process, the supranational institutions helped to keep peace among Europe's national states and to hold open cross-national economic exchange. At the same time, these national states consolidated their national authority, and the general legitimacy of politics, through the welfare state. In effect, there was a partial but important separation of roles between the European and national levels. Legitimacy was primarily generated through the national state, while the supranational level enjoyed a secondary legitimacy. While many influential scholars still see a functional differentiation as the (potential) basis of Europe's legitimacy,[3] I make a different argument.

Rather than requiring a fundamentally different form of legitimacy, the EU increasingly faces similar challenges to those developing at the state level—or indeed, they may be facing the same challenges jointly. Since the

---

[1] S Rokkan, *State Formation, Nation-Building and Mass Politics in Europe* (1999).
[2] A Milward, *The European Rescue of the Nation State* (1993).
[3] G Majone, 'Europe's "democratic deficit": the question of standards' (1998) 4 ELJ 5.

'golden age' of the welfare state, both the national and supranational levels have changed such that they increasingly face common dilemmas of legitimacy, such as declining participation in and engagement with politics. For example, neither motivated by a passionate objection to Europe nor a proxy for crucial issues in domestic politics, the referendum result rejecting the Nice Treaty in Ireland may mainly illustrate a disengagement from politics. Increasing multiculturalism, individualism, changes to the welfare state and political party systems are altering the allegiance of people to their national states. These changes are making states less 'national' in the classic sense. At the same time the inherently multicultural supranational polity is increasing in its range and authority. Moreover, as the Union increases in size, the ability of its members to use 'Europe' to achieve national ends has declined.

The historical context

At the start of the 21st century traditional forms of political, legal and economic organization are severely challenged. Whether cast in the fashionable, but usually misleading language of globalization, or disaggregated into a series of particular trends and tendencies, the 'order' associated with the epoch of the consolidating national states is, it seems, coming to an end. From the end of the 1770s until the 1970s, the tendential cultural homogenization of the (west) European national-states was reflected in a developing system of political representation and general citizenship.[4] Around the turn of the 19th–20th century, western Europe's political party systems stabilized into forms that allowed a broad range of society access to and involvement in surprisingly effective forms of political participation. States were also increasingly deeply involved in *securing* the welfare of their citizens, especially after 1945. More and more, formal equality before the law was coming to rest on a foundation of social security. Although it was hardly a smooth process, economic growth over these two centuries was spectacular and unprecedented.

Of course, Europe's 'states system' was not free from conflict. The interplay of statist nationalism and (sometimes catastrophic) economic rivalry had gruesome consequences, culminating in the monstrosity of Nazism and the 1939–45 War. It is the European Union's paradoxical historical mission

---

[4] Rokkan (n 1 above). See also S Bartolini, *The Political Mobilisation of the European Left, 1860–1980. The Class Cleavage* (2000), especially ch 4.

to have been first the saviour of the democratic national state in Europe, the means by which an increasingly 'universalist' national welfarism could be squared with, and prevented from degenerating into (internecine war or) protectionist national mercantilism;[5] but then apparently to have become its antithesis (whether in the form of the 'federalist superstate' that terrorizes the imaginations of some Eurosceptics or a complex multi-level polity or system of governance).

European integration was the means by which French and German post-war reconstruction could be reconciled. It provided the framework within which a series of traditional sectors of economic activity from coal and steel to agriculture could be organized and rationalized on a European scale. In parallel to the development of the supranational polity, western Europe's somewhat ramshackle states could reconstruct themselves whilst securing the affiliation[6] of their national populations by combining increased economic affluence with a deepened sense of social security, delivered in part through the welfare state. During the thirty years after 1945, economic affluence based on full male employment was matched by social security for the vulnerable provided by 'homemaker' wives (caring for the young and old) as much as by state welfare (although the role of the state here was also crucial). Political stability was found alongside social order. During this period Europe's party systems settled into a form that appeared to reflect stable cleavages,[7] allowing the seemingly 'essential' social structure of each state to be represented politically and hence to legitimize the state. Together these elements allowed the western European national-state to reach its (peaceful) apotheosis. During the same period, of course, the countries of east-central and south-eastern Europe were largely cut off from their own historical legacies and from the west. Economic integration in the eastern bloc took a quite different form, and one which hardly facilitated the development of the nation state.

[5] Milward (n 2 above).

[6] K van Kersbergen, 'Political allegiance and European integration' (2000) 37 European Journal of Political Research 1. This discussion is much influenced by Milward's historical work. In it 'affiliation' is used as a term of art, to identify the character of the attachment between peoples and states developed in post-war Europe. To me it suggests a form of attachment that is fairly deep, while not being a species of unthinking loyalty (say, based directly on ethnicity). It might potentially become somewhat 'taken for granted', without losing a slightly instrumental character.

[7] Indeed, in comparison with other periods before and since, the post-war period appears astonishingly stable in terms of socio-political cleavages and party systems, see S Bartolini and P Mair, *Identity, Competition and Electoral Availability* (1990).

Integration and the national states after 1980

Yet as the Union developed it became increasingly interwoven with its Member States, subtly changing them internally. As a result European integration contributed to shifts in the relative power of executives and legislatures, heads of government and ministers and various ministries. The law is the site, par excellence, of such change, with a complex and multi-dimensional legal system emerging from the interplay between, and increasing integration of, European and national law. During its first thirty years the European Community remained a somewhat obscure political entity, largely hidden beyond the horizon of popular politics, but by the end of the 1980s the Single Market programme and the political leadership of Jacques Delors had thrust it into the forefront of political debate. Initially this new profile was mainly associated with economic opportunities. However, if 'Europe' had once provided the context within which national states had been able to develop their welfare systems, increasingly it became identified as a potential threat to them, as Euro-liberalization undercut national social and economic 'models', triggering fears of social dumping and a 'race to the bottom'.

But if the Union contributes to changes in the political, legal and economic environment, Europe's national states are changing for other reasons as well. Partly due to economic changes and a shift in dominant economic ideas, full employment has become the Holy Grail that Europe's policy-makers have failed to find. Equally, however, gender roles have changed in ways that make full employment a much more challenging ideal, encompassing mass employment of women as well as men. As a consequence of mass female employment, the unpaid social service provided by women for the young, old and infirm has, if not vanished, certainly been fundamentally transformed, massively increasing the demands on state welfare provision (and in the process exposing the true nature of the post-war welfare state). At the same time Europe's party systems are no longer stable. They do not even appear to provide the primary and robust channels of political representation and legitimacy, that once they did. Compounding these changes the tendential cultural homogenization of the era of the national state in Europe has been replaced by an emerging multi-culturalism. Together, the European Union and its Member States face profound challenges of legitimacy. Of course, the EU sometimes exacerbates dilemmas of legitimacy for Europe's states, just as national politicians sometimes shift the blame for unpopular decisions to the European level. Equally, however, the EU has ameliorated some national legitimacy problems, as its historic role in Franco–German relations illustrates.

Both the national state and the (global) regional polity have reached their fullest development in Europe. Although it reached its apotheosis in Europe, at some times inspired by its model and at others imposed by its power, something like the national state became the dominant model of political order across the globe. Equally, outside Europe, states facing some of the same trends and tendencies (and sometimes reacting to the challenge of the EU's own success) seem increasingly to turn to (global) regional solutions. Yet cursory comparative analysis shows that from NAFTA to ASEAN, by way of Mercosur and APEC, no other regional political entity has a political structure as deep as that of the European Union. Only the EU has a method of enforcing rules that is remotely worthy of designation as a 'legal system'. Indeed, when states elsewhere designed their regional organizations, the EU model of supranational legalism seems to have served as a warning, not an inspiration, to political leaders seeking to limit the degree of political power they were pooling, delegating or surrendering. Europe's remarkable legal system and unusual political order give it a much greater capacity to intrude into the politics and economics of Europe's states. By the same token they create a potential for European-level political and legal strategies that use the EU's own institutions to hold 'Europe' to account that simply does not exist in other global regions.

The uniquely authoritative character of the legal and political institutions of the EU means that questions of accountability are much more complex and require closer scrutiny than is necessary in other regional organizations. Procedural aspects of accountability and legitimacy bulk large in such debates, to which the chapters in the first two parts of this book make important contributions. Ultimately, however, it is impossible wholly to separate procedure from substance. In particular, as the substantive range of the Union widens, taking in issues of foreign policy, internal and external security policy, the administration of justice and the politics of money, choice of procedures will have an impact on the character and quality of substantive outcomes. These choices become structures that facilitate the achievement of some outcomes and make others much more difficult to attain. Thus, for example, both the best means of achieving the purposes of the Union and the question of what those purposes are or should be are at stake in debates about a European Constitution.

Legitimacy after the European national state

To what, then, can or should the Union aspire? Many analysts distinguish 'input' from 'output' forms of legitimacy. The first depends on the pre-existing legitimacy of the political community. It assumes that just and legitimate procedures will translate it into legitimacy for the political regime and system. According to these accounts, 'input' legitimacy typically depends on a 'thick' communal identity, whether grounded on a civic or ethnic basis. Our polity is legitimate because of the dense pattern of communal ties that bind us together (or at least because this is how we believe we are bound together). Most commentators agree that Europeans are not interconnected in this sort of a way, and certainly do not feel themselves to be so bound together, although some may hold out hope that European identity will become an increasingly important element of the identities of Europeans. The contrast here, whether or not explicitly made, is with national communities. Of course, not everyone feels fully part of their 'own' national community. Indeed, the discussion above suggests that the era of tendential national cultural homgenization may have come to an end. Moreover, patterns of interaction across national boundaries facili-tated by the EU may allow other aspects of identity to flourish, and even help to create such identities. Nonetheless, my own feeling is that even if it proved possible to do so, it is forlorn to hope that allowing various 'iden-tities' within Europe to feel 'represented' in the Union's political process will solve its legitimacy problems.

At first glance the 'outputs' on which the Union has traditionally staked much of its appeal might seem to provide a more obvious basis for its claims to legitimacy. As soon as we scratch the surface, however, 'outputs' also prove controversial and problematic. While certain sorts of 'outputs', such as economic success, appear to have a very widespread appeal (although note the claims of some 'deep' ecologists), as soon as we move from the highly abstract general concept towards any more specific form difficult issues are raised. Only if the outputs are indeed desired will producing them enhance legitimacy. The questions are 'who decides and how is it decided what counts as a desirable outcome?' Unless the 'inputs' into this (putative) decision and the procedures by which it is achieved are themselves legitim-ate we cannot be confident that the outcomes will enhance legitimacy. Moreover, of course, we should never expect wholesale agreement on these matters.

So far, the discussion of input and output legitimacy has been somewhat abstract. But it takes a concrete form in one of the deep dilemmas facing European politics at the start of the 21st century. The relationship between economic efficiency and social welfare is one of the key challenges facing the EU and its Member States. Across the west, economic success is a key objective of political leaders. Popular perception of economic vibrancy secures both the overall legitimacy of a political system and the success of a particular political regime. Yet what counts as economic success is not wholly straightforward. Perhaps more than elsewhere, Europeans have come to expect a significant degree of economic and social security to be guaranteed by political authority. This security is, indeed, one of the most valued results of economic success. Yet there is a widespread sense that the social welfare systems on which such security seemed to rest are coming unstuck. Challenged by globalization, ageing populations, new technologies, changing expectations, as well as by European integration itself, after 25 years of austerity, Europe's welfare states now face a new set of reform challenges.

The elements of identity and (input and output) legitimacy take a particular form in this discussion. It is widely agreed that however well developed it may be, European identity is simply not strong enough to support large-scale redistribution of resources between individuals. While wealthy Europeans might accept heavy taxation to support their fellow nationals, they will not bear this burden to support Europeans of other nations. In this context, by massively increasing the potential scale of such redistribution, enlargement to the east pushes much further beyond the horizon of the politically possible. The relatively 'thin' character of European identity, many agree precludes legally binding European level fiscal and welfare policies.[8] But the illegitimacy of EU-level redistribution does not itself *necessarily* make EU economic regulation legitimate. Such an argument depends on the additional claim that economic efficiency can be separated from politics.[9] But this claim can be challenged in at least two ways.

First, even leaving issues of redistribution to one side, considerable scope for political disagreement exists over the appropriate scope and form of regulatory policies. Employers' organizations regularly complain about the excessive 'red tape' of regulation, particularly objecting to socially oriented

[8] But see Menon and Weatherill in this volume.
[9] And is particularly associated with Majone (n 3 above).

regulation.[10] Equally, and secondly, if EU economic regulation constrains political choices at the national level, however 'efficient' the European regime, its legitimacy might still be called into question. While a 'European' welfare state probably remains impossible and might well be undesirable, new modes of governance emerging within the EU may build upon and enhance processes of reform and renewal in the national welfare systems of Europe's states.[11] The Open Method of Coordination (OMC), for example, explicitly eschews the legally binding forms of policy at the European level that would make impossible demands of what sense of cross-national solidarity Europeans share. Nonetheless, these modes of governance give welfare issues an unprecedented 'presence' at the European level, potentially changing the 'balance' of the Union as perceived by its institutions.

Because these new modes of governance do not require binding laws, they are, in one sense at least, perfectly compatible with the regulatory theory. However, quite the opposite of the claims of these theorists, the emerging consensus on welfare reform is rooted in an attempt to *integrate* the economic and political purposes of social policy, not to separate economics from politics. After a long period when discussion of social policy was wholly concerned with retrenchment, a new politics of welfare may be emerging. In this new politics, social provision is not regarded as a deadweight transfer of resources from the successful to those who have failed, but reconstructed as an active welfare policy presented a tool of economic efficiency as well as of social justice.

If a new agenda is emerging in which economic efficiency and social justice are intimately linked rather than juxtaposed, it is still in a fledgling condition. Moreover, such an approach may face an early formidable challenge from further enlargement and monetary union.[12] Just as cohesion becomes increasingly necessary it is also more difficult to achieve. While collective European-level puzzling about how to reform existing welfare states may be starting to bear fruit, it is much less clear such an approach will work well in the states to be brought into the Union by the next enlargement. These states have neither the administrative capacity to reform the welfare state, nor western style welfare systems to be reformed in the first place. Indeed, if the OMC is premised on the view that new large scale European level redistribution is politically impossible, this premise and (by

---

[10] Of the sort analysed by Ellis in this volume.
[11] See the chapters by Szyszczak and Wincott in this volume.
[12] As noted by Martin in this volume.

extension) the OMC itself are likely to prove deeply disappointing to Central and Eastern European states.

Migration, enlargement and legitimacy

Thus far European integration has proceeded without provoking large-scale flows of internal migration. Such flows, once started, are likely to have self-reinforcing qualities. Some analysts of monetary union hope that people will begin to move around Europe in large numbers, viewing such movement as a means of balancing other economic pressures within such a Union. In the absence of other means of making the diverse post-enlargement regions of Europe cohesive, significant 'flows' of people around the continent might begin. Large-scale movement of people around Europe might well unsettle the existing welfare systems of the Member States. However well new modes of welfare provision integrate economic and social priorities, this integration is largely premised on the assumption that national populations remain relatively stable, so such a scenario might also cause the emerging approach to welfare reform to founder.

The record of the current membership of the Union on the question of eastern enlargement does not provide much cause for optimism here. While the provisions negotiated at Nice perhaps provide a better basis for enlargement than previously existed,[13] that may amount to little more than damning with faint praise. The securitization of Europe's post-enlargement new eastern border represents a profound misreading of its character, with potentially damaging consequences for the populations on both of its sides, as well as the credibility of the European border regime.[14] It is hard to avoid the conclusion that the existing members have failed to grasp the scale of the commitment they have taken on with enlargement. Equally, even after several years marked by disappointment, the incoming members still retain expectations of the Union and its current members that are unlikely to be met.

The European Union faces profound challenges. States in east Central Europe that were cut off from their heritage are re-joining the 'European' family just at the moment when the national state is facing fundamental changes. European supranationalism helped to provide the conditions within which the national state could achieve its democratic apogee in the

---

[13] See Fowler in this volume.   [14] See Batt in this volume.

European welfare state. The expectations of Europe's citizens are that their living standards will improve continually, that opportunities are consistent with security. In the 1980s and 1990s the EU's economic agenda, centred on the single market and monetary union, seemed to set economic efficiency against social security, juxtaposing a European drive to realize the benefits of economic integration against the stubborn resilience of nationally based social regimes. Today, the fate of the national and supranational institutions of Europe are ultimately entwined, confronted as they are by the same demanding challenges of renegotiating and reconstructing legitimacy for the era after the national state.

SELECT BIBLIOGRAPHY

JT Addison, CR Barrett and WS Siebert, 'The economics of labour market regulation' in JT Addison and WS Siebert (eds), *Labour Markets in Europe* (1997) 62.

JT Addison and WS Siebert, *Regulating European Labour Markets: More Costs than Benefits* (Institute for Economic Affairs, 1999).

L Aggestam, 'Germany' in I Manners and R Whitman (eds), *The Foreign Policies of European Union Member States* (2000) 64.

M Ahtisaari, J Frowein and M Oreja, *Report on the Austrian Government's Commitment to the Common European Values, in Particular Concerning the Rights of Minorities, Refugees and Immigrants, and the Evolution of the Political Nature of the FPÖ* (2001) 40 ILM 101.

A Alesina and RJ Barro, 'Currency Unions' (2002) Quarterly Journal of Economics (forthcoming).

G Alfredsson and A Eide (eds), *The Universal Declaration of Human Rights* (1999).

TRS Allan, *Law, Liberty, and Justice* (1993).

—— *Constitutional Justice* (2001).

M Allen, 'Die Rechte der Arbeitnehmer in Deutschland und dem Vereinigten König-greich' (2002) 55 ifo Schnelldienst 19.

P Alston (ed), *The EU and Human Rights* (1999).

KJ Alter, *Establishing the Supremacy of European Law* (2001).

G Amato, *Antitrust and the Bounds of Power: The Dilemma of Liberal Democracy in the History of the Market* (1997).

G Amato and J Batt, *Final Report of the Reflection Group on the Long-Term Implications of EU Enlargement: the Nature of the New Border* (1999).

F Amtenbrink, *The Democratic Accountability of Central Banks—A Comparative Study of the European Central Bank* (1999).

M Anderson and E Bort, *The Frontiers of the European Union* (2001).

H Armstrong and R Vickerman (eds), *Convergence and Divergence among European Regions* (1995).

KA Armstrong, 'Governance and the single European market' in P Craig and G de Búrca (eds), *The Evolution of EU Law* (1999) 745.

—— 'The White Paper and the rediscovery of civil society' (2001) 14 EUSA Review 6.

AM Arnull, *The European Union and its Court of Justice* (1999).

—— 'Modernising the Community Courts' (2000) 3 CYELS 37.

—— 'Private applicants and the action for annulment since *Codorníu*' (2001) 38 CMLRev 7.

AM Arnull, AA Dashwood, MG Ross and DA Wyatt, *Wyatt and Dashwood's European Union Law* (4th edn, 2000).

V Arora and O Jeanne, 'Integration and the exchange rate regime: some lessons from Canada' IMF Policy Discussion paper 01/1.

KJ Arrow, *Barriers to Conflict Resolution* (1995).

G Bachelard, *La dialectique de la durée* (1989).

M Baddeley, RL Martin and P Tyler, 'European regional unemployment disparities: convergence or persistence?' (1998) 5 European Urban and Regional Studies 195.

R Baldwin and P Krugman, 'Agglomeration, Integration and Tax Harmonization' CEPR Discussion Papers No 2630 November (2000).

E Barendt, *An Introduction to Constitutional Law* (1998).

B Barry and RE Goodin (eds), *Free Movement: Ethical Issues in the Transnational Migration of People and Money* (1992).

S Bartolini, *The Political Mobilisation of the European Left, 1860–1980. The Class Cleavage* (2000).

S Bartolini and P Mair, *Identity, Competition and Electoral Availability* (1990).

J Batt and K Wolczuk (eds), *Region, State and Identity in Central and Eastern Europe* (2002).

M Baun, *A Wider Europe. The Process and Politics of European Union Enlargement* (2000).

T Bayoumi and B Eichengreen, 'Shocking aspects of European monetary integration' in F Torres and F Giavazzi (eds), *Adjustment and Growth in the European Monetary Union* (1993) 193.

K Becher, 'Reforming German defence' (2000) 42 *Survival* 164.

D Beetham, *Democracy and Human Rights* (1999).

D Beetham and C Lord, *Legitimacy and the European Union* (1998).

B Beinart, 'The rule of law' (1962) Acta Juridica 99.

M Bell, 'Article 13 EC: the European Commission's anti-discrimination proposals' (2000) 29 ILJ 79.

C Bellamy, *Knights in White Armour: The New Art of War and Peace* (updated edition 1997).

S Berger and R Dore, *National Diversity and Global Capitalism* (1996).

J Berghmann, 'Social protection in the European Union' in A Bosco and M Hutsebaut (eds), *Social Protection in Europe: Facing up to Changes and Challenges* (1997) 17.

C Bildt, 'Force and Diplomacy' (2000) 42 *Survival* 141.

L Bini-Smaghi and D Gros, *Open Issues in European Central Banking* (2000).

O Blanchard and L Katz, 'Regional evolutions' (1992) 1 Brookings Papers in Economic Activity 159.

A Bloed, *The Conference on Security and Co-operation in Europe* (1993).

M Boldrin and F Canova, *Inequality and Convergence: Considering European Regional Policies* (2000).

D Booß and J Forman, 'Enlargement: legal and procedural aspects' (1995) 32 CMLRev 95.

GJ Borjas, 'Economic research on the determinants of immigration: lessons for the European Union' (World Bank technical paper no 438, Europe and Central Asia Poverty Reduction and Economic Management Series, 1999).

J Böröcz, 'The fox and the raven: the European Union and Hungary renegotiate the margins of "Europe"' (2000) 42 Comparative Studies in Society and History 847.

F Bosvieux, 'A business perspective on the EU Charter' in K Feus (ed), *An EU Charter of Fundamental Rights. Text and Commentaries* (2001) 147.

K St C Bradley, 'La transparence de l'Union européenne: une évidence ou un trompe l'œil ?' (1999) Cahiers de Droit Européen 283.

P Braunerhjelm, R Faini, V Norman, F Rauner and P Seabright, 'Integration and the regions of Europe: how the right policies can prevent polarisation' (2000) Monitoring European Integration 10.

H Bribosia, 'Subsidiarité et répartition des compétences entre la Communauté et ses Etats membres' (1992) Revue du marché unique européen 165.

WH Buiter, 'Alice in Euroland' (1999) 37 JCMS 181.

H Bull, 'Civilian power Europe: a contradiction in terms?' (1982) 20 JCMS 149.

M Bungenberg, *Artikel 235 EGV nach Maastricht: die Auswirkungen der Einheitlichen europäischen Akte und des Vertrages über die europäische Union auf die Handlungsbefugnis des Artikel 235 EGV (Artikel 308 EGV nF)* (1999).

G Burghardt and F Cameron, 'The enlargement of the European Union' (1997) 2 EFA Rev 7.

K Button and E Pentecost, *Regional Economic Performance within the European Union* (1999).

F Capotorti, M Hilf, FG Jacobs and J-P Jacqué, *The European Union Treaty* (1986).

M Castells, *The Rise of the Network Society* (1996).

M Chanock, 'A post-Calvinist catechism or a post-Communist manifesto? Intersecting narratives in the South African bill of rights debate' in P Alston (ed), *Promoting Human Rights Through Bills of Rights* (1999) 392.

R Cichowski, 'Western dreams, eastern realities. Support for the European Union in Central and Eastern Europe' (2000) 33 Comparative Political Studies 1243.

J Cloos, G Reinesch, D Vignes and J Weyland, *Le Traité de Maastricht: Genèse, Analyse, Commentaires* (2nd edn, 1994).

P Collier and D Dollar, 'Can the world cut poverty in half? How policy reform and effective aid can meet international development goals' (World Bank, Development Research Group, Policy Research Working Paper 2403, 2000).

V Constantinesco, *Compétences et pouvoirs dans les Communautés européennes* (1974).

P Cornish and G Edwards, 'Beyond the EU/NATO dichotomy: the beginnings of a European strategic culture' (2001) 77 International Affairs 587.

P Craig, 'Formal and substantive conceptions of the rule of law: an analytical framework' [1997] PL 467.

—— 'The nature of the Community: integration, democracy, and legitimacy' in P Craig and G de Búrca (eds), *The Evolution of EU Law* (1999) 1.

—— 'Constitutions, constitutionalism, and the European Union' (2001) 7 ELJ 125.

J Crawford, *Democracy in International Law* (1994).

D Curtin, 'Postnational democracy: the European Union in search of a political philosophy' (Universiteit Utrecht, 1997).

D Curtin, 'Citizens' fundamental right of access to EU information: an evolving digital *passepartout?*' (2000) 37 CMLRev 7.

I Daalder, 'Are the United States and Europe heading for divorce?' (2001) 77 International Affairs 553.

P Dagtoglou, 'The southern enlargement of the European Community' (1984) 21 CMLRev 149.

RA Dahl and ER Tufte, *Size and Democracy* (1973).

T Daintith (ed), *Implementing EC Law in the UK: Structures for Indirect Rule* (1995).

AA Dashwood, 'The limits of European Community powers' (1996) 21 ELRev 113.

—— 'States in the European Union' (1998) 23 ELRev 201 (reprinted in B Rider (ed), *Law at the Centre* (1999) 235).

—— 'European Community legislative procedures after Amsterdam' (1998) 1 CYELS 25.

—— 'The constitution of the European Union after Nice: law-making procedures' (2001) 26 ELRev 215.

RW Davis, 'The Court of Justice and the right of public access to Community-held documents' (2000) 25 ELRev 303.

S Deakin, 'Social rights and the market' in U Mückenberger (ed), *Manifesto Social Europe* (2001) 17.

G de Búrca, 'The quest for legitimacy in the European Union' (1996) 59 MLR 349.

—— 'Reappraising subsidiarity's significance after Amsterdam' (Harvard Jean Monnet Working Paper 7/1999). http://www.jeanmonnetprogram.org/

G de Búrca and J Scott (eds), *Constitutional Change in the EU: From Uniformity to Flexibility?* (2000).

P de Grauwe, *The Economics of Monetary Union* (4th edn, 2000).

J de Haan and SCW Eijffinger, 'The democratic accountability of the European Central Bank: a comment on two fairy-tales' (2000) 38 JCMS 393.

R Dehousse, 'European institutional architecture after Amsterdam: parliamentary system or regulatory structure' (1998) 35 CMLRev 595.

A Deighton (ed), *Western European Union 1954–1997: Defence, Security, Integration* (1997).

C de la Porte, P Pochet and G Room, 'Social benchmarking and EU governance' (2001) 11 JSP 291.

F de la Serre and H Wallace, 'Flexibility and enhanced cooperation in the European Union: placebo rather than panacea' (Notre Europe Research and Policy Papers No 2, September 1997).

C Delcourt, 'The *acquis communautaire* has the concept had its day?' (2001) 38 CMLRev 829.

C Dent, *The European Economy* (1997).

B de Witte, 'The pillar structure and the nature of the European Union: Greek temple or French gothic cathedral?' in T Heukels, N Blokker and M Brus (eds), *The European Union After Amsterdam* (1998) 57.

—— 'Chameleonic Member States: differentiation by means of partial and parallel international agreements' in B de Witte, D Hanf and E Vos (eds), *The Many Faces of Differentiation in EU Law* (2001) 231.

AV Dicey, *Introduction to the Study of the Law of the Constitution* (10th edn, 1959).

D Dimitrakopoulos and J Richardson, 'Implementing EU public policy' in J Richardson (ed), *European Union: Power and Policy-Making* (2nd edn, 2001) 335.

TJ Doleys, 'Member States and the European Commission: theoretical insights from the new economics of organization' (2000) JEPP 532.

A Dowty, *Closed Borders: The Contemporary Assault on Freedom of Movement* (1987).

P Drzemczewski, 'The Council of Europe's position with respect to the EU Charter of Fundamental Rights' (2001) 22 HRLJ 14.

S Duke, 'CESDP: Nice's overtrumped success?' (2001) 6 EFA Rev 155.

M Dunford and A Smith, 'Catching up or falling behind? Economic performance and the trajectories of economic development in an enlarged Europe' (2001) Economic Geography (forthcoming).

R Dworkin, *A Matter of Principle* (1985).

D Dyzenhaus, 'Form and substance in the rule of law: a democratic justification for judicial review?' in C Forsyth (ed), *Judicial Review and the Constitution* (2000) 141.

C-D Ehlermann, 'Differentiation, flexibility, closer co-operation: the new provisions of the Amsterdam Treaty" (1998) ELJ 246.

R Elgie and E Jones, 'Agents, principals and the studies of institutions: constructing a principal-centered account of delegation' (University of Nottingham, Working Documents in the Study of European Governance, no 5, December 2000).

KA Eliassen (ed), *Foreign and Security Policy in the European Union* (1998).

J Elster, *Deliberative Democracy* (1998).

TAO Endicott, 'The impossibility of the rule of law' (1999) 19 OJLS 1.

European Policy Centre, 'Beyond the delimitation of competences: implementing subsidiarity' (*The Europe We Need* Working Paper, 25 September 2001).

European University Institute/Robert Schuman Centre for Advanced Studies, *A Basic Treaty for the European Union—A Study of the Reorganisation of the Treaties* (2000).

M Ferrera, A Hemerijk and M Rhodes, *The Future of Social Europe: Recasting Work and Welfare in the New Economy* (2001).

K Feus, *A Simplified Treaty for the European Union?* (2001).

A Follesdal, 'Democracy, legitimacy and majority rule in the European Union' in M Nentwich and A Weale (eds), *Political Theory and the European Union: Legitimacy, Constitutional Choice and Citizenship* (1998) 34.

J Forman 'The equal pay principle under Community law' (1982) 1 LIEI 17.

B Fowler, 'Fuzzing citizenship, nationalising political space: a framework for interpreting the Hungarian "status law" as a new form of kin-state policy in Central and Eastern Europe' (Sussex European Institute, University of Sussex, One Europe or Several Programme, Working Paper 40/02, 2002).

B Fowler, 'Patterns of political conflict over territorial-administrative reform in Hungary', (2002) 12 Regional and Federal Studies 15.

G Fox and B Roth (eds), *Democratic Governance and International Law* (2000).

L Freedman (ed), *Military Intervention in European Conflicts* (1994).

——(ed) *Strategic Coercion* (1998).

GP Freeman, 'Migration and the political economy of the welfare state' (1986) *Annals of the American Academy of Political and Social Science* 51.

LL Fuller, *The Morality of Law* (1969).

L Funk, 'The "Storm before the Calm" thesis re-examined' in J Leonhard and L Funk (eds), *Ten Years of German Unification: Transfer, Transformation, Incorporation?* (2002) 183.

D Galloway, *The Treaty of Nice and Beyond* (2001).

G Garrett 'International cooperation and institutional choice: the European Community's internal market' (1992) 46 International Organization 533.

M-A Gaudissart and A Sinnaeve, 'The role of the White Paper' in M Maresceau (ed), *Enlarging the European Union* (1997) 41.

O Gerstenberg, 'The new Europe: part of the problem—or part of the solution to the problem?' (2002) 22 OJLS 563.

AJ Gil Ibáñez, *El control y la ejecución del Derecho Comunitario* (1998).

U Goll and M Kenntner, 'Brauchen wir ein europäisches Kompetenzgericht?' (2002) Europäische Zeitschrift für Wirtschaftsrecht 101.

LW Gormley, 'Public interest litigation in Community law' (2001) 7 EPL 51.

J Gow, *Triumph of the Lack of Will: International Diplomacy and the Yugoslav War* (1997).

J Gower, 'The Charter of Fundamental Rights and EU enlargement: consolidating democracy or imposing new hurdles?' in Federal Trust (ed), *The EU Charter of Fundamental Rights, Text and Commentaries* (2000).

H Grabbe, 'A partnership for accession? The implications of EU conditionality for Central and East European applicants' (European University Institute, Robert Schuman Centre, Working Paper 12/99, 1999).

—— 'How does Europeanization affect CEE governance? Conditionality, diffusion and diversity' (2001) 8 Journal of European Public Policy 1013.

T Gries, 'Soziales Marktmodell Europa versus liberales Marktmodell Amerika' (2001) 8 Wirtschaftsdienst 462.

E Guild, 'The constitutional consequences of law-making in the third pillar of the European Union' in P Craig and C Harlow (eds), *Law-Making in the European Union* (1988) 65.

E Guild and C Harlow (eds), *Implementing Amsterdam: Immigration and Asylum Rights in EC Law* (2001).

V Guiraudon, 'European integration and migration policy: vertical policy-making as venue shopping' (2000) 38 JCMS 251.

J Habermas, 'Remarks on Dieter Grimm's "Does Europe need a constitution?"' (1995) 1 ELJ 303.

C Haerpfer, 'Public opinion on European Union enlargement' (Centre for the Study of Public Policy, University of Strathclyde, Studies in Public Policy No 343, 2001).

P Hall and D Soskice, *Varieties of Capitalism: Institutional Foundations of Comparative Advantage* (2001).

W Hallstein, *Europe in the Making* (1972).

J Handoll, *Free Movement of Persons in the EU* (1995).

H Hannum (ed), *Guide to International Practice* (2nd edn, 1992).

C Harlow, 'Freedom of information and transparency as administrative and constitutional rights' (1999) 2 CYELS 285.

D Harris and J Darcy, *The European Social Charter* (2nd edn, 2001).

D Harris, M O'Boyle and C Warbrick, *Law of the European Convention on Human Rights* (1995).

TC Hartley, *Constitutional Problems of the European Union* (1999).

FA Hayek, *The Road to Serfdom* (1944).

P Hébraud, 'Obervations du temps dans le droit civil' in *Etudes offertes à Pierre Kayser* (1979) Vol 2, 1.

M Hedemann-Robinson, 'An overview of recent legal developments at Community level in relation to third country nationals resident within the European Union, with particular reference to the case law of the European Court of Justice' (2001) 38 CMLRev 525.

F Heisbourg (ed), 'European defence: making it work' (Chaillot Paper 42, Paris, WEU Institute for Security Studies, 2000).

K Henderson, 'Euroscepticism or europhobia: opposition attitudes to the EU in the Slovak Republic' (Sussex European Institute, University of Sussex, Working Paper No 50, 2001).

T Hervey, 'Social solidarity: a buttress against internal market law? in J Shaw (ed), *Social Law and Policy in an Evolving European Union* (2001) 31.

C Hill, 'The EU's Capacity for Conflict Prevention' (2001) 6 EFA Rev 315.

—— (ed), *The Actors in Europe's Foreign Policy* (1996).

C Hill and K Smith (eds), *European Foreign Policy: Key Documents* (2000).

D Hodson and I Maher, 'The open method as a new mode of governance: the case of soft law economic policy co-ordination' (2001) 39 JCMS 16.

S Hoffmann, 'The European process at Atlantic crosspurposes' (1964) 3 JCMS 85.

JR Hollingsworth and R Boyer, *Contemporary Capitalism: The Embeddedness of Institutions* (1997).

P Holmes, U Sedelmeier, A Smith, E Smith, H Wallace and A Young, 'The European Union and Central and Eastern Europe: pre-accession strategies' (Sussex European Institute, Working Paper No 15, March 1996).

N Hopkinsons, 'Migration into Western Europe' (Conference on political and economic migrants: pressures from the South and East and West European responses, London, HMSO, 1991).

M Höreth, 'No way out for the beast? The unsolved legitimacy problem of European governance' (1999) 6 JEPP 249.

J Howorth, 'European integration and defence: the ultimate challenge?' (Chaillot Paper 43, Paris, WEU Institute for Security Studies, 2000).

G Hunya and A Telegdi, 'Hungarian-Romanian cross-border economic cooperation' (Countdown project of the Vienna Institute for International Economic Studies (WIIW), 2001). http://eu-enlargement.org/discuss/default.asp?topic=research/.

J Huysmans, 'The European Union and the securitization of migration' (2000) 38 JCMS 751.

A Hyde-Price, *European Security Beyond the Cold War: Four Scenarios for the Year 2010* (1991).

—— *Germany and European Order: Enlarging NATO and the EU* (2000).

P Ifestos, *European Political Cooperation* (1987).

K Inglis, 'The Europe Agreements compared in the light of their pre-accession reorientation' (2000) 37 CMLRev 1173.

O Issing 'The Eurosystem: transparent and accountable, or "Willem in Euroland"' (1999) 37 JCMS 503.

C Joerges, Y Mény and JHH Weiler (eds), *What Kind of Constitution for What Kind of Polity? Responses to Joschka Fischer* (2000).

C Joerges and R Dehousse (eds), *Good Governance in Europe's Integrated Market* (2002).

C Joppke, 'Why liberal states accept unwanted migration' (1998) 50 World Politics 266.

M Jopp, *European Defence Policy: The Debate on the Institutional Aspects* (1999).

M Jopp and H Ojanen (eds), *European Security Integration: Implications for Non-alignment and Alliances* (1999).

J Jowell, 'The rule of law today' in J Jowell and D Oliver (eds), *The Changing Constitution* (4th edn, 2000) 3.

PJG Kapteyn, 'The Court of Justice after Amsterdam: taking stock' in T Heukels, N Blokker and M Brus (eds), *The European Union after Amsterdam* (1998) 139.

PJG Kapteyn and P VerLoren van Themaat (ed LW Gormley), *Introduction to the Law of the European Communities* (3rd edn, 1998).

H Kassim and A Menon, 'Rethinking the application of principal-agent models to the EU: Member States and the European Commission' (2002) JEPP (forthcoming).

G Klosko, *Democratic Procedures and Liberal Consensus* (2000).

B Kohler-Koch and R Eising, *The Transformation of Governance in the European Union* (1999).

M Kohnstamm and W Hager (eds), *A Nation Writ Large? Foreign-policy Problems before the European Community* (1973).

J Kokott, 'Federal States in federal Europe: the German *Länder* and problems of European integration' (1997) EPL 607.

D Kostakopoulou, 'The "protective union": change and continuity in migration law and policy in post-Amsterdam Europe' (2000) 38 JCMS 497.

HG Krenzler and C Pitschas, 'Progress or stagnation? The common commercial policy after Nice' (2001) 6 EFA Rev 291.

HC Krüger and J Polakiewicz, 'Proposals for a coherent human rights protection system in Europe' (2001) 22 HRLJ 1.

P Krugman, 'The lessons of Massachusetts for EMU' in F Torres and F Giavazzi (eds), *Adjustment and Growth in the European Monetary Union* (1993) 241.

T Kuhn, *Structures of Scientific Revolutions* (2nd edn, 1970).

PJ Kuijper, 'Some legal problems associated with communitarization of policy on visa, asylum, and immigration under the Amsterdam Treaty and incorporation of the Schengen acquis' (2000) 37 CMLRev 345.

B Laffan, 'The Nice Treaty: the Irish vote' http://www.notre-europe.asso.fr/Quoide-neuf.htm/.

A Lamfalussy, 'Reflections on the regulation of European securities markets' (SUERF Study No 14, October 2001).

A Landau and R Whitman (eds), *Rethinking the European Union: Institutions, Interests and Identities* (1997).

M la Torre, 'Legal pluralism as evolutionary achievement of Community law' (1999) 12 Ratio Juris 182.

RH Lauwaars, *Lawfulness and Legal Force of Community Decisions* (1973).

Sir John Laws, 'Judicial review and the meaning of law' in C Forsyth (ed), *Judicial Review and the Constitution* (2000) 173.

Z Layton-Henry, 'Citizenship and migrant workers in Western Europe' in U Vogel and M Moran (eds), *The Frontiers of Citizenship* (1991).

K Lenaerts, 'La Déclaration de Laeken: premier jalon d'une Constitution européenne?' (2002) 10 Journal des Tribunaux – Droit européen 29.

K Lenaerts and E De Smijter, 'A "Bill of Rights" for the European Union' (2001) 38 CMLRev 273.

A Lester, 'Age discrimination in equality' (2001) 100 Equal Opportunities Review 36.

M Libal, *Limits of Persuasion: Germany and the Yugoslav Crisis, 1991–1992* (1997).

C Lord, *Democracy in the European Union* (1998).

J-V Louis, 'A legal and institutional approach for building a monetary union' (1998) 35 CMLRev 33.

I Loveland, *Constitutional Law: A Critical Introduction* (2000).

TJ Lowi, *The End of Liberalism: The Second Republic of the United States* (1979).

P Luif, *On the Road to Brussels: The Political Dimension of Austria's, Finland's and Sweden's Accession to the European Union* (1995).

—— *The Common Foreign and Security Policy of the European Union: Theoretical and Empirical Issues* (1997).

N MacCormick, *Questioning Sovereignty* (1999).

Lord Mackenzie Stuart, *The European Communities and the Rule of Law* (1977).

C MacMaolain, 'Free movement of foodstuffs, quality requirements and consumer protection: have the Court and Commission both got it wrong?' (2001) 26 ELRev 413.

MP Maduro, *We, The Court* (1998).

MP Maduro, 'Europe and the constitution: what if this as good as it gets?' in J Weiler and M Wind (eds), *Rethinking European Constitutionalism* (forthcoming).

G Magnifico, *European Monetary Unification* (1973).

G Majone, *Regulating Europe* (1996).

—— 'Europe's "democratic deficit": the question of standards' (1998) 4 ELJ 5.

—— 'The credibility crisis of Community regulation' (2000) 38 JCMS 273.

I Manners and R Whitman (eds), *The Foreign Policies of European Union Member States* (2000).

M Maresceau, 'On association, partnership, pre-accession and accession' in M Maresceau (ed) *Enlarging the European Union* (1997) 3.

—— 'The EU pre-accession strategies: a political and legal analysis' in M Maresceau and E Lannon (eds), *The EU's Enlargement and Mediterranean Strategies* (2001).

—— 'From Europe Agreements to accession negotiations' in G Venturini (ed) *Europa di Domani* (2002).

G Marks, L Hooghe and K Blank, 'European integration from the 1980s: State-centric v multi-level governance' (1996) 34 JCMS 341.

S Marks, *The Riddle of all Constitutions* (2000).

R Martin, 'EMU versus the regions? Regional convergence and divergence in Euroland' (2001) 1 Journal of Economic Geography 51.

R Martin and P Sunley, 'Slow convergence? New endogenous growth theory and regional development' (1998) 74 Economic Geography 201.

R Martin and P Tyler, 'Regional employment evolutions in the European Union: a preliminary analysis' (2000) 34 Regional Studies 601.

P Masson and MP Taylor (eds), *Policy Issues in the Operation of Currency Unions* (1993).

A Mattera, 'La procédure en manquement et la protection des droits des citoyens et des opérateurs lésés' (1995) Revue du Marché Unique Européen 137.

F Mayer, 'Die drei Dimensionen der europäischen Kompetenzdebatte' (2001) 61 Zeitschrift für ausländisches öffentliches Recht und Völkerrecht 577.

A Mayhew, *Recreating Europe* (1998).

—— 'Enlargement of the European Union: an analysis of the negotiations with the Central and Eastern European candidate states' (Sussex European Institute, University of Sussex, Working Paper No 39, 2000).

R Miles, *Racism after Race Relations* (1993).

A Milward, *The European Rescue of the Nation State* (1993).

J Monar, 'Justice and Home Affairs in the Treaty of Amsterdam – reform at the price of fragmentation' (1998) 23 ELRev 320.

A Moravcsik, 'Preferences and power in the European Community: a liberal intergovernmentalist approach' (1993) 31 JCMS 509.

—— 'If it ain't broke, don't fix it!' (*Newsweek International*, 4 March 2002).

K Mortelmans, 'The common market, the internal market and the single market, what's in a market?' (1998) 35 CMLRev 101.

R Mudambi, P Navarra and G Sovvrio (eds), *Rules and Reason. Perspectives on Constitutional Political Economy* (2001).

R Mulgan, '"Accountability": an ever-expanding concept' (2000) 78 Public Administration 555.

P-C Müller-Graff, 'The legal framework for the enlargement of the internal market to Central and Eastern Europe' (1999) 6 MJ 192.

R Mundell, 'The Nobel monetary duel': http://www.nationalpost.com/features/duel/index.html/(2000).

—— 'The euro in the new economic order': http://www.ceps.be/Events/111401.htm/ (2001).

—— 'Nobel prize winner proposes new currency—— "intor"' (2001): http://english.peopledaily.com.cn/200110/20/eng20011020_82798.html/.

MC Munger, *Analyzing Policy. Choices, Conflicts and Practices* (2000).

C Munro, *Studies in Constitutional Law* (2nd edn, 1999).

G Munuera, 'Preventing armed conflict in Europe: lessons from recent experience' (Chaillot Paper 15–16, Paris, WEU Institute for Security Studies, 1994).

Sir Patrick Neill, 'The European Court of Justice: a case study in judicial activism' (European Policy Forum, 1995).

P Nicolaides, SR Boean, F Bollen and P Pezaros, *A Guide to the Enlargement of the European Union* Vol II (1999).

G Nodia, 'Nationalism and democracy' in L Diamond and M Plattner (eds), *Nationalism, Ethnic Conflict and Democracy* (1994).

S Nuttall, *European Political Cooperation* (1992).

U Öberg, 'EU citizens' right to know: the improbable adoption of a European Freedom of Information Act' (1999) 2 CYELS 303.

D Obradovic, 'Repatriation of powers in the European Community' (1997) 34 CMLRev 59.

D Oliver, *Government in the United Kingdom* (1991).

D O'Keeffe and P Twomey (eds), *Legal Issues of the Amsterdam Treaty* (1999).

Sir Con O'Neil, *Britain's Entry into the European Community* (2000).

M Ortega, 'Military intervention and the European Union' (Chaillot Paper 45, Paris, WEU Institute for Security Studies, 2001).

KH Paqué, 'Structural unemployment in Europe: a bird's-eye view' in JT Addison and PJJ Welfens (eds), *Labor Markets and Social Security. Wage Costs, Social Security Financing and Labor Market Reforms in Europe* (1998) 17.

M Pechstein and C Koenig, *Die Europäische Union* (1998).

S Peers, 'Who's judging the watchmen? The judicial system of the area of freedom, security and justice' (2000) 18 YEL 337.

I Pernice, 'Multi-level constitutionalism and the Treaty of Amsterdam: European constitution-making revisited' (1999) 36 CMLRev 703.

—— 'Kompetenzabgrenzung im europäischen Verfassungsverbund' (2000) Juristen Zeitung 866.

—— 'Rethinking the methods of dividing and controlling the competencies of the Union' in European Commission, *Europe 2004. Le grand débat* (2001) 96.

—— *The European Constitution* (2002).

J Peterson, 'Decision-making in the European Union: towards a framework for analysis' (1995) 2 JEPP 69.

J Peterson and H Sjursen, (eds), *A Common Foreign Policy for Europe? Competing Visions of the CFSP* (1998).

D Phinnemore, 'The Treaty of Nice, EU enlargement and the implications for Romania' (2001) 1 Romanian Journal of Society and Politics 5.

M Pollack, 'Delegation, agency and agenda setting in the European Community' (1997) 1 International Organization 51.

C Preston, 'Obstacles to EU enlargement: the classical method and the prospects for a wider Europe' (1995) 33 JCMS 451.

—— *Enlargement and Integration in the European Union* (1997).

G Pridham, 'EU accession and domestic politics: policy consensus and interactive dynamics in Central and Eastern Europe' (2001) 1 Perspectives on European Politics and Society 49.

J-P Puissochet, *L'Elargissement des Communautés Européennes* (1974).

D Quah, 'Galton's Fallacy and tests of the convergence hypothesis' (1993) 95 Scandinavian Journal of Economics 427.

H Ragnemalm, 'The Community Courts and openness within the European Union' (1999) 2 CYELS 19.

I Ramonet, *Géopolitique du chaos* (1999).

H Rasmussen, *On Law and Policy in the European Court of Justice* (1986).

J Rawls, *Justice as Fairness: A Restatement* (2001).

J Raz, *The Authority of Law* (1979).

—— *Ethics in the Public Domain* (1994).

W Rees, *The Western European Union at the Crossroads: Between Transatlantic Solidarity and European Integration* (1998).

E Regelsberger, P de Schoutheete de Tervarent and W Wessels (eds), *Foreign Policy of the European Union: From EPC to CFSP and Beyond* (1997).

N Reich, 'Union citizenship – metaphor or source of rights' (2001) 7 ELJ 4.

S Rokkan, *State Formation, Nation-Building and Mass Politics in Europe* (1999).

B Rosamond, 'Discourses of globalization and the social construction of European identities' (1999) 6 JEPP 652.

AK Rose, 'One money, one market: estimating the effect of common currency on trade' (2000) 30 Economic Policy: A European Forum 7.

U Roth and V Thomas, 'Europe on the path to a common social policy' (2000) 34 Inter Nationes Basis-Info 13.

M Rutten (ed), 'From St-Malo to Nice. European defence: core documents' (Chaillot Paper 47, Paris, WEU Institute for Security Studies, 2001).

X Sala-i-Martin and J Sachs, 'Fiscal federalism and optimum currency areas: evidence for Europe from the United States' (Working Paper 3855, National Bureau of Economic Research, Cambridge MA, 1991).

J Salt, J Clarke, S Schmidt, J Hogarth, P Densham and P Compton, 'Assessment of possible migration pressure and its labour market impact following EU enlargement to Central and Eastern Europe, part 1' (Research Brief No 138, Department for Education and Employment, 1999).

W Sandholtz and A Stone Sweet (eds), *European Integration and Supranational Governance* (1998).

F Scharpf, 'Community and autonomy: multi-level policy-making in the European Union' (1994) 1 JEPP 219.

—— *Games Real Actors Play* (1997).

—— 'Economic integration, democracy and the welfare state' (1997) 4 JEPP 18.

—— *Governing in Europe: Effective and Democratic?* (1999).

—— 'European governance: common concerns vs the challenge of diversity' in M Jachtenfuchs and M Knodt (eds), *Regieren in Internationalen Institutionen* (2002) 271.

H-E Scharrer, 'Single market or national industrial policies?' (2002) 37 Intereconomics 66.

E Schmidl and R Oakley (eds), *Peace Operations Between War and Peace* (2000).

R Schobben ' "New Governance" in the European Union: a cross-disciplinary comparison' (2000) 10 Regional and Federal Studies 35.

C Scott, 'Accountability in the regulatory state' (2000) 27 Journal of Law and Society 38.

J Scott and D Trubek, 'Mind the gap: law and new approaches to governance in Europe' (2002) ELJ (forthcoming).

J Shaw, 'The Treaty of Amsterdam: challenges of flexibility and legitimacy' (1998) ELJ 63.

—— 'Postnational constitutionalism in the European Union' (1999) 6 JEPP 579.

H Siebert, 'The assignment problem' in SK Berninghaus and M Braulke (eds), *Beiträge zur-Mikro und Makroökonomik* (2001) 439.

P Skidmore, 'EC Framework Directive on equal treatment in employment: towards a comprehensive Community anti-discrimination policy?' (2001) 30 ILJ 126.

B Skyrms, *The Dynamics of Rational Deliberation* (1990).

R Smits, *The European Central Bank: Institutional Aspects* (1997).

B Soetendorp, *Foreign Policy in the European Union* (1999).

D Soskice, B Hancké, G Trumbull and A Wren, 'Wage bargaining, labour markets and macroeconomic performance in Germany and the Netherlands' in L Delsen and E de Jong (eds), *The German and Dutch Economies. Who Follows Whom?* (1998) 39.

J Štebe, 'Support for the European Union from a comparative perspective: stability and change in the period of transition' (2001) 2 Central European Political Science Review 92.

P Stone, *Civil Jurisdiction and Judgments in Europe* (1998).

CR Sunstein, *Legal Reasoning and Political Conflict* (1996).

A Szczerbiak, 'Polish public opinion: explaining declining support for EU membership' (2001) 39 JCMS 105.

E Szyszczak, 'Free trade as a fundamental value in the European Union' in K Economides, L Betten, J Bridge, A Tettenborn and V Shrubsall (eds), *Fundamental Values* (2000) 159.

—— 'The evolving European Employment Strategy' in J Shaw (ed), *Social Law and Policy in an Evolving European Union* (2000) 197.

—— 'The new paradigm for social policy: a virtuous circle?' (2001) 38 CMLRev 1125.

AP Thirlwall, *The Euro and Regional Divergence in Europe* (2000).

—— 'European unity could flounder on regional neglect' (*Guardian*, 31 January 2000) 23.

B Tierney, *The Idea of Natural Rights* (1997).

C Tilly, *The Formation of National States in Western Europe* (1975).

C Timmermans, 'Judicial protection against the Member States: Articles 169 and 177 revisited' in D Curtin and T Heukels (eds), *Institutional Dynamics of European Integration—Essays in Honour of Henry G Schermers* Vol II (1994) 391.

—— 'How can one improve the quality of Community legislation?' (1997) 34 CMLRev 1229.

Y Tolias, 'Has the problem concerning the delimitations of the Community's competence been resolved since the Maastricht judgement of the Bundesverfassungsgericht?' (2002) EBLR (forthcoming).

A Tomkins, 'Transparency and the emergence of a European administrative law' (1999/2000) 19 YEL 217.

C Turpin, *British Government and the Constitution: Texts, Cases and Materials* (1999).

F Tuytschaever, *Differentiation in European Union Law* (1999).

RM Unger, *Law in Modern Society* (1976).

J Usher, *EC Institutions and Legislation* (1998).

—— 'Flexibility and enhanced cooperation' in T Heukels, N Blokker and M Brus (eds), *The European Union after Amsterdam* (1998) 253.

—— 'Economic and Monetary Union – a model for flexibility?' (1998) 1 CYELS 39.

P van den Bossche, 'In search of remedies for non-compliance: the experience of the EC' (1996) 3 MJ 371.

P van Ham, 'Europe's new defense ambitions: implications for NATO, the US and Russia' (the Marshall Center Papers, no1, 2000).

K van Kersbergen, 'Political allegiance and European integration' (2000) 37 European Journal of Political Research 1.

R Vaubel, *Europa-Chauvinismus. Der Hochmut der Institutionen* (2001).

Venice Commission, *Report on the Preferential Treatment of National Minorities by their Kin-States* (European Commission for Democracy through Law, Strasbourg, 2001). http://www.venice.coe.int/site/interface/english.htm

A Verhoeven, 'How democratic need European Union members be? Some thoughts after Amsterdam' (1998) 23 ELRev 217.

B Vesterdorf, 'Transparency—not just a vogue word' (1999) 22 Fordham International Law Journal 902.

P Veyne, *Comment on écrit l'histoire* (1996).

F Vibert, *Europe: A Constitution for the Millenium* (1995).

—— *Europe Simple, Europe Strong: The Future of European Governance* (2001).

S Voigt, 'What constitution for Europe? The constitutional question from the point of view of (positive) constitutional economics' in T Bruha, JJ Hesse and C Nowak (eds), *Welche Verfassung für Europa?* (2001) 41.

A von Bogdandy and J Bast, 'Die Vertikale Kompetenzordnung der europäischen Union' (2001) europäische Grundrechte Zeitschrift 441, 447–450; (2002) 39 CMLRev (forthcoming).

T von Danwitz, 'The EU Charter of Fundamental Rights' (2001) 2 Internationale Politik—Transatlantic Edition 23.

J Waldron, *Law and Disagreement* (1999).

H Wallace, 'Experiments in European governance' in M Jachtenfuchs and M Knodt (eds), *Regieren in Internationalen Institutionen* (2002) 255.

H Wallace and AR Young, *Participation and Policy Making in the European Union* (1997).

H Wallace and W Wallace (eds), *Policy-Making in the European Union* (4th edn, 2000).

M Walzer, *Spheres of Justice: A Defence of Pluralism and Equality* (1983).

S Weatherill, *Law and Integration in the European Union* (1995).

—— 'Recent case law concerning the free movement of goods: mapping the frontiers of market deregulation' (1999) 36 CMLRev 51.

—— 'Flexibility or fragmentation: trends in European integration' in J Usher (ed), *The State of the European Union* (2000).

—— 'New strategies for managing the EC's internal market' (2000) 53 CLP 595.

J Weiler 'The transformation of Europe' (1991) 100 Yale Law Journal 2403.

—— 'Does Europe need a constitution? Reflections on demos, telos and the German Maastricht decision' (1995) 1 ELJ 219.

—— 'The European Union belongs to its citizens: three immodest proposals' (1997) 22 ELRev 150.

—— *The Constitution of Europe* (1999).

W Wessels, 'Nice results: the millennium IGC in the EU's evolution' (2001) 39 JCMS 192.

S Wheatley, 'Democracy in international law: a European perspective' (2002) 51 ICLQ 225.

B White, *Understanding European Foreign Policy* (2001).

A Wiener, 'The constitutional significance of the charter of fundamental rights' (2001) 18 German Law Journal 7, http://www.germanlawjournal.com/print.php?id=113/.

MB Williams, 'Exporting the democratic deficit. Hungary's experience with EU integration' (2001) 48 Problems of Post-Communism 27.

R Williams, 'The European Commission and the enforcement of environmental law: an invidious position' (1994) 14 YEL 351.

OE Williamson, *Markets and Hierarchies* (1975).

D Wincott, 'Does the European Union pervert democracy? Questions of democracy in new constitutionalist thought on the future of Europe' (1998) 4 ELJ 411.

—— 'Looking forward or harking back? The Commission and the reform of governance in the EU' (2001) 39 JCMS 897.

—— 'Beyond social regulation? Social policy at Lisbon: new instruments or a new agenda?' (2003) Public Administration (forthcoming).

K Wolczuk, 'Polish-Ukrainian borderlands: the case of Lviv and Przemysl' in K Krzys-tofek and A Sadowski (eds), *Ethnic Borderlands in Europe: Harmony or Conflict?* (2001) 213.

K Wolczuk and R Wolczuk, *Poland and Ukraine. A Strategic Partnership in a Changing Europe?* (2002).

J Wouters, 'Institutional and constitutional challenges for the European Union—some reflections in the light of the Treaty of Nice' (2001) 26 ELRev 342.

J Ziller, 'European models of government: towards a patchwork with missing pieces' (2001) 54(1) Parliamentary Affairs 102.

—— 'L'Etat composé et son avenir en France' (2001) 103 Revue politique et parlemen-taire 151.

P Zimmermann-Steinhart, 'Der Konvent: die neue Methode? (2002) 51 Gesellschaft-Wirtschaft-Politik 65.

INDEX

Please note that references to flow charts, figures or tables are in italics